D0290539

Productivity
Volume 1: Postwar U.S.
Economic Growth

Productivity
Volume 1: Postwar U.S.
Economic Growth

Dale W. Jorgenson

The MIT Press
Cambridge, Massachusetts
London, England

Second printing, 1996

This book was printed and bound in the United States of America.

Library of Congress Cataloging-in-Publication Data

Jorgenson, Dale Weldeau, 1933–
Productivity / Dale W. Jorgenson.
p. cm.
Includes bibliographical references and index.
Contents: v. 1. Postwar U.S. economic growth—v. 2. International comparisons of economic growth.
ISBN 0-262-10049-5 (v. 1).—ISBN 0-262-10050-9 (v. 2).
1. Industrial productivity—United States. 2. Capital investments—United States. 3. United States—Economic conditions—1945– 4. Industrial productivity—Japan. 5. Japan—Economic conditions—1945– 6. Industrial productivity—Germany (West) 7. Capital investments—Germany (West)—Economic conditions. I. Title.
HC110.I52J668 1995 94-22733
338.9—dc20 CIP

Contents

List of Tables ix
Preface xv
List of Sources xxix

1. Productivity and Postwar U.S. Economic Growth **1**
D.W. Jorgenson
1.1. Introduction 1
1.2. Sources of U.S. Economic Growth 2
1.3. Aggregation over Sectors 7
1.4. Econometric Modeling of Production 11
1.5. Conclusion 16
1.6. Appendix: Methodology and Data Sources 17

2. The Embodiment Hypothesis **25**
D.W. Jorgenson
2.1. Introduction 25
2.2. Theory 27
2.3. Measurement 29
2.4. Explanation 33
2.5. Prediction 39
2.6. Mathematical Appendix 42

3. The Explanation of Productivity Change **51**
D.W. Jorgenson and Z. Griliches
3.1. Introduction 51
3.2. Theory 53
3.3. Measurement 68
3.4. Summary and Conclusion 83
3.5. Statistical Appendix 90

4. Issues in Growth Accounting: A Reply to Edward F. Denison **99**
D.W. Jorgenson and Z. Griliches
4.1. Introduction 99
4.2. Measurement of Output 103
4.3. Measurement of Capital Input 109
4.4. Relative Utilization of Capital 124
4.5. Measurement of Labor Input 130
4.6. Measurement of Total Factor Productivity 138

4.7. Major Issues in Growth Accounting 144
4.8. Final Reply 167

5. Measuring Economic Performance in the Private Sector 175
L.R. Christensen and D.W. Jorgenson
5.1. Introduction 175
5.2. Income and Wealth 179
5.3. Index Numbers 198
5.4. Perpetual Inventory 205
5.5. Production Account 223
5.6. Income and Expenditure, Accumulation, and Wealth Accounts 246
5.7. Extending the Accounting Framework 268

6. The Accumulation of Human and Nonhuman Capital, 1948–84 273
D.W. Jorgenson and B.M. Fraumeni
6.1. Introduction 273
6.2. Methodology 277
6.3. Production 281
6.4. Income and Expenditure 296
6.5. Accumulation and Wealth 314
6.6. Conclusion 328

7. The Output of the Education Sector 333
D.W. Jorgenson and B.M. Fraumeni
7.1. Introduction 333
7.2. Market and Nonmarket Labor Incomes 335
7.3. Investment in Education 345
7.4. Conclusion 360
7.5. Appendix 364

8. Investment in Education and U.S. Economic Growth 371
D.W. Jorgenson and B.M. Fraumeni
8.1. Introduction 371
8.2. Sources of Growth 373
8.3. Conclusion 385

9. Productivity Growth in U.S. Agriculture: A Postwar Perspective 389
D.W. Jorgenson and F.M. Gollop
9.1. Introduction 389

9.2. Patterns of Productivity Growth 391
9.3. Input Quality 397
9.4. Conclusion 399

References 401
Index 417

List of Tables

1.1	Growth in output and its sources, 1948–1979	3
1.2	Growth in sectoral output and its sources, 1948–1979	6
1.3	Growth in aggregate productivity and its sources, 1948–1979	10
1.4	Classification of industries by biases of productivity growth	15
2.1	Value shares and rates of growth	35
2.2	Indexes of embodied and disembodied technical change	36
2.3	Index of embodied technical change	38
2.4	Rates of growth and indexes of capital and surrogate capital	41
3.1	Total output, input, and factory productivity, U.S. private domestic economy, 1945–1965, initial estimates	69
3.2	Total output, input, and factor productivity, U.S. private domestic economy, 1945–1965, errors of aggregation eliminated	70
3.3	Alternate investment deflators	72
3.4	Total output, input, and factor productivity, U.S. private domestic economy, 1945–1965, errors in investment goods prices eliminated	74
3.5	Total input and factor productivity, U.S. private domestic economy, 1945–1965, errors in relative utilization eliminated	77
3.6	Total input and factor productivity, U.S. private domestic economy, 1945–1965, errors in aggregation of capital input eliminated; implicit rate of return after taxes	79
3.7	Relative prices, changes in distribution of the labor force, and indices of labor-input per man-hour, U.S. males, the civilian labor force, 1940–1964	82
3.8	Total input and factor productivity, U.S. private domestic economy 1945–1965, errors in aggregation of labor input eliminated	83
3.9	Total output, input, and factor productivity, U.S. private domestic economy, 1945–1965, average annual rates of growth	84
3.10	Relative utilization of electric motors, manufacturing, 1954 and 1962	92
3.11	Civilian labor force, males 18 to 64 years old, by educational attainment percent distribution by years of school completed	94
3.12	Mean annual earnings of males, 25 years and over by school years completed, selected years	95
4.1	Production account, gross private domestic product and factor outlay, United States, 1958	105

4.2 Gross private domestic product and factor outlay, 1950–1962 107
4.3 Gross private domestic product, 1950–62 108
4.4 Relative proportions of capital stock by sector, 1958 109
4.5 Benchmarks, rates of replacement, and price indices employed in estimating capital 111
4.6 Price indices by class of asset, 1950–1962 112
4.7 Evidence on drift in components of WPI 116
4.8 A comparison of OBE producers' durables investment deflators with census unit value indexes, 1962 117
4.9 Effective tax rates and rates of return, household and noncorporate sectors, 1950–1962 120
4.10 Tax structure and rate of return, corporate sector, 1950–1962 123
4.11 Potential gross private domestic capital input, 1950–1962 125
4.12 Relative utilization of electric motors, U.S. manufacturing, 1962 127
4.13 Equipment utilization indexes, mining industries, 1963 128
4.14 Selected utilization measures 129
4.15 Actual gross private domestic capital input, 1950–1962 131
4.16 Gross private domestic capital input, 1950–1962 132
4.17 Average hours worked per week by employed persons at work 135
4.18 Average weeks worked by males in the experienced civilian labor force 136
4.19 Private domestic labor input, 1950–1962 137
4.20 Gross private domestic factor input, 1950–1962 139
4.21 Sources of growth in factor input, 1950–1962 140
4.22 Total factor productivity, 1950–1962 141
4.23 Growth in total factor productivity, 1950–1962 142
4.24 The relative importance of productivity change, 1950–1962 143
4.25 Reconciliation of alternative estimates of growth in total factor productivity, 1950–1962 165

5.1 Production account, gross private domestic product and factor outlay, United States, 1958 182
5.2 Gross private domestic product and factor outlay, 1929–1969 184
5.3 Gross private national receipts and expenditures, 1958 187
5.4 Gross private national receipts and expenditures, 1929–1969 190
5.5 Gross private national capital formation, saving, and revaluation, 1958 191
5.6 Gross private national capital formation, saving, and revaluation, 1929–1969 193
5.7 Private national wealth, 1958 195
5.8 Private national wealth 1929–1969 196
5.9 Gross private domestic product, 1929–1969 226

5.10 Private domestic labor input, 1929–1969 229
5.11 Benchmarks, rates of replacement, and price indices employed in estimating capital 231
5.12 Relative proportions of capital stock by asset class and sector, 1958 235
5.13 Gross private domestic capital input, 1929–1969 241
5.14 Gross private domestic factor input, 1929–1969 243
5.15 Total factor productivity, 1929–1969 244
5.16 Relative importance of productivity change, 1929–1969 246
5.17 Private national consumption expenditures, consumer outlays, and national labor compensation, 1929–1969 249
5.18 Gross private national property compensation, rates of return, and effective rates of taxation, 1929–1969 252
5.19 Gross private national property compensation, 1929–1969 256
5.20 Gross private national capital formation, 1929–1969 259
5.21 Gross private national saving, depreciation, and revaluation, 1929–1969 262
5.22 Gross private national expenditures, receipts, and standard of living, 1929–1969 264
5.23 Private national wealth, 1929–1969 266

6.1 Production account, gross private domestic product and factor outlay, United States, 1982 283
6.2 Full investment (current dollars) 284
6.3 Full investment (constant dollars) 285
6.4 Full gross private domestic product (current dollars) 287
6.5 Full gross private domestic product (constant dollars) 288
6.6 Full gross private domestic product, rates of growth, 1949–1984 289
6.7 Full labor outlay (current dollars) 291
6.8 Full labor outlay (constant dollars) 292
6.9 Full gross private domestic factor outlay (current dollars) 293
6.10 Full gross domestic factor outlay (constant dollars) 294
6.11 Gross private national labor and property income, rates of growth, 1949–1984 295
6.12 Gross private national labor and property income, 1982 297
6.13 Full labor income (current dollars) 299
6.14 Full labor income (constant dollars) 300
6.15 Full private national income (current dollars) 301
6.16 Full private national Income (constant dollars) 302
6.17 Full private national income, rates of growth, 1949–1984 304
6.18 Gross private national receipts and expenditures, 1982 305
6.19 Full consumer outlays (current dollars) 306

6.20 Full consumer outlays (constant dollars) 307
6.21 Full gross private national saving (current dollars) 309
6.22 Full gross private national saving (constant dollars) 310
6.23 Full private national expenditures (current dollars) 311
6.24 Full private national expenditures (constant dollars) 312
6.25 Full private national expenditures, rates of growth, 1949–1984 313
6.26 Gross private national capital accumulation 1982 315
6.27 Full gross private national saving (current dollars) 316
6.28 Full gross private national saving (constant dollars) 317
6.29 Full gross private national saving, rates of growth, 1949–1984 319
6.30 Gross private national capital accumulation 320
6.31 Private national wealth, 1982 321
6.32 Full private national wealth (current dollars) 322
6.33 Full private national wealth (constant dollars) 323
6.34 Full private national wealth, rates of growth, 1949–1984 325
6.35 Private national human wealth, 1949–1969 326
6.36 Private national nonhuman wealth, 1949–1969 327
6.37 Full private national wealth, 1949–1969 328

7.1 School enrollment by sex and level, United States, 1947–1986 336
7.2 Value of market activities by sex and educational attainment, 1948–1987 (current dollars) 338
7.3 Value of market labor activities by sex and educational attainment, 1949–1987 (constant dollars) 339
7.4 Value of nonmarket activities by sex and educational attainment, 1948–1987 (current dollars) 341
7.5 Value of nonmarket labor activities by sex and educational attainment, 1949–1987 (constant dollars) 343
7.6 Investment in formal education by sex and level of environment, 1947–1986 (current dollars) 347
7.7 Investment in formal education by sex and level of enrollment, 1948–1986 (constant dollars) 348
7.8 Investment in formal education by sex and level of enrollment, 1947–1986 (current dollars) 350
7.9 Investment per student by sex and level of enrollment, 1947–1986 (current dollars) 352
7.10 Investment in formal education by sex and level of enrollment, market and nonmarket labor activities, 1948–1986 (constant dollars) 353
7.11 Percentage of investment based on market activities to total educational investment, 1947–1986 355
7.12 Human wealth by sex and educational attainment, 1947–1986 (current dollars) 356

7.13 Human wealth by sex and educational attainment, 1948–1986 (constant dollars) 357
7.14 Human wealth per person by sex and educational attainment, 1947–1986 (current dollars) 358
7.15 Human wealth per person by sex and educational attainment, (constant dollars) 359
7.16 Percentage of human wealth based on market labor activities to total human wealth by sex and educational attainment, 1947–1986 360
7.17 Comparison with other results 362

8.1 Sources of economic growth, noneducation sector, 1948–1986 373
8.2 Output, input, and productivity, noneducation sector, 1948–1986 374
8.3 Sources of economic growth, education sector, 1948–1986 377
8.4 Output, input, and productivity, education sector, 1948–1986 379
8.5 Sources of economic growth, U.S. economy, 1948–1986 381
8.6 Output, input, and productivity, U.S. economy, 1948–1986 382

9.1 Total factor productivity growth 390
9.2 Postwar trends: Agriculture and the private nonfarm economy 392
9.3 Contributions to economic growth 394
9.4 Input quality 396

Preface

Dale W. Jorgenson

This volume is devoted to postwar growth in the United States and is the first of two volumes containing my empirical studies of economic growth. Although the level of U.S. per capita output was higher than that of any other industrialized economy at the end of World War II, U.S. output has increased by more than four times and per capita output has more than doubled. By either measure the postwar growth performance of the U.S. economy has been outstanding. This volume documents in detail that investment is the predominant source of postwar U.S. economic growth.

A second volume, *International Comparisons of Economic Growth*, focuses on comparisons between the U.S. and Japan. This volume shows that the Asian model of economic growth exemplified by Japan gives even greater weight to investment and that investment is especially critical during periods of exceptionally rapid growth. Although the U.S. and Japan are often portrayed as economic adversaries, postwar experiences in both countries support policies that give high priority to stimulating and rewarding capital formation.

Jan Tinbergen (1942) was the first to divide the sources of economic growth between the two broad categories of investment and productivity. The comparative significance of these two components has dominated the voluminous literature on U.S. economic growth created during the postwar period. During the much discussed growth slowdown after 1973 it became apparent that protracted and sometimes acrimonious professional debates had failed to produce a consensus that could serve as a guide to economic policy.

Profound differences in policy implications militate against any simple resolution of the debate on the relative importance of investment and productivity. Proponents of income redistribution will not easily abandon the search for a "silver bullet" that will generate economic growth without the necessity of providing incentives for investment in tangible assets and human capital. Advocates of growth strategies based on capital formation will not readily give credence to claims of the importance of external benefits that "spill over" to beneficiaries that are difficult or impossible to identify.

To avoid the semantic confusion that pervades popular discussions of economic growth it is essential to be precise in distinguishing between investment and productivity. Investment is the commitment of current resources in the expectation of future returns and can take a multiplicity of forms. The distinctive feature of investment as a source of economic growth is that the returns can be internalized by the investor. The most straightforward application of this definition is to investments that create property rights, including rights to transfer the resulting assets and benefit from incomes that accrue to the owners.

Empirical research has gradually broadened the meaning of sources of growth to include investments that do not create property rights. For example, a student enrolled in school or a worker participating in a training program can be viewed as an investor. Although these investments do not create assets that can be bought or sold, the returns to higher educational qualifications or better skills in the workplace can be internalized. The contribution of investments in education and training to economic growth can be identified in the same way as for tangible assets.

The mechanism by which tangible investments are translated into economic growth is well understood. For example, an investor in a new industrial facility adds to the supply of assets and generates a stream of rental income. The investment and the income are linked through markets for capital assets and capital services. The income stream can be divided between the increase in capital input and the marginal product of capital or rental price. The increase in capital contributes to output growth in proportion to the marginal product.

Similarly, an individual who completes a course of education or training adds to the supply of people with higher qualifications or skills. The resulting income stream can be decomposed into a rise in labor input and the marginal product of labor or wage rate. The increase in labor contributes to output growth in proportion to the marginal product. Although there are no asset markets for human capital, investments in human and nonhuman capital have the common feature that returns are internalized by the investor.

The defining characteristic of productivity as a source of economic growth is that the incomes generated by higher productivity are external to the economic activities that generate growth. These benefits "spill over" to income recipients not involved in these activities, severing the connection between the creation of growth and the incomes that result. Since the benefits of policies to create externalities cannot be appropriated, these policies typically involve government programs or activities supported through public subsidies.

Publicly supported research and development programs are a leading illustration of policies to stimulate productivity growth. These programs can be conducted by government laboratories or financed by public subsidies to private laboratories. The justification for public financing is most persuasive for aspects of technology that cannot be fully appropriated, such as basic science and generic technology. The benefits of the resulting innovations are external to the economic units conducting the research and development.

Similarly, public investments in infrastructure can be justified by appealing to externalities associated with the use of public facilities. Improvement of public roads may relieve traffic congestion, but the returns can be appropriated only by limiting access to public facilities or monitoring the use of these facilities. This can be done for bridges, tunnels, and high density highways, but is more difficult for urban streets and low density highways. If access is unlimited, the benefits are external to the authority undertaking the investment.

Tangible investments are the most important sources of postwar U.S. economic growth. These investments appear on the balance sheets of firms, industries, and the nation as a whole as buildings, equipment, and inventories. The benefits of these investments appear on the income statements of these same economic units as profits, rents, and royalties. Investments in tangible assets are the primary focus of Chapters 1–5 and 9 below. My empirical studies of these investments and tax policies that affect them are presented in two companion volumes, *Capital Theory and Investment Behavior* and *Tax Policy and the Cost of Capital.*

Investments in human capital, especially through formal education, provide highly significant sources of postwar U.S. economic growth and are the focus of Chapters 6–8. These investments do not appear on the balance sheets of individuals receiving the education or the institutions providing it. However, increases in labor incomes make it possible to measure the investments and assess their contributions to economic growth. Chapter 1 summarizes the evidence that investments in tangible assets and human capital, taken together, account for the great preponderance of U.S. economic growth.

The starting point for my research on postwar U.S. economic growth was the aggregate production function employed by Paul Douglas (1928, 1948) and his associates. Tinbergen (1942) took a critical step beyond Douglas's original concept by adding a time trend interpreted as the level of "efficiency." Tinbergen analyzed the sources of U.S. economic growth over the period 1870–1914 and found that productivity accounted for slightly more than a quarter of U.S. economic growth during the period 1870–1914, while growth in capital and labor inputs accounted for about three-quarters. These proportions are very similar to those for postwar U.S. economic growth summarized in Chapter 1.

The notion of efficiency or total factor productivity was introduced independently by George Stigler (1947) and became the starting point for a major research program at the National Bureau of Economic Research. The National Bureau program resulted in important contributions by Moses Abramovitz (1956) and Solomon Fabricant (1959) and culminated in the monograph by John Kendrick (1961a), *Productivity Trends in the United States*. The conceptual framework of Douglas and Tinbergen was combined with data generated by Kendrick (1956) in Robert Solow's (1957) justly celebrated article, "Technical Change and the Aggregate Production Function."

The distinction between substitution and technical change emphasized by Solow parallels the distinction between investment and productivity as sources of economic growth. However, Solow's definition of investment was limited to tangible assets. He specifically excluded investments in human capital by omitting substitution among different types of labor inputs. Furthermore, Solow identified the contribution of tangible assets with increases in the stock, omitting substitution among different types of capital inputs. As a consequence, Solow attributed almost all of U.S. economic growth to "residual" growth in productivity.

My paper, "The Embodiment Hypothesis," published in 1966 and reprinted as Chapter 2 of this volume, took an initial step beyond the aggregate production function. I introduced a production possibility frontier, allowing for joint production of consumption and investment goods from capital and labor services, and employed this framework in generalizing Solow's (1960) concept of embodied technical change. I showed that economic growth could be interpreted, equivalently, as "embodied" in investment or "disembodied" in productivity growth.

My paper with Zvi Griliches, "The Explanation of Productivity Change," published in 1967 and reprinted as Chapter 3, identified embodiment empirically by introducing constant quality price indices for investment goods. This removed the indeterminacy in Solow's (1960) model. As a natural extension of Solow's (1956) one sector neoclassical model of economic growth, his model of embodiment had only a single output and did not allow for the introduction of a separate price index for investment goods.

Constant quality price indices for capital goods of different ages or vintages were developed by Robert Hall (1971). This important innovation made it possible for Hulten and Frank Wykoff (1981) to estimate relative efficiencies by age for all types of tangible assets included in the U.S. National Income and Product Accounts. The Hulten-Wykoff relative efficiencies were incorporated into capital stocks that I employed in the introductory chapter to this volume, "Productivity and Postwar U.S. Economic Growth."

For each type of investment Griliches and I defined the price of capital input as a rental price rather than an asset price, using a model of capital as a factor of production I had introduced in 1963. This made it possible to measure the marginal products of capital inputs directly. We incorporated differences in returns due to the tax treatment of capital income into a constant quality index of capital input and modeled the flow of capital services, relative to the stock, as the consequence of substitution among capital inputs.

Finally, Griliches and I combined different types of labor inputs, reflecting wage rates for workers with different levels of educational attainment, into a constant quality index of labor input. The methodology was based on a similar index that Griliches (1960) had developed for U.S. agriculture. Our index of labor input became the point of departure for a far more elaborate set of constant quality indices of labor input that I subsequently constructed with Frank Gollop (1980, 1983). These included characteristics of workers such as age, sex, occupation, class of employment and industry, as well as educational attainment.

In measuring productivity growth Griliches and I allowed for substitution between investment and consumption goods as outputs and capital and labor services as inputs. Our model of capital as a factor of production provided the conceptual framework for modeling substitution among capital inputs and permitted a detailed treatment of differences in returns on tangible assets. Finally, the parallel model of labor input encompassed substitution among labor inputs from workers with different levels of educational attainment.

The conclusion of the first phase of my research on postwar U.S. economic growth was that investments in human and nonhuman capital greatly predominated as sources of growth, while productivity played a clearly subordinate role. These findings were confirmed in my subsequent research with Laurits Christensen, described below, my 1987 book with Gollop and Fraumeni, *Productivity and U.S. Economic Growth*, summarized in Chapter 1, and my 1992 paper with Gollop, reprinted as Chapter 9.

The second stage of my research on postwar U.S. growth began with two papers I published in 1969 and 1970 with Laurits Christensen. These studies provided a much more detailed implementation of the concept of capital as a factor of production. We utilized a model of the tax structure for corporate capital income that I had developed in a series of papers with Hall (1967, 1971), reprinted in the volume *Tax Policy and the Cost of Capital*. Christensen and I extended this model to noncorporate and household capital incomes in order to capture differences in returns due to taxation.

In 1973 Christensen and I incorporated estimates of the sources of economic growth into a complete system of U.S. national accounts in our paper, "Measuring Economic Performance in the Private Sector," reprinted as Chapter 5 of this volume. The critical innovation in this accounting system was the construction of internally consistent income, product, and wealth accounts. The integration of income and product accounts is the major achievement of the United Nations System of National Accounts; however, this system does not include wealth accounts that are consistent with the income and product accounts.

Christensen and I distinguished two approaches to the analysis of economic growth. We identified the production possibility frontier with the production account. We identified a social welfare function with the income and expenditure account. We utilized data on inputs and outputs of production to allocate sources of economic growth between investment and productivity. We divided the uses of economic growth between current consumption and future consumption through saving by means of data on incomes and expenditures.

Saving is linked to the asset side of the wealth account through capital accumulation equations for each type of asset. These equations provide a perpetual inventory of assets accumulated at different points of time or different vintages. Prices for different vintages are linked to rental prices of capital inputs through a parallel set of capital asset pricing equations. The complete system of vintage accounts gives stocks of assets of each vintage and their prices. The stocks are cumulated to obtain asset quantities, while the prices are used to evaluate the stocks and derive rental prices.

Christensen and I implemented our vintage accounting system for the U.S. on an annual basis for the period 1929–1969. We constructed an internally consistent system of income, product, and wealth accounts, paralleling the U.S. National Income and Product Accounts. This generated the information required to implement both production and welfare approaches to the analysis of economic growth. Our system of vintage accounts also provides the conceptual underpinnings for measurements of investment in human capital described in more detail below.

An important objective of the Christensen-Jorgenson accounting system was to provide the data for econometric modeling of producer and consumer behavior. In collaboration with Lawrence Lau, Christensen and I introduced an econometric model of producer behavior based on the translog production possibility frontier in a paper published in 1973 and reprinted in the companion volume, *Econometrics and Producer Behavior*. We modeled joint production of consumption and investment goods from inputs of capital and labor services, utilizing data on these outputs and inputs from the production account.

Subsequently, Christensen, Lau, and I constructed an econometric model of consumer behavior based on the translog indirect utility function. We estimated this model on the basis of data from the income and expenditure account of the Christensen-Jorgenson accounting system. Diewert (1976) showed that the Tornqvist (1936) index numbers employed in the this system are "exact" for the translog production possibility frontier and indirect utility function.

Yun and I constructed a complete econometric model for postwar

U.S. economic growth in a paper published in 1986 and reprinted in the companion volume, *Tax Policy and the Cost of Capital*. We based our model of producer behavior on the translog production possibility frontier and our model of consumer behavior on the translog indirect utility function. Finally, we derived a social welfare function for evaluating alternative tax policies and analyzed the consequences of the Tax Reform Act of 1986 on U.S. economic growth in a paper published in 1990 and also reprinted in *Tax Policy and the Cost of Capital*.

Griliches and I utilized the production estimates from my papers with Christensen for the period 1950–1962 in our reply to a critique of our 1967 paper by Denison (1969). This reply was published in 1972 and is reprinted as Chapter 4 of this volume. We showed that Denison had confounded the production and welfare approaches to economic growth. He employed the concept of income, constructed from the welfare approach, as a measure of output. This concept is appropriate for analyzing the uses of economic growth, but inappropriate for analyzing the sources of growth.

The most important innovation of the second phase of my research on postwar U.S. economic growth was the development of two separate perspectives on the analysis of economic growth. The production approach requires data on outputs and inputs and allocates the sources of growth of output between investment and productivity. The welfare approach requires data on income and expenditure and allocates the uses of growth of income between consumption and saving. Once these two approaches are distinguished, the data to implement them can be generated within the accounting system Christensen and I have presented in Chapter 4.

The implementation of the welfare and production approaches to economic growth required the solution of a long-standing problem in national accounting. This is the integration of wealth accounts with income and product accounts. The solution of this problem was achieved by means of the vintage accounting system presented in my paper with Christensen. This system provided the data on assets and asset prices that underly production, income and expenditure, and wealth accounts.

The third stage in my research on postwar growth was to disaggregate the sources of U.S. economic growth to the level of individual industries. This was accomplished in my papers with Gollop (1980,

1983) and Fraumeni (1980, 1986). These papers dispensed with the aggregate production function, giving value added as a function of capital and labor inputs as well as productivity. We defined industry output as a function of productivity and capital, labor, and intermediate inputs, avoiding the artificial construct of value added at the industry level employed, for example, by Kendrick (1961a).

Gollop and I (1980) presented production accounts for fifty-one industrial sectors of the U.S. economy, including output for each sector and capital, labor, and intermediate inputs in both current and constant prices. Intermediate input consists of goods and services produced by other sectors, while capital and labor inputs are defined in the same way as at the aggregate level. We disaggregated intermediate input by industry of origin, integrating the U.S. inter-industry transactions accounts with the U.S. national product accounts.

Gollop and I disaggregated the model of capital services employed in my work with Christensen to include twenty categories of producers' durable equipment and fourteen categories of nonresidential structures and generated this information for individual industries. We also disaggregated labor input by two sexes, eight age groups, five educational attainment levels, two employment classes, and ten occupational categories within each sector. Our data on labor input combined the establishment surveys underlying the U.S. National Income and Product Accounts with household surveys from the Census of Population and the Current Population Survey.

My 1980 paper on "Accounting for Capital" extended the vintage accounting system I had developed with Christensen to include both sectoral and aggregate production accounts. Fraumeni and I implemented this new accounting system for the U.S., covering the period 1948–1973. In 1987 we published updated data on sectoral and aggregate production accounts in our book with Gollop, *Productivity and U.S. Economic Growth*. This book contains by far the most detailed data ever compiled on productivity in the U.S. economy. The results are summarized in Chapter 1.

Given the relative importance of intermediate input in the value of output in most industrial sectors, it is not surprising that this is the predominant source of growth at the sectoral level, exceeding both productivity growth and the contributions of capital and labor inputs. The contributions of these two inputs are substantially more important than productivity growth for almost every sector. The data from *Productivity and U.S. Economic Growth* have been updated through 1985 in my 1992 paper with Gollop, reprinted as Chapter 9.

My 1992 paper with Gollop is devoted to comparisons between sources of growth in the outputs of U.S. agriculture and nonagricultural industries over the period 1947–1985. This comparison showed that agriculture is an important exception to the findings presented in Chapter 1. Productivity clearly predominates among the sources of growth of this industry, accounting for eighty-two percent of postwar growth. By contrast productivity accounts for only thirteen percent of growth in the private nonfarm sector of the U.S. economy.

My 1980 paper also presented a methodology for aggregating over sectors. The existence of an aggregate production function imposes very stringent conditions on production patterns at the industry level. In addition to value added functions for each sector, an aggregate production function posits that these functions must be identical. Furthermore, the functions relating sectoral capital and labor inputs to their components must be identical and each component must receive the same price in all sectors. Aggregation over sectors has also been discussed by Evsey Domar (1961) and Hulten (1978).

The data for sectoral production accounts can be generated in a way that avoids the highly restrictive assumptions that underly the aggregate production function. These data can then be compared with those from the aggregate production account to test for the existence of an aggregate production function. In Chapter 1 I show that this hypothesis is inconsistent with empirical evidence. Gollop, Fraumeni, and I have also presented statistical tests of the much weaker hypothesis that value added functions exist for industrial sectors, but this hypothesis is also rejected.

An important objective of my book with Gollop and Fraumeni was to generate data for econometric modeling of producer behavior at the sectoral level. In 1981 I developed a general equilibrium model of production with Fraumeni, including econometric models of production for thirty-five industrial groups. These models represented the rate of productivity growth in each sector as well as the technical coefficients as functions of relative prices. Production models with these features were incorporated into an econometric model of the U.S. economy I constructed with Peter Wilcoxen and presented in papers reprinted in the accompanying volume, *Econometric General Equilibrium Modeling*.

The conclusion of my research on production at the sectoral level is that specifications of technology such as the aggregate production function and sectoral valued added functions result in substantial oversimplifications of the empirical evidence. However, these specifications are useful for particular but limited purposes. The aggregate production function is a worthwhile simplification in modeling long-run growth at the aggregate level and sectoral value added functions are essential for aggregating over sectors.

A satisfactory analysis of the sources of postwar U.S. economic growth at the sectoral level requires a flexible approach. Rather than imposing the assumptions required for an aggregate production function, capital, labor, and intermediate inputs must be treated symmetrically. This framework is also the most appropriate starting point for econometric modeling of producer behavior at the sectoral level. Studies presenting models of this type are summarized in my 1986 survey paper, "Econometric Methods for Modeling Producer Behavior," reprinted as Chapter 1 in the companion volume, *Econometrics and Producer Behavior*.

An important limitation of the framework of Abramovitz, Kendrick, and Solow is that the implied definition of investment specifically excludes investments in human capital. Increases in labor inputs resulting from investments by individuals in their own education and training are allocated to productivity growth. This has some intuitive appeal within a framework based on welfare rather than production, since effort is related to hours worked at the individual level. However, a constant quality measure of labor input is essential for the production approach to economic growth.

Constant quality indices of labor input were developed by Griliches (1960) for U.S. agriculture and Denison (1962) for the U.S. economy as a whole. My 1967 paper with Griliches presented a constant quality index for labor input focusing on differences in educational attainment among workers. My subsequent papers with Gollop (1980, 1983) gave constant quality indices of labor input for fifty-one industrial sectors of the U.S. economy. We disaggregated labor input for each industry by age, sex, educational attainment, class of employment, and occupation. This required the creation of an extensive data base giving hours worked and hourly compensation for individual categories of labor input.

Constant quality indices of labor input are an essential first step in incorporating investments in human capital into empirical studies of economic growth. However, completion of this task requires the measurement of these investments as an output of the U.S. economy. In 1989 Fraumeni and I extended the vintage accounting system developed in my work with Christensen to incorporate investments in human capital in a paper reprinted as Chapter 6 below. Our essential idea was to treat individual members of the U.S. population as human assets with "prices" given by their lifetime labor incomes.

The starting point for our measurements of lifetime labor incomes was the data base on market labor activities assembled in my papers with Gollop (1980, 1983). We first integrated our labor data base with a system of demographic accounts for the U.S. population constructed by Marilyn McMillen and Kenneth Land (1980). Our system of demographic accounts included the enrollment status for all individuals between five and thirty-four years of age and employment status for individuals between fourteen and seventy-four years of age.

We derived annual estimates of hours worked and hourly labor compensation classified by two sexes, individual years of age, and individual years of educational attainment. For each of these categories we constructed estimates of lifetime incomes from market labor activities. We then estimated hours devoted to nonmarket activities by allocating the total time available among work, schooling, household production and leisure, and maintenance. Finally, we imputed hourly labor compensation for nonmarket activities by reducing market wage rates by marginal tax rates on labor incomes and estimated lifetime incomes for nonmarket activities as well.

Fraumeni and I implemented our vintage accounting system for both human and nonhuman capital for the U.S. on an annual basis for the period 1948–1984. Asset prices for tangible assets can be observed directly from market transactions in investment goods; capital asset pricing equations are used to derive rental prices for capital services. For human capital wage rates correspond to rental prices and can be observed directly from transactions in the labor market. Lifetime labor incomes are derived by applying asset pricing equations to these wage rates. These incomes are analogous to the asset prices used in accounting for tangible assets.

Given our vintage accounts for human and nonhuman capital, Fraumeni and I constructed a system of income, product, and wealth accounts, paralleling the system I had developed with Christensen. In these accounts the value of human wealth was more than ten times the value of nonhuman wealth, while investment in human capital was five times investment in tangible assets. We defined "full" investment in the U.S. economy as the sum of these two types of investment. Similarly, we added the value of nonmarket labor activities to personal consumption expenditures to obtain "full" consumption. Our product measure included these new measures of investment and consumption.

Since our complete accounting system included a production account with "full" measures of capital and labor inputs, we were able to generate a new set of accounts for the sources of U.S. economic growth. Our system also included an income and expenditure account with income from labor services in both market and nonmarket activities. We combined this with income from capital services and allocated "full" income between consumption and saving. This provided a new set of accounts for the uses of U.S. economic growth. Our system was completed by a wealth account containing human wealth and tangible assets.

In 1992 Fraumeni and I developed a measure of the output of the U.S. education sector in a paper reprinted as Chapter 7. Our point of departure was that while education is a service industry, its output is investment in human capital. We estimated investment in education from the impact of increases in educational attainment on the lifetime incomes of all individuals enrolled in school. We found that investment in education, measured in this way, is similar in magnitude to the value of working time for all individuals in the labor force. Furthermore, the growth of investment in education during the postwar period exceeded the growth of market labor activities.

Second, we measured the inputs of the education sector, beginning with the purchased inputs recorded in the outlays of educational institutions, in a paper reprinted as Chapter 8. A major part of the value of the output of educational institutions accrues to students in the form of increases in their lifetime incomes. Treating these increases as compensation for student time, we evaluated this time as an input into the educational process. Given the outlays of educational institutions and the value of student time, we allocated the growth of the education sector to its sources.

We aggregated the growth of education and noneducation sectors of the U.S. economy to obtain a new measure of U.S. economic growth. Combining this with measures of input growth, we obtained a new set of accounts for sources of growth of the U.S. economy. Productivity contributes almost nothing to the growth of the education sector and only a modest proportion to output growth for the economy as a whole. Our overall conclusion is that investment in human and nonhuman capital accounts for an overwhelming proportion of postwar U.S. economic growth.

The accumulation of empirical evidence presented in this volume has gradually shifted the terms of the professional debate over the importance of investment and productivity as sources of postwar U.S. economic growth. My paper, "Productivity and Postwar U.S. Economic Growth," reprinted as Chapter 1 of this volume, summarizes the findings in my 1987 book with Frank Gollop and Barbara Fraumeni, *Productivity and U.S. Economic Growth.* This chapter shows that productivity accounts for less than a quarter of the growth of U.S. economy during the period 1948–1979, while growth of capital and labor inputs accounts for more than three-quarters.

I would like to thank June Wynn of the Department of Economics at Harvard University for her excellent work in assembling the manuscripts for this volume in machine-readable form. Renate d'Arcangelo of the Editorial Office of the Division of Applied Sciences at Harvard edited the manuscripts, proofread the machine-readable versions and prepared them for typesetting. Warren Hrung, a senior at Harvard College, checked the references and proofread successive versions of the typescript. Gary Bisbee of Chiron Inc. typeset the manuscript and provided the camera-ready copy for publication. The staff of the MIT Press, especially Terry Vaughn, Ann Sochi, and Michael Sims, has been very helpful at every stage of the project. I am also grateful to William Richardson and his associates for providing the index. Financial support from the Program on Technology and Economic Policy at the Kennedy School of Government, Harvard University, is gratefully acknowledged. As always, the author retains sole responsibility for any remaining deficiencies in the volume.

List of Sources

1. Dale W. Jorgenson 1988. Productivity and Postwar U.S. Economic Growth. *Journal of Economic Perspectives* 2, No. 4 (Fall): 23–42.

2. Dale W. Jorgenson 1966. The Embodiment Hypothesis. *Journal of Political Economy* 74, No. 1 (February): 1–17. Reprinted with permission of the University of Chicago Press.

3. Dale W. Jorgenson and Zvi Griliches 1967. The Explanation of Productivity Change. *Review of Economic Studies* 34, No. 99 (July): 249–280.

4. Dale W. Jorgenson and Zvi Griliches 1972. Issues in Growth Accounting: A Reply to Edward F. Denison. *Survey of Current Business* 52, No. 5, Part II (May): 65–94.

5. Laurits R. Christensen and Dale W. Jorgenson 1973. Measuring Economic Performance in the Private Sector. In *The Measurement of Economic and Social Performance*, ed. M. Moss. Studies in Income and Wealth, vol. 37. New York, NY: Columbia University Press.

6. Dale W. Jorgenson and Barbara M. Fraumeni 1989. The Accumulation of Human and Nonhuman Capital, 1948–84. *The Measurement of Saving, Investment, and Wealth*, eds. R. E. Lipsey and H. S. Tice. Studies in Income and Wealth, vol. 52. Chicago, IL: University of Chicago Press. Reprinted with permission of the University of Chicago Press.

7. Dale W. Jorgenson and Barbara M. Fraumeni 1992. The Output of the Education Sector. *Output Measurement in the Services Sector*, ed. Z. Griliches. Studies in Income and Wealth, vol. 55. Chicago, IL: University of Chicago Press. Reprinted with permission of the University of Chicago Press.

8. Dale W. Jorgenson and Barbara M. Fraumeni 1992. Investment in Education and U.S. Economic Growth. *Scandinavian Journal of Economics* 94, Supplement: 51–70.

9. Dale W. Jorgenson and Frank M. Gollop 1992. Productivity Growth in U.S. Agriculture: A Postwar Perspective. *American Journal of Agricultural Economics* 74, No. 3 (August): 745–750. Reprinted with permission of the American Journal of Agricultural Economics.

1 Productivity and Postwar U.S. Economic Growth

Dale W. Jorgenson

1.1 Introduction

The purpose of this chapter is to analyze the sources of postwar U.S. economic growth. The analysis of sources of economic growth originated in a notable but neglected article by Tinbergen (1942).[1] Among the many remarkable features of Tinbergen's study was an international comparison of growth of output, primary factor input, and total factor productivity for France, Germany, the United Kingdom, and the United States for the period 1870–1914. For the United States, Tinbergen found that the growth of output averaged 4.1 percent per year, the growth of input was 3.0 percent, while productivity growth averaged 1.1 percent. Productivity accounted for only 27 percent of U.S. economic growth during the period 1870–1914.

The findings presented here allocate more than three-fourths of U.S. economic growth during the period 1948–1979 to growth of capital and labor inputs and less than one-fourth to productivity growth. These findings coincide with those of Christensen and Jorgenson (1973a) for the period 1929–1969 and the much earlier findings of Tinbergen (1942) for the period 1870–1914. Perhaps surprisingly, many studies of aggregate U.S. economic growth, such as those of Abramovitz (1956) and Solow (1957), have placed greater emphasis on productivity growth than mobilization of capital and labor resources. This is in spite of the fact that the studies have generally allocated about half of economic growth to resource mobilization and half to productivity growth.

To provide additional insight into the sources of U.S. economic growth, this chapter then analyzes the sources of growth for individual industrial sectors. The rate of output growth for individual industries is decomposed between the contributions of capital, labor, and intermediate inputs and the growth of sectoral productivity. We find that the contributions of the three inputs account for an overwhelming proportion of the growth of industry output. The final step in this analysis of sources of economic growth is to integrate the sources of output growth for individual industries with sources of growth for the economy as a whole. This enables us to decompose the rate of aggregate productivity growth into a weighted sum of sectoral productivity growth rates and the contributions of reallocations of output and inputs among sectors.

Denison (1985) has analyzed the slowdown in U.S. economic growth since 1973, using an aggregate model of production. He has attributed the slowdown primarily to the decline in aggregate productivity growth. The results presented here bear out his conclusion. The decline in the rate of aggregate productivity growth accounts for 80 percent of the decline in the rate of growth of output. In addition, we find that the slowdown in productivity growth for the economy as a whole is fully explained by the decline in productivity growth at the sectoral level.

However, the decline in economic growth would be left unexplained without an econometric model to determine the rate of productivity growth. Thus, the final objective of this chapter is to complete the explanation of the slowdown in U.S. economic growth that took place after 1973. For this purpose we examine econometric models for individual industrial sectors that make the rate of productivity growth for each sector into an endogenous variable. In addition, these models incorporate inputs of energy and materials along with inputs of capital and labor. The models show that higher energy prices are important in explaining the slowdown in U.S. economic growth. An aggregate model of production would fail to establish the critical role of the increase in energy prices after 1973, since energy is excluded as an input at the aggregate level by assumption.

1.2 Sources of U.S. Economic Growth

Table 1.1 allocates aggregate output growth between growth in capital and labor inputs and changes in productivity. The growth rate of output is the sum of the contributions of capital and labor inputs and the rate of productivity growth. The contribution of each input is the

Table 1.1
Growth in output and its sources, 1948–1979 (measured by average annual rates of growth)

	1948–1979	1948–1953	1953–1957	1957–1960	1960–1966	1966–1969	1969–1973	1973–1979
Value added	.0342	.0404	.0302	.0274	.0444	.0326	.0308	.0283
Contribution of capital input	.0156	.0195	.0153	.0105	.0145	.0190	.0156	.0144
Contribution of labor input	.0105	.0124	.0035	.0084	.0141	.0134	.0095	.0105

Source: Jorgenson, Gollop, and Fraumeni (1987).

product of the value share of the input and its growth rate. The first panel of table 1.1 compares growth of output with the contributions of the two primary factor inputs and with productivity growth for the period 1948–1979 and for seven subperiods—1948–1953, 1953–1957, 1957–1960, 1960–1966, 1966–1969, 1969–1973, and 1973–1979.

The endpoints of the periods identified in table 1.1 are years in which a cyclical peak occurred. The growth rate presented for each period is the average annual growth rate between cyclical peaks. Capital and labor inputs combined contributed 2.6 percent per year to the output growth rate of 3.4 percent from 1948 to 1979. These two inputs accounted for more than three-fourths of output growth. By contrast, productivity advances contributed only 0.8 percent per year, or only 24 percent of output growth, during this period. The contribution of capital and labor inputs is the predominant source of U.S. economic growth for the period as a whole and all seven subperiods.

Comparing the contribution of capital input with other sources of output growth for the period 1948–1979 as a whole makes clear that capital input is the most significant source of growth. The contribution of capital input is also the most important source of growth for six of the seven subperiods, while productivity growth is the most important source for only one, 1960–1966. The contribution of capital input exceeds the contribution of labor input for all seven subperiods, while the contribution of labor input exceeds productivity growth in four of the seven subperiods.

In 1979, the output of the civilian economy stood at almost three times the level of output in 1948. The overall conclusion from this evidence is that the driving force behind the expansion of the U.S. economy between 1948 and 1979 has been the growth in capital and labor inputs. Growth in capital input is the most important source of growth in output, growth in labor input is the next most important source, and productivity growth is least important. Clearly, this perspective focuses attention on the mobilization of capital and labor resources rather than advances in productivity.

Table 1.1 allocates the sources of U.S. economic growth among contributions of growth in capital and labor inputs, and changes in productivity at the aggregate level. However, a major accomplishment of recent research on the sources of U.S. economic growth is the integration of the growth of intermediate, capital, and labor inputs at the level of individual industrial sectors into the analysis of the sources of growth for the economy as a whole. This makes it possible to attribute U.S. economic growth to its sources at the level of individual industries.

The analysis of sources of growth at the industry level is based on the decomposition of the growth rate of sectoral output into the sum of the contributions of intermediate, capital and labor inputs and the growth of sectoral productivity. The contribution of each input is the product of the value share of the input and its growth rate. Table 1.2 compares the growth rate of output with the contributions of the three inputs and the growth of productivity for the period 1948–1979. The sum of the contributions of intermediate, capital, and labor inputs is the predominant source of growth of output for 46 of the 51 industries included in table 1.2.

Comparing the contribution of intermediate input with other sources of output growth demonstrates that this input is by far the most significant source of growth. The contribution of intermediate input exceeds productivity growth and the contributions of capital and labor inputs. If we focus attention on the contributions of capital and labor inputs alone, excluding intermediate input from consideration, these two inputs are a more important source of growth than changes in productivity.

The perspective on U.S. economic growth suggested by the results presented in table 1.2 emphasizes the contribution of mobilization of resources within individual industries rather than productivity growth. The explanatory power of this perspective is overwhelming at the sectoral level. For 46 of the 51 industrial sectors included in table 1.2, the contribution of intermediate, capital, and labor inputs is the predominant source of output growth. Changes in productivity account for the major portion of output growth in only five industries.

An important feature of productivity growth at the sectoral level is that rates of productivity growth are negative over the period 1948–1979 for a number of industries. These negative growth rates represent a decline in the overall efficiency of production. Some of these declines may be the consequence of the drastic changes in relative prices of capital, labor, and intermediate inputs, especially after the energy crisis of 1973. Cost minimizing firms may have conserved energy by reverting to much earlier vintages of technology for energy utilization. Thus, energy conservation to minimize cost could have resulted in a decline in overall efficiency.

Table 1.2
Growth in sectoral output and its sources, 1948–1979 (average annual rates of growth)

		Contributions to Growth in Output			
Industry	Output	Intermediate Input	Capital Input	Labor Input	Rate of Productivity Growth
Agricultural production	.0216	.0128	.0040	−.0097	.0146
Agricultural services	.0297	.0173	.0068	.0111	−.0055
Metal mining	.0142	.0075	.0127	−.0004	−.0056
Coal mining	.0038	.0112	.0069	−.0116	−.0027
Crude petroleum and natural gas	.0213	.0291	.0104	.0031	−.0214
Nonmetallic mining and quarrying	.0409	.0153	.0178	.0039	.0038
Contract construction	.0271	.0169	.0022	.0074	.0006
Food and kindred products	.0281	.0134	.0018	−.0002	.0131
Tobacco manufacturers	.0072	.0116	.0039	−.0015	−.0068
Textile mill products	.0345	.0157	.0026	−.0030	.0192
Apparel and other fabricated textile products	.0264	.0130	.0016	.0009	.0109
Paper and allied products	.0401	.0322	.0054	.0041	−.0016
Printing and publishing	.0323	.0176	.0023	.0066	.0058
Chemicals and allied products	.0591	.0329	.0091	.0050	.0121
Petroleum and coal products	.0271	.0422	.0024	.0005	−.0179
Rubber and miscellaneous plastic products	.0477	.0259	.0062	.0113	.0043
Leather and leather products	−.0047	−.0023	.0005	−.0054	.0025
Lumber and wood products, except furniture	.0288	.0245	.0045	−.0011	.0009
Furniture and fixtures	.0373	.0281	.0029	.0038	.0026
Stone, clay, and glass products	.0382	.0281	.0057	.0038	.0007
Primary metal industries	.0128	.0154	.0023	.0110	−.0059
Fabricated metal industries	.0350	.0200	.0037	.0062	.0050
Machinery, except electrical	.0417	.0240	.0062	.0080	.0036
Electrical machinery, equipment, and supplies	.0580	.0262	.0058	.0102	.0158
Transportation equipment, except motor vehicles	.0559	.0408	.0013	.0100	.0039
Motor vehicles and equipment	.0451	.0285	.0053	.0022	.0091
Professional photographic equipment and watches	.0569	.0217	.0102	.0170	.0081
Miscellaneous manufacturing industries	.0340	.0243	.0037	.0015	.0046
Railroads and railway express service	.0053	−.0046	.0019	−.0108	.0187
Street railways, bus lines, and taxicabs	−.0217	−.0063	.0036	−.0044	−.0147

Table 1.2 (continued)

Industry	Output	Contributions to Growth in Output: Intermediate Input	Capital Input	Labor Input	Rate of Productivity Growth
Trucking services and warehousing	.0488	.0222	.0072	.0078	.0116
Water transportation	.0040	.0058	.0011	–.0019	–.0009
Air transportation	.0957	.0421	.0103	.0153	.0281
Pipelines, except natural gas	.0493	.0133	.0282	–.0014	.0093
Transportation services	.0268	.0488	.0034	.0049	–.0304
Telephone, telegraph, and miscellaneous communications services	.0688	.0077	.0234	.0087	.0290
Radio broadcasting and television	.0132	–.0064	.0185	.0216	–.0205
Electric utilities	.0628	.0227	.0275	.0034	.0092
Gas utilities	.0531	.0403	.0106	.0024	–.0001
Water supply and sanitary services	.0328	–.0031	–.0001	.0048	.0312
Wholesale trade	.0425	.0064	.0090	.0127	.0145
Retail trade	.0293	.0091	.0043	.0056	.0103
Finance, insurance, and real estate	.0493	.0341	.0031	.0076	.0044
Services, excluding private households and institutions	.0377	.0286	.0064	.0078	–.0052
Private households	.0491		.0499	–.0008	
Institutions	.0373	.0146	.0105	.0182	–.0059
Federal public administration	.0173			.0173	
Federal government enterprises	.0141			.0141	
State and local educational services	.0457			.0457	
State and local public administration	.0362			.0362	
State and local enterprises	.0363			.0363	

Source: Jorgenson, Gollop, and Fraumeni (1987).

1.3 Aggregation over Sectors

The measures of aggregate output, input, and productivity presented in table 1.1 are derived by explicit aggregation over the industrial sectors listed in table 1.2. However, the analysis of sources of growth for the U.S. economy as a whole presented in table 1.1 is based on a much more restrictive methodology for productivity measurement than the analysis of sources of growth for individual industries given in table 1.2. By comparing the two sets of results we can assess the validity of the more restrictive approach employed at the aggregate level.

The methodology we have employed for the economy as a whole is based on an aggregate production function. The existence of an aggregate production function implies very stringent limitations on the underlying sectoral models of production. In particular, we must introduce the concept of value added at the sectoral level.[2] The first step is to define value added as a function of capital and labor inputs and the level of productivity. We then express the output of each industrial sector as a function of value added and intermediate input. The separate effects of changes in capital and labor inputs and changes in productivity are transmitted to the level of output through changes in value added. The concept of value added is implicit in the analysis of sources of economic growth for the U.S. economy as a whole presented in table 1.1 and all studies at the aggregate level, beginning with Tinbergen (1942).

One can combine value added functions for all industrial sectors with market equilibrium conditions for each factor of production to obtain an aggregate model of production. Aggregate value added is the sum of quantities of value added in all sectors. Market equilibrium conditions take the form of equalities between the supplies of each type of labor and the sums of demands for that type of labor by all sectors. Similarly, market equilibrium implies equalities between the supplies of each type of capital and the sums of demands for that type of capital by all sectors.

The existence of an aggregate production function imposes additional requirements on the underlying sectoral models or production, too.[3] All sectoral value added functions must be identical to the aggregate production function.[4] In addition, the functions giving capital and labor inputs for each sector in terms of their components must be identical to the corresponding functions at the aggregate level. In essence, the value added function and the capital and labor input functions for each sector must be replicas of the aggregate functions.

The measures of value added, capital input, and labor input presented in table 1.1 are constructed from unweighted sums of value added, components of capital input, and components of labor input over all industries. An alternative measure of aggregate value added can be constructed by weighting value added in each industry by the price of value added in that industry. Similarly, alternative measures of aggregate capital and labor inputs can be constructed by weighting individual components of these inputs in each industry by the prices of these components in that industry.

Differences between growth rates of measures of output and input that reflect differences in prices among industries and measures that do not reflect these differences are presented in table 1.3. Differences in these growth rates can be interpreted as the contributions of reallocations of value added, capital input, and labor input among sectors to aggregate productivity growth. For example, if labor input is reallocated from a sector with high wages to a sector with low wages, the rate of aggregate productivity growth increases with no corresponding increase in the rates of sectoral productivity growth. The rate of aggregate productivity growth can be represented as a weighted sum of sectoral productivity growth rates and the reallocations of value added and capital and labor inputs.

Reallocations of value added incorporate differences in value added functions among industries. The reallocation also incorporates departures from the assumptions required for the existence of a value added function for each industrial sector. Similarly, reallocations of capital and labor inputs incorporate differences in these aggregates among sectors as well as departures from the assumptions required for the existence of these aggregates within each sector. If the prices of value added, capital input, and labor input were the same for all industries or if value added and all capital and labor inputs were to grow at the same rate, all the reallocations would vanish.

The data presented in table 1.3 make it possible to asses the significance of departures from the assumptions that underlie the aggregate model of production. Over the period 1948–1979 the reallocations are very small relative to the growth of capital and labor inputs and productivity growth. These results show that an aggregate production model may be appropriate for study of long-term U.S. economic growth. However, an aggregate model can be seriously misleading for relatively short time periods, such as the individual business cycles 1948–1953, 1966–1969, and 1973–1979.[5]

More specifically, the rate of aggregate productivity growth is 0.81 percent per year, while the weighted sum of sectoral productivity growth rates is 0.83 percent per year for the period 1948–1979 as a whole. The difference between the aggregate productivity growth rate and the weighted sum of sectoral productivity growth rates provides a measure of departures from the stringent assumptions that underlie the aggregate production model. This difference is equal to the sum of the reallocations of outputs and inputs among sectors. The difference is small, but not negligible, for the period 1948–1979.

Table 1.3
Growth in aggregate productivity and its sources, 1948–1979 (average annual rates of growth)

Variable	1948–1979	1948–1953	1953–1957	1957–1960	1960–1966	1966–1969	1969–1973	1973–1979
Rate of productivity growth	.0081	.0085	.0113	.0084	.0159	.0002	.0058	.0034
Rate of sectoral productivity growth	.0083	.0177	.1470	.0115	.0162	.0013	.0044	–.0072
Reallocation of value added	–.0009	–.0088	–.0040	–.0016	–.0022	–.0019	.0014	.0087
Reallocation of capital input	.0009	–.0001	.0020	.0015	.0018	.0012	.0009	–.0001
Reallocation of labor input	–.0002	–.0002	–.0014	–.0030	.0000	–.0004	–.0009	.0021

Source: Jorgenson, Gollop, and Fraumeni (1987).

1.3.1 Departures from the Aggregate Production Model

To illustrate the limitations of the aggregate production model, consider the slowdown in U.S. economic growth since 1973. For the period 1948–1979 the annual growth rate averages 3.42 percent. During the subperiod 1973–1979 the average growth rate is only 2.83 percent, a decline of 0.59 percent. The contribution of capital input declined 0.12 percent per year between the two periods, while the contribution of labor input was unchanged at 1.05 percent. By contrast, the decline in the productivity growth rate was 0.47 percent, almost four-fifths of the decline in the growth rate of output. We conclude that the most important factor in the slowdown is the decline in productivity growth.

We can decompose the decline in the aggregate productivity growth rate into the weighted sum of sectoral productivity growth rates and the reallocations of value added, capital input, and labor input. The decline in sectoral productivity growth between the period 1948–1979 and the subperiods 1973–1979 was 1.55 percent per year. This decline is more than sufficient to account for the slowdown in U.S. economic growth. The precipitous fall in sectoral productivity growth was masked at the aggregate level by increases in the reallocations of value added and labor input of 0.96 percent and 0.23 percent, respectively. The reallocations of capital input declined by 0.10 percent.

The conclusion should be clear: The assumptions that underlie the aggregate model of production fail to hold during the period 1973–1979. Unfortunately, this model has been used by Denison and other analysts as the sole basis for assessing the determinants of the slowdown in U.S. economic growth during this period. Since the stringent assumptions required for the validity of the model fail to hold during the period, this assessment of the causes of the slowdown can be seriously misleading.

1.4 Econometric Modeling of Production

The previous section shows that the slowdown in U.S. economic growth since 1973 can be attributed to a decline in aggregate productivity growth. Closer analysis reveals that this decline can be traced, in turn, to slower growth in productivity at the level of individual industries. However, in the absence of an econometric model to explain the rate of productivity growth at the sectoral level, the decline in U.S. economic growth would be left unexplained.

A wide variety of alternative production models are available for both aggregate and sectoral production modeling. The aggregate production model introduced by Cobb and Douglas (1928) and developed by Tinbergen (1942) retains its usefulness in modeling long-term growth trends. However, the critical evidence provided by the energy crises of the 1970s has exposed important empirical limitations of aggregate production modeling. These limitations cannot be overcome by introducing additional complexity at the aggregate level. In short, sectoral production models are essential in assimilating the important new evidence on patterns of production made available by the energy crisis of the 1970s and its aftermath.

The benefits of an aggregate production model must be weighed against the costs of departure from the highly restrictive assumptions that underlie the existence of an aggregate production function. We have shown that these assumptions are inappropriate during the period 1973–1979. Where an aggregate model of production is inappropriate, an econometric approach based on sectoral models of production can be employed in analyzing patterns of production for the economy as a whole.

1.4.1 Sectoral Production Modeling

I will argue that the decline in productivity growth at the level of individual industries is the main culprit in the slowdown of U.S. economic growth since 1973. Thus, to provide an explanation of this decline requires identifying the determinants of productivity growth at the sectoral level. To illustrate the econometric approach to productivity growth we summarize the results of fitting an econometric model to data on output and inputs for industrial sectors of the U.S. economy.

Index numbers for intermediate, capital, and labor inputs and rates of productivity growth are employed in the analysis of sources of economic growth presented in table 1.2. Production functions can be used in specifying econometric models of production. These models determine the distribution of the value of output among the inputs and the rate of productivity growth. In estimating the parameters of the econometric models the quantity indexes of inputs, the corresponding price indexes, and indexes of productivity growth can be employed as data.

The econometric study summarized here is based on sectoral models of production for each of 35 industries. These industries represent a consolidation of the 51 sectors included in table 1.2. Although production functions contain all the available information about producer behavior, it is useful here to express the sectoral models of production in an alternative and equivalent form. Under the assumption of constant returns to scale we can introduce price functions for each industry.[6] The price function gives the price of output as a function of the prices of all inputs and of time, the variable that represents the level of technology. These price functions just summarize the available information about producer behavior in a more convenient form.

To explain the cause of the productivity slowdown, it is also useful to disaggregate intermediate inputs between energy and materials inputs. Given the price function for each industry, we express the shares of each of the four inputs in the industry—capital, labor, energy, and materials inputs—in the value of output as functions of the prices of inputs and the level of technology. Finally, the model is completed with an equation that gives the rate of productivity growth as a function of the prices of the inputs and the level of technology. This equation is our econometric model of sectoral productivity growth.

As in any econometric model, the relationships determining the rate of productivity growth and the value shares of capital, labor energy, and materials inputs involve unknown parameters. Included among these parameters are biases of productivity growth. For example, the bias for capital input gives the change in the value share of capital in response to changes in technology.[7] We say that productivity growth is *capital using* if the bias for capital input is positive. Similarly, we say that productivity growth is *capital saving* if the bias for capital input is negative. The sum of the biases for all four inputs must be precisely zero, since the changes in all four value shares must sum to zero.

The biases of productivity growth appear as coefficients of time, representing the level of technology, in the equations for the value shares of the four inputs. The biases appear with the opposite sign as coefficients of the prices in the equation for productivity growth. This feature makes it possible to use information about changes in productivity growth with prices and changes in value shares with technology in estimating the biases of productivity growth as unknown parameters of an econometric model.[8]

Capital using productivity growth implies that an increase in the price of capital input diminishes the rate of productivity growth. Similarly, capital saving productivity growth implies that productivity growth increases with the price of capital input. Jorgenson and Fraumeni (198l) have fitted econometric models based on translog price functions to data for the aforementioned 35 industrial sectors. Since our primary concern is with the determinants of sectoral productivity growth, table 1.4 presents a classification of industries by biases of productivity growth.

The pattern of productivity growth that occurs most frequently in table 1.4 is capital using, labor using, energy using, and materials saving productivity growth. This pattern occurs for 19 of the 35 industries. For this pattern the biases of productivity growth for capital, labor, and energy inputs are positive and the bias of productivity growth for materials input is negative. This pattern implies that increases in the prices of capital, labor and energy inputs diminish the rate of productivity growth, while an increase in the price of materials input enhances productivity growth.

1.4.2 The Slowdown in Productivity Growth

The most striking change in the relative prices of capital, labor, energy, and materials inputs that has taken place since 1973 is the substantial increase in the price of energy. Reversing historical trends toward lower real prices of energy in the United States, the Arab oil embargo of late 1973 and early 1974 resulted in a dramatic increase in oil import prices. Real energy prices to final users increased by 23 percent in the United States during the period 1973–1975, despite price controls on domestic petroleum and natural gas. In 1978 the Iranian revolution sent a second wave of oil import price increases through the U.S. economy. Real energy prices climbed by 34 percent over the following two years.[9]

This evidence provides part of the solution of the problem of disappointing U.S. economic growth since 1973. Higher energy prices are associated with a decline in sectoral productivity growth for 29 of the 35 industries included in table 1.4. The resulting slowdown in sectoral productivity growth is more than sufficient to explain the decline in U.S. economic growth. The results of Jorgenson and Fraumeni (1981) have been corroborated by Jorgenson (1984) by further disaggregating energy between electricity and nonelectrical energy.

Table 1.4
Classification of industries by biases of productivity growth

Pattern of biases	Industries
Capital Using Labor Using Energy Using Material Saving	Agriculture, metal mining, crude petroleum and natural gas, nonmetallic mining, textiles, apparel, lumber, furniture, printing, leather, fabricated metals, electrical machinery, motor vehicles, instruments, miscellaneous manufacturing, transportation, trade, finance, insurance and real estate, services
Capital Using Labor Using Energy Saving Material Saving	Coal mining, tobacco manufactures, communications, government enterprises
Capital Using Labor Saving Energy Using Material Saving	Petroleum refining
Capital Using Labor Saving Energy Saving Material Using	Construction
Capital Saving Labor Saving Energy Using Material Saving	Electric utilities
Capital Saving Labor Using Energy Saving Material Saving	Primary metals
Capital Saving Labor Using Energy Using Material Saving	Paper, chemicals, rubber, stone, clay and glass, machinery except electrical, transportation equipment and ordnance, gas utilities
Capital Saving Labor Saving Energy Using Material Using	Food

Source: Jorgenson and Fraumeni (1981, p. 44).

It is important to emphasize once again that an econometric model of sectoral productivity growth is essential to solving the problem of the slowdown in U.S. economic growth since 1973. An aggregate model of production excludes energy and materials inputs by definition, since deliveries to intermediate demand are offset by receipts of intermediate inputs.

1.5 Conclusion

The analysis of sources of economic growth is an essential component of any study of economic growth. However, a theory of growth must also include an explanation of the growth in supplies of capital and labor inputs. In the neoclassical model of economic growth presented by Tinbergen (1942), saving generates growth in capital input and population growth generates growth in labor input. These features of the theory of economic growth have been retained in the neoclassical growth models developed by Solow (1956) and Tobin (1955).

The theoretical underpinnings of an analysis of growth in factor supplies are to be found in the theory of consumer behavior. For example, the study of saving requires modeling saving-consumption decisions. Similarly, the analysis of labor supplies requires modeling demographic behavior and labor-leisure choices. A theory of economic growth must incorporate the sources of economic growth and the modeling of producer behavior. The analysis of growth of factor supplies and the modeling of consumer behavior are required to complete the theory. Future research should give additional attention to growth of factor supplies and the modeling of consumer behavior. This focus characterized the classic studies of economic growth by Kuznets (1971) and Schultz (1961b).

Recent research on economic growth has emphasized the sources of economic growth and the modeling of producer behavior. This has proved to be very fruitful, as suggested by the research summarized above. The steps outlined here—disaggregating the sources of economic growth to the sectoral level, decomposing sectoral output growth between productivity growth and the growth of capital, labor, energy, and materials inputs, and modeling the rate of growth of sectoral productivity growth rate econometrically—have been taken only recently. Much additional research will be required to provide an exhaustive explanation of the slowdown of U.S. economic growth and the implications for the future growth of the economy.

1.6 Appendix: Methodology and Data Sources

An excellent overview of research on sources of economic growth, including alternative data sources and methodologies, is provided by the Rees Report to the National Research Council (1979). Tinbergen's methodology has dominated subsequent research on the sources of economic growth. This methodology was based on an aggregate production function for each country. Capital and labor inputs were weighted by their marginal products in determining an index of productivity ("efficiency" in Tinbergen's terminology).[10] Christensen, Cummings, and Jorgenson (1980) and Maddison (1987) have reviewed international comparisons of sources of economic growth among industrialized countries.

The methodology that underlies the data presented in table 1.2 is based on sectoral production functions of the translog form introduced by Christensen, Jorgenson, and Lau (1973).[11] Given translog production functions for all sectors, the corresponding price and quantity index numbers can be generated for all three inputs. The growth rate of each input is a weighted average of growth rates of its components. Similarly, the translog index of productivity growth is the difference between the growth rate of output and a weighted average of growth rates of intermediate, capital and labor inputs.[12]

The critical innovation in the methodology that underlies table 1.2 is to distinguish among components of intermediate, capital, and labor inputs that differ in marginal productivity. For each sector, intermediate input is represented as a function of deliveries from all other sectors. Capital input is broken down by class of asset and legal form of organization. Finally, labor input is broken down by characteristics of individual workers such as sex, age, education, employment status, and occupation.

1.6.1 Measuring Labor Input

A novel feature of the quantity indexes of labor input presented in table 1.2 is that these indexes incorporate data from both establishment and household surveys. Estimates of employment, hours worked, and labor compensation for each industrial sector are controlled to totals based on establishment surveys that underlie the U.S. national income accounts. These totals are allocated among categories of the work force cross-classified by the characteristics of individual workers on the basis of household surveys. The resulting estimates of hours worked and average compensation per hour for each sector provide the basis for the indexes of labor input presented in table 1.2.

For each of 51 industrial sectors listed in table 1.2 prices and quantities of labor input are cross-classified by the two sexes, eight age groups, five educational groups, two employment classes, and ten occupational groups. Annual data from 1948 to 1979 on hours worked and average labor compensation per hour are required for 1,600 components of the work force in each industry. For this purpose employment, hours, weeks, and labor compensation within each sector are allocated on the basis of the available cross-classifications. This methodology make it possible to exploit all the published detail on labor input from the decennial Census of Population and the Current Population Survey.

Quantity indexes of labor input are presented in table 1.2 for 51 industrial sectors. The data on labor input that underlie table 1.2 are cross-classified by sex, and education, class of employment, occupation, and industry for a total of 81,600 types of labor input. The growth of labor input can be decomposed to obtain the contribution of all six industrial, occupational, and demographic characteristics.[13]

1.6.2 Measuring Capital Input

The approach to the construction of the data on capital input presented in table 1.2 is strictly analogous to the approach for data on labor input. Capital service represent the quantity of capital input, just as labor services represent the quantity of labor input. Measures of capital services for depreciable assets are derived by representing capital stock at each point of time as a weighted sum of past investments The weights correspond to the relative efficiencies of capital goods of different ages, so that all components of capital stock have the same efficiency when appropriately weighted.

Rental rates for capital services provide the basis for property compensation, just as wage rates provide the basis for labor compensation. Information on rental transactions would be required to employ data sources for capital input that are analogous to those we have used for labor input. These data are not available in a readily accessible form, even for the substantial proportion of assets with active rental markets. However, rental value can be imputed on the basis of estimates of capital stocks and property compensation.

Data on rental prices for depreciable assets are generated by allocating property compensation for return to capital, depreciation, and taxes among assets. Depreciation is the decline in value of a capital good with age at a given point in time, so that estimates of depreciation depend on the relative efficiencies of capital goods of different ages. The estimates of capital input presented in table 1.2 incorporate the same data on relative efficiencies of capital goods into estimates of both capital stock and rental prices.

Data on capital input are unavailable for the five government sectors listed in table 1.2. For each of the 45 private industrial sectors listed in this table, capital input is cross-classified by four asset classes (producers' durable equipment, nonresidential structures, inventories, and land) and two legal forms of organization (corporate and noncorporate business). Households and institutions are treated as a separate sector with prices and quantities of capital input cross-classified by producers' and consumers' durable equipment, residential and nonresidential structures, and land.

Data on producers' durable equipment can be further subdivided among 20 categories, while data on nonresidential structures can be subdivided among 14 categories. Finally, data for each category of assets can be distinguished by age. On average, 43.5 vintages are distinguished for each category of producers' durable equipment and 73.5 vintages are distinguished for nonresidential structures. For each of the 45 private industrial sectors listed in table 1.2, annual data from 1948 to 1979 of capital stock and its rental price are required for an average of as many as 3802 components of the capital stock.

The first step in developing sectoral measures of capital input is to construct estimates of capital stock by industry for each year from 1948 to 1979. Investment data for producers' durable equipment and structures are distributed among industries on an establishment basis. Estimates of investment for all sectors are controlled to totals from the U.S. national product accounts. For residential structures, investment data are taken directly from the U.S. national product accounts. Investment goods prices from the U.S. national product accounts are employed to obtain estimates of investment in equipment and structures in constant prices.

The second step in developing sectoral measures of capital input is to construct estimates of prices of capital services from data on property compensation. For each asset the price of investment goods is a weighted sum of future rental prices, discounted by a factor that incorporates future rates of return. Weights are given by the relative efficiencies of capital goods of different ages. The same weights are used in constructing estimates of rental prices and capital stocks. For depreciable assets the weights decline with age; for nondepreciable assets the weights are constant.

1.6.3 Measuring Output, Intermediate Input, and Productivity

An important innovation embodied in the data on productivity presented in table 1.2 is that intermediate, capital, and labor inputs are treated symmetrically at the sectoral level. The value of output at the sectoral level includes the value of intermediate input as well as capital and labor inputs. All three inputs are employed in analyzing the sources of growth in sectoral output. The industry definitions employed in the U.S. national income accounts are used in measuring output. These definitions are based on establishments within each industry.

Data on output in current and constant prices are available from the Interindustry Economics Division of the Bureau of Economic Analysis (BEA, 1974b) for the manufacturing sectors and from a study by Jack Faucett Associates (1975) for the Bureau of Labor Statistics (BLS) for nonmanufacturing sectors. To calculate output from the point of view of the producing sector, excise and sales taxes must be subtracted and subsidies must be added to the value of output. The resulting price of output from the producers' point of view is equal to the ratio of the value of output in current prices to the value of output in constant prices.

Data on interindustry transactions published by (BEA) must be employed to disaggregate intermediate input by sector of origin. These data are based on industry definitions employed in the U.S. interindustry accounts. To bring measures of intermediate input into conformity with industry definitions from the U.S. national income accounts, interindustry transactions must be reallocated among sectors. To construct prices and quantities of intermediate input by sector of origin the value of intermediate input originating in each sector must be deflated by an index of purchasers' prices for the output of that sector.

For the five government sectors included in table 1.2 output is equal to labor input by definition; for private households output is equal to an index or capital and labor input. For these six sectors productivity growth is zero by definition. Rates of productivity growth for the remaining 45 sectors are presented on an annual basis for the period 1948–1979 in table 1.2.

1.6.4 Aggregation over Sectors

Aggregate data on prices and quantities of capital input, cross-classified by sex, age, education, employment class, and occupation, but not by industry, underlie the indexes of labor input presented in table 1.1. For the economy as a whole hours worked and labor compensation for each of 1600 categories of the work force are added over all industries. Labor compensation is divided by annual hours worked to derive labor compensation per hour worked for each category. Finally, price and quantitiy data are combined into price and quantity indexes of aggregate labor input.

Aggregate data on prices and quantities of capital input, cross-classified by asset class, legal form of organization, and age, but not by industry, underlie the indexes of capital input presented in table 1.1. For the economy as a whole, capital stock and property compensation for each category are added over all industries. Property compensation is divided by capital stock to derive property compensation per unit of capital stock for each category. Finally, price and quantity data are combined into price and quantity indexes of aggregate capital input.

The methodology we have outlined for the economy as a whole can be implemented by considering specific forms for the aggregate production function and for capital and labor inputs as functions of their components. We take these functions to be translog in form, so that we can generate a translog index of the rate of productivity growth. The average rate of productivity growth is the difference between the growth rate of value added and a weighted average of growth rates of capital and labor inputs. Similarly, we can generate translog indexes of capital and labor inputs, giving the growth rate of each input as a weighted average of growth rates of its components.

At a methodological level, the integration of data generation and econometric modeling is an important achievement of recent research on the sources of economic growth. The extensive data development we have outlined is firmly rooted in the economic theory of production. The conceptual basis for the measures of intermediate, capital, and labor inputs in tables 1.1 and 1.2 is provided by the theory of exact index numbers employed by Diewert (1976). Diewert showed that the index numbers utilized, for example, by Christensen and Jorgenson (1969) could be generated from the translog production function introduced by Christensen, Jorgenson, and Lau (1973).

The application of the theory of index numbers to the measurement of labor input requires weighting the components of labor input by wage rates. This was first carried out for all industrial sectors of the U.S. economy by Gollop and Jorgenson (1980). Similarly, the measurement of capital as a factor of production involves weighting the components of capital input by rental rates. The conceptual basis for imputing rental prices for capital goods was established by Jorgenson (1963). These rental prices were employed in aggregate productivity measurement by Jorgenson and Griliches (1967) and at the sectoral level by Fraumeni and Jorgenson (1986) and Gollop and Jorgenson (1980).

The final step in the methodology for analyzing sources of economic growth is to aggregate over industrial sectors. This step is critical in integrating the sources of growth for individual industries into the sources of growth for the economy as a whole. The methodology for aggregation over sectors originated by Domar (1961) has been generalized by Hulten (1978) and Jorgenson (1980). This methodology was implemented for the U.S. by Fraumeni and Jorgenson (1986) and underlies that data on aggregate productivity change presented in table 1.3.

Notes

1. An English translation appeared in Tinbergen's Selected Papers (1959).
2. The value added approach is utilized by Kendrick (1983).
3. The implications of aggregation over industrial sectors for the existence of an aggregate production function was a central issue in the "reswitching controversy" initiated by Samuelson (1962).
4. This condition for the existence of an aggregate production function is due to Hall (1973).
5. Gollop (1985) has surveyed the literature on the role of intersectoral shifts.
6. The price function was introduced by Samuelson (1953).
7. This definition of the bias of productivity growth is due to Hicks (1963). Alternative definitions of biases of productivity growth are compared by Binswanger (1978).
8. Further details on econometric modeling of sectoral productivity growth are given by Jorgenson (1986a).
9. Trends in energy prices since 1973 are discussed in greater detail by Jorgenson (1986b). Bruno (1984) has discussed the impact of higher raw materials prices after 1973. However, the bias of productivity growth for materials is positive for 33 of the 35 industries listed in table 1.4. For these industries an increase in the price of materials is associated with higher rather than lower productivity growth.

10. The concept of total factor productivity was developed independently of Tinbergen's work by Stigler (1947).
11. Detailed references to sectoral production studies incorporating intermediate input are given by Jorgenson (1986a).
12. Translog quantity indexes were employed by Christensen and Jorgenson (1969).
13. Chinloy (1981) provides such a decomposition for the U.S. economy.

2 The Embodiment Hypothesis

Dale W. Jorgenson

2.1 Introduction

In the study of total factor productivity two distinct approaches have been employed. First, total factor productivity may be treated as an index number, the ratio of indexes of total output and total input. Since the rates of growth of output and input vary from period to period, the rate of growth of total factor productivity may vary. Second, total factor productivity may be treated as a function of a particular form, for example, an exponential function of time. The parameters of such a function may be treated as unknowns to be estimated from data on output and input. Where total factor productivity grows exponentially, the rate of growth remains constant.

In either approach changes in the index of total factor productivity may be interpreted as shifts in an aggregate production function or as "disembodied" technical change. This interpretation of an index of total factor productivity with a constant rate of growth was first proposed by Tinbergen (1942, pp. 190–195). The corresponding interpretation of total factor productivity with a rate of growth that varies was first given by Solow (1957, pp. 312–113). More recently, changes in the index of total factor productivity have been interpreted by Solow as technical change "embodied" in new capital goods (1960, p. 91). Solow assumes that embodied technical change takes place at a constant exponential rate, but it is clear that the rate of growth could be treated as varying from period to period. Solow also assumes, implicitly, that consumption goods and investment goods as conventionally measured are perfect substitutes in production. The first objective of this paper is to provide a model of embodied technical change free of these two restrictive assumptions.

It has frequently been suggested that embodied and disembodied technical change are two different aspects of reality. For example, in commenting on Denison's study of total factor productivity (1962), based on disembodied technical change, Abramovitz says: "The economic model which underlies Denison's calculations stand in sharp contrast to the model with which Robert Solow has been experimenting.... The *factual gap* between the two views is profound and not really usefully attacked by speculation" (1962, p. 773).

Denison takes Abramovitz to task for stressing the importance of the question of embodiment, suggesting that "the whole embodiment question is of little importance for policy in the United States" (1964, p. 90). However, Denison does not dispute Abramovitz's basic presupposition that embodied and disembodied technical change may be distinguished by an appeal to evidence. The second objective of this paper is to examine this presupposition. After dropping the highly restrictive assumption that technical change proceeds at constant exponential rates, we are able to show that one can never distinguish a model of embodied technical change from a model of disembodied technical change on the basis of factual evidence such as that considered by Denison and Solow. Both types of technical change have precisely the same factual implications so that the "factual gap" suggested by Abramovitz is entirely illusory.

The conclusion that embodied and disembodied technical change have the same factual implications has importance for economic policy. In measuring potential economic growth it is often useful to calculate the amount of investment required for a given amount of economic growth. Calculations based on models of disembodied and embodied technical change give startlingly different results. Although differences in the results are often attributed to differences in the underlying models, the precise equivalence between the two models reveals that the source of the difference lies not in the models but, rather, in different assumptions about the facts. To illustrate: One can calculate the effects of investment for a model with a given rate of disembodied technical change. Using the correspondence between models of embodied and disembodied technical change, one can calculate the effects of investment for a model with the corresponding rate of growth of embodied technical change. The results for the two models will agree perfectly. On the other hand, one can do the second calculation for a model with a different rate of embodied technical change. Obviously, the results of the two calculations will differ. The difference in the results can be attributed to the fact that different assumptions are made concerning the rate of embodied technical change. In weighing the implications of calculations that differ, the problem is not to choose the correct model but rather to choose the correct factual assumption.

2.2 Theory

We first consider the simplest theoretical framework which encompasses both embodied and disembodied technical change. Within this framework we are able to eliminate the restrictive assumptions that consumption goods and investment goods are perfect substitutes in production and that technical change proceeds at constant exponential rates. To present the theoretical framework we let C and I represent the quantities of consumption and investment goods, K and L the quantities of capital and labor services, q_C and q_I the prices of consumption and investment goods, and p_K and p_L the prices of capital and labor services. The fundamental identity for each accounting period is that value of output is equal to value of input:

$$q_C C + q_I I = p_K K + p_L L \,. \tag{2.1}$$

This accounting identity is important in defining total factor productivity.

To define total factor productivity we first differentiate the fundamental identity (2.1) with respect to time and divide both sides by total value. (Time derivatives of variables are denoted by primes.) The result is an identity between weighted averages of rates of growth of output prices and quantities and rates of growth of input prices and quantities:

$$v_C\left(\frac{q'_C}{q_C}+\frac{C'}{C}\right)+v_I\left(\frac{q'_I}{q_I}+\frac{I'}{I}\right)=w_k\left(\frac{p'_K}{p_K}+\frac{K'}{K}\right)+w_L\left(\frac{p'_L}{p_L}+\frac{L'}{L}\right). \tag{2.2}$$

The weights v_C, v_I *and* w_K, w_L are relative value shares:

$$v_C=\frac{q_C C}{q_C C+q_I I}\,, \qquad v_I=\frac{q_I I}{q_C C+q_I I}\,;$$

$$w_K=\frac{p_K K}{P_K K+p_L L}\,, \qquad w_L=\frac{p_L L}{p_K K+p_L L}\,.$$

To verify that both sides of the identity (2.2) are weighted averages, we observe that:

$$v_C, v_I \geq 0, \qquad w_K, w_L \geq 0\,;$$
$$v_C + v_I = w_K + w_L = 1\,.$$

A useful index of total output is provided by the weighted average of rates of growth of output from (2.2); denoting this index of output by Y:

$$\frac{Y'}{Y} = v_C \frac{C'}{C} + v_I \frac{I'}{I}\,;$$

an analogous index of the quantity of total input, say X, is:

$$\frac{X'}{X} = w_K \frac{K'}{K} + w_L \frac{L'}{L}\,.$$

These quantity indexes are familiar as Divisia quantity indexes. In terms of Divisia index numbers a natural definition of total factor productivity, say P, is the ratio of the quantity of total output to the quantity of total input:

$$P = \frac{Y}{X}\,. \tag{2.3}$$

Using the definitions of Divisia quantity indexes, the rate of growth of total factor productivity may be expressed as:[1]

$$\frac{P'}{P} = \frac{Y'}{Y} - \frac{X'}{X} = v_C \frac{C'}{C} + v_I \frac{I'}{I} - w_K \frac{K'}{K} - w_L \frac{L'}{L}\,. \tag{2.4}$$

Divisia index numbers have the fundamental *reproductive property*, namely, a Divisia index of a group of Divisia indexes is also a Divisia index of the components of each group. This property assures us that no distinction need be made between a one-sector model with joint production of consumption and investment goods and a two-sector model with one sector corresponding to each output,[2] provided that the index of total output is a Divisia index of the outputs of the two sectors and the index of total inputs is a Divisia index of the inputs of the two sectors. If the price of an input is the same in both sectors, the appropriate index for this input may be constructed either as a Divisia index of the amounts of this input or as an ordinary sum of the amounts of the input.[3]

2.3 Measurement

Conceptually, the measurement of output and labor services is straightforward. Beginning with data on the value of transactions in each output and labor service, the value is separated into a price and a quantity. A quantity index may be constructed from the individual quantities, using relative value shares as weights.

If capital services were supplied and employed by distinct economic units, there would be no conceptual difference between construction of indexes for capital input and for labor input. Beginning with data on the value of transactions in each capital service, the value would be separated into a price and a quantity. A quantity index for capital input would be constructed from the quantities of each capital service, using as weights the relative value shares, that is, the shares of each capital service in the rental value of all capital services.

Measurement of capital services is less straightforward than measurement of labor services because the employer of a capital service is usually also the supplier of the service. Data on values of transactions in capital services are recorded only in the internal accounts of economic units. To extract the required information it is necessary to begin not with transactions in capital services but with transactions in investment goods. These values must first be separated into a price and a quantity. Second, the quantity of new investment goods reduced by the quantity of investment goods replaced must be added to accumulated stocks. Finally, the price and quantity of capital services for each stock must be calculated.

Calculation of an index of capital input from data on transactions in new investment goods depends on hypotheses about the rate of replacement of investment goods and about the quantity of capital services corresponding to a given capital stock. In this paper we assume that capital services are proportional to the cumulated stock of past investments. Second, we assume that the proportion of an investment replaced in an interval of time declines exponentially over time.[4] Under this assumption the cumulated stock of past investments, net of replacements, satisfies the well-known relationship:

$$I = K' + \delta K \ , \tag{2.5}$$

where δ is the instantaneous rate of replacement of investment goods.

Before considering alternative explanations of change in total factor productivity, we must discuss the effects of errors of measurement in the separation of transaction values into prices and quantities. Direct observations are usually available only for the values; the separation of these values into prices and quantities is based on much less complete information. It is important to consider the effects of systematic errors in this separation.

For consumption goods or labor services an error in separating the value of transactions into prices and quantities results in errors in the price and quantity of total output or total input. Errors in total output or input result in errors in total factor productivity. As an example, suppose that the price of a labor service is measured with error. Since all relative value shares are given data, the rate of growth of the error in the price of total input is equal to that of the error in the price of the labor service, multiplied by the relative value share of the service. The quantity of total input is measured with an error that is equal in magnitude but opposite in sign. The error in the rate of growth of total factor productivity is equal to the negative of the rate of growth of the error in total input. The effects of an error in the rate of growth of the price of consumer goods are entirely analogous; of course, an upward bias in the rate of growth of output increases the measured rate of growth of total factor productivity, while an upward bias in the rate of growth of input decreases the measured rate of growth.

Measurement of capital input is based, ultimately, on the separation of the value of transactions in new investment goods into a price and a quantity. An error in this separation will affect the measured prices and quantities of investment goods and capital services, and also measured total factor productivity. To examine these effects we let Q represent the relative error in the price of investment goods and I^* the "quantity" of investment goods calculated using the erroneous price. The bias in the rate of growth of investment goods output is then:

$$\frac{I'^*}{I^*} - \frac{I'}{I} = -\frac{Q'}{Q} . \tag{2.6}$$

The rate of growth of this bias is negative if the rate of growth of the error is positive, and *vice versa*. If we let K^* be the "quantity" of capital calculated using the erroneous price:

$$\begin{aligned} K^* &= \int_{-\infty}^{t} e^{-\delta(t-s)} I^*(s)\, ds \\ &= \int_{-\infty}^{t} e^{-\delta(t-s)} \frac{I(s)}{Q(s)}\, ds . \end{aligned}$$

The bias in the rate of growth of the quantity of capital services is then:

$$\frac{K'^*}{K^*} - \frac{K'}{K} = \frac{I}{QK^*} - \frac{I}{K}$$
$$= \frac{I}{\int_{-\infty}^{t} e^{-\delta(t-s)} \frac{Q(t)}{Q(s)} I(s)\, ds} - \frac{I}{\int_{-\infty}^{t} e^{-\delta(t-s)} I(s)\, ds} . \qquad (2.7)$$

The bias is negative if the rate of growth of the error is positive, and *vice versa*.

To calculate the error of measurement in total factor productivity, we represent the rate of growth of total factor productivity as before:

$$\frac{P'}{P} = v_I \frac{I'}{I} + v_C \frac{C'}{C} - w_K \frac{K'}{K} - w_L \frac{L'}{L} .$$

If we let P^* represent measured total factor productivity using the erroneous price of investment goods:

$$\frac{P'^*}{P} = v_I \frac{I'^*}{I^*} + v_C \frac{C'}{C} - w_K \frac{K'^*}{K^*} - w_L \frac{L'}{L} .$$

Subtracting the first of these expressions from the second, we obtain the bias in the rate of growth of total factor productivity:

$$\frac{P'^*}{P^*} - \frac{P'}{P} = v_I \left(\frac{I'^*}{I^*} - \frac{I'}{I} \right) - w_K \left(\frac{K'^*}{K^*} - \frac{K'}{K} \right) .$$

Substituting expression (2.7) and (2.6) for the biases in capital input and investment goods output, we have:

$$\frac{P'^*}{P^*} - \frac{P'}{P} = - v_I \frac{Q'}{Q}$$
$$- w_K \left[\frac{I}{\int_{-\infty}^{t} e^{-\delta(t-s)} \frac{Q(t)}{Q(s)} I(s)\, ds} - \frac{I}{\int_{-\infty}^{t} e^{-\delta(t-s)} I(s)\, ds} \right] . \qquad (2.8)$$

If investment and the error are growing at constant rates, the biases in the rates of growth of the quantity of investment goods produced and the quantity of capital services are equal; the net effect is equal to the rate of growth of the error, multiplied by the difference between the capital share in total input and the investment share in total output.[5]

We conclude that so long as the capital share is greater than the investment share and the investment share is not zero, one can produce any rate of growth in measured total factor productivity by introducing a sufficiently large error in the measured rate of growth of the price of investment goods. This conclusion is entirely independent of whether actual total factor productivity is changing or not. To be more specific, if the capital share in total input is greater than the investment share in total output, a positive rate of growth in total factor productivity can be produced by introducing an error in measurement of the price of investment goods with a positive rate of growth. The converse of this proposition is that one may reduce the rate of growth in measured total factor productivity by introducing a bias in the opposite direction in the measured rate of growth of the price of investment goods. In particular, one can eliminate growth in total factor productivity altogether by suitably "adjusting" the measured price of investment goods.[6] An explicit formula for the "adjustment" is obtained by setting the bias in the rate of growth of total factor productivity in (2.8) equal to the negative of the actual rate of growth, that is, by setting the erroneously measured rate of growth, P'^*/P^*, equal to zero. This results in the following relationship between total factor productivity, P, and the relative error in the measurement of the price of investment goods, Q:

$$\frac{P'}{P} = v_I \frac{Q'}{Q} + w_K \left[\frac{I}{\int_{-\infty}^{t} e^{-\delta(t-s)} \frac{Q(t)}{Q(s)} I(s)\, ds} - \frac{I}{\int_{-\infty}^{t} e^{-\delta(t-s)} I(s)\, ds} \right]. \tag{2.9}$$

The relationship (2.9) between total factor productivity, P, and the relative error in the measurement of investment goods, Q, may be interpreted in two ways. First, suppose that we have a relative error for which the measured rate of growth of total factor productivity is zero. Then, we may calculate the actual rate of growth of total factor productivity, P'/P, by treating the right-hand side of expression (2.9) as a given function of time. Alternatively, suppose that we have actual total factor productivity, P; then we may calculate the rate of growth of the corresponding relative error in the measurement of the price of investment goods, Q'/Q, by treating the left-hand side of expression (2.9) as a given function of time.

Our principal conclusion is that there is a one-to-one correspondence between indexes of total factor productivity, P, and errors in the price of investment goods, Q, that can make the rate of growth in measured total factor productivity equal to zero.[7] In view of this correspondence one can never distinguish a given rate of growth in total factor productivity from the corresponding rate of growth in the error in measurement of the price of investment goods. Given any observed index of total factor productivity, one can always relabel it as an error in the measurement of the price of investment goods. This relabeling is irrefutable on the basis of the data that underlie expressions (2.8) and (2.9) because the whole procedure is purely definitional. It amounts to computing two completely interchangeable quantities, P and Q, and giving each a different name.

2.4 Explanation

Up to this point we have interpreted expression (2.8) as a relationship between the relative error in the measurement of total factor productivity, P^*/P, and the relative error in the measurement of the price of investment goods, Q. Suppose we set the erroneously measured index of total factor productivity, P^*, equal to unity, so that the rate of growth of this index is zero. Then expression (2.9) becomes a relationship between the relative error in the measurement of the price of investment goods, Q, and total factor productivity.

Expression (2.8) has another interesting interpretation. We may interpret the rate of growth of total factor productivity, P, as the rate of disembodied technical change. Second, we may interpret the reciprocal of the relative error in the price of investment goods, $1/Q$, as an index of the quality of investment goods. The rate of growth of this index may be interpreted as the rate of embodied technical change. In this interpretation, the "erroneously" measured quantities of investment goods output, I^*, and capital input, K^*, are "surrogate" investment and "surrogate" capital, that is, investment and capital corrected for quality change.

We may interpret expression (2.9) as a relationship between the rate of disembodied technical change and the rate of embodied technical change. For any index of embodied technical change, we may calculate the corresponding index of disembodied technical change by treating the right-hand side of expression (2.9) as a given function of time. Alternatively, for any index of disembodied technical change, we may calculate the corresponding index of embodied technical change by treating the left-hand side of expression (2.9) as a given function of time. As before, we conclude that there is a one-to-one correspondence between indexes of embodied technical change and indexes of disembodied technical change. In view of this correspondence one can never distinguish a given rate of growth in embodied technical change from the corresponding rate of growth in disembodied technical change.

We conclude that one can always relabel any observed rate of growth in the index of disembodied technical change as a corresponding rate of growth in the index of embodied technical change. This relabeling is irrefutable on the basis of the data that underlie expressions (2.8) and (2.9) because the two indexes, P and $1/Q$, are completely interchangeable by means of expression (2.9). Any set of facts may be interpreted equivalently as embodied or disembodied technical change.

To illustrate the fact that any index of disembodied technical change, P, is completely interchangeable with an index of embodied technical change, $1/Q$, we compute an index of each type for the U.S. private domestic economy, 1939–1959. The data given at the outset include time series on prices and quantities of investment-goods output, consumption-goods output, and labor input, and the rate of replacement of capital goods. From these data the relative value shares of investment goods, consumption goods, capital services, and labor services, together with rates of growth of each of the output and input quantities, may be computed. The derived value shares and rates of growth for the U.S. private domestic economy are presented in table 2.1.[8]

Indexes of disembodied and embodied technical change for the U.S. private domestic economy are present in table 2.2.[9] Although the calculated indexes are meant to illustrate the equivalence of embodied and disembodied technical change, perhaps a comment on the empirical results is not entirely out of order. The average rate of growth of the index of disembodied technical change is approximately 0.024, which is roughly comparable with the results of previous studies.[10] On the other hand, the average rate of growth of the index of

Table 2.1
Value shares and rates of growth

Year	v_I	w_L	I'/I	C'/C	L'/L
1939	0.11191	0.64976	0.34259	0.05753	0.05225
1940	0.14224	0.62882	0.26552	0.12777	0.12077
1941	0.15573	0.60986	–0.48774	0.20639	0.09366
1942	0.06874	0.61325	–0.43085	0.09205	0.05157
1943	0.03362	0.62315	0.14953	0.04981	–0.01314
1944	0.03988	0.61705	0.38211	–0.03244	–0.05679
1945	0.05858	0.61815	1.49412	–0.12280	0.00941
1946	0.14860	0.64096	–0.02123	0.03679	0.03075
1947	0.14510	0.64437	0.20000	0.01060	0.01175
1948	0.17872	0.63651	–0.22691	0.04378	–0.04736
1949	0.13876	0.63765	0.45195	0.03539	0.03002
1950	0.19029	0.62931	0.03220	0.06371	0.04189
1951	0.18758	0.62349	–0.12652	0.06585	0.01136
1952	0.15846	0.63662	0.00397	0.05769	0.01297
1953	0.15148	0.64692	–0.03360	–0.01372	–0.04266
1954	0.14846	0.65048	0.27812	0.05672	0.04189
1955	0.17650	0.63869	–0.01280	0.03241	0.02138
1956	0.17693	0.65457	–0.05835	0.02518	–0.00838
1957	0.16466	0.65053	–0.15663	0.00893	–0.04476
1958	0.14144	0.64963	0.25918	0.04584	–0.04155
1959	0.16665	0.64713	–0.02431	0.03597	0.00594

embodied technical change is 0.101; this value may be compared with the experimental values of 0.01 and 0.05 employed by Solow.[11]

The conceptualization of embodied technical change that underlies expressions (2.6) and (2.7) above is not the only possible conceptualization. Solow has based his calculations on the assumption that consumption goods and investment goods as conventionally measured are perfect substitutes in production. This assumption implies that for investment goods of a fixed vintage, the output of consumption goods attainable from given quantities of capital and labor is the same at any point in time. However, for these same investment goods of fixed vintage the output of investment goods of a particular quality attainable from a given quantity of capital and labor varies over time. In effect, Solow assumes that investment goods *of a given vintage* progress technologically over time but only in the production of investment goods. In a two-sector model Solow's assumption would be equivalent to the assumption that all technical change is of the disembodied variety but that technical change is confined to the investment-goods sector.[12] The

Table 2.2
Indexes of embodied and disembodied technical change

Year	P'/P	$-Q'/Q$	P	$1/Q$
1939	0.05379	−0.23195	0.68852	2.32783
1940	0.06589	−0.27984	0.72556	1.78789
1941	0.03143	−0.05397	0.77337	1.28757
1942	0.02474	−0.14844	0.79768	1.21808
1943	0.06555	−0.97679	0.81741	1.03727*
1944	0.02255	−0.54131	0.87099	0.86328*
1945	−0.03288	1.01487	0.89063	0.71848*
1946	−0.00260	0.11596	0.86135	0.59797
1947	0.02060	−0.02590	0.85911	0.66731
1948	0.01209	0.04376	0.87681	0.65003
1949	0.06658	−0.28358	0.88741	0.67848
1950	0.01640	0.16137	0.94649	0.48608
1951	0.00768	0.22434	0.96201	0.56452
1952	0.03041	0.12228	0.96940	0.69116
1953	0.00112	0.28920	0.99888	0.77567
1954	0.05382	−0.00616	1.00000	1.00000
1955	0.00195	0.37577	1.05382	0.99384
1956	0.00421	0.42195	1.05587	1.36730
1957	0.00088	0.54246	1.06032	1.94422
1958	0.04265	0.45309	1.06125	2.99887
1959	0.01186	0.90646	1.10651	4.35761

* Calculated from $-Q'/Q$ by averaging values for 1943–1945.

further assumption that investment goods and consumption goods are perfect substitutes in production implies that the production functions in the two sectors are identical.

Solow adjusts the quantity of capital for quality change. He calls the resulting quantity of capital, K^* in our notation, a "surrogate" quantity of capital. To avoid the implication that disembodied technical change occurs for investment goods of a given vintage, at least in the production of new investment goods, it is necessary to adjust the quantity of investment goods produced as well. The resulting quantity of investment goods, I^* in our notation, would then be an appropriate "surrogate" quantity of investment goods. In the absence of this second adjustment, expression (2.9) reduces to:

$$\frac{P'}{P} = w_K \left[\frac{I}{\int_{-\infty}^{t} e^{-\delta(t-s)} \frac{Q(t)}{Q(s)} I(s)\, ds} - \frac{I}{\int_{-\infty}^{t} e^{-\delta(t-s)} I(s)\, ds} \right], \tag{2.10}$$

which corresponds to formulas (12) in Solow's first article on embodied technical change (1960, p. 94).

Expression (2.10) may be interpreted in the same way as formula (2.9). Given the index of the quality of investment goods, the corresponding index of disembodied technical change may be calculated by treating the right-hand side of expression (2.10) as a given function of time. Alternatively, for a given index of disembodied technical change, the rate of growth of the index of embodied technical change may be calculated by treating the left-side of expression (2.10) as a given function of time. As before, there is a one-to-one correspondence between indexes of embodied and disembodied technical change. In view of this correspondence one can never distinguish a given rate of growth in embodied technical change from the corresponding rate of growth in disembodied technical change.

We conclude that one can always relabel any observed rate of growth in the index of disembodied technical change as a corresponding rate of growth in the index of embodied technical change calculated on Solow's assumptions. This relabeling is irrefutable on the basis of the data that underlie expression (2.10), because the two indexes are completely interchangeable by means of this expression. To illustrate the fact that any index of disembodied technical change is completely interchangeable with an index of embodied technical change calculated on Solow's assumptions, an appropriate index of embodied technical change is presented for the U.S. private domestic economy, 1939–1959, in the first column of table 2.3.

Solow's assumption that consumption goods and investment goods as conventionally measured are perfect substitutes in production has at least one readily testable implication. This implication is that so long as both consumption goods and investment goods are produced in positive amounts, the prices of the two goods must be proportional to each other. In the present context this implies that the implicit deflators of consumption and investment goods must be proportional or that the rates of growth of these deflators must be equal. A careful and thoroughly documented test of this hypothesis has been carried out by R.A. Gordon (1961). Gordon's conclusions may be quoted in full:

> There has apparently been, for half a century or more, a secular tendency in the United States and some other countries for capital-goods prices to rise faster than those of consumers' goods.

Table 2.3
Index of embodied technical change

Year	$-Q'/Q$	q'_C/q_C	q'_I/q_I
1939	–0.00796	0.01542	0.05255
1940	–0.50671	0.09511	0.08554
1941	0.26828	0.13184	0.06669
1942	1.58115	0.10196	–0.00362
1943	–0.59978	0.01568	0.10759
1944	–2.17661	0.00915	0.05840
1945	–3.40897	0.09664	0.08174
1946	0.73106	0.10877	0.14219
1947	–0.26175	0.05709	0.14135
1948	1.69931	–0.00960	–0.01000
1949	–0.79225	0.00330	0.04363
1950	0.99485	0.07874	0.09219
1951	–0.02812	0.01828	0.01334
1952	–0.46928	0.00678	0.00558
1953	2.68494	0.00796	0.00459
1954	–0.80062	0.00558	0.02215
1955	0.10595	0.01906	0.06878
1956	–0.13054	0.04410	0.04240
1957	2.14949	0.01591	0.01565
1958	–0.59412	0.01134	0.01969
1959	–0.14750	0.01196	0.01126

If we can believe the figures, the contrast in the behavior of these sector price levels has been quite striking, particularly for the period since the 1920s. The contrast also shows up in earlier decades in the U.S. figures. The tendency for capital-goods prices to rise faster than those of consumers' goods is not confined to the United States. It is also evidenced in some, although not all, other advanced countries for which data are available (1961, p. 937).

The rates of growth of implicit deflators for consumption and investment goods for the U.S. private domestic economy, 1939–1959, are presented in table 2.3. In this table q'_C/q_C is the rate of growth of the implicit deflator for consumption goods, and q'_I/q_I is the rate of growth of the implicit deflator for investment goods. The hypothesis that the rates of growth are equal may be rejected, but only at a 0.25 level of significance. We conclude that the assumption that consumption goods and investment goods as conventionally measured are perfect substitutes in production is inconsistent with the evidence presented by Gordon and also weakly inconsistent with evidence for the U.S. private domestic economy, 1939–1959. The index of embodied technical change presented in the second column of table 2.2, unlike that given in the first column of table 2.3, does not require this assumption.

2.5 Prediction

We turn now to consideration of calculations of the amount of investment required to attain a given amount of economic growth. Many such calculations have been made and published; the results may be summarized, again in the words of Abramovitz: "It is an implication of Denison's analysis that we might do much to stimulate growth without raising our investment quotas. We might even permit them to sink, but in order to stimulate growth significantly through capital accumulation we should have to increase our investment quotas enormously. The moral of Solow's view is just the opposite. Pressed to the limit, nothing we might do to stimulate growth would be effective without a good deal of investment" (1962, p. 779).

Since embodied and disembodied technical change have the same factual implications, any statement based on one type of technical change can be translated into an entirely equivalent statement based on the other type of technical change. Expression (2.9) provides a means of making such translations. If the results of calculations based on embodied technical change differ from those based on disembodied technical change, the reason must be that the two statements, translated into the same framework, involve not two different models of technical change but, rather, two different factual assumptions within a given model of technical change. No one would knowingly deny that calculations based on a rate of disembodied technical change of, say, 4 percent per year will give different results than calculations based on a rate of 5 percent per year. However, it is easy to deny such a proposition inadvertently. One could calculate the effects of investment for a *disembodied* model with a rate of *disembodied* technical change of 4 percent per year and then calculate the effects of investment for an *embodied* model with a rate of *disembodied* technical change of 5 percent per year.

To check the consistency of two sets of factual assumptions, both sets of assumptions must be translated into the same framework and compared within that framework. In view of the one-to-one correspondence between indexes of embodied technical change and indexes of disembodied technical change, it is completely immaterial which framework is used for the comparison. If the two sets of factual assumptions are not consistent, the factual question that must be answered is not whether embodied or disembodied technical change is an appropriate model of reality. We have already demonstrated that both types of technical change imply the same model of reality, that is, both models have the same set of factual implications. The factual question to be answered is, in our example, whether disembodied change takes place at 4 percent per year or 5 percent per year.

We have already illustrated the equivalence of embodied and disembodied technical change by calculating indexes of each type from a given set of data. It may be useful to illustrate this equivalence further by calculating the amount of investment required to attain a given amount of economic growth using models of embodied and disembodied technical change, together with a set of assumptions that is factually consistent. This type of calculation can be done for very complicated sets of factual assumptions. The general procedure is to state the set of factual assumptions in such a way that the basic data that underlie expression (2.9) are specified. Then, for a given time path of the data and of the index of embodied technical change, expression (2.9) may be used to compute the equivalent time path of the index of disembodied technical change. Alternatively, for a given time path of the data and of the index of disembodied technical change, the equivalent time path of the index of embodied technical change may be computed using expression (2.9). In comparing factual assumptions about embodied technical change with factual assumptions about disembodied technical change, it is important to keep in mind that indexes of technical change and the corresponding indexes of capital input come in pairs. Choosing a particular index of the rate of technical change from among all those consistent with a given body of data implies the choice of a particular index of capital input. Indexes of capital input corresponding to the indexes of embodied and disembodied technical change of table 2.2 are presented in table 2.4. Table 2.4 contains the rates of growth of capital and surrogate capital, K'/K and K'^{*}/K^{*}, as well as the corresponding indexes of capital and surrogate capital, K and K^{*}, respectively.

To simplify the calculation of the amount of investment required for a given amount of economic growth, which is only intended to serve as an illustration, we assume that the calculation is to be done for a set of factual assumptions in which investment, capital, and indexes of technical change are growing at constant exponential rates. In the long run the rate of growth of investment and the rate of growth

Table 2.4
Rates of growth and indexes of capital and surrogate capital

Year	K'/K	K'^{*}/K^{*}	K	K^{*}
1939	0.00480	0.08426	701.68	63.60
1940	0.01493	0.08521	705.05	68.96
1941	0.02497	0.08400	715.58	74.84
1942	−0.00067	0.03692	733.45	81.13
1943	−0.01115	0.07565	732.96	84.13
1944	−0.00893	−0.00642	724.79	90.49
1945	−0.00267	0.06691	718.32	89.91
1946	0.03080	0.07155	716.40	95.93
1947	0.02787	0.07522	738.47	102.79
1948	0.03703	0.09180	759.05	110.52
1949	0.02062	0.09576	787.16	120.67
1950	0.04033	0.16741	803.39	132.22
1951	0.03984	0.17200	835.79	154.35
1952	0.02895	0.16597	869.09	180.90
1953	0.02759	0.15481	894.25	210.92
1954	0.02438	0.17576	918.92	243.57
1955	0.03692	0.22587	941.32	286.38
1956	0.03376	0.26208	976.07	351.06
1957	0.02836	0.28646	1009.02	443.07
1958	0.01849	0.32312	1037.64	569.99
1959	0.02896	0.49066	1056.83	754.16

of capital are equal; we assume that these rates of growth are equal at the outset. Finally, we assume that all value shares are constant.

For a model of disembodied technical change the rate of growth of output is a weighted average of the rates of growth of capital and labor plus the rate of growth of the index of disembodied technical change. The rate of growth of capital is equal to the ratio of investment to capital less the rate of replacement. Taking the value shares as those that prevailed in 1959, assuming that the rate of growth of labor is the same as in 1959 and taking the rate of replacement to be 0.025 per year, we suppose that the rate of disembodied technical change is 0.025 per year and the rate of growth of output is 0.03 per year. The implied ratio of gross investment to capital is 0.028. To raise the rate of growth of output by one percentage point to 0.04 per year, an increase of 33 percent, the required ratio of gross investment to capital is 0.056, an increase of 100 percent.

For a model of embodied technical change the rate of growth of output may be expressed in two ways. First, the rate of growth is a weighted average of the rates of growth of surrogate capital and labor. Alternatively, if the rate of embodied technical change is constant and the rates of growth of investment and capital stock are equal, the rate of growth of output is a weighted average of the rates of growth of capital and labor plus the relative share of capital less the relative share of investment multiplied by the rate of embodied technical change. Under the factual assumptions we have made, a rate of embodied technical change of 0.13 per year corresponds to a rate of disembodied technical change of 0.025 per year. At a rate of growth of output of 0.03 per year, the implied ratio of gross investment to capital is, of course, the same as before, 0.028. To raise the rate of growth of output by one percentage point, that is, to 0.04 per year, an increase of 33 percent, the required ratio of gross investment to capital is 0.056, an increase of 100 percent. This result illustrates the fact that calculations of the amount of investment required to attain a given amount of economic growth, using models of embodied and disembodied technical change together with a set of assumptions that is factually consistent, give identical results for the two models.

2.6 Mathematical Appendix

In this Appendix we present a formal analysis of the relationship between P, the index of total factor productivity, and Q, the relative error in measurement of the price of investment goods or the reciprocal of the index of the quality of investment goods. The data given at the outset include six basic time series and the rate of replacement of capital goods, δ. The six basic time series are prices and quantities of investment-goods output, consumption-goods output, and labor input. From these data the shares of investment goods, consumption goods, capital services, and labor services in the value of total output may be computed.

1. The first problem is to compute P, the index of total factor productivity, from the six basic time series. Beginning with the definition of the index of total factor productivity,

$$v_I \frac{I'}{I} + v_C \frac{C'}{C} = \frac{P'}{P} + w_K \frac{K'}{K} + w_L \frac{L'}{L},$$

and using the fact that

$$K' = I - \delta K ,$$

the definition may be written in the form:

$$v_I \frac{I'}{I} + v_C \frac{C'}{C} + w_K \delta - w_L \frac{L'}{L} - \frac{P'}{P} = \frac{e^{\delta t} w_K I}{\int_{-\infty}^{t} e^{\delta s} I(s)\, ds} .$$

Now, letting a, b, and c_P be given functions of time, defined as

$$a = v_I \frac{I'}{I} + v_C \frac{C'}{C} + w_K \delta - w_L \frac{L'}{L} ,$$
$$b = w_K I ,$$

and

$$c_P = -1 ,$$

we may rewrite the definition in the form:

$$\int_{-\infty}^{t} e^{\delta s} I(s)\, ds = \frac{b e^{\delta t} P}{aP + c_P P'} .$$

Differentiating with respect to time we obtain:

$$[Ia^2 - (b' + \delta b)a + a'b]P^2 + [2Iac_P - (b' + \delta b)c_P + bc'_P]PP' + [Ic_P^2 - bc_p]P'^2 + bc_P PP' = 0 .$$

Letting $R = P'/P$, we may write

$$R' = d_P + e_P R + f_P R^2 ,$$

where

$$d_P = a\left(I \frac{a}{b} - \frac{b'}{b} - \delta + \frac{a'}{a}\right),$$
$$e_P = -2I \frac{a}{b} + \frac{b'}{b} + \delta ,$$

and

$$f_P = \frac{1}{w_K} .$$

We conclude that the rate of growth of the index of total factor productivity satisfies an ordinary second-degree differential equation with variable coefficients that depend on the six basic time series.

2. The second problem is to compute Q, the relative error in the price of investment goods or the reciprocal of the index of quality of investment goods, from the six basic time series. Beginning with the definition of the index of the quality of investment goods,

$$v_I \frac{I'^*}{I^*} + v_C \frac{C'}{C} = w_K \frac{K'^*}{K^*} + w_L \frac{L'}{L} ,$$

where $QI^* = I$ and $K'^* = I^* - \delta K^*$, the definition may be written in the form:

$$v_I \frac{I'}{I} + v_C \frac{C'}{C} + w_K \delta - w_L \frac{L'}{L} - v_I \frac{Q'}{Q} = \frac{e^{\delta t} w_K I}{Q \int_{-\infty}^{t} e^{\delta s} \frac{I(s)}{Q(s)} ds} .$$

Letting a, b, and c_Q be given functions of time, with a and b defined as before and c_Q defined as $c_Q = - v_I$, we may rewrite the definition in the form:

$$\int_{-\infty}^{t} e^{\delta s} \frac{I(s)}{Q(s)} ds = \frac{be^{\delta t}}{aQ + c_Q Q'} .$$

Differentiating with respect to time we obtain:

$$[Ia^2 - a(b' + \delta b) + ab]Q^2 + [2Iac_Q - (b' + \delta b)c_Q + ab + bc'_Q]Q'Q$$
$$+ Ic_Q^2 Q'^2 + bc_Q QQ' = 0.$$

Letting $S = Q'/Q$, we may write

$$S' = d_Q + e_Q S + f_Q S^2 ,$$

where

$$d_Q = \frac{a}{v_I}\left(I \frac{a}{b} - \frac{b'}{b} - \delta + \frac{a'}{a}\right) = \frac{d_P}{v_I} ,$$

$$e_Q = - 2I \frac{a}{b} + \frac{b'}{b} + \delta + \frac{a - v'_I}{v_I} = e_P + \frac{a - v'_I}{v_I} ,$$

and

$$f_Q = \frac{v_I - w_K}{w_K} = (v_I - w_K) f_P.$$

We conclude that the rate of growth of the index of the quality of investment goods satisfies an ordinary second-degree differential equation with variable coefficients that depend on the six basic time series. The form of the equation is strictly analogous to that for the index of total factor productivity; the coefficients in both equations depend on the same basic time series.

3. To obtain the differential equation governing Q, the reciprocal of the index of the quality of investment goods, where "surrogate" capital is introduced but "surrogate" investment is not, we omit the term $-v_I(Q'/Q)$ from the definition of the index of the quality of investment goods. The resulting definition is

$$v_I \frac{I'}{I} + v_C \frac{C'}{C} + w_K \delta - w_K \frac{L'}{L} = \frac{e^{\delta t} w_K I}{Q \int\limits_{-\infty}^{t} e^{\delta s} \frac{I(s)}{Q(s)} ds},$$

or, employing the notation introduced above,

$$\int\limits_{-\infty}^{t} e^{\delta s} \frac{I(s)}{Q(s)} = \frac{b e^{\delta t}}{aQ}.$$

Differentiating with respect to time we obtain:

$$Q' + Q\left(I \frac{a}{b} - \frac{b'}{b} - \delta + \frac{a'}{a}\right) = 0.$$

Letting $S = Q'/Q$, as before, we may write

$$0 = d_Q + e_Q S,$$

where

$$d_Q = I \frac{a}{b} - \frac{b'}{b} - \delta + \frac{a'}{a} = \frac{d_P}{a}$$

and

$e_Q = 1$.

We conclude that in this case the rate of growth of the index of the quality of investment goods satisfies a linear equation with variable coefficients that depend on the six basic time series.

4. The final problem is to show that any pair of indexes, P and $1/Q$, constructed from the six basic time series, will satisfy equation (2.9) of the text, namely:

$$\frac{P'}{P} = v_I \frac{Q'}{Q} + w_K \left[\frac{I}{\int\limits_{-\infty}^{t} e^{-\delta(t-s)} \frac{Q(t)}{Q(s)} I(s)\, ds} - \frac{I}{\int\limits_{-\infty}^{t} e^{-\delta(t-s)} I(s)\, ds} \right].$$

To verify this equality we replace each of the integrals occurring on the right-hand side by the corresponding expression from the definitions of the indexes P and $1/Q$:

$$\frac{P'}{P} = v_I \frac{Q'}{Q} + w_K \left[\frac{I}{b} \left(a + c_Q \frac{Q'}{Q} \right) - \frac{I}{b} \left(a + c_P \frac{P'}{P} \right) \right].$$

Using the definitions of a, b, c_P, and c_Q, given above, the equality is easily verified.

We conclude that any pair of indexes, P and $1/Q$, constructed from the six basic time series, will satisfy equation (2.9) of the text. To be more precise: Both of the indexes satisfy ordinary second-order differential equations. Hence, the definition of each index generates a two-parameter family of indexes. The parameters that generate a given member of each family may be interpreted as the initial value of the index and the initial value of the corresponding capital stock. Any pair of indexes, P and $1/Q$, consisting of one member of each of the families, satisfies equation (2.9) of the text. There is a one-to-one correspondence between the families of indexes constructed from a given set of data.

5. Similarly, we may show that pairs of indexes, P and $1/Q$, where the index of the quality of investment goods, $1/Q$, is constructed omitting "surrogate" investment, will satisfy equation (2.10) of the text, namely:

$$\frac{P'}{P} = w_K \left[\frac{I}{\int_{-\infty}^{t} e^{-\delta(t-s)} \frac{Q(t)}{Q(s)} I(s)\, ds} - \frac{I}{\int_{-\infty}^{t} e^{-\delta(t-s)} I(s)\, ds} \right].$$

Using the definitions of the indexes P and Q as before,

$$\frac{P'}{P} = w_K \left[I \frac{a}{b} - \frac{I}{b} \left(a + c_P \frac{P'}{P} \right) \right].$$

This equality is easily verified directly from the definitions of a, b, and c_P.

Notes

1. These index numbers were first proposed by Divisia in 1925 (1925; 1926; 1928). Somewhat more accessible discussions of Divisia's work may be found in Frisch's survey article on the theory of index numbers (1936) and in Wold's book on demand analysis (1953). In a more recent publication, Divisia suggests the application of these indexes to the measurement of total factor productivity (1952, pp. 53–54). Even more recently, Solow has given an explicit derivation of the Divisia quantity index of total factor productivity (1957, p. 312) and has applied this index to data for the U.S. private nonfarm economy, 1909–1949.

The Divisia price indexes for total output and total input, say q and p are:

$$\frac{q'}{q} = w_C \frac{q'_C}{q_C} + w_I \frac{q'_I}{q_I},$$

$$\frac{p'}{p} = v_K \frac{p'_K}{p_K} + v_L \frac{p'_L}{p_L},$$

respectively. An alternative definition of total factor productivity, which may be somewhat less familiar than expression (2.3) given in the text, is the ratio of the price of a unit of input to the price of a unity of output: $P = p/q$.

Using the definitions of Divisia price indexes, p and q, the rate of growth of total factor productivity may be expressed as:

$$\frac{P'}{P} = w_K \frac{p'_K}{p_K} + w_L \frac{p'_L}{p_L} - v_C \frac{q'_C}{q_C} - v_I \frac{q'_I}{q_I},$$

which corresponds to expression (2.4) of the text. These two expressions for the rate of growth of total factor productivity are dual to each other; by itself each provides a complete definition of total factor productivity; the two definitions are equivalent by the identity (2.2).

Any index of total factor productivity may be computed either from quantity indexes of total output and total input or from the corresponding price indexes. The whole analysis that follows could be carried out in an entirely equivalent way, using price indexes instead of quantity indexes.

For present purposes we do not consider explicitly other explanations of change in total factor productivity, such as economies of scale, external economies, or economic disequilibrium. In both embodiment and disembodiment explanations of change in total factor productivity, these additional explanatory factors can be lumped together with pure technical change or treated separately. To simplify the following discussion, such factors will not be distinguished from technical change.

2. The analysis of total factor productivity can be carried out equivalently through index-number formulas or through production functions. From a purely formal point of view, both index-number formulas and production functions may be interpreted as mean value functions (Hardy, Littlewood, and Polya, 1952, pp. 12–14). Production functions have been discussed from this point of view by Arrow, Chenery, Minhas, and Solow (1961, pp. 230–231), while index-number formulas have been discussed from the same point of view by Wold (1953, pp. 132–239, esp. p. 133).

Tinbergen (1942, pp. 190–195) interprets the geometric quantity index of total factor productivity as a Cobb-Douglas production function. As further examples of index-number formulas that have been interpreted as production functions, a fixed-weight Laspeyres quantity index of total factor productivity may be interpreted as a "linear" production function, that is, as a production function with infinite elasticity of substitution, as Solow (1957, p. 317) and Clemhout (1963, pp. 358–360) have pointed out. In a sense, output-capital or output-labor ratios correspond to Leontief-type production functions, that is, to production functions with zero elasticity of substitution, as Domar points out (1961, p. 712–713).

To date, no attempt has been made to utilize the index-number formula which may be interpreted as a production function with arbitrary elasticity of substitution; of course, all the index-number formulas we have mentioned are special cases or limiting cases of such a formula.

3. This condition corresponds to Hicks's condition for aggregation of commodities in demand analysis (1946, pp. 312–313). Wold (1953, p. 109) calls this result the Leontief-Hicks Theorem.

4. A theoretical justification for this assumption is that replacement of investment goods is a recurrent event. An initial investment generates an infinite series of replacement investments over time. The distribution of replacements for such an infinite stream approaches a constant fraction of the accumulated stock of investment goods for any "survival curve" of individual pieces of equipment; but this is precisely the relationship between replacement and accumulated stock if an exponentially declining proportion of any given investment is replaced in a given interval of time.

5. This result does not agree with Domar's result on a closely related problem (1963, p. 587, formula [5]), because Domar assumes that capital input into the production of investment goods "is imported from the outside." Using the condition that capital input commands the same rental value in both sectors, the need for this specialization may be eliminated as previously indicated in text. The correct result for the general case is that given in the text.

6. This appears to be what Denison has in mind in stating that: "The frequently advanced proposition that inputs should be measured in units of constant quality, as determined by their ability to contribute to production is tantamount to making the index of [total input] identical with that of [total output]" (1961, pp. 349–350). For example, it is always possible to "adjust" the price of investment goods so that total factor productivity is constant. However, Denison's conclusion is false in general; not every adjustment for quality change will eliminate total factor productivity. Whether a

particular adjustment will have this effect is generally a refutable proposition and can be tested quite simply by appealing to the evidence. However, every adjustment computed from a formula like (2.9), in text, will eliminate total factor productivity; this is true by definition and is not refutable by any appeal to the evidence.

7. See the Mathematical Appendix. More precisely, we may say that the definition of each index generates a two-parameter family of indexes. The parameters that generate a given member of each family may be interpreted as initial values of the index of technical change and the corresponding index of capital stock. For a given set of data any pair of indexes consisting of one member of each of the families satisfies expression (2.9). There is a one-to-one correspondence between the families of indexes constructed from a given set of data. In this paper we leave open the question of whether disembodied technical change is an explanation of change in total factor productivity or simply a relabeling of Our Ignorance, as some have suggested. For those who prefer to call disembodied technical change a relabeling of Our Ignorance, expression (2.9) says that the relative error in the price of investment goods is an alternative and entirely equivalent relabeling of Our Ignorance. This is certainly a valid interpretation of the relative error in the price of investment goods. An alternative interpretation of the error is suggested below.

8. These data are based on those of Kendrick (1961a; Kendrick and Sato, 1963, pp. 996–1002). For the period 1939–1959 Kendrick's data on the output of consumption and investment goods are based on the Office of Business Economics accounts for gross national product. In all of the calculations given in table 2.2, the rate of replacement is assumed to be 0.025.

9. For details of the method of calculation, consult the Mathematical Appendix.

10. A comparison of the principal alternative estimates is provided by Abramovitz (1962, p. 765).

11. This empirical result may explain the seeming anomaly that the goodness of fit of a production function based on embodied technical change increases throughout the range of values considered by Solow. Further light is thrown on this question by the index of embodied technical change presented in table 2.4 below.

12. Solow points out that: "This [rate of gross investment] is not a wholly unambiguous notion. By the same rate of gross investment I mean the same physical output of 'machines.' But machines behave differently in the two economies [with embodied and disembodied technical change] and so must asset valuation. Production of identical numbers of machines may have quite different implications in value terms" (1960, p. 93, n. 5).

3 The Explanation of Productivity Change

Dale W. Jorgenson and
Zvi Griliches

But part of the job of economics is weeding out errors. That is much harder than making them, but also more fun. — R.M. Solow

3.1 Introduction

Measurement of total factor productivity is based on the economic theory of production. For this purpose the theory consists of a production function with constant returns to scale together with the necessary conditions for producer equilibrium. Quantities of output and input entering the production function are identified with real product and real factor input as measured for social accounting purposes. Marginal rates of substitution are identified with the corresponding price ratios. Employing data on both quantities and prices, movements along the production function may be separated from shifts in the production function. Shifts in the production function are identified with changes in total factor productivity.

Our point of departure is that the economic theory underlying the measurement of real product and real factor input has not been fully exploited. As a result a number of significant errors of measurement have been made in compiling data on the growth of real product and the growth of real factor input. The result of these errors is to introduce serious biases in the measurement of total factor productivity. The allocation of changes in real product and real factor input between movements along a given production function and shifts of the production function must be corrected for bias due to errors of concept and measurement.

The purpose of this paper is to examine a hypothesis concerning the explanation of changes in total factor productivity. This hypothesis may be stated in two alternative and equivalent ways. In the terminology of the theory of production, if quantities of output and input are measured accurately, growth in total output is largely explained by growth in total input. Associated with the theory of production is a system of social accounts for real product and real factor input. The rate of growth of total factor productivity is the difference between the rate of growth of real product and the rate of growth of real factor input. Within the framework of social accounting the hypothesis is that if real product and real factor input are accurately accounted for, the observed growth in total factor productivity is negligible.

We must emphasize that our hypothesis concerning the explanation of real output is testable. By far the largest portion of the literature on total factor productivity is devoted to problems of measurement rather than to problems of explanation. In recognition of this fact changes in total factor productivity have been given such labels as *The Residual* or *The Measure of Our Ignorance*. Identification of measured growth in total factor productivity with embodied or disembodied technical change provides methods for measuring technical change, but provides no genuine explanation of the underlying changes in real output and input.[1] Simply relabelling these changes as *Technical Progress* or *Advance of Knowledge* leaves the problem of explaining growth in total output unsolved.

The plan of this paper is as follows: We first discuss the definition of changes in total factor productivity from the point of view of the economic theory of production. Second, we provide operational definitions for the measurement of price and quantities that enter into the economic theory of production. These definitions generate a system of social accounts for real product and real factor input and for the measurement of total factor productivity. Within this system we provide an operational definition of total factor productivity. This definition is fundamental to an empirical test of the hypothesis that if real product and real factor input are accurately accounted for, the observed rate of growth of total factor productivity is negligible.

Within our system of social accounts for real product and real factor input we can assess the consequences of errors of measurement that arise from conceptual errors in the separation of the value of transactions into price and quantity. Errors in making this separation may effect real product, real factor input, or both; for example, an error in the measurement of the price of investment goods results in a bias in total output and a bias in the capital accounts that underlie the measurement of total input. Within this system of social accounts we can suggest principles for correct aggregation of inputs and outputs and indicate the consequences of incorrect aggregation. Many of the most important errors of measurement in previous compilations of data on real product and real factor input arise from incorrect aggregation.

Given a system of social accounts for the measurement of total factor productivity we attempt to correct a number of common errors of measurement of real product and real factor input by introducing data that correspond more accurately to the concepts of output and input of the economic theory of production. After correcting for errors of measurement we examine the validity of our hypothesis concerning changes in total factor productivity. We conclude with an evaluation of past research and a discussion of implications of our findings for further research.

3.2 Theory

Our definition of changes in total factor productivity is the conventional one. The rate of growth of total factor productivity is defined as the difference between the rate of growth of real product and the rate of growth of real factor input. The rates of growth of real product and real factor input are defined, in turn, as weighted averages of the rates of growth of individual products and factors. The weights are relative shares of each product in the value of total output and of each factor in the value of total input. If a production function has constant returns to scale and if all marginal rates of substitution are equal to the corresponding price ratios, a change in total factor productivity may be identified with a shift in the production function. Changes in real product and real factor input not accompanied by a change in total factor productivity may be identified with movements alongs a production function.

Our definition of change in total factor productivity is the same as that suggested by Abramovitz (1962), namely, "... the effect of 'costless' advances in applied technology managerial efficiency, and industrial organization (cost—the employment of scarce resources with alternative uses—is, after all, the touchstone of an 'input')...."[2] Of course, changes in total factor productivity or shifts in a given production function may be accompanied by movements along a production function. For example, changes in applied technology may be associated with the construction of new types of capital equipment. The alteration in patterns of productive activity must be separated into the part which is "costless," representing a shift in the production function, and the part which represents the employment of scarce resources with alternative uses, representing movements along the production function.

On the output side the quantities that enter into the economic theory of production correspond to real product as measured for the purposes of social accounting. Similarly, on the input side these quantities correspond to real factor input, also as measured for the purposes of social accounting. The prices that enter the economic theory of production are identified with the implicit deflators that underlie conversion of the value of total output and total input into real terms. The notion of real product is a familiar one to social accountants and has been adopted by most Western countries as the appropriate measure of the level of aggregate economic activity. The notion of real factor input is somewhat less familiar, since social accounting for factor input is usually carried out only in value terms or current prices. However, it is obvious that income streams recorded in value terms correspond to transactions in the services of productive factors. The value of these transactions may be separated into price and quantity and the resulting data may be employed to construct social accounts for factor input in constant prices. This type of social accounting is implicit in all attempts to measure total factor productivity.

The prices and quantities that enter into the economic theory of production will be given in terms of social accounts for total output and total input in current and constant prices. We observe that our measurement of total factor productivity is subject to all the well-known limitations of social accounting. Only the results of economic activities with some counterpart in market transactions are included in the accounts. No attempt is made to measure social benefits or social costs if these diverge from the corresponding private benefits or private costs. Throughout this study we adhere to the basic framework of social accounting. The measurement of both output and input is based entirely on market transactions; all prices reflect private benefits and private costs. That part of any alteration in the pattern of productive activity that is "costless" from the point of view of market transactions is attributed to change in total factor productivity. Thus the social accounting framework provides a definition of total factor productivity as the ratio of real product to real factor input.

To represent the system of social accounts that provides the basis for measuring total factor productivity, we introduce the following notation:

Y_i — quantity of the ith output, X_j — quantity of the jth input, q_i — price of the ith output, p_j — price of the jth input,

where there are m outputs and n inputs, the fundamental identity for each accounting period is that the value of output is equal to the value of input:

$$q_1Y_1 + q_2Y_2 + \cdots + q_mY_m = p_1X_1 + p_2X_2 + \cdots + p_nX_n \, . \tag{3.1}$$

This accounting identity is important in defining an appropriate method for measuring total factor productivity; it also provides a useful check on the consistency of any proposed definitions of total output and total input.

To define total factor productivity we first differentiate (3.1) totally with respect to time and divide both sides by the corresponding total value. The result is an identity between a weighted average of the sum of rates of growth of output prices and quantities and a weighted average of the sum of rates of growth of input prices and quantities:

$$\Sigma w_i \left[\frac{\dot{q}_i}{q_i} + \frac{\dot{Y}_i}{Y_i} \right] = \Sigma v_j \left[\frac{\dot{p}_j}{p_j} + \frac{\dot{X}_j}{X_j} \right], \tag{3.2}$$

with weights $\{w_i\}$ and $\{v_j\}$ given by the relative shares of the value of the ith output in the value of total output and the value of jth input in the value of total input:

$$w_i = \frac{q_iY_i}{\Sigma q_iY_i} , \quad v_j = \frac{p_jX_j}{\Sigma p_jX_j} \, .$$

To verify that both sides of (3.2) are weighted averages, we observe that:

$$w_i \geqq 0 \, , \quad i = 1 \cdots m \, ;$$
$$v_j \geqq 0 \, , \quad j = 1 \cdots n \, ;$$
$$\Sigma w_i = \Sigma v_j = 1 \, .$$

A useful index of the quantity of total output may be defined in terms of the weighted average of the rates of growth of the individual outputs from (3.2); denoting this index of output by Y, the rate of growth of this index is

$$\frac{\dot{Y}}{Y} = \Sigma w_i \frac{\dot{Y}_i}{Y_i} ;$$

an analogous index of the quantity of total input, say X, has rate of growth

$$\frac{\dot{X}}{X} = \Sigma v_j \frac{\dot{X}_j}{X_j} .$$

These quantity indexes are familiar as Divisia quantity indexes; the corresponding Divisia price indexes for total output and total input, say q and p, have rates of growth:

$$\frac{\dot{q}}{q} = \Sigma w_i \frac{\dot{q}_i}{q_i} ,$$
$$\frac{\dot{p}}{p} = \Sigma v_j \frac{\dot{p}_j}{p_j} ,$$

respectively.[3]

In terms of Divisia index numbers a natural definition of total factor productivity, say P, is the ratio of the quantity of total output to the quantity of total input:

$$P = \frac{Y}{X} . \tag{3.3}$$

Using the definitions of Divisia quantity indexes, Y and X, the rate of growth of total factor productivity may be expressed as:

$$\frac{\dot{P}}{P} = \frac{\dot{Y}}{Y} - \frac{\dot{X}}{X} = \Sigma w_i \frac{\dot{Y}_i}{Y_i} - \Sigma v_j \frac{\dot{X}_j}{X_j} . \tag{3.4}$$

or, alternatively, as:

$$\frac{\dot{P}}{P} = \frac{\dot{p}}{p} - \frac{\dot{q}}{q} = \Sigma v_j \frac{\dot{p}_j}{p_j} - \Sigma w_i \frac{\dot{q}_i}{q_i} .$$

These two definitions of total factor productivity are dual to each other and are equivalent by (3.2). In general, any index of total factor productivity can be computed either from indexes of the quantity of total output and total input or from the corresponding price indexes.[4]

Up to this point we have defined total factor productivity as the ratio of certain index numbers of total output and total input. An economic interpretation of this definition may be obtained from the theory of production. The theory includes a production function characterized by constant returns to scale; writing this function in implicit form, we have:

$$F(Y_1, Y_2,...,Y_m;\ X_1, X_2,...,X_n) = 0\ .$$

Shifts in the production function may be defined in terms of appropriate weighted average rates of growth of outputs and inputs,

$$G\dot{F} = \Sigma\left(\frac{F_i Y_i}{\Sigma F_i Y_i} \cdot \frac{\dot{Y}_i}{Y_i}\right) - \Sigma\left(\frac{F_j X_j}{\Sigma F_j X_j} \cdot \frac{\dot{X}_j}{X_j}\right), \tag{3.5}$$

where $F_i = \dfrac{\partial F}{\partial Y_i}$, $F_j = \dfrac{\partial F}{\partial X_j}$ and

$$\frac{1}{G} = \Sigma F_i Y_i = -\Sigma F_j X_j .$$

Changes in total factor productivity may be identified with shifts of the production function as opposed to movements along the production function by adding the necessary conditions for producer equilibrium—all marginal rates of transformation between pairs of inputs and outputs are equal to the corresponding price ratios—

$$\frac{\partial Y_i}{\partial X_j} = -\frac{F_j}{F_i} = \frac{p_j}{q_i}\ ; \qquad \frac{\partial Y_t}{\partial Y_k} = -\frac{F_k}{F_i} = \frac{q_i}{q_k}\ ;$$

$$\frac{\partial X_j}{\partial X_l} = -\frac{F_l}{F_j} = \frac{p_l}{p_j}\ ; \qquad (i, k = 1 \cdots m\ ;\ j, l = 1 \cdots n)\ .$$

Combining these conditions with the definition (3.5) of shifts in the production function, we obtain the definition (3.4) of total factor productivity:

$$G\dot{F} = \frac{\dot{P}}{P}\ .$$

The rate of growth of total factor productivity is zero if and only if the shift in the production function is zero.

The complete theory of production consists of a production function with constant returns to scale together with the necessary conditions for producer equilibrium. This theory of production implies the existence of a factor price frontier relating the prices of output to the prices of input. The dual to the definition (3.4) of total factor productivity may be identified with shifts in the factor price frontier.[5]

The economic interpretation of the index of total factor productivity is essential in measuring changes in total factor productivity by means of Divisia index numbers. As is well-known,[6] the Divisia index of total factor productivity is a line integral so that its value normally depends on the path of integration; even if the path returns to its initial value the index of total factor productivity may increase or decrease. However, if price ratios are identified with marginal rates of transformation of a production function with constant returns to scale, the index will remain constant if the shift in the production function is zero.[7]

From either of the two definitions of the index of total factor productivity we have given it is obvious that the rate of growth of this index is not zero by definition. Even for a production function characterized by constant returns to scale with all factors paid the value of their marginal products, the rate of growth of real product may exceed or fall short of the rate of growth of real factor input; similarly, the rate of growth of the price of real factor input may exceed or fall short of the rate of growth of the price of real product.[8]

The economic theory of production on which our interpretation of changes in total factor productivity rests is not the only possible theory of production. From the definition of shifts in the production function (3.5) it is clear that the production function may be considered in isolation from the necessary conditions for producer equilibrium, provided that alternative operational definitions of the marginal rates of transformation are introduced. Such a production function may incorporate the effects of increasing returns to scale, externalities, and disequilibrium. Changes in total factor productivity in our sense could then be interpreted as movements along the production function in this more general sense.

To provide a basis for assessing the role of errors of measurement in explaining observed changes in total factor productivity, we first set out principles for measuring total output and total input. The measurement of flows of output and labor services, is, at least conceptually, straightforward. Beginning with data on the value of transactions in each type of output and each type of labor service, this value is separated into a price and a quantity. A quantity index of total output is constructed from the quantities of each output, using the relative shares of the value of each output in the value of total output as weights. Similarly, a quantity index of total labor input is constructed from the quantities of each labor service, using the relative shares of the value of each labor service in the value of all labor services as weights.

If capital services were bought and sold by distinct economic units in the same way as labor services, there would be no conceptual or empirical difference between the construction of a quantity index of total capital input and the construction of the corresponding index of total labor input. Beginning with data on the value of transactions in each type of capital service, this value could be separated into a price of capital service or rental and a quantity of capital service in, say, machine hours. These data would correspond to the value of transactions in each type of labor service which could be separated into a price of labor service or wage and a quantity of labor service in, say, man-hours. A quantity index of total capital input would be constructed from the quantities of each type of capital service, using the relative shares of the rental value of each capital service in the rental value of all capital services as weights.

The measurement of capital services is less straightforward than the measurement of labor services because the consumer of a capital service is usually also the supplier of the service; the whole transaction is recorded only in the internal accounts of individual economic units. The obstacles to extracting this information for purposes of social accounting are almost insuperable; the information must be obtained by a relatively lengthy chain of indirect inference. The data with which the calculation begins are the values of transactions in new investment goods. These values must be separated into a price and quantity of investment goods. Second, the quantity of new investment goods reduced by the quantity of old investment goods replaced must be added to accumulated stocks. Third, the quantity of capital services corresponding to each stock must be calculated.[9]

Paralleling the calculation of quantities of capital services beginning with the quantities of new investment goods, the prices of capital services must be calculated beginning with the prices of new investment goods. Finally, a quantity index of total capital input must be constructed from the quantities of each type of capital service, using the relative shares of the implicit rental value of each capital service in the implicit rental value of all capital services as weights. The implicit rental value of each capital service is obtained by simply multiplying the quantity of that service by the corresponding price. At this final stage the construction of a quantity index of total capital input is formally identical to the construction of a quantity index of total labor input or total output. The chief difference between the construction of price and quantity indexes of total capital input and any other aggregation problem is in the circuitous route by which the necessary data are obtained.

The details of the calculation of a price and quantity of capital services from data on the values of transactions in new investment goods depend on empirical hypotheses about the rate of replacement of old investment goods and the quantity of capital services corresponding to a given stock of capital. In studies of total factor productivity it is conventional to assume that capital services are proportional to capital stock. Where independent data on rates of utilization of capital are available, this assumption can be dispensed with. A number of hypotheses about the rate of replacement of old investment goods have been used in the literature: (1) Accounting depreciation measured by the straight-line method is set equal to replacement possibly with a correction for changes in prices. (2) Gross investment in some earlier period is set equal to replacement. (3) A weighted average of past investment with weights derived from studies of the "survival curves" of individual pieces of equipment[10] is set equal to replacement. From a formal point of view, the last of these hypotheses includes the first two as special cases.

We assume that the proportion of an investment replaced in a given interval of time declines exponentially over time. A theoretical justification for this assumption is that replacement of investment goods is a recurrent event. An initial investment generates a series of replacement investments over time; each replacement generates a new series of replacements, and so on; this process repeats itself indefinitely. The appropriate model for replacement of investment goods is not the distribution over time of replacements for a given investment, but rather the distribution over time of the infinite stream of replacements generated by a given investment. The distribution of replacements for such an infinite stream approaches a constant fraction of the accumulated stock of investment goods for any "survival curve" of individual pieces of equipment and for any initial age distribution of the accumulated stock, whether the stock is constant or growing. But this is precisely the relationship between replacement and accumulated stock if an exponentially declining proportion of any given investment is replaced in a given interval of time.

The quantity of capital services corresponding to each stock could be measured directly, at least in principle. The stock of equipment would be measured in numbers of machines while the service flow would be measured in machine hours, just as the stock of labor is measured in numbers of men while the flow of labor services is measured in man-hours. While the stock of equipment may be calculated by cumulating the net flow of investment goods, the relative utilization of this equipment must be estimated in order to convert stocks into flows of equipment services. For the purposes of this study we assume that the relative utilization of all capital goods is the same; we estimate the relative utilization of capital from the relative utilization of power sources. An adjustment for the relative utilization of equipment is essential in order to preserve comparability among our measurements of output, labor input, and capital input.

To represent the capital accounts which provide the basis for measuring total capital input, we introduce the following notation:

I_k — quantity of output of the kth investment good,
K_k — quantity of input of the kth capital service.

As before, we use the notation:

q_k — price of the kth investment good,
p_k — price of the kth capital service.

Under the assumption that the proportion of an investment replaced in a given interval of time declines exponentially, the cumulated stock of past investments in the kth capital good, net of replacements, satisfies the well-known relationship:

$$I_k = \dot{K}_k + \delta_k K_k \,, \tag{3.6}$$

where δ_k is the instantaneous rate of replacement of the kth investment good. Similarly, in the absence of direct taxation the price of the kth capital service satisfies the relationship:

$$p_k = q_k \left[r + \delta_k - \frac{\dot{q}_k}{q_k} \right], \tag{3.7}$$

where r is the rate of return on all capital, δ_k is the rate of replacement of the kth investment good, and $\dot{q}_k/q_k$ is the rate of capital gain on that good. Given these relationships between the price and quantity of investment goods and the price and quantity of the corresponding capital services, the only data beyond values of transactions in new investment goods required for the construction of price and quantity indexes of total capital input are rates of replacement for each distinct investment good and the rate of return on all capital. We turn now to the problem of measuring the rate of return.

First, to measure the values of output and input it is customary to exclude the value of capital gains from the value of input rather than to include the value of such gains in the value of output. This convention has the virtue that the value of output may be calculated directly from the values of transactions. Second, to measure total factor productivity, depreciation is frequently excluded from both input and output; this convention is adopted, for example, by Kendrick (1961a). Exclusion of depreciation on capital introduces an entirely arbitrary distinction between labor input and capital input, since the corresponding exclusion of depreciation of the stock of labor services is not carried out.[11] To calculate the rate of return on all capital, our procedure is to subtract from the value of output plus capital gains the value of labor input and of replacement. This results in the rate of return multiplied by the value of accumulated stocks. The rate of return is calculated by dividing this quantity by the value of the stock.[12] The implicit rental value of the kth capital good is:

$$p_k K_k = q_k \left[r + \delta_k - \frac{\dot{q}_k}{q_k} \right] K_k \,.$$

To calculate price and quantity indexes for total capital input, the prices and quantities of each type of capital service are aggregated, using the relative shares of the implicit rental value of each capital service in the implicit rental value of all capital services as weights.

An almost universal conceptual error in the measurement of capital input is to confuse the aggregation of capital stock with the aggregation of capital service. This error may be exemplified by the following passage from a recent paper by Kendrick (1961b) devoted to theoretical aspects of capital measurement:

> . . . the prices of the underlying capital goods, as established in markets or imputed by owners, can be appropriately combined (with variable quantity

weights) to provide a deflator to convert capital values into physical volumes of the various types of underlying capital goods at base-period prices. Or, the result can be achieved directly by weighting quantities by constant prices.

As I view it, this is the most meaningful way to measure "real capital stock," since the weighted aggregate measures the physical complex of capital goods in terms of its estimated ability to contribute to production as of the base period.[13]

The "ability to contribute to production" is, of course, measured by the price of capital services, not the price of investment goods.[14]

We have already noted that direct observations are usually available only for values of transactions; the separation of these values into prices and quantities is based on much less complete information and usually involves indirect inferences; the presence of systematic errors in this separation is widely recognized. For output of consumption goods or input of labor services an error in separating the value of transactions into price and quantity results in an error in measurement of the price and quantity of total output or total labor input and in the measurement of total factor productivity. For example, suppose that the rate of growth of the price of a particular type of labor service is measured with an error; since all relative value shares remain the same, the resulting error in the price of total labor input has a rate of growth equal to the rate of growth of the error multiplied by the relative share of the labor service. The quantity of total labor input is measured with an error which is equal in magnitude but opposite in sign. The error in measurement of the rate of growth of total factor productivity is equal to the negative of the rate of growth of the error in the quantity of total labor input multiplied by the relative share of labor. The effects of an error in the rate of growth of the price of a particular type of consumption good are entirely analogous, of course, an upward bias in the rate of growth of output increases the measured rate of growth of total factor productivity, while an upward bias in the rate of growth of input decreases the measured rate of growth.

An error in the separation of the value of transactions in new investment goods into the price and quantity of investment goods will result in errors in measurement of the price and quantity of investment goods, of the price and quantity of capital services and of total factor productivity. To measure the bias in the rate of growth of the quantity of investment goods, we let Q^* be the relative error in the measurement of the price of investment goods, I^* the "quantity" of investment goods output, calculated using the erroneous "price" of investment goods, and I the actual quantity of investment goods output. The bias in the rate of growth of investment goods output is then:

$$\frac{\dot{I}^*}{I^*} - \frac{\dot{I}}{I} = - \frac{\dot{Q}^*}{Q^*} . \tag{3.8}$$

The rate of growth of this bias is negative if the rate of growth of the error in measurement of the price of investment goods is positive, and *vice versa*. If we let K^* be the "quantity" of capital calculated using the erroneous "price" of investment goods and K the actual quantity of capital:

$$K^* = \int_{-\infty}^{t} e^{-\delta(t-s)} I^*(s)\, ds = \int_{-\infty}^{t} e^{-\delta(t-s)} \frac{I(s)}{Q^*(s)}\, ds .$$

The bias in the rate of growth of the quantity of capital services is then:

$$\begin{aligned} \frac{\dot{K}^*}{K^*} - \frac{\dot{K}}{K} &= \frac{I}{Q^* K^*} - \frac{I}{K} \\ &= \frac{I}{\int_{-\infty}^{t} e^{-\delta(t-s)} \frac{Q^*(t)}{Q^*(s)} I(s)\, ds} - \frac{I}{\int_{-\infty}^{t} e^{-\delta(t-s)} I(s)\, ds} , \end{aligned} \tag{3.9}$$

which is negative if the rate of growth of the error in measurement of the price of investment goods is positive, and *vice versa*.

To calculate the error of measurement in total factor productivity, we let C represent the quantity of consumption goods and L the quantity of labor input; second, we let w_I represent the relative share of the value of investment goods in the value of total output and w_C the relative share of consumption goods; finally, we let v_K represent the relative share of the value of capital input in the value of total input and v_L the relative share of labor. The rate of growth of total factor productivity may be represented as:

$$\frac{\dot{P}}{P} = w_I \frac{\dot{I}}{I} + w_C \frac{\dot{C}}{C} - v_K \frac{\dot{K}}{K} - v_L \frac{\dot{L}}{L} .$$

If we let P^* represent the measured index of total factor productivity using the erroneous "price" of investment goods:

$$\frac{\dot{P}*}{P*} = w_I \frac{\dot{I}*}{I*} + w_C \frac{\dot{C}}{C} - v_K \frac{\dot{K}*}{K*} - v_L \frac{\dot{L}}{L}.$$

Subtracting the first of these expressions from the second we obtain the bias in the rate of growth of total factor productivity:

$$\frac{\dot{P}*}{P*} - \frac{\dot{P}}{P} = w_I \left[\frac{\dot{I}*}{I*} - \frac{\dot{I}}{I} \right] - v_K \left[\frac{\dot{K}*}{K*} - \frac{\dot{K}}{K} \right].$$

Substituting expressions (3.9) and (3.8) for the biases in the measured rates of growth of capital input and the output of investment goods, we have:

$$\frac{\dot{P}*}{P*} - \frac{\dot{P}}{P} = - w_I \frac{\dot{Q}*}{Q*}$$
$$-v_K \left(\frac{I}{\int_{-\infty}^{t} e^{-\delta(t-s)} \frac{Q*(t)}{Q*(s)} I(s)\, ds} - \frac{I}{\int_{-\infty}^{t} e^{-\delta(t-s)} I(s)\, ds} \right). \tag{3.10}$$

If investment and the error in measurement are growing at constant rates, the biases in the rates of growth of the quantity of investment goods produced and the quantity of capital services are equal, so that the net effect is equal to the rate of growth in the error in measurement of the price of investment goods multiplied by the difference between the capital share in total input and the investment share in total output.[15]

A second source of errors in measurement arises from limitations on the number of separate inputs that may be distinguished empirically. The choice of commodity groups to service as distinct "inputs" and "outputs" involves aggregation within each group by simply adding together the quantities of all commodities within the group and aggregation among groups by computation of the usual Divisia quantity index. The resulting price and quantity indexes are Divisia price and quantity indexes of the individual commodities only if the rates of growth either of prices or of quantities within each group are identical.

Errors of aggregation in studies of total factor productivity have not gone unnoticed; however, these errors are frequently mislabelled as "quality change." Quality change in this sense occurs whenever the rates of growth of quantities within each separate group are not identical. For example, if high quality items grow faster than items of low quality, the rate of growth of the group is biased downward relative to an index treating high and low quality items as separate commodities. To eliminate this bias it is necessary to construct the index of input or output for the group as a Divisia index of the individual items within the group. Elimination of "quality change" in the sense of aggregation bias is essential to accurate social accounting and to measurement of changes in total factor productivity. Separate accounts should be maintained for as many product and factor input categories as possible. An attempt should be made to exploit available detail in any empirical measurement of real product, real factor input, and total factor productivity.

In some contexts the choice of an appropriate unit for the measurement of quantities of real product or real factor input is not obvious. For example, fuel may be measured in tons or in B.T.U. equivalents, tractor services may be measured in tractor hours or in horsepower hours, and so on. Measures of real product and real factor input may be adjusted for "quality change" by converting one unit of measurement to another. This procedure conforms to the principles of social accounting we have outlined and their interpretation in terms of the economic theory of production if the adjustment for quality change corrects errors of aggregation. In the examples we have given, if the marginal products of different types of fuel always move in proportion when fuel is measured in B.T.U. equivalents but fail to do so when fuel is measured in tons, the appropriate unit for the measurement of fuel is the B.T.U. Similarly, if the marginal products of tractor services measured in horsepower hours always move in proportion, but when measured in tractor hours fail to do so, tractor services should be measured in horsepower hours.

The appropriateness of any proposed adjustment for quality change may be confronted with empirical evidence on the marginal products of individual items within a commodity group. Under the assumption that these products are equal to the corresponding price ratios this evidence takes the form of data on relative price movements for the individual items. Under a more general set of assumptions the marginal products might be calculated from an econometric production function. The latter treatment would be especially useful for "linking in" new factors and products since the relevant prices cannot be observed until the new factors and products appear in the market. Any change in measured total factor productivity resulting from adjustments for quality change is explained by evidence on the movement of marginal products and is not the result of an arbitrary choice of definitions. The choice of appropriate units for measurement of real product and real factor input may go beyond selection among alternative scalar measured such as B.T.U. equivalents or tons; a commodity may be regarded as multi-dimensional and an appropriate unit of measurement may be defined implicitly by taking prices as given by so-called "hedonic" price indexes. The critical property of such price indexes is that when prices are given by a "hedonic" price index for the commodities within a group, all such commodities have marginal rates of transformation *vis-à-vis* commodities outside the group that move in proportion to each other. Insofar as this property is substantiated by empirical evidence, adjustment of the commodity group for "quality change" by means of such a price index is entirely legitimate and amounts to correcting an error of aggregation.[16] This is not to say that any proposed adjustment for quality change is legitimate. The appropriateness of each adjustment must be judged on the basis of the evidence. If no fresh evidence is employed, the choice of appropriate units is entirely arbitrary and any change in measured total factor productivity resulting from adjustment for "quality change" is simply definitional.

"Quality change" is sometimes used to describe a special type of aggregation error, namely, the error that arises in aggregating investment goods of different vintages by simply adding together quantities of investment goods of each vintage. If the quality of investment goods, as measured by the marginal productivity of capital, is not constant over all vintages, this procedure results in aggregation errors. An appropriate index of capital services may be constructed by treating each vintage of investment goods as a separate commodity. To construct such an index empirically, data on the marginal productivity of capital of each vintage at each point of time are required. If independent data on relative prices of capital services of different vintages are used in the construction of such a capital services index, any resulting reduction in measured productivity growth is not tautological. Only where the change in quality is measured indirectly from the resulting increase in total factor productivity, as suggested by Solow (1960), does such a procedure result in the elimination of productivity change by definition.[17]

3.3 Measurement

3.3.1 Initial Estimates

We can now investigate the extent to which measured changes in total factor productivity are due to errors of measurement. We begin by constructing indexes of total output and total input for the United States for the twenty-year period following World War II, 1945–1965, without correcting for errors of measurement. As an initial index of total output we take U.S. private domestic product in constant prices as measured in the U.S. national product accounts (Office of Business Economics, 1966). As an index of total input we take the sum of labor and capital services in constant prices. Labor and capital services are assumed to be proportional to stocks of labor and capital, respectively. The stock of labor is taken to be the number of persons engaged in the private domestic sector of the U.S. economy. The stock of capital is the sum of land, plant, equipment, and inventories employed in this sector.[18] The rate of growth of total factor productivity is equal to the difference in the rates of growth of total output and total input.

Indexes of total output, total input, and total factor productivity are given in table 3.1. The average annual rate of growth of total output over the period 1945–1965 is 3.49 percent. The average rate of growth of total input is 1.83 percent. The average rate of growth of total factor productivity is 1.60 percent. The rate of growth of total input explains 52.4 percent of the growth in output; the remainder is explained by changes in total factor productivity.

3.3.2 Errors of Aggregation

The first error of measurement to be eliminated is an error of aggregation. This error results from aggregating labor and capital services by summing quantities in constant prices. To eliminate the error, we replace our initial index of total input by a Divisia index of labor and capital input, as suggested by Solow (1957). A similar error results from aggregating consumption and investment goods output by adding together quantities in constant prices. This error may be eliminated by replacing our initial index of total output by a Divisia index of consumption and investment goods output. Indexes of total output, total input, and total factor productivity with these errors of aggregation eliminated are presented in table 3.2.

Table 3.1
Total output, input, and factory productivity, U.S. private domestic economy, 1945–1965, initial estimates

	Output	Input	Productivity
1945	0.699	0.786	0.891
1946	0.680	0.817	0.836
1947	0.695	0.854	0.818
1948	0.729	0.876	0.836
1949	0.726	0.867	0.841
1950	0.801	0.891	0.901
1951	0.852	0.928	0.919
1952	0.873	0.947	0.924
1953	0.917	0.966	0.951
1954	0.904	0.954	0.949
1955	0.981	0.976	1.005
1956	0.999	1.001	0.998
1957	1.013	1.012	1.000
1958	1.000	1.000	1.000
1959	1.069	1.019	1.048
1960	1.096	1.036	1.057
1961	1.115	1.039	1.072
1962	1.189	1.057	1.123
1963	1.240	1.074	1.152
1964	1.307	1.097	1.188
1965	1.387	1.129	1.224

The average annual rate of growth of total output over the period 1945–1965 with the error in aggregation of consumption and investment goods output eliminated is 3.39 percent. The average rate of growth of total input with the error in aggregation of labor and capital services eliminated is 1.84 percent. The resulting rate of growth of total factor productivity is 1.49 percent. We conclude that these errors in aggregation result in an overstatement of the initial rate of growth of total factor productivity. With these errors eliminated total input explains 54.3 percent of the growth in total output. This result may be compared with the 52.4 percent of the growth in total output explained initially.

3.3.3 Investment Goods Prices

We have demonstrated that an error in the measurement of investment goods prices results in errors in the measurement of total output, total input, and total factor productivity. Roughly speaking, a positive

Table 3.2
Total output, input, and factor productivity, U.S. private domestic economy, 1945–1965, errors of aggregation eliminated

	Output	Input	Productivity
1945	0.713	0.783	0.912
1946	0.679	0.810	0.841
1947	0.694	0.847	0.824
1948	0.727	0.870	0.840
1949	0.727	0.864	0.845
1950	0.800	0.888	0.903
1951	0.851	0.925	0.921
1952	0.873	0.945	0.926
1953	0.918	0.964	0.953
1954	0.905	0.954	0.950
1955	0.981	0.976	1.005
1956	0.999	1.001	0.998
1957	1.013	1.012	1.000
1958	1.000	1.000	1.000
1959	1.070	1.019	1.049
1960	1.096	1.036	1.057
1961	1.115	1.038	1.073
1962	1.189	1.057	1.124
1963	1.240	1.073	1.153
1964	1.307	1.096	1.189
1965	1.387	1.128	1.225

bias in the rate of growth of the investment goods price index results in a positive bias in the rate of growth of total factor productivity, provided that the share of capital in the value of input exceeds the share of investment in the value of output. This condition is fulfilled for the U.S. private domestic sector throughout the period, 1945–1965. Hence, we must examine the indexes of investment goods prices that underlie our measurement for possible sources of bias.

Except for the price index for road construction the price indexes for structures that underlie the U.S. national accounts are indexes of the cost of input rather than the price of output. In the absence of changes in total factor productivity properly constructed price indexes for construction input would parallel the movements of price indexes for output. This is assured by the dual to the usual definition of total factor productivity (3.3). Dacy (1964) has shown that the rate of growth of the price of inputs in highway construction is considerably greater than that of the price of construction output. Dacy's output price index grows from 0.805 to 0.982 from 1947 through 1959, while the input price index grows from 0.615 to 1.024 in the same period, both on a base 1.000 in 1958.[19] This empirical finding is simply another way of looking at the positive residual between rates of growth of total output and total input where total factor productivity is measured with error. Input price indexes are subject to the same errors of aggregation as the corresponding quantity indexes. Since input quantity indexes grow too slowly, input price indexes grow too rapidly.

The use of input prices in place of output prices for structures results in an important error of measurement. To eliminate this error it is necessary to use an output price index in measuring prices of both investment goods output and capital services input. An index of this type has been constructed for the OBE 1966 Capital Stock Study (1966). Components of this index include the Bureau of Public Roads price index for highway structures, the Bell System price index for telephone buildings, and the Bureau of Reclamation prices indexes for pumping plants and power plants. The resulting composite index may be compared with the implicit deflator for new construction from the U.S. national accounts (1966). The implicit deflator grows from 0.686 to 1.029 during the period 1947 through 1959 while the OBE Capital Goods Study price index for new construction output grows from 0.762 to 0.958 during the same period. Thus the relative bias in the input price index for all new construction as a measure of the price of construction output is roughly comparable to the relative bias in Dacy's input price index for highway construction as a measure of the price of highway construction output. The input price index, labelled Structures I, and the output price index, labelled Structures II, are given in table 3.3.

The price indexes for equipment that underlie the U.S. national accounts are based primarily on data from the wholesale price index of the Bureau of Labor Statistics (various monthly issues). Since expenditures on the wholesale price index are less than those on the consumers' price index (various monthly issues), adjustments for quality change are less frequent and less detailed. A direct comparison of the durables components of the wholesale and consumers' price indexes gives some notion of the relative bias. The wholesale price index increases from 0.646 to 1.023 and the consumers' price index increases from 0.858 to 1.022 over the period 1947 to 1959, both on a base of 1.000 in 1958. A direct comparison of components common to both indexes reveals essentially the same relationship. To correct for bias in the implicit deflator for producers' durables, we

Table 3.3
Alternate investment deflators

	Structure II	Structures I	Equipment II	Equipment I	Inventories II	Inventories I
1945	0.616	0.510	0.759	0.517	0.633	0.357
1946	0.672	0.570	0.768	0.575	0.705	0.638
1947	0.762	0.686	0.827	0.646	0.786	2.310
1948	0.854	0.770	0.863	0.703	0.827	1.023
1949	0.824	0.755	0.868	0.736	0.818	0.788
1950	0.778	0.791	0.878	0.752	0.823	0.818
1951	0.955	0.847	0.942	0.809	0.879	0.945
1952	0.983	0.876	0.954	0.822	0.896	0.949
1953	0.947	0.889	0.943	0.835	0.903	0.497
1954	0.894	0.886	0.929	0.840	0.914	0.772
1955	0.868	0.910	0.919	0.859	0.921	0.931
1956	0.982	0.956	0.949	0.918	0.945	0.978
1957	1.025	0.992	0.984	0.975	0.978	1.113
1958	1.000	1.000	1.000	1.000	1.000	0.994
1959	0.958	1.029	1.014	1.020	1.012	0.991
1960	0.936	1.042	1.009	1.022	1.026	1.020
1961	0.944	1.053	1.006	1.021	1.037	1.011
1962	0.980	1.069	1.008	1.023	1.048	1.001
1963	1.004	1.089	1.004	1.023	1.059	1.011
1964	1.014	1.119	1.004	1.031	1.071	1.014
1965	1.051	1.149	0.995	1.038	1.089	1.032

substitute for this deflator the implicit deflator for consumers' durables. The deflator for producers' durables increased from 0.646 in 1947 to 1.020 in 1959. Over this same period the deflator for consumers' durables increased from 0.827 to 1.014, both on a base of 1.000 in 1958. Thus the relative bias in the producers' durables price index as revealed by a comparison with components common to the wholesale and consumers' price indexes may be corrected by simply substituting the implicit deflator for consumers' durables for the producers' durables deflator. Both indexes are given in table 3.3; the producers' durables index is labelled Equipment I while the consumers' durables index is labelled Equipment II.

The durables component of the consumers' price index was itself subject to considerable upward bias in recent years. The consumers' price index for new automobiles increased 62 percent from 1947 to 1959. It has been estimated that correcting this index for quality change would reduce this increase to only 31 percent in the same period.[20] In view of the upward bias in the consumers' price index our adjustment for bias in the producers' durables price index is conservative. In order to reduce the error of measurement further, detailed research like that already carried out for automobiles is required for each class of producers' durable equipment.

The price indexes for change in business inventories from the U.S. national accounts contain year-to-year fluctuations that result from changes in the composition of investment in inventories; these changes are much more substantial than the corresponding changes in the composition of inventory stocks. The implicit deflator for change in inventories is not published; however, it may be computed from data on change in inventories in current or constant dollars. Changes in that amount to nearly doubling or halving the index occur from 1946 to 1947, 1947 to 1948, and 1951 to 1952. The value of the index is 0.357 in 1945, 0.638 in 1946 and 2.310 in 1947, all on a base of 1.000 (or, to be exact, 0.994) in 1958. The index drops to 1.023 in 1948 and 0.788 in 1949. A less extreme but equally substantial movement in the index occurs from 1952 through 1957. Changes in the implicit deflator of this magnitude cannot represent movements in the price of all stocks of inventories considered as investment goods. To represent these movements more accurately, we replace the implicit deflator for change in inventories by the deflator for private domestic consumption expenditures. The level of this index generally coincides with that of the implicit deflator for change in business inventories; however, the fluctuations are much less. Both indexes are given in table 3.3; the implicit deflator for change in business inventories is labelled Inventories I while the implicit deflator for private domestic consumption expenditures is labelled Inventories II.

Indexes of total input, total output, and total factor productivity with errors in the measurement of prices of investment goods eliminated are presented in table 3.4. The average rate of growth of total output over the period 1945–1965 with these errors of measurement removed is 3.59 percent. This rate of growth may be compared with the original rate of growth of total output of 3.49 percent or with the rate of growth of 3.39 percent for total output with errors of aggregation removed. The average rate of growth of total input over this period is 2.19 percent. The original rate of growth of total input is 1.83 percent; with errors of aggregation removed the rate of growth of total input is 1.84 percent. The rate of growth of total factor productivity is 1.41 percent. With errors in measurement of the prices of investment goods eliminated the rate of growth of total input explains 61.0 percent of the rate of growth of total output.

Table 3.4
Total output, input, and factor productivity, U.S. private domestic economy, 1945–1965, errors in investment goods prices eliminated

	Output	Input	Productivity
1945	0.692	0.759	0.913
1946	0.662	0.786	0.846
1947	0.679	0.822	0.829
1948	0.718	0.845	0.853
1949	0.717	0.842	0.854
1950	0.798	0.867	0.922
1951	0.839	0.908	0.925
1952	0.858	0.930	0.925
1953	0.905	0.950	0.954
1954	0.900	0.942	0.957
1955	0.982	0.966	1.016
1956	0.995	0.996	0.999
1957	1.009	1.010	1.000
1958	1.000	1.000	1.000
1959	1.076	1.022	1.052
1960	1.107	1.042	1.061
1961	1.127	1.049	1.073
1962	1.199	1.071	1.117
1963	1.249	1.091	1.142
1964	1.319	1.117	1.177
1965	1.400	1.153	1.209

3.3.4 Measurement of Services

Up to this point we have assumed that labor and capital services are proportional to stocks of labor and capital. This assumption is obviously incorrect. In principle flows of capital and labor services could be measured directly. In fact it is necessary to infer the relative utilization of stocks of capital and labor from somewhat fragmentary data. Okun (1962) has attempted to circumvent the problem of direct observation of labor and capital services by assuming that the relative utilization of both labor and capital is a function of the unemployment rate for labor so that the gap between actual and "potential" output, that is, output at full utilization of both factors, may be expressed in terms of the unemployment rate. A similar notion has been used by Solow (1962) to adjust stocks of labor and capital for relative utilization. Most of the available capacity utilization measures are based on the relationship of actual output to output at full utilization of both labor and capital, so that these measures also attempt to adjust both labor and capital simultaneously.

Our approach to the problem of relative utilization is somewhat more direct in that we attempt to adjust capital and labor for relative utilization separately. Of course, this adjustment gives rise to a new concept of "potential" or capacity output, but we do not pursue this notion further in this paper. Our first assumption is that the relative utilization of capital is the same for all capital goods; while this is a very strong assumption it is weaker than the assumption underlying the Okun-Solow approach in which the relative utilization of capital and labor depends on that of labor. We estimate the relative utilization of capital from the relative utilization of power sources.[21] Data on the relative utilization of electric motors provides an indicator of the relative utilization of capital in manufacturing, since electric motors are the predominant source of power there. We assume that relative utilization of capital goods in the manufacturing and nonmanufacturing sectors is the same. When more complete data become available, this assumption can be replaced by less restrictive assumptions. Unfortunately, this adjustment allows only for the trend in the relative utilization of capital; it does not adjust for short-term cyclical variations in capacity utilization. Thus we are unable to attain the objective of complete comparability between measures of labor and capital input.

The assumption that labor services are proportional to the stock of labor is obviously incorrect. On the other hand, the assumption that labor services can be measured directly from data on man-hours is equally incorrect, as Denison (1961) has pointed out. The intensity of effort varies with the number of hours worked per week, so that the labor input can be measured accurately only if data on man-hours are corrected for the effects of variations in the number of hours per man on labor intensity. Denison (1962) suggests that the stock of labor provides an upper bound for labor services while the number of man-hours provides a lower bound. He estimates labor input by correcting man-hours for variations in labor intensity. We employ Denison's correction for intensity, but we apply this correction to actual hours per man rather than potential hours per man. Thus, our measure of labor input reflects short-run variations in labor intensity.

The assumption that labor and capital services are proportional to stocks of labor and capital results in an error in separating a given value of transactions into a price and a quantity. To correct this error we multiply the number of persons engaged by hours per man. The resulting index of man-hours is then corrected for variations in labor intensity. The corresponding error for capital is corrected by multiplying the stock of capital by the relative utilization of capital. Indexes of total input and total factor productivity after these errors have been eliminated are presented for the period 1945–1965 in table 3.5. The average annual rate of growth of total output is the same as before these corrections, 3.59 percent per year. The average rate of growth of total input is 2.57 percent. The resulting average rate of growth of total factor productivity is 0.96 percent. Total input now explains 71.6 percent of the rate of growth in total output.

3.3.5 Capital Services

In converting estimates of capital stock into estimates of capital services we have disregarded an important conceptual error in the aggregation of capital services. While investment goods output must be aggregated by means of investment goods or asset prices, capital services must be aggregated by means of service prices.

The prices of capital services are related to the prices of the corresponding investment goods; in fact, the asset price is simply the discounted value of all future capital services. Asset prices for different investment goods are not proportional to service prices because of

Table 3.5
Total input and factor productivity, U.S. private domestic economy, 1945–1965, errors in relative utilization eliminated

	Input	Productivity
1945	0.716	0.968
1946	0.742	0.895
1947	0.777	0.877
1948	0.801	0.899
1949	0.802	0.897
1950	0.830	0.963
1951	0.873	0.963
1952	0.899	0.956
1953	0.924	0.980
1954	0.923	0.976
1955	0.959	1.023
1956	0.994	1.001
1957	1.009	1.000
1958	1.000	1.000
1959	1.035	1.038
1960	1.057	1.046
1961	1.067	1.054
1962	1.089	1.098
1963	1.114	1.118
1964	1.146	1.147
1965	1.189	1.172

differences in rates of replacement and rates of capital gain or loss among capital goods. Implicitly, we have assumed that these prices are proportional; to eliminate the resulting error in measurement, it is necessary to compute service prices and to use these prices in aggregating capital services.

We have already outlined a method for computing the price of capital services in the absence of direct taxation of business income. In the presence of direct taxes we may distinguish between the price of capital services before and after taxes. The expression (3.7) given above for the price of capital services is the price after taxes. The price of capital services before taxes is:

$$p_k = q_k \left[\frac{1 - uv}{1 - u} r + \frac{1 - uw}{1 - u} \delta_k - \frac{1 - ux}{1 - u} \frac{\dot{q}_k}{q_k} \right] \tag{3.11}$$

where u is the rate of direct taxation, v the proportion of return to capital allowable as a charge against income for tax purposes, w the proportion of replacement allowable for tax purposes, and x the proportion of capital gains included in income for tax purposes.

We estimate the variables describing the tax structure as follows: The rate of direct taxation is the ratio of profits tax liability to profits before taxes. The proportion of the return to capital allowable for tax purposes is the ratio of net interest to the total return to capital. Total return to capital is the after tax rate of return, r, multiplied by the current value of capital stock. The proportion of replacement allowable for tax purposes is the ratio of capital consumption allowances to the current value of replacement. The proportion of capital gains included in income is zero by the conventions of the U.S. national accounts. Given the value of direct taxes we estimate the after tax rate of return by subtracting from the value of output plus capital gains the value of labor input, replacement, and direct taxes. This results in the total return to capital. The rate of return is calculated by dividing this quantity by the current value of the stock of capital. Given data on the rate of return and the variables describing the tax structure, we calculate the price of capital services before taxes for each investment good.[22] These prices of capital services are used in the calculation of indexes of capital input, total input, and total factor productivity.

For the U.S. private domestic economy it is possible to distinguish five classes of investment goods—land, residential and nonresidential structures, equipment, and inventories. Although it is also possible to distinguish a number of subclasses within each of these groupings, we will employ only the five major groups in calculating an index of total capital input. For each group we first compute a before tax service price analogous to (3.11). We then compute an index of capital input as a Divisia index of the services of land, structures, equipment and inventories. In constructing this index we eliminate the conceptual error that arises from the implicit assumption that service prices are proportional to asset prices for different investment goods. In eliminating this conceptual error we also eliminate the error of aggregation that results from adding together capital services in constant prices to obtain an index of total capital input. To eliminate the corresponding error in our index of investment goods output we replace our initial index by a Divisia index of investment in structures, equipment, and inventories. Indexes of total output, total input and total factor productivity resulting from the elimination of these errors are presented in table 3.6. The after tax rate of return implicit in the new index of capital input is also given in table 3.6.

The average rate of growth of total output over the period 1945–1965 with the error in aggregation of investment goods eliminated is 3.59. This rate of growth is essentially the same as for total output with errors in the aggregation of consumption and investment goods and errors in the measurement of investment goods prices eliminated. The average rate of growth of total input with errors in aggregation of capital services eliminated is 2.97 percent. This rate of growth may be compared with the initial rate of growth of 1.83 percent.

The resulting rate of growth of total factor productivity is 0.58 percent. The index of total factor productivity with these errors eliminated is presented in table 3.6. With these errors eliminated total input explains 82.7 percent of the growth of total output. The original index of total input explains 52.4 percent of this growth.

Table 3.6
Total input and factor productivity, U.S. private domestic economy, 1945–1965, errors in aggregation of capital input eliminated; implicit rate of return after taxes

	Output	Input	Productivity	Rate of return
1945	0.692	0.671	1.030	0.158
1946	0.661	0.698	0.950	0.198
1947	0.678	0.735	0.926	0.237
1948	0.717	0.765	0.940	0.223
1949	0.716	0.773	0.930	0.126
1950	0.797	0.804	0.992	0.095
1951	0.837	0.850	0.986	0.242
1952	0.857	0.880	0.976	0.143
1953	0.905	0.908	0.997	0.091
1954	0.900	0.911	0.988	0.078
1955	0.982	0.951	1.032	0.113
1956	0.995	0.987	1.008	0.175
1957	1.009	1.005	1.004	0.138
1958	1.000	1.000	1.000	0.107
1959	1.077	1.039	1.035	0.097
1960	1.107	1.063	1.040	0.105
1961	1.127	1.076	1.046	0.118
1962	1.199	1.099	1.089	0.138
1963	1.250	1.126	1.107	0.131
1964	1.320	1.160	1.134	0.127
1965	1.401	1.206	1.157	0.141

3.3.6 Labor Services

We have eliminated errors of aggregation that arise in combining capital services into an index of total capital input. Similar errors arise in combining different categories of labor services into an index of total labor input. Implicitly, we have assumed that the price per man-hour for each category of labor services is the same; to eliminate the resulting error of measurement it is necessary to use prices per man-hour for each category in computing an index of total labor input. Second, to eliminate the error of aggregation that results from adding together labor services in constant prices, we replace our initial index of labor input by a Divisia index of the individual categories of labor services.

The Divisia index of total labor input is based on a weighted average of the rates of growth of different categories of labor, using the relative shares in total labor compensation as weights. To represent our index of total labor input, we let L_l represent the quantity of input of the lth labor service, measured in man-hours. The rate of growth of the index of total labor input, say L, is:

$$\frac{\dot{L}}{L} = \Sigma v_l \frac{\dot{L}_l}{L_l}$$

where v is the relative share of the lth category of labor in the total value of labor input. The number of man-hours for each labor service is the product of the number of men, say n_l, and hours per man, say h_l; using this notation the index of total labor input may be rewritten:

$$\frac{\dot{L}}{L} = \Sigma v_l \frac{\dot{n}_l}{n_l} + \Sigma v_l \frac{\dot{h}_l}{h_l} .$$

For comparison with our initial indexes of labor input we separate the rate of growth of the index of labor input into three components—change in the number of men, change in hours per man, and change in labor input per man-hour. We have assumed that the number of hours per man is the same for all categories of labor services, say H. Letting N represent the total number of men and e_l the proportion of the workers in the lth category of labor services, we may write the index of total labor input in the form:

$$\frac{\dot{L}}{L} = \frac{\dot{H}}{H} + \frac{\dot{N}}{N} + \Sigma v_l \frac{\dot{e}_l}{e_l} . \tag{3.12}$$

Our initial index of labor input was simply N, the number of persons engaged; we corrected this index by taking into account the number of hours per man, H. To eliminate the remaining errors of aggregation we must correct the rate of growth of man-hours by adding to it an index of labor input per man-hour. The third term in the expression (3.12) for total labor input given above provides such an index. We will let E represent this index, so that:

$$\frac{\dot{E}}{E} = \Sigma v_l \frac{\dot{e}_l}{e_l} . \tag{3.13}$$

For computational purposes it is convenient to note that the index may be rewritten in the form:

$$\frac{\dot{E}}{E} = \sum \frac{p_l}{\Sigma p_l e_l} \dot{e}_l = \Sigma p_l' \dot{e}_l ,$$

where p_l is the price of the lth category of labor services and p_l' is the relative price. The relative price is the ratio of the price of the lth category of labor services to the average price of labor services, $\Sigma p_l e_l$.

In principle it would be desirable to distinguish among categories of labor services classified by age, sex, occupation, number of years schooling completed, industry of employment, and so on. An index of labor input per man-hour based on such a breakdown requires detailed research far beyond the scope of this study. We will compute such an index only for males and only for categories of labor broken down by the number of school years completed. The basic computation is presented in table 3.7. Data on relative prices for labor services are available for the years 1939, 1949, 1956, 1958, 1959 and 1963.[23] Combining these prices with changes in the distribution of the labor force provides a measure of the change in labor input per man-hour.[24]

Indexes of total input and total factor productivity with errors in the aggregation of labor services eliminated are presented in table 3.8. The average rate of growth of total input over the period 1945–1965 with the error in aggregation of labor services eliminated is 3.47. The rate of growth may be compared with the initial rate of growth of total input of 1.83 percent. The resulting rate of growth of total factor productivity is 0.10 percent. With these errors eliminated total input explains 96.7 percent of the growth in total output.

Table 3.7
Relative prices,* changes in distribution of the labor force, and indices of labor-input per man-hour, U.S. males, the civilian labor force, 1940–1964

School year completed	p'_l	Δe_l	p'_l	Δe_l	p'_l	Δe_l	p'_l	Δe_l	p'_l	Δe_l	p'_l	Δe_l
	1939	1940–48	1949	1948–52	1956	1952–57	1958	1957–59	1959	1959–62	1963	1962–65
Elementary 0–4	0.497	−2.3	0.521	−0.3	0.452	−1.3	0.409	−0.8	0.498	−0.8	0.407	−0.8
5–6 or 5–7	0.672	−3.1	0.685	−0.5	0.624	−0.2	0.565	−1.0	0.688	−0.9	0.562	−1.5
7–8 or 8	0.887	−6.8	0.813	−1.8	0.796	−3.3	0.753	−1.2	0.801	−1.9	0.731	−1.2
High school 1–3	1.030	2.4	0.974	−1.3	0.955	0.7	0.923	0.6	0.912	−0.6	0.886	−0.3
4	1.241	7.0	1.143	1.0	1.159	2.6	1.113	0.9	1.039	1.6	1.087	3.2
College 1–3	1.442	1.4	1.336	1.2	1.356	0.2	1.392	0.7	1.255	1.3	1.269	0.0
4+ or 4	1.947	1.3	1.866	1.6	1.810	1.3	1.840	0.9	1.569	1.0	1.571	0.2
5+	—	—	—	—	—	—	—	—	1.888	0.3	1.730	0.4
Percentage change in labor input per man-hour		6.45		2.50		2.97		2.39		2.36		2.13
Annual percentage change		0.78		0.62		0.59		1.20		0.79		0.72

Source: Derived from tables 2.11 and 2.12, Statistical Appendix.
* The relative prices are computed using the appropriate beginning period distribution of the labor force as weights.

Table 3.8
Total input and factor productivity, U.S. private domestic economy 1945–1965, errors in aggregation of labor input eliminated

	Input	Productivity
1945	0.634	1.090
1946	0.661	1.001
1947	0.700	0.971
1948	0.732	0.981
1949	0.743	0.966
1950	0.776	1.026
1951	0.823	1.017
1952	0.857	1.002
1953	0.887	1.020
1954	0.894	1.007
1955	0.936	1.048
1956	0.976	1.019
1957	0.997	1.012
1958	1.000	1.000
1959	1.047	1.027
1960	1.077	1.027
1961	1.096	1.027
1962	1.125	1.064
1963	1.158	1.076
1964	1.200	1.096
1965	1.255	1.112

3.4 Summary and Conclusion

3.4.1 Summary

The purpose of this paper has been to examine the hypothesis that if quantities of output and input are measured accurately, growth total output may be largely explained by growth in total input. The results are given in table 3.9 and charts 1, 2 and 3. We first present our initial estimates of rates of growth of output, input, and total factor productivity. These estimates include many of the errors made in attempts to measure total factor productivity without fully exploiting the economic theory underlying the social accounting concepts of real product and real factor input. We begin by eliminating errors of aggregation in combining investment and consumption goods and labor and capital services. We then eliminate errors of measurement in the prices of investment goods arising from the use of prices for inputs

Table 3.9
Total output, input, and factor productivity, U.S. private domestic economy, 1945–1965, average annual rates of growth

	Output	Input	Productivity
1. Initial estimates	3.49	1.83	1.60
Estimates after correction for:			
2. Errors of aggregation	3.39	1.84	1.49
3. Errors in investment good prices	3.59	2.19	1.41
4. Errors in relative utilization	3.59	2.57	0.96
5. Errors in aggregation of capital services	3.59	2.97	0.58
6. Errors in aggregation of labor services	3.59	3.47	0.10

into the investment goods sector rather than outputs from this sector. We remove errors arising from the assumption that the flow of services is proportional to stocks of labor and capital by introducing direct observations on the rates of utilization of labor and capital stock. We present rates of growth that result from correct aggregation of investment goods and capital services. Finally, we give rates of growth that result from correcting the aggregation of labor services.

The rate of growth of input initially explains 52.4 percent of the rate of growth of output. After elimination of aggregation errors and correction for changes in rates of utilization of labor and capital stock the rate of growth of input explains 96.7 percent of the rate of growth of output; change in total factor productivity explains the rest. In the terminology of the theory of production, movements along a given production function explain 96.7 percent of the observed changes in the pattern of productivity activity; shifts in the production function explain what remains.

This computation is based on the 1945–1965 period, measuring total factor productivity peak to peak. If one were to choose a different set of years, the numerical results would be slightly different, but their main thrust would be the same. For example, starting with the Post-Korean peak year of 1953, the rate of growth of input initially explains only 37.3 percent of the rate of growth of output. After all the corrections the rate of growth of input explains 79.2 percent of the growth in output between 1953 and 1965, reducing the estimated rate of change in total factor productivity from 2.12 percent per year to 0.72. We conclude that our hypothesis is consistent with the facts. If the economic theory underlying the measurement of real product and real factor input is properly exploited, the role to be assigned to growth in total factor productivity is small.

3.4.2 Evaluation of Past Research

Our conclusion that most of the growth in total output may be explained by growth in total input is just the reverse of the conclusion drawn from the great body of past research on total factor productivity, the research of Schmookler (1952), Mills (1952), Fabricant (1959), Abramovitz (1956), Solow (1957), and Kendrick (1961a). These conclusions, stated by Abramovitz, are ". . . that to explain a very large part of the growth of total output and the great bulk of output *per capita*, we must explain the increase in output per unit of conventionally measured inputs. . . ."[25] This conclusion results from inadequacies in the basic economic theory underlying the social accounts employed in productivity measurements. The increase in output per unit of conventionally measured inputs is characterized by very substantial errors of measurement, equal in magnitude to the alleged increase in productivity. We have given a concrete and detailed list of errors of this type.

Our results differ from those of Denison (1962) in that we correct changes in total factor productivity for errors in the measurement of output, capital services, and labor services, while Denison corrects only for errors in the measurement of labor services. To get some idea of the relative importance of errors in the measurement of labor and errors in the measurement of output and capital, we may observe that the rate of growth of total factor productivity is reduced from 1.60 percent per year to 0.10 percent per year. Of the total reduction of 1.50 percent per year errors in the measurement of output and capital account for 1.17 percent per year while errors in the measurement of labor account for 0.33 percent per year. We conclude that errors of measurement of the type left uncorrected by Denison are far more important than the type of errors he corrects.[26]

Our results suggest that the residual change in total factor productivity, which Denison attributes to Advance in Knowledge, is small. Our conclusion is not that advances in knowledge are negligible, but that the accumulation of knowledge is governed by the same economic laws as any other process of capital accumulation. Costs must be incurred if benefits are to be achieved. Although we have made no attempt to isolate the effects of expenditures on research and development from expenditures on other types of current inputs or investment goods, our results suggest that social rates of return to this type of investment are comparable to rates of return on other types of

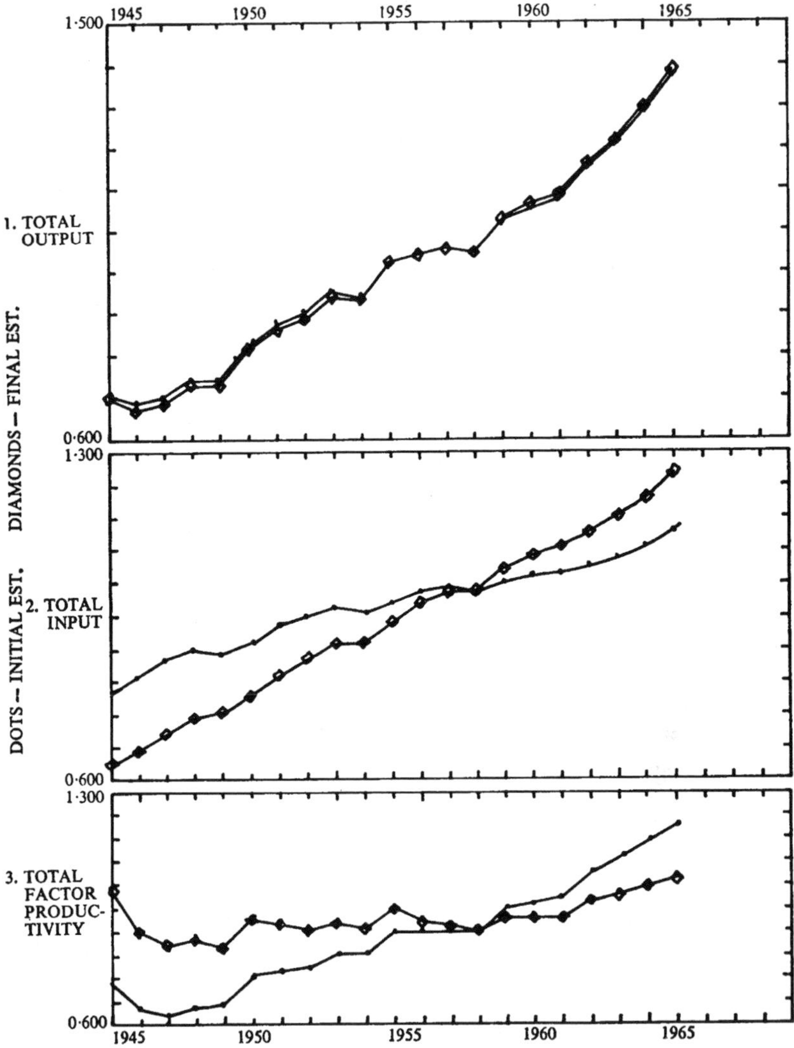

Figure 3.1. Indexes of Total Output, Total Input and Total Factor Productivity (1958 = 1.0), U.S. Private Domestic Economy, 1945–1965.

investment. Of course, our inference is indirect and a better test of this proposition could be provided by direct observation of private and social rates of return to investment in scientific research and development activities. Unfortunately, many of the direct observations on these rates of return available in the literature attribute all or part of the measured increase in total factor productivity to investment in research and development;[27] since these measured increases are subject to all the errors of measurement we have enumerated, satisfactory direct tests of the hypothesis that private and social rates of return to research and development investment are equal to private rates of return to other types of investment are not yet available.

Another limitation of our results is that discrepancies between private and social returns to investment in physical capital may play a relatively minor role in explaining economic growth. Under the operational definitions of total factor productivity we have adopted, a positive discrepancy between social and private rates of return would appear as a downward bias in the rate of growth of input, hence an upward bias in the rate of growth of total factor productivity. The effects of such discrepancies are lumped together with the effects of other sources of growth in total factor productivity we have measured. The fact that the growth of the resulting index is small indicates that the contribution of investment to economic growth is largely compensated by the private returns to investment. This implication of our findings is inconsistent with explanations of economic growth such as Arrow's model of learning by doing (Arrow, 1962), which are based on a higher social than private rate of return to physical capital.[28]

Of course, ours is not the first explanation of productivity change that does not rely primarily on discrepancies between private and social rates of return. An explanation of this type has been proposed by Solow (1960), namely, embodied technical change. As Solow (1964) points out, explanation of measured changes in total factor productivity as embodied technical change does not require discrepancies between private and social rates of return: ". . . the fact of expectable obsolescence reduces the private rate of return on saving below the marginal product of capital as one might ordinarily calculate it. But this discrepancy is fully reflected in a parallel difference between the marginal product of capital and the social rate of return on saving. So . . . the private and social rates of return coincide."[29] In referring to "capital as one might ordinarily calculate it," Solow explicitly does not identify quality-corrected or "surrogate" capital with capital input and "surrogate" investment with investment goods output. In Solow's framework the marginal product of "surrogate" capital is precisely equal to the private and social rate of return on saving. The difference between Solow's point of view and ours is that the private and social rates of return are equal by definition in his framework, where the equality between private and social rates of return is a testable hypothesis within our framework.[30]

3.4.3 Implications for Future Research

The problem of measuring total factor productivity is, at bottom, the same as the estimation of national product and national factor input in constant prices. The implication of our findings is that the predominant part of economic growth may be explained within a conventional social accounting framework. Of course, precise measurement of productivity change requires attention to reliability as well as accuracy. Our catalogue of errors of measurement could serve as an agenda for correction of errors in the measurement of output and for incorporation of the measurement of input into a unified social accounting framework. Given time and resources we could attempt to raise all of our measurements to the high standards of the U.S. National Product Accounts in current prices. This could be done with some difficulty for rates of relative utilization of labor and capital stock and the prices of investment goods, which require the introduction of new data into the social accounts. The elimination of aggregation errors in measuring capital services and investment goods requires a conceptual change to bring these concepts into closer correspondence with the economic theory of production. The measurement of appropriate indexes of labor input, corrected for errors of aggregation, necessitates fuller exploitation of existing data on wage differentials by education, occupation, sex, and so on.

The most serious weakness of the present study is in the use of long-term trends in the relative utilization of capital and labor to adjust capital input and labor input to concepts appropriate to the underlying theory of production. As a result of discrepancies between these trends and year-to-year variations in relative utilization of capital and labor, substantial errors of measurement have remained in the resulting index of total factor productivity. Examination of any of the alternative indexes we have presented reveals substantial unexplained cyclical variation in total factor productivity. An item of highest priority in future research is to incorporate more accurate data on annual variations in relative utilization. Hopefully, elimination of these remaining errors will make it possible to explain cyclical changes in total factor productivity along the same lines as our present explanation of secular changes. Cyclical changes are very substantial so that even our secular measurements could be improved with better data. For example, the use of the period 1945–1958, a peak in total factor productivity to a trough, reveals a drop in total factor productivity of nine percent; the use of the period 1949–1965, a trough to a peak, yields an increase in total factor productivity of eleven and a half percent.

In compiling data on labor input we have relied upon observed prices of different types of labor services. Given a broader accounting framework it would be possible to treat human capital in a manner that is symmetric with our measurement of physical capital. Investment in human capital could be cumulated into stocks along the lines suggested by Schultz (1961a). The flow of investment could be treated as part of total output. The rate of return to this investment could then be measured and compared with the rate of return to physical capital. Similarly, investment in scientific research and development could be separated from expenditures on current account and cumulated into stocks. The rate of return to research activity could then be computed. In both of these calculations it would be important not to rely on erroneously measured residual growth in total output for measurement of the social return to investment.

It is obvious that further disaggregation of our measurements would be valuable in order to provide a more stringent test of the basic hypothesis that growth in output may be explained by growth in input. The most important disaggregation of this type is to estimate levels of output and input by individual industries. The statistical raw material for disaggregation by industry is already available for stocks of labor and capital and levels of output. However, data for relative utilization of labor and capital and for disaggregation of different types of labor and capital within industry groups would have to be developed. Once these data are available, it will be possible to estimate rates of return to capital for individual industries and to study the effects of the distribution of productive factors among industries along the lines suggested by Massell (1961). The fact that past observations do not reveal significant changes in productivity does not imply that the existing allocation of productive resources is efficient relative to allocations that could be brought about by policy changes. In such a study it might be useful to extend the scope of productivity measurements to include the government sector. This would be particularly desirable if educational investment, which is largely produced in that sector, is to be incorporated into total output.

Finally, our results suggest a new point of departure for econometric studies of production function at every level of aggregation. While some existing studies (Griliches, 1967) employ data on output, labor, and capital corrected for errors of measurement along the lines we have suggested, most estimates of production functions are based on substantial errors of measurement. Econometric production functions are not an alternative to our methods for measuring total factor productivity, but rather supplement these methods in a number of important respects. Such production functions provide one means of testing the assumptions of constant returns to scale and equality between price ratios and marginal rates of transformation that underlie our measurement. A complete test of the hypothesis that growth in total output may be explained by growth in total input requires the measurement of input within a unified social accounting framework, the measurement of rates of return to both human and physical capital, further disaggregation, and new econometric studies of production functions. A start has been made on this task, but much interesting and potentially fruitful research remains to be done.

3.5 Statistical Appendix

1. As our initial estimate of output we employ gross private domestic product which is defined as gross national product less gross product, general government, and gross product, rest of the world, all in constant prices of 1958. These data are obtained from the U.S. national accounts. Our second estimate of output requires data on gross private domestic investment and gross private domestic consumption, defined as gross private domestic product less gross private domestic investment, in both current and constant prices of 1958. These data are also obtained from the U.S. national accounts.

As our initial estimate of labor input we employ private domestic persons engaged, defined as persons engaged for the national economy less persons engaged, general government, and persons engaged, rest of the world. These data are obtained from the U.S. national accounts (1966). Our initial estimate of capital input is obtained by the perpetual inventory method based on double declining balance estimates of replacement. For structures and equipment the lifetimes of individual assets are based on the "Bulletin F lives" employed by Jaszi, Wasson and Grose (1962). Data for gross private domestic investment prior to 1929 are unpublished estimates that underlie the capital stock estimates of Jaszi, Wasson and Grose (1962). For inventories and land, the initial values of capital stock in constant prices of 1958 are derived from Goldsmith (1955). The stock of land in constant prices is assumed to be unchanged throughout the period we consider. Estimates of the value of land in current prices are obtained from Goldsmith (1955).

The estimates of gross private domestic investment are subsequently revised by introducing alternative deflators to those employed in the U.S. national accounts. These deflators are given in table 3.3 of the text. Gross private domestic consumption is left unchanged in this calculation. We compute stocks of land, structures, residential and nonresidential, equipment, and inventories separately for each set of deflators. The basic formula is:

$$K_{t+1} = I_t + (1 - \delta)K_t \,, \tag{3.14}$$

where I_t is the value of gross private domestic investment for each category in constant prices. The initial (1929) value of capital stock in constant prices of 1958 and the depreciation rates are as follows:

	National accounts deflators		Alternative deflators	
	K_{1929}	δ	K_{1929}	δ
Land	254,700	0	254,700	0
Structures				
Residential	183,234	0.0386	162,708	0.0384
Nonresidential	163,205	0.0513	142,670	0.0509
Equipment	74,851	0.1325	51,701	0.1226
Inventories	48,504	0	48,504	0

2. In dropping the assumption that services are proportional to stock for both labor and capital, we require data on hours/man and hours/machine. The data on hours/man are derived from Kendrick's data on man-hours in the U.S. private domestic economy, extended through 1965.

To estimate hours/machine we first estimate the relative utilization of electric motors in manufacturing. Estimates have been given by Foss (1963) for 1929, 1939 and 1954. We have updated these estimates to 1962. The basic computation is given in table 3.10. The 1954 data and the basic method of computation are taken from Foss (1963, table

Table 3.10
Relative utilization of electric motors, manufacturing, 1954 and 1962

	Unit	1954	1962
1. Horsepower of electric motors, total	Thousand horsepower	91,505.000	126,783.000
2. Available kilowatt-hours of motors (line 1 × 7261)	Billions of kilowatt-hours	664.400	920.600
3. Electric power actually consumed, all purposes	Billions of kilowatt-hours	222.100	336.700
4. Percent power used for electric motors	—	64.600	65.600
5. Power consumed by motors (line 3 × line 4)	Billions of kilowatt-hours	143.500	220.900
6. Percent utilization (line 5/line 2 × 100)	—	21.600	24.000
7. Number of equivalent 40 hour weeks (line 6 × 4.2/100)	—	0.907	1.008
8. Index	1954 = 100	100.000	111.100

Line 2: The adjustment is derived as follows: It is assumed "that each electric motor could work continuously throughout the year . . . , 8760. . . . Horsepower hours are converted to kilowatt hours; . . . 1 horsepower hour = 0.746 kilowatt hours. The result [is] . . . adjusted upward by dividing through 0.9, since modern electric motors have an efficiency of approximately 90 percent. . . ." Foss (1963, p. 11). 8760 × 0.746/0.9 = 7261.

Line 4: Percent power used for electric motors in 1962 computed using the industry distribution in 1945 given by Foss (1963) in table 2.1, and the 1962 consumption of total electric power by industries from the 1962 *Survey of Manufacturers* (1962, Chapter 6).

Line 7: There are 4.2 forty-hour shifts in a full week of 168 hours.

II, p. 11). The 1954 data differ from the figures given by Foss due to a revision of the 1954 horsepower data by the Bureau of the Census and omission of the "fractional horsepower motors" adjustment. The latter, applied to both 1954 and 1962, would not have affected the estimated change in relative utilization. The horsepower data for 1962 and 1954 are from the 1963 *Census of Manufactures*, "Power Equipment in Manufacturing Industries," MC63(1)–6. Consumption of electric energy is taken from the 1962 *Survey of Manufactures*, Chapter 6. The 1962 total (388.2) is reduced by the consumption of electric power for nuclear energy (51.5) as shown in Series S81–93 of Bureau of the Census, *Continuation to* 1962 *of Historical Statistics of the U.S.* (1963c).

3. To estimate service prices for capital from the formula (3.11) given in the text we require data on the tax structure and on the rate of return. The variable u, the rate of direct taxation, is the ratio of profits tax liability to profits before taxes for the corporate sector. These data are from the U.S. national accounts. The variable v, the proportion of return to capital allowable as a charge against income for tax purposes, is the ratio of private domestic net interest to the after tax rate of return, r, multiplied by the current value of capital stock. Private domestic net interest is net interest less net interest for the rest of the world sector. These data are taken from the U.S. national accounts. We discuss estimation of the after tax rate of return below. The current value of capital stock is the sum of stock in land, structures, equipment, and inventories. Each of the four components is the product of the corresponding stock in constant prices of 1958, multiplied by the investment deflator for the component. Finally, the variable w, the proportion of replacement allowable for tax purposes, is the ratio of capital consumption allowances to the current value of replacement. Capital consumption allowances are taken from the U.S. national accounts. The current value of replacement is the sum of replacement in current prices for structures and equipment. Replacement in current prices is the product of replacement in constant prices of 1958 and the investment deflator for the corresponding component. Replacement in constant prices is a by-product of the calculation of capital stock by formula (3.14) given above. Replacement is simply δK_t, where K_t is capital stock in constant prices.

To estimate the rate of return we define the value of capital services for land, structures, equipment and inventories as the produce of the service price (3.11) and the corresponding stock in constant prices. Setting this equal to total income from property, we solve for the rate of return. Total income from property is gross private domestic product in constant prices less private domestic labor income. Private domestic labor income is private domestic compensation of employees from the U.S. national accounts multiplied by the ratio of private domestic persons engaged in production to private domestic full-time equivalent employees, both from *The National Income and Product Accounts of the United States*, 1929–1965 (1966). This amounts to assuming that self-employed individuals have the same average labor income as employees.

The final formula for the rate of return is then the ratio of total income from property less profits tax liability less the current value of replacement plus the current value of capital gain to the current value of capital stock. The current value of capital gain is the sum of capital gains for all assets; the capital gain for each asset is the product of the rate of growth of the corresponding investment deflator and the value of the asset in constant prices of 1958.

4. The basic sources of data underlying table 3.7 of the text are summarized in tables 3.11 and 3.12. Table 3.11 presents estimates of

Table 3.11
Civilian labor force, males 18 to 64 years old, by educational attainment percent distribution by years of school completed

School year completed	1940	1948	1952	1957	1959	1959†	1962†	1965†
Elementary 0–4	10.2	7.9	7.6	6.3	5.5	5.9	5.1	4.3
5–6 or 5–7*	10.2	7.1	6.6 11.6	11.4	10.4	10.7	9.8	8.3
7–8 or 8*	33.7	26.9	25.1 20.1	16.8	15.6	15.8	13.9	12.7
High School 1–3	18.3	20.7	19.4	20.1	20.7	19.8	19.2	18.9
4	16.6	23.6	24.6	27.2	28.1	27.5	29.1	32.3
College 1–3	5.7	7.1	8.3	8.5	9.2	9.4	10.6	10.6
4+ or 4	5.4	6.7	8.3	9.6	10.5	6.3	7.3	7.5
5+	—	—	—	—	—	4.7	5.0	5.4

Source: The basic data for columns 1, 3, 4, 5 and 6 are taken from U.S. Department of Labor, *Special Labor Force Report*, No. 1, "Educational Attainment of Workers, 1959." The 5–8 years class is broken down into the 5–7 and 8 (5–6 and 7–8 for 1940, 1948, and 1952) on the basis of data provided in *Current Population Report*, Series P-50, Nos. 14, 49, 78. The 1940 data were broken down using the 1940 *Census of Population*, Vol. III, Part 1, table 13. The 1952 breakdown for translating the single years of school completed from the 1950 *Census of Population*, Detailed Characteristics, U.S. Summary (1950). The 1962 data are from *Special Labor Force Report*, No. 30, and the 1965 figures are from *Special Labor Force Report*, No. 65, "Educational Attainment of Workers, March 1965."

* 5–6 and 7–8 for 1940, 1948 and the first part of 1952, 5–7 and 8 thereafter.

†Employed, 18 years and over.

Table 3.12
Mean annual earnings of males, 25 years and over by school years completed, selected years

School year completed	1939	1949	1956	1958	1959	1963
Elementary 0–4	665	1,724	2,127	2,046	2,935	2,465
5–6 or 5–7	900	2,268	2,927	2,829	4,058	3,409
7–8 or 8	1,188	2,693 2,839	3,732	3,769	4,725	4,432
High School 1–3	1,379	3,226	4,480	4,618	5,379	5,370
4	1,661	3,784	5,439	5,567	6,132	6,588
College 1–3	1,931	4,423	6,363	6,966	7,401	7,693
4+ or 4	2,607	6,179	3,490	9,206	9,255	9,523
5+	—	—	—	—	11,136	10,487

Source: Columns 1, 2, 3, 4, H.P. Miller (1960a, table 1, p. 966). Column 5 from 1960 *Census of Population*, PC(2)-7B, "Occupation by Earnings and Education." Column 6 computed from *Current Population Reports*, Series P-60, No. 43, Table 32, using midpoints of class intervals and $44,000 for the over $25,000 class. The total elementary figure in 1940 broken down on the basis of data from the 1940 *Census of Population*. The "less than 8 years" figure in 1949 split on the basis of data given in H.S. Houthakker (1959). In 1956, 1959, 1959 and 1963, split on the basis of data on earnings of males 25–64 from the 1959 1-in-a-1000 Census sample. We are indebted to G. Hanoch for providing us with this tabulation.
Earnings in 1939 and 1959; total income in 1949, 1958, and 1963.

the distribution of the male labor force by school years completed for 1940, 1948, 1952, 1957, 1959, 1962 and 1964. These data are taken from various issues of the *Special Labor Foce Reports* and *Current Population Reports*, with some additional data from the 1940, 1950 and 1960 *Census of Population* used to break down several classes into subclasses. We could have used data from the 1950 and 1960 Censuses on educational attainment. The increase in the number of links did not seem to offset the decrease in comparability that would be introduced by the use of different sources of data. Table 3.2 presents estimates of the mean incomes of males (25 years and over) for these classes. These data are largely taken from Miller (1960a), supplemented by Census and *Current Population Reports* data. Table 3.7 of the text presents the relative incomes, the first differences of the educational distribution, and the computation of an appropriate index of the change in the average education per man.

Notes

1. See Jorgenson (1966) for details.
2. Abramovitz (1962, p. 764).
3. Divisia (1925, 1928). Application of these indexes to the measurement of total factor productivity is suggested by Divisia in a later publication (1952, pp. 53–54). The economic interpretation of Divisia indexes of total factor productivity has been discussed by Solow (1957) and Richter (1966).
4. The basic duality relationship for indexes of total factor productivity has been discussed by Siegel (1952, 1961).
5. The notion of a factor price frontier has been discussed by Samuelson (1962); the factor price frontier is employed in defining changes in total factor productivity by Diamond (1965) and by Phelps and Phelps (1966).
6. See, for example, Wold (1953).
7. See Richter (1966). We are indebted to W.M. Gorman for bringing this fact to our attention.
8. It is essential to distinguish our basic hypothesis from a misinterpretation of it recently advanced by Denison: Since advances in knowledge cannot increase national product without raising the marginal product of one or more factors of production, they of course disappear as a source of growth if an increase in a factor's marginal product resulting from the advance of knowledge is counted as an increase in the quantity of factor input (1961, p. 76). In terms of our social accounting framework Denison suggests that we measure factor input as the sum of the increase in both prices and quantities; denoting the index of input implied by Denison's interpretation by X^D, gives:

$$\frac{\dot{X}^D}{X^D} = \Sigma v_j \frac{\dot{p}_j}{p_j} + \Sigma v_j \frac{\dot{X}_j}{X_j} ;$$

the corresponding index of output, say Y^D, would then be defined as:

$$\frac{\dot{Y}^D}{Y^D} = \Sigma w_i \frac{\dot{q}_i}{q_i} + \Sigma w_i \frac{\dot{Y}_i}{Y_i} .$$

The resulting index of total factor productivity, say P^D, is constant by definition:

$$\frac{\dot{P}^D}{P^D} = \frac{\dot{Y}^D}{Y^D} - \frac{\dot{X}^D}{X^D} = 0 .$$

By comparing this definition with our definition (3.4), the error in Denison's interpretation of our hypothesis is easily seen.
9. Here we assume that the "quantity" of a particular type of capital as an asset is proportional to its "quantity" as a service, whatever the age of the capital. If this condition is not satisfied, capital of each distinct age must be treated as a distinct asset and service. Output at each point of time consists of the usual output plus "aged" capital stock.
10. Studies in which these three methods have been employed are (1) Jaszi, Wasson, and Grose (1962), Goldsmith (1955), and Kuznets (1961); (2) Meyer and Kuh (1957) and Denison (1962); (30) Terborgh (1960).
11. This point is made by Domar (1961).

12. Domar's procedure (1961, p. 717, fn. 3) fails to correct for capital gains. Implicitly, Domar is assuming either no capital gains or that all capital gains are included in the value of output, whether realized or not.
13. Kendrick (1961b, p. 106); see the comments by Griliches (1961, p. 129). Kendrick takes a similar position in a more recent paper; see the comments by Jorgenson (1966). The treatment of capital input outlined above is based on our earlier paper (Griliches and Jorgenson, 1966). The data have been revised to reflect recent revisions in the U.S. national accounts.
14. The answer to Mrs. Robinson's (1953–1954) rhetorical question, "what units is capital measured in?" is dual to the measurement of the price of capital services. Given either an appropriate measure of the flow of capital services or a measure of its price, the other measure may be obtained from the value of income from capital. Since this procedure is valid only if the necessary conditions for producer equilibrium are satisfied, the resulting quantity of capital may not be employed to *test* the marginal productivity theory of distribution, as Mrs. Robinson and others have pointed out.
15. Domar (1963, p. 587, formula (3.5)) considers a special case of this problem in which capital "is imported from the outside." This specialization is unnecessary, as suggested in the text. A more detailed discussion of this issue is presented by Jorgenson (1966). For constant rates of growth of the relative error in the investment goods price index and the level of investment, formula (3.10) may be expressed in closed form:

$$\frac{\dot{P}*}{P*} - \frac{\dot{P}}{P} = -w_I \frac{\dot{Q}*}{Q*} + v_K \frac{\dot{Q}*}{Q*},$$
$$= (v_K - w_I) \frac{\dot{Q}*}{Q*}.$$

16. See Griliches (1964) and the references given there.
17. Jorgenson (1966).
18. To make stocks of labor and capital precisely analogous, it would be necessary to go even further. Unemployed workers should be included in the stock of labor since unemployed machines are included in the stock of capital. Workers should be aggregated by means of discounted lifetime incomes since capital goods are aggregated by means of asset prices.
19. The growth of the output price index may be compared with that for personal consumption expenditures, which grows from 76.5 to 108.6 from 1947 through 1959. The close parallel between the output price index for construction and the price of consumption goods suggests an explanation for the difference in rates of growth of prices of consumption and investment goods described by Gordon (1961). This difference results from the error of measurement in using an input price index in place of an output price index for investment goods. If this error is corrected, the difference vanishes.
20. Griliches (1964, table 8, last column, p. 397).
21. Foss (1963). See the Statistical Appendix for further details.
22. Further details are given in the Statistical Appendix.
23. Additional details on relative prices for labor services are presented in the Statistical Appendix.
24. Additional details on the distribution of the labor force are presented in the Statistical Appendix, table 3.11.
25. Abramovitz (1962, p. 776).
26. Errors in the aggregation of labor services account for 0.48 percent per year, but this is offset by errors of measurement in the relative utilization of labor of –0. 15 percent per year so that the net correction for errors of measurement of labor is 0.33 percent

per year. An alternative interpretation of our results may be provided by analogy with the conceptual framework for technical change discussed by Diamond (1965). Errors of measurement in the growth of labor services may be denoted labor-diminishing errors of measurement; capital-diminishing errors of measurement may be separated into embodied and disembodied errors. Errors in capital due to errors in the measurement of prices of investment goods are analogous to embodied technical change. Finally, some of the errors in measurement affect levels of output; these errors may be denoted output-diminishing errors of measurement. A decomposition of total errors of measurement into labor-diminishing, capital-diminishing, embodied and disembodied, and output-diminishing is as follows: Labor-diminishing errors of measurement contribute 0.33 percent per year to the initial measured rate of growth of total factor productivity. Embodied capital-diminishing errors contribute 0.28 percent per year and disembodied capital-diminishing errors contribute 0.99 percent per year. Finally, output-diminishing erorrs of measurement of 0.10 percent per year must be set off against the input-diminishing errors totalling 1.60 percent per year.

27. See, for example, the studies of Minasian (1962) and Mansfield (1965).

28. See Levhari (1966a,b) for an elaboration of this point.

29. Solow (1964, p. 58–59).

30. For further discussion of this point, see Jorgenson (1966).

4 Issues in Growth Accounting: A Reply to Edward F. Denison

Dale W. Jorgenson and
Zvi Griliches

4.1 Introduction

In our paper, "The Explanation of Productivity Change" (Jorgenson and Griliches, 1967), we examine the measurement of total factor productivity from the perspective provided by the economic theory of production. From the accounting point of view the major innovation in our approach is in the integration of productivity measurement with national accounts for income, saving, and wealth. Our main substantive conclusion is that growth in real factor input rather than growth in total factor productivity is the predominant source of growth in real product.

Both our approach to productivity measurement and our substantive conclusions require much further analysis and testing. Edward F. Denison has made an important contribution to this further analysis and testing in his paper, "Some Major Issues in Productivity Analysis: An Examination of Estimates by Jorgenson and Griliches" (1969). In this paper Denison examines our approach from the vantage point of methods developed in his study, *Why Growth Rates Differ* (1967). Denison's contribution is especially valuable since his objectives are similar to ours and his approach is carefully articulated with national income and expenditure accounts.

Although Denison's objectives and our objectives are similar, any attempt to integrate his approach to productivity measurement into national accounts for saving and wealth gives rise to serious difficulties. The first important difficulty arises from a basic confusion between depreciation and replacement that underlies all of Denison's work. Denison measures net national product as gross product less replacement; the correct definition is gross product less depreciation. The error in measurement of total product carries over to Denison's measure of total factor input, since the value of total product is equal to the value of total factor input as an accounting identity.

A second important difficulty in Denison's approach arises from an inconsistency between his treatment of depreciation in the measurement of total product and his treatment of replacement in the measurement of capital input. This inconsistency results in a contradiction between the income accounts that underlie productivity measurement and the wealth accounts that underlie the measurement of capital input. Although Denison's measure of total factor productivity is consistent with national income and expenditure accounts, it is impossible to integrate his measure into national saving and wealth accounts.

Further difficulties arise in Denison's allocation of property income among assets. First, Denison employs nominal rates of return rather than real rates of return in measuring income from the supply of capital services. As a consequence his allocation of property income among assets is inconsistent with the integration of property income into accounts for saving and wealth. Second, Denison's classification of assets ignores important differences in direct taxation of property income by legal form of organization. His allocation of property income fails to reflect the impact of the tax structure on rates of return of different types of assets.

The purpose of this paper is to compare our approach to productivity measurement with Denison's. For this purpose we present a new set of estimates of total factor productivity for the period 1950–1962 covered in Denison's study, *Why Growth Rates Differ* (1967). These estimates, prepared by Christensen and Jorgenson,[1] implement our approach in much greater detail than the estimates given in our earlier study. The new estimates and the methods employed in obtaining them are presented in sections 4.2–4.6 below. In section 4.7 we compare these results with Denison's and our own earlier ones and assess the quantitative importance of the differences.

The first step in productivity measurement is to define measures of product and factor input in current prices. Product is divided between consumption and investment; factor input is divided between labor and capital input. Investment and capital input are linked through national accounts for saving and wealth. Investment in reproducible tangible capital assets is part of the national product and also part of saving. Investment less depreciation plus capital gains is equal to the change in the value of the corresponding capital asset from period to period.

Capital assets underlie capital services. The treatment of capital assets as part of wealth must be consistent with the the treatment of capital services as part of factor input. An important objective of our approach to productivity measurement is the integration of capital input into national accounts for income, saving, and wealth. Our estimates of product and factor input, consumption and investment, and labor and capital services are presented in section 4.2 below.

In section 4.3 we present estimates of capital input implementing our approach in much greater detail than in our original study. The new estimates permit us to distinguish among components of property income corresponding to sectors of the economy that differ in legal form of organization. These estimates provide for a much more satisfactory integration of direct taxation of property income into factor input accounts.

We have attempted to validate our original measures by checking our data against a more comprehensive body of supplementary evidence—especially evidence on investment goods prices in section 4.3 and data on changes in the relative utilization of capital in section 4.4. In constructing a new set of estimates Christensen and Jorgenson have been able to incorporate new data. In the most difficult area of empirical research, the measurement of relative utilization, they incorporate cyclical as well as secular changes in relative utilization into their measure of capital input.[2] In reviewing their work in section 4.4 and in response to Denison's comments we have reached the conclusion that the scope of our original adjustments for changes in relative utilization should be reduced.

In the measurement of real factor input, rates of growth of labor and capital input are averaged to obtain the rate of growth of total factor input, using relative factor shares as weights. The measurement of aggregate labor input as developed by Denison, Griliches, and others,[3] amounts to applying the same principle of aggregation to the individual components of labor input. Rates of growth of the components are averaged to obtain the rate of growth of total labor input, using relative shares in the value of labor input as weights. Our measure of labor input does not differ conceptually from the measure employed by Denison. Even though the details of the measurement procedure are quite different for the two estimates, the empirical results are very similar. Both measures of labor input differ substantially from measures based on unweighted man-hours, such as those of Abramovitz (1956), Kendrick (1961a, 1973) and Solow (1957). In section 4.5 we compare our measure of labor input with alternatives incorporating additional detail.

In section 4.6 we present revised estimates of total factor productivity. Revised estimates of capital input require data on property income by legal form of organization, an analysis of the tax structure for property income, and the incorporation of measures of relative utilization of capital stock. Estimates of capital stock already incorporated into productivity studies provide an important part of the empirical basis for revised estimates of capital input. Ultimately, satisfactory estimates will require the integration of productivity measurement with accounts for income, saving, and wealth. Productivity measures of this type are available for the United States for the period 1929–1967,[4] but much further work remains to be done in refining and extending these estimates.

Section 4.7 summarizes the results of these revisions, compares them with our original estimates, reviews Denison's objections to them, and explores some of the remaining unresolved issues. Our original conclusions are changed somewhat, primarily as the result of the reduction in the magnitude and scope of the relative utilization adjustment. The resulting estimates of growth in total factor productivity are closer to Denison's estimates than our original ones, but still significantly lower. Our revised estimates meet, we believe, all of Denison's valid objections to our original procedures. We have preserved, however, the major conclusion of our original paper: Growth in total input is a major rather than a minor source in the growth of national output. The estimated residual change in total factor productivity is smaller than asserted by other investigators but not so small as was implied by our original estimates. This requires a revision of the implication of our original paper that all of output growth could be accounted for by a corrected version of total input within the conventions of national income measurement. This does not seem to be the case.

Further progress in explaining productivity change will require allowing the rates of return to differ among different types of investment and among industries and not only among legal forms of organization. Returns to labor of comparable quality may also differ by age, race, sex, or occupation and these differences should be reflected in the measurement of labor input. Finally, a more detailed investigation of possible contributions to growth associated with externalities in the process of research and educational activities would be worthwhile. It is still our belief that the correct research strategy in this area is to refine and extend the accounts so as to minimize the contribution of the unexplained residual.

4.2 Measurement of Output

4.2.1 Introduction

We define the value of output and factor input from the point of view of the producer. For each sector of the economy we measure revenue as proceeds to the sector and outlay as expenditures of the sector. The value of output is net of taxes on output while the value of input is gross of taxes on input. The resulting concept of gross value added is intermediate between gross product at market prices, which is the concept of output employed in our earlier study, and gross product at factor cost.

For any concept of gross product the fundamental accounting identity for productivity measurement is that the value of output is equal to the value of input. Denoting the price of aggregate output by q, the quantity by Y, and the price and quantity of aggregate input input p and X, we may represent this identity in the form:

$$qY = pX \ .$$

In measuring total factor productivity we confine our attention to the private domestic economy. In the U.S. national income and product accounts the value of government services is equal to the value of labor services by definition.[5] The services of capital input in the government sector are ignored, so that product accounts for private and government sectors are not comparable. For the rest of the world sector investment is not included in investment goods output, as defined below, so that factor input accounts for domestic and foreign sectors are not comparable.

In the U.S. national income and product accounts the services of owner-occupied housing and structures utilized by nonprofit institutions are included in the product of the private sector. The value of the flow of services is imputed from data on rental values of comparable structures. Capital services from consumers' durables and producers' durables used by nonprofit institutions are not treated symmetrically with services from owner-occupied housing and institutional structures. Purchases of consumers' durables are included in personal consumption expenditures and purchases of producers' durables by nonprofit institutions are included in private investment, but the flow of capital services from this equipment is not included in the value of private product.

We treat the services of owner-utilized consumers' durables symmetrically with the the services of owner-occupied housing, and the services of producers' durables utilized by nonprofit institutions symmetrically with those of structures occupied by these institutions. Purchases of new consumers' durables and purchases of producers' durables by nonprofit institutions are transferred from personal consumption expenditures to private investment, leaving the value of total product unaffected. We impute the value of services of consumers' durables and producers' durables owned by institutions from rental values implied by the imputed service flow for owner-occupied housing and institutional structures. We add the resulting service flow to the product of the private sector, increasing the value of the total product. The value of gross private domestic product and factor outlay for the year 1958 are presented in table 4.1.

4.2.2 Consumption, Investment, Labor, and Capital

In measuring total factor productivity we find it useful to divide total product between consumption and investment goods and total factor outlay between capital and labor services. In the U.S. national income and product accounts total output is divided among durables and structures output (which we denote investment goods output) and nondurables and services output (which we denote consumption goods output). Our definition of services output includes the services of consumers' durables and institutional durables along with the services output included in the U.S. accounts.

The value of private domestic factor outlay includes labor compensation of employees in private enterprises and in private households and nonprofit institutions, plus the labor compensation of self-employed persons.[6] In measuring labor compensation of the self-employed we assume for each sector that average labor compensation of proprietors and unpaid family workers is equal to the average labor compensation of full-time equivalent employees in the same sector. Our estimates of nonfarm proprietors and employees are those of the Office of Business Economics. Our estimates of unpaid family

Table 4.1
Production account, gross private domestic product and factor outlay, United States, 1958 (current prices)[a] [billions of dollars]

Line		Product	Total
1		*Private gross national product* (table 1.7)	$405.2
2	–	Income originating in government enterprises (table 1.13)	4.8
3	–	Rest of the world gross national product (table 1.7)	2.0
4	+	Services of consumers' durables (our imputation)	39.6
5	+	Services of durables held by institutions (our imputation)	0.3
6	–	Federal indirect business tax and nontax accruals (table 3.1)	11.5
7	+	Capital stock tax (table 3.1, footnote 2)	—
8	–	State and local indirect business tax and nontax accruals (table 3.3)	27.0
9	+	Motor vehicle licenses (table 3.3)	0.8
10	+	Property taxes (table 3.3)	13.8
11	+	Other taxes (table 3.3)	2.9
12	+	Subsidies less current surplus of Federal government enterprises (table 3.1)	2.7
13	–	Current surplus of state and local government ent enterprises (table 3.3)	1.8
14	=	*Gross private domestic product*	418.2
		Factor outlay	
1		*Capital consumption allowances* (table 1.9)	38.9
2	+	Business transfer payments (table 1.9)	1.6
3	+	Statistical discrepancy (table 1.9)	1.6
4	+	Services of consumers' durables (our imputation)	39.6
5	+	Services of durables held by institutions (our imputation)	0.3
6	+	Certain indirect business taxes (product account above, 9 + 10 + 11)	17.4
7	+	Income originating in business (table 1.13)	312.2
8	–	Income originating in government enterprises (table 1.13)	4.8
9	+	Income originating in households and institutions (table 1.13)	11.4
10	=	*Gross private domestic factor outlay*	418.2

[a] All table references are to *The National Income and Product Accounts of the United States, 1929–1965* (1966).

workers are those of Kendrick, allocated among sectors in proportion to the number of proprietors in each sector.[7] Our estimates of persons engaged in the farm sector are from Kendrick.

All outlay on factors of production not allocated to labor is allocated to capital. Outlay on capital services includes property income of the self-employed; profits, rentals, and interest; capital consumption allowances; business transfer payments; the statistical discrepancy; indirect business taxes that are part of the outlay on productive factors, such as motor vehicle licenses, property taxes, and other taxes; and the imputed value of the services of consumers' durables and producers' durables utilized by institutions.[8] Gross private domestic product and factor outlay in current prices for 1950–1962 are given in table 4.2. Total product is divided between gross private domestic investment and gross private domestic consumption. Total factor outlay is divided between labor compensation and property compensation.

4.2.3 Price and Quantity of Output

We turn next to the measurement of real product. Product is allocated between consumption and investment goods. Consumption goods include nondurable goods and services and investment goods include durable goods and structures. We construct quantity index numbers of output for these two types of output from data for the corresponding components of gross national product in constant prices. The product of the rest of the world and government sectors is composed entirely of services. The price index for the product of each of these sectors is assumed to be the same as for services as a whole. Quantity index numbers for the services of consumers' durables and institutional durables are constructed as part of our imputation of the value of these services. The value of output from the point of view of the producing sector excludes certain indirect business taxes less subsidies. The price of output is implicit in the value of output and the quantity index of output described above. Price and quantity indexes for gross private domestic product are presented in table 4.3.

Table 4.2
Gross private domestic product and factor outlay, 1950–1962 (current prices) [billions of dollars]

Year	Gross Private Domestic Product	Investment Goods Product	Consumption Goods Product	Labor Compensation	Property Compensation
1950	269.0	91.2	177.8	156.3	112.7
1951	307.2	106.2	200.9	177.4	129.8
1952	323.0	108.2	214.7	188.9	134.0
1953	340.1	115.3	225.0	202.7	137.4
1954	343.0	110.9	232.0	200.8	142.1
1955	374.5	128.6	246.0	216.5	158.1
1956	396.3	135.3	260.9	234.0	162.3
1957	415.0	140.0	274.9	246.0	169.0
1958	418.2	130.4	287.8	245.1	173.1
1959	453.2	146.8	306.4	265.5	187.6
1960	472.3	148.8	323.5	278.7	193.6
1961	487.0	147.4	339.5	284.7	202.3
1962	523.3	163.5	359.8	302.6	220.7

Table 4.3
Gross private domestic product, 1950–62 (constant prices of 1958)

Year	Gross Private Domestic Product, Quantity Index (billions of 1958 dollars)	Gross Private Domestic Product, Price Index (1958 = 1.000)	Consumption Goods Product, Quantity Index (billions of 1958 dollars)	Consumption Goods Product, Price Index (1958 = 1.000)	Investment Goods Product, Quantity Index (billions of 1958 dollars)	Investment Goods Product, Price Index (1958 = 1.000)	Relative Share of Investment Goods Product (percent)
1950	328.8	0.818	214.766	0.828	113.904	0.801	0.339
1951	351.3	0.874	228.302	0.880	122.926	0.864	0.346
1952	360.3	0.896	237.211	0.905	122.962	0.880	0.335
1953	378.8	0.898	247.510	0.909	131.163	0.879	0.339
1954	375.7	0.913	250.210	0.927	125.154	0.886	0.323
1955	406.6	0.921	262.751	0.936	143.861	0.894	0.343
1956	416.2	0.952	272.847	0.956	143.261	0.945	0.341
1957	422.6	0.982	280.978	0.978	141.571	0.989	0.337
1958	418.2	1.000	287.791	1.000	130.419	1.000	0.312
1959	445.5	1.017	300.561	1.020	144.976	1.013	0.324
1960	457.1	1.033	309.834	1.044	147.261	1.010	0.315
1961	466.1	1.045	320.175	1.060	145.733	1.012	0.303
1962	495.1	1.057	334.799	1.075	160.428	1.019	0.312

4.3 Measurement of Capital Input

4.3.1 Introduction

Our original estimates of capital input distinguished among five categories of capital input—land, residential and nonresidential structures, equipment, and inventories. Our approach has now been extended by Christensen and Jorgenson (1969, 1970) to 16 classes of assets, separating inventories into farm and nonfarm categories and adding consumers' durables to the other asset categories. Each asset category has been allocated among corporate, noncorporate, household, and institutional sectors.[9] This classification of assets permits a much more satisfactory treatment of the taxation of income from capital services. The original classification of assets was not sufficiently detailed to permit a fully satisfactory treatment of the tax structure. The relative proportions of capital stock by asset class for each sector for 1958 are given in table 4.4.

We have divided assets among sectors of the private domestic economy that differ in the tax treatment of property income. Households and institutions utilize the services of consumers' and institutional durables, owner-occupied dwellings, institutional structures, and land. No direct taxes are levied on this property income, but part of the income is taxed indirectly through property taxes. To incorporate property taxes into the capital service price, we add the rate of property taxation to the rate of return, the rate of replacement, and the rate of capital loss. Noncorporate business utilizes services from residential and nonresidential structures, producers' durable equipment,

Table 4.4
Relative proportions of capital stock by sector, 1958

Asset Class	Sector		
	Corporate Business	Noncorporate Business	Households and Institutions
Consumers' durables	0.00	0.00	1.00
Nonresidential structures	0.72	0.18	0.10
Producers' durables	0.68	0.31	0.01
Residential structures	0.08	0.07	0.85
Nonfarm inventories	0.82	0.18	0.00
Farm inventories	0.00	1.00	0.00
Land	0.19	0.50	0.31

nonfarm and farm inventories, and land held by that sector. This property income is taxed directly through the personal income tax and indirectly through property taxes. We measure the noncorporate rate of return before personal income taxes.

Corporations utilize services from residential and nonresidential structures, producers' durable equipment, nonfarm inventories, and land. We employ the capital service prices for corporate capital input developed by Hall and Jorgenson (1967, 1971) for depreciable assets, modified to include indirect business taxes,[10] including property taxes. Corporate property income is taxed directly through the corporation income tax and through the personal income tax and indirectly through property taxes. We measure the corporate rate of return before personal income taxes but after corporation income taxes.

4.3.2 Perpetual Inventory Method

The starting point for a revised index of real capital input is the estimation of capital stock by the perpetual inventory method. In discrete time the perpetual inventory method may be represented in the form:

$$K_{it} = I_{it} + (1 - \mu_i) K_{i,t-1}$$

where K_{it} is the end-of-period capital stock, I_{it} the quantity of investment occurring in the period, and μ_i the rate of replacement, all for the ith investment good. For each type of investment good we follow these steps in estimating capital stock by the perpetual inventory method: (1) a benchmark is obtained, (2) the investment series in current prices from the U.S. national accounts is deflated to obtain a real investment series, (3) a rate of replacement is chosen, and (4) the stock series is computed using the perpetual inventory method described above. Benchmarks for 1958, rates of replacement, and price indexes for each capital good are given in table 4.5. Price indexes for each asset class for 1950–1962 are given in table 4.6.

Our method of separating price and quantity components of a flow of capital services is based on the correspondence between asset prices and service prices implied by the equality between the value of an asset and the value of its services. This correspondence is the counterpart in price estimation to the relationship between investment and changes in capital stock used in estimation of national wealth by the perpetual inventory method. Data on asset prices, rates of replacement, and investment are required for perpetual inventory estimates

Table 4.5
Benchmarks, rates of replacement, and price indexes employed in estimating capital

Asset Class	1958 Benchmark (billions of 1958 dollars)	Replacement Rate	Deflator (sources given below)
Consumers' durables	115.2	0.200	Implicit deflator, national product accounts[a]
Nonresidential structures	136.1	0.056	Constant cost 2 deflator[b]
Producers' durables	123.4	0.138	Implicit deflator, national product accounts[a]
Residential structures	226.2	0.039	Constant cost 2 deflator[b]
Nonfarm inventories	80.3	—	Investment: Implicit deflator, national product accounts[c] Assets: BLS wholesale price index, goods other than farm products and food[d]
Farm inventories	24.6	—	Investment: Implicit deflator, national product accounts[c] Assets: BLS wholesale price index, farm products[d]
Land	322.2	—	Goldsmith[e]

[a] NIP (1966), table 8.1.
[b] *Capital Stock Study* (Grose, Rottenberg and Wasson, 1969).
[c] NIP (1966), tables 1.1 and 1.2.
[d] BLS (1968).
[e] Goldsmith (1962), tables A–5 and A–6.

Table 4.6
Price indices by class of asset, 1950–1962 [1958 = 1.000]

Year	Consumers' Durables	Structures, Nonresidential and Residential	Producers' Durables	Investment, Nonfarm Inventories	Assets, Nonfarm Inventories	Investment, Farm Inventories	Assets, Farm Inventories	Land
1950	0.878	0.763	0.752	0.800	0.833	1.000	1.027	0.706
1951	0.942	0.836	0.809	0.919	0.920	1.200	1.195	0.760
1952	0.954	0.881	0.822	0.840	0.899	1.429	1.127	0.785
1953	0.943	0.895	0.835	0.786	0.906	1.500	1.022	0.786
1954	0.929	0.897	0.840	0.808	0.909	1.200	1.008	0.811
1955	0.919	0.902	0.859	0.917	0.929	1.250	0.945	0.850
1956	0.949	0.959	0.918	0.944	0.970	0.667	0.932	0.897
1957	0.984	1.001	0.975	1.143	0.997	1.000	0.958	0.951
1958	1.000	1.000	1.000	1.000	1.000	1.000	1.000	1.000
1959	1.014	1.006	1.020	1.000	1.018	(a)	0.938	1.069
1960	1.009	1.005	1.022	1.031	1.018	1.000	0.935	1.143
1961	1.006	1.008	1.021	0.944	1.013	1.500	0.924	1.222
1962	1.008	1.024	1.023	1.019	1.013	1.000	0.943	1.306

[a] Investment in constant prices is zero.

of capital stock.[11] Our method for separation of property compensation between the price of capital services and its quantity requires the same data as the perpetual inventory method for measurement of capital stock, together with data on property income and the tax structure. Data on property compensation by legal form of of organization, such as those presented in the U.S. national income and product accounts, are essential for incorporating the effects of the tax structure. This straightforward extension of the perpetual inventory method makes it possible to allocate property income among different classes of assets.

To make the correspondence between asset prices and service prices explicit we must specify the relationship between the quantity of an asset acquired at one date and the quantity of the service flow of the asset at future dates. In our perpetual inventory estimates of the stock of assets, we have assumed that the service flow from the ith investment good declines geometrically over time,

$$1\,,(1-\mu_i)\,,(1-\mu_i)^2\,\ldots\,.$$

To infer the capital service price from the sequence of asset prices, we first write the asset price as the discounted value of future services,

$$q_{it}^{A}=\sum_{r=t}^{\infty}\prod_{s=t+1}^{r+1}\frac{1}{1+r_s}\,p_{i,r+1}^{S}(1-\mu_i)^{r-t}$$

where r_s is the rate of return in period s, q_{it}^{A} is the price of the ith investment good at time t and p_{it}^{S} is service price of the ith investment good. Solving for the service price, we obtain

$$p_{it}^{S}=q_{i,t-1}^{A}r_t+q_{it}^{A}\mu_i-(q_{i,t}^{A}-q_{i,t-1}^{A})\,.$$

Given the sequence of asset prices $\{q_{it}^{A}\}$, the rate of replacement μ_i, and the rate of return r_t, we obtain the perpetual inventory estimate of the service price of the ith investment good p_{it}^{S}.

The correspondence between asset prices and service prices implied by the perpetual inventory method is precisely the same correspondence that underlies the measurement of net capital stock. As Denison points out, "... net stock measures ... the discounted value of future capital services."[12] The measurement of net capital stock is well established in social accounting practice; our formula for the perpetual inventory estimate of the capital service price is an immediate implication of accounting methods for net capital stock. This formula may be generalized to alternative assumptions about the time pattern of the service flow associated with an asset. The formula developed by Haavelmo (1960) for a constant service flow over the lifetime of the asset has been suggested as a means of aggregating capital services by Johansen and Sorsveen (1967). Arrow (1964) has provided formulas for the service price for an arbitrary sequence of replacements. In Arrow's formula the rate of replacement μ_i, which we have assumed constant for each class of assets, is replaced by a weighted average of rates of replacement over the lifetime of the asset.

4.3.3 Price of Investment Goods

The prices indexes used by Christensen and Jorgenson in constructing the capital stock series differ from our original ones in using the national income implicit deflator for producers' durable equipment and the WPI as the deflator of the *stock* of inventories. There is enough evidence that the various official capital deflator series are biased upward during this period for us to be unwilling to concede that our original attempt to substitute something else (the CPI durables index) for the official equipment investment deflator was an error. While this is not the place to go into great detail, there is ample evidence that the components of the WPI, which in turn are a major source of deflators for the producers' durables investment, are (or at least have been) rather poor measures of price change. The WPI is based almost entirely on company and trade papers and association reports. Moreover, for a variety of reasons, it has had much less resources devoted to it relative to the CPI. All this has combined to produce what we believe to be a significant upward drift in components of this index during the post-World War II period.[13]

Our example of consumer durables was not intended to claim that the particular items were representative of most of the producers' durables but rather that such a comparison allowed one to detect the magnitude of the drift in the WPI which was due to the particular way in which its data were collected. The difference between the movement of prices for these identical items in the two index sources was interpreted not as property of the particular items, but as an estimate of the bias introduced by the basic procedure used in collecting the wholesale price data. The latter, we assumed, was generalizable to most of the other WPI items.

Actually, there is quite a bit more evidence on this point than was alluded to in our original paper and some of it is presented in table 4.7. The first line recapitulates the CPI-WPI identical durables comparison. The other comparisons can be divided into three groups: (1) transaction price data (circuit breakers and power transformers from the Dean-DePodwin study and tubes and batteries prices from Flueck's staff report); (2) more detailed attention to quality change and/or more analysis of the changing specifications of the priced items, sometimes via regression techniques (Dean-DePodwin and Census on steam generators, Barzel on electric equipment, the Association of American Railroads on railroad equipment prices, and Fettig on tractor prices); and (3) wider coverage and transaction pricing (Census unit values data).

The last, Census based, set of data (summarized in table 4.8) is particularly interesting since one might have expected that unit values would themselves be upward biased due to the secular shift to more elaborate, higher "quality" models. In fact, they and all the other additional comparisons point strongly to the existence of an upward bias in the comparable WPI components, at least in the recent past. Our implied estimate of this upward drift of 1.4 percent per year between 1950 and 1962 is quite consistent with the new evidence presented in this table. While it is not used in the productivity computations we borrow from Christensen and Jorgenson we are willing to stand by this part of our original estimates.[14]

Our substitution of the new OBE "constant cost 2" construction deflator for the comparable implicit GNP deflator component is not ideal and could be improved on. The "constant cost 2" deflator is an average, implicitly, of the Bureau of Public Roads highway structures, the Bureau of Reclamation pumping and power plant indexes, and the A.T.&T. and Turner construction cost indexes. The latter two are basically input price rather than output price indexes with some feeble adjustment for productivity changes.[15] The Bureau of Reclamation indexes are hard to interpret and seem to be based, to a large extent, on list prices of raw materials. A recent study by Gordon (1968) indicates that the constant cost 2 index may also be biased upward to an unknown degree.[16] It is likely, therefore, that if a more accurate construction price index were used it would imply a higher rate of growth in the structures component of capital input than was estimated in our original paper and is also used in this one. In short, more remains to be done in this area but we believe that our original

Table 4.7
Evidence on drift in components of WPI

Item	Reference	Period	Approximate Drift in Percent Per Year[a]
Identical consumer durables[b]	CPI	1947–58	1.9
Circuit breakers	Dean-DePodwin[c]	1954–59	4.0
Power transformers	Dean-DePodwin	1954–59	0.7
Power transformers	Census[d]	1954–63	1.2
Steam generators	Dean-DePodwin	1954–59	1.9
Steam generators	Census[e]	1954–63	6.4
Electric equipment	Dean-DePodwin	1954–59	1.2
Electric equipment	Census[d]	1954–63	1.9
Electric equipment	Barzel[f]	1949–59	4.4
Railroad equipment	Assoc. of Am. Railroads[g]	1961–67	0.8
Tractors	Fettig[h]	1950–62	0.6
Tubes, automobiles	Flueck[i]	1955–59	1.4
Batteries, vehicle	Flueck[i]	1949–60	6.3
Storage batteries	Census[d]	1954–63	2.9
Plumbing and heating	Census[d]	1954–63	1.2
Oil burners	Census[d]	1954–63	2.8
Warm air furnaces	Census[d]	1954–63	1.1
Metal doors	Census[d]	1954–63	0.7
Bolts and nuts	Census[d]	1954–63	2.3
Internal combustion engines	Census[d]	1954–63	1.8
Elevators and escalators	Census[d]	1954–63	1.1
Pumps and compressors	Census[d]	1954–63	2.0
Integrating instruments	Census[d]	1954–63	3.1
Electric welding	Census[d]	1954–63	–1.1
Electric lamps	Census[d]	1954–63	1.1
Trucks	Census[d]	1954–63	0.3

[a] Last column is the average change, over the specified period, in the particular WPI component relative to the estimated price change over the same period in the alternative source.

[b] The following items were compared for this period: automobiles, tires, radios, refrigerators, sewing machines, ranges, washing machines, vacuum cleaners, toasters, and furniture.

[c] Dean and DePodwin (1961) and an unpublished appendix to the original General Electric version.

[d] 1963 *Census of Manufactures* (1963a), Vol IV, *Indexes of Production*, Appendix A.

[e] Census unit values, adjusted for capacity and horsepower differences, 1963 *Census of Manufactures* (1963a), Vol. IV, *Indexes of Production*, Appendix A.

[f] Barzel (1964). Indexes in table 3 holding size constant are essentially flat throughout this period. A similar story is also told by the indexes in table 6, where size is taken into account.

[g] Joint Equipment Committee Report (1968) shows no significant increase in the "cost" of locomotives and freight and passenger cars during this period.

[h] Fettig (1963), table 6, p. 609.

[i] J.K. Flueck (1961).

Table 4.8
A comparison of OBE producers' durables investment deflators with census unit value indexes, 1962 (1954 = 100)

Category	Percent Direct Coverage by Data from Census[a]	Census (cross weights)[a]	OBE[b]	Drift in Percent Per Year
Furniture and fixtures	42.0	110.9	119.1	0.8
Fabricated metal products	34.0	117.3	121.7	0.4
Engines and turbines	54.0	93.3	134.7	4.2
Construction machinery	20.0	126.2	132.0	0.5
Metalworking machinery	42.0	122.9	137.2	1.2
Special industry machinery	20.0	119.3	138.7	1.7
General industry machinery[c]	15.0	116.9	131.4	1.3
Service industry machinery	27.0	82.3	100.9	2.3
Electric machinery	27.0	98.7	112.0	1.4
Trucks and buses[d]	91.0	118.0	122.5	0.4
Ships and boats	27.0	100.1	116.6	1.7
Railroad equipment	46.0	132.1	128.3	–0.3

[a] 1963 *Census of Manufactures* (1963a), Vol. IV, *Indexes of Production*, Appendix A.

[b] NIP (1966), table 8.8. For tractors, agricultural machinery, mining and oil field machinery, office equipment, passenger cars, aircraft, and instruments Census unit values are based on less than 15 percent coverage from Census sources. For a comparison of tractor price or indexes see table 7.

[c] OBE definition includes also materials handling machinery.

[d] Four separate Census categories aggregated using 1963 shipments as weights.

procedures were on the right track. The estimates we borrow from Christensen and Jorgenson are conservative in their choice of investment deflators.

4.3.4 Price and Capital Services

4.3.4.1 *Introduction*

The second step in the construction of a revised index of real capital input is to divide the value of capital services between price and quantity with price corresponding to the rental rate and quantity as the amount of capital services utilized. This division is precisely analogous to the separation of the value of labor services between a wage rate and the quantity of labor services. For property with an active rental market the separation may be carried out by means of market data on rental rates and corresponding data on the employment of capital. This method may be extended from rental property to property utilized by its owners if market rental values reflect the implicit rentals paid by owners for the use of their property. An imputation of this type is employed in the U.S. national income and product accounts in the measurement of services of owner-occupied housing.[17] A precisely analogous imputation occurs in measuring labor services of the self-employed. Market wage rates are used as a basis for imputing the implicit wage rates paid to the self-employed.[18] The main obstacle to application of this method to capital services on a comprehensive basis is the lack of sufficient data on market rental values.

To impute capital service prices we must estimate rates of return for corporate business, noncorporate business, and households and institutions.[19] As an accounting identity for each sector the value of all capital services is equal to total property income. We measure the value of capital services for each sector before either corporate or personal income taxes, but we measure the rate of return after corporate income taxes and before personal income taxes. In each sector asset prices and stocks, rates of replacement, and parameters describing the tax structure are given as data. The rate of return for each sector is chosen at each point of time so as to maintain the identity between property income and the value of all capital services in the sector.

Each capital service flow may be expressed as the sum of four terms, depending on the rate of return, the rate of replacement, the rate of capital losses accrued, and the rate of property taxation. Since property taxes are deducted from corporate income in determining corporate profits for tax purposes, the component of each capital service flow corresponding to property taxes is simply added to the other components. Similarly, the property tax component of each capital service flow for the noncorporate and household sector is simply added to the rest. Accordingly, our first step in estimating rates of return for the three sectors is to deduct all property taxes from the value of property compensation.

4.3.4.2 *Household sector*

Our measurement of the flow of capital services for the household sector is independent of the measurement of flows of capital services for the corporate and noncorporate sectors. The value of services of owner-occupied farm and nonfarm dwellings is the space-rental value of dwellings less associated purchases of goods and services. We assume that the proportion of purchases is the same for farm as for nonfarm dwellings. The effective tax rate is the ratio of taxes as a component of total space-rental value to the asset value of owner-occupied dwellings, including both structures and land. The value of services of institutional structures is the space-rental value of institutional buildings. To estimate the rate of return we divide the space-rental values of owner-occupied dwellings and institutional buildings, less associated purchases of goods and services for dwellings, less current replacement values, accrued capital losses, and taxes as a component of total space-rental value for dwellings by the current asset value of owner-occupied dwellings and institutional structures, including land.

Our measurement of the output of the producing sector differs from that of the U.S. national income and product accounts in the treatment of consumers' and institutional durables. We assign personal consumption expenditures on durables to gross investment rather than to current consumption. We then add the service flow from consumers' and institutional durables to the value of output and the value of capital input. The value of each service flow is the product of the service price given above and the corresponding service quantity. The values of these service flows enter the product and factor outlay accounts given in table 4.1. We assume that the rate of return on durables is the same as that on structures for the household sector. The effective tax rate on consumers' durables is the ratio of the following State and local personal taxes—motor vehicle licenses, property taxes, and other taxes—plus Federal automobile use taxes to the current asset value of consumers' durables. The effective property tax rates on household property and the rate of return for the household sector are presented in table 4.9.

4.3.4.3 Noncorporate sector

In measuring the rate of return for the noncorporate business sector we first estimate the effective tax rate on noncorporate property. We deduct property taxes on owner-occupied residential real estate from State and local business property taxes to obtain State and property taxes for corporate and noncorporate sectors.[20] We allocate business motor vehicle licenses between corporate and noncorporate sectors in proportion to the value of producers' durables in each sector; similarly, we allocate other State and local business taxes and Federal capital stock taxes in proportion to the value of all assets in each sector. The effective tax rate on noncorporate property is the

Table 4.9
Effective tax rates and rates of return, household and noncorporate sectors, 1950–1962 (annual rates)

Year	Effective Tax Rate on Owner-occupied Residential Real estate	Effective Tax Rate on Owner-utilized Consumers' Durables	Effective Tax Rate on Noncorporate Property	Rate of Return, Household Sector	Rate of Return, Noncorporate Sector
1950	0.009	0.008	0.018	0.063	0.178
1951	0.009	0.007	0.017	0.103	0.214
1952	0.009	0.007	0.018	0.062	0.121
1953	0.009	0.007	0.019	0.030	0.089
1954	0.010	0.007	0.019	0.032	0.108
1955	0.011	0.007	0.020	0.040	0.114
1956	0.012	0.007	0.019	0.083	0.127
1957	0.012	0.007	0.020	0.069	0.127
1958	0.013	0.007	0.020	0.035	0.116
1959	0.013	0.007	0.020	0.047	0.103
1960	0.014	0.008	0.021	0.043	0.096
1961	0.015	0.008	0.022	0.047	0.099
1962	0.015	0.009	0.022	0.058	0.111

ratio of the sum of property taxes, motor vehicle licenses, and other business taxes allocated to the noncorporate sector to the value of all assets held by the sector, including producers' durables, residential and nonresidential structures, inventories, and land.

The value of capital services for the noncorporate sector is the sum of income originating in business, other than income originating in corporate business, income originating in government enterprises, and interest and net rent of owner-occupied dwellings and institutional structures, less labor compensation in the the noncorporate sector, including imputed labor compensation of proprietors and unpaid family workers, plus noncorporate capital consumption allowances, less capital consumption allowances of owner-occupied dwellings and institutional structures, and plus indirect business taxes allocated to the noncorporate sector, as outlined above. We also allocate the statistical discrepancy to noncorporate property income.[21] To obtain our estimate of the noncorporate rate of return we deduct property taxes and the current value of replacement, add accrued capital gains on noncorporate assets, and divide by the value of noncorporate assets. The effective tax rate on noncorporate property and the rate of return in the noncorporate sector are given in table 4.9.

4.3.4.4 *Corporate sector*

In measuring the rate of return for corporate business we begin by estimating the effective tax rate on corporate property. We add State and local business property taxes, business motor vehicle licenses, other business taxes, and Federal capital stock taxes for the corporate sector to obtain total property taxes. The effective tax rate on corporate property is the ratio of these taxes to the value of all assets held by the corporate sector, including producers' durables, residential and nonresidential structures, inventories, and land. We measure corporate property income less property taxes as income originating in corporate business, less compensation of employees, plus corporate capital consumption allowances, plus business transfer payments.[22] The value of corporate capital input, which is equal to corporate property income, depends on the effective corporate income tax rate, the rate of return in the corporate sector, the investment tax credit, and the present values of depreciation deductions for nonresidential structures, producers' durables, and residential structures.

Corporate income taxes less the investment tax credit are equal to the effective tax rate applied to corporate property income, less property taxes and less deductions for capital consumption, expressed as proportions of current capital service flows after taxes. Our estimate of the effective rate of the investment tax credit is based on estimates of investment tax credit for corporations by the Office of Business Economics. The effective rate is defined as the amount of the investment tax credit divided by gross private domestic investment in producers' durables by corporations. We assume that the effective rate of the investment tax credit is the same for corporations and for noncorporate business. Although the nominal rate of the investment tax credit is 7 percent, certain limitations on its applicability reduce the effective rate considerably below this level.[23]

The present values of depreciation deductions on new investment depend on depreciation formulas allowable for tax purposes, the lifetimes of assets used in calculating depreciation, and the rate of return.[24] A reasonable approximation to depreciation practice is provided by the assumption that the straight-line depreciation formula was the only one permitted for assets acquired up to 1953 and that an accelerated depreciation formula, sum of the years' digits, was employed for assets acquired during the period 1954–1962.[25] Given depreciation formulas and lifetimes for tax purposes, calculation of present values of depreciation deductions requires an estimate of the rate of return for discounting these deductions. We assume that this rate of return was constant at 10 percent.[26] Substituting the present values of depreciation deductions into expressions for capital service prices we reduce the unknown variables to two, the effective corporate tax rate and the rate of return in the corporate sector. Corresponding to these two unknowns, we have two equations. The first relates corporate property income and the sum of values of the individual capital services. The second relates corporate income taxes and the effective tax rate on corporate income, applied to the corporate income tax base, less the investment tax credit. We measure corporate income taxes as Federal and State corporate profits tax liability. Since the two equations are independent, we may solve for values of the effective corporate tax rate and the corporate rate of return in each time period. Variables describing the corporate tax structure and the corporate rate of return for 1950–1962 are presented in table 4.10.

4.3.5 Price and Quantity of Capital Services

In separating the value of capital input into price and quantity components our basic accounting identity is that for each sector the value of all capital services or property compensation is equal to the sum of the

Table 4.10
Tax structure and rate of return, corporate sector, 1950–1962 (proportions and annual rates)

Year	Effective Tax Rate on Corporate Property	Effective Rate of Investment Tax Credit	Statutory Rate of Investment Tax Credit	Effective Tax Rate on Corporate Income	Statutory Tax Rate on Corporate Income	Present Value of Depreciation Deductions, Nonresidential Structure	Present Value of Depreciation Deductions, Producers' Durables	Present Value of Depreciation Deductions, Residential Structures	Rate of Return, Corporate Sector
1950	0.015	0.000	0.000	0.481	0.420	0.273	0.397	0.262	0.107
1951	0.014	0.000	0.000	0.521	0.508	0.273	0.397	0.262	0.157
1952	0.014	0.000	0.000	0.462	0.520	0.273	0.397	0.262	0.079
1953	0.015	0.000	0.000	0.477	0.520	0.273	0.397	0.262	0.065
1954	0.015	0.000	0.000	0.476	0.520	0.413	0.543	0.400	0.061
1955	0.016	0.000	0.000	0.479	0.520	0.425	0.560	0.412	0.093
1956	0.016	0.000	0.000	0.477	0.520	0.438	0.579	0.426	0.124
1957	0.016	0.000	0.000	0.468	0.520	0.453	0.596	0.439	0.103
1958	0.016	0.000	0.000	0.465	0.520	0.469	0.614	0.456	0.059
1959	0.016	0.000	0.000	0.494	0.520	0.486	0.632	0.473	0.079
1960	0.016	0.000	0.000	0.487	0.520	0.486	0.632	0.473	0.063
1961	0.017	0.000	0.000	0.479	0.520	0.486	0.632	0.473	0.062
1962	0.017	0.037	0.070	0.480	0.520	0.486	0.632	0.473	0.085

values of the individual capital services. In constructing Divisia index numbers of capital service price and quantity we combine service prices and quantities by class of asset for all sectors. Finally, we combine service price and quantity indexes by class of asset into an overall capital service price index and potential service quantity index, again as Divisia index numbers. We note that the overall service price and quantity indexes include capital services from assets held by households and institutions as well as by business. Price and quantity indexes of potential capital services for corporate, noncorporate, and household sectors for 1950–1962 are given in table 4.11.

4.4 Relative Utilization of Capital

4.4.1 Introduction

It has been common to assume that one may be able to approximate the unemployment of capital by the unemployment of labor. Solow (1962) assumed that there is a proportionality relationship between these concepts (and his capital measure included land and buildings, too!) while Okun (1962) suggested a nonlinear relationship between the two. It appeared to us that the unemployment of capital can be better approximated by the "unemployment" of one kind of capital (power-driven equipment), implicitly assuming a proportionality relationship between this type of capital and other capital, than by the assumption of proportionality between the employment of all labor and of all capital.

It is our assumption, for which we have no explicit evidence, that our measure of utilization measures not only the the utilization of power-driven equipment but also the fraction of calendar time that establishments or plants are in actual operation. That is, machine-hours per week are interpreted as a proxy for total hours per week operated by an establishment or industry. This, of course, is not an unambiguous concept, but it does explain why we were and still are willing to apply this estimated utilization rate not only to equipment but also to buildings. We are also willing, for lack of any better evidence, to extrapolate this to all industrial and agricultural equipment and structures and also to structures and equipment in the service industries. There is some scattered evidence that the hours operated per week by various retail establishments have increased in recent years.

Table 4.15
Actual gross private domestic capital input, 1950–1962 (constant prices of 1958)

Year	Corporate Capital Input, Quantity Index (billions of 1958 dollars)	Corporate Capital Input, Price Index (1958 = 1.000)	Noncorporate Capital Input, Quantity Index (billions of 1958 dollars)	Noncorporate Capital Input, Price Index (1958 = 1.000)	Private Domestic Capital Input, Quantity Index (billions of 1958 dollars)	Private Domestic Capital Input, Price Index (1958 = 1.000)	Index of Relative Utilization (1958 = 1.000)
1950	49.5	0.981	35.9	0.870	124.1	0.908	1.065
1951	53.2	1.034	37.9	0.991	134.5	0.965	1.092
1952	55.2	0.977	38.5	0.947	139.7	0.959	1.046
1953	59.4	0.938	39.8	0.903	147.4	0.932	1.098
1954	58.4	0.958	39.3	0.920	148.9	0.955	1.020
1955	63.5	1.061	41.2	0.896	158.6	0.996	1.105
1956	66.6	1.024	42.1	0.827	167.1	0.971	1.105
1957	68.4	1.027	41.9	0.883	171.9	0.983	1.065
1958	67.8	1.000	41.2	1.000	173.1	1.000	1.000
1959	73.6	1.078	43.4	0.887	182.5	1.028	1.092
1960	76.3	1.040	44.2	0.850	189.0	1.024	1.098
1961	78.2	1.042	44.5	0.902	194.1	1.043	1.085
1962	83.0	1.097	46.0	0.962	202.3	1.091	1.137

4.4.2 Measurement of Relative Utilization

In measuring the change in utilization between 1945 and 1954 by the average estimated change in utilization (per annum) between 1939 and 1954, we overestimated the former. The estimates used in this paper (also taken from Christensen and Jorgenson) solve this problem by adding a cyclical adjustment to the previously computed secular one. The benchmark years are now used only to derive the ratio of installed horsepower to potential capital. This ratio is assumed to change slowly and is interpolated linearly between benchmarks. Installed horsepower is then estimated as the product of this ratio and our index of potential flow of (business) capital services. The ratio of electric power consumed by motors to this estimate of installed horsepower is our new measure of relative utilization. The resulting series grows at a significantly lower rate, 0.54 percent per year, during the 1950–1962 period than the utilization index used in our original study (which rose at 10.6 percent per year).

Denison suggests that the weighting of utilization estimates for industry groups should be done be something other than the total horsepower of electric motors. Since we use it as a proxy for the utilization of all capital, the appropriate weights would be estimates of the value of capital services at the two-digit level. The closest we can come to it is to use weights based on the distribution of total fixed assets in 1962. Recomputing our estimates separately for each two-digit industry and then weighting them with these weights doesn't really change the numbers significantly (see table 4.12). If anything, it makes them slightly higher. The same is also true for mining during the 1954 to 1963 period (see table 4.13). The resulting weighted utilization index is still quite high and of the same order of magnitude as the manufacturing one (if allowance is made for the cyclical difference between 1963 and 1962). We conclude, therefore, that the unweighted figures we used are rather close to what the weighted figures would have been had we computed them.

Thus, except for the overestimate of the rate of change of utilization from 1945 to 1954, our estimates appear to be reasonably good estimates of the rate of utilization of electric motors in manufacturing. Similar estimates were presented for mining in table 4.13. An entirely different set of estimates, based on actual machine-hours worked for three textile subindustries, is presented in table 4.14. They, too, indicate an upward trend in utilization in the post-World War II period of

Table 4.12
Relative utilization of electric motors, U.S. manufacturing, 1962

Industry[a]	Indexes, 1954 = 1,000			Total Fixed Assets Weight[e]
	Horsepower of Electric Motors[b]	Total Electricity Consumption[c]	Utilization[d]	
	(1)	(2)	(3)	(4)
20	1.420	1.539	1.084	0.103
21	1.446	1.794	1.241	0.004
22	1.155	1.229	1.064	0.036
24	1.543	1.289	0.835	0.023
25	1.247	1.438	1.153	0.008
26	1.616	1.624	1.005	0.070
27	1.833	2.385	1.301	0.034
28	1.552	1.769	1.140	0.122
29	1.537	1.765	1.148	0.069
30	1.554	1.579	1.016	0.024
31	1.158	1.335	1.153	0.004
32	1.529	1.447	0.944	0.055
33	1.289	1.394	1.081	0.165
34	1.289	1.488	1.154	0.049
35 and 36	1.344	1.713	1.275	0.119
37	1.173	1.505	1.283	0.076
38	1.234	2.187	1.773	0.012
39 and 19	1.082	1.336	1.235	0.014
Total[f]	1.386	1.567	1.131	—
Total Weighted[g]	—	—	1.135	—

[a] "Two digit" manufacturing industries. Industry 23 apparel, excluded because no horsepower figures were asked for in 1954.

[b] Horsepower of electric motors from 1963 *Census of Manufactures* (1963a), "Power Equipment in Manufacturing Industries as of December 31, 1962," MC 63 (1)—6, table 2.

[c] Electricity, total purchased and generated minus sold, from 1963 *Census of Manufactures* (1963a), "Fuels and Electric Energy Consumed in Manufacturing Industries: 1962," MC 63 (1)—7, table 3.

[d] Utilization: column 2/column 1.

[e] 1962 fixed assets weights computed from 1964 *Annual Survey of Manufactures* (various annual issues), M 65 (AS)—6.

[f] Numbers differ from table X in Jorgenson and Griliches (1967), because no allowance could be made at the two-digit level for electricity consumption in nuclear energy installations. The comparable utilization index for total manufacturing allowing for this is 1.111.

[g] Σ (column 3 $\times$ column 4)/0.987, where 0.987 = Σ column 4.

Table 4.13
Equipment utilization indexes, mining industries, 1963 (1954 = 100)

Industry	Horsepower of Electric Motors[a] (1)	Electricity Consumption[b] (2)	Utilization Index[c] (3)	Depreciable Assets Weights (4)
Metal mining	111.3	175.0	157.2	0.246
Anthracite	42.4	51.7	122.0	0.014[e]
Bituminous coal	99.4	134.5	135.3	0.134[e]
Oil and gas	224.0	229.6	102.5	0.432
Nonmetallic minerals	152.2	156.9	103.1	0.174
Total mining	126.6	149.3	117.9	—
Adjusted	—	—	117.6[f]	—
Weighted	—	—	120.7[g]	—

[a] *Census of Mining* (1963b), chapter 7, table 1.

[b] *Census of Mining* (1963b), chapter 6, table 1; purchased and used.

[c] Column 2/column 1.

[d] From U.S. Internal Revenue Service, *Statistics of Income* (1963), *Corporation Income Tax Returns*, table 37. col. 3, p. 264.

[e] Total "coal mining" weight allocated on the basis of 1954 data for total capital given in Creamer, Dobrovolsky and Berenstein (1960), table B–11, p. 318.

[f] Adjusted for a small implied change in percentage of electric power used by electric motors (from 93.5 to 93.3) using the 1945 percentages given by Foss (1963) and the 1954 and 1963 total electricity consumption as weights.

[g] Σ (column 3 $\times$ column 4).

about the same order of magnitude. Thus, there is something in these data. They are measuring something, at least as far as the utilization of electric motors in manufacturing and mining is concerned.

Given our data, it was an error on our part (and on the part of those who preceded us on this path) to adjust the residential housing, land, and inventories components by this measure of capacity utilization. Until better evidence comes along, however, we are willing to hazard the very strong assumption that the capacity utilization of all *business* equipment and structures may be approximated by our estimates of capacity utilization of power-driven equipment in manufacturing (and mining). Business equipment and structures account for about 46 percent of our total capital input. Applying this to the reduced rate of growth in utilization leads to a utilization adjustment on the order of 16 percent of our previous adjustment.

Table 4.14
Selected utilization measures

Year	Cotton Broad Woven Goods; Average Loom Hours Per Loom in Place[a]	Cotton-system Spindle Hours Per Spindle in Place[b]	Man-made Fiber Broadwoven Goods; Average Loom Hours Per Loom in Place[a]
1947	5,042	5,074	5,220
1948	5,161	5,305	5,408
1949	4,689	4,433	4,991
1950	5,547	5,048	5,532
1951	5,276	5,823	5,045
1952	5,046	4,919	4,970
1953	5,579	5,513	5,240
1954	5,431	5,141	4,802
1955	5,658	5,501	5,326
1956	5,837	5,783	5,036
1957	5,425	5,512	5,463
1958	5,499	5,311	5,397
1959	6,114	5,853	5,718
1960	6,145	6,216	5,844
1961	6,020	5,830	5,717
1962	6,061	6,283	6,042
1963	6,124	6,074	6,105
1964	6,450	6,243	6,412
1965	6,741	6,489	6,513
Rates of growth, percent per year:			
1950–62	0.8	1.8	0.7
1947–65	1.6	1.4	1.7

[a] Computed from various issues of *Current Industrial Reports*, series M22T.1 and M22T.2. 1947–1953: Looms in place are averages of quarterly data as of the end of the quarter; 1954–64: Looms in place are averages of beginning and of year figures; 1965 for cotton broadwoven goods extrapolated on the basis of averages of monthly data on average hours per loom per week from the American Textile Manufacturers Institute (various monthly issues), for man-made fibers based on looms in place at the end of 1964.

[b] Bureau of the Census, *Cotton Production and Distribution* (1966), page 37. This is a more variable series, since the denominator is available only once during each year.

4.4.3 Actual and Potential Capital Services

The index of relative utilization used in this paper is given in table 4.15. Since the value of the capital service flow as we have measured is independent of the rate of utilization, we define a price and quantity index of actual capital services as price and quantity indexes of potential capital services, divided and multiplied, respectively, by our index of relative utilization. Price and quantity indexes of actual capital services for corporate and noncorporate sectors and price and quantity indexes of actual capital services for the private domestic economy for 1950–1962 are also presented in table 4.15.

To provide the basis for comparison of sources of growth of capital input with those for labor input, we present data on capital stock, potential service flow per unit of capital stock, and the relative utilization of capital in table 4.16. Capital stock is a Divisia index of capital stock for each class of assets—consumers' durables, nonresidential structures, producers' durables, residential structures, nonfarm inventories, farm inventories, and land. The potential service flow per unit of capital stock is the ratio of the quantity of potential gross private domestic capital input from table 4.11 to the index of capital stock. The relative utilization of *capital* is the ratio of the quantity of actual to potential gross private domestic capital input.

4.5 Measurement of Labor Input

4.5.1 Introduction

The labor input series used in this paper have also been borrowed from Christensen and Jorgenson. They are very similar to our original series except for the correction of an error in our original persons engaged series (it did not contain unpaid family workers) and the use of quality adjustments as extended by Griliches.[27] The Christensen-Jorgenson series add Kendrick's estimates of unpaid family workers to the OBE data on full-time equivalent employees and proprietors to arrive at a total persons engaged measure. Total man-hours in the private domestic sector are also based on Kendrick's series.[28]

Christensen and Jorgenson incorporate our original adjustment for the quality of the labor force based on the changing distribution of the labor force by years of school completed. They do not adjust, however, for the changing age-sex distribution of the labor force. An

Table 4.15
Actual gross private domestic capital input, 1950–1962 (constant prices of 1958)

Year	Corporate Capital Input, Quantity Index (billions of 1958 dollars)	Corporate Capital Input, Price Index (1958 = 1.000)	Noncorporate Capital Input, Quantity Index (billions of 1958 dollars)	Noncorporate Capital Input, Price Index (1958 = 1.000)	Private Domestic Capital Input, Quantity Index (billions of 1958 dollars)	Private Domestic Capital Input, Price Index (1958 = 1.000)	Index of Relative Utilization (1958 = 1.000)
1950	49.5	0.981	35.9	0.870	124.1	0.908	1.065
1951	53.2	1.034	37.9	0.991	134.5	0.965	1.092
1952	55.2	0.977	38.5	0.947	139.7	0.959	1.046
1953	59.4	0.938	39.8	0.903	147.4	0.932	1.098
1954	58.4	0.958	39.3	0.920	148.9	0.955	1.020
1955	63.5	1.061	41.2	0.896	158.6	0.996	1.105
1956	66.6	1.024	42.1	0.827	167.1	0.971	1.105
1957	68.4	1.027	41.9	0.883	171.9	0.983	1.065
1958	67.8	1.000	41.2	1.000	173.1	1.000	1.000
1959	73.6	1.078	43.4	0.887	182.5	1.028	1.092
1960	76.3	1.040	44.2	0.850	189.0	1.024	1.098
1961	78.2	1.042	44.5	0.902	194.1	1.043	1.085
1962	83.0	1.097	46.0	0.962	202.3	1.091	1.137

Table 4.16
Gross private domestic capital input, 1950–1962 (constant prices of 1958)

Year	Private Domestic Capital Stock (billions of 1958 dollars)	Potential capital Input Per Unit of Capital Stock (percent)	Relative Utilization of Capital (1958 = 1.000)
1950	964.6	0.126	1.024
1951	1021.4	0.127	1.035
1952	1068.5	0.128	1.018
1953	1100.3	0.129	1.037
1954	1134.6	0.130	1.007
1955	1163.2	0.131	1.040
1956	1213.9	0.132	1.040
1957	1255.5	0.133	1.026
1958	1287.9	0.134	1.000
1959	1305.8	0.135	1.038
1960	1341.4	0.135	1.040
1961	1373.9	0.136	1.035
1962	1399.1	0.137	1.055

examination of the underlying labor force data indicates that there has been little relevant change in the age distribution of the employed in the 1950–1962 period. There has been some relative increase in the number of young people in the labor force which has been largely counterbalanced by a decline in the proportion of older (above 65) employees. A pure age adjustment would have been a very minor effect on our estimates.[29] There has been, however, an increase in the proportion of women in the labor force. We investigated the magnitude of an appropriate adjustment for this, using data on the average shares of men and women in total earnings during the years 1958–1964, and the number of men and women employed in 1950 and 1958. The resulting adjustment is somewhat smaller but of the same order of magnitude as that reported by Denison for 1950–1962.[30]

We also attempted to estimate a more detailed quality adjustment for men for the 1950–1962 period, allowing for changes in education, age, race, and region (South and non-South). The basic data for this calculation were taken from Miller's monograph (1960a) and the associated Census volumes and refer to the population of men "with income," between the ages of 25 and 65. For this population, using the average of 1950 and 1960 income shares as weights, a straight education adjustment using average incomes by education for the population as a whole leads to an estimated 8.7 percent improvement in "quality." Using separate weights by region, race, age, and education leads to an estimated 12 percent rise in total labor quality, of which about 11 percent is due to the average improvement in the educational distribution within each age-race-region category and about 1 percent to the changing mix of these categories. In this case, a more detailed quality calculation for men produced a higher correction than the simple overall measure used by us. All this is just intended to indicate our belief that if we had developed a really detailed age-sex-region-education correction, it would as likely as not result in a higher rate of growth of labor input than was estimated by us originally.

4.5.2 Hours of Work

Up to this point we have proceeded on the assumption that *hours per man* changed at the same rate for all categories of labor. If this is not the case, a more detailed labor input index is called for. The rate of growth in total labor should be measured by

$$\frac{\dot{L}}{L} = \sum v_i \frac{\dot{h}_i}{h_i} + \sum v_i \frac{\dot{n}_i}{n_i}$$

where n_i is the number of workers in the ith category, h_i are the hours per man worked by men in this category, and

$$v_i = w_i h_i n_i / \sum w_i h_i n_i = y_i n_i / \sum y_i n_i$$

is the share of the ith category of labor in total labor payments (w_i = wage per hour and $y_i = w_i h_i$ = total earnings per man-year). Adding and subtracting $\dot{N}/N$ and $\dot{H}/H$, the rate of growth in total employment and the rate of growth in average hours worked per man, respectively, we can write

$$\begin{aligned}\frac{\dot{L}_i}{L_i} &= \frac{\dot{N}}{N} + \frac{\dot{H}}{H} + \sum v_i\left(\frac{\dot{n}_i}{n_i} - \frac{\dot{N}}{N}\right) + \sum v_i\left(\frac{\dot{h}_i}{h_i} - \frac{\dot{H}}{H}\right) \\ &= \frac{\dot{N}}{N} + \frac{\dot{H}}{H} + \sum v_i \frac{\dot{e}_i}{e_i} + \sum v_i \frac{\dot{m}_i}{m_i} \\ &= \frac{\dot{N}}{N} + \frac{\dot{H}}{H} + \frac{\dot{E}}{E} + \frac{\dot{M}}{M}\end{aligned}$$

where $e_i = n_i/N$ is the relative fraction of employment accounted for by the ith category and $m_i = h_i/H$ is its relative employment intensity (per year). $\dot{E}/E$ is then the rate of growth of average labor "quality" per man while $\dot{M}/M$ is the rate of growth in the relative quality of the average hour. In our original computations we left out the $\dot{M}/M$ term, assuming that all hours changed proportionately. To the extent that there has been a secular improvement in the employment experience of the educated versus uneducated, our index actually underestimates the "quality" improvement in the total labor force.

Unfortunately, the published data on hours and weeks worked per man from the 1950 and 1960 Censuses of Population were not cross-classified by education and hence, we cannot construct a comparable $\dot{M}/M$ index. Some idea, however, of the direction and order of magnitude of such an adjustment can be gathered from scattered data on hours worked by occupation. These are summarized in table 4.17 and imply about a 0.2 percent rate of growth per annum in the quality of the average hour during the 1950–1965 period. This, however, is somewhat of an overestimate, since during the 1950–1960 period (the only one for which we have data) a similar measure of "quality" of weeks worked deteriorated at about -0.04 percent per year (see table 4.18). That is, while the decline of hours was relatively smaller for some of the "higher quality" categories, this was counterbalanced to some extent by the improved annual employment experience of several of the less well paid occupations. On net we would estimate $\dot{M}/M \cong 0.16$, which if multiplied by the average labor share would more than counterbalance (0.11 versus -0.09) the estimated decline in overall quality of the labor force due to the increased participation of females.

Many of these adjustments are small and well within the range of possible error in the data. We conclude, nevertheless, that our original estimate of the rate of growth of total labor input stands up rather well under reexamination and that a more thorough and detailed analysis would in all likelihood result in a higher rather than lower figure.

4.5.3 Price and Quantity of Labor Services

The assumption that effective labor services are proportional to the stock of labor is obviously incorrect. On the other hand the assumption that effective labor services can be measured directly from data on man-hours is equally incorrect, as Denison (1961) has pointed out. The intensity of effort varies with the number of hours worked per week, so that effective labor input can be measured accurately only if

Table 4.17
Average hours worked per week by employed persons at work

Occupation	1950[a]	1960[a]	1960[b]	1965[b]	1959 Weights[c]
Total	44.6	43.2	40.5	40.5	—
Professional, technical, and kindred	44.1	46.9	41.3	41.4	0.167
Farmers and farm managers	60.0	54.2	52.0	52.1	0.031
Managers, etc., except farm	51.7	49.3	49.5	49.4	0.192
Clerical and kindred	41.3	40.8	37.6	37.4	0.062
Sales workers	45.1	42.9	38.2	37.8	0.077
Craftsmen, etc.	41.6	42.1	41.0	42.3	0.214
Operatives and kindred	42.0	42.2	40.3	41.2	0.169
Private household workers	40.8	32.8	26.6	24.1	0.003
Service workers except private household	44.7	41.9	38.7	37.8	0.037
Farm laborers and foremen	48.5	43.2	39.3	39.4	0.007
Laborers except farm and mine	39.3	37.1	35.9	35.5	0.041

[a] Employed males. 1950 data computed from table 5, page 42, of Finegan (1960). The separate figures for self-employed and wage and salary workers were averaged using the numbers given in 1950 Census of Population (1950), *Occupational Characteristics*, tables 14 and 15. The 1960 data are from 1960 U.S. Census of Population (1960), *Occupational Characteristics*, table 13. Average hours for farm and service workers estimated for 1950 using Finegan's procedures. Both average hours figures are for the Census survey week.

[b] All persons at work, annual average, from Bureau of Labor Statistics, *Special Labor Force Reports*, 14 and 69.

[c] Computed from data on mean earnings of males 18 and 64 years of age and on the number of such males with earnings in 1959, from 1960 U.S. Census of Population (1960), *Occupation by Earnings and Education*. The service weight allocated between private household workers and other workers using median incomes from the *Occupational Characteristics* volume.

Rate of growth of quality of average hours per man:

$\Sigma w_i \dfrac{h_{it}}{h_{it-1}} - \dfrac{H_{Tt}}{H_{Tt-1}}$		per annum
1950–1960	2.30	0.23
1960–1965	0.79	0.16

Table 4.18
Average weeks worked by males in the experienced civilian labor force[a]

Occupation	1949	1959
Total	45.1	45.6
Professional	46.9	47.6
Farmers and farm managers	47.4	47.7
Managers	48.6	49.6
Clerical	46.7	46.5
Sales workers	46.0	46.3
Craftsmen	45.4	46.2
Operatives	44.1	44.9
Private household workers	41.7	37.4
Service, except private household	44.7	37.4
Farm laborers	40.2	38.6
Laborers, except farm	41.0	39.7

[a] Average for those who worked in the particular year. Computed from the *Occupational Characteristics* volumes of the 1950 and 1960 Censuses of Population (1950, 1960). Midpoints used: 50–52: 51; 40–49: 45; 27–39: 33; 14–26: 20; and 1–13: 7. Rate of growth of quality of average week worked, using weights from table 3.17, can be computed as follows:

$$\left(\Sigma w_i \frac{W_{i1959}}{W_{i1949}}\right) - \frac{W_{T1959}}{W_{T1949}} = -0.38.$$

data on man-hours are corrected for the effects of variations in the number of hours per man on effective labor input. Denison (1962) suggests that the stock of labor provides an upper bound for effective labor services while the number of man-hours provides a lower bound. He estimates effective labor input by correcting man-hours for variations in labor intensity. We employ Denison's correction for intensity, but we apply this correction to actual hours per man rather than potential hours per man, as in our original study.

Our current measure of labor services is based on the stock of labor as measured by persons engaged, adjusted for effective hours per person and for changes in the composition of the labor force by educational attainment. The cost of labor services index is calculated by dividing total labor compensation by the quantity index of labor services. The number of persons engaged, the index of quality change, actual hours per worker, effective labor input per man-hour, and the quantity of labor input for 1950–1962 are given in table 4.19. The price of labor services implicit in private domestic labor compensation is also given in table 4.19. It would obviously be desirable to incor-

Table 4.19
Private domestic labor input, 1950–1962

Year	Private Domestic Persons Engaged (millions)	Educational Attainment Per Person (index) (1958 = 1.000)	Private Domestic Hours Per Person (thousands per year)	Effective Labor Input Per Hour (1958 = 1.000)	Private Domestic Labor Input, Quantity Index (billions of 1958 dollars)	Private Domestic Labor Input, Price Index (1958 = 1.000)
1950	52.972	0.948	2.197	0.978	228.8	0.683
1951	55.101	0.954	2.185	0.981	239.0	0.742
1952	55.385	0.960	2.187	0.980	241.7	0.782
1953	56.226	0.965	2.159	0.986	245.2	0.827
1954	54.387	0.971	2.139	0.990	237.4	0.846
1955	55.718	0.977	2.161	0.986	245.9	0.880
1956	56.770	0.982	2.151	0.988	251.6	0.930
1957	56.809	0.988	2.121	0.995	251.5	0.978
1958	55.023	1.000	2.099	1.000	245.1	1.000
1959	56.215	1.012	2.122	0.995	254.9	1.042
1960	56.743	1.020	2.126	0.994	259.6	1.074
1961	56.211	1.028	2.110	0.998	258.1	1.103
1962	57.078	1.036	2.117	0.996	264.6	1.144

porate additional aspects of labor force composition in adjusting the stock of labor for quality change. It would also be desirable to adjust the number of hours per man for changes in the relative number of hours worked by persons differing in educational attainment. But as outlined above, this would require a data base that is much more detailed than anything currently available.

4.6 Measurement of Total Factor Productivity

4.6.1 Introduction

Total factor productivity is defined as the ratio of real product to real factor input, or equivalently, as the ratio of the price of factor input to the product price. Growth in total factor productivity has a counterpart in growth of the price of factor input relative to the price of output. We may define a Divisia index of total factor productivity say P, as:

$$\log \frac{P_t}{P_{t-1}} = \log \frac{Y_t}{Y_{t-1}} - \log \frac{X_t}{X_{t-1}},$$

where Y is the quantity index of total product and X is the quantity index of total factor input.

To obtain an estimate of real factor input for the U.S. private domestic economy we combine estimates of labor and capital input. The basic data on labor input—number of persons engaged, educational attainment per person, and hours per person—are presented in table 4.19. The corresponding data on capital input—capital stock, potential service flow per unit of stock, and the relative utilization of capital—are presented in table 4.15. The index of educational attainment per person provides an adjustment of persons engaged for the aggregation bias that results from combining different types of labor into an unweighted aggregate. Similarly, capital stock is an unweighted aggregate; the index of potential capital services per unit of the capital stock provides an adjustment for aggregation bias. Potential capital services must be adjusted for relative utilization to obtain the actual flow of capital services. We construct price and quantity index numbers of factor input by combining Divisia indexes of labor and capital input into a Divisia index of total factor input. Price and quantity indexes for 1950–1962 are given in table 4.20. The relative share of property compensation for the same period is also given in table 4.20.

To provide a detailed accounting for the sources of growth in real factor input, we can separate the growth of quantity indexes of labor and capital input into the growth of the stock, growth in the quantity of input due to shifts in composition of such unweighted aggregates as persons engaged and capital stock or "quality change,"[31] and growth in relative utilization. The growth in labor input is the sum of growth in the number of persons engaged, the quality of the labor force, and the effective number of hours per person. The growth in capital input is the sum of growth in capital stock, the quality of capital, and relative utilization. Geometric average annual rates of growth for 1950–1962 are given for each component of the growth of labor and capital input in table 4.21.

Price and quantity indexes of output are given above in table 4.3. The index of total factor productivity for 1950–1962 corresponding to the quantity index of output from table 4.3 and the quantity index of gross private domestic factor input from table 4.20 is given in table 4.22. The conventions for measurement of factor services underlying our concept of gross private domestic factor input were employed in

Table 4.20
Gross private domestic factor input, 1950–1962 (constant prices of 1958)

Year	Gross Private Domestic Factor Input, Quantity Index (billions of 1958 dollars)	Gross Private Domestic Factor Input, Price Index (1958 = 1.000)	Property Compensation, Relative Share (percent)
1950	350.0	0.768	0.419
1951	371.3	0.827	0.423
1952	379.8	0.850	0.415
1953	391.5	0.869	0.404
1954	385.6	0.889	0.414
1955	404.3	0.926	0.422
1956	418.7	0.947	0.410
1957	423.4	0.980	0.407
1958	418.2	1.000	0.414
1959	437.4	1.036	0.414
1960	448.5	1.053	0.410
1961	452.0	1.077	0.415
1962	466.5	1.122	0.422

Table 4.21
Sources of growth in factor input, 1950–1962

1. Capital input	
a. Stock	3.14
b. Quality change	0.70
c. Relative utilization	0.25
2. Labor input	
a. Stock	0.63
b. Quality change	0.75
c. Relative utilization	–0.16

our original study. Our revised estimates, based on those of Christensen and Jorgenson, differ in two significant respects: First, we have converted the index of relative utilization to an annual basis and reduced the scope of adjustments of potential flows of capital services for changes in relative utilization. Second, we have measured the flow of capital services for sectors distinguished by legal form of organization in order to provide a more detailed representation of the tax structure. These differences have an important impact on the estimate of total factor productivity.

4.6.2 Alternative Measures of Productivity Change

To provide a basis for comparison of our estimate of total factor productivity with estimates that result from alternative conventions for the measurement of real factor input, we present a number of variants based on alternative accounting conventions. We begin with an estimate of total factor productivity based on the actual flow of labor and capital services. We compare this estimate with alternatives based on potential flows of labor and capital services and on stocks of labor and capital. The services of consumers' durables and producers' durables used by institutions are allocated directly to final demand so that growth in the quantities of these services does not affect growth of total factor productivity. Similarly, the services of owner-occupied dwellings and institutional structures are allocated directly to final demand.

Kendrick and Solow use a stock concept of capital input, measuring neither changes in relative utilization nor changes in the quality of capital services due to changes in the composition of the capital

Table 4.22
Total factor productivity, 1950–1962 (1958 = 1.000)

Year	Labor and Capital Services	Actual Labor Services; Potential Capital Services	Potential Labor and Capital Services	Potential Labor Services; Capital Stock	Labor and Capital Stock	Actual Labor Services; Capital Stock	Unweighted Man-hours; Capital Stock
1950	0.939	0.948	0.961	0.935	0.906	0.922	0.882
1951	0.946	0.960	0.971	0.949	0.923	0.938	0.902
1952	0.949	0.956	0.967	0.949	0.927	0.938	0.904
1953	0.968	0.982	0.990	0.974	0.954	0.966	0.938
1954	0.974	0.977	0.982	0.969	0.953	0.964	0.942
1955	1.006	1.022	1.031	1.020	1.006	1.012	0.989
1956	0.994	1.010	1.018	1.011	1.001	1.004	0.986
1957	0.998	1.009	1.012	1.009	1.002	1.006	0.996
1958	1.000	1.000	1.000	1.000	1.000	1.000	1.000
1959	1.019	1.034	1.038	1.039	1.046	1.035	1.039
1960	1.019	1.036	1.040	1.043	1.056	1.039	1.048
1961	1.031	1.046	1.048	1.054	1.072	1.053	1.068
1962	1.062	1.086	1.088	1.097	1.120	1.094	1.114

stock.[32] Denison weights persons engaged by an index of labor quality that incorporates the effects of growth in educational attainment but differs in a number of important respects from the index we have used.[33] Denison also adjusts man-hours for changes in labor efficiency that accompany changes in hours per man.[34] Solow uses unweighted man-hours, omitting the effects of changes in the composition of the labor force on the quantity of labor input.[35] Kendrick adjusts labor and capital input for changes in the industrial composition of labor force and capital stock.[36] However, changes within an industrial sector due to shifts in composition are not included in his measures of real factor input.

We present measures of total factor productivity based on potential service flows and on stocks of labor and capital in table 4.22. The first variant on our estimate of total factor productivity omits the relative utilization adjustment for capital, the second the relative utilization adjustment for labor; the second variant is based on potential service flows for both labor and capital input. The third variant omits the quality adjustment for capital, while the fourth omits the quality adjustment for labor, providing a stock measure of total factor productivity. Two final variants provide combinations of alternative measures of labor input with the stock measure of capital. The fifth combines actual labor input with the stock of capital, while the sixth combines unweighted actual man-hours with capital stock. It is obvious from a comparison of the alternative estimates of total factor productivity given in table 4.22 that the results are highly sensitive to the choice of conventions for measuring real factor input. The effects of varying the convention are summarized for the period 1950–1962 in table 4.23; geometric average annual rates of growth are given for each variant of total factor productivity.

Table 4.23
Growth in total factor productivity, 1950–1962

1. Actual labor and capital services	1.03
2. Actual labor services; potential capital services	1.14
3. Potential labor and capital services	1.04
4. Potential labor services; capital stock	1.34
5. Labor and capital stock	1.78
6. Actual labor services; capital stock	1.44
7. Man-hours and capital stock	1.96

4.6.3 Sources of U.S. Economic Growth, 1950–1962

Finally, to evaluate the relative importance of growth in real factor input and growth in total factor productivity as sources of economic growth, we consider the relative proportion of growth in real factor input. Geometric average annual rates of growth are given for real product and real factor input for 1950–1962 in table 4.24. The relative proportion of growth in total factor productivity in the growth of real product is also provided.

We find that the growth in real factor input predominates in the explanation of the growth of real product for the period 1950–1962. These findings are directly contrary to those of Abramovitz (1956), Kendrick (1961a, 1973) and Solow (1957) in earlier studies of productivity change. We have estimated real factor input on the basis of capital stock and actual man-hours, the conventions used by Solow and subsequently adopted by Arrow, Chenery, Minhas, and Solow (1961), 1950–1962. The resulting estimates of the distribution of the growth of real product between growth in real factor input and total factor productivity are comparable to those of Solow's earlier study. On the basis of our data and Solow's conventions total factor productivity grows at the average rate of 1.96 percent per year while real factor input grows at 1.51 percent per year. Our estimates, given in table

Table 4.24
The relative importance of productivity change, 1950–1962
(average annual rates of growth)

Gross private domestic product:	
Real product	3.47
Real factor input	2.42
Capital input:	
Stock	1.30
Quality change	0.30
Relative utilization	0.11
Labor input:	
Stock	0.37
Quality change	0.44
Relative utilization	–0.10
Total factor productivity	1.03
Relative proportion of productivity change	0.30

4.24, are that total factor productivity grows at 1.03 percent per year and real factor input at the rate of 2.42 percent per year.

We also present estimates of real factor input based on capital stock and actual labor input, which provide the best approximation to the conventions adopted by Denison (1967). Denison finds that total factor productivity grows at 1.37 percent per year, not adjusted for intensity of demand. We find that estimates of real factor input based on our data suggest that total factor productivity grows at the average rate of 1.44 percent per year while real factor input grows at 2.03 percent per year. The discrepancy between estimates based on our conventions, given in table 4.23, and those based on capital stock and actual labor input is accounted for almost entirely by our adjustments of the measure of capital input for quality change and relative utilization. Denison has incorporated about half the growth in real factor input over and above the growth of capital stock and actual manhours into his estimates of real factor input.

4.7 Major Issues in Growth Accounting

4.7.1 Introduction

Denison has examined our approach to productivity measurement in his paper, "Some Major Issues in Productivity Analysis: An Examination of Estimates by Jorgenson and Griliches" (1969). Denison's detailed examination of our estimates contributes significantly to the definition of unresolved issues in the measurement of total factor productivity. This contribution is especially valuable in view of the underlying agreement between our objectives and Denison's objectives in his pathbreaking studies of productivity change (1962, 1967). Although the basic agreement between our objectives in productivity measurement and Denison's is reassuring, important differences in methods of measurement and in substantive conclusions remain.

We have attempted to indicate the quantitative magnitude of disagreement between Denison's estimates of total factor productivity and ours by reworking our estimates in order to provide a direct comparison among the results of three different approaches to the measurement of total factor productivity—the conventional approach, Denison's approach, and our own approach. We have concentrated on the period 1950–1962 employed by Denison in his most recent study, *Why Growth Rates Differ* (1967). For convenience of the reader we follow the order of topics in Denison's paper (1969).

4.7.2 Scope of Product

We begin our examination of the issues raised by Denison with an analysis of the effects of the concept of real product on the measurement of productivity change. Denison regards both gross and net product measures as legitimate for productivity analysis,[37] but gives priority to the net product measure: "Insofar as a larger output is a proper goal of society and objective of policy, it is net product that measures the degree of success in achieving this goal. Gross product is larger by the value of capital consumption. There is no more reason to wish to maximize capital consumption—the quantity of capital goods used up in production—than there is to maximize the quantity of any other intermediate product. . . ."[38]

The first problem with Denison's argument is that the difference between gross product and net product is equal to depreciation, while the quantity of capital goods used up in production is equal to replacement. Depreciation is equal to replacement if and only if the decline in efficiency of capital goods is geometric. Under Denison's characterization of decline in efficiency, depreciation is not equal to replacement, so that Denison's argument is internally contradictory.[39] This contradiction can be removed by defining net product as gross product less depreciation.

In the estimates of productivity change given in section 4.6 above, the decline in efficiency of capital goods is assumed to be geometric so that depreciation and replacement are equal. Our product measure is gross product from the producer's point of view. Under our assumptions, Denison's argument justifying net product as a product measure is irrelevant to productivity measurement. Net product is associated with precisely the same measure of the absolute contribution of productivity change as gross product from the producers' point of view. Denison's argument provides no basis for discriminating between net and gross product as a basis for productivity measurement. Furthermore, the measure of the absolute contribution of productivity change is the same for our measure of gross product and for gross product at factor cost, the gross product concept Denison prefers for productivity analysis.[40]

The contribution of productivity change may be expressed as the absolute amount of growth in real product accounted for by changes in productivity.[41] This contribution is equal to the difference between period to period changes in real product and changes in real factor input. The contribution of productivity change may be expressed relative to any of the alternative concepts of real product, gross product from the producers' point of view, gross product at factor cost, and net product. Alternative measures of relative productivity change differ only in the concept of real product employed, not in the measure of the absolute contribution of productivity change.

We first demonstrate that the absolute contribution of productivity change is the same for gross product from the producers' point of view, gross product at factor cost, and net product. The difference between gross product from the producers' point of view and gross product at factor cost is indirect taxes on factors of production, such as property taxes. These taxes appear as part of both output and input and leave the absolute contribution of productivity change unaffected. The difference between gross product and net product is depreciation. Depreciation also appears as part of both output and input, leaving the contribution of productivity change unaffected. Problems that arise in measuring the depreciation component of gross capital input also arise in measuring depreciation to convert gross product to net product. The data required for measurement of gross product from the producers' point of view, gross product at factor cost, and net product are identical.

The absolute contribution of productivity change to the growth of real output is the difference between changes in output and changes in input, both evaluated at current prices; this is equal to the difference between changes in the prices of output and input, each multiplied by the corresponding quantity:

$$q\dot{Y} - p\dot{X} = \dot{p}X - \dot{q}Y \, .$$

The relative contribution of productivity change, say $\dot{P}/P$, is obtained by dividing the absolute contribution by the value of output (or input):

$$\frac{\dot{P}}{P} = \frac{q\dot{Y} - p\dot{X}}{qY} = \frac{q\dot{Y}}{qY} - \frac{p\dot{X}}{pX} = \frac{\dot{Y}}{Y} - \frac{\dot{X}}{X} \, .$$

Dividing output between consumption and investment goods and input between capital and labor services, the identity between the value of output and the value of input may be written:

$$q_C C + q_I I = p_K K + p_L L \, ,$$

where C and I are quantities of consumption and investment goods and K and L are quantities of capital and labor input. The corresponding prices are denoted q_C, q_I, p_K, and p_L. To represent gross value added from the producers' point of view we suppose for simplicity that tax depreciation and economic depreciation are the same. Under this simplifying assumption the price of capital services may be written:[42]

$$p_K = q_I\left(\rho + \mu + \tau - \frac{\dot{q}_I}{q_I}\right),$$

where ρ is the (before-tax) rate of return, μ the rate of depreciation, and τ the rate of indirect taxation of property. The accounting identity may then be rewritten:

$$q_C C + q_I I = q_I\left(\rho + \mu + \tau - \frac{\dot{q}_I}{q_I}\right)K + p_L L \,.$$

Identifying the change in the aggregate quantity of output with the sum of changes in consumption and investment goods output, evaluated at current prices, and defining the change in aggregate input similarly, the absolute contribution of productivity change may be represented in the form:

$$q_C\dot{C} + q_I\dot{I} - q_I\left(\rho + \mu + \tau - \frac{\dot{q}_I}{q_I}\right)\dot{K} - p_L\dot{L} \,.$$

To obtain corresponding measures of the contribution of productivity change for alternative concepts of social product, we first derive gross product at factor cost by subtracting the value of property taxes from both sides of the basic accounting identity, obtaining:

$$q_C C + q_I(I - \tau K) = q_I\left(\rho + \mu - \frac{\dot{q}_I}{q_I}\right)K + p_L L \,.$$

Defining the absolute contribution of productivity change as before we obtain:

$$\begin{aligned} q_C\dot{C} + q_I(\dot{I} - \tau\dot{K}) - q_I\left(\rho + \mu - \frac{\dot{q}_I}{q_I}\right)\dot{K} - p_L\dot{L} \\ = q_C\dot{C} + q_I\dot{I} - q_I\left(\rho + \mu + \tau - \frac{\dot{q}_I}{q_I}\right)\dot{K} - p_L\dot{L} \,. \end{aligned}$$

which is identical to the contribution of productivity change for gross product from the producers' point of view.

Second, we derive net product by subtracting the value of depreciation from both sides of the identity given above:

$$q_C C + q_I[I - (\tau + \mu)K] = q_I\left(\rho - \frac{\dot{q}_I}{q_I}\right)K + p_L L\ .$$

The resulting measure of the absolute contribution of productivity change is the same as for gross value added:

$$\begin{aligned} &q_C\dot{C} + q_I[I - (\tau + \mu)\,\dot{K}] - q_I\left(\rho - \frac{\dot{q}_I}{q_I}\right)\dot{K} - p_L\dot{L} \\ &\quad = q_C\dot{C} + q_I I - q_I\left(\rho + \mu + \tau - \frac{\dot{q}_I}{q_I}\right)\dot{K} - p_L\dot{L}\ . \end{aligned}$$

We conclude that the measure of productivity change in absolute terms is the same for all three concepts of real product we have considered—gross product from the producers' point of view, gross product at factor cost, and net product. The absolute contribution of productivity change may be expressed relative to any measure of output. Alternative measures of relative productivity change differ in the concept of output employed as a standard of comparison, but not in the measure of the absolute contribution of productivity change.

The absolute contribution of productivity change has the important property that the contribution to the growth of the economy as a whole is the sum of contributions to the growth of individual sectors. This property is maintained for measures of output of an economic sector that include intermediate goods purchased from other sectors, as in interindustry studies. Intermediate goods appear as real output in the sector of origin and real input in the sector of destination. Changes in the output of intermediate goods cancel out in any measure of the contribution of productivity change to the economy as a whole.

In our original estimates we used gross product at market prices; we now employ gross product from the producers' point of view, which includes indirect taxes levied on factor outlay, but excludes indirect taxes levied on output. Denison employs net product, which excludes all indirect taxes and depreciation along with a number of minor items. Our revised product measure covers the private domestic economy, incorporating the services of durables used by households and institutions along with the services of structures used in this sector. Our original product measure did not include the services of durables used by households and institutions. Denison covers the entire national economy. Our revised product measure provides for a more satisfactory treatment of indirect taxes. It also treats durables symmetrically with structures in the household sector.

To reconcile our revised product measure with Denison's it would be necessary to exclude the services of durables used by households and institutions and to eliminate indirect taxes and depreciation at replacement cost. The product of government and rest of the world sectors would have to be added. None of these changes would alter our estimate of the absolute contribution of productivity change. Any difference in percentage rates of growth of total factor productivity would be due to the product measure relative to which productivity change is expressed. The more comprehensive the product measure the less the relative rate of growth of total factor productivity associated with any absolute contribution of productivity change. To adjust estimates of the relative growth of total factor productivity based on our data to a net national product basis, percentage rates of growth should be multiplied by the ratio of gross product to net national product in each period. A similar adjustment can be made to convert relative rates of growth of total factor productivity to any other product measure.

4.7.3 Index Numbers

To separate flows of product and factor outlay into prices and quantities, we introduce price and quantity index numbers. As an example, suppose that there are m components to the value of output,

$$qY = q_1Y_1 + q_2Y_2 + \ldots + q_mY_m \, .$$

Index numbers for the price of output q and the quantity of output Y may be defined in terms of the prices $[q_i]$ and quantities $[Y_i]$ of the m components. Differentiating the value of output totally with respect to time and dividing both sides by total value,

$$\frac{\dot{q}}{q} + \frac{\dot{Y}}{Y} = \sum w_i \left[\frac{\dot{q}_i}{q_i} + \frac{\dot{Y}_i}{Y_i} \right];$$

weights $[w_i]$ are the relative shares of the value of the ith output:

$$w_i = \frac{q_i Y_i}{\sum q_i Y_i} .$$

We define the price and quantity indexes of output as weighted averages of rates of growth of prices and quantities of individual components:

$$\frac{\dot{q}}{q} = \sum w_i \frac{\dot{q}_i}{q_i} , \qquad \frac{\dot{Y}}{Y} = \sum w_i \frac{\dot{Y}_i}{Y_i} ,$$

obtaining Divisia price and quantity indexes.[43] Rates of growth of the Divisia indexes of prices and quantities add up to the rate of growth of the value (factor reversal test) and are symmetric in different directions of time (time reversal test). A Divisia index of Divisia indexes is a Divisia index of the components.

For application to data for discrete points of time an approximation to the continuous Divisia indexes is required. Price and quantity index numbers originally discussed by Fisher (1922) have been employed for this purpose by Törnqvist (1936)

$$\log q_t - \log q_{t-1} = \sum \bar{w}_{it} [\log q_{it} - \log q_{i,t-1}] ,$$
$$\log Y_t - \log Y_{t-1} = \sum \bar{w}_{it} [\log Y_{it} - \log Y_{i,t-1}] ,$$

where the weights $\bar{w}_{it}$ are arithmetic averages of the relative shares in the two periods,

$$\bar{w}_{it} = \frac{1}{2} w_{it} + \frac{1}{2} w_{i,t-1} .$$

A discrete Divisia index of discrete Divisia indexes is a discrete Divisia index of the components. Divisia index numbers for discrete time are also symmetric in data of different time periods (time reversal). Theil (1967) has demonstrated that the sum of changes in logarithms of discrete Divisia indexes of price and quantity is approximately equal to the change in the logarithm of the value (factor reversal). It is convenient to have the product of price and quantity indexes equal to the value of transactions, so that we construct discrete Divisia price indexes as the value in current prices divided by the discrete Divisia quantity index.

The estimates of Christensen and Jorgenson (1969, 1970) are based on a different discrete approximation to Divisia index numbers from that employed in our original estimates; the results are essentially unaffected for the period 1950–1962. Denison's estimates are based on an alternative discrete approximation. The three approximations appear to produce essentially similar results. Our approximation satisfies both time reversal and, approximately, factor reversal tests for index numbers.

4.7.4 Capital and Labor Weights

The value of labor input includes labor compensation of employees and the self-employed. Our estimates of the labor compensation of the self-employed are based on the assumption that average labor compensation of the self-employed in each sector is equal to average labor compensation of full-time equivalent employees in each sector. This method of imputation of the labor compensation of the self-employed is only one of many that have been proposed. Our original method did not separate labor and property components of noncorporate income by industrial sector. Our new method, discussed in detail by Christensen (1971), has the effect of allocating a larger share of factor outlay to capital, overcoming Denison's objection to our original method.[44] The resulting rates of return in corporate and noncorporate sectors are essentially the same, taking into account the effect of the corporate income tax. The revised allocation of noncorporate income seems to us to be superior to our original allocation and to Denison's allocation.[45]

Second, the concept of gross product from the producers' point of view enables us to eliminate an error in our original allocation of indirect tax liability.[46] Our original concept of gross product at market prices included sales and excise taxes and customs duties in the earnings of capital. Our present estimates include only taxes levied on income from property. This measure of capital earnings is the appropriate one, given our concept of gross product from the producers' point of view. The implied weights for labor and capital meet Denison's objections to our original treatment of indirect business taxes.[47]

4.7.5 Weights for Components of Capital and Land

The major difference between our measure of total factor input and Denison's is in the assignment of relative weights to components of land and capital input. An ideal measure of capital is strictly analogous to an ideal measure of labor input. Both measures combine rates of growth of individual components into an overall rate of growth, using relative shares of the individual components as weights. While factor shares for components of labor can be estimated from data on wages and employment, factor shares for components of capital must be imputed from accounting data on total property income. The problem for productivity measurement is to provide a practical method for carrying out this accounting imputation. Our method of imputation is described in detail in section 4.3 above.

Our original estimates, like those of Denison, distinguished alternative capital inputs by class of asset. For the private domestic economy we distinguished among five categories of assets—land, residential structures, nonresidential structures, equipment, and inventories. For this sector of the economy Denison distinguishes between residential and nonresidential land; otherwise the breakdown of assets is the same. Neither of these breakdowns is fully satisfactory for the incorporation of the effects of the tax structure on property income.

In our revised estimates inventories are allocated between farm and nonfarm sectors and consumers' durables are introduced as a new and separate class of assets. Each of the seven classes of assets is then allocated among sectors that differ in legal form of organization—corporate, noncorporate, and households and institutions. We assume, following Christensen and Jorgenson (1969), that the rates of return on all assets held within a given sector are the same. Property income in the corporate sector is subject to both corporate and personal income taxes. Noncorporate property income is subject only to the personal income tax. The property income of households and institutions is subject to neither tax. This new, more detailed, asset classification enables us to meet a number of valid objections Denison has raised to our original treatment of the tax structure.[48]

Our new estimates incorporate the tax structure for property income in a more satisfactory way than our original estimates. Property taxes are separated from other earnings from capital and treated as tax deductible for income tax purposes. Depreciation for tax purposes is incorporated at its present value for the the lifetime of an asset, so that the effects of accelerated depreciation are simultaneous with the adoption of the depreciation provisions of the Internal Revenue Act of 1954. Our revised estimates also incorporate the investment tax credit adopted in 1962. The rate of the investment tax credit and the rate of the corporate income tax are effective rates, measured from national accounting data.

Denison incorporates part of the tax structure implicitly by excluding property taxes from his measure of social product. This procedure is equivalent to our treatment of property taxes for the purposes of measuring absolute productivity change. Denison's estimates do not take explicit account of direct taxation of income from property. He distinguishes among property income in housing, agricultural, and all other sectors of the economy, but this breakdown of the economy does not coincide with the breakdown associated with the structure of taxation of property income. The availability of data on property income by legal form of organization from the U.S. national accounts makes it possible to improve on Denison's treatment of property income and on our original estimates. We conclude that Denison's classification of assets, like our original classification, fails to capture differences in direct taxation of property income for enterprises that differ in legal form of organization. Denison's estimates of property income fail to incorporate depreciation for tax purposes and the investment tax credit in a satisfactory way.

The rates of return included in our capital service prices are real rates of return rather than nominal rates of return. Nominal rates are assumed to be the same for all assets within a given sector. Real rates differ by differentials between rates of growth of asset prices for different classes of assets. The allocation of property income among asset classes depends on differentials among rates of growth of prices. If all asset prices are growing at the same rate, real rates of return are the same for all assets within each sector. Denison objects to the use of real rates of return on the grounds that price changes in assets other than land are always unanticipated.[49] His proposed procedure would amount to ignoring differentials among assets other than land and to setting the differential between land and other assets equal to the rate of growth of land prices. For the 1950–1962 period land prices grow more rapidly than other asset prices, but there is substantial inflation in the price of structures and producers' durables. On the other hand the price of farm inventories actually falls. It is clear that Denison's proposed procedure, or his actual practice of ignoring differential rates of inflation,[50] introduces distortions in the allocation of property income among asset classes.

A serious accounting problem arises in attempting to integrate Denison's proposed allocation of property income among assets into national accounts for saving and wealth. Changes in the value of national wealth are equal to saving plus capital gains from the revaluation of assets. Saving is equal to labor income less consumption plus property income less depreciation. These definitions hold for individual wealth holders as well as for the economy as a whole. Capital gains from the the revaluation of assets must be taken into account in allocating property income among capital assets and, implicitly, among individual wealth holders. The changes in the value of assets that enter individual and national wealth accounts must be consistent with the property income attributed to those assets in individual and national income accounts. The use of real rates of return is necessitated by internal consistency of the complete system of national accounts. Capital gains should be incorporated into the allocation of property income among classes of assets. Denison is in error, not only in failing to take capital gains into account in measuring income from land, but in omitting capital gains in measuring income from other assets.[51] We conclude that Denison's proposed allocation of property income among assets is inconsistent with the integration of property income into individual and national accounts for saving and wealth.

Finally, Denison defends Kendrick's exclusion of depreciation on the grounds that Kendrick uses net product and net earnings from capital in measuring total factor productivity.[52] Actually, Kendrick employs both net and gross measures of output and uses net earnings for allocating property income for both, which is the error we originally pointed out.[53] Denison is in error in asserting that we recommend the inclusion of depreciation in weights for the analysis of net product and in associating with himself with Kendrick's weighting scheme.[54]

The most serious problem with Denison's treatment of depreciation is the lack of consistency between depreciation as it enters his measure of real product and the corresponding treatment of capital assets in his measure of real factor input. In section 4.3.2 above we have outlined a perpetual inventory method for measurement of depreciation and capital assets based on the assumption that the service flow from an investment good declines geometrically. To describe Denison's method, we must generalize our treatment to alternative assumptions about the time pattern of the service flow. We assume that the relative efficiency of the ith investment good may be described by a sequence of nonnegative numbers,

$$d_{i0}\,,\ d_{i1}\,\ldots\,.$$

Denison points out, correctly, that a capital input measure depends on the relative efficiency of capital goods of different ages:

In principle, the selection of a capital input measure should depend on the changes that occur in the ability of a capital good to contribute to net production as the good grows older (within the span of its economic life). Use of net stock, with depreciation computed by the straight-line formula, would imply that this ability drops very rapidly—that it is reduced by one-fourth when one-fourth of service life has passed, and by nine-tenths when nine-tenths of the service life has passed. Use of gross stock would imply that this ability is constant throughout the service life of a capital good.[55]

Denison argues, further, that:

I believe that net value typically declines more rapidly than does the ability of a capital good to contribute to production. . . . On the other hand, the gross stock assumption of constant services throughout the life of an asset is extreme.[56]

Under our assumption, that decline in efficiency is geometric:

$$d_{i\tau} = (1 - \mu_i)^{\tau}\,, \quad (\tau = 0\,, 1\,, \ldots)\,.$$

Under Denison's gross stock assumption relative efficiency is constant over the economic lifetime of the equipment:

$$d_{i\tau} = 1\,, \quad (\tau = 0\,, 1\,, \ldots\,, T_i - 1)\,,$$

where T_i is economic lifetime of the ith investment good. Under Denison's net stock assumption, efficiency declines linearly

$$d_{i\tau} = 1 - \frac{1}{T_i}\tau\,, \quad (\tau = 0\,, 1\,, \ldots\,, T_i - 1)\,,$$

where $1/T_i$ is the rate of decrease in efficiency of the ith investment good from period to period.

Capital stock at the end of the period, say K_{it}, is the sum of past investments, say $\{I_{i,t-\tau}\}$ each weighted by its relative efficiency:

$$K_{it} = \sum_{r=0}^{\infty} d_{i\tau}\, I_{i,t-\tau}\,.$$

With a geometric decline in efficiency we obtain the capital stock measures used in section 4.3 above. With constant relative efficiency we obtain Denison's gross stock measure; with linear decline in relative efficiency, we obtain Denison's net stock measure. In Denison's study, *Sources of Economic Growth* (1962), gross stock is employed as a measure of capital input. In *Why Growth Rates Differ* (1967, p. 141) an arithmetic average of gross stock and net stock is employed; the implied relative efficiency of capital goods is an average of constant and linearly declining relative efficiency,

$$d_{i\tau} = 1 - \frac{1}{2T_i}\tau\,, \quad (\tau = 0, 1, \ldots, T_i - 1)\,,$$

where $1/2\ T_i$ is the rate of decrease in efficiency.

Replacement requirements, say R_{it}, are a weighted average of past investments with weights given by the mortality distribution:

$$R_{it} = \sum_{r=1}^{\infty} m_{i\tau} I_{i,t-\tau}\,,$$

where

$$m_{i\tau} = -(d_{i\tau} - d_{i,\tau-1})\,, \quad (\tau = 1, 2, \ldots)\,.$$

For geometric decline in efficiency, replacement requirements are proportional to capital stock,

$$R_{it} = \mu_i K_{i,t-1}\,.$$

Turning to asset and service prices, the price of the ith asset is equal to the discounted value of future services:

$$q_{it}^{A} = \sum_{r=t}^{\infty} \prod_{s=t+1}^{r+1} \frac{1}{1+r_s}\, p_{i,r+1}^{S} d_{i,r-t}\,.$$

Depreciation on a capital good is a weighted average of future rental price with weights given by the mortality distribution:

$$q_{it}^{D} = \sum_{r=t+1}^{\infty} \prod_{s=t+1}^{r+1} \frac{1}{1+r_s}\, p_{i,r+1}^{S} m_{i,r-t}\,.$$

For geometric decline in efficiency depreciation is proportional to the asset price:

$$q_{it}^D = \mu_i q_{it}^A .$$

Depreciation and replacement must be carefully distinguished in order to preserve consistency between the treatment of capital services and the treatment of capital assets. Depreciation is a component of the price of capital services. The value of capital services is equal to property income, including depreciation. Replacement is the consequence of a reduction in the efficiency of capital assets or, in Denison's language, the ability of a capital good to contribute to production. The value of depreciation is equal to the value of replacement if and only if decline in efficiency is geometric:

$$q_{it}^D K_{i,t-1} = \mu_i q_{it}^A K_{i,t-1} = q_{it}^A R_{it} .$$

Otherwise, replacement and depreciation are not equal to each other. Replacement reflects the current decline in efficiency of all capital goods acquired in the past. Depreciation reflects the current value (present discounted value) of all future declines in efficiency on all capital goods.

A confusion between depreciation and replacement pervades Denison's treatment of real product, real factor input, and capital stock. The first indication of this confusion is Denison's definition of net product: "Net product measures the amount a nation consumes plus the addition it makes to its capital stock. Stated another way, it is the amount of its output a nation could consume without changing its stock of capital."[57] The correct definition of net product is gross product less depreciation; this is the definition suggested by Denison's second statement quoted above. The first statement defines net product as gross product less replacement, since the addition to capital stock is equal to investment less replacement. The two definitions are consistent if and only if depreciation is equal to replacement, that is, if and only if decline in efficiency is geometric.

Denison measures capital consumption allowances on the basis of Bulletin F lives and the straight-line method.[58] Under the assumption that relative efficiency (Denison's "ability to contribute" to production) declines linearly, this estimate corresponds to replacement rather than depreciation. To measure net product Denison reduces gross product by his estimate of capital consumption allowances.[59] Since his estimate of capital consumption allowances is a measure of replacement, this procedure employs the incorrect definition of net product as consumption plus investment less replacement. This inappropriate measure of net product is reduced by labor compensation to obtain property income net of capital consumption allowances. Thus, Denison's measure of property income is also net of replacement rather than depreciation. This erroneous measure is allocated among capital inputs to obtain weights employed in measuring capital input as a component of real factor input; Denison's weights for different components of capital input are measured incorrectly. These weights should reflect property income less depreciation; in fact, they reflect property income less replacement.

The final confusion in Denison's treatment of capital in *Why Growth Rates Differ* (1967) arises in the adoption of an arithmetic average of gross and net stock as a measure of capital input. As indicated above, this measure of capital input implies that efficiency declines linearly up to the end of an asset's economic lifetime; at that point half the asset's "ability to contribute" to production remains so that all the remaining decline in efficiency takes place in one year. Denison's measure of capital consumption allowances by the straight-line method fails to measure either replacement or depreciation. We conclude that Denison's treatment of capital consumption allowances in the measurement of net product and net factor input is inconsistent with his treatment of capital assets in the measure of real capital input that is incorporated into his measure of real factor input. A similar problem arises in Denison's earlier study, *Sources of Economic Growth* (1962). There gross product is employed as a measure of capital input.[60] Denison's measure of capital consumption allowances corresponds to replacement rather than depreciation so that his measures of net product and net factor input are inconsistent with his measure of capital input.

We assume that the decline in efficiency of capital goods is geometric; under this assumption depreciation and replacement are equal, so that the inconsistencies in Denison's procedure outlined above do not arise. If we were to assume that the decline in efficiency is linear, as in Denison's arithmetic average of net and gross stock, depreciation would be measured differently from replacement. The first step would be to estimate the value of capital assets of each age at each point of time as the discounted value of future capital services. This is the definition of net stock suggested by Denison,[61] but not the definition used in his measure of net stock, which is net of replacement rather than net of depreciation.[62] The second step would be to estimate depreciation on capital goods of each age by discounting the mortality distribution, as indicated above in the definition of depreciation q_{it}^{D}. The third step would be to obtain total depreciation as the sum over all types of capital goods and all ages. Only at this point would it be possible to measure net product as gross product less depreciation.

It is clear that the selection of an appropriate assumption about the decline in efficiency of capital goods is both important and difficult. We selected geometrically declining efficiency on the basis of its convenience and consistency with scattered empirical evidence. The available evidence arises from two sources—studies of replacement investment and studies of depreciation in the market prices of capital goods. Geometric decline in efficiency has been employed by Hickman and by Hall and Jorgenson in studies of investment.[63] This assumption has been tested by Meyer and Kuh, who find no effect of the age distribution of capital stock in the determination of replacement investment.[64] Geometric decline in efficiency has been employed in the study of depreciation on capital goods by Cagan, Griliches, and Wykoff.[65] This assumption has been tested by Hall, who finds no effect of the age of a capital good in the determination of depreciation as measured from the prices of used capital goods.[66] The power of these tests is not high and some contrary evidence is presented by Griliches.[67] Nevertheless, the weight of the evidence suggests that Denison's treatment of capital could be radically simplified and made internally consistent by adopting our assumption of geometric decline in efficiency of capital goods. Any alternative assumption about the decline in efficiency requires redefinition of Denison's measures of replacement, depreciation, and capital stock to make them consistent.

A conceptual issue that can be clarified at this point is the role of disaggregation in the measurement of real product and real factor input. Our original presentation included an extensive discussion of two alternative concepts of "quality change" in productivity analysis.[68] We indicated that quality change in the sense of "aggregation error" should be eliminated by disaggregating product and factor input measures so as to treat distinct products and factors as separate commodities wherever possible. The term quality change is often used in a different sense. Estimates of quality change are sometimes made by attributing changes in productivity to changes in the quality of a particular factor *without disaggregation*.

A particularly graphic example of inappropriate use of quality change occurs in the analysis of the "vintage" model of capital. The correct measure of quality change across vintages would require data on the price and quantity of capital services for each vintage at each point in time. Aggregation over vintages could then be carried out in the same way as any other type of aggregation and biases due to quality change could be eliminated.[69] In the absence of the required data, productivity change itself has been employed to estimate the quantity of capital input corrected for quality change.[70] Denison registers disagreement with this approach to the problem of quality change;[71] in fact, our view of this problem is identical to Denison's.

If it were possible to implement our original suggestion that different vintages of capital goods be weighted in measuring capital input by their marginal products, this would not have the effect of incorporating "embodied" technical progress, as Denison (1969, p. 26) suggests. In fact the position attributed to us by Denison, the use of "unmeasured" quality change to correct capital input for changes in quality by vintage, is precisely the position we originally rejected (Jorgenson and Griliches, 1967, p. 206). Of course implementation of our suggestion would require data on service prices by vintage at each point of time.

4.7.6 Measurement of Capital and Land

Our estimates of the value of land are revised considerably from the Goldsmith estimates employed in our original paper.[72] While we have assumed that nonresidential land has remained constant, this assumption could be improved upon. There are scattered data on types of land, their relative value, and the changing composition of land actually in use in the private economy. Very little of the investment related to shifts of land from one category of use to another is captured in the standard investment series. Some of these investments are directly expensed and others are government subsidized. A rough measure of the effects of shifts in the use of land to higher valued urban uses from 1945 to 1958 can be constructed from Goldsmith's data. Land input rises 1.4 percent per year by this measure.[73] If this figure were extrapolated to the 1950–1962 period it would raise our estimated growth of total factor input by 0.14 percent per year.

Our estimates of the stocks of inventories and depreciable assets are based on those of OBE. Estimates of depreciable assets for corporate and noncorporate sectors are based on the OBE Capital Goods Study (Grose, Rottenberg and Wasson, 1969). Our perpetual inventory estimates of stocks of residential structures and durables used by households are based on methods similar to those employed in the Capital Goods Study. The main difference between our estimate of capital stocks and Denison's is in our use of declining balance depreciation. Denison uses a mixture of the one-hoss-shay and the straight-line method,[74] which gives rise to the problems in maintaining internal consistency among depreciation, replacement and capital stock outlined above.

Our original estimates of capital input were based on price indexes that attempted to correct for various biases in the deflators employed in the U.S. national accounts. Since a positive bias in the investment goods price index results in underestimation of the growth of both product and capital input, correction of biases does not affect estimates of total factor productivity substantially. Our present estimates, based on those of Christensen and Jorgenson (1969, 1970) are conservative in the choice of price deflators. We use national accounts deflators except for structures; for both residential and nonresidential structures we employ OBE "constant cost 2" as a price deflator.[75] We also incorporate both asset and investment deflators for inventories, overcoming another of Denison's objections to our original estimates.[76] Finally, we did not replace the producers' durable equipment price index by the comparable consumers' durable series, a practice Denison objects to but which we have defended above.[77] Thus, there is no practical difference between the price series we use and those recommended by Denison.

4.7.7 Utilization Adjustment

Denison directs his strongest criticisms, and correctly so, against what is probably the weakest link in our chain. While we have most of his criticism, we still believe that the question posed by our utilization adjustment is interesting, the numbers used are not all that bad, and something has been learned from this exercise.

Denison's criticisms can be summarized under the following headings:

1 the basic numbers are faulty (because of cyclical and weighting problems);

2 they are extrapolated too widely, from electric motors in manufacturing to "everything";

3 they are misused by not allowing for double counting, i.e., these changes are due to other inputs and hence have already been measured;

4 they are misinterpreted as an increase in input rather than an advancement in knowledge.

We have reviewed our adjustment for relative utilization in section 4.4 above. Our revised estimates differ very substantially from our original estimates. In the original estimates we estimated the contribution of utilization to the explanation of growth in total factor productivity at 0.58 percent per year. By reducing the scope of the adjustment to business structures and equipment and by incorporating annual estimates of horsepower or capacity, we have reduced the contribution of utilization to 0.11 percent per year for the period 1950–1962. This may be contrasted with Denison's estimate of –0. 04 percent per year for the same period.

Denison points out that we do not discuss the "sources" of changes in utilization rates and wonders if there has been some double counting. We do not see why the possibility of change in machine-hours per year per machine is more mysterious than a change in man-hours per man-year. Obviously, there is a need for an explanation of the sources of such changes and an analysis of the prospects for additional such changes in the future. Although we have not provided such an explanation, we did point out and localize what may be an important source of observed growth in output. An attribution of growth to investment, education, research and development, economies of scale, or capacity utilization is always just the beginning of a relevant line of analysis. But that is as far as one can go within the framework of national income accounting. A more "causal" analysis requires different models, tools, and data.

As to the actual points enumerated by Denison, we see no evidence that the sources of such utilization changes have already been counted in the other inputs. There is no evidence that our rather faulty machinery price deflators have allowed for such improvements in the quality of capital. Nor is there any evidence that this has been already counted in the contribution of labor or inventory input. For example, the ratio of inventories to shipments in manufacturing has remained virtually unchanged between 1947 and 1965.[78]

From our point of view, the main difficulty with the capacity utilization adjustment is that it is not articulated well with our theory and measurement of capital services and their rental prices. We lack an explicit theory of capacity utilization. It is either a disequilibrium phenomenon, or is related to differential costs of working people and machines at different hours of the day and different days of the year. Neither case fits well into the equilibrium, all-prices-are-equalized, framework of national income accounts. One possible basis for such a theory is to make depreciation a function of utilization. Thus, industries where machines worked a higher number of hours per year would have a higher rate of depreciation. In such a world, a mix change such as discussed by Denison would show up as an increase in aggregate capital input, with the weight of industries with higher δ's increasing in the total. And from our point of view, this would be a correct interpretation of the data. An economy that succeeded in recovering its capital in a shorter period would in fact experience a growth in output, and our measure would provide an "explanation" for it.

The issue whether this growth should be attributed to "advances in knowledge" or to increase in "inputs," is ultimately a semantic one. What is important is to know whence it has come, not what its name is. We don't think it very fruitful to put utilization into the "advances in knowledge" category because (a) the latter is already a "residual" category and throwing something more into it will just muddle up its meaning further, and (b) the types of change which are likely to be the sources of the increased rates of utilization, be they institutional or a consequence of changing relative scarcities of machine versus human time, are only very vaguely and probably misleadingly related to the ideas associated with the concept of "advances in knowledge." In any case, our contribution was to isolate and identify a potentially important source of growth. Since we have not really "explained" it, and we agree that this is the important next task, we are unwilling to argue too much over "naming" it. We find it more convenient to work within a broader definition of "input," minimizing thereby the role of the amorphous "residual." But we concede that the same questions can be also asked in a different language.

4.7.8 Labor Input

Our methods for measuring labor input are similar to Denison's, except that Denison reduces the observed income differentials among components of the labor force classified by years of school completed to allow for the correlation between education and "ability." At the same time, Denison also makes an adjustment for the increase in the length of the school year over time. We have made neither of these adjustments and have come out to about the same numbers as Denison, indicating that these two adjustments just about cancel out. Elsewhere one of us has argued that Denison's "ability" adjustment may be too large.[79] Thus, if we had made a smaller ability adjustment and had accepted Denison's "days per school year" adjustment our total labor input would probably grow somewhat faster over most of this period.

Our labor input measure is very similar to Denison's. Careful examination of the issues raised by Denison leads us to the conclusion that our original estimate of labor input can be left unchanged. This estimate has been incorporated into our measure of total factor productivity, but with a relative weight that differs due to changes in our method for allocating noncorporate income between labor and capital. We have also corrected the error of omitting unpaid family workers from our estimates of persons engaged; this leaves the final results unaffected.

4.7.9 Conclusions and Suggestions for Further Research

We have summarized the differences among our estimates of the rate of growth of total factor productivity for the period 1950–1962, based on the results of Christensen and Jorgenson (1970), our original estimates (1967), and Denison's estimates (Jorgenson and Griliches, 1967). At this point it is useful to compare these alternative estimates and to attempt a reconciliation among them; a partial reconciliation is given in table 4.25. From this comparison it is apparent that our new estimates represent a compromise between our original position and Denison's position. Referring to table 4.25, we may now summarize our conclusions. From an empirical point of view the greatest differences among our original estimates, our revised estimates, and Denison's estimates are in the adjustment for utilization of resources. Denison estimates that the utilization of resources declines between 1950 and 1962. We estimate that utilization increased, but by considerably less than we originally suggested. The revision in our adjustment for relative utilization accounts for 0.47 percent per year of the total discrepancy of 0.73 percent per year between our original estimate of the rate of growth of total factor productivity and our revised estimate.

Table 4.25
Reconciliation of alternative estimates of growth in total factor productivity, 1950–1962 (percent per year)

Denison, adjusted for utilization, his data		1.41
Denison's utilization adjustment	–0.04	
Denison, unadjusted, his data		1.37
Unexplained difference	.07	
Denison, unadjusted, our data		1.44
Capital input:		
Quality change	.30	
Our utilization adjustment	.11	
Jorgenson-Griliches, adjusted, revised		1.03
Revision in utilization adjustment	.47	
Other revisions	.26	
Jorgenson-Griliches, adjusted, original		.30

From a conceptual point of view the greatest difference among alternative procedures is in the allocation of income from property among its components. Except for our assumption that replacement requirements should be estimated by the double declining balance formula, our estimates of capital stock for each class of assets are very similar to Denison's estimates. Our estimates of capital input differ very substantially from his due to differences in treatment of the tax structure for property income, the use of real rates of return rather than nominal rates for each class of assets, and the use of declining balance depreciation and replacement. Part of the unexplained residual between our version of Denison's estimate of total factor productivity and his own is accounted for by his separation of assets among those held by housing, agricultural, and all other sectors of the economy. This separation goes part of the way toward a satisfactory treatment of the tax structure, but should be replaced, in our view, by a breakdown by legal form of organization.

In revising our original computations we have made a number of conservative assumptions and did not correct for some obvious errors in the data where the data base for such adjustments appeared to be too scanty. This is particularly true of the deflators of capital expenditures that we used and of our measure of land input. More research is needed on these and on the magnitude and sources of changes in utilization rates, on capital deterioration and replacement rates, and on the changing characteristics of the labor force.

While better data may decrease further the role of total factor productivity in accounting for the observed growth in output, they are unlikely to eliminate it entirely. It is probably impossible to achieve our original program of accounting for all the sources of growth within the current conventions of national income accounting. But this is no reason to accept the current estimates of total factor productivity as final. Their residual nature makes them intrinsically unsatisfactory for the understanding of actual growth processes and useless for policy purposes.

To make further progress in explaining productivity change will require the extension of such accounts in at least three different directions: (1) allowing rates of return to differ not only by legal form of organization but also by industry and type of asset; (2) incorporating the educational sector into a total economy-wide accounting framework; and (3) constructing measures of research (and other intangible) capital and incorporating them into such productivity accounts.

To allow rates of return to differ among industries and assets would require a much more detailed data base than is currently available and would introduce the notion of disequilibrium (at least in the short and intermediate runs) into such accounts. Such a framework would be consistent with a more general view of sources of growth[80] and would introduce explicitly the changing industrial composition of output as one such source.

In measuring labor input, OBE data on persons engaged should include estimates of the number of unpaid family workers, such as those of Kendrick (1961a, 1973). Estimates of man-hours for different components of the labor force should be compiled on a basis consistent with data on persons engaged as Kendrick has done. Although Denison (1967) has given additional evidence in support of his adjustment of labor input for intensity of effort, a satisfactory treatment of this adjustment requires data on income by hours of work, holding other characteristics of the labor force constant. Until such data become available it may be best to exclude this adjustment from the measure of real labor input incorporated into the national accounts. Quality adjustments for labor input based on such characteristics of the labor force as age, race, sex, occupation, and education should be incorporated into the labor input measure.

The basic accounting framework should also be expanded to incorporate investment in human capital along with investment in physical capital. Investment in human capital is primarily a product of the educational sector, which is not included in the private domestic sector of the economy. In addition to data on education already incorporated into the national accounts, data on physical investment and capital stock in the educational sector would be required for incorporation of investment in human capital into growth accounting.

Another issue for long-term research is the incorporation of research and development into growth accounting. At present research and development expenditures are treated as a current expenditure. Labor and capital employed in research and development activities are commingled with labor and capital used to produce marketable output. The first step in accounting for research and development is to develop data on factors of production devoted to research. The second step is to develop measures of investment in research and development.[81] The final step is to develop data on the stock of accumulated research. A similar accounting problem arises for advertising expenditures, also currently treated as a current expenditure.

Both education and investment in research and development are heavily subsidized in the United States, so that private costs and returns are not equal to social costs and returns. The effects of these subsidies would have to be taken into account in measuring the effects of human capital and accumulated research on productivity in the private sector. If the output of research activities is associated with external benefits in use, these externalities would not be reflected in the private cost of investment in research. Some way must be found to measure these externalities. Once such measures are developed and the growth accounts expanded accordingly, this would result in a significant departure from the conventions of national accounting, more far-reaching than the departures contemplated in our original paper. A new accounting system is required to comprehend the whole range of possible sources of economic growth.

4.8 Final Reply

In our paper, "The Explanation of Productivity Change" (Jorgenson and Griliches, 1967),[82] we showed that earlier estimates of total factor productivity by Edward F. Denison and other productivity analysts contained serious conceptual flaws. Most analysts weight total labor and total capital input by estimates of their marginal products to obtain a measure of total factor input. We argued that the same principle should have been applied consistently to the subcomponents of labor and capital as well.

In our paper, "Issues in Growth Accounting: A Reply to Edward F. Denison," we demonstrate in much greater detail that capital input and total factor productivity measures employed by Denison in his monographs, *Sources of Economic Growth* ... (1962) and *Why Growth Rates Differ* (1967), are permeated by internal contradictions. Although Denison agrees that subcomponents of capital input should be weighted by their marginal products, he fails to apply this principle in an internally consistent way.

The force of our criticism is easy to appreciate, even for someone who does not wish to enter into the details of the argument. Economic depreciation plays a crucial role in any measurement of capital input and total factor productivity. Depreciation depends on the decline in efficiency of capital goods. In Denison's two monographs two different assumptions about decline in efficiency are employed, but the same basic method for calculating depreciation, the straight-line method, is employed in both.[83] At a minimum it is obvious that if one of Denison's calculations is correct the other is wrong. In our reply to Denison we demonstrate that both sets of calculations are internally inconsistent.

Denison's paper "... Major Issues ..." (1969) is devoted to an examination of our procedures for estimating total factor productivity in "The Explanation of Productivity Change" (Jorgenson and Griliches, 1967). All of Denison's valid objections to these procedures have been met and several major improvements have been made in our new estimates, based on those of Christensen and Jorgenson (1969, 1970).[84]

Specifically, capital input has been disaggregated so as to incorporate the effects of direct and indirect taxation in a more satisfactory way. Second, our estimate of the effects of changes in a relative utilization has been revised downward. As before, our conclusion is that total factor input, not productivity change, predominates in the explanation of growth of output.

In our discussion of quality change we distinguish between measures of "quality change" which make it equal to one or another version of the "residual" tautologically, and quality change estimated from current differences in marginal products. To us, this latter type is "measured" quality change, provided that it can in fact be measured with some precision from observed market prices and rents of different commodity groups, including different vintages, and we would wish to count it as part of input in the capital-using sector. This procedure will not eliminate productivity change by definition since it will result in higher productivity growth in the capital-producing sector. It will only attribute it where it belongs.

Various other issues raised by Denison deal with the semantic problem of what to include in "input" and what to include in "productivity." Since at the aggregate level the idea of an input is at best rather vague while the idea of "productivity" does not hide anything more than the "residual" from all other calculations, it has been our tendency to take out most of the measurable sources of growth (such as intersectoral shifts) from the wastebasket of the "residual" and include them perforce in our concept of input. We have no objection, however, to a more complex classification scheme.

The major portion of Denison's "Final Comments" is devoted to defending the procedures used in *Why Growth Rates Differ* (1967).[85] To state our criticism of these procedures as succinctly as possible: We do not insist that Denison adopt our assumption of geometric decline in efficiency, let alone our depreciation rates; this is one way of solving the problem of maintaining internal consistency, but it is not the only solution. We simply urge him to adopt a single assumption about decline in efficiency and to employ this assumption in measuring both depreciation and capital input. Denison's procedures in *Why Growth Rates Differ* (1967) employ one assumption for depreciation and another for capital input.

Denison's defense of the methods employed in *Why Growth Rates Differ* fails to meet the basic issue of inconsistency. Unlike Denison's paper, his accompanying "Final Comments" do not really advance the discussion of the methods of measuring total factor productivity further. We are prepared to leave this exchange of views with Denison at this point and continue with the work of improving our estimates in both scope and quality.

Notes

1. Estimates of real capital input are presented in Christensen and Jorgenson (1969); estimates of total factor productivity are given in Christensen and Jorgenson (1970). Our original estimates are presented in Griliches and Jorgenson (1966) and Jorgenson and Griliches (1967).
2. Christensen and Jorgenson (1969), pp. 314–319.
3. Denison (1962), pp. 35–87, and Griliches (1960), pp. 1414–1417.
4. Accounts are given by Christensen and Jorgenson (1970).

5. All references to data from the U.S. national income and product accounts are to *The National Income and Product Accounts of the United States, 1929–1965, Statistical Tables, A Supplement to the Survey of Current Business*, August 1966, henceforward NIP (Office of Business Economics, 1966).
6. Self-employed persons include proprietors and unpaid family workers. The method for imputation of labor compensation of the self-employed that underlies our estimates is discussed in detail by Christensen (1971). Alternative methods for imputation are reviewed by Kravis (1959).
7. Kendrick (1961a, 1973). Office of Business Economics data on nonfarm proprietors and employees are from NIP (1966), tables 6.4 and 6.6.
8. Christensen and Jorgenson (1970) assume that the statistical discrepancy reflects errors in reporting property income rather than labor income.
9. This allocation is described by Christensen and Jorgenson (1970), pp. 297–301.
10. A derivation of prices of capital services is given by Hall and Jorgenson (1971, 1967) for continuous time. Christensen and Jorgenson (1969) have converted this formulation to discrete time, added property taxes, and introduced alternative measurements for the tax parameters. Similar formulas have been developed by Coen (1968).
11. The perpetual inventory method is discussed by Goldsmith (1951) and employed extensively in his *Study of Saving* (1955) and more recent studies of U.S. national wealth (1965, 1962, 1963). This method is also used in the OBE *Capital Goods Study* (Griliches, 1963) and in the study of capital stock for the United States by Tice (1967).
12. Denison (1967), p. 140.
13. Detailed evidence on the quality of the price quotations underlying the WPI is presented by Flueck (1961).
14. See Gordon (1971) for additional evidence supporting this position.
15. The A.T.&T. structures index uses American Appraisal Company indexes with essentially negligible productivity adjustments since 1955.
16. Gordon's "final Price of Structures" index rises by 11 percent less between 1950 and 1965 than the constant cost 2 deflator. See Gordon (1968), table A-1, pp. 427–428. Gordon errs, in a paper published a year later than ours, in failing to notice that the final version of our paper did not incorporate the Bureau of Public Roads index as a deflator but used the more representative but still imperfect OBE constant cost 2 index.
17. The imputation of the value of services from owner-occupied dwellings and structures is imputed by this method in the U.S. national accounts. NIP (1966), table 7.3.
18. See footnote 6.
19. This division of the private domestic economy follows the U.S. national accounts; see NIP (1966), table 1.13. Other sectors included in the accounts are government and rest of the world.
20. These data were provided by the Office of Business Economics.
21. Christensen and Jorgenson (1970) assume that errors in reporting property income occur mainly in noncorporate business.
22. Christensen and Jorgenson (1970) assume that business transfer payments are taken mainly from corporate income.
23. Alternative provisions for the investment tax credit are discussed by Hall and Jorgenson (1971).
24. Christensen and Jorgenson (1969) assume that no depreciation is taken during the year of acquisition of an asset.
25. Formulas for the present values of depreciation deductions are:

straight-line:

$$\frac{1}{rt}\left[1-\left(\frac{1}{1+r}\right)^{t}\right]$$

sum of the years' digits:

$$\frac{2}{rt}\left[1-\frac{1+r}{r(t+1)}\left(1-\frac{1}{1+r}\right)^{t+1}\right]$$

where r is the discount rate and t is the lifetime of assets allowable for tax purposes. Depreciation practices have adapted to the use of accelerated methods only gradually, as Wales (1966) has demonstrated.

26. The appropriate rate of return for this purpose is the long-term expected rate of return; 10 percent is close to the average of corporate after-tax rates of return for the period 1929–1967. See Christensen and Jorgenson (1969), table 5, pp. 312–313.

27. Griliches (1970), pp. 77–78.

28. See footnote 7.

29. See for example (Bureau of the Census, *Current Population Reports*, 1968), p. 7, where it is estimated that the quality of men deteriorated by less than 1 percent over the 10-year period between 1956 and 1966 due to changes in their age distribution.

30. *Index Numbers*; 1958 = 100

	Men	*Women*	*Total*	*Weighted total*
1964	107.7	120.8	112.1	110.2
1950	99.1	81.9	93.8	95.7

The weights used were 0.805 for males and 0.195 for females. The share of men in total earnings was 0.81 in 1958 and 0.80 in 1964. These figures imply a –0. 13 percent per year decline in the quality of the labor force due to the increase in the female population. Given our average labor share, this would imply a –0. 09 percent contribution to the rate of growth of total input. These numbers are taken from (Bureau of the Census, *Trends in Income of Families and Persons*, 1967b).

31. "Quality change" in this sense is equivalent to aggregation bias. For further discussion, see Jorgenson and Griliches (1967), especially pp. 259–260.

32. Kendrick (1961a), pp. 252–289, and Solow (1957), p. 315.

33. Denison (1962), especially pp. 67–72.

34. Denison (1962), especially pp. 35–41.

35. Solow (1957), p. 315.

36. Kendrick (1961a), especially pp. 252–289.

37. Denison (1969), p. 4.

38. Denison (1969), p. 2.

39. See section 4.7.5 below for further discussion.

40. Denison (1971), fn. 1, p. 2.

41. The absolute contribution of productivity change is discussed by Denison (1969), pp. 2–3.

42. See Hall and Jorgenson (1971); see also (1967). We assume here that the decline in efficiency of capital goods with age is geometric so that capital consumption allowances are proportional to capital stock. If decline in efficiency is not geometric,

capital consumption allowances are not proportional to capital stock and depreciation is not equal to replacement. Since Denison assumes that decline in efficiency is linear rather than geometric (1967, p. 140), serious difficulties arise in preserving internal consistency in his accounts for gross product, net product, net product, factor input, and capital stock. See section 4.7.5 below for further discussion.

43. The interpretation of Divisia indexes is discussed by Solow (1957), Richter (1966), and Jorgenson and Griliches (1967).

44. Denison (1969), p. 4.

45. Denison (1969), p. 4, bases his allocation of noncorporate income on relative shares in the nonfinancial corporate sector. This procedure has the effect of ignoring the impact of the corporate income tax. For further discussion, see Christensen (1971).

46. See Denison (1969), p. 5.

47. In fact, our revised estimates can be regarded as solving the problem of simultaneously incorporating both property taxation and the corporate income tax posed by Denison as follows:

For one tax classified as indirect, that on real property, this assumption [that the tax be included in the earnings of capital] may be preferable. Indeed, in the context of considering the effect of taxes on the allocation of resources among sectors of the economy, I have myself suggested that one should not consider the impact of the corporate income tax, which bears only on the corporate sector, without simultaneously considering the property tax, which bears most heavily on the principal noncorporate sectors of the private economy: housing and farming (Denison, 1969 , p. 5).

48. Denison (1969), pp. 6–13.

49. Denison (1969), p. 8.

50. Denison (1969), p. 8, suggests adjusting the weight of land, but not that of other capital, for inflation. His actual procedure (1962, 1967) for allocating property income ignores the effects of inflation for all assets. Denison (1969), p. 8, argues that:

Their [our] idea is that current asset values are proportional to . . . the discounted value of the anticipated stream of earnings and capital gains. . . .

He then states that prices of depreciable assets

. . . are firmly anchored to the present price level and present production costs of capital goods and are not affected by capital gains.

Actually, the contradiction between our view and his is only apparent. From the point of view of producers of capital goods the prices are anchored to present production costs. From the point of view of purchasers of capital goods these prices are related to the discounted value of future earnings, including capital gains or losses. Thus prices are simultaneously anchored ot the current price level and to anticipations of future earnings.

51. Denison (1969), pp. 8, 13, acknowledges the possibility that his results could be improved by taking capital gains into account in measuring earnings from land.

52. Denison (1969), p. 13.

53. Jorgenson and Griliches (1967), p. 257. See Kendrick (1961a, 1973).

54. Denison (1969), p. 13.

55. Denison (1967), p. 140

56. Denison (1967), p. 140.

57. Denison (1967), p. 14.

58. Denison (1967), p. 351.

59. Denison (1967), p. 14.

60. Denison (1962), pp. 112–113.

61. Denison (1967), p. 140.
62. Denison (1967), p. 351.
63. Hickman (1965), pp. 223–248; Hall and Jorgenson (1971), pp. 28–31. Many other references could be given. Geometrically declining efficiency is the standard assumption in econometric studies of investment behavior.
64. Meyer and Kuh (1957), pp. 91–94.
65. Cagan (1965), pp. 222–226; Griliches (1960), pp. 197–200; Wykoff (1970), pp. 171–172.
66. Hall (1971), pp. 19–20.
67. Griliches (1963), pp. 121–123 and 129–131.
68. Jorgenson and Griliches (1967), pp. 259–260; see also (Griliches, 1960).
69. Jorgenson and Griliches (1967), p. 260.
70. See Solow (1957, 1960); for an interpretation of the resulting measure of capital input, see Jorgenson (1966).
71. Denison (1969), p. 26.
72. For a detailed discussion, see Christensen and Jorgenson (1969), p. 296.
73. Our calculations are based on data from Goldsmith (1962), table A-13:

Category of private land	In constant prices (1947–49 = 100)			Average (1945–58) relative weight in total value of private land
	1945 (1)	1958 (2)	Rate of change per year 1945–58 (3)	(4)
Agricultural	53.8	52.9	−0.15	0.40
Residential	31.3	44.6	2.77	.23
Nonresidential	47.7	64.6	2.37	.33
Forests	6.4	6.9	.60	.04

Note. — Rate of Growth of private stock of land per year =
$\sum[\text{column } 3 \times \text{column } 4] = 1.38$

74. Denison employs OBE estimates of inventory stocks (1969, p. 13); we have employed the same estimates of inventory stocks. We also incorporate estimates of stocks of depreciable assets from the OBE Capital Goods Study (Grose, Rottenberg and Wasson, 1969). Although Denison did not employ these estimates, he indicates that:

Had the OBE study been completed, I would have used OBE capital stock series based on Bulletin F lives, on the use of the Winfrey distribution for retirements, and on the use of the OBE "price deflation II" (Denison, 1969, p. 14).

This accords with our estimates except for the use of the Winfrey distribution.
75. See Grose, Rottenberg and Wasson (1969).
76. Denison (1969), pp. 12–14.
77. Denison (1969), p. 16.
78. There is also some confusion about the measurement of marginal contributions in some of Denison's examples. These examples seem to imply that if higher skill workers are required to run new machines, the contribution of such machines cannot be measured separately and is already included in the contribution of labor input. But this is clearly wrong.
79. Griliches (1970) and Griliches and Mason (1972).
80. See Johnson (1964) for an outline of a similar position.

81. See Griliches (1973) for further discussion of this topic and for some order of magnitude estimates.
82. All reference numbers are from the list of references given in our accompanying paper, "Issues in Growth Accounting: A Reply to Edward F. Denison."
83. Here we adopt Denison's interpretation of his estimates based on replacement, as measures of depreciation. Denison's two "views" of depreciation in his "Final Comments," pages 104–107, are definitions of two distinct concepts—*replacement* as defined on page 213 of our accompanying paper and *depreciation* as defined on page 213. The use of a single term for the two concepts is the source of Denison's error in the definition of net product and of inconsistencies in his accounting for depreciation and capital input. See our accompanying paper, "Issues in Growth Accounting: A Reply to Edward F. Denison," p. 213, for an elaboration of these points.
84. Denison's objections to our deflation of government and rest of the world product have already been met in a revised and extended set of estimates for the period 1929–1969; see: D.W. Jorgenson, "Measuring Economic Performance," in M. Moss (ed.), *The Measurement of Economic and Social Performance*, Studies in Income and Wealth, No. 37, New York, Columbia University Press, 1973. Reprints are available from the author.
85. See Denison (1972), pp. 99–109.

5 Measuring Economic Performance in the Private Sector

Laurits R. Christensen and
Dale W. Jorgenson

5.1 Introduction

The problem of measuring economic performance involves comparisons. The output of an economic system is greater or less than its output at some previous point in time. The input of factors of production is greater or less in one industry than another. The standard of living in one region is greater or less than in another. Systems of economic accounts have provided a useful framework for organizing the information required for comparisons of this type.

Comparisons between the performance of two economies or the performance of an economic system at two points of time are of great interest from a scientific point of view. They are also of interest for the evaluation of economic policies. Evaluation of alternative policies involves comparison of the present state of affairs and possible alternative states associated with changes in policy.

The description of alternative states of an economic system involves the value of accounting magnitudes associated with each state. Changes from one state to another must be separated into price and quantity components. For example, the measurement of inflation involves an analysis of price changes, while the measurement of real output involves changes in quantity.

In view of the importance of the separation of changes in accounting magnitudes into price and quantity components, it is not surprising that much attention has been given to the measurement of real product. The scope of the product measure—whether and how to include activities internal to households, institutions, and governments, or services of the external environment—has been discussed in great detail.

Denison has recently drawn attention to the limitations inherent in a one-dimensional view of economic performance (1971, pp. 1–8). In comparing economic systems or alternative states of an economy it is impossible to summarize all the relevant information in a single measure of economic welfare. Real output is important, but the composition of output—by end use, industry of origin, and so on—is equally important in interpreting economic events and evaluating performance.

A complete economic system includes a production account, incorporating data on output and factor input, and income and expenditure account—giving data on factor incomes, expenditures, and saving—and an accumulation account, allocating saving to its uses in various types of capital formation.[1] In addition, a complete system contains data on national wealth from both asset and liability points of view. All of these accounting magnitudes are of interest in evaluating economic performance.

Although the separation of changes in accounting magnitudes into price and quantity components is of fundamental importance for the evaluation of economic performance, only the measurement of real product and real assets is well established in accounting practice. For the evaluation of economic performance, measures of factor input, income, expenditures, saving, and capital formation in both current and constant prices are essential.

In this paper we present a complete accounting system in constant prices that comprehends all the aspects of economic performance we have listed above. This system is implemented in detail for the private sector of the U.S. economy. Although it would be desirable to implement the system for a detailed breakdown of the economy by sectors, our presentation is limited to national aggregates.

In measuring economic performance, our basic framework consists of a production account for the U.S. private domestic economy and a consolidated income and expenditure account for the U.S. private national economy. The income and expenditure account is consolidated with the accumulation account to provide a complete summary of the income of the private sector and its disposition in the form of consumer expenditures and capital formation.

For the production account, the fundamental accounting identity is that the value of output is equal to the value of factor input. Changes in the values of product and factor input are separated into price and quantity components. A summary measure of performance is based on the level of productivity defined as the ratio of real product to real factor input or the ratio of the price of input to the price of output.

For the consolidated income and expenditure account the fundamental accounting identity is that the value of consumer receipts is equal to consumer outlays plus capital formation. Consumer receipts, consumer outlays, and capital formation can be separated into price and quantity components. A summary measure of performance is based on the standard of living, defined as the ratio of real expenditures to real receipts or the ratio of the price of factor services to the price of expenditures.

The interpretation of real product, real factor input, and total factor productivity requires the notion of a social production possibility frontier.[2] In each period the inputs of factors of production are transformed into outputs. In an extended description of the production possibilities, the inputs may include durable goods of various ages, inventories and financial claims, as well as the services of labor and natural agents.[3] The outputs would include used durable goods, unspent inventories, and goods and services for private or public consumption.

The interpretation of real consumer receipts and outlays and the standard of living requires the notion of a social welfare function.[4] An extended description of the determinants of social welfare must include all "goods" and "bads" relevant to social choice. Within the conventional framework the "goods" would include deliveries to final consumption in every future period and the "bads" would include deliveries of labor services in every future period. Evaluation would involve comparisons of "wealth-like" magnitudes.[5]

In this paper, we concentrate on the development of a complete accounting system in both current and constant prices. We limit the transactions included to those that can be measured or imputed from presently available primary data sources—income tax returns, populations and production censuses and surveys, and so on. We present data for the period 1929–1969 for each of the accounting magnitudes we discuss.

The first step in constructing an accounting system for the measurement of economic performance is to develop accounts in current prices. We present income and wealth accounts, including production, income and expenditure, accumulation and wealth accounts for the U.S. private economy for 1929–1969 in section 5.2 below.

In section 5.3, we introduce the problem of constructing accounts in constant prices with a description of our system of index numbers for prices and quantities. In section 5.4, we present an extension of the perpetual inventory method, familiar from national wealth accounting, to incorporate prices as well as quantities of capital goods. The price counterpart of the perpetual inventory method involves the estimation of prices of capital goods of every vintage at each point of time.

The presentation of a system of accounts in constant prices begins in section 5.5 with the production account. The product side of the account includes consumption and investment goods output in constant prices. The factor outlay side includes labor and capital input. The ratio of output in constant prices to factor input is equal to total factor productivity. We present estimates of product, factor input, and total factor productivity for the U.S. private domestic economy for 1929–1969.

In section 5.6, we present income and expenditure, accumulation, and wealth accounts in constant prices for the U.S. private national economy, 1929–1969. Consolidating the income and expenditure accounts we obtain a single account giving income and its disposition in constant prices.

We conclude with a discussion of possible extensions of the accounting framework in section 5.7. The educational sector of the U.S. economy, which is largely governmental rather than private, could be incorporated into our accounting system by compiling data on educational investment, capital and labor input used in the educational sector, and the stock of human capital. Research and development expenditures in the private sector are treated on current account; expenditures on research should be capitalized.

Many other extensions of our accounting framework can be suggested. Activities internal to the household and government sectors could be incorporated into the accounting system by making appropriate imputations for nonmarket activities. Accounts for the educational sector could serve as a prototype for complete accounts for the household and government sectors.

A different range of extensions, not discussed in section 5.7, would involve the compilation of accounts in constant prices for individual sectors in the economy. The production account could be disaggregated and complete interindustry accounts in constant prices could be incorporated into the system. The wealth account could be extended to include both assets and liabilities. Accumulation and wealth accounts could be disaggregated to incorporate complete flow of funds accounts.

As a basis for comparison we contrast our approach with two alternative accounting systems. The first is the U.S. national accounts, augmented by Denison's *Sources of Economic Growth*, which extends the framework of the U.S. accounts considerably.[6] The second is the United Nations System of National Accounts, as revised in 1968. In both systems, efforts have been made to develop accounts in both current and constant prices.

Despite the severe self-imposed limitations of our accounting system, concentrating on national aggregates of transactions that are already included in present accounting systems, our accounts differ very substantially from current practice. In comparing our system with available alternatives we focus attention on these differences. The basic similarities between our approach and current accounting practice can be recognized through the heavy reliance we have placed on data derived from the U.S. national accounts.

5.2 Income and Wealth

5.2.1 Introduction

The first problem in accounting for economic performance is the measurement of income and wealth in current prices. The solution of this problem requires a system of four accounts. First, the production account includes data on the output of the producing sector and the outlay of that sector on factor services, both expressed in current prices. Second, the income and expenditure account contains data on transfer payments and income from factor services, consumer outlays, and saving. Third, the accumulation account includes data on saving, capital formation, revaluation of existing assets, and the change in wealth from period to period. Finally, successive values of wealth are contained in the wealth account.

5.2.2 Production Account

The production account contains data on the value of output and the value of input. As an accounting identity, the value of output is equal to the value of input. The two sides of the production account are linked through production of investment goods and compensation for the services of capital. Investment goods output enters the change in wealth from period to period through capital formation. Accumulated wealth generates factor incomes that arise as compensation for the services of capital. Investment goods output and property compensation must be defined in a consistent manner.

In the U.S. national income and product accounts, total output is divided among services, nondurable goods, durable goods, and structures.[7] The output of services includes the services of owner-occupied dwellings; the output of structures includes the production of new residential housing. Capital formation in the form of residential housing is a component of the change in wealth from period to period; property compensation includes the imputed value of compensation for the use of owner-occupied dwellings. The output of durables includes consumer durables and producer durables used by nonprofit institutions. However, property compensation, as defined in the U.S. national accounts, does not include the imputed value of the services of these durables.

In the U.S. national accounts, the value of the services of owner-occupied residential real estate, including structures and land, is imputed from market rental prices of renter-occupied residential real estate. The value of these services is allocated among net rent, interest, taxes, and capital consumption allowances. A similar imputation is made for the services of real estate used by nonprofit institutions, but the imputed value excludes net rent.

To preserve consistency between the accounts for investment goods production and for property compensation we introduce imputations for the value of the services of consumer durables and durables used by nonprofit institutions and the net rent of real estate used by institutions. The value of the services of these assets is included in the output of services, together with the services of owner-occupied dwellings. Property compensation also includes the value of these services. This imputation preserves the accounting identity between the value of output and the value of input.

We implement the production account for the U.S. private domestic economy, including the production activities of U.S. business and household sectors.[8] In principle, similar accounts could be constructed for government and rest of world sectors of the economy. Wealth accounts for the government sector would be required for construction of a production account for government comparable to our production account for the private domestic sector.

We define revenue as proceeds to the sector from the sale of output, and outlay as gross outlays by the sector on purchases of input. Our concept of output is intermediate between gross output at market prices and gross output at factor cost, as these terms are usually employed. Output at market prices includes all indirect taxes in the value of output; output at factor cost excludes all indirect taxes. We distinguish between taxes charged against revenue, such as excise or sales taxes, and taxes that are part of the outlay on factor services, such as property taxes. We exclude taxes on output from the value of gross output since these taxes are not included in the proceeds to the sector. We include taxes on input since these taxes are included in the outlay of the sector.

Taxes on output reduce the proceeds of the sector and subsidies increase these proceeds; accordingly, the value of output includes production subsidies. To be more specific, we exclude excise and sales taxes, business nontax payments, and customs duties from the value of output and include other indirect business taxes plus subsidies and less current surplus of federal and state and local government enterprises. The resulting production account is given for 1958 in table 5.1.

As an accounting identity, the value of gross private domestic factor outlay is equal to the value of gross private domestic product. Factor outlay is the sum of income originating in private enterprises and private households and institutions, plus the imputed value of consumer durables, producer durables utilized by institutions, and the net rent on institutional real estate, plus indirect taxes included in factor outlay. Factor outlay includes capital consumption allowances, business transfer payments, and the statistical discrepancy. Capital consumption allowances are part of the rental value of capital services. We include business transfer payments and the statistical discrepancy in factor outlay on capital. The value of gross private domestic factor outlay for the year 1958 is presented in table 5.1.

Product and income accounts are linked through capital formation and the corresponding compensation of property. To make this link explicit we must divide the total product between consumption and investment goods and total factor outlay between labor and property compensation. Investment goods production in the private domestic sector is equal to the total output of durable goods and structures included in the gross national product. Consumption goods production in the private domestic sector is equal to the output of nondurable goods and services in the gross national product, less the

Table 5.1
Production account, gross private domestic product and factor outlay, United States, 1958 (billions of current dollars)

Line		Product	Total
1		*Private gross national product* (table 1.7)	$405.2
2	−	Income originating in government enterprises (table 1.13)	4.8
3	−	Rest of the world gross national product (table 1.7)	2.0
4	+	Services of consumers' durables (our imputation)	40.3
5	+	Services of durables held by institutions (our imputation)	0.3
6	+	Net rent on institutional real estate (our imputation)	0.8
7	−	Federal indirect business tax and nontax accruals (table 3.1)	11.5
8	+	Capital stock tax (table 3.1, footnote 2)	—
9	−	State and local indirect business tax and nontax accruals (table 3.3)	27.0
10	+	Business motor vehicle licenses (table 3.3)	0.8
11	+	Business property taxes (table 3.3)	13.8
12	+	Business other taxes (table 3.3)	2.9
13	+	Subsidies less current surplus of Federal government enterprises (table 3.1)	2.7
14	−	Current surplus of state and local government enterprises (table 3.3)	1.8
15	=	*Gross private domestic product*	419.7
		Factor outlay	
1		*Capital consumption allowances* (table 1.9)	38.9
2	+	Business transfer payments (table 1.9)	1.6
3	+	Statistical discrepancy (table 1.9)	1.6
4	+	Services of consumers' durables (our imputation)	40.3
5	+	Services of durables held by institutions (our imputation)	0.3
6	+	Net rent on institutional real estate (our imputation)	0.8
7	+	Certain indirect business taxes (product account above, lines 8 + 10 + 11 + 12)	17.4
8	+	Income originating in business (table 1.13)	312.2
9	−	Income originating in government enterprises (table 1.13)	4.8
10	+	Income originating in households and institutions (table 1.13)	11.4
11	=	*Gross private domestic factor outlay*	419.7

Note: All table references are to OBE (1966).

output of the foreign and government sectors, plus our imputation for the services of consumer durables and institutional durables and the net rent of institutional real estate. The output of the foreign and government sectors consists entirely of services.

The imputed value of the services of consumer and institutional durables and the net rent on institutional real estate is included in the value of output and the value of capital input. The value of outlay on capital services also includes the property income of self-employed persons; profits, rentals, and interest; capital consumption allowances; business transfer payments; the statistical discrepancy; and indirect taxes included in outlay on capital services, such as motor vehicle licenses, property taxes, and other taxes. The value of labor input includes the compensation of employees in private enterprises and in private households and nonprofit institutions, plus the labor compensation of the self-employed.

We estimate labor compensation of the self-employed by assuming that the compensation per full-time equivalent employee is equal to the labor compensation of proprietors and unpaid family workers.[9] This method is only one of many that have been proposed. Denison has suggested that the results are biased in the direction of allocating too large a proportion of the income of the self-employed to labor compensation.[10] However, Christensen has shown that the method produces results consistent with the assumption that rates of return to property used by the self-employed are comparable to rates of return in the corporate business sector when appropriate corrections are made for taxation and accrued capital gains or losses.[11] Gross private domestic product and factor outlay in current prices for 1929–1969 are given in table 5.2. Total product is divided between investment and consumption goods output. Total factor outlay is divided between labor and property compensation.

5.2.3 Income and Expenditure Account

The income and expenditure account includes data on transfer payments and the value of income from factor services, the value of consumer outlays, and saving. As an accounting identity, the value of consumer receipts is equal to the value of consumer outlays plus saving. The two sides of the income and expenditure account are linked through property compensation and saving. Saving results in the accumulation of tangible assets and financial claims; the accumulated

Table 5.2
Gross private domestic product and factor outlay, 1929–1969 (billions of current dollars)

Year	Gross Private Domestic Product	Investment Goods Product	Consumption Goods Product	Labor Outlay	Property Outlay
1929	104.2	28.5	75.7	60.5	43.7
1930	91.0	20.3	70.8	55.6	35.5
1931	76.6	14.1	62.5	47.3	29.3
1932	55.7	7.2	48.5	37.2	18.6
1933	54.5	7.5	47.0	34.8	19.7
1934	62.3	10.4	51.9	39.3	23.0
1935	67.9	12.7	55.2	42.6	25.3
1936	77.6	17.1	60.5	47.4	30.2
1937	85.3	19.6	65.7	53.7	31.6
1938	79.1	15.3	63.8	49.6	29.6
1939	85.4	19.3	66.1	53.0	32.4
1940	94.0	23.9	70.1	57.1	36.9
1941	115.9	36.9	79.0	69.6	46.3
1942	140.9	47.6	93.3	86.9	54.0
1943	167.8	60.5	107.3	102.3	65.5
1944	178.6	61.2	117.4	108.7	69.9
1945	177.7	52.8	124.9	108.4	69.3
1946	190.3	49.7	140.6	119.5	70.8
1947	218.3	64.1	154.2	137.8	80.6
1948	244.4	72.8	171.7	151.0	93.4
1949	235.1	72.1	162.9	148.9	86.1
1950	270.4	91.1	179.3	162.6	107.8
1951	305.8	106.0	199.8	183.8	122.0
1952	320.7	108.2	212.5	196.0	124.7
1953	340.6	115.1	225.5	210.5	130.1
1954	341.6	111.0	230.6	209.2	132.4
1955	377.7	128.5	249.2	225.0	152.7
1956	395.5	135.3	260.2	242.6	152.9
1957	413.4	140.0	273.4	254.1	159.3
1958	419.7	130.6	289.2	252.8	166.9
1959	458.1	146.8	311.3	273.6	184.5
1960	475.5	148.8	326.7	286.5	189.1
1961	488.1	147.5	340.6	292.3	195.8
1962	524.6	163.4	361.2	310.7	213.9
1963	553.4	173.2	380.2	325.0	228.4
1964	592.7	186.6	406.1	346.8	245.9
1965	640.5	204.5	436.0	371.4	269.1
1966	703.5	224.1	479.4	405.8	297.7
1967	739.8	229.3	510.4	429.9	309.8
1968	798.3	251.3	546.9	469.8	328.5
1969	863.7	270.7	593.0	514.8	348.9

wealth generates future property income. Saving must be defined in a way that is consistent with accounts for property income. Income must include all payments for factor services that result in consumption expenditures or in the accumulation of assets that result in future income.

We implement the income and expenditure account for the U.S. private national economy.[12] For this purpose we consolidate the accounts of private business with those of private households and institutions. Financial claims on the business sector by households and institutions are liabilities of the business sector; in the consolidated accounts these assets and liabilities cancel out. The assets of the private national economy include the tangible assets of the business sector. We treat social insurance funds as part of the private national economy. The claims of these funds on other governmental bodies are treated as assets of the private sector.

In the U.S. national accounts the income and expenditure account of the government sector does not include income from tangible assets owned by governmental bodies. If capital accounts were available for the government sector, we could construct income and expenditure accounts for that sector analogous to our accounts for the private sector. The income and expenditure account of the rest of the world sector of the U.S. national accounts is comparable to our account for the private sector.

We define income of the private national economy as proceeds from the sale of factor services. We define expenditure of the sector as consumer outlays plus saving. Our concept of income is closer to that underlying the concept of gross private saving in the U.S. national accounts than to the more commonly employed concept of personal disposable income. Accordingly, we refer to our income concept as gross private national income. Outlay on factor services by the production sector includes indirect taxes such as property taxes and motor vehicle licenses. This outlay also includes direct taxes such as corporate and personal income taxes. Our concept of gross private national income excludes both indirect and direct taxes.

To be specific, gross private national income includes labor and property income originating in the private domestic economy and the rest of the world sectors, labor income originating in the government sector, net interest paid by government, and the statistical discrepancy. Income is net of indirect taxes on factor outlay and all direct taxes on incomes. Gross private national income excludes interest paid by consumers and personal transfer payments to foreigners. Income also includes the investment income of social insurance funds, less transfers to general government by these funds. Contributions to social insurance are included and transfers from social insurance funds are excluded from income. The value of gross private national income and expenditures for the year 1958 are presented in table 5.3.

Consumption is equal to personal consumption expenditures on services and nondurable goods plus our imputation for the services of consumer and institutional durables and the net rent of institutional real estate. Purchases of consumer durables, included in personal consumption expenditures in the U.S. national accounts, are treated as part of saving in our income and expenditure account. The value of consumption includes taxes and excludes subsidies on output; these taxes are excluded from the value of consumption goods output in the production account. Our concept of saving differs from gross private saving as defined in the U.S. national accounts in the treatment of social insurance and statistical discrepancy. The expenditure account for the consuming sector for the year 1958 is presented in table 5.3.

Our definition of income is similar to the concept of income underlying the U.S. national accounts concept of gross private saving. Our concept of income differs from the national accounts concept in the treatment of social insurance and transfer payments, the inclusion of the services of consumer and institutional durables, the net rent on institutional real estate, and the statistical discrepancy. Transfer payments are treated as a nonincome receipt of the consumer sector. The services of durables, net rent, and the statistical discrepancy are treated as part of outlays on capital services. The services of durables are included in output and capital input in order to preserve consistency between the definition of investment goods in the production account and the definition of property compensation in the factor outlay account. Net rent is included in output and factor outlay to preserve consistency between the treatment of owner-occupied residential real estate and institutional real estate. The statistical discrepancy is assigned to factor outlay so that the accounting identity between the value of output and the value of factor outlay is preserved.

Our treatment of social insurance can be compared with the treatment that underlies the U.S. national accounting concepts of personal disposable income and gross private saving. In these income concepts the social insurance funds are treated as part of the government sector rather than the private sector. Contributions to social insurance are

Table 5.3
Gross private national receipts and expenditures, 1958 (billions of current dollars)

		Receipts	
1.		Gross private domestic factor outlay[a]	419.7
2.	+	Income originating in general government (table 1.13)[b]	42.1
3.	+	Income originating in government enterprises (table 1.13)	4.8
4.	+	Income originating in rest of world (table 1.13)	2.0
5.	+	Investment income of social insurance funds (table 3.7)	1.8
6.	−	Transfers to general government from social insurance funds (table 3.7)	0.6
7.	+	Net interest paid by government (tables 3.1, 3.3)	6.2
8.	−	Corporate profits tax liability (table 1.10)	19.0
9.	−	Business propoerty taxes[c]	17.4
10.	−	Personal tax and nontax payments (table 2.1)	42.3
11.	+	Personal nontax payments (tables 3.1, 3.3)	2.3
12.	=	Gross private national income	399.5
13.	+	Government transfer payments to persons other than benefits from social insurance funds	8.1
14.	=	Gross private national consumer receipts	407.7
		Expenditures	
1.		Personal consumption expenditures (table 1.1)	290.1
2.	−	Personal consumption expenditures, durable goods (table 1.1)	37.9
3.	+	Services of consumer durables (our imputation)[d]	40.3
4.	+	Services of institutional durables (our imputation)[d]	0.3
5.	+	Opportunity cost of equity capital, institutional real estate (our imputation)[e]	0.8
6.	=	Private national consumption expenditure	293.6
7.	+	Personal transfer payments to foreigners (table 2.1)	0.6
8.	+	Personal nontax payments (tables 3.1, 3.3)	2.3
9.	=	Private national consumer outlays	296.5
10.	+	Gross private national saving[f]	111.2
11.	=	Private national expenditures	407.7

[a] Christensen and Jorgenson (1970, table 1, p. 23]. This series has been revised to include a net rent imputation to institutional structures. Our other imputations have also been slightly modified. See expenditure items 3, 4, and 5 below.

[b] All table references are to OBE (1966).

[c] Christensen and Jorgenson (1970, table 1, p. 23, line 6, in factor outlay).

[d] Christensen and Jorgenson (1970, Section 5).

[e] We have computed an implicit rental value for institutional structures and land based on our estimate of the rate of return to owner-occupied real estate. The opportunity cost of equity capital is the difference between the implicit rental value and the net rent figure OBE (1966, table 7.3). This imputation was suggested to us by Edward F. Denison

[f] See table 4.5, line 10, below.

treated as a tax, benefits paid by these funds are treated as a transfer payment, and the claims of these sectors on other governmental bodies are treated as claims on the government by itself that cancel out in a consolidated government wealth account. Our concept of income focuses on the separation of contributions to social insurance from other taxes and on the effects of a future stream of benefits on saving decisions by individuals. The national accounts treatment focuses on the involuntary nature of contributions to social insurance.

The differences between our concept of income and the national accounts concept of personal disposable income are very substantial. In addition to the differences we have already outlined, our concept of income includes undistributed corporate profits, the corporate inventory valuation adjustment, corporate and noncorporate capital consumption allowances, and wage accruals less disbursements. All of these components of factor outlay are excluded from personal disposable income. We also exclude government transfer payments and net interest paid by consumers, which are included in personal disposable income. These differences between gross private national income, as we have defined it and personal disposable income are primarily attributable to our consolidation of the accounts of the private business sector with those of private households and institutions. The income of the private sector includes all property compensation whether paid out in the form of dividends and interest or retained by the business sector.

Income and expenditure accounts are linked through saving and the resulting income from the services of property. To make this link explicit we must divide income between labor and property compensation and expenditure between saving and consumption. The measurement of labor and property compensation gross of taxes is straightforward. We have already described the allocation of private domestic factor outlay between the value of capital input and the value of labor input. Corresponding allocations for government and rest of the world sectors are available from the U.S. national accounts. The problem is to allocate taxes on factor services between labor services and capital services. We allocate indirect business taxes on factor services and the corporate income tax to income from capital. The problem that remains is to allocate personal income tax payments between income from labor and income from capital.

To allocate personal income tax payments between labor and property compensation we employ a method developed by Frane and

Klein (1953) and applied by Ando and Brown (1963) to U.S. data on the personal income tax for 1929–1958. Personal income taxes on income from labor services are a remarkably stable proportion of total personal income tax receipts. The data for 1929 to 1958 show that the proportion of taxes on labor income in total personal taxes for the latter part of the period is 0.755 with a negligible variation. We have extended the estimates of personal income taxes on labor income by Ando and Brown to 1969 by assuming that the proportion of these taxes in total personal income taxes is constant at 0.755. Personal income taxes not allocated to labor income are allocated to property income. Gross private national receipts and expenditures in current prices for 1929–1969 are given in table 5.4. Income is divided between labor and property compensation, net of taxes. Expenditure is divided between consumer outlays and saving.

5.2.4 Accumulation Account

The accumulation account includes data on saving, capital formation, revaluation of existing assets, and the change in wealth from period to period. Gross private national saving is reduced by depreciation to obtain saving as it enters the accumulation account. As an accounting identity, the value of saving is equal to the value of capital formation. The change in wealth from period to period is equal to saving plus the revaluation of existing assets. Although revaluations are part of the change in wealth, they are excluded from income and from saving. In measuring the return from investment in different types of assets, both returns in the form of income and returns from revaluations must be considered.

We implement the accumulation account for the U.S. private national economy.[13] Sources of saving include gross private saving, as defined in the U.S. national accounts, the surplus of federal and state and local social insurance funds, personal consumption expenditures on durable goods, and the statistical discrepancy. Capital formation includes gross private domestic investment, personal consumption expenditures on durable goods, deficits of the federal, state, and local governments excluding social insurance funds, and net foreign investment. Private national saving and capital formation are given for 1958 in table 5.5.

In the U.S. national accounts depreciation on tangible assets in the business sector is set equal to depreciation claimed for tax purposes.

Table 5.4
Gross private national receipts and expenditures. 1929–1969 (billions of current dollars)

Year	Gross Private National Income	Labor Compen-sation	Property Compen-sation	Gross Private National Receipts and Expenditures	Consumption Expenditures	Consumer Outlays	Gross Private National Savings
1929	102.7	65.5	37.1	103.5	77.0	78.1	25.4
1930	90.1	60.8	29.3	91.0	71.4	72.4	18.6
1931	76.9	52.7	24.1	78.8	63.5	64.4	14.3
1932	56.2	42.3	13.9	57.4	50.0	50.8	6.7
1933	55.3	39.9	15.3	56.5	49.3	50.0	6.5
1934	63.8	45.4	18.4	65.1	53.9	54.6	10.5
1935	69.2	49.1	20.1	70.7	56.4	57.1	13.7
1936	79.0	55.2	23.8	81.7	62.8	63.5	18.2
1937	85.6	61.0	24.6	87.2	66.5	67.2	20.0
1938	80.6	57.6	23.1	82.3	65.4	66.0	16.3
1939	86.8	61.1	25.8	88.5	67.6	68.2	20.3
1940	94.1	65.3	28.8	95.7	70.6	71.3	24.4
1941	112.1	79.3	32.8	113.8	78.7	79.4	34.4
1942	136.7	100.7	35.9	138.4	87.1	87.8	50.6
1943	160.3	118.3	41.9	162.0	103.0	103.9	58.1
1944	178.5	130.1	48.4	180.7	111.6	112.6	68.1
1945	181.8	132.0	49.8	185.9	123.1	124.3	61.6
1946	185.2	130.7	54.5	193.4	142.8	144.1	49.4
1947	204.1	142.1	62.0	212.7	158.6	159.9	52.8
1948	230.0	156.9	73.1	238.0	171.0	172.6	65.4
1949	227.0	159.3	67.6	234.7	166.6	168.1	66.6
1950	254.0	174.1	79.9	261.8	184.8	186.3	75.5
1951	282.9	194.6	88.3	289.6	200.7	202.2	87.4
1952	299.4	206.9	92.4	306.0	215.3	216.9	89.0
1953	317.1	221.2	96.0	323.6	227.6	229.4	94.2
1954	324.3	223.6	100.7	331.0	235.2	237.2	93.8
1955	354.7	239.3	115.4	361.9	252.8	254.8	107.1
1956	370.5	256.7	113.8	377.7	265.9	268.3	109.4
1957	388.6	269.2	119.5	396.2	278.7	281.4	114.9
1958	399.5	271.5	128.1	407.7	293.6	296.5	111.2
1959	431.9	292.3	139.7	440.3	315.6	318.7	121.6
1960	448.5	305.8	142.7	456.9	331.8	334.9	122.0
1961	462.0	314.7	147.3	471.0	343.0	346.4	124.6
1962	496.2	333.9	162.3	505.4	360.4	364.2	141.2
1963	522.8	350.0	172.8	532.5	380.8	385.0	147.5
1964	567.2	379.2	188.0	577.4	406.5	411.3	166.1
1965	609.9	404.9	205.0	621.1	433.9	439.1	181.9
1966	669.4	442.2	227.2	681.3	470.8	476.6	204.8
1967	708.0	470.4	237.6	721.8	499.0	505.7	216.1
1968	756.0	511.0	245.0	771.5	536.2	543.7	227.8
1969	807.8	551.8	256.0	825.7	583.5	591.9	233.8

Table 5.5
Gross private national capital formation, saving, and revaluation, 1958 (billions of current dollars)

		Saving	
1.		Personal saving (table 2.1)	22.3
2.	+	Undistributed corporate profits (table 5.1)	10.8
3.	+	Corporate inventory valuation adjustment (table 5.1)	–0.3
4.	+	Corporate capital consumption allowances (table 5.1)	22.0
5.	+	Noncorporate capital consumption allowances (table 5.1)	16.9
6.	+	Wage accruals less disbursements (table 5.1)	0.0
7.	+	Personal consumption expenditures, durable goods (table 1.1)	37.9
8.	+	Surplus, social insurance funds (table 3.7)	0.0
9.	+	Statistical discrepancy (table 1.9)	1.6
10.	=	Gross private national saving	111.2
11.	–	Depreciation (our imputation)	80.8
12.	=	Net private national saving	30.4
13.	+	Revaluation (our imputation)	31.6
14.	=	Change in private national wealth	62.1
		Capital Formation	
1.		Gross private domestic investment (table 1.2)	60.9
2.	+	Personal consumption exxpenditures, durable goods (table 1.1)	37.9
3.	+	Deficit of federal government (table 3.1)	10.2
4.	+	Deficit of state and local governments (table 3.3)	2.3
5.	–	Deficit, federal social insurance funds (table 3.7)	–1.6
6.	–	Deficit, state and local social insurance funds (table 3.7)	1.7
7.	+	Net foreign investment (table 5.1)	–0.2
8.	=	Gross private national capital formation	111.2

Note: All table references are to OBE (1966).

We replace this estimate of depreciation by our own imputation, described in detail in section 5.4 below. No depreciation for consumer for consumer durables and durables used by institutions is included in the U.S. national accounts. Our imputed value of depreciation includes depreciation for both these classes of assets.

To estimate the change in wealth from period to period we require estimates of saving net of depreciation and estimates of the revaluation of existing assets due to price changes. Revaluations are not included in the U.S. national accounts, so that an essential link between income and expenditure accounts and wealth accounts is missing. We have estimated the revaluations for private domestic tangible assets as part of our perpetual inventory of capital goods, described in section 5.4 below. Our estimates of revaluations for financial claims are based on accounts for stocks of these claims in current prices. We estimate revaluations as the difference between the period to period changes in these stocks and the deficits of the government and the rest of world sectors. Private national saving and capital formation in current prices for 1929–1969 are given in table 5.6.

5.2.5 Wealth Account

All of the accounts we have considered up to this point contain data on flows. The production account includes flows of output and input; the income and expenditure account includes the corresponding flows; the flow of saving and changes in wealth from period to period are included in the accumulation account. The wealth account contains data on the stock of wealth in successive periods. The wealth account can be presented in balance sheet form with the value of assets equal to the value of liabilities as an accounting identity. We present only the asset side of the wealth account.

We implement the wealth account for the U.S. private national economy.[14] The wealth accounts of private business are consolidated with those of private households and institutions. Our wealth account includes data on assets in the consolidated account. These assets include the tangible assets of private households and institutions and the tangible assets of private business. In addition, they include net claims on the foreign and government sectors by the private sector. Social insurance funds are treated as part of the private sector rather than as part of government.

Our estimate of the stock of private domestic tangible assets is based on a perpetual inventory of capital goods, as described in section 5.4. Our estimate of net claims on foreigners and governments is based on the flow of funds accounts of the Board of Governors of the Federal Reserve System and on *Studies in the National Balance Sheet of the United States* (Goldsmith, Lipsey and Mendelson, 1963) and *The National Wealth of the United States in the Postwar Period* (Goldsmith, 1962).[15] We distinguish between monetary and nonmonetary claims on the federal government by the private sector. Monetary claims include vault cash of commercial banks, member bank reserves, and currency outside banks. Nonmonetary claims on the federal government include U.S. government total liabilities, less U.S. government financial assets, plus net liabilities of federally sponsored credit agencies and financial assets of included social insurance funds, less U.S.

Table 5.6
Gross private national capital formation, saving, and revaluation, 1929–1969 (billions of current dollars)

Year	Gross Private National Saving and Capital Formation	Replacement and Depreciation	Net Private National Saving and Capital Formation	Revaluation	Change in Wealth
1929	25.4	19.2	6.2	3.4	9.7
1930	18.6	19.0	–0.4	–22.0	–22.4
1931	14.3	17.2	–2.8	–39.9	–42.7
1932	6.7	14.7	–8.0	–38.7	–46.7
1933	6.5	13.3	–6.7	1.7	–5.0
1934	10.5	13.5	–2.9	19.8	16.9
1935	13.7	12.9	0.7	3.4	4.2
1936	18.2	12.9	5.3	8.0	13.3
1937	20.0	14.1	5.9	17.4	23.2
1938	16.3	14.8	1.4	–2.1	–0.7
1939	20.3	14.5	5.8	–1.5	4.3
1940	24.4	15.0	9.4	6.2	15.7
1941	34.4	16.8	17.6	30.2	47.8
1942	50.6	20.3	30.3	41.7	72.0
1943	58.1	20.9	37.2	27.6	64.7
1944	68.1	21.7	46.5	21.8	68.3
1945	61.6	21.7	39.9	12.9	52.9
1946	49.4	22.9	26.4	52.5	79.0
1947	52.8	28.4	24.4	83.2	107.6
1948	65.4	33.9	31.5	46.4	77.9
1949	66.6	37.9	28.8	–10.8	17.9
1950	75.5	41.8	33.7	45.4	79.0
1951	87.4	49.6	37.8	64.9	102.7
1952	89.0	53.8	35.2	15.7	50.9
1953	94.2	56.5	37.7	5.2	42.9
1954	93.8	59.2	34.6	5.3	39.9
1955	107.1	62.3	44.8	21.4	66.2
1956	109.4	69.8	39.6	58.1	97.8
1957	114.9	76.5	38.4	51.9	90.3
1958	111.2	80.8	30.4	32.4	62.8
1959	121.6	83.7	37.9	39.3	77.2
1960	122.0	86.7	35.3	32.1	67.4
1961	124.6	89.7	34.9	29.5	64.4
1962	141.2	92.4	48.8	40.8	89.6
1963	147.5	96.3	51.2	37.6	88.7
1964	166.1	101.5	64.6	45.7	110.4
1965	181.9	107.5	74.5	52.4	126.8
1966	204.8	115.7	89.0	64.1	153.1
1967	216.1	127.2	88.9	79.1	168.1
1968	227.8	138.5	89.3	98.6	187.9
1969	233.8	152.0	81.8	120.7	202.5

government liabilities to rest of world, plus U.S. government credits and claims abroad, less monetary liabilities. Private sector claims on state and local government include state and local government total liabilities, less state and local government financial assets, plus assets of cash sickness compensation funds. Net private claims on the rest of the world include private U.S. assets and investments abroad less private U.S. liabilities to foreigners. Private national wealth in 1958 is presented in table 5.7. Annual data on the components of private national wealth are presented in table 5.8.

5.2.6 The Accounting System

The production and income and expenditure accounts are related through markets for commodities and factor services. Factor outlay by the producing sector is the most important component of income from the supply of factor services by the consuming sector. Income also includes the value of factor services supplied to the government and rest of the world sectors. The expenditure account is linked to the production account through the market for consumption goods and services. The production of consumption goods also includes goods consumed by the government and the rest of the world sectors. Expenditure on consumption goods includes goods supplied by the rest of the world sector. The expenditure account is also linked to the production indirectly through saving.

The accumulation account allocates saving among its sources and uses. The uses of saving include capital formation through investment in reproducible tangible assets. Expenditure on investment in these assets is linked to the production account through the market for investment goods output. The production of investment goods is partly consumed by government and rest of the world sectors; part of the supply of these goods originates in the rest of the world sector. The accumulation account is linked to the wealth account through the accounting identity between period to period changes in wealth and the sum of saving and revaluations of existing assets.

The structure of this accounting system can be compared with that of the U.S. national accounts. The production account is for gross national product and includes income generated in the government and rest of the world sectors. Our production account is for gross private domestic product and excludes these two sectors. The income and expenditure account in the U.S. national accounts is for personal

Table 5.7
Private national wealth, 1958 (billions of current dollars)

1. Private domestic tangible assets[a]			1,300.1
2. + Net claims on the federal, state, and local governments			280.9
3. a. Federal, monetary[b]		50.6	
(i) + Vault cash of commercial banks	3.2		
(ii) + Member bank reserves	18.5		
(iii) + Currency outside banks	28.9		
b. Federal, nonmonetary		195.2	
(i) U.S. government total liabilities[b]	256.4		
(ii) – U.S. government financial assets[b]	50.0		
(iii) + Net liabilities, federally-sponsored credit agencies[b]	0.5		
(iv) + Assets of included social insurance funds[c]	30.4		
(v) – U.S. government liabilities to the rest of world[d]	8.8		
(vi) + U.S. government credits and claims abroad[d]	18.3		
(vii) – Monetary liabilities[b]	50.6		
c. State and local		35.1	
(i) State and local government total liabilities[b]	62.6		
(ii) – State and local government financial assets[b]	27.7		
(iii) + Assets of cash sickness compensation fund	0.2		
3. + Net claims on the rest of world			13.8
a. Private U.S. assets and investments abroad		41.1	
b. – Private U.S. liabilities to foreigners		27.3	
4. = Private national wealth			1,594.9

[a] See Christensen and Jorgenson (1970, pp. 294–301) for a discussion

[b] Haavelmo (1960)

[c] U.S. Department of Treasury, *Treasury Bulletin*, (February issues)

[d] OBE, Survey of Current Business ("The International Investment Position of the United States," in October issues)

Table 5.8
Private national wealth 1929–1969 (current prices)

Year	Corporate Tangible Assets	Noncorporate Tangible Assets	Household and Institutional Tangible Assets	Net Claims on Governments and Rest of World	Private National Wealth
1929	116.7	106.7	158.1	33.0	414.6
1930	110.3	97.9	150.0	34.0	392.2
1931	97.7	85.1	131.5	35.2	349.5
1932	84.1	73.3	108.1	37.3	302.7
1933	80.4	73.4	104.4	39.4	297.6
1934	83.1	76.3	109.5	45.2	314.2
1935	83.7	79.4	107.9	47.4	318.3
1936	86.6	82.7	112.5	50.0	331.8
1937	95.0	88.1	120.5	51.7	355.2
1938	92.2	85.6	122.2	54.4	354.3
1939	91.9	85.3	123.6	57.8	358.6
1940	96.6	88.7	129.2	59.9	374.4
1941	109.7	98.6	143.7	70.5	422.5
1942	121.1	108.6	155.1	110.3	495.0
1943	126.4	115.1	163.6	155.2	560.2
1944	130.4	121.2	173.9	202.9	628.5
1945	133.1	127.2	181.2	239.0	680.8
1946	159.6	148.5	206.7	244.6	759.4
1947	199.1	175.0	252.6	240.3	867.0
1948	224.2	192.2	291.8	236.0	944.2
1949	226.6	190.4	302.1	242.8	962.0
1950	248.2	212.7	341.8	238.8	1,041.5
1951	286.9	234.4	384.9	238.1	1,144.3
1952	303.0	237.5	408.7	245.9	1,195.0
1953	315.5	238.6	427.8	256.5	1,238.4
1954	323.1	244.4	442.9	267.6	1,278.0
1955	344.3	253.5	477.6	268.8	1,344.1
1956	381.8	269.7	518.8	271.6	1,441.9
1957	411.9	287.8	553.8	278.5	1,532.0
1958	422.2	303.9	574.0	294.8	1,594.9
1959	443.7	315.4	612.8	300.5	1,672.4
1960	461.9	330.6	640.7	306.4	1,739.7
1961	476.6	347.3	663.8	316.7	1,804.3
1962	500.1	367.0	698.6	328.3	1,893.9
1963	524.4	384.7	737.9	335.5	1,982.6
1964	556.4	404.8	785.1	346.9	2,093.2
1965	598.9	433.9	831.1	355.8	2,219.7
1966	660.0	464.2	880.6	367.9	2,372.7
1967	714.8	494.0	943.0	389.1	2,540.9
1968	771.4	529.5	1,022.9	404.5	2,728.3
1969	839.8	570.8	1,109.5	410.5	2,930.6

income and outlay. Factor outlay in the producing sector taking the form of undistributed corporate profits is excluded from personal income. Our concept of gross private national income is more closely related to the concept of income underlying the U.S. national accounts concept of gross private saving than to the concept of personal disposable income.

The accumulation account of the U.S. national accounts is based on national saving and investment rather than private saving and investment. However, the most serious problem with the accumulation account is the absence of two types of data that are essential in linking income and wealth accounts. The first is an estimate of economic depreciation. Estimates of capital consumption allowances in the U.S. national accounts are based on depreciation reported for tax purposes. As tax laws have evolved over time, these estimates have come to reflect widely varying depreciation formulas and lifetimes of assets for tax purposes.[16] No attempt has been made to replace estimates of depreciation for tax purposes with estimates based on an economic concept of depreciation.[17] We have attempted to remedy this deficiency. The second important omission in the accumulation account is an estimate of the revaluation of assets. Data on revaluations are essential for the construction of an integrated system of national income and wealth accounts.

The structure of our accounting system can also be compared with the United Nations *System of National Accounts* (1968). The principal difference between our system and the U.N. system is that we confine the accounts to the private sector. In the U.N. system the production account is based on the domestic economy rather than the private domestic sector; the income and expenditure account and the accumulation account are based on the national economy rather than the private sector. We have combined the accumulation and revaluation accounts of the U.N. system into a single accumulation account, which also includes period to period changes in national wealth. We have presented only the asset side of the national wealth accounts, while the U.N. system includes a balance sheet with data on both assets and liabilities.

5.3 Index Numbers

5.3.1 Introduction

The second problem in accounting for economic performance is the measurement of income and wealth in constant prices. Preliminary to the solution of this problem we must consider the selection of an appropriate system of index numbers. To express any accounting magnitude in constant prices we must separate the change in value from period to period into components associated with change in price and change in quantity. As an illustration, the change in the value of output entering the production account can be separated into a change in the quantity of output and a change in the price of output. Changes in other flows—factor outlay, income, expenditure on consumer goods, and investment—can be decomposed into price and quantity changes in the same way. As a second illustration, the change in the value of wealth entering the wealth account can be separated into a change in the quantity of assets and a change in the price of assets. We identify the change in quantity with saving and the change in price with revaluation of assets.

5.3.2 Divisia Index Numbers

Our system of index numbers is based on a discrete approximation to continuous index numbers. To illustrate the construction of index numbers of prices and quantities we consider the value of output as it enters the production account. Suppose that m components of output are distinguished in the accounts; the value of output, say qY, may be written:

$$qY = q_1Y_1 + q_2Y_2 + \cdots + q_mY_m \, .$$

Our system of index numbers consists of an index for the price of output q and the quantity of output Y, defined in terms of the prices (q_i) and quantities (Y_i) of the m components. The first step in defining these indexes is to differentiate the value of output with respect to time, obtaining:

$$\dot{q}Y + q\dot{Y} = \sum \dot{q}_iY_i + \sum q_i\dot{Y}_i \, .$$

We may define the relative shares of the value of the ith output in the value of total output, say w_i, as follows:

$$w_i = \frac{q_i Y_i}{\sum q_i Y_i} .$$

Dividing both sides of the total derivative of the value of output with respect to time by the value of output, we obtain:

$$\frac{\dot{q}}{q} + \frac{\dot{Y}}{Y} = \sum w_i \left(\frac{\dot{q}_i}{q_i} + \frac{\dot{Y}_i}{Y_i} \right).$$

We define the price and quantity indexes for output in terms of the prices and quantities of individual components; the rates of growth of the price index q and the quantity index Y are:

$$\frac{\dot{q}}{q} = \sum w_i \frac{\dot{q}_i}{q_i} , \qquad \frac{\dot{Y}}{Y} = \sum w_i \frac{\dot{Y}_i}{Y_i} ,$$

respectively. These index numbers are Divisia price and quantity indexes.[18] The indexes are defined in terms of rates of growth of price and quantity components of the rate of growth of the value of output. To obtain the price and quantity indexes themselves we choose a base for the indexes and integrate the rates of growth with respect to time. For the index numbers given below we choose the base for all price indexes as 1.000 in 1958. The base for the quantity indexes is equal to the value of the corresponding accounting magnitude in 1958.

The principal advantages of Divisia index numbers for social accounting purposes are, first, that rates of growth of these indexes of prices and quantity are symmetrical and add up to the rate of growth of the value of output (factor reversal test). Second, Divisia indexes are unaffected by a change in the direction of time (time reversal test). Finally, these indexes have the important reproductive property that a Divisia index of Divisia indexes is a Divisia index of the components. As an illustration, if the quantity index of total product is a Divisia index of quantity indexes of consumption and investment goods output and if the consumption and investment goods indexes are each Divisia indexes of individual consumption and investment goods, then the total product index is a Divisia index of the individual consumption and investment goods. The Divisia index numbers provide a convenient framework for national accounting since the principles of aggregation for data from subsectors of the economy are the same as those for construction of data for the subsectors. The results for the economy as a whole are independent of the structuring of the subaggregates.

For application to data for discrete points of time an approximation to the Divisia indexes for continuous time is required. Price and quantity index numbers originally discussed by Fisher (1922) may be employed for this purpose. Approximating rate of growth by the period-to-period changes in logarithms, we obtain:

$$\log q_t - \log q_{t-1} = \sum \bar{w}_{it}(\log q_{it} - \log q_{i,t-1}),$$
$$\log Y_t - \log Y_{t-1} = \sum \bar{w}_{it}(\log Y_{it} - \log Y_{i,t-1}),$$

where the weights ($\bar{w}_{it}$) are arithmetic averages of the relative shares in the two periods,

$$\bar{w}_{it} = \frac{1}{2} w_{it} + \frac{1}{2} w_{i,t-1} .$$

These index numbers have been suggested as a discrete approximation to the Divisia index by Törnqvist (1936). Obviously, the discrete and continuous index numbers are equal if and only if relative shares are constant. If shares are not constant, the discrete approximation involves an error that depends on the variability of the relative shares and the length of the time period.

Divisia index numbers for discrete time are symmetric in data of different time periods (time reversal). They also have the basic reproductive property that a discrete Divisia index of discrete Divisia indexes is a discrete Divisia index of the components. This property implies that the indexes for the economy as a whole are independent of the structuring of subsectors from which the aggregate data are constructed. The discrete Divisia price and quantity indexes are symmetrical. Theil (1967) has demonstrated that the sum of changes in the logarithms of discrete Divisia indexes of price and quantity is approximately equal to the change in the logarithm of the corresponding value (factor reversal). The factor reversal test is satisfied exactly if relative shares are constant; the accuracy of the approximation depends on the change in relative shares.

As a practical matter the approximation of changes in value by the sum of changes in discrete Divisia price and quantity indexes is extremely accurate. For the annual rate of growth in value of personal consumption expenditures in the Netherlands for the period

1921–1963, Theil shows that the error averages only 0.01 percent of the annual growth rate. It is convenient to have the product of price and quantity indexes equal to the value of transactions so that standard accounting identities hold for variables defined as price and quantity index numbers. Accordingly, we construct discrete Divisia price indexes as the value of the corresponding accounting magnitude divided by the discrete Divisia quantity index. The resulting price indexes are approximately equal to Divisia price indexes and have the reproductive property of Divisia indexes. They also satisfy, approximately, the time reversal and factor reversal tests for index numbers.

5.3.3 Taxes

At a number of points in our accounting system transactions data are presented net and gross of taxes. As one illustration, consumer purchases of goods and services in the income and expenditure accounts include sales and excise taxes. Sales of the same goods and services in the production account exclude these taxes. As a second illustration, outlay on factor services in the production account includes direct taxes and certain indirect taxes such as property taxes. Income from factor services in the income and expenditure accounts excludes these taxes. We treat sales and excise taxes as part of the price paid by consumers. We treat property taxes and income taxes as part of the price paid by producers. We can separate the change in the value of transactions into three components—change in price, change in quantity, and change in tax. The tax change is a component of the change in the price paid by the sector making an expenditure; the tax change is excluded from the change in the price received by the sector receiving income.

To illustrate the construction of price, quantity, and tax indexes we consider the value of consumer expenditure as it enters the income and expenditure account. Again, suppose that m components of consumer expenditure are distinguished in the accounts; the value of output, gross of tax, say $q^{+}Y$, may be written:

$$q^{+}Y = q_1^{+}Y_1 + q_2^{+}Y_2 + \cdots + q_m^{+}Y_m \,.$$

The prices (q_i^{+}) include sales and excise taxes; the quantities (Y_i) are measured in the same way as in the production accounts. Price and quantity indexes based on these prices and quantities may be defined in the same way as before.

To introduce taxes into the system of index numbers we let the market price of output q^+ be equal to the price received by the producer, say q, multiplied by unity plus the effective tax rate, t; the value of output at market price is:

$$q^+Y = (1 + t)qY \ .$$

The value of output at market prices may be expressed in terms of prices received by producers, each multiplied by unity plus the corresponding tax rate:

$$(1 + t)qY = \sum(1 + t_i)q_iY_i \ ,$$

where the prices paid by the consumers (q_i^+) are expressed in terms of prices received by producers (q_i) and tax rates (t_i).

Proceeding as before, we express the rate of growth of the value of consumer expenditure as the sum of rates of growth of taxes, prices, and quantities:

$$\frac{(1 + \dot{t}\,)}{1 + t} + \frac{\dot{q}}{q} + \frac{\dot{Y}}{Y} = \sum w_i \left[\frac{(1 + \dot{t}_i)}{1 + t_i} + \frac{\dot{q}_i}{q_i} + \frac{\dot{Y}_i}{Y_i} \right].$$

The rate of growth of the tax index, $1 + t$, is:

$$\frac{(1 + \dot{t}\,)}{1 + t} = \sum w_i \ \frac{(1 + \dot{t}_i)}{1 + t_i} \ ;$$

rates of growth of price and quantity indexes are analogous to those for the production account described above. To construct a tax index from the rate of growth we choose an appropriate base and integrate the rates of growth with respect to time. For the index numbers given below we choose the base for all tax indexes as the ratio of the corresponding accounting magnitude before taxes to this magnitude after taxes for 1958. To obtain the effective tax rate, we subtract unity from the resulting tax index.

For application to data for discrete points of time we approximate Divisia indexes for continuous time as before. It is convenient to preserve accounting identities for variables defined as price, quantity, and tax index numbers. Accordingly, we construct an index of taxes $1 + t$ by dividing the value of transactions at market prices by the value of transactions at producer prices. The resulting tax index is approximately equal to the Divisia tax index. It should be noted that Divisia price and quantity indexes at market prices differ from the corresponding indexes at producer prices since taxes enter the weights (w_i) employed in constructing the indexes.

5.3.4 Index Number Systems

In the U.S. national accounts only the output side of the production account is measured in current and constant prices. The index number system employed for the measurement of output in constant prices is based on a Laspeyres index number for the quantity of output and a Paasche index number for the price of output. In the Laspeyres index of output, prices of a base year are employed as weights for quantities of output. The Laspeyres index of quantity of output, say Y^L, is defined by:

$$Y_1^L = \frac{\Sigma q_{i0} Y_{i1}}{\Sigma q_{i0} Y_{i0}} ,$$

where the base prices (q_{i0}) are prices of 1958. Dividing the ratio of the values of transactions in period 1 to those in period 0 by the Laspeyres quantity index, we obtain the Paasche index of the price of output, q^P:

$$q_1^P = \frac{\Sigma q_{i1} Y_{i1}}{\Sigma q_{i0} Y_{i1}} ,$$

where the quantities (Y_{i1}) are quantities of the current year.

To compare the Divisia index numbers with the system of index numbers used in the U.S. national accounts we consider the rate of growth of the Laspeyres index of real product:

$$\frac{Y_1^L - Y_0^L}{Y_0^L} = \frac{\Sigma q_{i0} Y_{i1}}{\Sigma q_{i0} Y_{i0}} - \frac{\Sigma q_{i0} Y_{i0}}{\Sigma q_{i0} Y_{i0}} = \frac{\Sigma q_{i0} Y_{i1}}{\Sigma q_{i0} Y_{i0}} - 1 .$$

Next we consider the Laspeyres approximation to the rate of growth of the Divisia quantity index:

$$\frac{Y_1^D - Y_0^D}{Y_0^D} = \Sigma \frac{q_{i0} Y_{i0}}{\Sigma q_{i0} Y_{i0}} \frac{Y_{i1} - Y_{i0}}{Y_{i0}} = \frac{\Sigma q_{i0} Y_{i1}}{\Sigma q_{i0} Y_{i0}} - 1 .$$

The rate of growth of the Laspeyres approximation to the Divisia index is identical with the rate of growth of the usual Laspeyres quantity index.

The first difference between our system of index numbers and the system employed in the U.S. national accounts is that we approximate the underlying continuous index numbers by price and quantity indexes that satisfy the time reversal and factor reversal tests for index numbers. The Laspeyres approximation given above satisfies neither test since the corresponding price index number is a Paasche approximation to the underlying continuous price index number and since the Laspeyres and Paasche formulas are not symmetric in data of different time periods. These differences do not produce large variations in the price and quantity index numbers.

The second difference between our system of index numbers and the system of the U.S. national accounts is that our indexes are chain-linked. For each year, current prices are used as weights in estimating the rate of growth of quantity to the following year and current quantities are used as weights in estimating the rate of growth of price. This process is followed for each pair of years, and the resulting indexes are chain-linked. In effect the base of the index numbers is moved continually. The main advantage of a continually changing base is in the reduction of errors of approximation as the economy moves from one production or expenditure configuration to another. Chain-linked index numbers reduce the errors of approximation to a minimum. The use of a chain-linked index alters price and quantity indexes substantially for periods in which relative prices and relative quantities are shifting.

Denison (1962) has augmented the quantity and price indexes of the production account of the U.S. national accounts to provide quantity and price indexes of factor input. Although he uses the quantity and price indexes of output based on the national accounts, he employs chain-linked indexes of input with weights changing every five years. The Laspeyres approximation to the Divisia indexes of input and output is employed by Jorgenson and Griliches (1967), while Christensen and Jorgenson (1970) have used the approximation described above, satisfying factor and time reversal tests for index numbers. The main differences between the price and quantity indexes for these alternative systems of index numbers result from the use of chain-linked indexes. Alternative approximations to continuous indexes produce substantially similar results.

In the United States *System of National Accounts* (1968), systems of index numbers like that employed in the U.S. national accounts are recommended as a basis for constructing price and quantity indexes for the output side of the production account. As the base period is changed from time to time, chain-linking of the resulting price and quantity indexes is recommended. Continual chain-linking is not recommended for general adoption "mainly because the amount of data it requires is altogether greater than the amount required by the alternative."[19] The index numbers we employ in constructing accounts for output in constant prices are chain-linked indexes of component indexes obtained from the U.S. national accounts. They represent a mixture of chain-linked and fixed weights indexes. The index numbers we employ in constructing accounts for input, income, and expenditure are chain-linked indexes based on price and quantity data.

5.4 Perpetual Inventory

5.4.1 Introduction

Measurement of the output side of the production account and the asset side of the wealth account in constant prices is well established in social accounting practice. Index numbers of the price and quantity of output are constructed from data on prices and quantities of individual outputs. Index numbers of the price and quantity of capital assets are constructed from data on prices and quantities of individual assets. Quantities of individual assets are estimated from data on past levels of investment, and investment goods prices by the perpetual inventory method.[20]

Our objective is to develop a complete system of accounts in constant prices, linking output in constant prices to assets in constant prices. The most important obstacle to development of a complete accounting system is the lack of appropriate data on capital. To estimate the necessary data we extend the perpetual inventory method to encompass data on prices as well as quantities of capital goods by vintage. An accounting system of this type can be implemented only in a highly simplified form. However, even a simplified accounting system makes it possible to avoid inconsistencies in the treatment of capital that frequently occur in studies of total factor productivity.

5.4.2 Relative Efficiency

We begin the construction of a complete system of income and wealth accounts in constant prices with a description of the price and quantity data required for a single capital good. As in the perpetual inventory method, our characterization of a capital good is based on the relative efficiency of capital goods of different ages.[21] In the perpetual inventory method, the relative efficiency of a capital good depends on the age of the good and not on the time it is acquired. Replacement requirements are determined by losses in efficiency of existing capital goods as well as actual physical disappearance or retirement of capital goods. When a capital good is retired its relative efficiency drops to zero. The relative efficiency of capital goods of different ages can be described by a sequence of nonnegative numbers, $d_0, d_1, \ldots$.

We normalize the relative efficiency of a new capital good at unity and assume that relative efficiency is nonincreasing so that:

$$d_0 = 1 ; \quad d_\tau - d_{\tau-1} \leqq 0 ; \quad \tau = 0, 1, \ldots .$$

We also assume that every capital good is eventually retired or scrapped so that relative efficiency eventually drops to zero:

$$\lim_{\tau \to \infty} d_\tau = 0 .$$

Subject to these restrictions, a wide variety of patterns of decline in efficiency may be employed in the perpetual inventory method.

For illustration we consider three patterns of decline in efficiency "one-hoss shay," straight-line, and declining balance. In the "one-hoss shay" pattern, efficiency is constant over the lifetime of the capital good. Where T is the lifetime, relative efficiency is:

$$d_\tau = 1 ; \quad \tau = 0, 1, \ldots, T - 1 .$$

In the straight-line pattern, efficiency declines linearly over the lifetime of the capital good:

$$d_\tau = 1 - \frac{1}{T}\tau ; \quad \tau = 0, 1, \ldots, T - 1 .$$

In the declining balance pattern, efficiency declines geometrically:

$$d_\tau = (1 - \delta)^\tau ; \quad \tau = 0, 1, \ldots .$$

These patterns of decline in efficiency and many others may be treated as special cases within the framework of our extension of the perpetual inventory method.

Capital goods decline in efficiency at each point of time, giving rise to needs for replacement to maintain productive capacity. The proportion of an investment to be replaced during the τth period after its acquisition is equal to the decline in efficiency during that period. We refer to the decline in relative efficiency as the mortality distribution of a capital good, say m, where:

$$m_\tau = -(d_\tau - d_{\tau-1}) \; ; \qquad \tau = 1, 2, \ldots .$$

By our assumption that relative efficiency is nonincreasing, the mortality distribution may be represented by a sequence of nonnegative numbers, $m_1, m_2, \ldots$, where:

$$\sum_{\tau=1}^{\infty} m_\tau = \sum_{\tau=1}^{\infty} (d_{\tau-1} - d_\tau) = d_0 = 1 .$$

For the patterns of decline in efficiency considered above, we can derive the corresponding mortality distributions. If efficiency is constant over the lifetime of the capital good, the mortality distribution is zero except for period T: $m_T = 1$. For linear decline in efficiency, the mortality distribution is constant throughout the lifetime of the capital good:

$$m_\tau = \frac{1}{T} \; ; \qquad \tau = 1, 2, \ldots, T .$$

For geometric decline in efficiency, the mortality distribution declines geometrically:

$$m_\tau = \delta(1 - \delta)^{\tau-1} \; ; \qquad \tau = 0, 1, \ldots .$$

Replacement requirements can be expressed in terms of the mortality distribution for capital goods. Requirements can also be expressed in terms of the proportion of an initial investment replaced τ periods after the initial acquisition. This proportion includes replacement of the initial investment and subsequent replacements of each succeeding replacement. We refer to the sequence of these proportions as the replacement distribution of a capital good; each coefficient, say δ_τ is the rate of replacement of an investment replaced τ periods after initial acquisition. The sequence of replacement rates (δ_τ) can be computed recursively for the sequence of mortality rates (m_τ). The proportion of an initial investment replaced at time v and again at time $\tau > v$ is $m_v \delta_{\tau-v}$. The proportion of the stock replaced in the τth period is the sum of proportions replaced first in periods 1, 2, ..., and later at period τ; hence,

$$\delta_\tau = m_1 \delta_{\tau-1} + m_2 \delta_{\tau-2} + \cdots + m_\tau \delta_0 \; ; \qquad \tau = 1, 2, \ldots .$$

This equation is referred to as the renewal equation.[22]

For constant relative efficiency over the lifetime of a capital goods, the replacement distribution is periodic with the period equal to the lifetime of the capital good:

$$\delta_\tau = 1 \; ; \qquad \tau = T, 2T, \ldots .$$

For linear decline in efficiency, the replacement distribution may be represented in the form:

$$\delta_1 = \frac{1}{T} \; ;$$

$$\delta_2 = \frac{1}{T}\left(1 + \frac{1}{T}\right); \qquad \text{etc.}$$

For geometric decline in efficiency, the replacement distribution is constant:

$$\delta_\tau = \delta \; ; \qquad \tau = 1, 2, \ldots .$$

5.4.3 Quantities and Prices

The relative efficiency of capital goods of different ages and the derived mortality and replacement distributions are useful in estimating the data required for income and wealth accounts in constant prices. We begin our description of the required capital data with quantities estimated by the perpetual inventory method. First, capital stock at the end of each period, say K_t, is the sum of past investments, say $A_{t-\tau}$, each weighted by its relative efficiency:

$$K_t = \sum_{\tau=0}^{\infty} d_\tau A_{t-\tau} .$$

For a complete system of accounts, both capital stock and investments in every preceding period are required. For this purpose a system of vintage accounts containing data on investments of every age in every period is essential.

Taking the first difference of the expression for capital stock in terms of past investments, we obtain:

$$\begin{aligned} K_t - K_{t-1} &= A_t + \sum_{\tau=1}^{\infty} (d_\tau - d_{\tau-1})A_{t-\tau} ; \\ &= A_t - \sum_{\tau=1}^{\infty} m_\tau A_{t-\tau} \\ &= A_t - R_t ; \end{aligned}$$

where:

$$R_t = \sum_{\tau=1}^{\infty} m_\tau A_{t-\tau}$$

is the level of replacement requirements in period t. The change in capital stock from period to period is equal to the acquisition of investment goods less replacement requirements.

Replacement requirements may also be expressed in terms of present and past changes in capital stock, using the replacement distribution:

$$R_t = \sum_{\tau=1}^{\infty} \delta_\tau (K_{t-\tau} - K_{t-\tau-1}) .$$

The average replacement rate for capital stock at the beginning of the period,

$$\hat{\delta}_t = \frac{R_t}{K_{t-1}} = \sum_{\tau=1}^{\infty} \delta_\tau \, \frac{(K_{t-\tau} - K_{t-\tau-1})}{K_{t-1}} ,$$

is a weighted average of replacement rates with weights given by the relative proportions of changes in capital stock of each vintage in beginning-of-period capital stock.

We turn next to a description of the price data required for construction of income and wealth accounts in constant prices. These accounts require an extension of the perpetual inventory method to incorporate data on prices of capital goods of each vintage. Our extension of the perpetual inventory method is dual to the usual method in the sense that there is a one-to-one correspondence between the quantities that appear in the perpetual inventory method and the prices that appear in our extension of it.[23] To bring out this correspondence and to simplify the notation we use a system of present or discounted prices. Taking the present as time zero, the discounted price of a commodity, say p_t, is the discounted value of the future price, say q_t:

$$p_t = \prod_{s=1}^{t} \frac{1}{1+r_s} q_t \,.$$

The notational convenience of present or discounted prices results from dispensing with explicit discount factors in expressing prices for different time periods.

In the correspondence between the perpetual inventory method and its dual or price counterpart, the price of acquisition of a capital good is analogous to capital stock. The price acquisition, say p_{At}, is the sum of future rental prices of capital services, say $p_{K,t}$, weighted by the relative efficiency of the capital good in each future period:

$$p_{A,t} = \sum_{\tau=0}^{\infty} d_\tau p_{K,t+\tau+1} \,.$$

This expression may be compared with the corresponding expression giving capital stock as weighted sum of past investments. The acquisition price of capital goods enters the production account through the price of investment goods output. This price also appears as the price component of capital formation in the accumulation account. Vintage accounts, containing data on the acquisition prices of capital goods of every age at every point of time, are required for a complete system of accounts.

Taking the first difference of the expression for the acquisition price of capital goods in terms of future rentals, we obtain:

$$\begin{aligned} p_{A,t} - p_{A,t-1} &= -\, p_{K,t} - \sum_{\tau=1}^{\infty} (d_\tau - d_{\tau-1}) p_{K,t+\tau} \\ &= -\, p_{K,t} + \sum_{\tau=1}^{\infty} m_\tau p_{K,t+\tau} \\ &= -\, p_{K,t} + p_{D,t} \,; \end{aligned}$$

where

$$p_{D,t} = \sum_{\tau=1}^{\infty} m_\tau p_{K,t+\tau}$$

is depreciation on a capital good in period t. The period to period change in the price of acquisition of a capital good is equal to depreciation less the rental price of capital. In the correspondence between the perpetual inventory method and its price counterpart, investment corresponds to the rental price of capital and replacement corresponds to depreciation.

We can rewrite the expression for the first difference of the acquisition price of capital goods in terms of undiscounted prices:

$$q_{K,t} = q_{A,t-1} r_t + q_{D,t} - (q_{A,t} - q_{A,t-1}) ,$$

where $q_{A,t}$ is the undiscounted price of acquisition of capital goods, $q_{K,t}$ the price of capital services, $q_{D,t}$ depreciation, and r_t the rate of return, all in period t. The price of capital services $q_{K,t}$ is the sum of return per unit of capital $q_{A,t-1} r_t$, depreciation $q_{D,t}$, and the negative of revaluation $-(q_{A,t} - q_{A,t-1})$. The service price enters the production and the income and expenditure accounts through the price component of capital input and property compensation. Depreciation enters the accumulation account as the price component of depreciation on existing capital assets. Revaluation enters the accumulation account as the price component of revaluation of existing assets.

Depreciation may also be expressed in terms of present and future changes in the price of acquisition of investment goods, using the replacement distribution:

$$p_{D,t} = -\sum_{\tau=1}^{\infty} \delta_\tau (p_{A,t+\tau} - p_{A,t+\tau-1}) .$$

The average depreciation rate on the acquisition price of a capital good,

$$\bar{\delta}_t = \frac{p_{D,t}}{p_{A,t}} = -\sum_{\tau=1}^{\infty} \delta_\tau \frac{(p_{A,t+\tau} - p_{A,t+\tau-1})}{p_{A,t}} ,$$

is a weighted average of replacement rates with weights given by the relative proportions of changes in futures prices in the acquisition price of investment goods in the current period. This expression may be compared with that for the average replacement rate, $\hat{\delta}_t$, given above. For a complete system of accounts, vintage data on the depreciation of capital goods of every age at every point of time are required.

In the perpetual inventory method, data on the quantity of investment goods of every vintage are used to estimate capital formation, replacement requirements, and capital stock. In the price counterpart of the perpetual inventory method, data on the acquisition prices of investment goods of every vintage are required. The price of acquisition of an investment good of age v at time t, say $p_{A,t,v}$, is the weighted sum of future rental prices of capital prices. The weights are relative efficiencies of the capital good in each future period, beginning with age v:

$$p_{A,t,v} = \sum_{\tau=0}^{\infty} d_{\tau+v}\, p_{K,t+\tau+1}\,.$$

A new investment good has age zero so that:

$$p_{A,t,0} = p_{A,t}\,.$$

Given the acquisition prices, we require estimates of depreciation and the rental price for goods of each vintage.

To calculate depreciation on capital goods of each vintage we take the first difference of the acquisition prices across vintages at a given point in time:

$$\begin{aligned} p_{A,t,v} - p_{A,t,v+1} &= -\sum_{\tau=1}^{\infty} (d_{\tau+v} - d_{\tau+v-1}) p_{K,t+v+\tau} \\ &= \sum_{\tau=1}^{\infty} m_{\tau+v}\, p_{K,t+v+\tau} \\ &= p_{D,t,v}\,; \end{aligned}$$

where $p_{D,t,v}$ is depreciation on a capital good of age v at time t. Again a new investment good has age zero so that:

$$p_{D,t,0} = p_{D,t}\,.$$

To obtain depreciation in terms of future prices or undiscounted prices, we observe that acquisition prices across vintages at a given point in time and the corresponding depreciation are associated with the same discount factor, so that:

$$q_{A,t,v} - q_{A,t,v+1} = q_{D,t,v} \ .$$

To calculate the capital service price for goods of each vintage, we first observe that the rental of a capital good of age v at time t, say $q_{K,t,v}$, is proportional to the rental of a new capital good,

$$q_{K,t,v} = d_v q_{K,t} \ ,$$

with the constant of proportionality given by the efficiency of a capital good of age v relative to that of a new capital good. New and used capital goods are perfect substitutes in production. To calculate the service price for new capital goods, we use the formula derived above:

$$q_{K,t} = q_{A,t-1} r_t + q_{D,t} - (q_{A,t} - q_{A,t-1}) \ .$$

To apply this formula we require a series of undiscounted acquisition prices for capital goods ($q_{A,t}$), rates of return (r_t), depreciation on new capital goods ($q_{D,t}$), and revaluation of existing capital goods ($q_{A,t} - q_{A,t-1}$).

To calculate the rate of return in each period, we set the formula for the rental price $q_{K,t}$ times the quantity of capital K_{t-1} equal to property compensation. All of the variables entering this equation—current and past acquisition prices for capital goods, depreciation, revaluation, capital stock, and property compensation -- except for the rate of return, are known. Replacing these variables by the corresponding data we solve this equation for the rate of return. To obtain the capital service price itself we substitute the rate of return into the original formula along with the other data. This completes the calculation of the service price.

We conclude that acquisition prices for capital goods of each vintage at each point of time provide sufficient information to enable us to calculate depreciation and rental value for capital goods of each vintage. These data together with current investment, capital stock, replacement, and investments of all vintages at each point of time constitute the basic data on quantities and prices required for an extended perpetual inventory system. The problem that remains is to describe the role of each set of data in a complete accounting system. From this point we consider an accounting system for any number of investment goods. Price and quantity data that we have described above for a single investment good are required for each investment good in the system. The data for all investments goods are used to derive price and quantity indexes that play the role of the price and quantity data for a single investment good outlined above.

5.4.4 Accounting System

The quantities of investment goods (A_t) enter the production account in the period the investment is made through the quantity of investment goods output. An analogous quantity appears as part of capital formation in the accumulation account. The prices associated with investment in the production and accumulation accounts are prices of acquisition of new investment goods ($q_{A,t}$). The value of investment goods output is price times quantity, say $q_{A,t}A_t$. The value of capital formation is also equal to price times quantity; the price includes taxes on investment goods output. For several investment goods the values of investment goods output and capital formation are sums of prices times quantities for the individual investment goods. The price and quantity components of these accounts are derived by application of the Divisia index number formulas to the underlying price and quantity data for the individual investment goods.

Capital stock enters the production account through the quantities of capital service input (K_{t-1}); the quantity of capital service input also appears in the income and expenditure account as the quantity component of property compensation. The prices associated with capital services in the production and the income and expenditure accounts are rental prices ($q_{K,t}$). The value of capital input and property compensation is price times quantity, say $q_{K,t}K_{t-1}$. The service prices entering the production account are gross of taxes while the prices entering the property compensation account are net of taxes; these service prices will be discussed in more detail in sections 5.5 and 5.6 below. For several capital goods the values of capital services input and property compensation are sums of prices times quantities for each capital good. The price and quantity components of these accounts are derived by application of the Divisia index number formulas to the rental price and service quantity data for the individual capital goods.

Capital stock enters the accumulation account as the quantity component of depreciation. In the accumulation account capital stock must be distinguished by vintage so that vintage accounts containing data on investment of every age (A_{t-v-1}) may be regarded as part of the accumulation account in constant prices. The prices associated with capital stock in the accumulation account are the levels of depreciation ($q_{D,t,v}$). The value of depreciation for capital goods of age v is price times quantity, say $q_{D,t,v}A_{t-v-1}$; to obtain the total value of depreciation we sum over vintages, obtaining

$$\sum_{v=0}^{\infty} q_{D,t,v}A_{t-v-1} \ .$$

Even for a single capital good the separation of prices and quantities of depreciation requires application of an index number formula to the underlying vintage data. For several capital goods, the appropriate price and quantity index numbers can be constructed by applying the Divisia index number formulas to prices and quantities for each capital good derived from vintage data.

Capital stock also enters the accumulation account as the quantity component of revaluation. The prices associated with capital stock in measuring revaluation are the price changes $q_{A,t,v} - q_{A,t-1,v}$. Revaluation for capital goods of age v is price times quantity, say $(q_{A,t,v} - q_{A,t-1,v})A_{t-v-1}$; to obtain total revaluation we sum over vintages, obtaining

$$\sum_{v=0}^{\infty} (q_{A,t,v} - q_{A,t-1,v})A_{t-v-1} \ .$$

Separation of price and quantity components of revaluation for a single capital good or for several goods requires the application of Divisia index number formulas to prices and quantities for each vintage of each capital good, just as in the depreciation account. The prices used for depreciation and revaluation in the accumulation account must be consistent with those used for capital service prices in the production and the income and expenditure accounts.

Replacement appears in the accumulation account as part of capital formation. Gross capital formation is equal to investment. Net capital formation is equal to gross capital formation less replacement. Net capital formation is equal to the period to period change in capital stock. Replacement represents the change in the quantity of existing capital goods due to a decline in relative efficiency. Depreciation represents the change in the price of existing capital goods due to present and all future declines in efficiency. We have already described the separation of price and quantity components of gross capital formation. The methods for separation of these components of net capital formation and replacement are strictly analogous; quantities of gross capital formation or investment are replaced by quantities of net capital formation and replacement in index number formulas that also depend on prices of acquisition of investment goods.

Finally, capital stock appears in the wealth account as the quantity component of capital assets. In the wealth account, capital stock must be distinguished by vintage so that vintage accounts containing investment of every age in every time period may be regarded as part of both accumulation and wealth accounts. The prices associated with capital stock in the wealth account are the acquisition prices ($q_{A,t,v}$). The value of wealth for capital goods of age v is price times quantity, say $q_{A,t,v}A_{t-v}$; to obtain the total value of wealth we sum over vintages, obtaining

$$\sum_{v=0}^{\infty} q_{A,t,v}A_{t-v} \, .$$

For a single capital good or for several capital goods, price and quantity index numbers of wealth can be constructed by applying the Divisia index number formulas to prices and quantities of capital assets of each vintage at each point of time.

For capital goods with a full set of data for every time period, including investment of every vintage and the price of acquisition for every vintage, accounts can be compiled for capital input, property compensation, depreciation, capital formation, replacement, and wealth in current and constant prices. Price data corresponding to each of the accounts in constant prices can also be compiled. For capital goods with a less complete set of data, a simplified system of accounts can be constructed on the basis of the assumption that decline in efficiency is geometric. Under this assumption the rate of replacement and the rate of depreciation are constant and equal to the rate of decline in efficiency:

$$\hat{\delta}_t = \bar{\delta}_t = \delta \, .$$

Constant rates of replacement and depreciation lead to substantial simplifications in our system of income and wealth accounts in constant prices. Vintage accounts can be dispensed with since replacement is proportional to capital stock and depreciation is proportional to the current acquisition price of investment goods.

As a first step in construction of a simplified accounting system for income and wealth in constant prices we estimate capital stock at the end of each period as a weighted sum of past investments:

$$K_t = \sum_{\tau=0}^{\infty} (1 - \delta)^{\tau} A_{t-\tau} .$$

With a constant rate of replacement, replacement becomes:

$$R_t = \delta K_{t-1} .$$

The price of acquisition of new investment goods is a weighted sum of future rentals:

$$p_{A,t} = \sum_{\tau=0}^{\infty} (1 - \delta)^{\tau} \, p_{K,t+\tau+1} .$$

With a constant rate of depreciation, depreciation becomes:

$$q_{D,t} = \delta q_{A,t} .$$

The acquisition price of investment goods of age v at time t is:

$$q_{A,t,v} = (1 - \delta)^{v} \, q_{A,t} .$$

The service price for new capital goods becomes:

$$q_{K,t} = q_{A,t-1} r_t + \delta q_{A,t} - (q_{A,t} - q_{A,t-1}) .$$

In the complete accounting system for income and wealth in constant prices outlined above, vintage accounts for capital are required for calculating replacement, depreciation, capital formation, revaluation, and wealth. With constant replacement rates (δ_τ) the values of replacement and depreciation are equal and depend only on the price of acquisition of new capital goods and the stock of capital:

$$q_{A,t} R_t = \delta q_{A,t} K_{t-1} = q_{D,t} K_{t-1} .$$

Similarly, the value of wealth is the product of the price acquisition and the stock of capital, $q_{A,t} K_t$. The change in wealth from period to period,

$$q_{A,t}K_t - q_{A,t-1}K_{t-1} = q_{A,t}(K_t - K_{t-1}) + (q_{A,t} - q_{A,t-1})K_{t-1} ,$$

is the sum of capital formation and revaluation. No vintage accounts for capital goods are required under the assumption of constant replacement rates. For several capital goods the Divisia index number formulas must be employed to separate replacement, depreciation, capital formation, revaluation, and wealth into price and quantity components.

Geometric decline in efficiency is among the patterns most commonly employed in estimating capital stock by the perpetual inventory method.[24] For geometric decline in efficiency, depreciation is proportional to the acquisition price of new capital goods and replacement is proportional to capital stock. These properties result from the constancy of the sequence of replacement rates (δ_τ). Neither property holds for any other representation of the relative efficiency of capital goods of different ages. A fundamental result of renewal theory is that δ_τ tends to a constant value for almost any pattern of decline in efficiency.[25] Geometric decline in efficiency, resulting in a constant rate of replacement δ, may provide a useful approximation to replacement requirements and depreciation for a wide variety of patterns of decline in efficiency. Where this approximation is unsatisfactory, a complete accounting system for income and wealth in constant prices requires vintage accounts for capital goods quantities and prices.

Many different retirement distributions have been found useful in describing the retirement of physical disappearance of capital goods.[26] Considerably less evidence is available on the decline in efficiency of existing capital goods.[27] The available evidence arises from two sources—studies of replacement investment and studies of depreciation on capital goods. Geometric decline in efficiency has been employed by Hickman (1965) and by Hall and Jorgenson (1967, 1971) in studies of investment. This assumption is tested by Meyer and Kuh, who find no effect of the age distribution of capital stock in the determination of replacement investment.[28] Geometric decline in efficiency has been employed in the study of depreciation on capital goods by Cagan, Griliches, and Wykoff.[29] This assumption has been tested by Hall, who finds no effect on the age of a capital good in the determination of the rate of depreciation as measured from prices of capital goods of different vintages.[30] The available empirical evidence supports the use of geometric decline in efficiency as a useful approximation to replacement requirements and depreciation.

5.4.5 Alternative Accounting Systems

We have outlined the development of a complete system of income and wealth accounts in constant prices. Only the measurement of the output side of the production account and the asset side of the wealth account in constant prices are well established in social accounting practice. In the study of total factor productivity, attempts have been made to measure the input side of the production account in constant prices. Christensen and Jorgenson (1969, 1970) have applied the methods we have described for a simplified accounting system to the measurement of factor input in constant prices and the measurement of total factor productivity.

It is very useful to compare our accounting system with an alternative approach developed by Denison in his path-breaking monograph, *Sources of Economic Growth* (1962). Denison's monograph deals with output and input sides of the production account for the United States. Similar methods have been applied to data for a number of other countries in his book, *Why Growth Rates Differ* (1967). Denison takes gross national product in constant prices from the U.S. national accounts as a point of departure. He measures labor input along lines similar to those we outline below, weighting rates of growth of each type of labor input by relative shares in the values of total labor input to obtain the rate of growth of an index of labor input.[31] In comparing Denison's approach with our own, we concentrate on the measurement of capital input.

Denison points out that the construction of a capital input measure depends on the relative efficiency of capital goods of different ages:

In principle, the selection of a capital input measure should depend on the changes that occur in the ability of a capital good to contribute to net production as the good grows older (within the span of economic life). Use of net stock, with depreciation computed by the straight-line formula, would imply that this ability drops very rapidly—that it is reduced by one-fourth when one-fourth of the service life has passed and by nine-tenths when nine-tenths of the service life has passed. Use of gross stock would imply that this ability is constant throughout the service life of a capital good.[32] Denison adds: "I believe that net value typically declines more rapidly than does the ability of a capital good to contribute to production. . . On the other hand, the gross stock assumption of constant services throughout the life of an asset is extreme."[33]

Under Denison's gross stock assumption, relative efficiency is constant over the economic lifetime of the equipment:

$$d_\tau = 1 \, ; \quad \tau = 0, 1, \ldots, T - 1;$$

where T is the economic lifetime of the capital good. Under Denison's net stock assumption, efficiency declines linearly:

$$d_\tau = 1 - \frac{1}{T}\tau \, ; \quad \tau = 0, 1, \ldots, T - 1.$$

In Denison's *Sources of Economic Growth* gross stock is employed as a measure of the quantity of capital input. In *Why Growth Rates Differ* an arithmetic average of gross stock and net stock is employed;[34] the implied relative efficiency of capital goods is an average of constant and linearly declining relative efficiency:

$$d_\tau = 1 - \frac{1}{2T}\tau \, ; \quad \tau = 0, 1, \ldots, T - 1 \, .$$

Since Denison does not assume that the relative efficiency of capital goods declines geometrically, depreciation and replacement must be carefully distinguished in order to preserve consistency among production, income and expenditure, accumulation, and wealth accounts in constant prices. Depreciation is a component of the price of capital services. The value of capital services is equal to property income including depreciation. Replacement is the consequence of a decline in the efficiency of capital assets or, in Denison's language, the ability of a capital good to contribute to production. Unfortunately, a confusion between depreciation and replacement pervades Denison's treatment of the output and input sides of the production account and the measurement of capital stock. This confusion leads to a series of inconsistencies, making it impossible to incorporate Denison's measures of product and factor input in constant prices into a complete accounting system.

The first indication of confusion between depreciation and replacement is Denison's definition of net product: "Net product measures the amount a nation consumes plus the addition it makes to its capital stock. Stated another way, it is the amount of its output a nation could consume without changing its stock of capital."[35] The correct definition of net product is gross product less depreciation; this is the definition suggested by the second statement quoted above. The first statement defines net product as gross product less replacement, since the addition to capital stock or net capital formation is equal to investment less replacement. The two definitions are consistent if and only if depreciation is equal to replacement. Under any of Denison's assumptions about decline in relative efficiency, depreciation and replacement are not equal, so that his definition of net product is self-contradictory.

In *Why Growth Rates Differ* Denison measures capital consumption allowances on the basis of Bulletin F lives and the straight-line method.[36] Even under the assumption that relative efficiency or Denison's "ability to contribute to production" declines linearly, this estimate corresponds to replacement rather than depreciation. Denison reduces gross product by his estimate of capital consumption allowances to obtain his measure of net product.[37] This procedure employs the incorrect definition of net product as gross product less replacement. A similar procedure for calculating capital consumption allowances is employed in *Sources of Economic Growth.* Denison's confusion between depreciation and replacement carries over to the input side of the production account. His measure of net product is reduced by labor compensation to obtain property compensation net of capital consumption allowances. Thus, Denison's measure of property compensation is also calculated net of replacement rather than net of depreciation. This erroneous measure is allocated among capital inputs to obtain weights employed in measuring capital input as a component of factor input in constant prices. Denison's weights for different components of capital input are measured incorrectly; these weights should reflect property compensation less depreciation rather than property compensation less replacement.

A further difficulty with Denison's estimate of capital consumption allowances in *Why Growth Rates Differ* is that in estimating capital stock Denison assumes that the decline in efficiency is linear, but at half the straight-line rate. He uses the straight-line method to estimate capital consumption allowances; the resulting estimate is equal to neither depreciation nor replacement for the pattern of decline in efficiency he uses in estimating capital. In *Sources of Economic Growth* Denison assumes that relative efficiency is constant over the lifetime of a capital good.[38] Again, the straight-line estimates of capital consumption allowances are equal to neither depreciation nor replacement for the pattern of decline in efficiency underlying his estimate of capital. In both *Sources of Economic Growth* and *Why Growth Rates*

Differ the price and quantity components of the input side of the production account are mutually contradictory.

In our accounting system for capital input and property compensation, the price component of the flow of capital services is the sum of return per unit of capital, depreciation, and revaluation. In estimating the rate of return Denison omits revaluations of existing capital goods and fails to measure depreciation correctly.[39] His implied estimate of return per unit capital is erroneous. Denison omits capital gains and losses from the revaluation of assets in allocating property income among capital assets; so the weights for different components of capital input are measured incorrectly. The revaluation are required as part of the accumulation account for an accounting system that includes accumulation and wealth accounts. If Denison's measure of capital input were to be incorporated into a complete accounting system, the omission of revaluations from the price component of capital services would introduce an inconsistency between the production and the income and expenditure accounts on the one hand and the accumulation and wealth accounts on the other.

Denison's assumption about the decline in relative efficiency of capital goods can be incorporated into a complete accounting system along the lines we have suggested. Since he does not assume that efficiency declines geometrically, vintage accounts for quantities and prices of capital goods of every age at every point of time are required. Vintage data are essential even for the relatively limited objective of measuring net product; net product measurement requires an estimate of depreciation and estimation of depreciation requires vintage prices. The first step in implementing Denison's assumptions would be to assemble data on the acquisition prices of capital goods of every age at every point in time. The second step would be to estimate depreciation for goods of every vintage at every point of time from the vintage data on prices. This estimate of depreciation would replace Denison's estimate of capital consumption allowances in measuring net product and property compensation net of depreciation. The third step would be to estimate capital service prices by combining estimates of the return per unit of capital, depreciation, and revaluation of assets. These prices could be combined with Denison's estimates of capital stock to construct index numbers of the price and quantity of capital input.

We conclude that Denison's assumptions about the relative efficiency of capital goods of different ages can be incorporated into a complete accounting system for income and wealth in constant prices. A broader data base than that Denison has employed would be required. Denison's estimates of both the output and input sides of the production account would have to be revised substantially. To employ an approach that dispenses with vintage accounts for capital goods prices and quantities, like the approach Denison actually uses, it is necessary to assume that the decline in efficiency of capital goods is geometric. In the absence of vintage data the use of Denison's assumptions about relative efficiency leads to a series of inconsistencies in the construction of even a single account, the production account, in current and constant prices. If Denison's estimates of the production accounts were to be incorporated into a complete accounting system, these inconsistencies would ramify throughout the system.

In the United Nations *System of National Accounts*,[40] the construction of a production account in constant prices is discussed at some length. In the United Nations system capital stock is measured as gross stock, following Denison's practice in *Sources of Economic Growth*. Capital consumption allowances are measured by the straight-line method, again following Denison's practice. We conclude that the United Nations system of accounts in constant prices incorporates a production account similar to Denison's. We have already outlined the internal contradictions in Denison's production account; an accounting system incorporating a production account like Denison's would give rise to inconsistencies between the production and the income and expenditure accounts on the one hand and the accumulation and wealth accounts on the other. We conclude that the United Nations system provides a satisfactory solution to the problem of constructing accounts in constant prices only for the output side of the production account. Measurement of the other accounting magnitudes of the system in constant prices requires an extension of the perpetual inventory method like that we have outlined above.

5.5 Production Account

5.5.1 Introduction

In sections 5.3 and 5.4 our objective has been to develop methods for measuring income and wealth in constant prices. The task that remains is to present production, income and expenditure, accumulation, and wealth accounts in constant prices. To complete this task we must separate the values included in the accounts presented in section 5.2 into price and quantity components. For this purpose we employ the system of price and quantity index numbers discussed in section 5.3. This system is based on a discrete approximation to continuous Divisia index numbers of prices and quantities.

To construct a complete system of accounts in constant prices we must account for investment goods output, capital input, property compensation, capital formation, and wealth in a way that is internally consistent. For this purpose we have extended the perpetual inventory method to incorporate data on prices as well as quantities of capital goods by vintage. We have also presented a simplified version of the perpetual inventory method and its price counterpart, based on approximation of replacement rates for individual capital goods by a constant rate of replacement for each good. Our extension of the perpetual inventory method is presented in section 5.4.

In this section we present the production account for the U.S. private domestic sector in constant prices. In the following section we present income and expenditure, accumulation, and wealth accounts for the U.S. private national economy in constant prices. In section 5.7 we discuss possible extensions of our accounting system.

In constructing the production account in constant prices changes in the value of product and the value of factor outlay must be separated into price and quantity components. The ratio of the quantity of total product to the quantity of total factor input or, alternatively, the ratio of the price of total factor input to the price of total product is equal to total factor productivity. In addition to data on output and input the production account in constant prices includes data on total factor productivity.

5.5.2 Output and Labor Input

To construct a quantity index for gross product we first allocate the value of output between consumption and investment goods. Investment goods include durable goods and structures. Consumption goods include nondurable goods and services. Data for prices and quantities of both consumption and investment goods are included in the U.S. national accounts as part of gross national product. The product of the rest of the world and government sectors consists entirely of services. Price and quantity index numbers for the services of consumer and institutional durables are constructed as part of our imputation for the value of the services, described below.

The value of output from the point of view of the producing sector excludes certain indirect taxes and includes subsidies. Sales excise taxes must be allocated between consumption and investment goods output. Since a portion of each of these taxes is levied on intermediate goods, a completely satisfactory allocation would require a detailed interindustry analysis. We have allocated these taxes in proportion to the value of consumption and investment goods output. The price index for each type of output is implicit in the value and quantity of output included in gross national product. We construct price and quantity indexes of gross output by applying Divisia index numbers formulas to price and quantity data for consumption and investment goods product. The results are given in table 5.9.

To construct a quantity index for gross factor input we allocate the value of factor outlay between labor and capital input. The construction of a quantity index of labor input begins with data on the number of persons engaged in the private domestic sector. Persons engaged include full-time equivalent employees and proprietors. Our estimates for the nonfarm business sector are identical to those of the Office of Business Economics for full-time equivalent employees and proprietors. We add Kendrick's estimates of employment in agriculture to obtain total persons engaged.[41] To obtain a measure of labor input our next step is to estimate the number of man-hours worked. For this purpose we employ Kendrick's estimates of man-hours for the private domestic sector.[42]

Denoting the index of man-hours by L and the wage index by p_L, we first represent the value of labor input as the sum of the values of labor input for each category of labor:

$$p_L L = \sum p_{L,j} L_j,$$

where $p_{L,j}$ is the price of the jth type of labor, and L_j is the number of man-hours worked by workers of this type. Divisia indexes of the wage rate and man-hours worked are:

$$\frac{\dot{p}_L}{p_L} = \sum v_j \frac{\dot{p}_{L,j}}{p_{L,j}}, \quad \frac{\dot{L}}{L} = \sum v_j \frac{\dot{L}_j}{L_j},$$

where the weights (v_j) are the relative shares of each type of labor in the value of total labor input.

Table 5.9
Gross private domestic product, 1929–1969 (constant prices of 1958)

	Gross Private Domestic Product		Consumption Goods Product		Investment Goods Product		
Year	Price Index	Quantity Index	Price Index	Quantity Index	Price Index	Quantity Index	Relative Share
1929	0.556	187.5	0.566	133.7	0.508	56.1	.278
1930	0.536	169.8	0.547	129.5	0.489	41.5	.227
1931	0.489	156.6	0.497	125.8	0.453	31.2	.188
1932	0.420	132.5	0.423	114.6	0.407	17.8	.134
1933	0.418	130.3	0.421	111.6	0.403	18.6	.143
1934	0.440	141.7	0.445	116.6	0.414	25.2	.176
1935	0.447	151.8	0.453	121.8	0.418	30.5	.197
1936	0.455	170.3	0.465	130.2	0.414	41.3	.231
1937	0.471	181.1	0.476	137.8	0.441	44.5	.241
1938	0.460	171.8	0.461	138.4	0.448	34.2	.203
1939	0.458	186.4	0.460	143.7	0.441	43.8	.236
1940	0.463	202.8	0.465	150.7	0.446	53.5	.266
1941	0.503	230.6	0.497	159.1	0.504	73.2	.333
1942	0.563	250.3	0.545	171.2	0.588	80.9	.351
1943	0.626	268.3	0.625	171.7	0.617	98.1	.375
1944	0.631	283.0	0.647	181.4	0.594	103.1	.358
1945	0.636	279.5	0.667	187.4	0.569	92.7	.312
1946	0.701	271.5	0.728	193.0	0.643	77.3	.276
1947	0.787	277.5	0.807	191.2	0.748	85.8	.309
1948	0.826	295.8	0.851	201.8	0.778	93.6	.312
1949	0.796	295.3	0.800	203.6	0.791	91.2	.323
1950	0.827	326.9	0.843	212.8	0.800	114.0	.354
1951	0.876	349.1	0.884	226.0	0.862	123.0	.364
1952	0.897	357.7	0.907	234.4	0.879	123.0	.354
1953	0.906	375.9	0.922	244.6	0.878	131.1	.355
1954	0.915	373.2	0.932	247.5	0.886	125.3	.341
1955	0.932	405.4	0.953	261.5	0.893	144.0	.357
1956	0.951	415.8	0.956	272.3	0.943	143.4	.359
1957	0.978	422.6	0.974	280.8	0.988	141.7	.355
1958	1.000	419.7	1.000	289.2	1.000	130.6	.326
1959	1.023	447.8	1.028	302.8	1.012	145.1	.336
1960	1.034	459.8	1.046	312.5	1.009	147.4	.329
1961	1.039	469.6	1.052	323.6	1.011	145.8	.317
1962	1.051	499.3	1.066	338.9	1.018	160.5	.327
1963	1.062	521.0	1.081	351.6	1.021	169.5	.329
1964	1.074	551.6	1.096	370.6	1.029	181.3	.330
1965	1.090	587.5	1.113	391.5	1.041	196.5	.335
1966	1.121	627.4	1.149	417.1	1.062	210.9	.333
1967	1.146	645.6	1.170	436.2	1.095	209.5	.324
1968	1.177	678.2	1.202	455.1	1.125	223.4	.330
1969	1.228	703.4	1.258	471.3	1.164	232.5	.329

For each category of labor, total man-hours is the product of persons engaged, say n_j, and hours per person say h_j. Where N is the total number of persons engaged and H is the number of hours per man, the quantity index of labor input may be rewritten in the form:

$$\frac{\dot{L}}{L} = \sum v_j \left(\frac{\dot{n}_j}{n_j} - \frac{\dot{N}}{N} \right) + \sum v_j \left(\frac{\dot{h}_j}{h_j} - \frac{\dot{H}}{H} \right) + \left(\frac{\dot{N}}{N} + \frac{\dot{H}}{H} \right).$$

The first term in this expression represents the change in labor input per person engaged due to changes in the composition of the labor force. The second term represents the change in labor input per hour due to changes in the relative number of hours worked per man among components of the labor force. The last term is the change in total man-hours. Adjustments for changes in the composition of the labor force and the relative number of hours worked per man are required to convert an index of man-hours into an index of the quantity of labor input.

Price and quantity indexes of output require data on the prices and quantities of individual outputs. Similarly, price and quantity indexes of labor input require data on the wages and hours worked for different types of workers. It would be desirable to distinguish among hours worked by workers classified by sex, race, years of schooling, occupation, age, and so on. Price and quantity indexes of labor input would be obtained by applying Divisia index number formulas to price and quantity data for different types of workers. The data available for construction of price and quantity indexes of labor input are very limited. We distinguish among different categories of labor by years of schooling completed. We employ the data compiled by Jorgenson and Griliches and extended by Griliches to estimate the change in labor input due to changes in the educational composition of the labor force.[43]

Kendrick distinguishes among different categories of labor by industry of employment (1961a). Jorgenson and Griliches distinguish among different categories by years of schooling completed (1967). Our adjustment of the index of man-hours is limited to changes in the quality of labor input due to changes in the educational composition of the labor force. Adjustments for changes in the distribution of the labor force by age and sex would require more detailed data. We have made no adjustment for changes in the relative number of hours worked by different types of workers. Estimates of the likely effect of additional adjustments of each type are given by Jorgenson and Griliches (1972a).

Denison (1961, 1962) has observed that the intensity of effort may vary with the number of hours worked per week. Correction of the quantity index of labor input to reflect changes in intensity of effort would require estimates of wages and man-hours, classified by the number of hours worked per week. Denison suggests that the stock of labor input provides an upper bound for labor input corrected for variations in intensity while the number of man-hours provides a lower bound. He estimates effective labor input by correcting man-hours for variations in labor intensity. We have employed Denison's adjustment for the intensity of effort applied to actual hours per man rather than potential hours per man. The number of persons engaged and hours per worker, together with price and quantity indexes of labor input for 1929–1969, are given for the private domestic economy in table 5.10.

5.5.3 Capital Input

Our estimates of capital input, property compensation, depreciation, replacement, and capital assets are based on an extension of the perpetual inventory method to incorporate data on prices as well as quantities of investment goods by vintage. We estimate capital service prices, depreciation, and acquisition prices for capital goods of different vintages on the basis of the assumption that the decline in efficiency of capital goods is geometric in form. We estimate capital stock, replacement, and quantities of capital goods of different vintages on the basis of the same assumption. Estimates of capital input, property compensation, depreciation, and capital assets in constant prices require data on both prices and quantities of capital goods by vintage. We continue our discussion of the production account for the U.S. private domestic economy in constant prices by describing the construction of prices and quantities of capital input.[44]

The starting point for a quantity index of capital input is a perpetual inventory estimate of the stock of each type of capital, based on past investments in constant prices. At each point of time the stock of each type of capital is the sum of stocks remaining from past investments of each vintage. Under the assumption that efficiency of capital goods declines geometrically, the rate of replacement, say δ, is a constant. Capital stock at the end of every period may be estimated from investment and capital stock at the beginning of the period:

Table 5.10
Private domestic labor input, 1929–1969 (constant prices of 1958)

Year	Private Domestic Persons Engaged (millions)	Private Domestic Hours per Person (thousands per year)	Private Domestic Labor Input	
			Price Index	Quantity Index
1929	43.0	2.645	0.338	178.8
1930	40.8	2.600	0.326	170.6
1931	37.6	2.579	0.290	163.2
1932	34.2	2.512	0.254	146.1
1933	34.2	2.488	0.238	146.0
1934	36.7	2.281	0.257	152.6
1935	37.9	2.327	0.267	159.3
1936	39.8	2.380	0.281	168.7
1937	41.6	2.420	0.303	177.4
1938	39.1	2.350	0.298	166.6
1939	40.5	2.389	0.305	174.0
1940	42.2	2.391	0.314	182.1
1941	45.8	2.402	0.351	198.6
1942	48.1	2.458	0.411	211.6
1943	48.7	2.517	0.472	216.7
1944	47.5	2.549	0.505	215.5
1945	46.0	2.487	0.520	208.5
1946	48.6	2.372	0.543	220.1
1947	50.9	2.314	0.597	230.7
1948	52.0	2.287	0.640	236.0
1949	50.2	2.279	0.651	228.9
1950	51.7	2.250	0.689	236.0
1951	53.7	2.242	0.746	246.5
1952	54.1	2.239	0.786	249.3
1953	54.9	2.208	0.832	252.9
1954	53.2	2.185	0.854	244.9
1955	54.5	2.210	0.887	253.7
1956	55.6	2.197	0.935	259.5
1957	55.5	2.170	0.979	259.4
1958	53.7	2.150	1.000	252.8
1959	54.8	2.175	1.040	263.0
1960	55.4	2.177	1.070	267.8
1961	54.9	2.160	1.098	266.3
1962	55.8	2.163	1.138	272.9
1963	56.3	2.160	1.173	277.0
1964	57.4	2.163	1.221	284.1
1965	59.2	2.166	1.262	294.4
1966	61.3	2.152	1.323	306.8
1967	62.3	2.154	1.366	314.7
1968	63.8	2.151	1.447	324.6
1969	65.6	2.139	1.537	334.9

$$K_t = A_t + (1 - \delta)K_{t-1} ,$$

where K_t is end of period capital stock, A_t the quantity of investment and K_{t-1} the capital stock at the beginning of the period.

For each type of capital included in our accounts we prepare perpetual inventory estimates of the stock as follows: First, we obtain a benchmark estimate of capital stock from the data on national wealth in constant prices. Second, we deflate the investment series from the U.S. national accounts to obtain investment in constant prices. Third, we choose an estimate of the rate of replacement from data on the lifetimes of capital goods. Finally, we estimate capital stock in every period by applying the perpetual inventory method described above. We have prepared estimates for the stocks of consumer durables, nonresidential structures, producer durables, residential structures, nonfarm inventories, farm inventories, and land. Benchmark estimates of capital stocks in 1929, expressed in constant prices of 1958, rates of replacement, and price indexes for each type of capital are presented in table 5.11.

Our price indexes for consumer and producer durables and for farm and nonfarm inventories are taken directly from the U.S. national accounts. These indexes are the implicit deflators for investment in each category from estimates of gross private domestic investment in current and constant prices. We replace the deflators from the national accounts for residential and nonresidential structures by the "constant cost 2" construction price index employed in the *Capital Stock Study* of the Office of Business Economics.[45] This index results from an attempt to correct implicit deflators for structures for changes in the quality of structures produced. In the *Capital Stock Study* the "constant cost 2" price index is employed to deflate data on investment in nonresidential structures. We employ Goldsmith's price index for land through 1958, extrapolating this index from 1958 to 1969 by assuming a constant rate of growth of the price of land at 6.9 percent per year.[46] Our price indexes for farm and nonfarm inventory stocks[47] are based on unpublished estimates of the Office of Business Economics.[48]

Rates of replacement for inventories and land are zero by definition. To estimate rates of replacement for structures and durables we employ double declining balance replacement rates from the *Capital Stock Study*. For each asset the rate of replacement is $\delta = 2/T$ where T is the mean service life for the asset given in the *Capital Stock Study*.[49]

Table 5.11
Benchmarks, rates of replacement, and price indexes employed in estimating capital

Asset Class	1929 Benchmark (billions of 1958 dollars)	Replace-ment Rate	Deflator
1. Consumer Durables	74.9	.200	Implicit deflator, national product accounts[a]
2. Nonresidential structures	148.2	.056	Constant cost 2 deflator[b]
3. Producer durables	77.5	.138	Implicit deflator, national product accounts[a]
4. Residential structures	214.0	.039	Implicit deflator, national product accounts[a]
5. Nonfarm inventories	57.1	—	Investment: Implicit deflator, national product accounts[c] Assets: Implicit deflator, OBE[d]
6. Farm inventories	21.9	—	Investment: Implicit deflator, national product accounts[c] Assets: Implicit deflator, OBE[d]
7. Land	321.6	—	Goldsmith[e]

[a] OBE, NIP (1966, table 8.1)

[b] Haavelmo (1960)

[c] OBE, NIP (1966, tables 1.1 and 1.2)

[d] Unpublished OBE sources

[e] Goldsmith (1965, tables A–5 and A–6)

Our estimates of replacement rates incorporate both retirements of capital goods and the decline in efficiency of existing capital goods. In the *Capital Stock Study* investment in nonresidential structures is divided into fifty-two categories. Although it would be possible to compile data on capital input for each of these categories separately, we have limited our estimates to total producer durables and total nonresidential structures. The replacement rate for each group is estimated as weighted average of replacement rates for the individual components, using relative shares of the value of each category in the total value of capital stock as weights.

Residential structures may be divided into farm and nonfarm components. We estimate service lives for each component on the basis of Bulletin F lifetimes; the replacement rate for residential structures is a weighted average of double declining balance replacement rates with weights based on the relative shares of farm and nonfarm residential structures in the total.[50] We assume that the rate of replacement for consumer durables is 0.200; this estimate was developed by de Leeuw in estimating stocks of consumer durables (undated memorandum).

We have described the measurement of capital stocks for each category of capital goods by the perpetual inventory method. Our next step is to describe the measurement of capital service prices by the price counterpart of the perpetual inventory method. For property with an active rental market the price of capital services may be observed directly as the rental price of the corresponding asset. A substantial portion of the range of capital goods employed in the U.S. private domestic sector has an active rental market; most classes of structures can be rented and a rental market exists for many types of equipment, especially large pieces of equipment such as aircraft, trucks, construction equipment, computers, and so on. Unfortunately, very little effort has been devoted to compiling data on rental rates for either structures or equipment. Data on the flow of rent payments among industrial sectors have been compiled by Creamer (1971). However, both current price and constant price flows are required for direct measurement of the price and quantity of capital services by class of asset.

Given market rental prices by class of asset, the implicit rental values paid by owners for the use of their property may be imputed by applying rental rates to capital stocks employed by owner-users. This method for imputation is used to estimate the price and quantity of capital services from owner-occupied dwellings in the U.S. national accounts. Data on rental prices of dwellings occupied by renters are employed to impute the rental value of dwellings occupied by owners. The total rental value of owner-occupied dwellings is divided among taxes, capital consumption allowances, interest payments, and net rent. A somewhat similar but not identical method of imputation is used for the space rental value of institutional buildings. Capital consumption allowances and interest payments by institutions are estimated as components of imputed space rental value. Net rent is omitted from the imputation, but this component of space rental value could be estimated from the market rental prices of space comparable to that used by institutions. The main obstacle to broader application of this method of imputation is the lack of appropriate data on market rental prices.

An alternative method for imputation of the rental value of owner-utilized assets is included in our extension of the perpetual inventory method to incorporate data on prices of capital goods by vintage. For each type of capital included in our accounts we prepare perpetual inventory estimates of acquisition prices, service prices, depreciation, and revaluation by vintage. Under our assumption of geometrically declining relative efficiency of capital goods, perpetual inventory estimates of prices can be simplified considerably. First, beginning with acquisition prices for new capital goods of each type, the acquisition prices for goods of each vintage decline geometrically with vintage. The formula for the value of capital stock,

$$q_{A,t}K_t = \sum q_{A,t}(1-\delta)^{\tau} A_{t-\tau} = \sum q_{A,t,\tau} A_{t-\tau} \, ,$$

may be regarded as the sum of past investments weighted by relative efficiency and evaluated at the acquisition price for new capital goods or, equivalently, as the sum of the past investments evaluated at the acquisition price for the corresponding vintage of capital.

Second, under our assumption that replacement rates are constant, depreciation is proportional to the value of beginning of period capital stock:

$$q_{D,t}K_{t-1} = \delta q_{A,t} K_{t-1} \, .$$

This measure of depreciation can also be obtained by estimating depreciation separately for each vintage and summing over vintages:

$$\sum q_{D,t,\tau} A_{t-\tau-1} \parallel \sum \delta q_{A,t,\tau} A_{t-\tau-1} = \delta q_{A,t} K_{t-1} \, .$$

Similarly, revaluation is equal to the change in the acquisition price of new capital goods multiplied by beginning of period capital stock. This measure can also be obtained by estimating revaluation separately for each vintage and summing over vintages:

$$(q_{A,t} - q_{A,t-1})K_{t-1} = \sum (q_{A,t,\tau} - q_{A,t-1,\tau-1})A_{t-\tau-1} .$$

In the absence of taxation, the value of capital services is the sum of the cost of capital and depreciation, less revaluation:

$$q_{K,t}K_{t-1} = [q_{A,t-1}r_t + q_{A,t}\delta - (q_{A,t} - q_{A,t-1})]K_{t-1} .$$

We can obtain this expression by estimating the capital service price for capital goods of each vintage and summing over vintages:

$$q_{K,t}K_{t-1} = \sum (1-\delta)^{\tau} q_{K,t}A_{t-\tau-1} = \sum q_{K,t,\tau}A_{t-\tau-1} .$$

Given the quantity of each type of asset held, the acquisition price, and the rate of replacement, only the rate of return remains to be determined in compiling data on the price and quantity of capital services. In measuring the rate of return, differences in the tax treatment of property compensation from different sectors must be taken into account.

For tax purposes the private domestic sector of the U.S. economy can be divided into corporate business, noncorporate business, and households and nonprofit institutions. Households and institutions are not subject to direct taxes on the flow of capital services they utilize. Noncorporate business is subject to personal income taxes on income generated from capital services, while corporate business is subject to both corporate and personal income taxes. Households and corporate and noncorporate business are subject to indirect taxes on property income through taxes levied on the value of property. In order to take these differences in taxation into account we first allocate each class of assets among the four sectors of the U.S. private domestic economy—corporations, noncorporate business, households, and institutions. The relative proportions of capital stock by asset class for each sector for 1958 are given in table 5.12.

For a sector not subject to either direct or indirect taxes on property income, the value of property compensation is equal to the value of capital services, i.e., property compensation = $q_{K,t}K_{t-1}$. This formula is appropriate for a single class of assets. For several classes of assets, property compensation is the sum of price times quantity of capital

Table 5.12
Relative proportions of capital stock by asset class and sector, 1958

Asset Class	Sector			
	Corporate Business	Non-corporate Business	House-holds & Insti-tutions	Total
1. Consumer Durables	—	—	.138	0.138
2. Nonresidential structures	.104	.027	.014	0.145
3. Producer durables	.090	.041	.002	0.132
4. Residential structures	.019	.009	.211	0.238
5. Nonfarm inventories	.065	.013	—	0.078
6. Farm inventories	—	.021	—	0.021
7. Land	.047	.124	.077	0.247
Total	.325	.234	.442	1.000

services for all classes of assets. We assume that the rate of return is the same for all assets held by a given sector; rates of return can be estimated for each flow of property compensation that can be measured separately. Flows of property compensation can be separately measured for industry groups or even for individual firms.

Given property compensation, the acquisition prices of new capital goods ($q_{A,t}$), the rate of replacement (δ), and capital stocks estimated by the perpetual inventory method (K_{t-1}), we can solve for the rate of return by substituting the capital service price,

$$q_{K,t} = q_{A,t-1}r_t + q_{A,t}\delta - (q_{A,t} - q_{A,t-1}),$$

into the expression for property compensation. In this expression only the rate of return is unknown and we may solve for the rate of return in terms of the observed data, obtaining:

$$r_t = \frac{\text{Property compensation} - q_{A,t}\delta K_{t-1} + (q_{A,t} - q_{A,t-1})K_{t-1}}{q_{A,t-1}K_{t-1}}.$$

The rate of return is the ratio of property compensation less depreciation plus revaluation of capital assets to the value of capital stock at the beginning of the period. For more than one capital good we estimate depreciation, revaluation, and the value of capital stock by summing over all capital goods.

The formula for the rate of return given above is appropriate only with no direct or indirect taxes on property compensation. For the

U.S. private domestic economy, this formula can be applied only to nonprofit institutions. We discuss the imputation of the value of the capital services utilized by these institutions below. Households hold consumer durables and owner-occupied dwellings. The property compensation associated with these assets is not taxed directly; however, part of the income is taxed indirectly through property taxes. To incorporate property taxes into our estimates of the price and quantity of capital services we add taxes to the cost of capital, depreciation, and revaluation, obtaining the capital service price:

$$q_{K,t} = q_{A,t-1}r_t + q_{A,t}\delta - (q_{A,t} - q_{A,t-1}) + q_{A,t}\tau_t ,$$

where τ_t is the rate of property taxation. To estimate the rate of return we proceed as before, substituting the capital service price including property taxes into the expression for property compensation. The rate of return is the ratio of property compensation less depreciation plus revaluation of capital assets less taxes to the value of capital stock at the beginning of the period.

In measuring the capital service flow utilized by households and institutions we first estimate the value of the services of owner-occupied residential real estate, including both land and structures. This value is obtained directly from the U.S. national accounts. Using prices of acquisition for land and residential structures, the corresponding stocks in constant prices, the rate of replacement for structures, and the value of owner-occupied housing services, we estimate the implicit rate of return for the household sector. We assume that rates of return for consumer durables and for producer durables, nonresidential structures, and land utilized by institutions are the same as for owner-occupied residential real estate. This assumption results in a single rate of return for households and institutions. Adding the cost of capital and depreciation, subtracting revaluation for assets held by households and institutions, and adding property taxes for the household sector, we obtain the imputed value of property compensation, gross of taxes, for households and institutions. The imputed value of the services of owner-occupied dwellings is identical to the value of the flow of services from these dwellings from the U.S. national accounts.

Given the rate of return for households and institutions, we can construct estimates of capital service prices for each class of assets held by households and institutions—land held by households and institutions, residential structures, nonresidential structures, producer durables, and consumer durables. These estimates require acquisition prices for each capital good, rates of replacement, rates of taxation for assets held by households, and the rate of return for the sector as a whole. We employ separate effective tax rates for owner-occupied residential property, both land and structures, and for consumer durables. Corresponding to these price data we can construct estimates of capital service quantities for each class of assets. Price and quantity measures of capital input by class of asset can be combined into price and quantity index numbers of capital input by households and institutions, utilizing the Divisa index number formulas presented in section 5.3 above.

Our measure of the gross output of the private domestic sector of the U.S. economy differs from that of the U.S. national accounts in the treatment of consumer and institutional durables and institutional real estate. We assign personal consumption expenditures on durables to gross investment rather than consumption. This change leaves the product of the private domestic sector unchanged. We add the service flow from consumer and institutional durables to the value of output and the value of capital input. We also add the net rent component of the services of institutional real estate to values of both output and input. The values of these service flows enter the product and factor outlay accounts given in table 5.1 above and represent net additions to the value of gross product of the private domestic sector from the U.S. national accounts.

Our method for estimating the prices and quantities of capital services in the noncorporate sector is similar to the method we have described for households and institutions. For the noncorporate sector we estimate property compensation directly as the sum of income originating in business, other than income originating in corporate business and government enterprises and net rent of owner-occupied dwellings, less labor compensation in the noncorporate sector, including imputed labor compensation of proprietors and unpaid family workers, plus noncorporate capital consumption allowances, less allowances for owner-occupied dwellings and institutional structures, and plus indirect business taxes allocated to the noncorporate sector. We also allocate the statistical discrepancy to noncorporate property compensation.

To obtain an estimate of the noncorporate rate of return we deduct property taxes from noncorporate property compensation, add revaluation of assets, subtract depreciation, and divide the result by the value of noncorporate assets at the beginning of the period. The noncorporate rate of return is gross of personal income taxes on noncorporate property compensation. Property compensation of households and institutions is not subject to the personal income tax.

The value of property compensation in the noncorporate sector is equal to the value of the flow of capital services from residential and nonresidential structures, producer durable equipment, farm and nonfarm inventories, and land held by the sector. All farm inventories are assigned to the noncorporate sector. Given the noncorporate rate of return, estimated from noncorporate property compensation by the method outlined above, and given data on prices of acquisition, stocks, tax rates, and replacement rates for each class of assets, we can estimate capital service prices for each class of assets held by the noncorporate sector. Quantity data on capital services for each class of assets are constructed by the perpetual inventory method. Price and quantity measures of capital input by class of asset can be combined into price and quantity index numbers of capital input by noncorporate business, using Divisia index number formulas as before.

We next consider the measurement of prices and quantities of capital services for corporate business. We measure corporate property compensation as income originating in corporate business, less compensation of employees, plus corporate capital consumption allowances, plus business transfer payments, plus the indirect business taxes allocated to the corporate sector. To obtain an estimate of the corporate rate of return we must take into account the corporate income tax. The capital service price, modified to incorporate income tax and indirect business taxes, becomes:

$$q_{K,t} = \left[\frac{1 - u_t z_t - k_t + y_t}{1 - u_t}\right] [q_{A,t-1} r_t + q_{A,t}\delta - (q_{A,t} - q_{A,t-1})] + q_{A,t}\tau_t ,$$

where indirect business taxes $q_{A,t}\tau_t$ are deducted from corporate property compensation before taxes as an expense, u_t is the corporate tax rate, z_t is the present value of depreciation allowances on one dollar's worth of investment, k_t the investment tax credit, and $y_t = k_t u_t z_t$.[51] The variable y_t is set equal to zero for all years but 1962 and 1963; it is used in accounting for the fact that the investment tax credit was deducted from the value of an asset for depreciation in those years. The tax credit is different from zero only for producer durables. Depreciation allowances are different from zero only for durables and structures.

Our method for estimating the corporate rate of return is the same as for the noncorporate rate of return. Property compensation in the corporate sector is the sum of the value of services from residential and nonresidential structures, producer durable equipment, nonfarm inventories, and land held by that sector. To estimate the rate of return in the corporate sector we require estimates of the variables that describe the corporate tax structure—the effective corporate tax rate, the present value of depreciation allowances, and the investment tax credit. We obtain estimates of all the variables—acquisition prices and stocks of assets, rates of replacement, and variables describing the tax structure—that enter the value of capital services except, of course, for the rate of return. We then solve for the rate of return in terms of these variables and total property compensation.

Our estimate of the effective rate of the corporate income tax is obtained as the ratio of federal and state and local corporate profits tax liability plus the investment tax credit to corporate property income less taxes on corporate property and the imputed value of depreciation allowances for tax purposes. Imputed depreciation differs from depreciation for tax purposes in reflecting changes in the present value of future depreciation allowances as well as the current flow of depreciation allowances. The present value of depreciation deductions on new investment depends on depreciation formulas allowed for tax purposes, the lifetimes of assets used in calculating depreciation, and the rate of return. We assume that the rate of return used for discounting future depreciation allowances in the corporate sector is constant at 10 percent. Our estimate of the effective rate of the investment tax credit is based on estimates of the tax credit claimed by corporations. The effective rate is the investment tax credit divided by investment in producer durable equipment by corporations.

To estimate the rate of return in the corporate sector our first step is to subtract property taxes from total property compensation before taxes. The second step is to subtract federal and state and local corporate profits tax liability. We then add revaluation of assets, subtract depreciation, and divide the result by the value of corporate assets at the beginning of the period. The corporate rate of return is gross of personal income taxes, but net of the corporate income tax. We estimate the price of capital services for each asset employed in the corporate sector by substituting the corporate rate of return into the corresponding formula for the price of capital services. These formulas also depend on acquisition prices of capital assets, rates of replacement, and variables describing the tax structure. Quantity data for each class of assets are constructed by the perpetual inventory method. Price and quantity indexes of capital input by class of asset are combined into price and quantity indexes of capital input for the corporate sector, utilizing Divisia index number formulas.

In separating changes in the value of capital input into price and quantity components we preserve the accounting identity that property compensation for each sector of the U.S. private domestic economy is equal to the value of all capital services utilized in that sector. Denoting the index of capital input by K and the capital service price index by p_K, total property compensation is the sum of values of capital input for each category of capital:

$$p_K K = \sum p_{K,j} K_j ,$$

where $p_{K,j}$ is the price of the jth type of capital service and K_j is the quantity of capital of this type. Divisia indexes of the capital service price and capital input are:

$$\frac{\dot{p}_K}{p_K} = \sum v_j \frac{\dot{p}_{K,j}}{p_{K,j}}, \qquad \frac{\dot{K}}{K} = \sum v_j \frac{\dot{K}_j}{K_j},$$

where the weights are the relative shares of each type of capital input in total property compensation.

We assume that the rate of return is the same for all assets within a given sector. This rate of return is inferred from the value of property compensation, acquisition prices and stocks of capital goods, rates of replacement, and variables describing the tax structure. To obtain price and quantity indexes of capital input for the private domestic sector as a whole we apply the Divisia index formulas to Divisia price and quantity indexes for each of the three subsectors—corporations, noncorporate business, and households and institutions. By the reproductive property of Divisia index numbers the resulting price and quantity indexes are equivalent to Divisia indexes computed from data on prices and quantities of capital goods distinguished by class of asset and sector. Price and quantity indexes of capital services for corporations, noncorporate business, households and institutions, and the U.S. private domestic sector as a whole are given for 1929–1969 in table 5.13.

Table 5.13
Gross private domestic capital input, 1929–1969 (constant prices of 1958)

	Corporate Capital Input		Noncorporate Capital Input		Household Capital Input		Private Domestic Capital Input	
Year	Price Index	Quantity Index	Price Index	Quantity Index	Price Index	Quantity Index	Price Index	Quantity Index
1929	.070	261.7	.052	204.6	.053	280.9	.057	765.8
1930	.056	268.2	.029	210.2	.050	285.1	.045	782.4
1931	.039	267.9	.025	210.9	.048	279.8	.038	776.2
1932	.026	260.0	.011	216.9	.035	270.2	.024	758.1
1933	.025	242.6	.013	211.2	.043	254.1	.028	714.3
1934	.040	228.0	.017	204.5	.044	240.5	.034	676.6
1935	.048	220.8	.025	209.6	.041	232.5	.038	661.5
1936	.059	216.8	.031	210.3	.047	231.6	.046	655.9
1937	.063	219.3	.032	213.2	.046	238.1	.047	667.6
1938	.053	224.9	.029	220.6	.046	244.6	.043	686.4
1939	.060	220.6	.034	220.3	.048	242.6	.048	678.7
1940	.076	220.7	.038	221.9	.048	247.3	.054	684.5
1941	.099	227.3	.051	225.0	.048	256.8	.066	704.0
1942	.119	239.6	.065	230.2	.040	269.5	.073	735.7
1943	.137	239.0	.074	228.5	.061	261.6	.090	728.3
1944	.139	234.5	.094	224.6	.065	250.4	.098	710.8
1945	.123	231.1	.103	223.6	.075	239.0	.099	697.4
1946	.110	234.5	.103	223.9	.094	232.0	.102	695.8
1947	.133	252.9	.095	229.3	.099	255.9	.108	744.1
1948	.155	272.1	.100	235.1	.098	285.4	.117	799.3
1949	.143	288.1	.089	245.9	.074	313.3	.101	852.4
1950	.165	295.0	.098	254.0	.101	341.6	.121	891.0
1951	.177	310.6	.117	266.2	.093	383.5	.128	955.7
1952	.163	331.0	.107	274.6	.101	408.2	.123	1,010.0
1953	.162	344.3	.101	279.4	.108	426.8	.124	1,047.1
1954	.157	357.0	.098	284.1	.108	452.8	.121	1,090.2
1955	.184	365.3	.098	288.2	.119	476.6	.136	1,125.4
1956	.178	382.5	.089	294.7	.114	514.5	.129	1,187.1
1957	.175	402.5	.096	298.3	.112	540.2	.129	1,239.5
1958	.162	418.1	.111	302.0	.117	562.0	.130	1,282.0
1959	.187	423.7	.100	304.6	.130	574.0	.142	1,302.2
1960	.182	437.2	.096	309.1	.133	598.7	.140	1,346.1
1961	.180	452.6	.104	313.4	.132	620.9	.141	1,389.8
1962	.197	463.1	.114	316.9	.136	637.5	.150	1,421.3
1963	.202	479.7	.115	323.5	.142	663.5	.155	1,471.5
1964	.214	497.4	.115	330.8	.146	695.0	.161	1,528.8
1965	.231	520.1	.125	338.8	.146	731.2	.168	1,597.5
1966	.239	549.5	.140	349.7	.152	775.7	.177	1,684.1
1967	.224	590.0	.145	359.6	.153	819.7	.174	1,783.9
1968	.232	620.9	.140	368.8	.155	856.4	.176	1,864.0
1969	.230	650.2	.136	379.3	.164	903.2	.179	1,952.4

5.5.4 Total Factor Productivity

We construct price and quantity index numbers for total factor input by combining Divisia indexes of labor and capital input into a Divisia index of total factor input. The weights for labor and capital are the relative shares of labor and property compensation in the value of total factor outlay. Price and quantity index numbers for gross private domestic product may be represented in the form:

$$\frac{\dot{p}}{p} = v_L \frac{\dot{p}_L}{p_L} + v_K \frac{\dot{p}_K}{p_K},$$

$$\frac{\dot{X}}{X} = v_L \frac{\dot{L}}{L} + v_K \frac{\dot{K}}{K},$$

where p is the price index for total factor input, X is the quantity index, v_L is the relative share of labor, and v_K the relative share of capital. Discrete approximations to these continuous Divisia indexes for the price and quantity of total factor input for the U.S. private domestic economy are given for 1929–1969 in table 5.14.

Total factor productivity is defined as the ratio of real product to real factor input or, equivalently, as the ratio of the price of factor input to the product price.[52] Growth in total factor productivity may be regarded as an increase in the efficiency of the use of input to produce output or as a decline in the cost of input required to produce a given value of output. We may define a Divisia index of total factor productivity, say P, as :

$$\frac{\dot{P}}{P} = \frac{\dot{Y}}{Y} - \frac{\dot{X}}{X},$$

where Y is the quantity index of total output and X is the quantity index of total factor input. Equivalently, the index of total factor productivity may be defined as:

$$\frac{\dot{P}}{P} = \frac{\dot{p}}{p} - \frac{\dot{q}}{q},$$

where p is the price index of total factor input and q is the price index of output. A discrete approximation to the Divisia index of total factor productivity is given in table 5.15. For comparison, indexes of total factor productivity for a number of alternative conventions for the measurement of total factor input are also included in this table.

Table 5.14
Gross private domestic factor input, 1929–1969 (constant prices of 1958)

	Gross Private Domestic Factor Input		
Year	Price Index	Quantity Index	Property Outlay, Relative Share
1929	0.376	277.5	.419
1930	0.335	272.1	.389
1931	0.290	264.0	.382
1932	0.228	243.8	.333
1933	0.228	238.7	.362
1934	0.259	240.7	.370
1935	0.277	245.2	.373
1936	0.306	253.2	.389
1937	0.324	263.1	.370
1938	0.310	255.5	.374
1939	0.327	261.4	.379
1940	0.348	269.7	.392
1941	0.403	287.3	.399
1942	0.464	303.8	.383
1943	0.546	307.2	.390
1944	0.589	303.2	.391
1945	0.602	295.0	.390
1946	0.624	304.8	.372
1947	0.678	321.8	.369
1948	0.729	335.3	.382
1949	0.698	337.0	.366
1950	0.774	349.3	.399
1951	0.829	368.7	.399
1952	0.845	379.4	.389
1953	0.878	388.1	.382
1954	0.884	386.4	.388
1955	0.945	399.8	.404
1956	0.955	413.9	.387
1957	0.982	420.8	.385
1958	1.000	419.7	.398
1959	1.059	432.5	.403
1960	1.073	443.0	.398
1961	1.091	447.2	.401
1962	1.145	458.0	.408
1963	1.181	468.6	.413
1964	1.226	483.2	.415
1965	1.275	502.4	.420
1966	1.337	526.2	.423
1967	1.352	547.1	.419
1568	1.407	567.3	.412
1969	1.467	589.0	.404

Table 5.15
Total factor productivity, 1929–1969 (1958 = 1.000)

Year	Labor Services and Capital Services	Labor Services and Capital Stock	Unweighted Man-hours and Capital Stock
1929	0.674	0.637	0.519
1930	0.623	0.590	0.487
1931	0.592	0.560	0.475
1932	0.543	0.512	0.438
1933	0.545	0.511	0.439
1934	0.589	0.547	0.489
1935	0.619	0.575	0.511
1936	0.673	0.624	0.549
1937	0.688	0.641	0.560
1938	0.673	0.629	0.560
1939	0.713	0.667	0.591
1940	0.752	0.704	0.625
1941	0.802	0.754	0.669
1942	0.823	0.777	0.686
1943	0.873	0.823	0.722
1944	0.933	0.878	0.773
1945	0.948	0.892	0.796
1946	0.891	0.841	0.773
1947	0.863	0.819	0.765
1948	0.882	0.847	0.798
1949	0.877	0.847	0.802
1950	0.936	0.909	0.867
1951	0.947	0.924	0.887
1952	0.943	0.924	0.890
1953	0.969	0.952	0.924
1954	0.966	0.953	0.930
1955	1.014	1.003	0.980
1956	1.005	0.998	0.980
1957	1.004	1.001	0.991
1958	1.000	1.000	1.000
1959	1.036	1.036	1.040
1960	1.038	1.042	1.050
1961	1.050	1.057	1.073
1962	1.091	1.100	1.120
1963	1.112	1.125	1.151
1964	1.142	1.160	1.191
1965	1.169	1.195	1.230
1966	1.192	1.227	1.270
1967	1.180	1.224	1.274
1968	1.196	1.247	1.305
1969	1.195	1.254	1.319

Solow (1960) uses a stock concept of capital input, omitting changes in the quantity of capital due to changes in the composition of capital input. Denison (1962) distinguishes among residential real estate, farm capital, and all other capital input. Since this breakdown of capital input does not coincide with sectors distinguished by a legal form of organization, Denison's measure fails to take account of differences in rates of return due to differences in the tax structure. Denison omits revaluation of assets in estimating rates of return and fails to account for the quantity of capital and depreciation in an internally consistent way. Kendrick (1961a) adjusts capital input for changes in the industrial composition of capital stock. This breakdown of capital input also fails to capture differences in rates of return due to the tax structure.

Solow employs unweighted man-hours as a measure of labor input, omitting the effects of changes in the composition of the labor force on the quantity of labor input. Denison weights persons engaged by an index of labor quality that incorporates the effects of growth in educational attainment, but differs in a number of details from the index we have used. Kendrick adjusts labor input for changes in the industrial composition of man-hours worked. For comparison with our index of total factor productivity we present indexes based on man-hours and capital stock and based on our index of labor input and capital stock. The first of these indexes provides an approximation to the conventions for measuring total factor productivity used by Solow. The second provides an approximation to the conventions employed by Denison. It is obvious from a comparison of the alternative estimates of total factor productivity given in table 5.15 that the results are very sensitive to the choice of methods for measuring real factor input.

Finally, to evaluate the relative importance of growth in real factor input and growth in total factor productivity as sources of economic growth, we present the relative productivity as sources of economic growth, we present the relative proportion of growth in real factor input. Geometric average annual rates of growth are given for real product and real factor input for 1929–1949 and 1949–1969 in table 5.16. The relative proportion of growth in total factor productivity in the growth of real product is also given.

Table 5.16
Relative importance of productivity change, 1929–1969 (average annual rates of growth)

	1929–49	1949–69	1929–69
Gross private domestic product			
Real product	2.28	4.34	3.31
Real factor input	0.97	2.79	1.88
Total factor productivity	1.31	1.55	1.43
Relative proportion of productivity change	0.57	0.36	0.43

5.6 Income and Expenditure, Accumulation, and Wealth Accounts

5.6.1 Introduction

In section 5.5 we presented the production account for the U.S. private domestic economy in constant prices. We gave data in constant prices for both product and factor input sides of the production account. In this section we present income and expenditure, accumulation, and wealth accounts for the U.S. private national economy in constant prices. In constructing these accounts in constant prices we must separate changes in income, consumer outlays, and capital formation into price and quantity components.

The fundamental accounting identity for the income and expenditure account is that consumer receipts are equal to consumer outlays plus saving. The corresponding identity for the accumulation account is that saving is equal to capital formation. The income and expenditure account is linked directly to the production account through factor income and consumer outlays. The income and expenditure and production accounts are linked indirectly through the accumulation account. The accumulation account is linked to the production account through capital formation. Capital formation includes expenditures on investment goods. Through the accumulation account, production and income and expenditure are linked to wealth. The change in wealth from period to period is equal to capital formation less depreciation plus revaluation of assets.

The accumulation account is also linked to production through net capital formation, defined as capital formation less replacement. If the decline in efficiency of capital goods is geometric, replacement is equal to depreciation and net capital formation is equal to the change in wealth from period to period less the revaluation of assets. If decline in efficiency is not geometric, a perpetual inventory of prices and quantities of capital goods is required. Net capital formation is linked to changes in capital input, while net saving is linked to changes in wealth.

Consumption expenditures in the income and expenditure account include sales and excise taxes and customs duties on consumption goods. Taxes are excluded from the value of consumption goods output in the production account. Factor outlay in the production account includes both direct taxes on factor in come and indirect taxes that form a part of outlay on factors of production. In the income and expenditure account factor incomes exclude both direct and indirect taxes. Similarly, capital formation in the accumulation account includes sales and excise taxes and customs duties on investment goods. Taxes are excluded from the value of investment goods output in the production account.

5.6.2 Labor Income and Consumer Outlays

We begin by presenting estimates of labor income and consumer outlays in constant prices for the U.S. private national economy. To construct price and quantity indexes of consumer outlays, we obtain data for consumption expenditures on nondurable goods and services, excluding the services of institutional real estate, in constant prices from the U.S. national accounts. We combine these data with imputed values of the services of consumer and institutional durables, and the services of institutional real estate in constant prices. Prices of services and nondurable goods are implicit in the data on personal consumption expenditures in current prices from the U.S. national accounts. Price indexes for the services of consumer and institutional durables, and institutional real estate are the capital service prices described in section 5.5 above.

The value of consumption expenditures includes customs duties, excise and sales taxes, and excludes subsidies. In section 5.5 we have outlined the method for allocating excise and sales taxes between investment and consumption goods output. We construct a quantity index of consumption expenditures as a Divisia index of the quantity indexes of nondurables, services and our estimate of imputed capital services. The price index is then computed as the ratio of consumption expenditures to the quantity index. We deflate consumer outlays by the price index of consumption expenditures and consumer outlays in table 5.17.

Labor services offered are not identified with hours actually worked. Unemployment is a measure of the number of persons willing to offer labor at the current wage rate who do not have a demand for their labor. We include a "normal workday" for the unemployed in working time. All nonworking time is considered to be leisure. A case could be made for including even more in working time offered on the grounds that there is an interaction between labor force participation and unemployment rates. As unemployment is reduced, people previously discouraged from entering the labor force by high unemployment are induced to enter. We include in working time offered only the time of the unemployed, assuming that the average workweek is the same as for the employed.

Our data for man-hours are from Kendrick.[53] Kendrick provides total man-hours for the farm sector, the general government sector, and the total private domestic sector. Hours for proprietors and unpaid family workers are included in his estimates. We provide our own hours estimate only for the rest of world sector. We assume that hours per man employed are equal to hours per man for the private domestic nonfarm economy. We adjust the total time endowment and the quantity of working time offered for quality change as measured by educational attainment. Both work and leisure are composed of quantities of labor services of varying qualities. Quantities of the different categories of labor services offered are combined into a Divisia quantity index of labor offered. In principle, a quantity index of labor supply could be built up from man-hours worked, classified by sex, race, years of schooling, occupation, age, and so on. Wage rates net of tax could be estimated for each class of worker. Our adjustment of the quantity of man-hours for changes in the educational composition of the labor force fails to take into account differences in taxes paid by workers at different levels of income.

Our concept of labor income is net of personal income taxes. The effective tax rate on labor income is computed as the ratio of taxes on labor income to labor income including taxes. Price, quantity, and tax indexes for labor income are presented in table 5.17.

Table 5.17
Private national consumption expenditures, consumer outlays, and national labor compensation, 1929–1969 (constant prices of 1958)

Year	Consumption Expenditures and Consumer Outlays (price index)	Consumption Expenditures (quantity index)	Consumer Outlays (quantity index)	Private National Labor Compensation		
				Price Index	Quantity Index	Effective Tax Rate
1929	0.546	141.0	142.9	0.278	235.8	.001
1930	0.527	135.5	137.5	0.260	234.0	.001
1931	0.481	132.0	133.9	0.226	233.8	.001
1932	0.411	121.5	123.4	0.185	229.0	.001
1933	0.414	119.1	120.8	0.171	233.1	.004
1934	0.437	123.3	124.8	0.203	224.0	.004
1935	0.447	126.3	127.7	0.212	231.6	.005
1936	0.458	137.2	138.7	0.227	243.5	.005
1937	0.469	141.9	143.4	0.248	246.3	.007
1938	0.457	143.0	144.4	0.237	242.7	.009
1939	0.457	147.9	149.3	0.246	248.1	.008
1940	0.460	153.6	155.1	0.261	250.5	.009
1941	0.487	161.5	162.9	0.304	260.8	.011
1942	0.526	165.6	166.9	0.367	274.6	.024
1943	0.602	171.0	172.4	0.392	301.7	.086
1944	0.630	177.1	178.6	0.424	306.8	.086
1945	0.660	186.7	188.4	0.456	289.3	.090
1946	0.730	195.5	197.3	0.505	259.2	.081
1947	0.804	197.2	198.9	0.553	257.1	.092
1948	0.840	203.7	205.5	0.606	258.9	.081
1949	0.799	208.6	210.5	0.620	256.9	.068
1950	0.845	218.7	220.5	0.670	260.0	.065
1951	0.881	227.7	229.4	0.723	269.1	.092
1952	0.909	236.9	238.7	0.759	272.7	.103
1953	0.926	245.7	247.7	0.811	272.7	.101
1954	0.932	252.3	254.5	0.831	269.0	.089
1955	0.953	265.4	267.5	0.874	273.7	.090
1956	0.957	277.8	280.2	0.928	276.7	.094
1957	0.974	286.0	288.7	0.981	274.3	.095
1958	1.000	293.6	296.5	1.000	271.5	.094
1959	1.031	306.0	309.0	1.059	275.9	.095
1960	1.052	315.4	318.4	1.093	279.7	.099
1961	1.057	324.3	327.6	1.123	280.2	.098
1962	1.071	336.4	340.0	1.180	283.0	.101
1963	1.090	349.2	353.1	1.224	286.0	.102
1964	1.106	367.5	371.8	1.306	290.4	.090
1965	1.121	386.9	391.6	1.360	297.7	.094
1966	1.157	407.0	412.0	1.441	306.8	.099
1967	1.178	423.7	429.3	1.496	314.4	.102
1968	1.214	441.9	448.0	1.591	321.2	.111
1969	1.271	459.1	465.7	1.678	328.8	.123

5.6.3 Property Income

The starting point for estimating price and quantity components of property income is a set of perpetual inventory estimates of stocks of each type of capital employed in measuring capital input in constant prices in the production account. We assume that the flow of capital services from each type of tangible asset is proportional to the stock. Real property compensation for each asset is equal to the real service flow. Similarly, real property compensation from the government and rest of world sectors is proportional to the quantity of net claims on governments and foreigners.

Prices of capital input from the point of view of the producer include both direct and indirect taxes. To obtain prices for capital input from the point of view of the owner of the asset we exclude all taxes. Excluding both direct and indirect taxes, the price of capital services becomes:

$$q_{K,t} = q_{A,t-1} r_t + q_{A,t} \delta - (q_{A,t} - q_{A,t-1}),$$

where r_t is the after-tax rate of return. The depreciation rate δ is different from zero only for structures, equipment, and consumer durables employed in the private domestic sector. For inventories, land, and financial claims on the government and rest of world sectors the capital service price reduces to the cost of capital $q_{A,t-1} r_t$ less revaluation of assets $q_{A,t} - q_{A,t-1}$. For a financial asset the value of capital services is equal to earnings on the asset, for example, interest payments on a bond.

To construct price and quantity indexes of property compensation for the income and expenditure account our procedure is analogous to the methods we have used for the production account, except for the treatment of taxes. Property compensation before taxes includes the property share of gross private domestic factor outlay, corporate profits and net interest originating in the foreign sector, net interest paid by government, and investment income of social insurance funds net of transfers to general government. We have described effective rates of business property taxation and corporate income taxation in our presentation of the production account. We compute an effective rate of personal income taxation on property compensation net of business property taxes and the corporate income tax, and an effective rate of estate, death, and gift taxation on wealth.

We allocate federal estate and gift taxes and state and local death and gift taxes proportionally to all the components of private national wealth. Property income from assets in the households sector is not subject to personal income taxation; thus we must allocate personal income taxes attributed to property compensation among the corporate, noncorporate, government, and foreign sectors. A detailed allocation of personal income taxes to the various types of property compensation would be desirable; we simply allocate the taxes proportionately to all nonhousehold property compensation after corporate and property taxes but before personal taxes. The effective rate of personal income taxation on property compensation is estimated as the ratio of personal income taxes to property compensation before personal taxes other than household and institutional property compensation.

The after-tax return to capital in each sector includes property compensation, net of all taxes; it also includes capital gains and excludes economic depreciation. Our estimates of capital gains and economic depreciation for corporate and noncorporate tangible assets are discussed in detail in Christensen and Jorgenson (1969). Depreciation is zero for the financial assets which constitute net claims on governments and foreigners. Capital gains on net claims on foreigners are computed as the yearly increase in net claims less net private foreign investment. Capital gains on net claims on governments are computed as the yearly increase in net claims on governments less the current government deficit. These items are discussed in greater detail below.

The after-tax rate of return in each sector is computed by dividing the after-tax return to capital by the value of assets. These rates of return are nominal or money rates. We can also compute the real or own rates of return by excluding capital gains from the return to capital. Nominal and own rates of return for each sector and for the private national economy are presented in table 5.18, together with effective tax rates on property compensation. We can now estimate the price of capital services for each asset from the formula above as a function of the rate of return, the depreciation rate, and the current and lagged acquisition price. Real property income for each sector and the private national economy is obtained as a Divisia quantity index of real property income from each asset. The price indexes for property income are computed as the ratios of property income to the

Table 5.18
Gross private national property compensation, rates of return, and effective rates of taxation, 1929–1969

a. Nominal Rates of Return

Year	Corporate Sector	Noncorporate Sector	Households and Institutions	Net Claims on Governments and Rest of World	Private National Economy
1929	.076	.056	.029	.078	.053
1930	−.008	−.067	−.031	.042	−.028
1931	−.065	−.117	−.092	−.017	−.084
1932	−.091	−.141	−.151	.036	−.113
1933	−.005	.010	.017	.043	.012
1934	.082	.062	.090	.108	.083
1935	.062	.049	.002	.032	.034
1936	.078	.071	.059	.009	.060
1937	.131	.073	.078	.034	.084
1938	.029	−.005	.032	−.001	.017
1939	.052	.027	.019	.007	.027
1940	.096	.070	.041	.002	.056
1941	.154	.159	.092	.088	.123
1942	.181	.187	.079	.109	.136
1943	.129	.156	.096	.010	.098
1944	.124	.172	.103	−.025	.087
1945	.077	.170	.080	−.017	.066
1946	.158	.265	.125	.027	.123
1947	.243	.253	.186	.008	.154
1948	.140	.141	.114	.018	.099
1949	.055	.036	−.021	.024	.020
1950	.096	.152	.074	.042	.087
1951	.136	.161	.085	.028	.100
1952	.062	.065	.040	.024	.047
1953	.048	.048	.027	.034	.038
1954	.048	.067	.017	.030	.037
1955	.076	.073	.055	.029	.058
1956	.103	.092	.071	.034	.076
1957	.086	.096	.054	.032	.066
1958	.049	.097	.037	.037	.051
1959	.065	.064	.064	.041	.060
1960	.050	.069	.051	.042	.053
1961	.050	.076	.046	.031	.050
1962	.068	.082	.056	.040	.061
1963	.067	.073	.061	.034	.060
1964	.080	.075	.069	.030	.067
1965	.094	.092	.060	.039	.072
1966	.104	.100	.069	.035	.079
1967	.095	.094	.085	.023	.080
1968	.089	.092	.088	.034	.081
1969	.087	.087	.093	.041	.082

Table 5.18 (continued)

b. Own Rates of Return

Year	Corporate Sector	Noncorporate Sector	Households and Institutions	Net Claims on Governments and Rest of World	Private National Economy
1929	.074	.058	.012	.052	.044
1930	.050	.016	.008	.047	.025
1931	.022	.010	.014	.044	.018
1932	−.002	−.019	−.001	.035	−.002
1933	−.004	−.012	.019	.033	.007
1934	.026	−.002	.015	.036	.017
1935	.042	.017	.009	.031	.023
1936	.060	.031	.020	.027	.034
1937	.063	.027	.013	.026	.031
1938	.040	.020	.011	.026	.023
1939	.056	.033	.015	.025	.032
1940	.075	.042	.014	.027	.038
1941	.076	.069	.008	.025	.043
1942	.074	.089	−.020	.024	.037
1943	.067	.085	.011	.018	.042
1944	.075	.115	.008	.018	.048
1945	.057	.119	.016	.016	.045
1946	.046	.115	.037	.018	.046
1947	.057	.086	.034	.019	.044
1948	.070	.079	.025	.021	.045
1949	.060	.061	−.003	.023	.032
1950	.054	.068	.025	.022	.040
1951	.049	.081	.010	.024	.037
1952	.042	.062	.017	.024	.034
1953	.037	.054	.024	.023	.033
1954	.040	.051	.024	.025	.033
1955	.056	.051	.036	.024	.042
1956	.045	.036	.026	.025	.033
1957	.040	.039	.019	.027	.030
1958	.034	.048	.022	.026	.031
1959	.043	.035	.033	.027	.035
1960	.039	.029	.034	.028	.033
1961	.039	.033	.032	.028	.033
1962	.050	.038	.035	.030	.039
1963	.051	.036	.039	.031	.040
1964	.059	.035	.041	.035	.044
1965	.068	.039	.040	.035	.047
1966	.070	.046	.045	.036	.050
1967	.058	.044	.043	.037	.047
1968	.052	.036	.039	.038	.042
1969	.042	.027	.042	.036	.038

Table 5.18 (continued)

c. Effective Tax Rates

Year	Effective Corporate Income Tax Rate	Effective Personal Income Tax Rate on Property Compensation	Effective Rate of Wealth Taxation
1929	.108	.070	.000
1930	.083	.106	.000
1931	.074	.098	.000
1932	.113	a	.000
1933	.207	a	.000
1934	.136	.092	.000
1935	.139	.065	.001
1936	.172	.063	.001
1937	.156	.101	.001
1938	.133	.112	.001
1939	.167	.054	.001
1940	.243	.051	.001
1941	.440	.061	.001
1942	.492	.089	.001
1943	.531	.208	.001
1944	.495	.157	.001
1945	.492	.183	.001
1946	.470	.170	.001
1947	.443	.150	.001
1948	.391	.123	.001
1949	.331	.123	.001
1950	.486	.163	.000
1951	.520	.155	.000
1952	.463	.182	.000
1953	.477	.195	.001
1954	.481	.187	.001
1955	.481	.173	.001
1956	.476	.212	.001
1957	.469	.212	.001
1958	.472	.198	.001
1959	.497	.206	.001
1960	.495	.230	.001
1961	.488	.222	.001
1962	.467	.200	.001
1963	.477	.201	.001
1964	.479	.173	.001
1965	.470	.165	.001
1966	.463	.169	.001
1967	.449	.186	.001
1968	.504	.222	.001
1969	.511	.282	.001

[a] Income base is zero or negligible.

quantity indexes. The price and quantity indexes of property income are presented in table 5.19.

5.6.4 Accumulation Account

The fundamental accounting identity for the accumulation account is that gross private national saving, taken from the income and expenditure account, is equal to gross private national capital formation. Gross private national saving may be expressed as the sum of depreciation and net private national saving. Net private national saving is equal to the change in wealth from period to period less revaluation of assets. Gross private national capital formation can be expressed as the sum of replacement and net private national capital formation. We present data in constant prices for saving and capital formation, both gross and net, and for depreciation, replacement, and revaluation. Gross private national capital formation is equal to gross private domestic investment, as defined in the U.S. national accounts, plus personal consumption expenditures on durable goods, plus the current deficits of the federal and state and local social insurance funds, plus the current surpluses of federal and state and local social insurance funds, plus net foreign investment.

We divide the components of gross private national capital formation into prices and quantities using the following deflators: The implicit deflators from the U.S. national income and product accounts are used for investment in producer and consumer durables, and for farm and nonfarm inventories. For residential and nonresidential structures we use the "constant cost 2" price index for structures from the Bureau of Economic Analysis (formerly the Office of Business Economics) *Capital Stock Study* for both capital formation and replacement.[54] We have constructed price index for claims on the government and rest of world sectors from data on changes in the value of claims from period to period and data on the corresponding components of capital formation from the U.S. national accounts. We set the price of claims of each type equal to 1.000 in 1958 and the quantity in 1958 equal to the value of outstanding claims in that year. These price indexes are then used to deflate the government deficit and net foreign investment.

To construct an index of the quantity of gross private national capital formation we first construct a Divisia index of the quantities of investment in producer and consumer durables, residential and

Table 5.19
Gross private national property compensation, 1929–1969 (constant prices of 1958)

	Corporate Property Compensation		Noncorporate Property Compensation		Households and Institutions, Property Compensation	
Year	Price Index	Quantity Index	Price Index	Quantity Index	Price Index	Quantity Index
1929	.056	257.9	.039	200.9	.048	273.9
1930	.044	264.0	.017	212.2	.045	278.2
1931	.029	263.4	.013	216.0	.044	272.8
1932	.018	255.5	.000	214.9	.031	263.0
1933	.016	237.2	.003	208.6	.039	246.3
1934	.029	221.5	.007	202.6	.039	232.5
1935	.036	213.8	.015	197.6	.036	224.4
1936	.043	209.5	.020	197.5	.042	223.6
1937	.046	211.6	.020	201.8	.041	230.6
1938	.038	216.9	.017	211.4	.041	237.5
1939	.045	212.8	.022	211.3	.043	235.5
1940	.053	212.8	.026	213.4	.043	240.5
1941	.056	219.2	.038	216.7	.043	250.2
1942	.060	230.9	.051	221.9	.034	263.4
1943	.061	229.7	.053	219.5	.055	255.3
1944	.069	225.0	.073	215.3	.059	243.9
1945	.061	222.2	.079	214.2	.069	232.4
1946	.057	227.0	.081	214.8	.088	225.4
1947	.073	245.2	.073	220.6	.093	249.7
1948	.092	266.1	.079	227.3	.092	279.5
1949	.089	282.8	.069	238.6	.067	307.9
1950	.085	290.6	.074	248.0	.094	337.0
1951	.086	306.0	.090	261.4	.086	379.7
1952	.084	326.0	.079	270.6	.094	404.9
1953	.082	339.8	.072	276.1	.100	423.7
1954	.085	353.3	.070	281.4	.099	450.2
1955	.100	363.1	.071	286.2	.110	474.3
1956	.095	380.4	.061	293.6	.104	513.2
1957	.095	401.0	.066	297.9	.101	539.5
1958	.091	418.1	.078	302.0	.105	562.0
1959	.102	424.7	.068	305.0	.118	574.0
1960	.098	438.1	.062	310.3	.120	599.3
1961	.098	454.3	.067	315.7	.117	622.3
1962	.111	465.2	.074	319.9	.121	639.4
1963	.113	482.2	.073	328.1	.126	666.5
1964	.122	500.6	.073	337.4	.130	699.5
1965	.133	525.0	.080	347.8	.129	737.9
1966	.138	556.8	.090	361.5	.134	785.4
1967	.129	599.7	.092	374.3	.134	832.8
1968	.125	634.3	.084	386.3	.135	872.6
1969	.119	667.8	.076	400.9	.143	923.3

Table 5.19 (continued)

Year	Government and Rest of World, Property Compensation		Private National Property Compensation	
	Price Index	Quantity Index	Price Index	Quantity Index
1929	.048	35.1	.045	834.0
1930	.044	35.0	.034	854.7
1931	.041	36.3	.028	849.8
1932	.031	40.0	.017	830.7
1933	.029	42.3	.020	784.7
1934	.032	44.2	.025	745.3
1935	.030	47.3	.028	725.8
1936	.025	49.5	.033	721.3
1937	.025	53.2	.033	738.2
1938	.024	54.6	.030	760.9
1939	.023	59.0	.034	756.2
1940	.024	63.8	.038	766.8
1941	.022	67.8	.041	791.3
1942	.023	75.1	.043	828.7
1943	.018	108.4	.050	831.1
1944	.018	153.7	.059	823.6
1945	.016	209.8	.061	822.7
1946	.017	255.8	.066	831.1
1947	.018	259.0	.070	888.5
1948	.020	257.2	.076	956.5
1949	.021	253.7	.066	1,019.7
1950	.020	260.5	.074	1,074.0
1951	.022	250.9	.077	1,154.3
1952	.023	249.2	.076	1,216.0
1953	.022	257.3	.076	1,262.9
1954	.024	265.9	.076	1,320.0
1955	.024	275.5	.084	1,369.8
1956	.024	275.5	.079	1,447.5
1957	.026	276.0	.079	1,510.0
1958	.026	282.3	.082	1,564.2
1959	.027	294.7	.088	1,594.1
1960	.028	296.6	.087	1,548.7
1961	.029	298.4	.086	1,703.1
1962	.031	307.0	.093	1,744.9
1963	.032	315.3	.095	1,809.8
1964	.036	321.4	.100	1,884.3
1965	.037	333.8	.104	1,975.9
1966	.037	340.9	.109	2,088.6
1967	.039	353.0	.107	2,215.5
1968	.039	378.6	.105	2,326.9
1969	.037	395.4	.104	2,450.2

nonresidential structures, and the quantity indexes of net foreign investment and government deficits. Real investment in inventories of durable and nondurable goods is added to the Divisia index to obtain the quantity index of gross private national capital formation. The price index of replacement is computed as the ratio of the value of replacement to the Divisia index of replacement. A quantity index of net private national capital formation is computed as the quantity index of gross private national capital formation less the quantity index of replacement. The price of net private national capital formation is computed as the ratio of the value in current prices to the quantity index. The price and quantity indexes of gross private national capital formation, replacement, and net private national capital formation are presented in table 5.20.

Net private national capital formation in constant prices is equal to the change in the quantity of capital for each type of capital utilized in the U.S. private domestic economy. Capital input and net capital formation in a given period are combined in the perpetual inventory formula to obtain capital input from each capital good in the following period. Changes in the value of capital input can be decomposed into price and quantity components. The quantity component must be carefully distinguished from the quantity of net capital formation. The quantity of capital input is weighted by capital service prices, while the quantities of gross and net capital formation are weighted by capital asset prices.

The value of gross private national saving is taken from the income and expenditure account. To construct the saving side of the accumulation account in constant prices we begin with gross private national capital formation in constant prices. The capital formation and saving sides of the accumulation account are equal in both current and constant prices. To complete the saving side of the accumulation account in constant prices we must construct accounts for depreciation and revaluation of assets in constant prices. We outline methods for constructing these accounts from a perpetual inventory of prices and quantities of capital goods; we then specialize to the case of geometric decline in efficiency of capital goods.

For a single capital good the value of wealth is the sum of values of investment goods of each vintage, summed over all vintages:

$$W_t = \sum_{v=0}^{\infty} q_{A,t,v} \, A_{t-v} \, .$$

Table 5.20
Gross private national capital formation, 1929–1969 (constant prices of 1958)

Year	Gross Private National Capital		Replacement		Effective Sales Tax Rate of Investment Goods
	Price Index	Quantity Index	Price Index	Quantity Index	
1929	0.474	53.6	0.463	41.3	.017
1930	0.473	39.3	0.449	42.3	.019
1931	0.471	30.5	0.411	41.8	.021
1932	0.441	15.2	0.365	40.2	.029
1933	0.423	15.5	0.352	37.7	.042
1934	0.483	21.8	0.379	35.5	.048
1935	0.429	31.8	0.379	34.1	.047
1936	0.436	41.8	0.381	33.8	.045
1937	0.434	46.1	0.408	34.6	.044
1938	0.490	33.2	0.416	35.7	.045
1939	0.467	43.4	0.410	35.3	.044
1940	0.460	53.2	0.418	35.8	.044
1941	0.510	67.5	0.453	37.2	.044
1942	0.765	66.1	0.516	39.2	.039
1943	0.848	68.5	0.551	38.0	.037
1944	0.861	79.1	0.595	36.4	.042
1945	0.822	75.0	0.617	35.2	.048
1946	0.661	74.6	0.655	35.0	.053
1947	0.728	72.5	0.741	38.3	.049
1948	0.798	82.0	0.792	42.9	.047
1949	0.809	82.4	0.799	47.4	.050
1950	0.803	94.1	0.817	51.2	.048
1951	0.885	98.8	0.880	56.3	.046
1952	0.906	98.3	0.898	59.9	.048
1953	0.903	104.2	0.901	62.7	.048
1954	0.906	103.6	0.895	66.2	.046
1955	0.904	118.4	0.901	69.2	.045
1956	0.949	115.3	0.945	73.9	.046
1957	0.989	116.2	0.986	77.6	.046
1958	1.000	111.2	1.000	80.8	.045
1959	1.017	119.5	1.017	82.2	.046
1960	1.020	119.5	1.018	85.2	.048
1961	1.018	122.4	1.017	88.2	.047
1962	1.027	137.5	1.023	90.3	.047
1963	1.030	143.2	1.026	93.8	.048
1964	1.040	159.8	1.035	98.1	.047
1965	1.048	173.6	1.040	103.4	.046
1966	1.059	193.4	1.051	110.2	.043
1967	1.081	199.9	1.080	117.7	.043
1968	1.117	204.0	1.115	124.2	.046
1969	1.164	200.9	1.155	131.6	.047

The change in wealth from period to period may be written:

$$\begin{aligned} W_t - W_{t-1} &= \sum_{v=0}^{\infty} q_{A,t,v} A_{t-v} - \sum_{v=0}^{\infty} q_{A,t-1,v} A_{t-v-1} \\ &= q_{A,t,0}\, A_t + \sum_{v=0}^{\infty} q_{A,t,v-1}\, A_{t-v-1} - \sum_{v=0}^{\infty} q_{A,t-1,v} A_{t-v-1} \\ &= q_{A,t} A_t + \sum_{v=0}^{\infty} (q_{A,t,v-1} - q_{A,t,v}) A_{t-v-1} + \sum_{v=0}^{\infty} (q_{A,t,v} - q_{A,t-1,v}) A_{t-v-1} \,. \end{aligned}$$

In this expression for change in the value of wealth, the first term is the value of gross capital formation, the second is the negative of depreciation on capital goods of all vintages, and the third is the revaluation of assets of all vintages.

We have already described the construction of price and quantity index numbers for gross capital formation. Treating the change in prices across vintages, $q_{A,t,v} - q_{A,t,v-1}$, as the price component of depreciation and A_{t-v-1} as the quantity component, we may apply Divisia index number formulas to perpetual inventory data on prices and quantities of each vintage of a capital good to obtain price and quantity index numbers for depreciation on a single capital good. To obtain index numbers for several capital goods we again apply Divisia index number formulas, this time to the price and quantity indexes for each capital good. Similarly, treating the change in prices across time periods, $q_{A,t,v} - q_{A,t-1,v}$, as the price component of revaluation, we may obtain price and quantity index numbers of revaluation for any number of capital goods.

The value of gross saving is equal to change in wealth plus depreciation less revaluation of assets. We may define the quantity of gross saving as the sum of quantities of change in wealth and depreciation less the quantity of revaluation. The quantity of change in wealth itself is the sum of quantities of gross capital formation and revaluation less the quantity of depreciation. The quantity of net saving is equal to the quantity of gross saving less the quantity of depreciation. Quantities of gross saving and gross capital formation are, of course, identical.

If the decline in efficiency of capital goods is geometric the change in wealth from period to period for a single capital good may be written:

$$\begin{aligned} W_t - W_{t-1} &= q_{A,t}K_t - q_{A,t-1}K_{t-1} \\ &= q_{A,t}(K_t - K_{t-1}) + (q_{A,t} - q_{A,t-1})K_{t-1} \\ &= q_{A,t}A_t - q_{A,t}\delta K_{t-1} + (q_{A,t} - q_{A,t-1})K_{t-1} \,. \end{aligned}$$

Gross saving is represented by $q_{A,t}A_t$, which is equal to gross capital formation and has the same price and quantity components. Depreciation is represented by $q_{A,t}\delta K_{t-1}$ and is equal to replacement; the price and quantity components of depreciation differ from the price and quantity components of replacement. We construct the quantity index of depreciation as a Divisia index of the various lagged stocks, K_{t-1}, with depreciation shares as weights. The quantity index of replacement is a Divisia index of the δK_{t-1} with replacement shares as weights. The weights are, of course, the same for replacement and depreciation under geometric decline in efficiency; so the quantity indexes for depreciation and replacement are proportional. The price index of depreciation is computed as the ratio of depreciation to the quantity index of depreciation.

Revaluation is represented by $(q_{A,t} - q_{A,t-1})K_{t-1}$. We construct a quantity index of revaluation as a Divisia index of the various lagged capital stocks with revaluation shares as weights. The price index of revaluation is computed as the ratio of revaluation to the quantity index of revaluation. Price and quantity index numbers of private national saving, depreciation, and revaluation are presented in table 5.21.

5.6.5 Standard of Living

At this point we can consolidate the receipt and expenditure account with the accumulation account to obtain a consolidated receipt and expenditure account. In the consolidated account consumer receipts are equal to the sum of consumer outlays and gross capital formation. Price and quantity index numbers for factor income can be constructed by combining Divisia index numbers of labor and property income into a Divisia index of factor income. The weights for labor and property are the relative shares of labor and property compensation in the value of total factor income. We use the price index of factor income to deflate government transfer payments to persons, except for social insurance benefits. Adding deflated transfer payments to the quantity index of factor income provides an index of total

Table 5.21
Gross private national saving, depreciation, and revaluation, 1929–1969 (constant prices of 1958)

Year	Gross Private National Saving		Depreciation		Revaluation	
	Price Index	Quantity Index	Price Index	Quantity Index	Price Index	Quantity Index
1929	0.474	53.6	.046	418.3	.003	1,200.3
1930	0.473	39.3	.044	428.3	−.018	1,214.8
1931	0.471	30.5	.041	422.8	−.033	1,212.2
1932	0.441	15.2	.036	407.1	−.032	1,200.5
1933	0.423	15.5	.035	381.3	.001	1,293.4
1934	0.483	21.8	.037	359.2	.015	1,361.8
1935	0.429	31.8	.037	345.4	.003	1,298.2
1936	0.436	41.8	.038	342.1	.008	1,301.3
1937	0.434	46.1	.040	350.3	.013	1,299.7
1938	0.490	43.2	.041	361.3	−.002	1,384.7
1939	0.467	43.4	.041	357.6	−.001	1,445.9
1940	0.460	53.2	.041	362.6	.004	1,491.5
1941	0.510	67.5	.045	376.3	.020	1,514.1
1942	0.765	66.1	.051	396.8	.026	1,581.3
1943	0.848	68.5	.054	384.6	.017	1,598.6
1944	0.861	79.1	.059	368.4	.015	1,470.6
1945	0.822	75.0	.061	355.7	.010	1,260.3
1946	0.661	74.6	.065	354.4	.044	1,188.0
1947	0.728	72.5	.073	387.8	.067	1,235.3
1948	0.798	82.0	.078	433.9	.036	1,287.3
1949	0.809	82.4	.079	479.4	−.008	1,317.4
1950	0.803	94.1	.081	518.1	.035	1,314.2
1951	0.885	98.8	.087	570.0	.048	1,367.2
1952	0.906	98.3	.089	606.5	.011	1,411.0
1953	0.903	104.2	.089	634.2	.004	1,456.7
1954	0.906	103.6	.088	670.0	.003	1,469.6
1955	0.904	118.4	.089	699.7	.015	1,446.6
1956	0.949	115.3	.093	747.6	.039	1,489.3
1957	0.989	116.2	.097	785.1	.034	1,534.5
1958	1.000	111.2	.099	817.7	.020	1,564.2
1959	1.017	119.5	.101	832.1	.025	1,581.2
1960	1.020	119.5	.101	862.1	.020	1,599.1
1961	1.018	122.4	.101	892.3	.018	1,603.7
1962	1.027	137.5	.101	913.9	.025	1,613.3
1963	1.030	143.2	.101	949.4	.023	1,627.5
1964	1.040	159.8	.102	992.2	.028	1,641.8
1965	1.048	173.6	.103	1,045.7	.032	1,659.1
1966	1.059	193.4	.104	1,114.7	.038	1,684.7
1967	1.081	199.9	.107	1,190.9	.046	1,721.1
1968	1.117	204.0	.110	1,256.4	.056	1,751.6
1969	1.164	200.9	.114	1,331.9	.067	1,791.3

real consumer receipts. The construction of an index of total real consumer receipts is analogous to the construction of an index of total factor input in the production account; the scope of transactions covered by the two indexes is different and consumer receipts are net of both direct and indirect taxes in the consolidated consumer receipts and expenditures account.

Price and quantity index numbers for total expenditures can be constructed by combining Divisia index numbers of consumer outlays and capital formation into a Divisia index of total expenditures. The weight for consumer outlays and capital formation are the relative shares of these components of expenditure in the value of total expenditure. The price and quantity indexes of expenditures are analogous to indexes for total product in the production account; the scope of transactions is different and expenditures include sales and excise taxes, while the value of total product excludes such taxes.

The standard of living may be defined as the ratio of real expenditures to real receipts or, equivalently, the ratio of the price of factor income to the price of expenditures. A Divisia index of the standard of living may be defined as the ratio of Divisia indexes of the quantity of expenditures to the quantity of consumer receipts or, equivalently, the ratio of Divisia indexes of the price of factor income to the price of consumer expenditures. Divisia price and quantity indexes of consumer receipts and total expenditures and the standard of living for the U.S. private national economy are given in table 5.22 for 1929–1969.

5.6.6 Wealth Account

In section 5.2 we described the asset side of the wealth account for the U.S. private national economy in current prices. Changes in the value of wealth from period to period may be separated into price and quantity components. The price component is equal to gross saving less depreciation or net saving. Capital formation is related to the change in capital input, but not to the change in capital assets, except where the decline in efficiency of capital goods is geometric. Under this assumption depreciation is equal to replacement so that net saving is equal to net capital formation. Net capital formation, like net saving, may be interpreted as the quantity component of the change in the value of wealth, but only under the assumption of geometric decline in efficiency of capital goods.

Table 5.22
Gross private national expenditures, receipts, and standard of living, 1929–1969 (constant prices of 1958)

Year	Gross Private National Expenditures		Gross Private National Consumer Receipts		Standard of Living
	Price Index	Quantity Index	Price Index	Quantity Index	
1929	0.531	194.8	0.346	298.8	0.652
1930	0.516	176.3	0.303	300.4	0.587
1931	0.479	164.3	0.259	304.3	0.540
1932	0.416	138.1	0.193	297.1	0.465
1933	0.416	135.8	0.191	296.7	0.458
1934	0.444	146.5	0.230	283.6	0.517
1935	0.443	159.6	0.245	288.8	0.553
1936	0.453	180.4	0.271	301.9	0.598
1937	0.461	189.2	0.289	301.7	0.627
1938	0.464	177.4	0.273	301.8	0.588
1939	0.459	192.9	0.290	305.6	0.631
1940	0.459	208.5	0.310	308.6	0.676
1941	0.493	230.9	0.356	319.7	0.722
1942	0.594	233.0	0.413	335.1	0.695
1943	0.672	241.0	0.451	358.8	0.672
1944	0.695	259.9	0.498	363.0	0.716
1945	0.704	263.9	0.529	351.1	0.752
1946	0.710	272.3	0.582	332.5	0.819
1947	0.782	272.0	0.632	336.6	0.808
1948	0.827	287.7	0.693	343.5	0.837
1949	0.801	293.1	0.674	348.4	0.841
1950	0.832	314.6	0.736	355.6	0.885
1951	0.882	328.3	0.783	369.9	0.887
1952	0.908	337.1	0.808	378.9	0.890
1953	0.919	352.0	0.846	382.6	0.920
1954	0.924	358.2	0.861	384.3	0.932
1955	0.938	385.8	0.920	393.3	0.981
1956	0.955	395.6	0.937	402.9	0.982
1957	0.978	405.0	0.977	405.7	0.998
1958	1.000	407.7	1.000	407.7	1.000
1959	1.027	428.6	1.063	414.2	1.035
1960	1.043	438.0	1.081	422.5	1.037
1961	1.047	450.0	1.101	427.6	1.052
1962	1.059	477.3	1.166	433.5	1.101
1963	1.074	496.0	1.205	441.9	1.123
1964	1.088	530.9	1.277	452.2	1.174
1965	1.101	564.3	1.329	467.2	1.208
1966	1.128	603.9	1.404	485.4	1.244
1967	1.150	627.7	1.432	504.1	1.245
1968	1.186	650.7	1.483	520.2	1.251
1969	1.240	665.9	1.534	538.2	1.237

To construct price and quantity indexes of wealth we require a perpetual inventory of prices and quantities of capital goods. We first outline methods for constructing these indexes from perpetual inventory data; we then specialize to the case of geometric decline in efficiency of capital goods. For a single capital good, the value of wealth, as given above, is the sum of values of investment goods of all vintages:

$$W_t = \sum_{v=0}^{\infty} q_{A,t,v} A_{t-v}.$$

Price and quantity indexes of wealth may be constructed from price and quantity data for each vintage, treating $q_{A,t,v}$ as the price and A_{t-v} as the quantity. Price and quantity indexes for several capital goods may be constructed by applying Divisia index numbers to price and quantity indexes of wealth for each capital good.

With geometric decline in efficiency the expression for the value of wealth reduces to:

$$W_t = q_{A,t} K_t \ .$$

For several capital goods the acquisition price $q_{A,t}$ and quantity of capital K_t for each capital good can be combined into price and quantity indexes for wealth. Our wealth account for the U.S. private national economy includes tangible assets held by private households and institutions, and by corporate and noncorporate business, and net claims on the government and foreign sectors, including the claims of social insurance funds. We estimate the price and quantity of assets for each of the five sectors by applying Divisia index number formulas to price and quantity data for each class of capital assets held by the sector. We construct price and quantity index numbers for the U.S. private national economy by applying these index number formulas to Divisia price and quantity indexes for the five sectors. Price and quantity indexes of wealth for 1929–1969 are given in table 5.23.

Table 5.23
Private national wealth, 1929–1969 (constant prices of 1958)

Year	Corporate Tangible Assets		Noncorporate Tangible Assets		Household and Institutional Tangible Assets	
	Price Index	Quantity Index	Price Index	Quantity Index	Price Index	Quantity Index
1929	0.424	275.3	0.417	256.2	0.427	370.7
1930	0.399	276.4	0.382	256.0	0.410	366.1
1931	0.364	268.2	0.333	255.1	0.366	358.8
1932	0.332	253.5	0.293	250.4	0.312	346.7
1933	0.331	242.6	0.299	245.6	0.311	335.3
1934	0.350	237.5	0.318	240.3	0.335	327.5
1935	0.357	234.6	0.328	242.2	0.332	324.5
1936	0.363	238.6	0.341	242.5	0.345	325.9
1937	0.388	244.8	0.356	247.0	0.368	327.9
1938	0.384	240.2	0.348	246.2	0.375	325.6
1939	0.382	240.6	0.345	247.1	0.376	328.4
1940	0.390	247.7	0.355	249.7	0.387	334.3
1941	0.420	260.9	0.387	254.7	0.419	342.9
1942	0.465	260.3	0.425	255.3	0.461	336.5
1943	0.494	255.8	0.456	252.5	0.500	327.2
1944	0.518	251.6	0.482	251.6	0.547	317.7
1945	0.528	251.8	0.506	251.2	0.582	311.4
1946	0.587	271.7	0.582	255.0	0.633	326.7
1947	0.696	286.0	0.680	257.5	0.728	346.9
1948	0.746	300.8	0.722	266.2	0.793	368.1
1949	0.742	305.5	0.705	270.2	0.778	388.3
1950	0.773	321.2	0.764	278.6	0.816	418.9
1951	0.840	341.5	0.824	284.4	0.877	439.0
1952	0.857	353.4	0.827	287.2	0.897	455.4
1953	0.866	364.2	0.822	290.3	0.900	475.4
1954	0.873	370.0	0.835	292.7	0.894	495.4
1955	0.891	386.5	0.853	297.1	0.911	524.5
1956	0.942	405.2	0.901	299.2	0.952	545.0
1957	0.985	418.1	0.953	302.0	0.985	562.0
1958	1.000	422.2	1.000	303.9	1.000	574.0
1959	1.021	434.5	1.028	306.7	1.031	594.2
1960	1.033	447.4	1.069	309.2	1.049	611.0
1961	1.044	456.5	1.115	311.3	1.063	624.5
1962	1.062	470.8	1.164	315.2	1.086	643.6
1963	1.079	486.0	1.207	318.7	1.109	665.4
1964	1.101	505.3	1.255	322.4	1.140	688.7
1965	1.129	530.5	1.322	328.3	1.162	715.3
1966	1.167	565.4	1.393	333.2	1.190	739.9
1967	1.210	590.7	1.462	337.8	1.240	760.4
1968	1.255	614.5	1.545	342.7	1.300	786.9
1969	1.312	640.3	1.638	348.5	1.366	812.2

Table 5.23 (continued)

Year	Net Claims on Governments and Rest of World		Private National Wealth	
	Price index	Quantity Index	Price index	Quantity Index
1929	0.943	35.0	0.572	725.3
1930	0.938	36.3	0.532	736.7
1931	0.881	40.0	0.475	736.3
1932	0.882	42.3	0.414	732.0
1933	0.891	44.2	0.417	714.0
1934	0.955	47.3	0.450	698.2
1935	0.956	49.5	0.460	691.9
1936	0.940	53.2	0.478	693.6
1937	0.947	54.6	0.504	705.4
1938	0.922	59.0	0.494	717.6
1939	0.905	63.8	0.498	720.6
1940	0.883	67.8	0.511	732.8
1941	0.938	75.1	0.562	752.2
1942	1.018	108.4	0.629	787.3
1943	1.010	153.7	0.653	857.8
1944	0.967	209.8	0.669	939.4
1945	0.935	255.8	0.660	1,031.0
1946	0.944	259.0	0.693	1,096.0
1947	0.934	257.2	0.763	1,136.8
1948	0.931	253.7	0.806	1,171.4
1949	0.932	260.5	0.794	1,211.1
1950	0.951	250.9	0.835	1,247.9
1951	0.956	249.2	0.885	1,293.0
1952	0.956	257.3	0.893	1,337.6
1953	0.966	265.9	0.899	1,377.9
1954	0.971	275.5	0.899	1,421.6
1955	0.976	275.5	0.920	1,460.9
1956	0.984	276.0	0.954	1,512.0
1957	0.989	282.3	0.986	1,555.0
1958	1.000	294.7	1.000	1,594.7
1959	1.014	296.6	1.029	1,625.8
1960	1.028	298.4	1.046	1,664.0
1961	1.032	307.0	1.062	1,698.6
1962	1.042	315.3	1.093	1,732.5
1963	1.045	321.4	1.115	1,778.5
1964	1.039	333.8	1.146	1,825.9
1965	1.044	340.9	1.178	1,884.7
1966	1.043	353.0	1.217	1,950.4
1967	1.028	378.6	1.254	2,026.8
1968	1.023	395.4	1.299	2,100.7
1969	1.028	399.2	1.350	2,171.5

5.7 Extending the Accounting Framework

5.7.1 Introduction

As a long-term objective the basic accounting framework must be expanded to incorporate investment in human capital. Investment in human capital is primarily a product of the educational sector, which is not included in the private domestic sector of the economy. In addition to data on education already incorporated into the national accounts, data on physical investment and capital stock in the educational sector would be required for incorporation of investment in human capital into a complete accounting system.[55] We outline methods for incorporation of the education sector into the basic accounting framework below.

A second objective for long-term research is the incorporation of research and development into a complete system of accounts.[56] At present research and development expenditures are treated as a current expenditure. Labor and capital employed in research and development activities are commingled with labor and capital used to produce marketable output. The first step in accounting for research and development is to develop data on factors of production devoted to research. The second step is to develop measures osf investment in research and development. The final step is to develop data on the stock of accumulated research. A similar accounting problem arises for advertising expenditures, also treated as a current expenditure.

Both education and investment in research and development are heavily subsidized in the United States, so that private costs and returns are not equal to social costs and returns. The effects of these subsidies would have to be taken into account in measuring the effects of human capital and accumulated research on productivity in the private sector. If the output of research activities is associated with external benefits in use, these externalities would not be reflected in the private cost of investment in research.

5.7.2 Investment in Human Capital

To illustrate the design of a system of accounts incorporating the educational sector, we suppose that the stock of human capital at any point of time, say E, can be imputed from past investment in education, say I_E:

$$I_E = \dot{E} + \delta E ,$$

where δ is the rate of required replacement of human capital. Total labor compensation in the private domestic economy, $q_L L$, may be divided between the value of services of human capital, say $q_E E$, and the value of labor services, $q_{N \cdot H} N \cdot H$, where N is number of persons engaged, H is effective man-hours per person engaged, and $N \cdot H$ is the number of effective man-hours:

$$q_L L = q_E E + q_{N \cdot H} N \cdot H .$$

Our present measure of real labor input, corrected for quality change, is an estimate of the services of both labor, $N \cdot H$, and human capital, E.

Next, we suppose that the value of the product of the private domestic sector is equal to the value of factor outlay, as before:

$$p_I I + p_c C = q_K K + q_E E + q_{N \cdot H} N \cdot H .$$

The product of the educational sector consists entirely of investment in human capital, produced with physical capital, human capital, and labor in the educational sector:[57]

$$p_E I_E = q_K K_E + q_E E_E + q_{N \cdot H} N_E H_E ,$$

where p_E is the unit value of investment in human capital, K_E, E_E, N_E, and H_E are physical capital, human capital, persons engaged, and effective man-hours per person, all in the education sector.[58]

An important obstacle to implementation of a consolidated system of accounts is the need to compile data on the stock of physical capital in the educational sector. In compiling data on the stock of human capital and its service flow the procedure we have followed for physical capital would be reversed. Data on the flow of services is readily available; from these data we would infer an appropriate implied rate of return on educational investment.

5.7.3 Research and Development

To incorporate investment in the form of research into our accounting framework, we may suppose, as in our analysis of investment in education, that accumulated research and development can be treated as a stock, say R, with a corresponding investment flow, I_R. The value of output, including research and development investment, is equal to the value of factor outlay, including the services of accumulated research:

$$p_R I_R + p_I I + p_C C = q_K K + q_R R + q_L L \,,$$

where p_R is the unit value of investment in research and development and q_R is the service price of accumulated research. The value of labor and capital employed in producing research are, of course, included in the value of factor outlay. The absolute contribution of productivity change is the sum of productivity changes in research and in ordinary production activities.

Now, suppose that research and development are treated, erroneously, as a current expenditure so that no investment is recorded as an output. The value of output may then be written:

$$p_I I + p_C C = q_K K + q_R R + q_L L - p_R I_R \,.$$

If factor outlay on capital is computed as a residual equal to the value of output less the value of outlay on labor, the service price of capital is estimated, erroneously, as:

$$q_K{}^* = \frac{q_K K + q_R R - p_R I_R}{K} \,.$$

Notes

1. For a description of a complete accounting system, see Statistical Office of the United Nations (1968).
2. This interpretation is developed by Solow (1960), Richter (1966), and Jorgenson and Griliches (1967).
3. An extended description is presented by Malinvaud (1953) and Hicks (1961).
4. This interpretation is developed by Samuelson (1950, 1961), and many others; detailed references to the literature are given in Samuelson (1961, pp. 44–52).
5. See Samuelson (1961, pp. 53–56).
6. All references to data from the US national income and product accounts are to NIP (1966) and Denison (1962).
7. See NIP (1966, tables 1.4 and 1.5).

8. Our estimates are based on thos of Christensen and Jorgenson (1970).
9. Self-employed persons include proprietors and unpaid family workers. The method for imputation of labor compensation of the self-employed that underlies our estimates is discussed in detail by Christensen (1971). Alternative methos for imputation are reviewed in Kravis (1959).
10. See Denison (1969, p. 4).
11. See Christensen (1971).
12. Our estimates are based on those of Christensen and Jorgenson (1973b).
13. Our estimates are based on Christensen and Jorgenson (1973b).
14. Our estimates are based on Christensen and Jorgenson (1973b).
15. Data on flow of funds are based on estimates of *FFA* (1970), Goldsmith (1955, 1962, 1965), and Goldsmith, Lipsey and Mendelson (1963).
16. A detailed discussion of tax provisions affecting depreciation and amortization for tax purposes is given in Young (1968).
17. Estimates of replacement based on the straight-line method and estimates of depreciation and replacement based on the declining balance method for producer durables and nonresidential structures are contained in the Office of Business Economics *Capital Goods Study*. See Grose, Rottenberg and Wasson (1969).
18. The economic interpretation of Divisia indexes of total factor productivity has been discussed in Solow (1960), Richter (1966), and Jorgenson and Griliches (1967).
19. See System of National Accounts (1968, p. 58).
20. The perpetual inventory method is discussed by Goldsmith (1951), and employed extensively in his *Study of Saving* (1955), and more recent studies of U.S. national wealth (1962, 1965; Goldsmith, Lipsey and Mendelson, 1963). This method is also used in the OBE *Capital Goods Study* and in the study of capital stock for the United States by Tice (1967).
21. A more detailed discussion of the economic theory of replacement and depreciation is given by Jorgenson (1973).
22. See Feller (1957).
23. The dual to the durable goods model was developed by Arrow (1964), and Hall (1968), on the basis of earlier work by Hotelling (1925).
24. A representative study is the OBE *Capital Goods Study:* in this research straight-line and double-declining balance methods are employed. See Grose, Rottenberg and Wasson (1969).
25. For detailed discussion of the application of renewal theory to replacement and depreciation, see Jorgenson (1973).
26. A relatively recent work on capital equipment lifetimes is Marston, Winfrey, and Hempstead (1953). The classic work in the field is E.B. Kurtz (1930), which provides other references.
27. When a capitald good is retired, relative efficiency drops to zero.
28. See Meyer and Kuh (1957, pp. 91–100).
29. See Cagan (1965, pp. 222–226), Griliches (1960, pp. 197–200), and Wykoff, (1970, pp. 171–172).
30. See Hall (1968, pp. 19–20).
31. A detailed comparison of our estimates of labor input and those of Denison is given by Jorgenson and Griliches (1972a); see section 5.5.2 below for further discussion.
32. Denison (1967, p. 140).
33. Denison (1967, p. 140).

34. Denison (1967, p. 141).
35. Denison (1967, p. 14).
36. Denison (1967, p. 351).
37. Denison (1967, p. 14).
38. Denison (1962, pp. 112–113).
39. Denison (1969, p.8).
40. Statistical Office of the United Nations (1968, pp. 52–70).
41. These data have been compiled for John W. Kendrick's study (1961a). We are indebted to Kendrick for providing us with these data in advance of publication. The conceptual basis for compilation of the data is the same as in Kendrick's (1961a). The Office of Business Economics data on nonfarm proprietors and employees are from OBE (1966, tables 6.4 and 6.6).
42. See note 41, above.
43. See Jorgenson and Griliches (1967) and Griliches (1970). We have extended Griliches' estimates back to 1929, using relative earnings for 1939 and estimates of the educational attainment of the labor force for 1930 and 1940 by Folger and Nam (1964).
44. Our estimates are based on those of Christensen (1970).
45. The Office of Business Economics *Capital Stock Study* is reported in a series of articles. See Grose, Rottenberg and Wasson (1969), and the references given there. We are indebted to Robert Wasson for permission to use the underlying data on investment in current and constant prices.
46. See Goldsmith (1962, tables A-40 and A-41, pp. 186–189).
47. Asset deflators are weighted by the relative proportion of assets of each type in total assets; investment deflators are weighted by the relative proportion of investment goods of each type in total investment. See Denison (1969, p. 12). Asset deflators are appropriate for deflating asset values and for estimating rental values of capital services.
48. We are indebted to Shirley Loftus for providing us with these estimates.
49. These lifetimes have been compiled for the Office of Business Economics *Capital Stock Study*; we are indebted to Robert Wasson for providing us with data on service lives.
50. Bulletin F (1942) lives have been compared with alternative lifetimes by Wasson (1964).
51. A detailed derivation of prices of capital services is given by Hall and Jorgenson (1967, 1971) for continuous time. We have converted their formulation to discrete time, added property taxes, and introduced alternative measurements for the tax parameters. Similar formulas have been developed by Coen (1968).
52. For further discussion of this index of total factor productivity, see Jorgenson and Griliches (1967), especially pp. 250–254. The Divisia index of total factor productivity described in the text is a discrete approximation to the continuous Divisia index discussed by Jorgenson and Griliches.
53. See footnote 41, above.
54. See footnote 45, above.
55. Estimates of the stock of educational capital have been compiled by Schultz (1971); see especially pp. 123–131.
56. The incorporation of research and development into a complete system of accounts has been discussed by Griliches (1973).
57. Labor may include the imputed value of the time of students as well as the market value of the time of teachers.

6 The Accumulation of Human and Nonhuman Capital, 1948–1984

Dale W. Jorgenson and
Barbara M. Fraumeni

6.1 Introduction

The objective of this paper is to present a new system of national accounts for the U.S. economy. The purpose of this accounting system is to provide a comprehensive perspective on the role of capital formation in U.S. economic growth. The distinctive feature of our system is that we include fully comparable measures of investment in human and nonhuman capital. We have implemented this system of accounts for the private sector of the U.S. economy, covering the period 1948–1984.

The concept of human capital is based on an analogy between investment in physical capital and investment in human beings. The common element is that present expenditures yield returns over the future. In order to construct comparable measures of investment in human and nonhuman capital, we define human capital in terms of lifetime labor incomes for all individuals in the U.S. population. Lifetime labor incomes correspond to the asset values for investment goods used in accounting for physical or nonhuman capital. We present a summary of our methodology in section 6.2.

The U.S. national income and product accounts (NIPAs) contain a great deal of valuable information on capital formation. For example, these accounts provide data on investment in physical or nonhuman capital that are both comprehensive and detailed;[1] however, the national accounts are closely tied to market transactions, avoiding imputations for nonmarket activities wherever possible. Not surprisingly, investment in human capital is not included in the U.S. national accounts.

The perspective on capital formation provided by the U.S. national accounts is seriously incomplete, as a consequence of the fact that these accounts are limited to market transactions. Our measures of capital formation show that investment in human capital is at least four times the magnitude of investment in nonhuman capital; moreover, the value of wealth in the form of human capital is over eleven times the value of physical or nonhuman capital.

The total product of an economic system includes investment in human and nonhuman capital and consumption of market and nonmarket goods and services. We define full consumption as the sum of goods and services supplied by market and nonmarket activities. Similarly, we define full investment as the sum of investments in human and nonhuman capital. Finally, we define full product as the sum of investment and consumption. We present measures of full product, investment and consumption in section 6.3.

Our system of accounts assigns an equal role to consumption and investment as proportions of the national product; however, the relative importance of investment is much greater in our system than in the U.S. national accounts. Full investment is around 50 percent of full product, where human and nonhuman capital are treated on a comparable basis. Full consumption is about half of full product, where both market and nonmarket goods and services are included in consumption.

The value of full product is equal to the value of outlays on the services of human and nonhuman capital. These outlays take the form of labor and property compensation. We define full labor compensation as the sum of market labor compensation for activities involving employment through the labor market and nonmarket labor compensation for activities resulting in investment in education and direct consumption of labor services. Similarly, we define full property compensation as the sum of market and nonmarket property compensation. Finally, we define full factor outlay as the sum of labor and property compensation. We present measures for full factor outlay, labor compensation, and property compensation in section 6.3.

Nonmarket labor compensation is more than 80 percent of labor compensation, since full compensation includes the value of nonmarket activities such as investment in education, household production, and leisure time. Full labor compensation is around 90 percent of factor outlay, while property compensation is close to 10 percent of the total. In our system of national accounts the relative importance of labor compensation is much greater than in the U.S. national accounts.

Both property and labor compensation must be reduced by taxes and increased by subsidies to obtain incomes accruing to individuals. We define full labor income as the sum of market and nonmarket labor compensation after taxes. Similarly, we define full property income as the sum of market and nonmarket property compensation after taxes. Full income is defined as the sum of labor income and property income. We present measures for full income, labor income, and property income in section 6.4.

Receipts accruing to individuals include full income and government transfer payments to persons. Receipts are divided between consumption of market and nonmarket goods and services and saving in the form of human and nonhuman capital. We define full personal consumption expenditures as the sum of market goods and services consumed by households and nonprofit institutions, the services of human capital consumed directly through household production and leisure, and the services of nonhuman capital consumed directly in the form of services of consumers' durables and owner-occupied housing. We define full consumer outlays as the sum of personal consumption expenditures, personal transfer payments to foreigners, and personal nontax payments. We present measures for full consumer outlays and saving in the form of human and nonhuman capital in section 6.4.

Since our system of accounts includes the consumption of both market and nonmarket goods and services, consumer outlays are much greater than in the U.S. national accounts. The market share of consumer outlays averages around 35 percent of total outlays. Similarly, our concept of human and nonhuman saving is much more comprehensive than the concept of saving in the U.S. national accounts. Human saving is between 80 and 90 percent of full saving. Nonhuman saving, the only portion included in the U.S. national accounts, is between 10 and 20 percent of the total.

The proportion of full saving to national expenditure ranges from 45 to 50 percent in our accounting system. This is far greater than the proportion of national saving to national expenditure in the U.S. national accounts. The saving proportion in our accounts rose to a peak in the year 1971 and has been gradually declining since then. The saving rate is lower in 1983 and 1984 than at any previous time in the postwar period.

To integrate our measures of income and expenditure with measures of human and nonhuman wealth, we require concepts of depreciation and revaluation for human and nonhuman capital. We define depreciation of human capital in terms of changes in the lifetime labor incomes of individuals with age. Depreciation on human capital is the sum of changes in lifetime labor incomes with age for all individuals who remain in the population and lifetime labor incomes of all individuals who die or emigrate. Similarly, we define depreciation for nonhuman capital in terms of changes in asset values with age. Depreciation on nonhuman capital is the sum of changes in asset values for all investment goods remaining in the capital stock and the asset values of all investment goods that are retired from the capital stock. We define full depreciation as the sum of depreciation for human and nonhuman capital.

Depreciation is a very large component of saving in the form of both human and nonhuman capital. Depreciation was a fairly stable proportion of full gross saving at around 35 percent until the mid-1960s. Since that time the relative importance of depreciation has risen steadily to almost 50 percent of saving. By contrast net saving has declined from nearly 65 percent of saving at the beginning of the postwar period to slightly over 50 percent at the end of the period.

We define revaluation for human capital in terms of changes in lifetime labor incomes from period to period for individuals with a given set of demographic characteristics—age, sex and education. Revaluation of human wealth is the sum of changes in lifetime incomes for all individuals initially in the population, holding age, sex and education for each individual constant. Similarly, we define revaluation for nonhuman capital in terms of changes in asset values from period to period for individual investment goods. Revaluation of nonhuman capital is the sum of changes in asset values for all investment goods initially in the capital stock, holding the age of each investment good constant. We define full revaluation as the sum of revaluation for human and nonhuman capital.

We conclude the development of a new system of national accounts for the United States by defining full wealth as the sum of human and nonhuman wealth. The change in wealth from period to period is the sum of investment in human and nonhuman capital, net of depreciation, and the revaluation of human and nonhuman capital. We present measures of full investment, depreciation, revaluation and changes in wealth in section 6.5 below. Finally, we present measures of full wealth in section 6.5.

Human wealth greatly predominates in the value of wealth, amounting to more than 90 percent of the total throughout the postwar period. The U.S. national accounts do not include wealth accounts. Only investment in the form of physical or nonhuman wealth is included in the national accounts. Wealth accounts consistent with the U.S. national accounts would exclude human wealth altogether. Obviously, the exclusion of investment in the form of human wealth is an extremely important omission.

It is necessary to emphasize that our study is exploratory in character. Unlike the U.S. national accounts, which are firmly rooted in market transactions, our system of accounts involves very sizable imputations for the value of nonmarket activities. This disadvantage must be weighed against the important advantage that we provide a comprehensive view of capital formation. Judgments about the relative importance of investment and consumption, labor and property income, or different forms of saving require information of the type presented in our new system of national accounts.

6.2 Methodology

The implementation of our system of accounts for human capital requires a new data base for measuring lifetime labor incomes for all individuals in the U.S. population.[2] Our system includes demographic accounts that incorporate population data from the U.S. Bureau of the Census. Our demographic accounts include annual estimates of mid-year population by sex and age for individuals under 75 years of age. Using data from the censuses of population for 1940, 1950, 1960, 1970, and 1980, we have distributed the population of each sex by individual years of age and individual years of educational attainment. The estimation of changes in the numbers of individuals classified by age, sex and education from year to year requires data on enrollment in formal schooling and births, deaths and migration.[3]

The starting point for the measurement of lifetime labor incomes for all individuals in the U.S. population is the data base on market labor activities assembled by Gollop and Jorgenson (1980, 1983). This data base includes the number of employed persons, hours worked, and labor compensation for the United States on an annual basis, cross-classified by sex, age, education, employment class, occupation and industry. We have derived annual estimates of hours worked and labor compensation required for measuring incomes from market labor activities by summing over employment class, occupation and industry and by distributing the work force of each sex by individual years of age from 14 to 74 and individual years of educational attainment from no education to 1 to 17 or higher. We obtain average hourly labor compensation annually for individuals classified by the two sexes, sixty-one age groups, and eighteen education groups for a total of 2,196 groups by dividing market labor compensation by hours worked by each group.

The second step in the measurement of lifetime labor incomes is to impute labor compensation and hours devoted to nonmarket activities. Six types of nonmarket activities are commonly distinguished in studies of time allocation—production of goods and services within the household unit, volunteer work outside the household unit, commuting to work, formal education, leisure, and the satisfaction of physiological needs such as eating and sleeping.[4] We classify time spent satisfying physiological needs as maintenance and exclude this time from our measure of time spent in nonmarket activities. We assume that the time available for all market and nonmarket activities has been constant over time and is equal to fourteen hours per day for all individuals.

We allocate the annual time available for all individuals in the population among work, schooling, household production and leisure, and maintenance. Our system of demographic accounts includes the enrollment status for individuals of each sex between 5 and 34 years of age. We estimate the time spent in formal schooling for all individuals by assigning 1,300 hours per year to each person enrolled in school. We allocate time spent in schooling to investment. Similarly, our demographic accounts include employment status for individuals of each sex between 14 and 74 years of age. Hours worked for all employed individuals, classified by sex, age and education, are included in our data base for market labor activities. We allocate time that is not spent working or in formal schooling directly to consumption. For all individuals this time is equal to the difference between fourteen hours per day and time spent working or in school.

The third step in the measure of lifetime labor incomes is to impute the value of labor compensation for nonmarket activities.[5] For this purpose we first obtain average hourly labor compensation for all employed persons classified by sex, age and education from our data base for market labor activities. Second, we estimate marginal tax rates for all employed persons, again classified by sex, age and education. We multiply compensation per hour by one minus the marginal tax rate to obtain imputed hourly labor compensation for nonmarket activities other than formal schooling. Since individuals under 14 years of age do not participate in the labor force, their imputed hourly labor compensation is set equal to zero. Individuals over 74 years of age are also assigned zero as their hourly labor compensation.

To estimate lifetime labor incomes for all individuals in the U.S. population, we distinguish among three stages in the life cycle. In the first stage individuals may participate in formal schooling but not in the labor market. In the second stage, individuals may enroll in school and also work. In the third stage, individuals may participate in the labor market but not in formal schooling. For individuals in the third stage of the life cycle, total labor compensation is the sum of compensation for market labor activities after taxes and imputed compensation for nonmarket labor activities. For individuals in the second stage of the life cycle, total labor compensation also includes imputed labor compensation for schooling. For individuals in the first stage of the life cycle, labor compensation includes only the imputed value of time spent in schooling.

For an individual in the third stage of the life cycle, we assume that expected incomes in future time periods are equal to the incomes of individuals of the same sex and education, but with the age that the individual will have in the future time period, adjusted for increases in real income. We assume that real incomes rise over time at the rate of Harrod-neutral technical change, which we estimate at 2 percent per year. We weight income for each future year by the probability of survival, given the initial age of the individual. We obtain these probabilities by sex from publications of the National Center for Health Statistics. Where necessary, these survival functions, giving probability of survival by age and sex, are interpolated by means of standard demographic techniques. Finally, we discount expected future incomes at a real rate of return of 4 percent per year to obtain the lifetime labor income of an individual of a given sex, age and education.

For an individual at the second stage of the life cycle, combining formal schooling with the possibility of participation in the labor market, we impute the value of time spent in schooling through its effect on lifetime labor income. For an individual of a given sex and age who is completing the highest level of schooling, grade 17 or higher, lifetime labor income is the discounted value of expected future labor incomes for a person of that sex and age and seventeen or more years of schooling. The imputed labor compensation for the time spent in formal schooling is equal to the difference between the lifetime labor incomes of an individual with seventeen or more years of education and an individual with the same sex and age and one less year of education, less tuition and fees for that grade of schooling. Total labor compensation is equal to the value of time spent in formal schooling plus labor compensation for market and nonmarket activities other than formal schooling.

For an individual completing grade 16, lifetime labor income is equal to the lifetime labor income of an individual of the same sex and education, but one year older, plus expected labor compensation for one year, discounted back to the present and multiplied by the probability of survival for one year. Expected labor compensation is equal to the probability of enrollment in grade 17 or higher, multiplied by market and nonmarket labor compensation for a person enrolled in that grade, and one minus the probability of enrollment, multiplied by market and nonmarket labor compensation for a person with sixteen years of education, not enrolled in school. As before, the imputed labor compensation for the time spent in formal schooling is equal to the difference between the lifetime incomes of an individual with sixteen years of education and an individual with the same sex and age and one less year of education, less tuition and fees. Using the same approach to defining lifetime labor incomes for individuals completing earlier grades, lifetime incomes and imputed labor compensation for the time spent in formal schooling can be determined for individuals completing fifteen years of education, fourteen years of education, and so on.

For an individual in the first stage of the life cycle, where participation in the labor market is ruled out, the value of labor compensation is limited to the imputed value of schooling. Lifetime incomes for individuals at this stage of the life cycle can be determined for individuals completing one year of education, two years of education, and so on, working back from higher levels of education as outlined above. For individuals too young to be enrolled in school, imputed labor compensation is zero, but lifetime labor incomes are well defined. The value of a newborn entrant into the population is equal to the lifetime labor income of that individual at age zero. Investment in human capital in any year is the sum of lifetime incomes for all individuals born in that year and all immigrants plus the imputed labor compensation for formal schooling for all individuals enrolled in school.

The implementation of our new system of national accounts for the United States begins with the accounting system presented by Fraumeni and Jorgenson (1980). That accounting system includes a production account, an income and expenditure account, and accumulation account, and a wealth account—all in current and constant prices;[6] however, their accounts for capital services, investment, and wealth are limited to nonhuman capital. We have incorporated their estimates for nonhuman capital into our system of U.S. national accounts. We have added estimates of the services of human capital, investment in human capital, and human wealth.

Our system of U.S. national accounts includes a production account that divides the national product between investment and consumption and divides national factor input between the services of human and nonhuman capital. The system also includes an income and expenditure account that divides income between compensation for human and nonhuman capital services and divides expenditures between saving and current consumption. Changes in wealth are divided between investment and revaluation of human and nonhuman capital in an accumulation account. The system is completed by a wealth account incorporating human and nonhuman wealth.

As a basis for comparison of measurements of human capital based on lifetime labor incomes with alternative approaches, we can compare our estimates of human wealth and investment in human capital with those of Kendrick (1976). Like Machlup (1962), Nordhaus and Tobin (1972), Schultz (1961b) and others, Kendrick employs costs of education, including earnings foregone by students, as a basis for measuring investment through education. He employs costs of rearing as a basis for measuring investment through addition of new members of the population. Since his estimates of human capital are based on costs of education and rearing rather than lifetime labor incomes, he omits the value of nonmarket activities from his estimates of human capital. Our estimates of human capital are much larger than those of Kendrick. Our estimates of nonhuman wealth are also higher than Kendrick's and our estimates of total wealth are much higher than his.[7]

6.3 Production

In implementing our production account for the United States, we limit our attention to the private domestic sector of the U.S. economy, following Fraumeni and Jorgenson (1980). The total product of the private domestic sector of the U.S. economy includes investment in human and nonhuman capital and consumption of market and nonmarket goods and services. We add to consumption of market goods and services, as defined by Fraumeni and Jorgenson, our estimates of consumption of nonmarket goods and services. Similarly, we add to their estimates of investment in nonhuman capital our estimates of investment in human capital.

The value of total product is equal to the value of total factor outlay for the production account. Total factor outlay in the U.S. economy includes market labor compensation for activities involving employment through the labor market and nonmarket labor compensation for activities resulting in investment in education and direct consumption of labor services. We add to market labor compensation, as defined by Fraumeni and Jorgenson (1986), our estimates of the value of nonmarket labor compensation. We incorporate their estimates of property compensation into our factor outlay account.

We present the production account in current prices for the private domestic sector of the U.S. economy for the year 1982 in table 6.1. We first observe that the value of time spent in household production and leisure, which is assigned to consumption, is larger than the gross private domestic product, as defined by Fraumeni and Jorgenson. The value of investment in human capital is comparable in magnitude to gross private domestic product. Considering the value of time spent in household production and leisure and investment in human capital together, we find that outlay on human capital services is more than twice the size of gross private domestic factor outlay, as defined by Fraumeni and Jorgenson.

Our next objective is to allocate the value of total product for the private domestic sector of the U.S. economy between consumption and investment for the period 1948–1984. We first estimate the value of investment in human and nonhuman capital for all years. The value of investment in human capital is equal to the value of investment in education and the value of new members of the population resulting from births and migration. Our estimates of investment in nonhuman capital are based on those of Fraumeni and Jorgenson. We present estimates of investment in human capital, investment in nonhuman capital, and full investment in current prices in table 6.2 and in constant prices in table 6.3.

The value of investment in human capital is by far the largest part of full investment, varying from 0.812 to 0.869 as a proportion of

Table 6.1
Production account, gross private domestic product and factor outlay, United States, 1982 (billions of current dollars)

		Product	
1.		Private gross national product (table 1.7, line 1 minus line 12)	2,822.1
2.	−	Compensation of employees in government enterprises (table 6.4, lines 81 and 86)	39.6
3.	−	Rest-of-the-world gross national product (table 1.7, line 15)	51.2
4.	−	Federal indirect business tax and nontax accruals (table 3.2, line 9)	48.1
5.	+	Capital stock tax (table 3.1, n. 2)	—
6.	−	State and local indirect business tax and nontax accruals (table 3.3, line 7)	210.8
7.	+	Business motor vehicle licenses (table 3.5, line 25)	2.1
8.	+	Business property taxes (table 3.3, line 9)	85.3
9.	+	Business other taxes (table 3.5, lines 26, 27)	14.8
10.	+	Subsidies less current surplus of federal government enterprises (table 3.2, line 27)	16.0
11.	+	Subsidies less current surplus of state and local government enterprises (table 3.3, line 22)	−7.3
12.	+	Imputation for nonhuman capital services	338.7
13.	=	Gross private domestic product	2,921.9
14.	+	Time in household production and leisure	3,944.5
15.	+	Investment in human capital	4,568.6
16.	=	Full gross private domestic product	11,435.0
		Factor outlay	
1.		Capital consumption allowances (table 1.9, line 2)	383.2
2.	+	Business transfer payments (table 1.9, line 7)	14.3
3.	+	Statistical discrepency (table 1.9, line 8)	−0.1
4.	+	Certain indirect business taxes (product account above, 5 + 7 + 8 + 9)	102.2
5.	+	Income originating in business (table 1.12, line 14)	2,010.6
6.	−	Compensation of employees in government enterprises (table 6.4, line 81 and line 86)	39.6
7.	+	Income originating in households and institutions (table 1.12, line 19)	112.7
8.	+	Imputation for nonhuman capital services	338.7
9.	=	Gross private domestic factor outlay	2,921.9
10.	+	Imputations for human capital services (14 + 15 above)	8,513.1
11.	=	Full gross private domestic factor outlay	11,435.0

Note: All table references are to the NIPA tables in the March 1986 *Survey of Current Business*, with the exception of capital stock tax which refers to Bureau of Economic Analysis (1966).

Table 6.2
Full investment (billions of current dollars)

Year	Full investment	Human investment	Nonhuman investment	Human share	Nonhuman share
1948	471.0	392.9	78.1	0.834	0.166
1949	488.4	415.5	72.9	0.851	0.149
1950	536.5	441.3	95.2	0.823	0.177
1951	587.8	477.2	110.5	0.812	0.188
1952	619.9	508.9	111.0	0.821	0.179
1953	679.9	563.7	116.3	0.829	0.171
1954	720.7	607.6	113.0	0.843	0.157
1955	768.1	635.9	132.3	0.828	0.172
1956	816.7	678.6	138.1	0.831	0.169
1957	896.4	755.2	141.2	0.843	0.157
1958	951.4	819.5	132.0	0.861	0.139
1959	997.4	846.5	150.9	0.849	0.151
1960	1,034.5	884.7	149.8	0.855	0.145
1961	1,102.9	952.5	150.4	0.864	0.136
1962	1,163.8	996.1	167.7	0.856	0.144
1963	1,209.6	1,031.3	178.3	0.853	0.147
1964	1,331.1	1,140.5	190.6	0.857	0.143
1965	1,406.9	1,193.2	213.7	0.848	0.152
1966	1,504.6	1,268.3	236.3	0.843	0.157
1967	1,596.1	1,355.7	240.4	0.849	0.151
1968	1,728.5	1,466.7	261.8	0.849	0.151
1969	1,864.0	1,582.9	281.0	0.849	0.151
1970	2,074.1	1,796.2	277.9	0.866	0.134
1971	2,335.9	2,029.6	306.3	0.869	0.131
1972	2,413.7	2,068.3	345.5	0.857	0.143
1973	2,568.9	2,170.2	398.7	0.845	0.155
1974	2,809.0	2,397.1	411.9	0.853	0.147
1975	3,143.7	2,722.2	421.5	0.866	0.134
1976	3,316.0	2,817.4	498.5	0.850	0.150
1977	3,626.9	3,047.3	579.6	0.840	0.160
1978	3,794.1	3,121.1	673.0	0.823	0.177
1979	4,287.2	3,545.2	741.9	0.827	0.173
1980	4,724.9	3,974.7	750.1	0.841	0.159
1981	5,129.4	4,289.4	839.9	0.836	0.164
1982	5,354.4	4,568.6	785.8	0.853	0.147
1983	5,701.5	4,843.1	858.4	0.849	0.151
1984	6,153.2	5,123.2	1,030.0	0.833	0.167

Table 6.3
Full investment (billions of constant dollars)

	Full investment		Human investment		Nonhuman investment	
Year	quantity	price	quantity	price	quantity	price
1949	2,899.1	0.168	2,669.1	0.156	282.0	0.259
1950	3,025.0	0.177	2,686.5	0.164	353.8	0.269
1951	3,144.1	0.187	2,756.9	0.173	389.3	0.284
1952	3,207.0	0.193	2,812.6	0.181	396.8	0.280
1953	3,293.1	0.206	2,878.3	0.196	414.0	0.281
1954	3,349.0	0.215	2,956.1	0.206	400.5	0.282
1955	3,487.9	0.220	3,032.9	0.210	450.0	0.294
1956	3,552.8	0.230	3,106.6	0.218	446.1	0.310
1957	3,658.0	0.245	3,226.6	0.234	439.3	0.321
1958	3,706.2	0.257	3,312.7	0.247	412.5	0.320
1959	3,805.1	0.262	3,356.2	0.252	458.0	0.330
1960	3,872.9	0.267	3,438.3	0.257	448.9	0.334
1961	3,991.1	0.276	3,556.0	0.268	452.6	0.332
1962	4,091.0	0.284	3,606.4	0.276	495.2	0.339
1963	4,209.2	0.287	3,694.2	0.279	523.0	0.341
1964	4,338.5	0.307	3,790.0	0.301	553.9	0.344
1965	4,402.0	0.320	3,797.7	0.314	604.2	0.354
1966	4,443.3	0.339	3,786.3	0.335	652.6	0.362
1967	4,508.5	0.354	3,851.1	0.352	653.3	0.368
1968	4,625.5	0.374	3,941.8	0.372	679.2	0.385
1969	4,767.4	0.391	4,072.2	0.389	690.9	0.407
1970	4,876.0	0.425	4,218.3	0.426	654.6	0.425
1971	5,020.9	0.465	4,335.4	0.468	682.4	0.449
1972	5,010.3	0.482	4,268.6	0.485	741.0	0.466
1973	5,066.4	0.507	4,240.4	0.512	829.1	0.481
1974	5,045.1	0.557	4,253.6	0.564	792.4	0.520
1975	5,046.8	0.623	4,323.7	0.630	718.7	0.587
1976	5,124.4	0.647	4,328.4	0.651	794.7	0.627
1977	5,286.1	0.686	4,418.0	0.690	868.6	0.667
1978	5,385.0	0.705	4,447.7	0.702	938.0	0.718
1979	5,434.5	0.789	4,487.8	0.790	947.3	0.783
1980	5,439.3	0.869	4,560.3	0.872	878.7	0.854
1981	5,468.9	0.938	4,575.7	0.937	892.9	0.941
1982	5,354.4	1.000	4,568.6	1.000	785.8	1.000
1983	5,395.4	1.057	4,543.7	1.066	853.4	1.006
1984	5,501.4	1.118	4,510.4	1.136	1,002.9	1.027

investment during the period 1948–1984. The share of investment in nonhuman capital fell over the period from 0.166 in 1948 to 0.131 in 1971. The nonhuman share then rose to 0.167 in 1984, almost the same level as in 1948. The price of investment in human capital has risen much more rapidly than the price of investment in nonhuman capital. By contrast investment in human capital has grown much more slowly than investment in nonhuman capital. Investment in human capital reached a peak in 1971 that was not surpassed until 1977. The level of investment in human capital in 1984 was below the peak for the period as a whole, which was reached in 1981.

Our final step in allocating the value of total product of the private sector of the U.S. economy between consumption and investment for the period 1948–1984 is to estimate the value of consumption for all years. The value of full consumption is equal to the value of consumption of market goods and services plus the value of nonmarket consumption in the form of time spent in household production and leisure. Our estimates of consumption of market goods and services are based on those of Fraumeni and Jorgenson. We present estimates of full consumption, investment and product in current prices in table 6.4 and constant prices in table 6.5. The share of consumption in total product is almost the same as the share of investment, falling from 0.523 in 1948 to a low of 0.485 in 1971 and rising to a peak of 0.536 in 1984 at the end of the period. The price of investment has risen more rapidly than the price of consumption. By contrast investment has grown more slowly than consumption.

We next analyze changes in the structure of full gross private domestic product for the U.S. economy over the period 1948–1984. We present growth rates of full product, investment, and consumption for the period as a whole and for eight subperiods in table 6.6. We give growth rates for each measure of output in current and constant prices and a growth rate for the corresponding price index. We also provide growth rates for each output measure in per capita terms.

The growth rate of full investment was at its maximum during the period 1948–1953 at 3.19 percent per year. The growth rate of investment per capita was only 0.54 percent per year for the period as a whole and was negative for the last of the eight subperiods. By contrast the growth rate of full consumption per capita was positive for all eight subperiods with a rising trend, reaching a maximum in the period 1973–1979 at 1.87 percent. The growth rate of full product showed little trend through 1960–1966 after an initial burst of growth

Table 6.4
Full gross private domestic product (billions of current dollars)

Year	Full product	Full consumption	Full investment	Consumption share	Investment share
1948	988.4	517.4	471.0	0.523	0.477
1949	1,037.7	549.3	488.4	0.529	0.471
1950	1,113.3	576.8	536.5	0.518	0.482
1951	1,203.0	615.2	587.8	0.511	0.489
1952	1,262.8	642.9	619.9	0.509	0.491
1953	1,379.3	699.4	679.9	0.507	0.493
1954	1,462.0	741.3	720.7	0.507	0.493
1955	1,531.8	763.6	768.1	0.499	0.501
1956	1,617.5	800.8	816.7	0.495	0.505
1957	1,759.1	862.7	896.4	0.490	0.510
1958	1,877.6	926.2	951.4	0.493	0.507
1959	1,951.5	954.2	997.4	0.489	0.511
1960	2,027.8	993.3	1,034.5	0.490	0.510
1961	2,162.8	1,059.9	1,102.9	0.490	0.510
1962	2,273.7	1,109.9	1,163.8	0.488	0.512
1963	2,360.4	1,150.8	1,209.6	0.488	0.512
1964	2,587.4	1,256.2	1,331.1	0.486	0.514
1965	2,765.8	1,358.9	1,406.9	0.491	0.509
1966	2,980.1	1,475.5	1,504.6	0.495	0.505
1967	3,168.4	1,572.4	1,596.1	0.496	0.504
1968	3,401.3	1,672.8	1,728.5	0.492	0.508
1969	3,651.7	1,787.7	1,864.0	0.490	0.510
1970	4,056.9	1,982.8	2,074.1	0.489	0.511
1971	4,538.8	2,202.9	2,335.9	0.485	0.515
1972	4,785.5	2,371.8	2,413.7	0.496	0.504
1973	5,184.1	2,615.1	2,568.9	0.504	0.496
1974	5,670.2	2,861.2	2,809.0	0.505	0.495
1975	6,335.6	3,191.9	3,143.7	0.504	0.496
1976	6,790.7	3,474.7	3,316.0	0.512	0.488
1977	7,382.5	3,755.7	3,626.9	0.509	0.491
1978	7,911.4	4,117.3	3,794.1	0.520	0.480
1979	8,918.2	4,631.0	4,287.2	0.519	0.481
1980	9,731.1	5,006.2	4,724.9	0.514	0.486
1981	10,620.7	5,491.4	5,129.4	0.517	0.483
1982	11,435.0	6,080.6	5,354.4	0.532	0.468
1983	12,272.2	6,570.7	5,701.5	0.535	0.465
1984	13,254.7	7,101.5	6,153.2	0.536	0.464

Table 6.5
Full gross private domestic product (billions of constant dollars)

	Full product		Full consumption		Full investment	
Year	quantity	price	quantity	price	quantity	price
1949	5,597.2	0.185	2,696.7	0.204	2,899.1	0.168
1950	5,755.8	0.193	2,736.6	0.211	3,025.0	0.177
1951	5,944.0	0.202	2,809.1	0.219	3,144.1	0.187
1952	6,062.9	0.208	2,865.2	0.224	3,207.0	0.193
1953	6,234.7	0.221	2,950.5	0.237	3,293.1	0.206
1954	6,321.0	0.231	2,982.3	0.249	3,349.0	0.215
1955	6,524.7	0.235	3,051.4	0.250	3,487.9	0.220
1956	6,648.6	0.243	3,110.6	0.257	3,552.8	0.230
1957	6,830.7	0.258	3,188.7	0.271	3,658.0	0.245
1958	6,943.8	0.270	3,252.6	0.285	3,706.2	0.257
1959	7,105.9	0.275	3,317.3	0.288	3,805.1	0.262
1960	7,240.1	0.280	3,383.7	0.294	3,872.9	0.267
1961	7,464.4	0.290	3,490.1	0.304	3,991.1	0.276
1962	7,643.6	0.297	3,570.3	0.311	4,091.0	0.284
1963	7,858.7	0.300	3,667.9	0.314	4,209.2	0.287
1964	8,101.9	0.319	3,782.4	0.332	4,338.5	0.307
1965	8,280.5	0.334	3,895.2	0.349	4,402.0	0.320
1966	8,444.5	0.353	4,014.5	0.368	4,443.3	0.339
1967	8,620.3	0.368	4,123.3	0.381	4,508.5	0.354
1968	8,833.0	0.385	4,219.7	0.396	4,625.5	0.374
1969	9,060.5	0.403	4,306.9	0.415	4,767.4	0.391
1970	9,286.4	0.437	4,424.0	0.448	4,876.0	0.425
1971	9,561.0	0.475	4,554.2	0.484	5,020.9	0.465
1972	9,700.9	0.493	4,701.3	0.504	5,010.3	0.482
1973	9,848.5	0.526	4,791.9	0.546	5,066.4	0.507
1974	9,929.0	0.571	4,890.0	0.585	5,045.1	0.557
1975	10,129.2	0.625	5,085.7	0.628	5,046.8	0.623
1976	10,345.4	0.656	5,223.9	0.665	5,124.4	0.647
1977	10,643.1	0.694	5,360.3	0.701	5,286.1	0.686
1978	10,872.9	0.728	5,490.7	0.750	5,385.0	0.705
1979	11,027.5	0.805	5,638.3	0.821	5,434.5	0.789
1980	11,223.5	0.867	5,783.3	0.866	5,439.3	0.869
1981	11,375.0	0.934	5,905.6	0.930	5,468.9	0.938
1982	11,435.0	1.000	6,080.6	1.000	5,354.4	1.000
1983	11,584.5	1.059	6,189.0	1.062	5,395.4	1.057
1984	11,811.5	1.122	6,310.0	1.125	5,501.4	1.118

Table 6.6
Full gross private domestic product, rates of growth, 1949–1984

	1949–1984	1949–1953	1953–1957	1957–1960	1960–1966	1966–1969	1969–1973	1973–1979	1979–1984
Full product:									
Current prices	7.28	7.11	6.08	4.74	6.42	6.77	8.76	9.04	7.93
Constant prices	2.13	2.70	2.28	1.94	2.56	2.35	2.08	1.95	1.29
Constant prices per capita	0.84	1.04	0.51	0.13	1.11	1.25	1.12	1.11	0.24
Price index	5.15	4.45	3.87	2.73	3.86	4.42	6.66	7.09	6.64
Full investment:									
Current prices	7.24	8.27	6.91	4.78	6.24	7.14	8.02	8.54	7.23
Constant prices	1.83	3.19	2.63	1.90	2.29	2.35	1.52	1.17	0.24
Constant prices per capita	0.54	1.52	0.86	0.10	0.84	1.25	0.55	0.33	–0.80
Price index	5.42	5.10	4.33	2.87	3.98	4.76	6.50	7.37	6.97
Full consumption:									
Current prices	7.31	6.04	5.25	4.70	6.60	6.40	9.51	9.52	8.55
Constant prices	2.43	2.25	1.94	1.98	2.85	2.34	2.67	2.71	2.25
Constant prices per capita	1.13	0.59	0.17	0.17	1.40	1.25	1.70	1.87	1.20
Price index	4.88	3.75	3.35	2.72	3.74	4.01	6.86	6.80	6.30

in full product at 2.70 percent per year in 1948–1953. Since 1966 the growth rate of full product has gradually declined, exhibiting the much-discussed slowdown in U.S. economic growth.

Our next objective is to allocate the value of total factor outlay for the private domestic sector of the U.S. economy between labor and property services for the period 1948–1984. We first estimate the value of outlay on the services of human capital for all years. The value of outlay on the services of human capital is the sum of outlay on market and nonmarket labor activities. Our estimates of market labor outlays are based on those of Fraumeni and Jorgenson. We present estimates of market labor outlay, nonmarket labor outlay and full labor outlay in current prices in table 6.7 and constant prices in table 6.8. The share of nonmarket labor outlay has been by far the largest part of labor outlay, varying relatively little from 0.835 at the beginning of the postwar period. The prices of market and nonmarket labor outlay move in parallel throughout the period, as do the corresponding quantities.

We combine our estimates of the services of human capital with estimates of the services of nonhuman capital, which are based on those of Fraumeni and Jorgenson. We present the value of full factor outlay, property outlay, and labor outlay in current prices in table 6.9 and constant prices in table 6.10. Labor has had a predominant share in full factor outlay, averaging around 90 percent throughout the period. The share of property has averaged close to 10 percent, rising slightly from 0.112 at the beginning of the period to 0.119 at the end of the period. The price of labor outlay has risen relative to the price of property outlay, while capital services have risen relative to labor services. Capital services have grown more rapidly than output throughout the period.

To analyze changes in the structure of gross private domestic factor outlay, we present growth rates of full factor output, labor outlay, and property outlay for the period 1948–1984 and for eight subperiods in table 6.11. The growth rate of labor input or full labor outlay at constant prices was only slightly greater than the growth of population. The per capita growth rate of labor input was only 0.38 per year for the period as a whole. This growth rate was negative or zero for two of the eight subperiods.

The growth rate of capital input or full property outlay at constant prices exceeded the growth of population by a considerable margin. The per capita growth rate of capital input was 2.02 percent per year. This growth rate was positive throughout the period. The growth rate

Table 6.7
Full labor outlay (billions of current dollars)

Year	Full labor outlay	Market labor outlay	Nonmarket labor outlay	Market share	Nonmarket share
1948	877.6	144.8	732.8	0.165	0.835
1949	929.5	144.1	785.3	0.155	0.845
1950	988.6	156.9	831.7	0.159	0.841
1951	1,062.7	180.5	882.2	0.170	0.830
1952	1,123.4	194.1	929.3	0.173	0.827
1953	1,235.2	208.9	1,026.3	0.169	0.831
1954	1,316.8	209.9	1,106.9	0.159	0.841
1955	1,360.7	219.2	1,141.5	0.161	0.839
1956	1,445.7	234.7	1,211.0	0.162	0.838
1957	1,585.2	250.6	1,334.6	0.158	0.842
1958	1,710.0	257.2	1,452.8	0.150	0.850
1959	1,756.6	270.1	1,486.5	0.154	0.846
1960	1,832.8	282.7	1,550.1	0.154	0.846
1961	1,961.8	292.4	1,669.3	0.149	0.851
1962	2,052.4	309.8	1,742.6	0.151	0.849
1963	2,118.4	320.5	1,797.9	0.151	0.849
1964	2,321.5	339.5	1,982.0	0.146	0.854
1965	2,465.1	363.0	2,102.1	0.147	0.853
1966	2,655.7	401.7	2,254.1	0.151	0.849
1967	2,838.7	427.3	2,411.4	0.151	0.849
1968	3,056.5	470.7	2,585.8	0.154	0.846
1969	3,296.7	519.1	2,777.6	0.157	0.843
1970	3,698.9	556.2	3,142.6	0.150	0.850
1971	4,145.7	594.2	3,551.5	0.143	0.857
1972	4,342.8	652.7	3,690.2	0.150	0.850
1973	4,706.6	745.2	3,961.4	0.158	0.842
1974	5,181.2	816.1	4,365.1	0.158	0.842
1975	5,763.2	858.8	4,904.4	0.149	0.851
1976	6,139.3	957.3	5,181.9	0.156	0.844
1977	6,630.6	1,063.0	5,567.6	0.160	0.840
1978	7,068.3	1,214.7	5,853.5	0.172	0.828
1979	8,010.9	1,375.3	6,635.6	0.172	0.828
1980	8,758.3	1,493.9	7,264.4	0.171	0.829
1981	9,485.9	1,635.5	7,850.4	0.172	0.828
1982	10,205.1	1,692.0	8,513.1	0.166	0.834
1983	10,908.4	1,790.5	9,117.8	0.164	0.836
1984	11,682.8	1,968.6	9,714.1	0.169	0.831

Table 6.8
Full labor outlay (billions of constant dollars)

	Full labor outlay		Market labor outlay		Nonmarket outlay	
Year	quantity	price	quantity	price	quantity	price
1949	5,739.7	0.162	1,000.7	0.144	4,743.8	0.166
1950	5,808.1	0.170	1,031.5	0.152	4,783.8	0.174
1951	5,939.0	0.179	1,087.3	0.166	4,862.6	0.181
1952	6,042.6	0.186	1,108.3	0.175	4,945.5	0.188
1953	6,150.2	0.201	1,100.2	0.190	5,059.5	0.203
1954	6,253.9	0.211	1,084.5	0.194	5,176.4	0.214
1955	6,381.8	0.213	1,119.4	0.196	5,270.7	0.217
1956	6,509.0	0.222	1,144.2	0.205	5,373.5	0.225
1957	6,675.1	0.237	1,141.7	0.220	5,539.6	0.241
1958	6,786.4	0.252	1,099.9	0.234	5,687.5	0.255
1959	6,885.2	0.255	1,140.0	0.237	5,748.2	0.259
1960	7,031.9	0.261	1,166.2	0.242	5,868.9	0.264
1961	7,208.8	0.272	1,150.6	0.254	6,057.9	0.276
1962	7,329.5	0.280	1,183.3	0.262	6,147.0	0.283
1963	7,476.7	0.283	1,191.6	0.269	6,284.7	0.286
1964	7,620.4	0.305	1,196.7	0.284	6,422.2	0.309
1965	7,708.4	0.320	1,238.4	0.293	6,470.9	0.325
1966	7,779.6	0.341	1,275.3	0.315	6,507.6	0.346
1967	7,919.3	0.358	1,286.4	0.332	6,635.2	0.363
1968	8,101.1	0.377	1,322.2	0.356	6,781.7	0.381
1969	8,331.4	0.396	1,371.5	0.379	6,963.6	0.399
1970	8,535.9	0.433	1,353.8	0.411	7,183.0	0.438
1971	8,728.4	0.475	1,328.5	0.447	7,397.1	0.480
1972	8,784.8	0.494	1,384.1	0.472	7,400.8	0.499
1973	8,867.1	0.531	1,443.4	0.516	7,425.8	0.533
1974	8,990.3	0.576	1,458.5	0.560	7,533.8	0.579
1975	9,132.7	0.631	1,405.9	0.611	7,726.1	0.635
1976	9,269.8	0.662	1,461.2	0.655	7,808.8	0.664
1977	9,493.2	0.698	1,527.9	0.696	7,965.7	0.699
1978	9,674.1	0.731	1,632.3	0.744	8,041.5	0.728
1979	9,851.9	0.813	1,672.3	0.822	8,179.2	0.811
1980	10,037.7	0.873	1,692.9	0.882	8,344.5	0.871
1981	10,150.4	0.935	1,718.3	0.952	8,431.7	0.931
1982	10,205.1	1.000	1,692.0	1.000	8,513.1	1.000
1983	10,254.0	1.064	1,710.4	1.047	8,543.6	1.067
1984	10,324.7	1.132	1,794.2	1.097	8,532.6	1.138

Table 6.9
Full gross private domestic factor outlay (billions of current dollars)

Year	Full factor outlay	Full property outlay	Full labor outlay	Property share	Labor share
1948	988.4	110.8	877.6	0.112	0.888
1949	1,037.7	108.3	929.5	0.104	0.896
1950	1,113.3	124.7	988.6	0.112	0.888
1951	1,203.0	140.3	1,062.7	0.117	0.883
1952	1,262.8	139.4	1,123.4	0.110	0.890
1953	1,379.3	144.1	1,235.2	0.104	0.896
1954	1,462.0	145.2	1,316.8	0.099	0.901
1955	1,531.8	171.1	1,360.7	0.112	0.888
1956	1,617.5	171.8	1,445.7	0.106	0.894
1957	1,759.1	173.9	1,585.2	0.099	0.901
1958	1,877.6	167.6	1,710.0	0.089	0.911
1959	1,951.5	195.0	1,756.6	0.100	0.900
1960	2,027.8	195.0	1,832.8	0.096	0.904
1961	2,162.8	201.0	1,961.8	0.093	0.907
1962	2,273.7	221.3	2,052.4	0.097	0.903
1963	2,360.4	242.0	2,118.4	0.103	0.897
1964	2,587.4	265.9	2,321.5	0.103	0.897
1965	2,765.8	300.7	2,465.1	0.109	0.891
1966	2,980.1	324.4	2,655.7	0.109	0.891
1967	3,168.4	329.8	2,838.7	0.104	0.896
1968	3,401.3	344.8	3,056.5	0.101	0.899
1969	3,651.7	354.9	3,296.7	0.097	0.903
1970	4,056.9	358.0	3,698.9	0.088	0.912
1971	4,538.8	393.1	4,145.7	0.087	0.913
1972	4,785.5	442.7	4,342.8	0.092	0.908
1973	5,184.1	477.5	4,706.6	0.092	0.908
1974	5,670.2	489.0	5,181.2	0.086	0.914
1975	6,335.6	572.3	5,763.2	0.090	0.910
1976	6,790.7	651.4	6,139.3	0.096	0.904
1977	7,382.5	752.0	6,630.6	0.102	0.898
1978	7,911.4	843.2	7,068.3	0.107	0.893
1979	8,918.2	907.3	8,010.9	0.102	0.898
1980	9,731.1	972.7	8,758.3	0.100	0.900
1981	10,620.7	1,134.9	9,485.9	0.107	0.893
1982	11,435.0	1,229.9	10,205.1	0.108	0.892
1983	12,272.2	1,363.8	10,908.4	0.111	0.889
1984	13,254.7	1,571.9	11,682.8	0.119	0.881

Table 6.10
Full gross domestic factor outlay (billions of constant dollars)

	Full factor outlay		Property outlay		Labor outlay	
Year	quantity	price	quantity	price	quantity	price
1949	6,081.7	0.171	399.0	0.271	5,739.7	0.162
1950	6,170.2	0.180	413.5	0.302	5,808.1	0.170
1951	6,334.3	0.190	437.8	0.320	5,939.0	0.179
1952	6,464.5	0.195	457.5	0.305	6,042.6	0.186
1953	6,586.8	0.209	470.4	0.306	6,150.2	0.201
1954	6,706.3	0.218	484.4	0.300	6,253.9	0.211
1955	6,847.2	0.224	496.8	0.344	6,381.8	0.213
1956	7,001.9	0.231	519.0	0.331	6,509.0	0.222
1957	7,188.8	0.245	538.2	0.323	6,675.1	0.237
1958	7,317.7	0.257	554.4	0.302	6,786.4	0.252
1959	7,423.3	0.263	561.7	0.347	6,885.2	0.255
1960	7,587.1	0.267	578.1	0.337	7,031.9	0.261
1961	7,777.2	0.278	591.9	0.340	7,208.8	0.272
1962	7,910.1	0.287	604.0	0.366	7,329.5	0.280
1963	8,075.3	0.292	621.1	0.390	7,476.7	0.283
1964	8,241.1	0.314	640.9	0.415	7,620.4	0.305
1965	8,357.3	0.331	664.0	0.453	7,708.4	0.320
1966	8,466.7	0.352	694.0	0.467	7,779.6	0.341
1967	8,645.3	0.366	727.2	0.453	7,919.3	0.358
1968	8,857.9	0.384	755.5	0.456	8,101.1	0.377
1969	9,120.3	0.400	786.1	0.452	8,331.4	0.396
1970	9,359.4	0.433	819.7	0.437	8,535.9	0.433
1971	9,577.8	0.474	845.7	0.465	8,728.4	0.475
1972	9,664.5	0.495	875.9	0.505	8,784.8	0.494
1973	9,785.1	0.530	914.0	0.522	8,867.1	0.531
1974	9,953.7	0.570	961.4	0.509	8,990.3	0.576
1975	10,130.2	0.625	997.6	0.574	9,132.7	0.631
1976	10,288.3	0.660	1,018.8	0.639	9,269.8	0.662
1977	10,543.0	0.700	1,050.2	0.716	9,493.2	0.698
1978	10,764.6	0.735	1,090.2	0.773	9,674.1	0.731
1979	10,988.1	0.812	1,135.5	0.799	9,851.9	0.813
1980	11,214.6	0.868	1,176.8	0.827	10,037.7	0.873
1981	11,353.6	0.935	1,203.2	0.943	10,150.4	0.935
1982	11,435.0	1.000	1,229.9	1.000	10,205.1	1.000
1983	11,502.6	1.067	1,248.5	1.092	10,254.0	1.064
1984	11,597.4	1.143	1,271.7	1.236	10,324.7	1.132

Table 6.11
Gross private national labor and property income, rates of growth, 1949–1984

	1949–1984	1949–1953	1953–1957	1957–1960	1960–1966	1966–1969	1969–1973	1973–1979	1979–1984
Full factor outlay:									
Current prices	7.28	7.11	6.08	4.74	6.42	6.77	8.76	9.04	7.93
Constant prices	1.84	1.99	2.19	1.80	1.83	2.48	1.76	1.93	1.08
Constant prices per capita	0.55	0.33	0.41	−0.01	0.38	1.38	0.79	1.09	0.03
Price index	5.43	5.02	3.97	2.87	4.61	4.26	7.04	7.11	6.84
Full labor outlay:									
Current prices	7.23	7.11	6.24	4.84	6.18	7.21	8.90	8.86	7.55
Constant prices	1.68	1.73	2.05	1.74	1.68	2.28	1.56	1.76	0.94
Constant prices per capita	0.38	0.07	0.28	−0.07	0.23	1.19	0.59	0.91	−0.11
Price index	5.55	5.39	4.12	3.22	4.46	4.98	7.33	7.10	6.62
Full property outlay:									
Current prices	7.64	7.14	4.70	3.82	8.48	3.00	7.42	10.70	10.99
Constant prices	3.31	4.12	3.37	2.38	3.05	4.15	3.77	3.62	2.27
Constant prices per capita	2.02	2.45	1.59	0.58	1.59	3.06	2.80	2.77	1.22
Price index	4.34	3.04	1.35	1.41	5.44	−1.09	3.60	7.09	8.73

of total input, full factor outlay in constant prices, is a weighted average of growth rates of labor and capital inputs and averaged 0.55 per year in per capita terms for the period as a whole.

Comparing the growth rates of input and output, we find that output grew at 2.13 percent per year for the period as a whole, while input grew at 1.84 percent. Input growth has accounted for 86 percent of output growth. This proportion has increased in recent subperiods. For example, input growth was 99 percent of output growth in the period 1973–1979 and 84 percent in 1979–1984.

6.4 Income and Expenditure

In this section we integrate the estimates of income and expenditure associated with market activities by Fraumeni and Jorgenson (1980) with our estimates of income and expenditure for nonmarket activities. Following Fraumeni and Jorgenson, we present accounts for the private national sector of the U.S. economy. The income of the private national sector includes compensation for the services of human and nonhuman capital in the private domestic sector, the government sector and the rest of the world. Income from the services of human capital for the private national sector includes all incomes generated from human capital for individuals in the U.S. population.

The value of income is equal to the value of expenditure for the income and expenditure account. Expenditure in the U.S. economy includes the consumption of market and nonmarket goods and services and saving in the form of human and nonhuman capital. We add to the consumption of market goods and services, as defined by Fraumeni and Jorgenson, our estimates of the value of consumption of nonmarket goods and services. Similarly, we add to estimates of saving in the form of nonhuman capital by Fraumeni and Jorgenson our estimates of saving in the form of human capital.

We present the income side of the income and expenditure account in current prices for the private national sector of the U.S. economy for the year 1982 in table 6.12. We have estimated labor compensation after taxes for individual workers cross-classified by sex, single year of education and single year of age. Labor compensation after taxes is the sum of labor compensation for all groups of individual workers. For market labor compensation, we estimate personal income taxes attributed to labor income by the methods of Jorgenson and Yun (1986). Income tax not allocated to labor income is allocated to

Table 6.12
Gross private national labor and property income, 1982 (billions of current dollars)

		Labor income	
1.		Private domestic outlay for labor services (table 6.4, line 3, plus our imputation for proprietors)	1,692.0
2.	+	Income originating in general government (table 1.7, line 12)	343.9
3.	+	Compensation of employees in government enterprises (table 6.4, lines 81 and 86)	39.6
4.	+	Compensation of employees, rest-of-world (table 6.4, line 87)	–.1
5.	–	Personal income taxes attributed to labor income (our imputation)	263.1
6.	=	Private national labor income	1,812.3
7.	+	Nonmarket labor income	8,513.1
8.	=	Full private national labor income	10,325.4
		Property income	
1.		Gross private domestic outlay for capital services (our imputation)	1,229.9
2.	+	Corporate profits and net interest, rest-of-world (table 6.1, line 82)	51.2
3.	+	Investment income of social insurance funds less transfers to general government (table 3.13, lines 7, 9, 18, 20)	33.0
4.	+	Net interest paid by government (table 1.9, line 16 plus line 12 minus table 3.1, line 18 and table 2.1, line 28)	39.0
5.	–	Corporate profits tax liability (tables 3.2, line 6 and 3.3, line 6)	63.0
6.	–	Business property taxes (table 3.5, lines 24–27)	102.2
7.	–	Personal income taxes attributed to property income (our imputation)	85.4
8.	–	Federal estate and gift taxes (table 3.2, line 4)	7.6
9.	–	State and local estate and gift taxes (table 3.4, line 11)	2.6
10.	–	State and local personal motor vehicle licences, property taxes, and other taxes (table 3.4, lines 12–14)	7.3
11.	=	Gross private national property income	1,085.1

Note: All table references are to the NIPA tables in the March 1986 *Survey of Current Business.*

property income to obtain property compensation after taxes. Following Fraumeni and Jorgenson, we treat social insurance funds as part of the private sector of the U.S. national economy. Contributions to social insurance are included and transfers from social insurance funds excluded from labor income. Property income includes the investment income of social insurance funds, less transfers to general government by these funds.

Our next objective is to allocate the value of income for the private national sector of the U.S. economy between labor and property income for the period 1948–1984. We first estimate the value of compensation for market and nonmarket labor activities for all years. The value of labor compensation for nonmarket activities is equal to the value of time spent in household production and leisure and the value of time spent on investment in human capital. Our estimates of market labor compensation after taxes are based on those of Fraumeni and Jorgenson. We present estimates of market labor income, nonmarket labor income, and full labor income in current prices in table 6.13 and in constant prices in table 6.14.

The share of nonmarket labor income is far larger than that of market labor income, varying from 0.817 to 0.842 as a proportion of full labor income during the period 1948–1984. The share of market labor income is nearly constant over the period. The prices of market and nonmarket components of labor income have risen in proportion with a slightly greater increase in the price of nonmarket income since around 1958.

Our final step in allocating the value of income for the private national sector of the U.S. economy between labor and property income for the period 1948–1984 is to estimate the value of property compensation for all years. Our estimates of property compensation are based on those of Fraumeni and Jorgenson. We present estimates of full labor income, property income, and income in current prices in table 6.15 and constant prices in table 6.16. The property share of national income has risen from a minimum of 0.066 in 1974 to a maximum for the period as a whole of 0.107 in 1984.

The price of property income rose less rapidly than the price of labor income until around 1960. The price of property income then fell during the period 1966–1969 and resumed its rise during 1969–1973. Since that time the price of property income has been rising more rapidly with a substantial acceleration, relative to the price of labor income, after 1979. The stability of the share of property

Table 6.13
Full labor income (billions of current dollars)

Year	Full labor income	Market labor income	Nonmarket labor income	Market share	Nonmarket share
1948	884.2	151.4	732.8	0.171	0.829
1949	940.5	155.2	785.3	0.165	0.835
1950	1,000.5	168.9	831.7	0.169	0.831
1951	1,073.8	191.7	882.2	0.178	0.822
1952	1,134.6	205.4	929.3	0.181	0.819
1953	1,246.3	220.0	1,026.3	0.177	0.823
1954	1,331.6	224.7	1,106.9	0.169	0.831
1955	1,375.4	233.9	1,141.5	0.170	0.830
1956	1,460.2	249.2	1,211.0	0.171	0.829
1957	1,600.7	266.2	1,334.6	0.166	0.834
1958	1,729.3	276.5	1,452.8	0.160	0.840
1959	1,775.6	289.1	1,486.5	0.163	0.837
1960	1,852.8	302.7	1,550.1	0.163	0.837
1961	1,984.6	315.3	1,669.3	0.159	0.841
1962	2,076.5	333.8	1,742.6	0.161	0.839
1963	2,144.6	346.7	1,797.9	0.162	0.838
1964	2,355.3	373.3	1,982.0	0.159	0.841
1965	2,500.2	398.1	2,102.1	0.159	0.841
1966	2,694.1	440.1	2,254.1	0.163	0.837
1967	2,881.9	470.5	2,411.4	0.163	0.837
1968	3,100.7	514.9	2,585.8	0.166	0.834
1969	3,339.0	561.4	2,777.6	0.168	0.832
1970	3,756.1	613.4	3,142.6	0.163	0.837
1971	4,216.1	664.5	3,551.5	0.158	0.842
1972	4,410.1	719.9	3,690.2	0.163	0.837
1973	4,781.5	820.1	3,961.4	0.172	0.828
1974	5,258.3	893.1	4,365.1	0.170	0.830
1975	5,864.1	959.7	4,904.4	0.164	0.836
1976	6,239.6	1,057.6	5,181.9	0.170	0.830
1977	6,730.2	1,162.6	5,567.6	0.173	0.827
1978	7,166.3	1,312.8	5,853.5	0.183	0.817
1979	8,102.0	1,466.5	6,635.6	0.181	0.819
1980	8,858.3	1,593.9	7,264.4	0.180	0.820
1981	9,583.9	1,733.5	7,850.4	0.181	0.819
1982	10,325.4	1,812.4	8,513.1	0.176	0.824
1983	11,055.7	1,937.9	9,117.8	0.175	0.825
1984	11,840.4	2,126.3	9,714.1	0.180	0.820

Table 6.14
Full labor income (billions of constant dollars)

	Full labor income		Market labor income		Nonmarket labor income	
Year	quantity	price	quantity	price	quantity	price
1949	5,692.5	0.165	948.0	0.164	4,743.8	0.166
1950	5,774.5	0.173	990.4	0.171	4,783.8	0.174
1951	5,900.3	0.182	1,037.5	0.185	4,862.6	0.181
1952	6,013.7	0.189	1,067.7	0.192	4,945.5	0.188
1953	6,146.3	0.203	1,086.4	0.202	5,059.5	0.203
1954	6,260.3	0.213	1,083.1	0.207	5,176.4	0.214
1955	6,369.1	0.216	1,097.5	0.213	5,270.7	0.217
1956	6,490.3	0.225	1,115.8	0.223	5,373.5	0.225
1957	6,660.5	0.240	1,119.6	0.238	5,539.6	0.241
1958	6,809.8	0.254	1,120.4	0.247	5,687.5	0.255
1959	6,894.3	0.258	1,144.4	0.253	5,748.2	0.259
1960	7,056.7	0.263	1,186.6	0.255	5,868.9	0.264
1961	7,244.0	0.274	1,183.7	0.266	6,057.9	0.276
1962	7,368.1	0.282	1,219.1	0.274	6,147.0	0.283
1963	7,522.8	0.285	1,235.8	0.281	6,284.7	0.286
1964	7,686.1	0.306	1,261.6	0.296	6,422.2	0.309
1965	7,768.0	0.322	1,295.7	0.307	6,470.9	0.325
1966	7,855.2	0.343	1,348.3	0.326	6,507.6	0.346
1967	8,010.2	0.360	1,375.8	0.342	6,635.2	0.363
1968	8,186.9	0.379	1,406.0	0.366	6,781.7	0.381
1969	8,402.5	0.397	1,439.7	0.390	6,963.6	0.399
1970	8,636.6	0.435	1,453.6	0.422	7,183.0	0.438
1971	8,858.5	0.476	1,460.1	0.455	7,397.1	0.480
1972	8,889.5	0.496	1,488.3	0.484	7,400.8	0.499
1973	8,966.5	0.533	1,540.9	0.532	7,425.8	0.533
1974	9,097.8	0.578	1,564.2	0.571	7,533.8	0.579
1975	9,313.6	0.630	1,587.3	0.605	7,726.1	0.635
1976	9,429.8	0.662	1,621.3	0.652	7,808.8	0.664
1977	9,624.0	0.699	1,658.6	0.701	7,965.7	0.699
1978	9,765.6	0.734	1,723.4	0.762	8,041.5	0.728
1979	9,903.9	0.818	1,725.1	0.850	8,179.2	0.811
1980	10,073.8	0.879	1,730.9	0.921	8,344.5	0.871
1981	10,213.6	0.938	1,782.2	0.973	8,431.7	0.931
1982	10,325.4	1.000	1,812.4	1.000	8,513.1	1.000
1983	10,401.6	1.063	1,858.3	1.043	8,543.6	1.067
1984	10,443.1	1.134	1,911.9	1.112	8,532.6	1.138

Table 6.15
Full private national income (billions of current dollars)

Year	Full income	Full property income	Full labor income	Property share	Labor share
1948	974.8	90.6	884.2	0.093	0.907
1949	1,030.7	90.2	940.5	0.087	0.913
1950	1,096.9	96.4	1,000.5	0.088	0.912
1951	1,180.3	106.5	1,073.8	0.090	0.910
1952	1,242.0	107.4	1,134.6	0.086	0.914
1953	1,356.3	110.1	1,246.3	0.081	0.919
1954	1,445.2	113.6	1,331.6	0.079	0.921
1955	1,509.2	133.8	1,375.4	0.089	0.911
1956	1,592.9	132.7	1,460.2	0.083	0.917
1957	1,735.0	134.3	1,600.7	0.077	0.923
1958	1,858.9	129.6	1,729.3	0.070	0.930
1959	1,926.5	150.9	1,775.6	0.078	0.922
1960	2,002.8	150.1	1,852.8	0.075	0.925
1961	2,138.0	153.4	1,984.6	0.072	0.928
1962	2,247.7	171.2	2,076.5	0.076	0.924
1963	2,332.8	188.2	2,144.6	0.081	0.919
1964	2,565.4	210.1	2,355.3	0.082	0.918
1965	2,739.3	239.1	2,500.2	0.087	0.913
1966	2,950.6	256.5	2,694.1	0.087	0.913
1967	3,141.8	259.9	2,881.9	0.083	0.917
1968	3,364.3	263.6	3,100.7	0.078	0.922
1969	3,605.2	266.2	3,339.0	0.074	0.926
1970	4,029.9	273.8	3,756.1	0.068	0.932
1971	4,517.6	301.6	4,216.1	0.067	0.933
1972	4,749.3	339.2	4,410.1	0.071	0.929
1973	5,149.4	367.9	4,781.5	0.071	0.929
1974	5,632.3	374.0	5,258.3	0.066	0.934
1975	6,319.3	455.2	5,864.1	0.072	0.928
1976	6,756.8	517.3	6,239.5	0.077	0.923
1977	7,331.1	600.9	6,730.2	0.082	0.918
1978	7,846.5	680.2	7,166.3	0.087	0.913
1979	8,846.1	744.1	8,102.0	0.084	0.916
1980	9,666.9	808.6	8,858.3	0.084	0.916
1981	10,555.8	972.0	9,583.9	0.092	0.908
1982	11,410.5	1,085.1	10,325.4	0.095	0.905
1983	12,268.7	1,212.9	11,055.7	0.099	0.901
1984	13,251.8	1,411.4	11,840.4	0.107	0.893

Table 6.16
Full private national Income (billions of constant dollars)

	Full income		Property income		Labor income	
Year	quantity	price	quantity	price	quantity	price
1949	6,013.2	0.171	338.6	0.266	5,692.5	0.165
1950	6,110.8	0.180	350.6	0.275	5,774.5	0.173
1951	6,243.7	0.189	358.1	0.297	5,900.3	0.182
1952	6,367.0	0.195	367.2	0.292	6,013.7	0.189
1953	6,511.1	0.208	377.8	0.291	6,146.3	0.203
1954	6,638.8	0.218	389.9	0.291	6,260.3	0.213
1955	6,761.8	0.223	402.1	0.333	6,369.1	0.216
1956	6,896.3	0.231	413.8	0.321	6,490.3	0.225
1957	7,076.3	0.245	424.0	0.317	6,660.5	0.240
1958	7,238.2	0.257	436.2	0.297	6,809.8	0.254
1959	7,333.4	0.263	446.0	0.338	6,894.3	0.258
1960	7,504.8	0.267	455.4	0.330	7,056.7	0.263
1961	7,700.4	0.278	464.5	0.330	7,244.0	0.274
1962	7,836.4	0.287	475.9	0.360	7,368.1	0.282
1963	8,007.2	0.291	490.7	0.384	7,522.8	0.285
1964	8,187.1	0.313	506.0	0.415	7,686.1	0.306
1965	8,295.0	0.330	526.7	0.454	7,768.0	0.322
1966	8,409.4	0.351	548.3	0.468	7,855.2	0.343
1967	8,595.2	0.366	574.6	0.452	8,010.2	0.360
1968	8,806.3	0.382	605.4	0.436	8,186.9	0.379
1969	9,049.6	0.398	631.6	0.421	8,402.5	0.397
1970	9,304.2	0.433	651.7	0.420	8,636.6	0.435
1971	9,553.2	0.473	678.9	0.444	8,858.5	0.476
1972	9,614.8	0.494	710.8	0.477	8,889.5	0.496
1973	9,717.0	0.530	736.7	0.499	8,966.5	0.533
1974	9,881.6	0.570	772.6	0.484	9,097.8	0.578
1975	10,130.2	0.624	807.0	0.564	9,313.6	0.630
1976	10,302.8	0.656	867.9	0.596	9,429.8	0.662
1977	10,540.1	0.696	913.0	0.658	9,624.0	0.699
1978	10,711.6	0.733	943.4	0.721	9,765.6	0.734
1979	10,877.8	0.813	971.8	0.766	9,903.9	0.818
1980	11,076.1	0.873	1,001.0	0.808	10,073.8	0.879
1981	11,257.5	0.938	1,043.8	0.931	10,213.6	0.938
1982	11,410.5	1.000	1,085.1	1.000	10,325.4	1.000
1983	11,552.4	1.062	1,151.1	1.054	10,401.6	1.063
1984	11,655.9	1.137	1,212.6	1.164	10,443.1	1.134

income through 1980 was the consequence of a steady increase in property income relative to labor income in constant prices. Property income in constant prices corresponds to the services of physical or nonhuman capital, while labor income corresponds to the services of human capital.

We next analyze the structure of full private national income over the postwar period. In table 6.17 we present growth rates of full income, labor income, and property income for the period 1949–1984 and for eight subperiods. We give growth rates for each measure of income in current and constant prices and in per capita terms. The growth rate of national income in constant prices was positive throughout the period, averaging 1.89 percent per year. The growth rate of property income in constant prices was considerably greater than that of labor income. The growth rate of property income averaged 3.64 percent per year, while the growth rate of labor income averaged only 1.73 percent.

To complete the income and expenditure account for the private national sector of the U.S. economy, we add government transfer payments to persons, other than benefits from social insurance funds, to full national income to obtain national receipts. To allocate the value of receipts between consumption and saving, we first estimate the value of full consumption. Full consumption is the sum of the consumption of market goods and services, as defined by Fraumeni and Jorgenson, and our estimates of the value of household production and leisure. Next, we estimate the value of full savings. Full saving is the sum of saving in the form of nonhuman capital, again as defined by Fraumeni and Jorgenson, and our estimates of saving in the form of human capital. We present estimates of full receipts and expenditures for the year 1982 in table 6.18.

Our next objective is to allocate the value of full receipts for the private national sector of the U.S. economy between consumption and saving for the period 1948–1984. We first estimate the value of consumer outlays for all years. We present estimates of market consumer outlays, nonmarket consumer outlays and full consumer outlays in current prices in table 6.19 and constant prices in table 6.20. The value of consumer outlays in nonmarket goods and services predominates in consumer outlays, averaging around 65 percent of outlays over the period 1948–1984. The market share of full consumer outlays reached a minimum of 0.315 in 1971 and has risen to a maximum of 0.361 in 1984 at the end of the period, a rise of 15 percent; however, there is

Table 6.17
Full private national income, rates of growth, 1949–1984

	1949–1984	1949–1953	1953–1957	1957–1960	1960–1966	1966–1969	1969–1973	1973–1979	1979–1984
Full national income:									
Current prices	7.30	6.86	6.16	4.78	6.46	6.68	8.91	9.02	8.08
Constant prices	1.89	1.99	2.08	1.96	1.90	2.45	1.78	1.88	1.38
Constant prices per capita	0.60	0.33	0.31	0.15	0.45	1.35	0.81	1.04	0.33
Price index	5.41	4.90	4.09	2.87	4.56	4.19	7.16	7.13	6.71
Full labor income:									
Current prices	7.24	7.04	6.26	4.88	6.24	7.15	8.98	8.79	7.59
Constant prices	1.73	1.92	2.01	1.93	1.79	2.25	1.62	1.66	1.06
Constant prices per capita	0.44	0.26	0.24	0.12	0.34	1.15	0.66	0.81	0.01
Price index	5.51	5.18	4.19	3.05	4.43	4.87	7.36	7.14	6.53
Full property income:									
Current prices	7.86	4.98	4.97	3.71	8.93	1.24	8.09	11.74	12.80
Constant prices	3.64	2.74	2.88	2.38	3.09	4.71	3.85	4.62	4.43
Constant prices per capita	2.35	1.08	1.11	0.57	1.64	3.62	2.88	3.77	3.38
Price index	4.22	2.25	2.14	1.34	5.82	−3.53	4.25	7.14	8.37

Table 6.18
Gross private national receipts and expenditures, 1982 (billions of current dollars)

		Receipts	
1.		Gross private domestic factor outlay	2,921.9
2.	+	Income originating in general government (table 1.7, line 12)	343.9
3.	+	Compensation of employees in government enterprises (table 6.4, lines 81 and 86)	39.6
4.	+	Income originating in rest-of-world (table 6.1, line 82)	51.2
5.	+	Investment income of social insurance funds (table 3.13, lines 7 and 18)	39.9
6.	−	Transfer to general government from social insurance funds (table 3.13, lines 9 and 20)	6.9
7.	+	Net interest paid by government (table 1.9, line 16 plus line 12 minus table 3.1, line 18 and table 2.1, line 28)	39.0
8.	−	Corporate profits tax liability (tables 3.2, line 6, and 3.3, line 6)	63.0
9.	−	Business property taxes (table 3.5, lines 24, 25, 26, 27)	102.2
10.	−	Personal tax and nontax payments (table 2.1, line 24)	409.3
11.	+	Personal nontax payments (tables 3.4, lines 8 and 15)	43.5
12.	=	Gross private national income	2,897.5
13.	+	Nonmarket labor income	8,513.1
14.	=	Full gross private national income	11,410.7
15.	+	Government transfer payment to persons other than benefits from social insurance funds (table 3.11, lines 1, 3, 29)	99.6
16.	=	Full gross private national consumer receipts	11,510.3
		Expenditures	
1.		Personal consumption expenditures (table 1.1, line 2)	2,050.7
2.	−	Personal consumption expenditures, durable goods (table 1.1, line 3)	252.7
3.	+	Imputation for nonhuman capital services	338.7
4.	=	Private national consumption expenditure	2,136.7
5.	+	Consumption of nonmarket goods and services	3,944.5
6.	=	Full private national consumption expenditure	6,081.2
7.	+	Personal transfer payments to foreigners (table 2.1, line 29)	1.3
8.	+	Personal nontax payments (table 3.4, lines 8 and 15)	43.5
9.	=	Full private national consumer outlays	6,126.0
10.	+	Full gross private national saving[a]	5,384.4
11.	=	Full private national expenditures	11,510.3

Note: All table references are to the NIPA tables in the March 1986 *Survey of Current Business*.
[a] See below, table 6.26, line 14.

Table 6.19
Full consumer outlays (billions of current dollars)

Year	Full consumer outlays	Market consumer outlays	Nonmarket consumer outlays	Market share	Nonmarket share
1948	522.0	182.1	339.9	0.349	0.651
1949	553.6	183.8	369.9	0.332	0.668
1950	585.9	195.6	390.4	0.334	0.666
1951	620.1	215.1	404.9	0.347	0.653
1952	647.8	227.5	420.3	0.351	0.649
1953	702.0	239.3	462.6	0.341	0.659
1954	747.5	248.3	499.3	0.332	0.668
1955	770.6	265.0	505.6	0.344	0.656
1956	808.8	276.3	532.5	0.342	0.658
1957	868.8	289.5	579.3	0.333	0.667
1958	933.1	299.8	633.3	0.321	0.679
1959	962.3	322.3	640.0	0.335	0.665
1960	1,000.6	335.3	665.3	0.335	0.665
1961	1,065.6	348.8	716.8	0.327	0.673
1962	1,115.3	368.8	746.5	0.331	0.669
1963	1,157.0	390.4	766.6	0.337	0.663
1964	1,263.0	421.6	841.5	0.334	0.666
1965	1,366.6	457.6	909.0	0.335	0.665
1966	1,480.7	495.0	985.7	0.334	0.666
1967	1,575.7	520.0	1,055.7	0.330	0.670
1968	1,678.9	559.8	1,119.1	0.333	0.667
1969	1,797.8	603.1	1,194.7	0.335	0.665
1970	1,998.8	652.4	1,346.5	0.326	0.674
1971	2,220.6	698.7	1,521.9	0.315	0.685
1972	2,390.8	768.9	1,621.9	0.322	0.678
1973	2,634.3	843.0	1,791.2	0.320	0.680
1974	2,888.1	920.1	1,968.1	0.319	0.681
1975	3,213.3	1,031.1	2,182.2	0.321	0.679
1976	3,510.6	1,146.1	2,364.5	0.326	0.674
1977	3,800.6	1,280.3	2,520.3	0.337	0.663
1978	4,162.2	1,429.8	2,732.5	0.344	0.656
1979	4,685.4	1,595.1	3,090.3	0.340	0.660
1980	5,064.9	1,775.2	3,289.7	0.350	0.650
1981	5,550.6	1,989.6	3,561.0	0.358	0.642
1982	6,126.0	2,181.5	3,944.5	0.356	0.644
1983	6,635.5	2,360.9	4,274.7	0.356	0.644
1984	7,184.5	2,593.6	4,590.9	0.361	0.639

Table 6.20
Full consumer outlays (billions of constant dollars)

	Full consumer outlays		Market consumer outlays		Nonmarket consumer outlays	
Year	quantity	price	quantity	price	quantity	price
1949	2,727.1	0.203	695.9	0.264	2,076.9	0.178
1950	2,784.7	0.210	725.5	0.270	2,098.9	0.186
1951	2,828.5	0.219	751.8	0.286	2,110.1	0.192
1952	2,885.0	0.225	776.1	0.293	2,138.2	0.197
1953	2,958.2	0.237	799.9	0.299	2,186.7	0.212
1954	3,014.8	0.248	816.4	0.304	2,226.8	0.224
1955	3,091.4	0.249	864.6	0.306	2,246.1	0.225
1956	3,152.1	0.257	891.8	0.310	2,276.4	0.234
1957	3,223.8	0.269	915.1	0.316	2,324.3	0.249
1958	3,295.0	0.283	926.6	0.324	2,386.5	0.265
1959	3,363.7	0.286	971.9	0.332	2,404.2	0.266
1960	3,424.6	0.292	992.8	0.338	2,443.7	0.272
1961	3,523.3	0.302	1,020.0	0.342	2,515.8	0.285
1962	3,606.9	0.309	1,061.7	0.347	2,554.6	0.292
1963	3,701.4	0.313	1,103.1	0.354	2,605.3	0.294
1964	3,815.9	0.331	1,169.7	0.360	2,648.0	0.318
1965	3,932.4	0.348	1,242.2	0.368	2,687.9	0.338
1966	4,044.1	0.366	1,305.9	0.379	2,733.8	0.361
1967	4,152.6	0.379	1,351.6	0.385	2,796.1	0.378
1968	4,258.3	0.394	1,400.5	0.400	2,852.6	0.392
1969	4,358.2	0.413	1,446.9	0.417	2,905.6	0.411
1970	4,487.3	0.445	1,501.3	0.435	2,980.4	0.452
1971	4,621.9	0.480	1,538.3	0.454	3,077.4	0.495
1972	4,771.3	0.501	1,623.7	0.474	3,144.0	0.516
1973	4,875.9	0.540	1,680.2	0.502	3,194.0	0.561
1974	4,964.4	0.582	1,673.9	0.550	3,285.3	0.599
1975	5,151.4	0.624	1,739.9	0.593	3,406.3	0.641
1976	5,312.1	0.661	1,826.1	0.628	3,483.1	0.679
1977	5,460.0	0.696	1,908.5	0.671	3,550.5	0.710
1978	5,584.0	0.745	1,989.1	0.719	3,596.0	0.760
1979	5,729.4	0.818	2,039.2	0.782	3,691.1	0.837
1980	5,841.7	0.867	2,058.4	0.862	3,783.5	0.869
1981	5,962.0	0.931	2,106.5	0.944	3,855.6	0.924
1982	6,126.0	1.000	2,181.5	1.000	3,944.5	1.000
1983	6,256.6	1.061	2,257.0	1.046	3,999.9	1.069
1984	6,398.0	1.123	2,378.5	1.090	4,022.1	1.141

almost no trend in this share for the period as a whole. The price of nonmarket consumer outlays has increased more rapidly than the price of market outlays. Constancy of the market share has been maintained by a more rapid growth at market consumer outlays in constant prices.

We combine our estimates of saving in the form of human capital with estimates of saving in the form of nonhuman capital, based on those of Fraumeni and Jorgenson, to obtain the value of full saving. We present estimates of saving in the form of human capital, saving in the form of nonhuman capital, and full saving in current prices in table 6.21 and constant prices in table 6.22. The share of saving in the form of human capital greatly predominates, ranging from 0.881 in 1961 to 0.829 in 1984, a very modest decline. The price of saving in the form of human capital has risen more rapidly than the price of nonhuman saving, but the growth of nonhuman saving in constant prices has been much more rapid than the growth of human saving.

We combine our estimates of full consumer outlays with our estimates of saving in the form of human and nonhuman capital to obtain the value of full expenditures. We present estimates of full consumer outlays, saving, and expenditures in current prices in table 6.23 and in constant prices in table 6.24. The share of consumer outlays slightly predominates in full expenditures for most of the period, ranging from 0.490 in 1964 to 0.538 in 1984. The share of saving has trended downward since 1970. The price of saving has risen relative to the price of consumer outlays, but the growth rate of outlays in constant prices has been considerably greater than the growth rate of saving.

We next analyze the structure of full private national expenditures by presenting growth rates of full expenditures, consumer outlays, and saving in current and constant prices for the period 1948–1984 and for eight subperiods in table 6.25. We also give growth rates of expenditures, outlays, and saving in constant prices per capita. The growth rate of consumer outlays per capita averaged 1.14 percent per year for the period as a whole. Especially rapid growth has characterized the period since 1960 with only modest retardation after 1979. By contrast the growth rate of saving per capita averaged only 0.58 percent per year for the period as a whole, with rapid growth in 1953–1957 and 1966–1969 and negative growth from 1979–1984.

Table 6.21
Full gross private national saving (billions of current dollars)

Year	Full saving	Nonhuman saving	Human saving	Nonhuman share	Human share
1948	460.3	67.4	392.9	0.146	0.854
1949	483.8	68.3	415.5	0.141	0.859
1950	518.6	77.3	441.3	0.149	0.851
1951	566.4	89.2	477.2	0.157	0.843
1952	600.2	91.3	508.9	0.152	0.848
1953	660.7	97.0	563.7	0.147	0.853
1954	704.1	96.5	607.6	0.137	0.863
1955	745.2	109.3	635.9	0.147	0.853
1956	791.0	112.4	678.6	0.142	0.858
1957	873.5	118.3	755.2	0.135	0.865
1958	933.9	114.4	819.5	0.122	0.878
1959	971.9	125.4	846.5	0.129	0.871
1960	1,010.4	125.7	884.7	0.124	0.876
1961	1,081.2	128.7	952.5	0.119	0.881
1962	1,141.4	145.3	996.1	0.127	0.873
1963	1,185.3	154.0	1,031.3	0.130	0.870
1964	1,312.7	172.2	1,140.5	0.131	0.869
1965	1,384.0	190.8	1,193.2	0.138	0.862
1966	1,482.0	213.7	1,268.3	0.144	0.856
1967	1,580.8	225.1	1,355.7	0.142	0.858
1968	1,702.7	236.0	1,466.7	0.139	0.861
1969	1,827.9	245.0	1,582.9	0.134	0.866
1970	2,056.0	259.8	1,796.2	0.126	0.874
1971	2,327.6	298.0	2,029.6	0.128	0.872
1972	2,392.7	324.4	2,068.3	0.136	0.864
1973	2,553.2	383.0	2,170.2	0.150	0.850
1974	2,789.8	392.7	2,397.1	0.141	0.859
1975	3,163.1	440.9	2,722.2	0.139	0.861
1976	3,306.7	489.3	2,817.4	0.148	0.852
1977	3,593.1	545.8	3,047.3	0.152	0.848
1978	3,752.7	631.6	3,121.1	0.168	0.832
1979	4,236.1	690.9	3,545.2	0.163	0.837
1980	4,691.4	716.7	3,974.7	0.153	0.847
1981	5,102.5	813.1	4,289.4	0.159	0.841
1982	5,384.4	815.8	4,568.6	0.152	0.848
1983	5,739.7	896.6	4,843.1	0.156	0.844
1984	6,178.7	1,055.5	5,123.2	0.171	0.829

Table 6.22
Full gross private national saving (billions of constant dollars)

	Full saving		Nonhuman saving		Human saving	
Year	quantity	price	quantity	price	quantity	price
1949	2,864.8	0.169	239.5	0.285	2,669.1	0.156
1950	2,975.7	0.174	299.4	0.258	2,686.5	0.164
1951	3,044.3	0.186	301.2	0.296	2,756.9	0.173
1952	3,073.8	0.195	287.4	0.318	2,812.6	0.181
1953	3,155.4	0.209	300.3	0.323	2,878.3	0.196
1954	3,224.9	0.218	298.0	0.324	2,956.1	0.206
1955	3,373.2	0.221	350.3	0.312	3,032.9	0.210
1956	3,433.0	0.230	343.2	0.328	3,106.6	0.218
1957	3,537.6	0.247	336.7	0.351	3,226.6	0.234
1958	3,589.4	0.260	315.6	0.363	3,312.7	0.247
1959	3,691.5	0.263	360.2	0.348	3,356.2	0.252
1960	3,761.6	0.269	353.7	0.355	3,438.3	0.257
1961	3,873.3	0.279	352.8	0.365	3,556.0	0.268
1962	3,973.6	0.287	392.8	0.370	3,606.4	0.276
1963	4,091.6	0.290	419.0	0.368	3,694.2	0.279
1964	4,229.9	0.310	455.7	0.378	3,790.0	0.301
1965	4,297.6	0.322	506.2	0.377	3,797.7	0.314
1966	4,336.2	0.342	549.4	0.389	3,786.3	0.335
1967	4,402.9	0.359	552.1	0.408	3,851.1	0.352
1968	4,514.8	0.377	572.6	0.412	3,941.8	0.372
1969	4,654.6	0.393	582.6	0.420	4,072.2	0.389
1970	4,789.1	0.429	572.9	0.453	4,218.3	0.426
1971	4,963.6	0.469	629.0	0.474	4,335.4	0.468
1972	4,944.6	0.484	676.9	0.479	4,268.6	0.485
1973	5,003.0	0.510	764.6	0.501	4,240.4	0.512
1974	4,973.5	0.561	720.9	0.545	4,253.6	0.564
1975	5,019.2	0.630	696.2	0.633	4,323.7	0.630
1976	5,076.7	0.651	748.6	0.654	4,328.4	0.651
1977	5,216.0	0.689	798.5	0.684	4,418.0	0.690
1978	5,305.7	0.707	857.6	0.737	4,447.7	0.702
1979	5,350.5	0.792	862.2	0.801	4,487.8	0.790
1980	5,379.2	0.872	818.9	0.875	4,560.3	0.872
1981	5,430.2	0.940	854.3	0.952	4,575.7	0.937
1982	5,384.4	1.000	815.8	1.000	4,568.6	1.000
1983	5,428.9	1.057	886.8	1.011	4,543.7	1.066
1984	5,527.8	1.118	1,028.4	1.026	4,510.4	1.136

Table 6.23
Full private national expenditures (billions of current dollars)

Year	Full expenditures	Full consumer outlays	Full saving	Outlays share	Saving share
1948	982.3	522.0	460.3	0.531	0.469
1949	1,037.4	553.6	483.8	0.534	0.466
1950	1,104.5	585.9	518.6	0.530	0.470
1951	1,186.5	620.1	566.4	0.523	0.477
1952	1,248.0	647.8	600.2	0.519	0.481
1953	1,362.6	702.0	660.7	0.515	0.485
1954	1,451.7	747.5	704.1	0.515	0.485
1955	1,515.8	770.6	745.2	0.508	0.492
1956	1,599.7	808.8	791.0	0.506	0.494
1957	1,742.3	868.8	873.5	0.499	0.501
1958	1,867.0	933.1	933.9	0.500	0.500
1959	1,934.2	962.3	971.9	0.498	0.502
1960	2,011.0	1,000.6	1,010.4	0.498	0.502
1961	2,146.8	1,065.6	1,081.2	0.496	0.504
1962	2,256.7	1,115.3	1,141.4	0.494	0.506
1963	2,342.3	1,157.0	1,185.3	0.494	0.506
1964	2,575.7	1,263.0	1,312.7	0.490	0.510
1965	2,750.5	1,366.6	1,384.0	0.497	0.503
1966	2,962.7	1,480.7	1,482.0	0.500	0.500
1967	3,156.5	1,575.7	1,580.8	0.499	0.501
1968	3,381.6	1,678.9	1,702.7	0.496	0.504
1969	3,625.7	1,797.8	1,827.9	0.496	0.504
1970	4,054.8	1,998.8	2,056.0	0.493	0.507
1971	4,548.2	2,220.6	2,327.6	0.488	0.512
1972	4,783.5	2,390.8	2,392.7	0.500	0.500
1973	5,187.5	2,634.3	2,553.2	0.508	0.492
1974	5,677.9	2,888.1	2,789.8	0.509	0.491
1975	6,376.4	3,213.3	3,163.1	0.504	0.496
1976	6,817.3	3,510.6	3,306.7	0.515	0.485
1977	7,393.7	3,800.6	3,593.1	0.514	0.486
1978	7,914.9	4,162.2	3,752.7	0.526	0.474
1979	8,921.5	4,685.4	4,236.1	0.525	0.475
1980	9,756.3	5,064.9	4,691.4	0.519	0.481
1981	10,653.1	5,550.6	5,102.5	0.521	0.479
1982	11,510.3	6,126.0	5,384.4	0.532	0.468
1983	12,375.3	6,635.5	5,739.7	0.536	0.464
1984	13,363.2	7,184.5	6,178.7	0.538	0.462

Table 6.24
Full private national expenditures (billions of constant dollars)

	Full expenditures		Consumer outlays		Full saving	
Year	quantity	price	quantity	price	quantity	price
1949	5,592.9	0.185	2,727.1	0.203	2,864.8	0.169
1950	5,756.8	0.192	2,784.7	0.210	2,975.7	0.174
1951	5,867.3	0.202	2,828.5	0.219	3,044.3	0.186
1952	5,955.5	0.210	2,885.0	0.225	3,073.8	0.195
1953	6,110.0	0.223	2,958.2	0.237	3,155.4	0.209
1954	6,235.4	0.233	3,014.8	0.248	3,224.9	0.218
1955	6,456.3	0.235	3,091.4	0.249	3,373.2	0.221
1956	6,576.9	0.243	3,152.1	0.257	3,433.0	0.230
1957	6,751.8	0.258	3,223.8	0.269	3,537.6	0.247
1958	6,875.7	0.272	3,295.0	0.283	3,589.4	0.260
1959	7,045.2	0.275	3,363.7	0.286	3,691.5	0.263
1960	7,175.9	0.280	3,424.6	0.292	3,761.6	0.269
1961	7,385.8	0.291	3,523.3	0.302	3,873.3	0.279
1962	7,569.1	0.298	3,606.9	0.309	3,973.6	0.287
1963	7,780.8	0.301	3,701.4	0.313	4,091.6	0.290
1964	8,032.8	0.321	3,815.9	0.331	4,229.9	0.310
1965	8,218.8	0.335	3,932.4	0.348	4,297.6	0.322
1966	8,371.8	0.354	4,044.1	0.366	4,336.2	0.342
1967	8,548.3	0.369	4,152.6	0.379	4,402.9	0.359
1968	8,765.7	0.386	4,258.3	0.394	4,514.8	0.377
1969	9,004.4	0.403	4,358.2	0.413	4,654.6	0.393
1970	9,267.8	0.438	4,487.3	0.445	4,789.1	0.429
1971	9,576.2	0.475	4,621.9	0.480	4,963.6	0.469
1972	9,709.0	0.493	4,771.3	0.501	4,944.6	0.484
1973	9,873.1	0.525	4,875.9	0.540	5,003.0	0.510
1974	9,934.8	0.572	4,964.4	0.582	4,973.5	0.561
1975	10,168.4	0.627	5,151.4	0.624	5,019.2	0.630
1976	10,386.6	0.656	5,312.1	0.661	5,076.7	0.651
1977	10,673.7	0.693	5,460.0	0.696	5,216.0	0.689
1978	10,887.9	0.727	5,584.0	0.745	5,305.7	0.707
1979	11,080.0	0.805	5,729.4	0.818	5,350.5	0.792
1980	11,221.6	0.869	5,841.7	0.867	5,379.2	0.872
1981	11,392.7	0.935	5,962.0	0.931	5,430.2	0.940
1982	11,510.3	1.000	6,126.0	1.000	5,384.4	1.000
1983	11,685.5	1.059	6,256.6	1.061	5,428.9	1.057
1984	11,925.9	1.121	6,398.0	1.123	5,527.8	1.118

Table 6.25
Full private national expenditures, rates of growth, 1949–1984

	1949–1984	1949–1953	1953–1957	1957–1960	1960–1966	1966–1969	1969–1973	1973–1979	1979–1984
Full expenditures:									
Current prices	7.30	6.82	6.15	4.78	6.46	6.73	8.96	9.04	8.08
Constant prices	2.16	2.21	2.50	2.03	2.57	2.43	2.30	1.92	1.47
Constant prices per capita	0.87	0.55	0.73	0.22	1.12	1.33	1.33	1.08	0.42
Price index	5.15	4.67	3.64	2.73	3.91	4.32	6.61	7.12	6.62
Full consumer outlays:									
Current prices	7.32	5.94	5.33	4.71	6.53	6.47	9.55	9.60	8.55
Constant prices	2.44	2.03	2.15	2.01	2.77	2.49	2.81	2.69	2.21
Constant prices per capita	1.14	0.37	0.38	0.21	1.32	1.40	1.84	1.85	1.16
Price index	4.89	3.87	3.17	2.73	3.76	4.03	6.70	6.92	6.34
Full saving:									
Current prices	7.28	7.79	6.98	4.85	6.38	6.99	8.35	8.44	7.55
Constant prices	1.88	2.42	2.86	2.05	2.37	2.36	1.80	1.12	0.65
Constant prices per capita	0.58	0.75	1.09	0.24	0.92	1.26	0.84	0.28	−0.40
Price index	5.40	5.31	4.18	2.84	4.00	4.63	6.52	7.34	6.89

6.5 Accumulation and Wealth

Our final objective is to integrate our measures of saving in the form of human and nonhuman capital with measures of human and nonhuman wealth. For this purpose we implement an accumulation account for the private national sector of the U.S. economy. This account includes saving in the form of human and nonhuman capital and depreciation on both forms of capital. Depreciation on human capital is due to aging, deaths, and emigration. Depreciation on nonhuman capital is due to deterioration and retirement of investment goods with age. The difference between saving and depreciation is the net saving of the private national sector.

The accumulation account also includes revaluation of human and nonhuman capital. Revaluation of human capital is due to changes in lifetime incomes for individuals of a given age, sex, and education. Revaluation of nonhuman capital is due to changes in asset values for investment goods of a given age. The change in the value of wealth from period to period is the sum of net saving and revaluation of capital. The value of saving in the form of human and nonhuman capital is equal to the value of capital formation in both forms. We add saving, depreciation and revaluation in the form of nonhuman capital, as defined by Fraumeni and Jorgenson (1980), to our estimates of saving, depreciation and revaluation in the form of human capital.

We present the accumulation account in current prices for the private national sector of the U.S. economy for the year 1982 in table 6.26. Human capital saving is very large by comparison with private national saving, which is very similar to the corresponding concept in the U.S. national accounts. Depreciation is a very large proportion of full gross private national saving, which includes human and nonhuman saving. Finally, in 1982 revaluation of human and nonhuman capital was far more important than net saving in the change in private national wealth. Saving in the accumulation account is equal to saving in the income and expenditure account; in the accumulation account saving is equal to capital formation.

Our next objective is to allocate change in wealth for the private national sector of the U.S. economy among revaluation, saving and depreciation for the period 1948–1984. We first estimate the value of saving and depreciation for all years. Our estimates of full gross saving, net saving and depreciation are given in current prices in table 6.27 and in constant prices in table 6.28. The share of net saving in

Table 6.26
Gross private national capital accumulation 1982 (billions of current dollars)

		Saving	
1.		Personal saving (table 5.1, line 3)	153.9
2.	+	Undistributed corporate profits (table 5.1, line 5)	39.6
3.	+	Corporate inventory valuation adjustment (table 5.1, line 6)	−10.4
4.	+	Capital consumption adjustment (table 5.1, line 7)	−9.2
5.	+	Corporate capital consumption allowances with capital consumption adjustment (table 5.1, line 8)	235.0
6.	+	Noncorporate capital consumption allowances with capital consumption adjustment (table 5.1, line 9)	148.2
7.	+	Private wage accruals less disbursements (table 5.1, line 10)	.0
8.	+	Personal consumption expenditures, durable goods (table 1.1, line 3)	252.7
9.	+	Surplus, social insurance funds (table 3.13, lines 11 and 22)	6.1
10.	+	Government wage accruals less disbursements (table 3.2, line 30 and table 3.3, line 25)	0.0
11.	+	Statistical discrepancy (table 1.9, line 8)	−.1
12.	=	Gross private national saving	815.8
13.	+	Human capital saving	4,568.6
14.	=	Full gross private national saving	5,384.4
15.	−	Depreciation	2,624.8
16.	=	Net private national saving	2,759.5
17.	+	Revaluation	10,643.0
18.	=	Change in private national wealth	13,402.5
		Capital formation	
1.		Gross private domestic investment (table 1.1, line 6)	447.3
2.	+	Personal consumption expenditures, durable goods (table 1.1, line 3)	252.7
3.	+	Deficit of federal government (table 3.2, line 31)	145.9
4.	+	Deficit of state and local governments (table 3.3, line 26)	−35.1
5.	−	Deficit, federal social insurance funds (table 3.13, line 11)	30.8
6.	−	Deficit, state and local social insurance funds (table 3.13, line 22)	−36.9
7.	+	Wage accruals less disbursement, federal government (table 3.2, line 30)	0.0
8.	+	Wage accruals less disbursement, state and local government (table 3.3, line 25)	0.0
9.	+	Net foreign investment (table 5.1, line 17)	−1.0
10.	=	Gross private national capital formation	815.8
11.	+	Gross private national human capital formation	4,568.6
12.	=	Full gross private national capital formation	5,384.4

Note: All table references are to the NIPA tables in the March 1986 *Survey of Current Business*.

Table 6.27
Full gross private national saving (billions of current dollars)

Year	Full gross saving	Full net saving	Depre- ciation	Net share	Depre- ciation share
1949	483.8	306.9	176.8	0.634	0.366
1950	518.6	327.6	191.0	0.632	0.368
1951	566.4	358.8	207.6	0.634	0.366
1952	600.2	379.7	220.5	0.633	0.367
1953	660.7	421.9	238.8	0.639	0.361
1954	704.1	451.3	252.8	0.641	0.359
1955	745.2	480.6	264.5	0.645	0.355
1956	791.0	508.5	282.4	0.643	0.357
1957	873.5	571.0	302.5	0.654	0.346
1958	933.9	614.7	319.2	0.658	0.342
1959	971.9	640.8	331.1	0.659	0.341
1960	1,010.4	670.4	340.1	0.663	0.337
1961	1,081.2	720.2	361.0	0.666	0.334
1962	1,141.4	762.8	378.6	0.668	0.332
1963	1,185.3	791.7	393.6	0.668	0.332
1964	1,312.7	882.7	430.0	0.672	0.328
1965	1,384.0	923.4	460.6	0.667	0.333
1966	1,482.0	980.1	501.9	0.661	0.339
1967	1,580.8	1,037.4	543.4	0.656	0.344
1968	1,702.7	1,109.1	593.6	0.651	0.349
1969	1,827.9	1,184.5	643.4	0.648	0.352
1970	2,056.0	1,339.9	716.1	0.652	0.348
1971	2,327.6	1,526.0	801.6	0.656	0.344
1972	2,392.7	1,515.0	877.7	0.633	0.367
1973	2,553.2	1,585.0	968.2	0.621	0.379
1974	2,789.8	1,689.6	1,100.2	0.606	0.394
1975	3,163.1	1,910.2	1,252.9	0.604	0.396
1976	3,306.7	1,929.9	1,376.9	0.584	0.416
1977	3,593.1	2,072.2	1,520.9	0.577	0.423
1978	3,752.7	2,099.5	1,653.2	0.559	0.441
1979	4,236.1	2,338.4	1,897.7	0.552	0.448
1980	4,691.4	2,514.9	2,176.5	0.536	0.464
1981	5,102.5	2,700.7	2,401.8	0.529	0.471
1982	5,384.4	2,759.5	2,624.8	0.513	0.487
1983	5,739.7	2,911.5	2,828.3	0.507	0.493
1984	6,178.7	3,107.6	3,071.0	0.503	0.497

Table 6.28
Full gross private national saving (billions of constant dollars)

	Full gross saving		Full net saving		**Full depreciation**	
Year	quantity	price	quantity	price	quantity	price
1949	2,864.6	0.169	1,815.2	0.169	1,073.1	0.165
1950	2,975.5	0.174	1,884.3	0.174	1,105.7	0.173
1951	3,044.2	0.186	1,932.8	0.186	1,136.3	0.183
1952	3,073.6	0.195	1,949.7	0.195	1,157.2	0.191
1953	3,155.3	0.209	2,017.4	0.209	1,174.0	0.203
1954	3,224.7	0.218	2,075.1	0.217	1,190.6	0.212
1955	3,373.1	0.221	2,206.4	0.218	1,202.7	0.220
1956	3,432.9	0.230	2,245.6	0.226	1,224.3	0.231
1957	3,537.5	0.247	2,339.4	0.244	1,241.5	0.244
1958	3,589.4	0.260	2,383.4	0.258	1,255.2	0.254
1959	3,691.4	0.263	2,460.7	0.261	1,266.3	0.261
1960	3,761.5	0.269	2,514.6	0.267	1,279.7	0.266
1961	3,873.2	0.279	2,602.0	0.277	1,305.0	0.277
1962	3,973.5	0.287	2,670.4	0.286	1,326.3	0.285
1963	4,091.4	0.290	2,752.8	0.288	1,353.2	0.291
1964	4,229.7	0.310	2,850.2	0.310	1,384.8	0.310
1965	4,297.4	0.322	2,869.1	0.322	1,423.9	0.323
1966	4,336.0	0.342	2,853.7	0.343	1,473.0	0.341
1967	4,402.6	0.359	2,866.5	0.362	1,526.8	0.356
1968	4,514.6	0.377	2,924.7	0.379	1,579.9	0.376
1969	4,654.4	0.393	3,011.4	0.393	1,634.4	0.394
1970	4,788.8	0.429	3,093.5	0.433	1,689.2	0.424
1971	4,963.3	0.469	3,210.0	0.475	1,746.4	0.459
1972	4,944.4	0.484	3,124.3	0.485	1,816.9	0.483
1973	5,002.8	0.510	3,116.9	0.508	1,893.3	0.511
1974	4,973.3	0.561	3,009.2	0.561	1,978.7	0.556
1975	5,019.1	0.630	2,977.0	0.642	2,056.3	0.609
1976	5,076.5	0.651	2,961.7	0.652	2,130.0	0.646
1977	5,215.8	0.689	3,017.7	0.687	2,212.1	0.688
1978	5,305.6	0.707	3,012.3	0.697	2,306.7	0.717
1979	5,350.3	0.792	2,950.5	0.793	2,407.0	0.788
1980	5,379.0	0.872	2,881.2	0.873	2,498.1	0.871
1981	5,430.0	0.940	2,869.7	0.941	2,560.4	0.938
1982	5,384.2	1.000	2,759.3	1.000	2,624.8	1.000
1983	5,428.7	1.057	2,743.4	1.061	2,686.0	1.053
1984	5,527.6	1.118	2,773.5	1.120	2,755.1	1.115

gross saving has declined from 0.672 in 1964 to 0.503 in 1984. The share of depreciation has risen from 0.328 to 0.497 between these two years. The prices of net saving and depreciation are nearly proportional to each other, so that the rise in the share of depreciation is due to a decline in net saving in constant prices from its peak level in 1971. Depreciation in constant prices has grown steadily throughout the postwar period.

We have analyzed the structure of full gross private national saving in table 6.29. We present gross saving, net saving, and depreciation in current and constant prices. We also give saving and depreciation in constant prices per capita. The growth rate of net saving in constant prices per capita has been slightly negative for the period as a whole. This growth rate was positive for the periods 1948–1953 through 1966–1969 and has been negative ever since. The growth rate of gross saving in constant prices per capita was only 0.58 percent per year for the period as a whole and has been negative for the period 1979–1984.

The final step in integrating our measures of saving with measures of human and nonhuman wealth is the estimate of revaluation of human and nonhuman capital for all years. We present estimates of saving, depreciation, net saving, revaluation and change in wealth for the period 1948–1984 in table 6.30. Revaluation rose to a peak in 1979 and has declined since then. Both revaluation and change in wealth fluctuate substantially from period to period, reflecting variations in the rate of change of lifetime labor incomes and asset values from period to period. Revaluation has exceeded net capital formation as a proportion of change in wealth in every year since 1963.

We conclude our presentation of a new system of national accounts for the United States with an account for the wealth of the private national sector of the U.S. economy. The value of full wealth is the sum of nonhuman wealth, as defined by Fraumeni and Jorgenson (1980), and our estimate of human wealth. We present estimates of full wealth, human wealth and nonhuman wealth for the year 1982 in table 6.31. The share of human wealth dwarfs the share of nonhuman wealth. We present estimates of full wealth, human wealth and nonhuman wealth for the period 1948–1984 in current prices in table 6.32 and in constant prices in table 6.33. The share of human wealth in full wealth ranges from 0.943 in 1971 to 0.921 in 1981. The price of human wealth rises more rapidly than that of nonhuman wealth, so that constancy of the human share is due to the slower growth of human wealth in constant prices.

Table 6.29
Full gross private national saving, rates of growth, 1949–1984

	1949–1984	1949–1953	1953–1957	1957–1960	1960–1966	1966–1969	1969–1973	1973–1979	1979–1984
Full gross saving:									
Current prices	7.28	7.79	6.98	4.85	6.38	6.99	8.35	8.44	7.55
Constant prices	1.88	2.42	2.86	2.05	2.37	2.36	1.80	1.12	0.65
Constant prices per capita	0.58	0.75	1.09	0.24	0.92	1.26	0.84	0.28	−0.40
Price index	5.40	5.31	4.18	2.84	4.00	4.63	6.52	7.34	6.89
Full net saving:									
Current prices	6.61	7.96	7.57	5.35	6.33	6.31	7.28	6.48	5.69
Constant prices	1.21	2.64	3.70	2.41	2.11	1.79	0.86	−0.91	−1.24
Constant prices per capita	−0.08	0.98	1.93	0.60	0.66	0.70	−0.11	−1.76	−2.28
Price index	5.40	5.31	3.87	3.00	4.17	4.54	6.42	7.42	6.91
Full depreciation:									
Current prices	8.16	7.52	5.91	3.91	6.49	8.28	10.22	11.22	9.63
Constant prices	2.69	2.25	1.40	1.01	2.34	3.47	3.68	4.00	2.70
Constant prices per capita	1.40	0.59	−0.37	−0.80	0.89	2.37	2.71	3.16	1.65
Price index	5.46	5.18	4.60	2.88	4.14	4.82	6.50	7.22	6.94

Table 6.30
Gross private national capital accumulation (billions of current dollars)

Year	Gross private national saving	Depreciation	Net capital formation	Revaluation	Change in wealth
1949	483.8	176.8	306.9	729.5	1,036.5
1950	518.6	191.0	327.6	739.5	1,067.1
1951	566.4	207.6	358.8	941.2	1,300.0
1952	600.2	220.5	379.7	623.3	1,003.0
1953	660.7	238.8	421.9	1,400.4	1,822.3
1954	704.1	252.8	451.3	798.5	1,249.8
1955	745.2	264.5	480.6	−63.3	417.3
1956	791.0	282.4	508.5	927.5	1,436.1
1957	873.5	302.5	571.0	1,744.1	2,315.1
1958	933.9	319.2	614.7	1,783.9	2,398.6
1959	971.9	331.1	640.8	−128.3	512.5
1960	1,010.4	340.1	670.4	838.7	1,509.1
1961	1,081.2	361.0	720.2	1,291.4	2,011.6
1962	1,141.4	378.6	762.8	743.3	1,506.1
1963	1,185.3	393.6	791.7	378.1	1,169.9
1964	1,312.7	430.0	882.7	2,360.0	3,242.7
1965	1,384.0	460.6	923.4	2,202.2	3,125.6
1966	1,482.0	501.9	980.1	2,925.1	3,905.2
1967	1,580.8	543.4	1,037.4	2,392.5	3,429.8
1968	1,702.7	593.6	1,109.1	2,312.3	3,421.4
1969	1,827.9	643.4	1,184.5	2,955.1	4,139.6
1970	2,056.0	716.1	1,339.9	5,424.9	6,764.8
1971	2,327.6	801.6	1,526.0	5,542.9	7,068.9
1972	2,392.7	877.7	1,515.0	3,378.8	4,893.8
1973	2,553.2	968.2	1,585.0	7,663.9	9,248.9
1974	2,789.8	1,100.2	1,689.6	5,834.0	7,523.6
1975	3,163.1	1,252.9	1,910.2	6,335.3	8,245.5
1976	3,306.7	1,376.9	1,929.9	6,937.3	8,867.2
1977	3,593.1	1,520.9	2,072.2	5,632.2	7,704.4
1978	3,752.7	1,653.2	2,099.5	11,069.9	13,169.4
1979	4,236.1	1,897.7	2,338.4	13,278.3	15,616.7
1980	4,691.4	2,176.5	2,514.9	5,053.2	7,568.1
1981	5,102.5	2,401.8	2,700.7	10,410.9	13,111.7
1982	5,384.4	2,624.8	2,759.5	10,643.0	13,402.5
1983	5,739.7	2,828.3	2,911.5	10,571.3	13,482.8
1984	6,178.7	3,071.0	3,107.6	12,048.5	15,156.1

Table 6.31
Private national wealth, 1982 (billions of current dollars)

1.			Private domestic tangible assets			12,791.8
2.	+		Net claims on the federal, state, and local governments			896.2
			a. Federal, monetary		182.6	
		(i) +	Vault cash of commercal banks[a]	19.5		
		(ii) +	Member bank reserves[a]	26.5		
		(iii) +	Currency outside banks[a]	136.6		
			b. Federal, nonmonetary		644.1	
		(i)	U.S. government total liabilities[a]	1,133.9		
		(ii) −	U.S. government financal assets[a]	292.0		
		(iii) +	Net liabilities, federally-sponsored credit agencies[a]	−5.9		
		(iv) +	Assets of social insurance funds[b]	65.7		
		(v) −	U.S. government liabilities to rest-of-world[c]	172.0		
		(vi) +	U.S. government credits and claims abroad[c]	97.1		
		(vii) −	Monetary liabilities	182.6		
			c. State and local		69.4	
		(i)	State and local government total liabilities[a]	315.8		
		(ii) −	State and local government financial assets[a]	246.5		
		(iii) +	Assets of cash sickness compensation fund (our imputation)	0.1		
3.	+		Net claims on the rest-of-world			199.9
			a. Private U.S. assets and investments abroad[c]	716.6		
			b. − Private U.S. liabilities to foreigners[c]	516.6		
4.	=		Private national nonhuman wealth			13,887.9
5.	+		Private national human wealth			166,990.4
6.	=		Full private national wealth			180,878.3

[a] Board of Governors of the Federal Reserve System, *Flow of Funds Accounts*, various issues.

[b] U.S. Department of Treasury, *Treasury Bulletin*, February issues.

[c] "The International Investment Position of the United States," *Survey of Current Business*, October issues.

Table 6.32
Full private national wealth (billions of current dollars)

Year	Full wealth	Human wealth	Nonhuman wealth	Human share	Nonhuman share
1949	16,710.1	15,536.7	1,173.5	0.930	0.070
1950	17,777.2	16,512.9	1,264.3	0.929	0.071
1951	19,077.2	17,687.9	1,389.3	0.927	0.073
1952	20,080.2	18,618.4	1,461.8	0.927	0.073
1953	21,902.5	20,372.5	1,530.0	0.930	0.070
1954	23,152.3	21,574.4	1,577.9	0.932	0.068
1955	23,569.7	21,904.1	1,665.5	0.929	0.071
1956	25,005.7	23,209.8	1,795.9	0.928	0.072
1957	27,320.9	25,417.2	1,903.7	0.930	0.070
1958	29,719.4	27,737.3	1,982.2	0.933	0.067
1959	30,232.0	28,174.9	2,057.1	0.932	0.068
1960	31,741.0	29,603.6	2,137.4	0.933	0.067
1961	33,752.7	31,551.9	2,200.8	0.935	0.065
1962	35,258.8	32,971.7	2,287.1	0.935	0.065
1963	36,428.7	34,056.3	2,372.4	0.935	0.065
1964	39,671.4	37,187.6	2,483.8	0.937	0.063
1965	42,797.0	40,171.4	2,625.6	0.939	0.061
1966	46,702.1	43,886.3	2,815.8	0.940	0.060
1967	50,132.0	47,137.4	2,994.6	0.940	0.060
1968	53,553.4	50,331.7	3,221.7	0.940	0.060
1969	57,693.0	54,184.1	3,508.9	0.939	0.061
1970	64,457.8	60,722.1	3,735.7	0.942	0.058
1971	71,526.6	67,478.3	4,048.3	0.943	0.057
1972	76,420.4	71,999.6	4,420.8	0.942	0.058
1973	85,669.3	80,686.5	4,982.7	0.942	0.058
1974	93,192.9	87,523.0	5,669.9	0.939	0.061
1975	101,438.4	95,046.5	6,391.9	0.937	0.063
1976	110,305.6	103,214.4	7,091.2	0.936	0.064
1977	118,010.0	110,041.7	7,968.2	0.932	0.068
1978	131,179.4	122,024.2	9,155.2	0.930	0.070
1979	146,796.0	136,287.5	10,508.5	0.928	0.072
1980	154,364.1	142,516.4	11,847.7	0.923	0.077
1981	167,475.8	154,259.9	13,215.9	0.921	0.079
1982	180,878.3	166,990.4	13,887.9	0.923	0.077
1983	194,361.1	179,555.3	14,805.8	0.924	0.076
1984	209,517.2	193,829.2	15,688.0	0.925	0.075

Table 6.33
Full private national wealth (billions of constant dollars)

	Full wealth		Human wealth		Nonhuman wealth	
Year	quantity	price	quantity	price	quantity	price
1949	96,884.8	0.172	91,689.0	0.169	5,213.6	0.225
1950	98,785.0	0.180	93,314.3	0.177	5,446.9	0.232
1951	100,730.0	0.189	95,024.7	0.186	5,650.5	0.246
1952	102,664.9	0.196	96,789.4	0.192	5,805.2	0.252
1953	104,650.1	0.209	98,603.6	0.207	5,962.4	0.257
1954	106,679.5	0.217	100,472.2	0.215	6,113.7	0.258
1955	108,896.9	0.216	102,441.8	0.214	6,338.5	0.263
1956	111,142.0	0.225	104,468.7	0.222	6,538.3	0.275
1957	113,477.8	0.241	106,624.7	0.238	6,708.3	0.284
1958	115,805.9	0.257	108,833.5	0.255	6,827.6	0.290
1959	118,302.2	0.256	111,134.8	0.254	7,013.7	0.293
1960	120,844.0	0.263	113,506.4	0.261	7,178.5	0.298
1961	123,408.8	0.274	115,910.1	0.272	7,335.6	0.300
1962	126,098.6	0.280	118,390.3	0.278	7,537.6	0.303
1963	128,874.3	0.283	120,934.3	0.282	7,760.7	0.306
1964	131,693.1	0.301	123,489.4	0.301	8,015.5	0.310
1965	134,505.5	0.318	125,992.3	0.319	8,319.8	0.316
1966	137,273.7	0.340	128,423.9	0.342	8,657.3	0.325
1967	140,060.0	0.358	130,911.8	0.360	8,959.3	0.334
1968	142,922.6	0.375	133,470.4	0.377	9,269.0	0.348
1969	145,801.8	0.396	136,048.7	0.398	9,575.7	0.366
1970	148,666.3	0.434	138,650.8	0.438	9,843.1	0.380
1971	151,669.2	0.472	141,342.5	0.477	10,170.0	0.398
1972	154,569.2	0.494	143,901.4	0.500	10,536.2	0.420
1973	157,173.3	0.545	146,113.0	0.552	10,970.0	0.454
1974	159,869.7	0.583	148,492.6	0.589	11,310.0	0.501
1975	162,721.7	0.623	151,071.3	0.629	11,593.2	0.551
1976	165,344.2	0.667	153,376.0	0.673	11,927.8	0.595
1977	168,111.2	0.702	155,791.4	0.706	12,295.5	0.648
1978	170,556.4	0.769	157,858.0	0.773	12,689.8	0.721
1979	173,039.8	0.848	159,991.9	0.852	13,049.7	0.805
1980	175,753.0	0.878	162,424.8	0.877	13,331.7	0.889
1981	178,384.4	0.939	164,751.3	0.936	13,634.3	0.969
1982	180,878.3	1.000	166,990.4	1.000	13,887.9	1.000
1983	183,323.4	1.060	169,120.6	1.062	14,204.0	1.042
1984	185,734.0	1.128	171,121.4	1.133	14,622.0	1.073

We have analyzed the structure of full private national wealth for the U.S. economy in table 6.34. We present growth rates of full wealth, human wealth, and nonhuman wealth in current and constant prices and constant prices per capita for the period 1949–1984. The growth rate of human wealth per capita in constant prices has been only 0.49 percent per year during the postwar period. By contrast, the growth rate of nonhuman wealth per capita in constant prices has averaged 1.65 percent per year. The behavior of full wealth closely parallels that of human wealth, which greatly predominates in the total.

Our final objective is to compare our estimates of human and nonhuman wealth with those of Kendrick (1976). We have defined human wealth in terms of lifetime labor incomes for all individuals in the U.S. population. We have also incorporated nonmarket activities into our measures of lifetime income. These two innovations result in important differences between our estimates and those of Kendrick. Kendrick, following the classic studies of Machlup (1962) and Schultz (1961b) employs costs of education, including income foregone by students, as a basis for measuring investment in education. Similarly, he employs costs of rearing as a basis for measuring investment in human capital through the addition of new members of the population. His estimates do not include measures of the returns to investment in education or additions to the population.

In table 6.35, we present estimates of private national human wealth in current and constant prices from the present study and the study by Kendrick (1976). For comparability between the two studies, we have used the same year as a base for the price system as that employed by Kendrick, namely, 1958. Our estimates range from 14.64 to 16.67 times those of Kendrick in current prices and from 13.15 to 18.68, those of Kendrick's in constant prices. It is important to note that Kendrick deflates his estimates on the basis of cost indexes for education and rearing of children, while our estimates are deflated by an index of lifetime incomes for all individuals in the U.S. population.

Our estimates of nonhuman wealth are based on those of Jorgenson and Fraumeni. In table 6.36 we compare our estimates with those of Kendrick in current and constant prices, using 1958 as the base year for the price system. Our estimates are a fairly constant proportion of Kendrick's, amounting to about twice the level of Kendrick's estimates. In table 6.37 we present a comparison of our estimates of full wealth and those of Kendrick in current and constant prices. Since

Table 6.34
Full private national wealth, rates of growth, 1949–1984

	1949–1984	1948–1953	1953–1957	1957–1960	1960–1966	1966–1969	1969–1973	1973–1979	1979–1984
Full wealth:									
Current prices	7.23	6.76	5.53	5.00	6.44	7.04	9.88	8.98	7.12
Constant prices	1.86	1.93	2.02	2.10	2.12	2.01	1.88	1.60	1.42
Constant prices per capita	0.56	0.27	0.25	0.29	0.67	0.91	0.91	0.76	0.37
Price index	5.37	4.87	3.56	2.91	4.28	5.08	7.98	7.37	5.71
Human wealth:									
Current prices	7.21	6.77	5.53	5.08	6.56	7.03	9.95	8.74	7.04
Constant prices	1.78	1.82	1.96	2.08	2.06	1.92	1.78	1.51	1.35
Constant prices per capita	0.49	0.16	0.18	0.28	0.61	0.82	0.82	0.67	0.30
Price index	5.44	5.07	3.49	3.07	4.50	5.05	8.18	7.23	5.70
Nonhuman wealth:									
Current prices	7.41	6.63	5.46	3.86	4.59	7.34	8.77	12.44	8.01
Constant prices	2.95	3.36	2.95	2.26	3.12	3.36	3.40	2.89	2.28
Constant prices per capita	1.65	1.69	1.18	0.45	1.67	2.26	2.43	2.05	1.23
Price index	4.46	3.32	2.50	1.60	1.45	3.96	5.39	9.55	5.75

Table 6.35
Private national human wealth, 1949–1969

	Billions of current dollars			Billions of 1958 dollars		
Year	Jorgenson and Fraumeni	Kendrick	Ratio	Jorgenson and Fraumeni	Kendrick	Ratio
1949	15,536.7	938.9	16.55	23,214.7	1,242.9	18.68
1950	16,512.9	991.3	16.66	23,576.8	1,280.5	18.41
1951	17,687.9	1,097.7	16.11	24,051.8	1,322.2	18.19
1952	18,618.4	1,172.6	15.88	24,412.9	1,366.9	17.86
1953	20,372.5	1,236.8	16.47	25,051.4	1,413.3	17.73
1954	21,574.4	1,294.4	16.67	25,551.2	1,460.0	17.50
1955	21,904.1	1,364.2	16.06	26,061.8	1,509.9	17.26
1956	23,209.8	1,462.7	15.87	26,510.7	1,565.6	16.93
1957	25,417.2	1,576.8	16.12	27,104.6	1,623.7	16.69
1958	27,737.3	1,682.6	16.48	27,737.3	1,682.6	16.48
1959	28,174.9	1,786.9	15.77	28,285.0	1,744.7	16.21
1960	29,603.6	1,901.4	15.57	28,928.2	1,615.1	17.91
1961	31,551.9	2,012.8	15.68	29,594.3	1,888.4	15.67
1962	32,971.7	2,137.4	15.43	30,263.3	1,962.5	15.42
1963	34,056.3	2,273.0	14.98	30,927.5	2,041.9	15.15
1964	37,187.6	2,423.9	15.34	31,751.5	2,126.8	14.93
1965	40,171.4	2,594.4	15.48	32,465.6	2,218.8	14.63
1966	43,886.3	2,818.7	15.57	33,172.9	2,323.4	14.28
1967	47,137.4	3,049.7	15.46	33,838.9	2,434.0	13.90
1968	50,331.7	3,344.4	15.05	34,494.0	2,550.1	13.53
1969	54,184.1	3,699.9	14.64	35,164.9	2,674.4	13.15

Table 6.36
Private national nonhuman wealth, 1949–1969

	Billions of current dollars			Billions of 1958 dollars		
Year	Jorgenson and Fraumeni	Kendrick	Ratio	Jorgenson and Fraumeni	Kendrick	Ratio
1949	1,173.5	571.1	2.05	1,512.5	717.6	2.11
1950	1,264.3	621.4	2.03	1,580.4	750.1	2.11
1951	1,389.3	711.3	1.95	1,637.8	789.6	2.07
1952	1,461.8	749.1	1.95	1,682.2	819.6	2.05
1953	1,530.0	771.4	1.98	1,726.5	844.5	2.04
1954	1,577.9	782.2	2.02	1,773.6	868.3	2.04
1955	1,665.5	827.2	2.01	1,836.5	899.8	2.04
1956	1,795.9	898.1	2.00	1,893.9	938.6	2.02
1957	1,903.7	958.2	1.99	1,943.9	971.3	2.00
1958	1,982.2	989.7	2.00	1,982.2	989.7	2.00
1959	2,057.1	1,031.4	1.99	2,036.0	1,005.9	2.02
1960	2,137.4	1,057.6	2.02	2,080.0	1,030.4	2.02
1961	2,200.8	1,077:7	2.04	2,127.4	1,049.4	2.03
1962	2,287.1	1,115.6	2.05	2,189.0	1,072.2	2.04
1963	2,372.4	1,164.3	2.04	2,248.4	1,102.8	2.04
1964	2,483.8	1,222.6	2.03	2,323.6	1,138.2	2.04
1965	2,625.6	1,292.4	2.03	2,409.6	1,183.5	2.04
1966	2,815.8	1,383.4	2.04	2,512.6	1,235.0	2.03
1967	2,994.6	1,475.5	2.03	2,600.1	1,274.6	2.04
1968	3,221.7	1,549.7	2.08	2,684.8	1,300.8	2.06
1969	3,508.9	1,644.1	2.13	2,780.3	1,332.4	2.09

Table 6.37
Full private national wealth, 1949–1969

	Billions of current dollars			Billions of 1958 dollars		
Year	Jorgenson and Fraumeni	Kendrick	Ratio	Jorgenson and Fraumeni	Kendrick	Ratio
1949	16,710.1	1,510.0	11.07	24,968.0	1,960.5	12.74
1950	17,777.2	1,612.7	11.02	25,381.9	2,030.8	12.50
1951	19,077.2	1,809.0	10.55	25,941.0	2,111.8	12.28
1952	20,080.2	1,921.7	10.45	26,329.6	2,186.5	12.04
1953	21,902.5	2,008.2	10.91	26,932.7	2,257.8	11.93
1954	23,152.3	2,076.6	11.15	27,420.0	2,328.3	11.78
1955	23,569.7	2,191.4	10.76	28,043.6	2,409.7	11.64
1956	25,005.7	2,360.8	10.59	28,562.1	2,504.2	11.41
1957	27,320.9	2,535.0	10.78	29,134.7	2,595.0	11.23
1958	29,719.4	2,672.3	11.12	29,719.4	2,672.3	11.12
1959	30,232.0	2,818.3	10.73	30,350.1	2,750.6	11.03
1960	31,741.0	2,959.0	10.73	31,016.9	2,845.5	10.90
1961	33,752.7	3,090.5	10.92	31,658.6	2,937.8	10.78
1962	35,258.8	3,253.0	10.84	32,362.5	3,034.7	10.66
1963	36,428.7	3,437.3	10.60	33,081.9	3,144.7	10.52
1964	39,671.4	3,646.5	10.88	33,872.3	3,265.0	10.37
1965	42,797.0	3,886.8	11.01	34,587.5	3,402.3	10.17
1966	46,702.1	4,202.1	11.11	35,301.3	3,558.4	9.92
1967	50,132.0	4,525.2	11.08	35,988.6	3,708.6	9.70
1968	53,553.4	4,894.1	10.94	36,701.9	3,850.9	9.53
1969	57,693.0	5,344.0	10.80	37,442.2	4,006.8	9.34

full wealth is dominated by human wealth, we find that our estimates greatly exceed those of Kendrick in both current and constant prices.

6.6 Conclusion

In this paper, we have presented a new system of national accounts for the United States, based on comparable measures of investment in human and nonhuman capital. Our accounting system incorporates four major innovations. First, we have defined human capital in terms of lifetime labor income for all individuals in the U.S. population. Second, we have integrated demographic accounts for the U.S. population with economic accounts for the private sector of the U.S. economy. Third, we have incorporated the value of nonmarket activities in our measures of labor incomes and human capital. Fourth, we have measured the services of both human and nonhuman capital in a comparable way.

To implement our system of accounts for the United States, we have constructed a new data base for measuring lifetime labor incomes for all individuals in the U.S. population. Our data base includes demographic accounts in each year for the population by each sex, cross-classified by individual years of age and individual years of educational attainment. Our demographic accounts include data on the number of individuals enrolled in formal schooling and births, deaths and migration. These accounts are based on annual population data from the U.S. Bureau of the Census. We have incorporated data from the decennial census of population to obtain estimates of the population cross-classified by sex, age, and education.

To measure lifetime labor incomes for all individuals in the U.S. population, we begin with the data base on market labor activities assembled by Gollop and Jorgenson (1980, 1983). We have derived estimates of hours worked and labor compensation for each sex by sixty-one age groups and eighteen education groups for a total of 2,196 groups for each year. We impute wage rates for nonmarket activities from wage rates for employed individuals. We allocate the total time endowment for all individuals in the population among work, schooling, household production and leisure, and maintenance. We exclude maintenance through the satisfaction of physiological needs from our accounts for lifetime labor incomes. We assign the value of time spent in household production and leisure to consumption and time spent in schooling to investment.

Our final step in measuring lifetime labor incomes for all individuals in the U.S. population is to project incomes for future years and to discount incomes for all future years back to the present, weighting income by the probability of survival. We combine estimates of lifetime labor incomes by sex, age and education with demographic accounts for the numbers of individuals to obtain estimates of human wealth, investment in human capital and human capital services. We have presented these estimates in current prices for the period 1948–1984 for all individuals in the U.S. population. Combining these estimates with measures of nonhuman capital services by Fraumeni and Jorgenson (1980, 1986), we obtain a complete system of national accounts for the United States.

Our new system of U.S. national accounts results in a dramatic change in perspective on the role of wealth, investment and capital services in economic activity. We have employed the resulting system of accounts to describe economic growth by means of a production account, the allocation of income between consumption and saving by means of an income and expenditure account, and the accumulation of wealth by means of accumulation and wealth accounts. Even as an accounting exercise our results have important limitations. Perhaps the most significant is the exclusion of the government sector, including public education, from the production account. This is an important gap that we hope to fill.[8]

Our system of accounts could be extended in the direction of a measure of economic welfare, taking the concept of consumption employed in our income and expenditure account as a point of departure. Our concept includes consumption of nonmarket goods and services, including household production and the enjoyment of leisure, as well as market goods and services. This concept of consumption could be augmented by consumption provided by the business sector, but not included in our expenditure account, and diminished by work-related outlays that are included in our account. Our concept could also be increased by government services, excluding instrumental or defensive outlays. Finally, additional imputations could be made for amenities and disamenities associated with changes in the social and physical environment.[9]

Another task that remains is to employ the new accounting framework in exploring the determinants of saving and wealth, including human and nonhuman capital. The production account could be modeled by means of a production function, giving output as a function of inputs of human and nonhuman capital services. The income and expenditure account could be modeled by means of a model of household behavior, generating income from the supply of human and nonhuman capital services, and allocating this income between consumption and saving. Current consumption would enter into an intertemporal utility function that also includes future consumption. Finally, the accumulation and wealth accounts could be modeled by means of a model of portfolio choice.

Notes

1. See, for example, Gorman, Musgrave, Silverstein, and Comins (1985) and Bureau of Economic Analysis (1976).
2. Estimates of lifetime labor incomes for men based on market labor activities have been presented by Weisbrod (1961), Miller (1965), Miller and Hornseth (1967), The Bureau of the Census (1968, 1974), and Graham and Webb (1979).
3. Demographic accounting is discussed in detail by Stone (1971) and the United Nations (1975). This approach and its relationship to economic accounts are reviewed

by Stone (1981). A system of demographic accounts has been implemented for the United States by McMillen and Land (1980) and by McMillen (1980). The results of this research are reviewed by Land and McMillen (1981).

4. An economic theory of time allocation is presented by Becker (1965). Detailed references to more recent literature on time allocation are given by Murphy (1980). Results of a comprehensive and recent empirical study for the United States are presented by Juster *et al.* (1978). Kendrick (1979) summarizes the results of an unpublished paper by Wehle (1979), comparing seventeen studies of time allocation for the United States, covering the period 1924–1976.

5. Nineteen empirical studies of the valuation of nonmarket labor activities for the United States are surveyed by Murphy (1980). Kendrick (1979) provides recent estimates covering the period 1929–1973. An excellent summary of current research on demographic and time use accounting is provided by a recent volume edited by Juster and Land (1981a). Overviews of research in both areas are provided by House (1981), Juster and Land (1981b), and Ruggles (1981), all of which appear in Juster and Land (1981a). Time use accounting has been discussed by Fox and Ghosh (1981), Juster, Courant, and Dow (1981a,b), and Terleckj (1981). Gates and Murphy (1982) presented detailed time use accounts for the United States for 1975–1976, based on data collected by the Survey Research Center of the University of Michigan.

6. A system of vintage accounts for nonhuman capital is presented by Jorgenson (1980). This system of accounts has been implemented for the U.S. economy by Fraumeni and Jorgenson (1980). A preliminary form of vintage accounts for human and nonhuman capital has been presented by Jorgenson and Pachon (1983a,b). Additional details are provided by Christensen and Jorgenson (1969, 1970, 1973a,b). Campbell and Peskin (1979) have summarized accounting systems developed by Kendrick (1976, 1979), Ruggles and Ruggles (1970, 1973), and Eisner (1978, 1980). Kendrick's accounting system is similar in scope to our own since it includes production, income and expenditure, accumulation and wealth accounts. Kendrick's accounting system is also discussed by Engerman and Rosen (1980). Further references to the literature are given by Campbell and Peskin (1979). Ruggles and Ruggles (1982) have recently presented a system of integrated economic accounts for the United States that combines income and product accounts, flow-of-funds accounts, and balance sheets for nonhuman capital.

7. Kendrick's estimates of human capital have been compared with estimates based on lifetime labor incomes for males between the ages of fourteen and seventy-four for the United States, excluding the value of nonmarket activities, for the year 1969 by Graham and Webb (1979). A very detailed survey of nonmarket labor time and its value has been presented by Murphy (1980). Murphy (1982) provides detailed estimates of the value of household work in the United States for 1976.

8. A complete account for the educational sector is needed to estimate rates of return to educational investment. Estimates of investment in education have been presented by Schultz (1961b). Rates of return are given by Becker (1975). Kendrick (1976) provides estimates covering the period 1929–1969. Detailed references to recent literature are provided by Campbell and Peskin (1979). Gates (1982) provides time-series estimates of education and training costs for 1965–1979.

9. Welfare measures of aggregate economic activity for the United States have been presented by Sametz (1968), Nordhaus and Tobin (1972). Proposals for measuring welfare have been reviewed by Campbell and Peskin (1979), the United Nations (1977), and Beckerman (1978). Measurement of environmental amenities and disamenities is discussed by Cremeans (1977) and by Peskin and Peskin (1978). Detailed references to the literature are given by Campbell and Peskin (1979).

7 The Output of the Education Sector

Dale W. Jorgenson and
Barbara M. Fraumeni

7.1 Introduction

In recent years educational expenditures have averaged around seven percent of the national product. This percentage doubled between 1950 and 1970 and has remained stable since then. Obviously, education is a very important economic activity. Excellent statistics exist on all aspects of education, except the one most fundamental from the economic point of view, namely, the output of the educational system. We need a measure of output to put the education industry on par with other industries producing goods and services. The purpose of this paper is to present a new approach to measuring the output of the education sector.

Our point of departure is that although education is a service industry, its product is investment in human capital. The effects of formal schooling on income endure throughout the lifetime of an educated individual. Accordingly, we employ the impact of education on an individual's lifetime income as a measure of educational output. A second important idea is that the benefits of schooling are not limited to time spent at work. Education also enhances the value of activities outside the labor market, such as parenting and the enjoyment of leisure time. Our estimates of the output of the education sector incorporate the value of time spent outside the labor market.

Beginning with the seminal contributions of Becker (1964), Mincer (1974), and Schultz (1961b), economists have found it useful to characterize the benefits of education by means of the notion of investment in human capital.[1] This idea captures the fact that investment in human beings, like investment in tangible forms of capital such as buildings and industrial equipment, generates a stream of future benefits. Education is regarded as an investment in human capital, because benefits accrue to an educated individual over a lifetime of activities. Of course, investment in education is only one of many forms of investment in human capital. Important investments are made by families in the rearing of their children and by employers and workers in on-the-job training.

The most common approach to compiling data on education investment is to measure the inputs, rather than the output, of the educational system.[2] Data on the expenditures of educational institutions for teachers and other personnel, buildings and equipment, and materials can be compiled from accounting records. This information can be supplemented by estimates of the value of time spent by students (and their parents) as part of the educational process. Costs of schooling and the value of the time spent by students can be used to measure the flow of resources into schools and universities.

Although the costs of education are highly significant in economic terms, the cost-based approach to measurement of educational investment ignores a fundamental feature of the process of education, the lengthy gestation period between the application of educational inputs—mainly the services of teachers and the time of their students—and the emergence of human capital embodied in the graduates of educational institutions. Furthermore, some of the benefits of investment in education, such as greater earning power, are reflected in transactions in the labor market; others—such as better parenting or more rewarding enjoyment of leisure—remain unrecorded.[3]

In measuring the output of the educational system our first step is to compile data on the economic value of labor market activities. In section 7.2 we show that the constant dollar value of time spent working has doubled in the postwar United States. The growth of this value has been greater—or the decline has been less—for women than for men at all levels of educational attainment and reflects the rapid increase in labor force participation by women relative to men. The proportional increase in the value of market labor time has been greatest for college-educated men and women and corresponds to the substantial growth in levels of educational attainment.

Our second step in measuring the output of the education sector is to estimate the value of nonmarket labor activities. These activities include both time spent in investment in education and time spent in the consumption of leisure. We infer rates of compensation for nonmarket activities from market wage rates. The value of nonmarket activities, measured in this way, exceeds the value of market activities, primarily because nonmarket time exceeds time in the labor market. However, the value of nonmarket labor activities has grown more slowly. The expansion of the value of nonmarket time has been more rapid for men than for women. We discuss these findings at greater length in section 7.2.

In section 7.3 we estimate lifetime labor incomes for all individuals in the U.S. population. These incomes include the value of both market and nonmarket labor time. We then estimate the effect of increases in educational attainment on the lifetime incomes of all individuals enrolled in school. We find that investment in education, measured in this way, is greater in magnitude than the value of working time for all individuals in the labor force. Furthermore, the growth of investment in education has exceeded the growth of market labor activities. Investment in education has increased much more rapidly for women than for men, especially at the college level.

We present the conclusions of our study in section 7.4. One of the most attractive aspects of cost-based estimates of investment in education from the accounting viewpoint is that these estimates can be derived primarily or even entirely from data on market transactions. Unfortunately, it is precisely this feature that leads to the undeserved neglect of nonmarket activities. The lifetime-income approach presented in this paper easily encompasses the value of time spent outside the labor market. When applied to education, this approach yields far greater estimates of the output of the education sector than do those based on costs of inputs.

7.2 Market and Nonmarket Labor Incomes

In order to measure investment in human capital as an output of the educational system we have constructed a new data base for measuring lifetime labor incomes for all individuals in the U.S. population. This data base includes demographic accounts for the population in each year, cross-classified by sex, age, and year of highest educational attainment. Our demographic accounts include data on the number of individuals enrolled in formal schooling and on the number employed. These demographic accounts are based on annual population data from the U.S. Bureau of the Census.[4]

Table 7.1 presents our estimates of numbers of students between 5 and 34 years old enrolled in school, cross-classified by sex and level of

Table 7.1
School enrollment by sex and level, United States, 1947–1986 (thousands)

		Male			Female		
Year	Total	Grade 1–8	High school	College	Grade 1–8	High school	College
1947	28,411	9,871	3,593	1,663	9,142	3,378	764
1948	28,876	10,120	3,570	1,694	9,387	3,341	764
1949	29,581	10,485	3,555	1,719	9,731	3,324	767
1950	30,318	10,840	3,562	1,741	10,069	3,333	773
1951	30,980	11,120	3,623	1,702	10,352	3,403	780
1952	31,721	11,407	3,712	1,669	10,639	3,503	791
1953	33,011	11,954	3,810	1,648	11,177	3,611	811
1954	34,433	12,545	3,922	1,644	11,751	3,731	840
1955	35,791	13,072	4,055	1,655	12,259	3,873	877
1956	37,166	13,551	4,232	1,685	12,718	4,055	925
1957	38,577	13,954	4,493	1,730	13,097	4,324	979
1958	40,028	14,368	4,756	1,788	13,497	4,579	1,040
1959	41,492	14,819	4,969	1,870	13,950	4,771	1,113
1960	43,198	15,382	5,157	1,999	14,497	4,943	1,220
1961	44,643	15,683	5,442	2,164	14,767	5,238	1,349
1962	46,121	15,929	5,797	2,335	15,002	5,588	1,470
1963	47,645	16,203	6,154	2,498	15,283	5,927	1,580
1964	49,140	16,496	6,475	2,668	15,580	6,229	1,692
1965	50,432	16,759	6,636	2,950	15,838	6,347	1,902
1966	51,665	16,991	6,756	3,271	16,072	6,458	2,117
1967	52,894	17,206	6,901	3,582	16,276	6,607	2,322
1968	54,068	17,358	7,080	3,899	16,417	6,788	2,526
1969	55,102	17,421	7,268	4,218	16,511	6,966	2,718
1970	55,907	17,392	7,434	4,567	16,450	7,130	2,934
1971	56,447	17,282	7,616	4,764	16,352	7,300	3,133
1972	56,717	17,048	7,783	4,957	16,129	7,451	3,349
1973	56,736	16,739	7,908	5,129	15,833	7,562	3,565
1974	56,554	16,389	7,989	5,273	15,503	7,638	3,762
1975	56,301	16,037	8,037	5,401	15,171	7,679	3,976
1976	55,996	15,723	8,048	5,499	14,878	7,677	4,171
1977	55,680	15,476	8,017	5,562	14,647	7,635	4,343
1978	55,200	15,202	7,968	5,577	14,381	7,565	4,507
1979	54,437	14,863	7,843	5,563	14,062	7,427	4,679
1980	53,552	14,560	7,644	5,511	13,775	7,214	4,848
1981	52,696	14,098	7,425	5,879	13,359	7,118	4,817
1982	52,648	13,989	7,361	5,940	13,308	7,088	4,962
1983	51,980	13,832	7,178	6,063	13,174	6,843	4,890
1984	51,664	13,722	7,149	6,058	13,005	6,757	4,973
1985	51,037	13,577	7,064	5,855	12,869	6,673	4,999
1986	51,110	13,612	7,177	5,744	12,908	6,779	4,890

education.[5] Enrollments in grades 1–8 and high school peaked during the late 1960s or the 1970s and have gradually drifted downward through 1986, the last year for which our data are available. Enrollments in college flattened in the 1980s for both men and women and have begun to decline. Enrollments in primary schools have increased over the period 1947–1986 as a whole; enrollments in secondary schools have nearly doubled. Enrollments in higher education have risen very dramatically, especially for women.

To measure lifetime labor incomes for all individuals in the U.S. population we begin with a data base on market activities constructed by Gollop and Jorgenson (1980, 1983). We derive estimates of hours worked and labor compensation for each sex by 61 age groups and 18 education groups for a total of 2,196 groups for each year. Table 7.2 presents our estimates of the value of time spent working, cross-classified by sex and educational attainment, for all individuals in the U.S. economy from 1948 to 1987. In this table we give estimates of the value of labor time in current prices. The corresponding estimates in constant prices are given for 1949–1987 in table 7.3.

Labor time in constant prices is a quantity-index number, defined in terms of annual hours worked for individuals cross-classified by age, sex, and educational attainment. To construct a quantity index of labor time, we weight these hours worked by average compensation per hour. We assume that labor time can be expressed as a translog function of its 2,196 components. The growth rate of the corresponding quantity index is a weighted average of growth rates of these components. The weights are given by the shares of each component in the value of market labor time. A quantity index of labor input is unaffected by inflation in rates of labor compensation; the current market value obviously reflects this inflation.

The current dollar value of market labor activities has increased seventeen-fold over the postwar period. The proportional increases were greatest for college-educated workers—almost forty times for men and sixty-five times for women. The proportional increase for women exceeds that for men for all levels of educational attainment. For the population as a whole the growth of labor compensation is due to a rise in employment and very substantial increases in rates of labor compensation per hour worked. The contrasting trends for men and women are due to a modest rise in employment for men and much greater increase in employment for women. Hours worked per employed person have declined for both sexes.

Table 7.2
Value of market activities by sex and educational attainment, 1948–1987 (billions of current dollars)

		Male			Female		
Year	Total	Grade 1–8*	High school	College	Grade 1–8*	High school	College
1948	147.3	44.2	51.6	24.1	7.9	13.6	5.9
1949	151.2	44.1	52.6	25.6	8.2	14.3	6.5
1950	164.5	47.6	56.0	29.2	8.7	15.1	7.9
1951	187.5	51.8	65.2	35.4	9.2	17.2	8.7
1952	201.4	53.6	70.5	40.0	9.5	18.6	9.3
1953	215.2	55.8	76.1	43.9	9.7	19.8	9.8
1954	220.6	54.3	79.1	47.3	9.4	20.3	10.2
1955	229.4	54.4	83.1	49.7	9.8	21.6	10.8
1956	245.6	56.4	89.6	54.3	10.2	23.5	11.7
1957	262.8	58.0	96.6	60.0	10.4	25.2	12.6
1958	274.1	56.9	101.9	65.4	10.5	26.1	13.5
1959	285.4	57.2	107.5	68.7	10.6	27.3	14.1
1960	299.4	58.4	113.8	70.8	11.0	30.2	15.3
1961	311.4	55.9	118.3	76.5	10.5	32.9	17.3
1962	328.8	55.8	125.2	81.7	10.5	36.3	19.3
1963	340.8	55.8	131.1	85.3	10.8	38.6	19.1
1964	365.9	56.6	141.5	92.2	11.3	43.2	21.0
1965	388.4	58.3	151.2	97.1	11.6	47.5	22.7
1966	429.1	62.4	167.5	106.8	12.5	54.4	25.6
1967	460.4	63.1	178.2	118.5	13.2	58.8	28.6
1968	504.2	65.4	195.5	131.0	13.8	65.6	32.8
1969	548.7	67.2	211.7	144.0	14.7	74.8	36.3
1970	602.3	68.1	230.2	160.3	15.4	85.5	42.7
1971	651.4	66.4	247.6	181.5	15.5	90.8	49.5
1972	701.5	66.0	267.3	201.7	15.3	97.9	53.4
1973	797.8	69.1	301.7	236.8	15.8	111.0	63.3
1974	870.1	71.5	323.5	262.7	16.2	121.0	75.3
1975	941.7	65.9	341.4	298.4	16.5	132.1	87.4
1976	1,036.0	67.8	370.5	335.3	17.3	145.0	100.1
1977	1,132.4	70.1	399.1	371.3	17.5	161.6	112.9
1978	1,273.4	74.8	441.6	423.5	19.8	183.7	130.0
1979	1,429.1	77.6	490.0	485.0	20.2	204.8	151.6
1980	1,560.8	77.6	518.8	533.8	21.4	231.4	177.8
1981	1,690.3	76.8	553.4	586.0	21.6	253.1	199.5
1982	1,757.6	69.2	554.1	617.7	21.1	268.9	226.5
1983	1,869.8	66.4	561.4	683.3	20.9	281.6	256.2
1984	2,047.3	69.2	620.7	752.2	21.6	303.9	279.6
1985	2,190.2	70.8	654.5	809.8	21.5	320.1	313.5
1986	2,350.9	71.5	686.5	875.6	22.3	347.6	347.4
1987	2,519.6	72.0	722.5	946.8	22.4	371.0	384.9

*The grade 1–8 column includes persons who have completed less than the first grade.

Table 7.3
Value of market labor activities by sex and educational attainment, 1949–1987 (billions of constant dollars)

		Male			Female		
Year	Total	Grade 1–8*	High school	College	Grade 1–8*	High school	College
1949	981.8	308.8	336.4	163.0	59.9	91.8	43.6
1950	1,021.1	318.1	343.8	176.8	60.8	93.2	50.5
1951	1,105.3	326.7	383.8	200.1	61.5	102.6	52.5
1952	1,134.8	324.9	399.6	212.2	60.0	106.2	53.1
1953	1,154.6	323.1	411.8	219.9	58.3	108.8	53.1
1954	1,130.1	302.6	409.4	223.2	54.1	106.9	52.0
1955	1,163.6	301.5	423.1	232.2	56.3	113.9	54.3
1956	1,187.3	297.5	434.3	240.3	56.5	119.4	56.2
1957	1,191.5	287.0	439.9	246.2	55.0	121.8	57.0
1958	1,169.2	267.8	436.5	248.2	52.6	120.3	56.9
1959	1,207.4	268.6	454.6	259.8	53.1	125.2	58.2
1960	1,221.2	259.8	464.6	266.9	52.0	129.0	59.6
1961	1,231.1	239.8	470.6	280.2	47.9	134.6	65.5
1962	1,268.1	231.4	487.3	295.3	45.9	142.7	71.1
1963	1,285.0	225.0	497.9	305.7	45.5	146.9	68.7
1964	1,312.8	214.4	510.7	318.6	44.4	155.6	72.5
1965	1,352.8	212.1	528.2	329.8	43.9	165.0	76.5
1966	1,399.6	208.6	549.2	342.5	43.5	176.9	81.1
1967	1,419.8	198.2	554.5	362.7	42.2	179.2	84.7
1968	1,450.2	190.2	569.1	375.2	40.7	185.6	90.7
1969	1,487.3	182.2	580.8	392.0	40.0	198.5	94.7
1970	1,467.9	164.4	571.1	393.0	37.3	204.6	97.9
1971	1,466.2	149.1	564.6	406.7	34.8	204.5	106.7
1972	1,508.1	142.2	579.2	432.1	33.0	211.4	110.2
1973	1,564.2	135.0	593.3	462.1	31.8	220.6	121.2
1974	1,568.1	127.7	583.4	471.0	29.9	221.5	134.0
1975	1,544.0	107.5	560.9	484.9	27.9	220.3	141.8
1976	1,587.7	103.0	568.2	510.5	27.0	225.8	152.3
1977	1,640.2	100.2	577.3	536.1	25.8	237.2	162.7
1978	1,713.2	98.6	593.2	570.0	26.9	249.2	174.5
1979	1,772.3	93.8	605.9	599.8	25.2	257.5	189.6
1980	1,764.8	86.1	587.0	601.7	23.9	263.7	202.2
1981	1,782.8	79.9	584.3	616.0	22.6	268.2	211.7
1982	1,757.6	69.2	554.1	617.7	21.1	268.9	226.5
1983	1,799.9	64.3	546.9	654.3	20.1	269.5	244.6
1984	1,897.8	64.9	583.4	693.4	19.9	279.9	256.1
1985	1,937.5	63.3	590.8	711.1	18.7	280.3	272.9
1986	1,953.2	60.1	584.0	718.9	18.3	286.1	284.9
1987	2,013.4	58.3	594.3	744.9	17.8	294.1	302.8

*The grade 1–8 column includes persons who have completed less than the first grade.

The constant dollar value of market labor activities has more than doubled over the postwar period. However, the quantity index for workers with eight or fewer years of educational attainment has declined substantially. For high-school-educated workers, quantity peaks in 1979 for males and rises throughout the period for females. Finally, working time in constant prices increases by more than four and a half times for college-educated males and almost seven times for college-educated females. The constant dollar value of working time for males with a college education exceeds that for high-school-educated males, beginning in 1980; the value for college-educated females exceeds that for females with a high school education at the end of the period in 1987.

Turning next to the task of evaluating labor time spent in nonmarket activities, we consider activities, such as formal schooling, that enter into investment in human capital and activities that result in consumption. The importance of evaluating time spent in nonmarket activities is widely recognized.[6] For example, Nordhaus and Tobin (1972) have incorporated measures of the value of these activities into their measure of economic welfare. Kendrick (1976) and Eisner (1989) have also imputed values for time spent outside the labor market. Five types of nonmarket activities are commonly distinguished in studies of time allocation—household work, human capital investment, travel, leisure, and maintenance—the satisfaction of physical needs such as eating and sleeping.[7]

We allocate the total time available for all individuals in the population among maintenance, work, school, and household production and leisure. Studies of time allocation show that maintenance time per capita has changed very little during the postwar period. We estimate that time spent in maintenance is ten hours per day per person and exclude this time from our measure of the value of nonmarket activities. We estimate the time spent in formal education for all individuals enrolled in school and allocate this time to investment. Finally, we allocate the time that is not spent on maintenance, work, or school to consumption. We impute rates of labor compensation for nonmarket activities from wage rates for employed individuals with the same age, sex, and educational attainment. Market wage rates are reduced by taxes on labor incomes estimated by Jorgenson and Yun (1990).

Table 7.4 gives the value of nonmarket activities in current prices, cross-classified by sex and educational attainment, for all individuals

Table 7.4
Value of nonmarket activities by sex and educational attainment, 1948–1987 (billions of current dollars)

		Male			Female		
Year	Total	Grade 1–8*	High school	College	Grade 1–8*	High school	College
1948	376.4	78.0	75.7	37.5	68.5	87.4	29.4
1949	401.7	80.8	84.1	41.8	69.3	93.8	32.0
1950	415.4	80.4	89.4	43.8	69.6	98.7	33.6
1951	425.3	81.5	89.4	45.8	70.3	102.3	36.0
1952	441.4	82.2	92.5	48.9	71.7	107.4	38.7
1953	465.6	84.4	98.2	53.4	73.9	114.0	41.8
1954	512.7	91.4	109.5	60.9	78.5	125.2	47.1
1955	519.1	90.2	113.3	63.3	76.5	127.3	48.3
1956	546.9	93.5	121.3	68.8	77.7	134.1	51.4
1957	590.8	100.0	132.7	76.8	80.8	144.4	56.1
1958	638.7	106.2	146.5	86.4	83.2	155.1	61.4
1959	644.4	102.9	149.8	88.1	80.8	159.0	63.8
1960	693.3	108.3	161.1	92.5	85.0	176.6	69.9
1961	739.5	116.0	170.4	99.5	90.7	188.4	74.5
1962	778.4	119.6	178.1	105.1	95.3	201.1	79.3
1963	804.2	118.4	184.4	109.4	96.6	210.7	84.7
1964	878.8	126.7	202.8	120.1	103.5	232.3	93.4
1965	953.7	132.6	220.9	131.9	110.6	255.0	102.6
1966	1,038.8	141.6	239.8	146.6	118.8	278.0	114.1
1967	1,127.4	148.2	260.8	158.4	127.5	305.5	126.9
1968	1,218.1	154.0	281.6	174.9	135.4	332.8	139.3
1969	1,317.7	160.7	306.5	190.9	143.9	361.6	154.1
1970	1,517.4	177.7	357.0	226.3	159.7	413.3	183.5
1971	1,676.3	190.8	397.9	261.0	173.9	448.6	204.1
1972	1,788.1	195.0	424.6	287.3	178.7	475.8	226.8
1973	1,937.9	206.8	463.7	322.6	181.8	511.9	251.1
1974	2,147.4	219.2	518.6	373.6	192.1	563.1	280.8
1975	2,365.3	234.6	575.7	426.1	201.3	612.5	315.2
1976	2,559.9	241.6	622.2	473.8	211.4	661.2	349.7
1977	2,725.3	243.7	661.8	519.1	216.7	701.1	382.8
1978	2,993.3	255.7	724.8	583.8	228.5	768.3	432.2
1979	3,294.1	270.0	795.6	665.0	243.3	837.5	482.7
1980	3,629.3	277.2	877.5	764.9	255.2	912.7	541.8
1981	3,930.1	287.8	972.4	832.6	271.9	987.1	578.2
1982	4,372.8	300.1	1,089.6	961.2	282.6	1,093.0	646.3
1983	4,706.9	309.1	1,145.9	1,071.8	287.6	1,149.6	742.8
1984	4,942.2	315.6	1,188.6	1,127.3	300.4	1,209.3	801.1
1985	5,346.6	343.6	1,259.9	1,242.9	323.7	1,281.8	894.7
1986	5,774.8	358.1	1,369.2	1,373.7	331.7	1,367.8	974.4
1987	6,536.0	381.4	1,557.8	1,583.9	356.0	1,525.5	1,131.3

*The grade 1–8 column includes persons who have completed less than the first grade.

in the U.S. population for the period 1948 to 1987. The corresponding estimates in constant prices are given for 1949–1987 in table 7.5. As before, nonmarket time in constant prices is a quantity-index number, defined in terms of hours of nonmarket time for all 2,196 categories of workers. Although nonmarket time in current prices reflects inflation in imputed rates of compensation, the quantity index number is unaffected by inflation.

The value of nonmarket activities in either current or constant prices exceeds the value of market activities by a factor of two. This is due to the fact that nonmarket time, as we measure it, is greater than time spent at work. For the population as a whole the growth of the value of nonmarket time is roughly comparable to the growth of the value of work time; however, the distribution of this growth is considerably different. Because each individual has a fixed time budget of 14 hours per day, allocated between market and nonmarket activities, the general pattern for nonmarket time is a mirror image of that for work time. For both men and women the value of nonmarket activities has grown considerably more slowly than the value of time spent working.

Given increased rates of labor force participation for women, the value of work time has grown more rapidly for women than for men. With fixed time budgets for both men and women, the value of nonmarket time has increased faster for men. For example, the value of nonmarket time for college-educated men has increased by forty-two times, whereas the value for college-educated women has grown by a factor of thirty-eight. The relative increase in the value of nonmarket time is greater for individuals of both sexes with higher education than for individuals with only secondary education. This increase is greater for individuals with secondary education than for those with only primary education. These trends reflect increases in levels of educational attainment for both men and women.

Our final step in measuring lifetime labor incomes for all individuals in the U.S. population is to project incomes for future years, discount these incomes back to the present, and weight income for each individual by the probability of survival.[8] We obtain these probabilities by sex from life tables published by the National Center for Health Statistics.[9] We combine estimates of lifetime labor incomes by sex, age, and educational attainment with demographic accounts for the numbers of individuals to obtain estimates of human capital, investment in this capital, and the flow of human capital services. The

Table 7.5
Value of nonmarket labor activities by sex and educational attainment, 1949–1987 (billions of constant dollars)

		Male			Female		
Year	Total	Grade 1–8*	High school	College	Grade 1–8*	High school	College
1949	2,438.5	524.2	484.4	238.0	508.6	554.5	191.4
1950	2,457.0	505.1	502.1	241.9	500.1	571.3	194.7
1951	2,434.7	489.5	489.3	239.2	493.2	579.6	200.2
1952	2,456.9	481.9	496.1	244.9	488.3	593.0	206.4
1953	2,484.0	473.6	504.7	253.8	483.0	607.2	212.8
1954	2,551.5	480.7	526.3	266.9	479.4	624.9	220.2
1955	2,570.6	471.5	535.2	275.0	470.4	636.5	224.5
1956	2,599.5	465.2	546.9	284.4	463.4	649.3	229.6
1957	2,647.5	465.4	563.2	295.2	458.1	666.1	235.6
1958	2,713.6	468.8	587.2	308.7	451.7	686.3	242.6
1959	2,730.0	455.9	594.9	314.9	441.5	701.8	248.0
1960	2,784.0	452.3	613.7	327.1	434.4	723.6	255.4
1961	2,849.9	461.3	630.7	340.9	434.6	738.4	263.5
1962	2,888.7	454.4	642.1	354.1	427.9	753.6	272.5
1963	2,942.6	442.9	659.4	370.9	417.7	773.7	288.5
1964	2,988.3	435.1	675.6	385.9	408.1	790.6	299.8
1965	3,030.0	421.6	689.5	403.2	398.7	808.8	311.7
1966	3,070.5	409.0	700.9	422.6	389.8	824.7	325.4
1967	3,136.1	402.1	725.2	437.6	381.4	849.1	340.6
1968	3,195.6	392.4	743.8	459.0	373.2	871.8	354.6
1969	3,250.5	382.2	766.1	477.5	363.8	890.0	370.3
1970	3,351.4	378.2	805.6	509.6	355.6	914.8	387.8
1971	3,447.7	380.1	830.8	542.0	352.5	934.7	407.9
1972	3,513.3	374.3	840.4	567.9	348.1	949.6	433.4
1973	3,563.8	367.4	849.2	591.0	341.5	961.5	453.2
1974	3,659.8	360.5	877.5	633.1	335.3	980.2	473.0
1975	3,782.8	364.1	916.3	673.6	329.4	1,000.5	498.1
1976	3,855.2	354.6	932.1	707.6	321.8	1,015.5	522.4
1977	3,921.5	343.0	946.2	743.9	313.8	1,025.4	547.7
1978	3,975.8	330.3	955.9	776.1	303.9	1,034.8	573.6
1979	4,040.4	319.1	967.6	813.8	295.2	1,046.1	598.0
1980	4,153.4	308.8	1,002.3	875.1	284.8	1,057.5	625.0
1981	4,240.0	305.6	1,045.6	897.0	290.5	1,073.2	628.1
1982	4,372.8	300.1	1,089.6	961.2	282.6	1,093.0	646.3
1983	4,468.1	295.3	1,094.6	1,016.0	271.8	1,086.6	703.3
1984	4,503.7	292.3	1,092.1	1,028.1	270.2	1,095.4	725.1
1985	4,578.9	295.2	1,096.5	1,067.2	268.9	1,090.4	760.0
1986	4,663.8	288.2	1,123.7	1,108.0	262.2	1,098.6	782.7
1987	4,731.4	274.9	1,151.5	1,140.4	252.5	1,099.7	812.4

*The grade 1–8 column includes persons who have completed less than the first grade.

value of the services of human capital is, of course, equal to the sum of the values of market and nonmarket time presented in tables 7.2–7.5 above.

In estimating lifetime labor incomes we distinguish among five stages of the life cycle. We assume that all individuals 75 or older are retired, so that the value of current labor time is set equal to zero. Lifetime labor income for these individuals is zero.[10] We assume that individuals between 35 and 74 may work, but do not attend school. Lifetime labor income is the discounted sum of future labor incomes through age 74, holding the level of educational attainment constant. We project future labor incomes for a person of given sex and educational attainment by taking these incomes equal to the current average for all individuals with the same age, sex, and educational attainment, increased by 1.32 percent per year to reflect future increases in real incomes.[11]

For example, we project future labor incomes for a male with a high school education at age 35 by first considering current labor incomes for males with high school education at ages 35, 36, and so on, up to age 74. We increase the labor income for a 36-year-old individual by 1.32 percent to reflect increase in real income. We increase labor income for an individual aged 37 by a further 1.32 percent, and so on. We then multiply labor incomes for ages 35–74 by the probabilities that the individual will survive to each of these ages, given that he or she has already reached the age of 35. Finally, we discount the labor incomes at 4.58 percent per year back to the present.[12]

For individuals between 14 and 34, we assume that an individual may work as well as enroll in school. For an individual of a given age and sex enrolled in the highest level of formal schooling, which is the 17th year of school or higher, lifetime labor income is the discounted value of labor incomes for a person with 17 or more years of education. For an individual enrolled in the 16th year of school, lifetime labor income includes the discounted value of labor incomes for a person with 17 years of formal education or more, multiplied by the probability of enrolling in the 17th year of school, given enrollment in the 16th year. This includes the time not spent in school during the 17th year. It also includes the discounted value of labor incomes for a person with 16 years of education, multiplied by one minus this probability, which is the likelihood of teminating formal schooling at 16 years.

By working backward from the lifetime incomes of individuals with the highest level of education we can derive the lifetime labor incomes for all individuals enrolled in school. At each level of formal education this is the lifetime labor income of an individual who teminates formal schooling at the end of the current level, multiplied by the probability of teminating at that level, plus the lifetime income of an individual with the next higher level of formal education, multiplied by one minus this probability, which is the likelihood of completing an additional year of schooling. In addition, lifetime labor income for each individual enrolled in school includes the value of time not spent in school.

Individuals between 5 and 13 years old are not pemitted to participate in the labor market, so that the value of time not spent in school is set equal to zero. However, lifetime labor incomes for these individuals are affected by formal schooling and are calculated in the same way as for individuals between 14 and 35 who are enrolled in school. Because the probabilities of continuing in school are very close to unity for people below the minimum age for leaving school, differences in lifetime labor incomes by age primarily reflect greater discounting of future labor incomes for younger individuals. For people younger than 5 years old, lifetime labor incomes are well defined, but are not affected by school enrollment. A summary of our methodology in algebraic form is presented in the appendix.

7.3 Investment in Education

To estimate investment in education we employ data on lifetime labor incomes, cross-classified by sex, single age, and single grade of highest educational attainment. We use increments in lifetime labor incomes and estimates of the number of individuals enrolled in school presented in table 7.1 above to measure the value of investment in education.[13] At this point our approach to measuring investment in education incorporates the crucial time dimension of the educational process. Lifetime incomes reflect the effect of educational attainment on the values of future market and nonmarket labor activities over the whole lifetime of an educated individual. These values are discounted back to the present in order to reflect the time value of money.

The gestation periods between educational outlays and the final emergence of human capital embodied in the graduates of educational institutions are very lengthy—8 years for individuals completing primary education, 12 years for secondary education, and 16 or more years for higher education. These long gestation periods imply that educational investment must reflect the increase in the value of previous investments in education that are due to the time value of money as well as to the current outlays of educational institutions. In measuring investment in education we focus on increments in lifetime labor incomes that are due to increases in educational attainment. These increments incorporate the time value of money for investments in education in earlier time periods. Of course, increments in lifetime labor incomes, as we define them, incorporate the effects of enhanced earning power on the values of both work time and nonmarket time.

In table 7.6 we present estimates of the value of educational investment in current prices for 1947–1986. We give the corresponding estimates in constant prices for 1948–1986 in table 7.7. Our most remarkable finding is that the value of investment in education is considerably greater in magnitude than the value of time spent at work, presented in table 7.2 above. The value of investment in education, as we measure it, accrues in the form of increments to the lifetime incomes of individuals enrolled in school. This value is greater than the value of the time spent at work by the whole labor force. However, the growth in the value of educational investment is almost twenty-one times the initial level, whereas the increase in the value of work is only seventeen times the initial level. This growth reflects the investment associated with rising levels of educational attainment.

The growth of investment in education is greater in relative terms for women than for men. Although the value of market activities for college-educated women has increased sixty-five times, the value of investment in higher education for women has grown by a factor of seventy-four. The corresponding growth in the value of market activities for college-educated men is forty times the initial level, and investment in higher education for men has increased by fifty-one times. The massive rise in investment in education by women is associated with the costs of substantially higher levels of educational attainment. These costs have preceded the entry of more highly educated women into the labor force.

Our estimates of investment in education incorporate a number of critical assumptions. We have assumed that the future growth of real incomes is constant at 1.32 percent per year. We have discounted future incomes by 4.58 percent per year to reflect the time value of money. Finally, we have estimated the value of nonmarket labor activities by subtracting time spent in market activities from a total time budget of 14 hours per day for both men and women. We obtain this

Table 7.6
Investment in formal education by sex and level of environment, 1947–1986 (billions of current dollars)

		Male			Female		
Year	Total	Grade 1–8	High school	College	Grade 1–8	High school	College
1947	181.1	66.7	32.0	21.4	33.3	18.0	9.7
1948	214.3	71.0	42.6	30.5	35.5	21.7	13.0
1949	231.6	76.2	44.4	33.6	39.6	23.1	14.8
1950	257.2	84.7	46.9	39.7	44.4	24.4	17.2
1951	293.2	98.5	51.2	43.0	53.7	27.4	19.3
1952	323.4	108.2	55.0	47.0	61.1	30.2	22.0
1953	372.7	123.2	62.1	52.7	73.2	35.3	26.2
1954	390.2	126.4	63.9	53.5	79.8	38.2	28.4
1955	433.8	139.4	69.5	57.9	92.2	42.7	32.2
1956	495.8	158.8	78.4	65.1	107.7	48.9	36.8
1957	570.8	182.8	90.7	73.7	125.0	56.4	42.1
1958	603.5	185.2	93.1	74.6	139.8	63.3	47.3
1959	616.9	177.9	93.3	72.1	151.1	72.0	50.5
1960	650.9	185.8	101.4	77.1	157.6	78.4	50.6
1961	678.3	185.4	107.4	81.4	163.8	84.4	55.8
1962	695.3	184.1	108.1	84.3	169.7	86.0	63.0
1963	738.6	186.4	113.7	90.3	181.5	95.5	71.2
1964	768.2	185.3	118.3	94.1	190.3	104.2	76.0
1965	832.3	193.3	129.4	101.1	207.1	118.0	83.4
1966	903.5	199.8	140.4	107.9	228.4	134.2	92.7
1967	985.3	209.6	151.0	125.9	244.7	143.0	111.0
1968	1,039.4	208.1	154.1	140.5	259.1	152.5	125.1
1969	1,252.5	232.1	176.9	169.0	323.4	191.4	159.6
1970	1,383.7	250.3	201.9	192.4	352.6	210.3	176.3
1971	1,458.4	252.5	210.0	206.9	374.2	227.1	187.8
1972	1,521.7	261.8	221.9	234.9	375.4	231.6	196.0
1973	1,594.5	265.5	237.1	265.2	373.1	241.5	212.1
1974	1,719.2	279.4	261.5	310.7	373.4	256.4	237.8
1975	1,792.7	284.5	276.0	342.7	360.5	262.8	266.2
1976	1,825.5	281.0	282.2	367.6	340.5	263.1	291.2
1977	1,883.6	278.7	294.7	405.4	319.9	263.4	321.5
1978	1,991.9	282.3	314.5	464.7	307.4	267.6	355.5
1979	2,113.1	283.1	330.5	525.3	304.2	275.2	394.8
1980	2,346.6	311.1	360.9	584.3	338.3	304.9	447.1
1981	2,515.9	335.0	374.9	601.0	383.7	341.0	480.3
1982	2,834.9	342.5	421.1	725.1	421.6	373.5	551.1
1983	2,975.4	360.3	419.2	800.3	422.1	371.2	602.3
1984	3,171.2	384.1	448.9	885.0	433.7	384.3	635.2
1985	3,359.3	413.4	487.6	981.2	435.2	382.6	659.4
1986	3,779.0	461.3	546.5	1,096.6	510.6	442.6	721.4

Table 7.7
Investment in formal education by sex and level of enrollment, 1948–1986 (billions of constant dollars)

		Male			Female		
Year	Total	Grade 1–8	High school	College	Grade 1–8	High school	College
1948	1,073.9	272.7	175.0	131.9	262.8	144.4	69.6
1949	1,087.6	278.6	174.5	133.6	270.9	143.3	69.9
1950	1,105.7	287.3	173.1	134.9	281.9	141.9	70.4
1951	1,128.2	300.5	171.7	132.0	297.9	142.0	70.3
1952	1,139.5	302.8	171.4	135.1	301.8	141.5	72.8
1953	1,153.0	305.3	171.5	138.2	305.5	142.7	75.4
1954	1,168.0	306.9	174.0	141.5	308.0	145.2	77.9
1955	1,204.2	316.3	176.8	146.3	320.7	148.4	81.2
1956	1,241.4	324.8	180.6	151.8	331.8	152.8	85.1
1957	1,281.3	333.2	185.6	158.0	342.4	158.1	89.5
1958	1,320.2	339.3	192.2	165.2	350.2	164.5	94.3
1959	1,360.6	342.2	202.6	172.7	354.9	175.4	99.1
1960	1,403.2	345.2	213.9	181.0	360.8	185.2	104.3
1961	1,481.5	351.0	234.4	195.8	369.6	195.5	123.1
1962	1,566.8	364.9	246.3	213.4	386.8	201.3	142.6
1963	1,642.8	372.8	261.0	230.7	396.0	214.4	157.9
1964	1,714.2	380.1	277.7	245.1	406.0	229.3	167.6
1965	1,788.9	387.6	298.3	256.3	417.9	246.1	175.2
1966	1,868.9	395.8	320.2	269.0	430.4	263.1	184.1
1967	1,967.9	403.5	335.3	301.6	442.3	268.8	214.1
1968	2,057.8	411.8	346.7	336.5	452.8	276.4	235.4
1969	2,129.5	417.5	360.9	358.1	462.7	286.1	248.6
1970	2,200.6	421.3	378.1	379.3	471.3	297.6	260.3
1971	2,246.1	422.2	382.2	401.1	476.8	306.7	266.5
1972	2,292.1	423.9	385.8	429.9	480.8	308.5	277.0
1973	2,363.0	422.5	399.9	456.5	480.5	323.7	296.2
1974	2,430.7	418.5	412.5	484.7	476.7	337.3	319.6
1975	2,504.4	413.6	421.4	509.6	471.6	349.6	357.1
1976	2,567.2	406.8	429.0	533.3	464.9	360.4	391.0
1977	2,627.7	398.2	434.2	556.9	457.1	369.8	427.7
1978	2,652.7	384.6	433.3	581.2	450.6	379.0	437.8
1979	2,707.1	378.0	431.5	606.8	445.7	385.0	468.3
1980	2,742.6	368.9	428.9	623.9	437.8	389.0	497.9
1981	2,720.7	359.2	418.8	640.4	429.1	380.5	494.5
1982	2,834.9	342.5	421.1	725.1	421.6	373.5	551.1
1983	2,861.7	337.2	402.4	767.6	416.4	365.0	572.9
1984	2,859.4	333.5	394.7	780.5	410.6	361.7	578.1
1985	2,833.5	331.4	394.1	785.4	403.8	350.1	566.9
1986	2,834.6	331.2	394.5	788.3	399.4	349.5	569.4

time budget by allocating 10 hours per day to maintenance for each individual. In order to assess the sensitivity of our estimates to these assumptions, we present a series of alternative estimates of investment in education in table 7.8.

In giving investment in education in current prices, we assume in the first panel of table 7.8 that real incomes grow at two percent per year and future incomes are discounted at four percent per year. We have used these assumptions in earlier estimates of investment in human capital, for example, in Jorgenson and Fraumeni (1989). Because the difference between the discount factor and the growth rate of real income is reduced from 3.26 for the estimates given in table 7.6 to only 2 percent for those in the first panel of table 7.8, we expect the resulting values of investment in education to be substantially larger. The differences decline from 43 percent in 1947 to 33 percent in 1986. These differences are greatest for primary education and reflect the longer gestation period between the investments and the resulting future incomes.

To consider the effect of an increase in the difference between the discount factor and the growth rate of real income, we present investment in education in the second panel of table 7.8 under the assumptions that real incomes grow at only one percent per year and future incomes are discounted at six percent per year. The difference between the discount factor and the growth rate is five percent by contrast with 3.26 percent in table 7.6. We anticipate a substantial reduction in the value of investment in education. The difference declines from 36 percent in 1947 to 29 percent in 1986. As in the first panel of table 7.8, estimates of investment in primary education are more strongly affected by this change in assumptions. Although our estimates of investment in education are affected by these assumptions, the qualitative features of the estimates remain the same.

An important feature of our estimates of investment in education is that they incorporate the values of both market and nonmarket labor activities. Whereas hours worked in the labor market can be measured directly, hours allocated to nonmarket activities depend on our assumption about the total time available. In the third panel of table 7.8 we reduce our estimate of maintenance time from ten to eight hours per day, and thereby increase the time allocated to nonmarket activities by two hours per day. In the fourth panel of table 7.8 we increase the estimate of daily maintenance to twelve hours, reducing our estimate of nonmarket time by two hours. These alternative

Table 7.8
Investment in formal education by sex and level of enrollment, 1947–1986 (billions of current dollars)

		Male			Female		
Year	Total	Grade 1–8	High school	College	Grade 1–8	High school	College
		Real Income Growth Rate = 2%; Discount Rate = 4%					
1947	259.0	99.6	45.3	28.4	48.4	24.3	13.0
1953	529.3	186.1	86.5	68.6	106.7	47.2	34.3
1957	811.1	276.3	125.9	95.6	182.9	75.6	54.9
1960	918.0	278.2	139.8	99.4	230.0	105.0	65.6
1966	1,262.7	295.8	190.0	138.8	336.3	181.5	120.3
1969	1,743.2	346.9	238.9	217.0	475.5	258.5	206.3
1973	2,209.6	399.8	320.2	340.7	550.0	326.5	272.5
1979	2,845.9	420.4	443.5	676.2	442.5	362.7	500.6
1986	5,030.2	682.6	726.6	1,387.7	744.3	582.0	907.0
		Real Income Growth Rate = 1%; Discount Rate = 6%					
1947	116.3	40.4	20.7	15.1	20.9	12.6	6.8
1953	241.9	73.0	41.0	38.2	45.9	24.9	18.9
1957	370.4	108.0	60.3	53.7	78.0	39.8	30.6
1960	427.2	111.7	68.2	56.6	98.6	55.2	36.9
1966	599.9	122.1	97.0	79.5	140.8	93.0	67.6
1969	835.5	139.2	122.5	124.7	199.4	132.7	117.1
1973	1,070.2	157.5	164.5	195.3	229.0	167.1	156.8
1979	1,474.3	172.6	231.9	385.6	190.3	197.7	296.2
1986	2,676.9	281.9	387.6	823.5	318.1	318.6	547.3
		8 Hours of Maintenance per Day					
1947	206.2	76.0	36.4	24.3	37.9	20.5	11.1
1953	423.2	139.6	70.4	59.8	83.4	40.2	29.9
1957	648.1	207.0	102.8	83.5	142.4	64.3	48.0
1960	739.1	210.5	114.9	87.3	179.6	89.3	57.6
1966	1,026.7	226.4	159.0	122.2	260.5	153.0	105.6
1969	1,422.0	262.4	199.7	191.2	368.8	218.0	181.9
1973	1,802.5	298.4	266.5	299.1	423.7	274.0	240.8
1979	2,373.4	315.9	368.8	590.0	342.6	309.5	446.6
1986	4,269.2	518.5	614.8	1,238.7	578.5	500.2	818.6
		12 Hours of Maintenance per Day					
1947	156.0	57.5	27.5	18.5	28.7	15.5	8.3
1953	322.1	106.7	53.7	45.7	63.0	30.4	22.5
1957	493.5	158.5	78.6	64.0	107.6	48.6	36.3
1960	562.7	161.2	88.0	67.0	135.5	67.4	43.5
1966	780.3	173.3	121.8	93.7	196.3	115.4	79.8
1969	1,083.1	201.9	154.1	146.8	278.1	164.8	137.4
1973	1,386.4	232.6	207.8	231.2	322.4	208.9	183.5
1979	1,852.9	250.3	292.2	460.7	265.8	241.0	343.0
1986	3,288.8	404.2	478.3	954.4	442.8	385.0	624.2

assumptions produce relatively modest changes in our estimates of investment in education. As before, the qualitative features of the estimates are unaffected.

Investment in education in constant prices is a quantity-index number, based on the school enrollments presented in table 7.1 above. The numbers of individuals in school are weighted by increments in lifetime labor incomes, cross-classified by age, sex, and level of schooling. Investment closely parallels school enrollments for each level of education. However, there are important differences for different levels of schooling. To analyze these differences in greater detail we present investment in education per student in current prices for 1947–1986 in table 7.9 and constant prices for 1948–1986 in table 7.10. These estimates make it possible to separate trends in the number of students from trends in per-capita levels of educational investment.

The value of educational investment per student is far greater than per capita income from market activities. This difference reflects the fact that investment in education includes the effect of formal schooling on the value of nonmarket as well as market activities.[14] For most of the period the values of investment for men and women are similar at all levels of education, despite differences in labor compensation between the sexes. For men the value of investment per student in higher education considerably exceeds that for secondary education, which exceeds in turn the value for primary education. These relationships also hold for women for most of the period. They reflect the lower differentials between wages of workers with secondary and primary education and the greater importance of time discounting for investments in primary education.

Investment per student in constant prices increases steadily throughout the period, reflecting the rising enrollments in secondary and higher education for both men and women. Although for men the values of investments in primary and secondary education are relatively constant throughout the period, the value of investment in higher education rises steadily. For women the value of investment in primary education increases, the value in secondary education rises and then falls, and the value in higher education remains almost the same throughout the period. The values of investment in primary and secondary education are higher for women than for men throughout the period, and the value of investment in higher education is greater for women than for men until 1979.

We have emphasized that our estimates of investment in education

Table 7.9
Investment per student by sex and level of enrollment, 1947–1986 (thousands of current dollars)

		Male			Female		
Year	Total	Grade 1–8	High school	College	Grade 1–8	High school	College
1947	8.6	8.8	11.6	16.4	5.2	7.7	15.3
1948	10.5	10.2	13.1	19.0	6.6	8.8	16.4
1949	11.1	10.7	13.7	20.5	7.2	9.4	18.5
1950	12.1	11.5	14.5	23.9	7.7	10.0	21.2
1951	13.4	12.8	15.9	26.2	8.9	11.1	23.8
1952	14.7	14.0	17.2	27.9	10.0	12.4	26.2
1953	16.8	15.8	19.4	30.5	11.9	14.4	30.1
1954	17.4	16.1	19.8	30.2	12.9	15.4	31.6
1955	18.8	17.2	21.2	31.7	14.4	16.9	34.5
1956	20.9	19.1	23.5	34.4	16.3	18.9	37.9
1957	23.4	21.5	26.5	37.4	18.3	21.1	41.6
1958	24.1	21.5	26.2	36.4	20.1	22.6	44.6
1959	24.0	20.4	25.0	33.8	21.4	24.3	45.5
1960	24.7	21.1	26.0	34.5	21.9	25.3	43.5
1961	24.8	20.7	25.3	34.6	22.7	26.0	42.2
1962	24.4	20.0	23.9	33.3	23.0	25.6	41.5
1963	25.0	19.9	23.7	33.2	24.2	26.9	43.3
1964	25.0	19.4	23.1	32.4	24.8	27.7	43.2
1965	26.1	19.9	23.7	32.8	26.4	29.6	44.8
1966	27.2	20.1	24.2	33.0	28.6	31.9	47.1
1967	28.7	20.8	24.8	35.2	30.0	33.1	51.1
1968	29.2	20.4	24.3	35.7	31.3	34.1	52.5
1969	34.1	22.5	26.6	39.8	38.6	41.4	62.5
1970	36.6	24.1	28.9	42.5	41.8	43.9	64.9
1971	37.9	24.3	29.9	43.3	44.1	46.7	64.2
1972	38.9	25.2	31.3	46.5	44.0	47.2	62.9
1973	39.8	25.6	32.3	50.0	43.8	46.1	63.7
1974	41.9	27.3	34.6	55.8	44.1	46.1	66.0
1975	42.9	28.2	35.8	59.2	43.0	44.8	68.2
1976	43.1	28.3	36.0	61.2	41.3	43.0	69.0
1977	43.9	28.6	37.2	65.2	39.5	41.4	70.8
1978	46.0	29.5	39.7	72.3	38.5	40.5	73.6
1979	48.4	30.0	41.9	79.9	38.6	40.6	77.7
1980	53.7	33.7	46.3	87.1	43.8	44.2	83.4
1981	57.9	37.1	49.3	85.0	50.8	50.9	87.0
1982	64.5	39.8	55.1	92.5	58.2	56.4	92.2
1983	68.2	42.5	57.4	99.9	58.7	57.1	98.4
1984	72.5	45.7	62.2	107.6	61.4	58.8	100.9
1985	77.8	49.5	68.0	118.8	62.6	60.5	107.9
1986	87.1	55.5	75.6	131.8	74.1	70.0	113.9

Table 7.10
Investment in formal education by sex and level of enrollment, market and nonmarket labor activities, 1948–1986 (thousands of constant dollars)

		Male			Female		
Year	Total	Grade 1–8	High school	College	Grade 1–8	High school	College
1948	52.4	39.1	53.7	82.1	48.9	58.4	88.1
1949	52.2	39.0	53.7	81.6	48.9	58.4	87.5
1950	51.9	38.9	53.6	81.2	48.9	58.2	86.9
1951	51.6	39.2	53.3	80.5	49.3	57.6	86.5
1952	51.8	39.2	53.5	80.3	49.5	57.9	86.5
1953	52.0	39.2	53.5	80.0	49.7	58.3	86.7
1954	52.1	39.1	53.8	79.8	49.7	58.6	86.7
1955	52.2	39.0	53.9	80.0	49.9	58.9	87.1
1956	52.4	39.1	54.1	80.2	50.1	59.1	87.7
1957	52.5	39.2	54.2	80.3	50.2	59.1	88.4
1958	52.7	39.3	54.2	80.6	50.3	58.8	88.9
1959	52.9	39.3	54.4	80.8	50.3	59.3	89.3
1960	53.1	39.1	54.8	81.1	50.2	59.7	89.6
1961	54.2	39.2	55.2	83.2	51.3	60.1	93.1
1962	55.0	39.7	54.6	84.4	52.5	60.0	93.9
1963	55.5	39.8	54.3	84.9	52.7	60.4	96.0
1964	55.8	39.8	54.3	84.4	53.0	61.0	95.3
1965	56.0	39.8	54.7	83.3	53.3	61.7	94.1
1966	56.4	39.9	55.1	82.4	53.9	62.6	93.5
1967	57.3	40.0	55.1	84.3	54.3	62.2	98.6
1968	57.8	40.3	54.6	85.6	54.8	61.9	98.9
1969	57.9	40.4	54.3	84.4	55.3	61.8	97.3
1970	58.2	40.6	54.2	83.8	55.9	62.2	95.8
1971	58.4	40.7	54.4	83.9	56.2	63.1	91.1
1972	58.6	40.8	54.5	85.0	56.4	62.9	88.8
1973	59.0	40.8	54.5	86.1	56.4	61.8	88.9
1974	59.3	40.9	54.5	87.0	56.3	60.6	88.7
1975	60.0	40.9	54.6	88.1	56.3	59.6	91.4
1976	60.6	40.9	54.7	88.8	56.4	58.8	92.7
1977	61.3	40.9	54.8	89.6	56.4	58.1	94.2
1978	61.2	40.2	54.6	90.5	56.5	57.3	90.6
1979	62.1	40.1	54.7	92.3	56.6	56.8	92.1
1980	62.8	40.0	55.0	93.0	56.7	56.4	92.9
1981	62.6	39.8	55.1	90.5	56.8	56.8	89.6
1982	64.5	39.8	55.1	92.5	58.2	56.4	92.2
1983	65.6	39.8	55.1	95.8	57.9	56.1	93.6
1984	65.4	39.7	54.7	94.9	58.1	55.3	91.8
1985	65.6	39.7	55.0	95.1	58.1	55.3	92.8
1986	65.3	39.8	54.6	94.7	58.0	55.3	89.9

incorporate the value of nonmarket labor activities. Estimates implicit in the rate of return calculations reported, for example, by Becker (1964) and Mincer (1974) exclude the value of nonmarket time. In order to bring out the significance of nonmarket time, we find it useful to consider estimates based on market time alone. To do so requires that we re-estimate lifetime incomes for all individuals in the U.S. population. For this purpose we include the values of work time given in table 7.2 above, but exclude the values of nonmarket time presented in table 7.4.

Investment in education including only market time is given as a percentage of investment also including nonmarket time in table 7.11. This percentage rises rapidly over the period 1948–1952, reflecting increases in labor force participation during this period. Since 1952 the percentage has varied around 40 percent of the estimates we present in table 7.6 and is higher for men than for women at every level of education. This percentage is rising for women and falling for men. We conclude that the magnitude of this bias is changing for both men and women. In order to capture trends accurately, both market and nonmarket activities must be included in estimates of the value of investment in education. Excluding nonmarket activities from these estimates produces a much more substantial downward bias for women than for men.

Human wealth is the sum of lifetime labor incomes for all individuals in the U.S. population. Table 7.12 presents estimates of human wealth in current prices by sex and level of educational attainment for 1947–1986. The corresponding estimates in constant prices are given for 1948–1986 in table 7.13. These estimates are obtained by multiplying lifetime labor incomes by numbers of individuals in the population, cross-classified by sex, age, and education. The totals presented in tables 7.12 and 7.13 are obtained by summing over age groups. The value of human wealth reflects the value of market and nonmarket activities given in tables 7.2–7.5 above. However, our estimates of human wealth incorporate not only investment in education, but also all forms of investment in human capital including, for example, investments in child rearing and the value of new individuals added to the population.

In table 7.14 we present the average values of human wealth per person in current prices for individuals cross-classified by sex and educational attainment for 1947–1986. We give the average values in constant prices for 1948–1986 in table 7.15. These values have

Table 7.11
Percentage of investment based on market activities to total educational investment, 1947–1986

		Male			Female		
Year	Total	Grade 1–8	High school	College	Grade 1–8	High school	College
1947	33.7	36.4	36.2	32.3	28.8	28.6	30.1
1953	40.5	46.8	48.5	45.2	29.4	27.8	29.9
1957	38.5	44.7	45.7	42.8	29.0	27.5	29.8
1960	37.7	44.5	46.9	42.6	29.2	28.9	29.0
1966	35.7	38.8	42.1	40.6	30.8	30.7	31.2
1969	31.1	32.4	39.5	35.4	27.2	28.3	25.6
1973	38.7	40.6	46.1	39.6	35.8	36.0	33.1
1979	42.6	46.0	49.9	47.3	37.6	37.4	32.4
1986	41.2	41.8	46.0	43.9	40.9	40.4	33.6

increased slightly for primary and higher education throughout the postwar period, but the relative values for men and women have remained fairly stable. By contrast human wealth per person in constant prices for secondary education has declined slightly for both men and women. Growth in human wealth for the population as a whole results from the increase in the population, the rise in average levels of educational attainment, and the growth in rates of labor compensation. Growth in compensation rates is by far the most important component of the increase in human wealth.

Our estimates of the value of human wealth, like our estimates of investment in education, are based on lifetime labor incomes that include both market and nonmarket activities. In table 7.16 we present measures of human wealth that exclude nonmarket time as a percentage of the estimates given in table 7.14. For the population as a whole the percentage of human wealth based on market labor activities alone is fairly stable, varying from 29.5 percent in 1947 to 32.5 percent from 1979 to 1986. However, this percentage has fallen slightly for men from the values of the 1960s. By contrast the percentage has grown very rapidly for women. The omission of nonmarket activities produces a downward bias for women that greatly exceeds the downward bias for men.

Table 7.12
Human wealth by sex and educational attainment, 1947–1986 (billions of current dollars)

		Male			Female		
Year	Total	Grade 1–8*	High school	College	Grade 1–8*	High school	College
1947	15,082	4,780	3,133	1,382	2,842	2,232	711
1948	16,081	5,052	3,344	1,517	3,000	2,388	778
1949	16,957	5,323	3,532	1,646	3,129	2,490	835
1950	18,055	5,660	3,780	1,832	3,271	2,607	902
1951	19,178	5,989	3,998	2,009	3,464	2,743	972
1952	20,513	6,403	4,270	2,193	3,693	2,905	1,046
1953	22,433	6,964	4,631	2,443	4,056	3,171	1,167
1954	23,176	7,237	4,790	2,537	4,174	3,234	1,202
1955	24,805	7,779	5,131	2,749	4,441	3,418	1,285
1956	27,105	8,515	5,626	3,066	4,803	3,688	1,404
1957	29,570	9,294	6,168	3,431	5,160	3,978	1,536
1958	30,492	9,527	6,383	3,505	5,348	4,122	1,604
1959	32,457	9,923	6,771	3,611	5,824	4,582	1,745
1960	34,672	10,521	7,214	3,851	6,258	4,969	1,857
1961	36,788	11,042	7,573	4,090	6,742	5,325	2,014
1962	38,067	11,249	7,855	4,273	6,967	5,587	2,134
1963	41,145	11,932	8,535	4,647	7,505	6,160	2,363
1964	44,096	12,524	9,198	5,014	8,032	6,734	2,591
1965	48,087	13,402	10,129	5,560	8,668	7,427	2,899
1966	51,788	14,062	10,911	6,107	9,309	8,132	3,264
1967	56,099	14,901	11,900	6,857	9,905	8,874	3,658
1968	60,327	15,606	12,876	7,555	10,511	9,696	4,081
1969	68,923	17,270	14,733	8,884	11,884	11,220	4,928
1970	75,554	18,487	16,544	10,266	12,427	12,271	5,558
1971	80,601	19,271	17,827	11,353	12,836	13,114	6,196
1972	88,245	20,642	19,855	13,011	13,415	14,337	6,984
1973	96,651	21,953	21,993	14,818	14,189	15,794	7,901
1974	106,010	23,271	24,296	16,988	15,051	17,389	9,012
1975	114,568	24,289	26,328	18,964	15,886	18,965	10,135
1976	121,760	24,939	28,074	20,777	16,455	20,330	11,182
1977	133,148	26,300	30,733	23,464	17,517	22,468	12,664
1978	146,260	27,992	33,898	26,888	18,547	24,605	14,327
1979	159,836	29,515	36,836	30,408	19,785	27,024	16,265
1980	171,254	30,877	39,317	33,759	20,492	28,762	18,043
1981	186,814	32,980	43,442	36,355	22,293	31,892	19,850
1982	198,951	34,558	45,827	39,518	23,707	33,724	21,615
1983	210,240	35,859	47,239	43,472	24,641	34,793	24,233
1984	225,320	38,203	50,255	47,162	26,036	37,222	26,439
1985	242,713	40,996	53,548	52,120	27,493	38,993	29,559
1986	268,567	44,683	58,966	58,215	30,229	43,206	33,265

*The grade 1–8 column includes persons who have completed less than the first grade.

Table 7.13
Human wealth by sex and educational attainment, 1948–1986 (billions of constant dollars)

		Male			Female		
Year	Total	Grade 1–8*	High school	College	Grade 1–8*	High school	College
1948	112,520	35,318	22,297	9,625	23,618	16,853	5,390
1949	114,719	35,758	22,756	10,021	23,931	17,233	5,578
1950	116,858	36,184	23,213	10,410	24,227	17,591	5,757
1951	119,151	36,733	23,641	10,815	24,621	17,932	5,905
1952	121,505	37,326	24,075	11,199	25,045	18,290	6,045
1953	123,879	37,942	24,522	11,572	25,474	18,663	6,176
1954	126,564	38,653	25,041	11,962	25,959	19,079	6,313
1955	129,203	39,355	25,557	12,345	26,433	19,492	6,451
1956	131,854	40,021	26,115	12,729	26,888	19,926	6,583
1957	134,705	40,714	26,752	13,120	27,347	20,437	6,731
1958	137,904	41,371	27,575	13,539	27,822	21,088	6,894
1959	140,923	41,934	28,432	13,963	28,172	21,740	7,056
1960	143,941	42,478	29,264	14,388	28,562	22,376	7,232
1961	147,149	43,073	29,883	15,071	29,021	22,813	7,596
1962	150,478	43,405	30,762	15,841	29,260	23,463	8,008
1963	153,503	43,488	31,720	16,604	29,346	24,166	8,417
1964	156,537	43,549	32,707	17,372	29,424	24,874	8,827
1965	159,346	43,491	33,685	18,155	29,432	25,565	9,241
1966	162,066	43,307	34,554	19,117	29,353	26,177	9,777
1967	164,712	43,016	35,390	20,177	29,195	26,802	10,354
1968	167,288	42,621	36,287	21,247	28,968	27,483	10,935
1969	169,624	42,097	37,211	22,283	28,677	28,149	11,490
1970	172,301	41,596	38,248	23,408	28,356	28,908	12,099
1971	175,200	41,341	39,044	24,630	28,190	29,464	12,827
1972	177,591	40,795	39,805	25,882	27,816	30,003	13,572
1973	179,806	40,111	40,561	27,181	27,343	30,521	14,338
1974	181,960	39,351	41,282	28,542	26,826	31,023	15,144
1975	184,167	38,618	41,958	29,955	26,326	31,495	15,983
1976	186,354	37,829	42,610	31,436	25,789	31,947	16,871
1977	188,420	37,047	43,168	32,959	25,257	32,337	17,753
1978	190,380	36,269	43,636	34,490	24,731	32,661	18,663
1979	192,372	35,540	44,042	36,068	24,244	32,927	19,589
1980	194,591	34,970	44,363	37,704	23,870	33,136	20,554
1981	196,836	34,834	45,569	38,070	23,799	33,732	20,838
1982	198,951	34,558	45,827	39,518	23,707	33,724	21,615
1983	201,208	34,346	45,299	41,646	23,547	33,225	23,133
1984	203,319	34,497	45,589	42,539	23,480	33,441	23,758
1985	205,415	34,622	45,538	43,717	23,483	33,006	25,023
1986	207,234	34,505	45,995	44,464	23,390	33,199	25,651

*The grade 1–8 column includes persons who have completed less than the first grade.

Table 7.14
Human wealth per person by sex and educational attainment, 1947–1986 (thousands of current dollars)

		Male			Female		
Year	Total	Grade 1–8*	High school	College	Grade 1–8*	High school	College
1947	101.1	102.3	148.4	195.7	65.6	90.7	111.8
1948	106.0	107.3	154.7	206.2	68.5	94.6	117.7
1949	110.0	112.2	159.7	215.0	70.8	96.2	121.7
1950	115.2	118.4	167.0	230.4	73.3	98.3	126.9
1951	120.4	124.0	173.1	243.5	76.7	101.2	133.0
1952	126.7	131.2	181.2	256.9	80.7	104.8	139.2
1953	136.4	141.3	192.6	277.0	87.6	111.8	151.5
1954	138.5	145.3	195.0	278.5	89.0	111.4	152.1
1955	145.7	154.4	204.3	292.3	93.6	114.9	158.5
1956	156.5	167.3	218.9	315.8	100.0	121.0	168.9
1957	167.8	180.8	234.1	342.6	106.2	127.1	180.0
1958	170.2	184.1	235.9	339.9	109.0	128.0	183.3
1959	178.3	190.6	243.3	339.8	118.0	138.3	194.4
1960	186.7	200.0	251.2	350.1	125.3	145.2	200.6
1961	194.9	208.9	257.6	355.3	134.0	152.0	208.1
1962	198.6	212.9	259.7	354.2	138.4	155.0	210.6
1963	211.6	226.7	273.8	368.3	149.3	165.9	223.1
1964	223.7	239.1	286.4	380.6	160.3	176.2	234.4
1965	241.0	257.6	306.5	404.5	173.8	188.9	251.5
1966	256.6	273.0	321.6	423.2	188.1	201.5	269.6
1967	275.0	292.8	341.9	452.0	202.2	214.1	287.7
1968	292.8	311.2	360.5	475.0	217.4	227.6	306.2
1969	331.2	349.9	401.7	533.9	249.1	256.4	353.6
1970	359.4	380.8	439.0	589.8	264.3	272.8	381.1
1971	379.5	401.4	464.8	620.7	275.7	286.4	402.5
1972	411.9	437.1	508.5	677.1	292.5	307.3	430.1
1973	447.9	474.2	553.6	734.9	315.1	332.6	462.1
1974	487.8	513.6	601.4	803.0	341.0	359.9	500.7
1975	523.1	547.2	641.2	854.6	366.9	386.0	535.1
1976	551.9	574.4	673.3	893.2	388.1	407.2	561.2
1977	598.7	618.7	726.6	962.5	421.4	443.1	605.1
1978	652.3	672.3	790.6	1,053.4	455.0	478.2	651.9
1979	706.8	723.0	848.6	1,138.8	494.5	518.4	705.8
1980	750.7	769.5	896.5	1,210.1	520.4	545.5	747.6
1981	810.4	825.9	969.0	1,283.9	562.0	597.9	812.1
1982	853.7	873.3	1,012.8	1,339.0	602.7	624.0	853.6
1983	893.4	911.5	1,048.9	1,398.1	634.6	647.7	887.8
1984	948.4	971.9	1,103.3	1,484.6	672.4	687.3	942.2
1985	1,011.5	1,038.0	1,173.2	1,593.4	711.6	722.7	1,001.8
1986	1,108.3	1,137.5	1,276.6	1,734.0	785.4	794.0	1,095.3

*The grade 1–8 column includes persons who have completed less than the first grade.

Table 7.15
Human wealth per person by sex and educational attainment, 1948–1986 (thousands of constant dollars)

		Male			Female		
Year	Total	Grade 1–8*	High school	College	Grade 1–8*	High school	College
1948	741.8	750.4	1,031.2	1,307.4	539.5	667.5	815.0
1949	743.9	753.5	1,028.6	1,308.7	541.0	665.8	812.4
1950	745.8	756.6	1,025.3	1,308.9	542.6	663.5	809.5
1951	748.2	760.6	1,023.4	1,310.9	544.8	661.5	807.4
1952	750.4	764.9	1,021.3	1,311.1	547.4	659.5	804.6
1953	752.9	769.9	1,019.9	1,312.0	550.2	657.9	801.4
1954	756.3	775.8	1,019.3	1,312.7	553.7	656.9	798.4
1955	759.0	781.3	1,017.7	1,312.3	556.8	655.3	795.4
1956	761.4	786.3	1,015.9	1,310.8	559.8	653.4	791.2
1957	764.4	791.9	1,015.3	1,310.0	562.7	652.7	788.3
1958	769.7	799.3	1,019.0	1,312.7	567.0	654.7	787.5
1959	774.3	805.3	1,021.8	1,313.9	570.6	656.1	785.8
1960	775.0	807.6	1,018.9	1,308.1	571.9	653.9	781.2
1961	779.4	814.8	1,016.2	1,309.0	576.9	651.2	784.6
1962	785.0	821.4	1,016.9	1,313.0	581.1	651.1	790.1
1963	789.5	826.2	1,017.5	1,315.7	583.9	650.8	794.3
1964	794.2	831.2	1,018.5	1,318.3	587.1	650.6	798.3
1965	798.6	836.1	1,019.2	1,320.5	590.2	650.1	801.5
1966	803.0	840.8	1,018.3	1,324.6	593.2	648.4	807.6
1967	807.3	845.2	1,016.8	1,330.0	596.0	646.5	814.1
1968	811.8	849.9	1,016.0	1,335.7	599.0	645.2	820.3
1969	815.1	853.0	1,014.4	1,339.0	601.0	643.3	824.2
1970	819.6	856.8	1,014.9	1,344.7	603.2	642.7	829.6
1971	824.9	861.1	1,017.9	1,346.5	605.5	643.4	833.2
1972	828.9	863.9	1,019.4	1,346.9	606.4	643.1	835.9
1973	833.2	866.4	1,020.9	1,348.0	607.2	642.7	838.5
1974	837.3	868.5	1,021.8	1,349.1	607.8	642.1	841.3
1975	840.9	870.0	1,021.9	1,350.0	608.0	641.0	843.8
1976	844.6	871.3	1,021.9	1,351.4	608.2	639.8	846.6
1977	847.3	871.6	1,020.5	1,351.9	607.6	637.8	848.2
1978	849.0	871.1	1,017.7	1,351.2	606.6	634.8	849.1
1979	850.7	870.6	1,014.5	1,350.8	605.9	631.6	850.1
1980	853.0	871.5	1,011.6	1,351.5	606.2	628.4	851.6
1981	853.9	872.3	1,016.5	1,344.5	600.0	632.4	852.6
1982	853.7	873.2	1,012.8	1,339.0	602.6	624.0	853.5
1983	855.1	873.0	1,005.8	1,339.4	606.4	618.5	847.5
1984	855.8	877.6	1,000.9	1,339.0	606.4	617.5	846.6
1985	856.1	876.6	997.7	1,336.5	607.8	611.7	848.0
1986	855.2	878.4	995.8	1,324.4	607.7	610.0	844.6

*The grade 1–8 column includes persons who have completed less than the first grade.

Table 7.16
Percentage of human wealth based on market labor activities to total human wealth by sex and educational attainment, 1947–1986

		Male			Female		
Year	Total	Grade 1–8*	High school	College	Grade 1–8*	High school	College
1947	29.5	38.4	40.5	39.7	13.3	13.4	16.9
1953	30.8	40.9	41.8	43.5	14.6	14.6	19.2
1957	31.6	41.1	42.2	43.9	15.2	15.2	19.3
1960	31.9	41.1	42.3	43.9	15.6	15.6	19.5
1966	32.3	41.0	42.7	43.9	16.5	16.7	20.2
1969	32.4	40.9	42.7	43.9	17.0	17.3	20.5
1973	32.4	40.5	42.2	43.1	17.5	17.9	20.7
1979	32.5	40.1	41.4	42.2	18.9	19.2	21.9
1986	32.5	39.0	39.2	40.1	20.6	20.5	23.3

*The grade 1–8 column includes persons who have completed less than the first grade.

7.4 Conclusion

Our new estimates of investment in education will help to bring the role of human capital in the process of economic growth into proper perspective.[15] Economic growth is measured through increments in the national product, as recorded in the U.S. National Income and Product Accounts.[16] These accounts are compiled by the Bureau of Economic Analysis of the U.S. Department of Commerce. The accumulation of human and nonhuman capital accounts for the predominant share of economic growth.[17]

Although both human and nonhuman capital accumulation are important sources of economic growth, the information required to measure investment in human capital is not available in standard data sources like the U.S. national accounts. For example, the Bureau of Economic Analysis publishes a great deal of valuable information on investment in nonhuman capital.[18] The national accounts provide nothing on investment in human capital.[19] The primary reason for this fact is that the accounts are limited to market transactions. Although there have been numerous attempts to augment the U.S. national accounts to incorporate human capital, none of them measures investment in education as an output of the education sector.[20]

Investment in education, which is a major portion of investment in human capital, is produced almost entirely outside the business sector of the economy.[21] Transmission of education from schools and universities to their students involves increases in educational attainment that are not evaluated in the marketplace, at least not initially. However, the economic value of these increases can be traced through their impact on the lifetime incomes of individuals enrolled in school. Fortunately, participation in schooling is recorded in enrollment statistics. Furthermore, levels of educational attainment are routinely collected for individuals as part of the census of population.

We have emphasized the critical importance of including both market and nonmarket incomes in estimating the value of investment in education. In section A of table 7.17 we present a comparison between our estimates of the value of nonmarket activities and the well-known estimates of Nordhaus and Tobin (1972). Their estimates are derived from rates of labor compensation before taxes: our estimates employ after-tax wage rates. The use of before-tax wage rates imparts a substantial upward bias to the estimates of Nordhaus and Tobin; however, the trend in these estimates is nearly identical to that in the estimates we have presented in table 7.4.

We have pointed out that existing estimates of the value of human wealth are based on the costs of education. Estimates of this type have been constructed by Kendrick (1976) for an augmented system of U.S. national accounts. We present a comparison of our estimates with those of Kendrick for the period 1948–1969 in section B of table 7.17. The ratio of our estimates in current prices to Kendrick's varies from 17.47 to 18.75 with very little trend from 1948 to 1969. The corresponding ratio for the two constant price estimates declines from 20.31 in 1948 to 14.29 in 1969. We conclude that Kendrick's cost-based estimates differ from our lifetime labor income-based estimates by more than an order of magnitude.[22] The trends in the two sets of estimates are broadly similar, but far from identical.

It is important to note that Kendrick's cost-based estimates of human capital include the accumulated costs of rearing within the family as well as the costs of formal schooling. However, our lifetime income-based estimates include all sources of lifetime labor income, including investment in education, the value of rearing—which is partly offset by depreciation of human capital with aging—and the lifetime incomes of individuals added to the population, prior to any investment in education or rearing. Nonetheless, the disparities between the two sets of estimates of human capital are very striking. These disparities provide a graphic demonstration of the conceptual

Table 7.17
Comparison with other results

A. Value of nonmarket activities selected years (billions of current dollars)

Year	Current Dollars J-F	Current Dollars Nordhaus-Tobin	Current Dollars Ratio
1954	512.7	637.0	0.805
1958	638.7	794.6	0.804
1965	953.7	1,096.9	0.869

B. Private national human wealth, 1948–1969 (billions of dollars)

	Current dollars			1958 dollars		
Year	J-F	Kendrick	Ratio	J-F	Kendrick	Ratio
1948	16,081.4	908.8	17.70	24,505.0	1,206.3	20.31
1949	16,957.9	938.9	18.06	25,156.1	1,242.9	20.24
1950	18,055.8	991.3	18.21	25,598.1	1,280.5	19.99
1951	19,178.6	1,097.7	17.47	26,036.4	1,322.2	19.69
1952	20,513.8	1,172.6	17.49	26,715.6	1,366.9	19.54
1953	22,433.3	1,236.8	18.14	27,310.1	1,413.3	19.32
1954	23,176.5	1,294.4	17.91	27,911.5	1,460.0	19.12
1955	24,805.7	1,364.2	18.18	28,494.8	1,509.9	18.87
1956	27,105.4	1,462.7	18.53	29,190.4	1,565.6	18.64
1957	29,570.6	1,576.8	18.75	29,837.0	1,623.7	18.38
1958	30,492.0	1,682.6	18.12	30,492.0	1,682.6	18.12
1959	32,457.5	1,786.9	18.16	31,203.8	1,744.7	17.88
1960	34,672.6	1,901.4	18.24	31,961.6	1,615.1	19.79
1961	36,788.8	2,012.8	18.28	32,701.2	1,888.4	17.32
1962	38,068.0	2,137.4	17.81	33,440.1	1,962.5	17.04
1963	41,145.1	2,273.0	18.10	34,262.1	2,041.9	16.78
1964	44,096.6	2,423.9	18.19	34,903.3	2,126.8	16.41
1965	48,087.5	2,594.4	18.54	35,667.5	2,218.8	16.08
1966	51,788.3	2,818.7	18.37	36,365.5	2,323.4	15.65
1967	56,099.5	3,049.7	18.40	36,959.7	2,434.0	15.18
1968	60,327.7	3,344.4	18.04	37,641.8	2,550.1	14.76
1969	68,923.4	3,699.9	18.63	38,215.0	2,674.4	14.29

differences between the cost-based approach and the income-based approach to the measurement of investment in human capital.

Although cost-based estimates of investment in education reflect the current flow of resources into educational institutions, they do not capture the crucial time dimension of educational investment. There is a lengthy gestation period between the current outlays of educational institutions and the emergence of human capital embodied in their graduates. A very substantial proportion of educational investment is attributable to the time value of money, applied to previous investments in the education of individuals who are still enrolled in school. This feature of investment in education is entirely disregarded in estimates limited to current educational outlays.

The availability of estimates of the output of the education sector has created an opportunity for important new research on educational productivity. By combining cost-based estimates of educational inputs with our estimates of educational output, it is possible to measure the productivity of the educational sector. A productivity measure for this sector requires estimates of capital, labor, and intermediate inputs in current and constant prices like those compiled by Jorgenson, Gollop, and Fraumeni (1987) for all the other industries that comprise the U.S. economy. An important issue that remains to be resolved is the appropriate valuation of the time spent in educational institutions by students. This time is an important input into the educational sector.

We conclude that the time scale for measuring human capital formation is given by the lifespan of an educated individual. The appropriate value of investment in education is given by its effect on the individual's lifetime income. The relevant concept of income must not be limited to market activities alone, because many of the benefits of education accrue in the form of enhanced value to nonmarket activities. Our estimates of investment in education incorporate the effect of higher educational attainment on the value of nonmarket activities such as parenting or enjoyment of leisure as well as the effect of increased education on earning power in the labor market.

Our estimates of investment in education are based on very detailed information on the value of working time. However, we have based our estimates of the value of nonmarket labor time on market wage rates. The valuation of nonmarket activities could be refined considerably, especially for individuals not in the labor force. An alternative approach is to infer the value of nonmarket time from labor supply behavior. Second, we have estimated the value of increments in lifetime incomes as a result of increases in educational attainment by comparing the incomes of individuals of the same age and sex with different levels of education. An important further refinement would base estimates of differences on lifetime incomes on the deteminants of educational attainment for a given individual. These limitations of our existing estimates suggest opportunities for significant new research on the benefits of education.

Finally, another important source of new research opportunities is the extension of our methods to encompass other forms of investment in human capital. We have already mentioned three extensions of this type. First, fertility behavior is influenced by the lifetime incomes of children added to the population and by the effects of childbearing on the lifetime incomes of parents. Second, investment in child rearing is an important component of investment in human capital and can be measured on the basis of its effect on lifetime incomes of children. Third, the value of on-the-job-training can be appraised by employers and workers in terms of its effect on lifetime labor incomes.[23]

7.5 Appendix

In this appendix we outline the methodology for measuring the output of the educational sector in algebraic form. To represent the use of time and the corresponding labor income we require the following notation:

$y = 1947, 1948, \ldots, 1987$—calendar year.
$s = 1, 2$—sex, male or female.
$a = 0, 1, \ldots, 74, 75, 75+$ —age.
$e = 1, 2, \ldots, 18$—educational attainment, none or less than grade one, ..., five years of college or more.

The variables required for estimates of the output of the educational sector are denoted as follows:

com—hourly compensation, net of taxes on labor income.

empr—employment rate.

life—lifetime labor income per capita.

mhrs—market labor time per capita.

mi—lifetime market labor income per capita.

nmhrs—nonmarket labor time per capita.

nmi—lifetime nonmarket labor income per capita.

senr—school enrollment rate, the probability that an individual with educational attainment e is enrolled in educational level $e + 1$.

shrs—school hours per capita; enrolled individuals are assumed to be in school 1300 hours per years.

si—investment in education per capita.

sr—probability of survival, specific to the year of birth.

tax—average tax rate on labor income.

taxam—average marginal tax rate on labor income.

whrs—annual market hours worked per person employed.

ymi—annual market income per capita, net of tax on labor compensation.

ynmi—annual nonmarket income per capita, net of tax on labor compensation, where the tax is calculated at the average marginal rate.

Our first set of equations provides estimates of annual hours of market and nonmarket components of labor time. The first equation gives school hours per capita

$$\text{shrs}_{y,s,a,e} = \text{senr}_{y,s,a,e} * 1300 .$$

The second equation gives market hours per capita

$$\text{mhrs}_{y,s,a,e} = \text{whrs}_{y,s,a,e} * \text{empr}_{y,s,a,e} .$$

Our third through eighth equations give nonmarket hours per capita for each of the five stages of the life cycle described in section 7.2. Stage 1 includes ages 0–4; stage 2 includes ages 5–13; stage 3 includes ages 14–34; stage 4 includes ages 35–74; stage 5 includes ages 75 and over. Maintenance time per capita is 10 hours per day, leaving 14 hours per day to be allocated between market and nonmarket time. The first stage is no school and no work

$$\text{nmhrs}_{y,s,a,e} = 14 * 7 * 52 .$$

The second stage is school but no work

$$\text{nmhrs}_{y,s,a,e} = 14 * 7 * 52 - \text{shrs}_{y,s,a,e} .$$

The third stage is school and work

$$\text{nmhrs}_{y,s,a,e} = 14 * 7 * 52 - \text{shrs}_{y,s,a,e} - \text{mhrs}_{y,s,a,e} \,.$$

The fourth stage is work but no school

$$\text{nmhrs}_{y,s,a,e} = 14 * 7 * 52 - \text{mhrs}_{y,s,a,e} \,.$$

The fifth and final stage is retirement or no school or work

$$\text{nmhrs}_{y,s,a,e} = 14 * 7 * 52 \,.$$

Our second set of equations provides estimates of market labor income. The first equation gives annual market labor income per capita

$$\text{ymi}_{y,s,a,e} = \text{mhrs}_{y,s,a,e} * \text{com}_{y,s,a,e} \,.$$

The second equation gives annual nonmarket labor income per capita

$$\text{ynmi}_{y,s,a,e} = \text{nmhrs}_{y,s,a,e} * \text{com}_{y,s,a,e} * (1 + \text{tax}_y) * (1 - \text{taxam}_y) \,.$$

Our third through eighth equations give lifetime market labor income per capita at the five stages of the life cycle described in section 7.2. Lifetime incomes are calculated by a backward recursion, starting with age 74, which is the oldest age before retirement. Future incomes are discounted back to the current age of the individual. The first stage is no school and no work

$$\text{mi}_{y,s,a,e} = \text{sr}_{y,s,a+1} * \text{mi}_{y,s,a+1,e} * \frac{1.0132}{1.0458} \,.$$

The second stage is school but no work

$$\begin{aligned}\text{mi}_{y,s,a,e} = {} & [\text{senr}_{y+1,s,a,e} * \text{sr}_{y,s,a+1} * \text{mi}_{y,s,a+1,e+1} \\ & + (1 - \text{senr}_{y+1,s,a,e}) * \text{sr}_{y,s,a+1} * \text{mi}_{y,s,a+1,e}] * \frac{1.0132}{1.0458} \,.\end{aligned}$$

The third stage is school and work

$$\begin{aligned}\text{mi}_{y,s,a,e} = {} & \text{ymi}_{y+1,s,a,e} + [\text{senr}_{y+1,s,a,e} * \text{sr}_{y,s,a+1} * \text{mi}_{y,s,a+1,e+1} \\ & + (1 - \text{senr}_{y+1,s,a,e}) * \text{sr}_{y,s,a+1} * \text{mi}_{y,s,a+1,e}] * \frac{1.0132}{1.0458} \,.\end{aligned}$$

The fourth stage is work but no school

$$\text{mi}_{y,s,a,e} = \text{ymi}_{y+1,s,a,e} + \text{sr}_{y,s,a+1} * \text{mi}_{y,s,a+1,e} * \frac{1.0132}{1.0458} \,.$$

The fifth and final stage is retirement or no school or work

$$\text{mi}_{y,s,a,e} = 0 .$$

Our third set of equations gives estimates of nonmarket labor income. The first through fifth equations give lifetime nonmarket labor income for the five stages of the life cycle described in section 7.2. The first stage is no school or work

$$\text{nmi}_{y,s,a,e} = \text{sr}_{y,s,a+1} * \text{nmi}_{y,s,a+1,e} * \frac{1.0132}{1.0458} .$$

The second stage is school but no work

$$\text{nmi}_{y,s,a,e} = [\text{senr}_{y+1,s,a,e} * \text{sr}_{y,s,a+1} * \text{nmi}_{y,s,a+1,e+1} + (1 - \text{senr}_{y+1,s,a,e}) * \text{sr}_{y,s,a+1} * \text{nmi}_{y,s,a+1,e}] * \frac{1.0132}{1.0458} .$$

The third stage is school and work

$$\text{nmi}_{y,s,a,e} = \text{ynmi}_{y+1,s,a,e} + [\text{senr}_{y+1,s,a,e} * \text{sr}_{y,s,a+1} * \text{nmi}_{y,s,a+1,e+1} + (1 - \text{senr}_{y+1,s,a,e}) * \text{sr}_{y,s,a+1} * \text{nmi}_{y,s,a+1,e}] * \frac{1.0132}{1.0458} .$$

The fourth stage is work but no school

$$\text{nmi}_{y,s,a,e} = \text{ynmi}_{y+1,s,a,e} + \text{sr}_{y,s,a+1} * \text{nmi}_{y,s,a+1,e} * \frac{1.0132}{1.0458} .$$

The fifth and final stage is retirement or no school or work

$$\text{nmi}_{y,s,a,e} = 0 .$$

Total lifetime labor income per capita, including market and nonmarket components is

$$\text{life}_{y,s,a,e} = \text{mi}_{y,s,a,e} + \text{nmi}_{y,s,a,e} .$$

Investment in education per capita is

$$\text{si}_{y,s,a,e} = \text{senr}_{y,s,a,e} * (\text{life}_{y,s,a,e+1} - \text{life}_{y,s,a,e}) .$$

Notes

1. Rates of return to investment in human capital are discussed by Becker (1964) and Mincer (1974). Welch (1979) presents estimates of relative rates of return for different age cohorts of the U.S. population. Murphy and Welch (1989) give estimates of rates of return for higher education. Surveys of different aspects of the literature are provided by Griliches (1977) and Rosen (1977).
2. In this context we employ the notion of output as the economic value produced within the educational sector. Outputs of the educational system can also be defined in terms of measures of educational achievement, such as performance in standardized tests. This definition is the basis for the literature on educational production functions reviewed by Hanushek (1986, 1989).
3. Nonmarket benefits of education are discussed by Haveman and Wolfe (1984) and Michael (1982).
4. See, for example, Bureau of the Census (1985). We employ a system of demographic accounts for the United States constructed by Land and McMillen (1981). Demographic accounting is discussed by Stone (1981).
5. See, for example, National Center for Education Statistics (1988). A compendium of educational statistics is given by O'Neill and Sepielli (1985).
6. An economic theory of time allocation is presented by Becker (1965). Detailed references to the literature are given by Murphy (1980). Gates and Murphy (1982) present time use accounts for the United States for 1975–1976, based on data collected by the Survey Research Center of the University of Michigan. A survey of time allocation is given by Juster and Stafford (1991).
7. See, for example, Gates and Murphy (1982) and Juster, Courant, and Dow (1981).
8. Estimates of lifetime labor incomes for men based on market labor activities are presented by Weisbrod (1961), Miller (1965), and Graham and Webb (1979).
9. See National Center for Health Statistics (various annual issues).
10. The proportion of the U.S. population 75 and over has risen from 2.4 percent in 1948 to 5.0 percent in 1987, so that omissions of lifetime labor incomes for this part of the population imparts a small but slowly increasing bias to our estimates of human wealth for the population as a whole.
11. Our estimate of the growth rate of real incomes is based on the rate of Harrod-neutral productivity growth for the United States estimated by Jorgenson and Yun (1990).
12. Our estimate of the discount rate is based on the long run rate of return for the private sector of the U.S. economy estimated by Jorgenson and Yun (1990).
13. Details are discussed in Jorgenson and Fraumeni (1989).
14. Kroch and Sjoblom (1986) give estimates of investment in education based on lifetime labor incomes from market activities for men and women.
15. Jorgenson, Gollop, and Fraumeni (1987), especially chap. 8, present estimates of the contribution of education to U.S. economic growth. In Jorgenson and Fraumeni (1989) we give a complete set of U.S. national accounts, incorporating the estimates of market and nonmarket labor time, investment in education, and human wealth given above. Surveys of the contribution of education to economic growth are presented by Dean (1984), Mincer (1984), and Murnane (1988).
16. See, for example, Bureau of Economic Analysis (1986).
17. See Jorgenson, Gollop, and Fraumeni (1987), especially chaps. 1 and 9.
18. See Bureau of Economic Analysis (1987), which gives and investment and capital stocks for 61 industries broken down by 72 categories of physical assets.
19. Gates (1982) provides time series estimates of education and training costs for 1965–1979. The compendium edited by Peskin (1982) includes other studies of nonmar-

ket activities at the Bureau of Economic Analysis. Unfortunately, the bureau has discontinued this line of investigation.

20. The cost-based approach to measuring investment in human capital was originated by Machlup (1962) and Schultz (1961b). Campbell and Peskin (1979) and Eisner (1988) survey augmented accounting systems, including those containing cost-based estimates of investment in human capital. Kendrick's (1976) accounting system is also discussed by Engerman and Rosen (1980).

21. The educational sector is discussed from the economic point of view in the collection of papers by Froomkin, Jamison, and Radner (1976).

22. Graham and Webb (1979) compare Kendrick's estimate of human wealth for 1969 with estimates on the basis of lifetime labor incomes for males, excluding the value of nonmarket activities. Kroch and Sjoblom (1986) compare their estimates of human capital accumulated through education, based on lifetime labor incomes from market activities for men and women, with Kendrick's estimates, based on costs of education and training.

23. A survey of recent research on the prevalence and impact of on-the-job training is presented by Mincer (1989a). Mincer (1989b) presents estimates of the annual costs of training in the United States for 1958, 1976, and 1987. For 1976 these costs amount to half of the costs of formal schooling.

8 Investment in Education and U.S. Economic Growth

Dale W. Jorgenson and
Barbara M. Fraumeni

Abstract

The purpose of this paper is to measure the impact of investment in education on U.S. economic growth. Education is treated as an investment in human capital, since benefits accrue to an educated individual over a lifetime of activities. One of the most important benefits is higher income from labor market participation. This is the key to understanding the link between investment in education and economic growth. Our most important finding is that investment in human and nonhuman capital accounts for an overwhelming proportion of the growth of the U.S. economy during the postwar period. Educational investment will continue to predominate in the investment requirements for more rapid growth.

8.1 Introduction

The purpose of this paper is to describe the impact of investment in education on U.S. economic growth. Beginning with the seminal contributions of Becker (1964), Mincer (1974), and Schultz (1961b), economists have found it useful to characterize the benefits of education by means of the notion of investment in human capital.[1] This idea captures the fact that investment in human beings, like investment in tangible forms of capital such as buildings and industrial equipment, generates a stream of future benefits. Education is regarded as an investment in human capital, since benefits accrue to an educated individual over a lifetime of activities.

One of the most important benefits of education is higher income from participation in the labor market. This increase in income is the key to understanding the link between investment in education and economic growth. People differ enormously in effectiveness on the job. Substituting more effective for less effective workers increases output per worker. More highly educated or better trained people are more productive than less educated or poorly trained people. However, education and training are costly, so that substitution of people with more education and training requires investment in human capital.

To quantify the impact of investment in education on economic growth we introduce a new approach for measuring the output of the education sector.[2] Since the effects of formal schooling endure through the lifetime of an educated individual, we utilize the impact of education on an individual's lifetime labor income as a measure of educational output. We define labor income for this purpose to include the value of time spent outside the labor market, since education also enhances the value of activities such as parenting and the value of leisure time.

Second, we measure the inputs of the education sector, beginning with the purchased inputs recorded in the outlays of educational institutions. We also measure the inputs of time for all students enrolled in formal education. A major part of the value of the output of educational institutions accrues to students in the form of increases in their lifetime labor incomes. Treating these increases as compensation for student time, we can evaluate this time as an input into the educational process. Given the outlays of educational institutions and the value of student time, we can allocate the growth of the education sector to its sources.

Finally, we aggregate the growth of education and noneducation sectors of the U.S. economy to obtain a new measure of U.S. economic growth. This includes the growth of the business and government sectors. It also includes the growth of the education sector. Combining these measures of output growth with the corresponding measures of input growth, we obtain a new set of accounts for the growth of the U.S. economy. In these accounts the scope of output is increased by investment in education and the scope of input is increased by the value of student time.

Our most important conclusion is that investment in human and nonhuman capital accounts for an overwhelming proportion of the growth of the U.S. economy during the postwar period. This finding characterizes the noneducation sector of the U.S. economy as well as the economy as a whole, including the education sector. Since 1973 the growth rate of the U.S. economy has slowed by almost four-fifths of a percentage point, relative to the postwar average. Education will continue to predominate in the investment requirements for the revival of more rapid U.S. economic growth.

Given the importance of investment in education for long term economic growth, economists and policy makers have devoted far too little attention to the implications of educational policy. The magnitude of investment in education dwarfs that of conventional forms of investment, such as investment in tangible assets. Educational policy can affect individual decisions by financing participation in the educational system and expanding the capacity of educational institutions.

While educational policy deserves much higher priority among policies for enhancing long term economic growth, other policies must be reevaluated in light of their impact on educational investment. For example, tax policy and labor market policy have major impacts on the decisions of individuals to enroll in educational institutions. A progressive tax on labor income has the unfortunate consequence of taxing away a portion of the benefits to individuals from these investments. This is an important justification for reducing marginal tax rates on labor incomes, as in recent tax reforms in both Sweden and the U.S.

More generally, redistributional policies have a highly distortionary impact on decisions to invest in education. From the perspective of individual choosing among alternative levels of educational attainment, such policies reduce the benefits of educational investment and increase the costs in terms of foregone earnings. For example, a "solidaristic" wage policy along Swedish lines has a depressing effect on educational investments similar to that of a progressive income tax. An undesirable side effect of such a policy is underinvestment in education.

8.2 Sources of Growth

Our objective is to assess the impact of investment in education on U.S. economic growth.[3] An analysis of the sources of growth of the noneducation sector of the U.S. economy is presented in table 8.1. The noneducation sector of the U.S. economy includes the business and government sectors, but excludes private and public educational institutions. Since outlays on education comprise about seven percent of the national product, this sector produces close to ninety-three percent of the product. Growth rates for the period 1948–1986 are given for output and the two inputs in the first column of table 8.1.

Value added grows at the rate of 3.29 percent per year, while capital grows at 3.34 percent and labor input grows at 1.60 percent. The contributions of capital and labor inputs to the growth of output of the noneducation sector are obtained by weighting the growth rates of these inputs by their shares in value added. This produces the familiar allocation of growth to its sources.[4] Capital input is the most important source of growth of the noneducation sector by a substantial margin, accounting for almost forty percent of growth during the period. Labor input accounts for twenty-nine percent of growth. Productivity growth accounts for thirty-one percent of the growth of the noneducation sector during the postwar period.

The findings summarized in table 8.1 are not limited to the period as a whole. In this table we compare the growth of output of the noneducation sector with the contributions of capital and labor inputs and productivity growth for eight subperiods. The end points of the periods identified in the table, except for the last period, are years in which a cyclical peak occurred. The growth rate presented for each subperiod is the average annual growth rate between cyclical peaks. The contributions of capital and labor inputs are the predominant sources of U.S. economic growth for the period as a whole and all eight subperiods. Annual data on the output of the noneducation sector and capital and labor inputs into the sector are presented in table 8.2.

In 1986 the output of the noneducation sector stood at more than three and a half times the level of output in 1948. Our overall conclusion is that the driving force behind the expansion of this sector between 1948 and 1986 has been the growth in capital and labor inputs. The findings we have summarized are consistent with a substantial body of research. For example, these findings coincide with those of Christensen and Jorgenson (1973a) for the U.S. economy for the period 1929–1969. Maddison (1987) gives similar results for six industrialized countries, including the United States, for the period 1913–1984. However, these findings contrast sharply with those of Abramovitz (1956), Kendrick (1956), and Solow (1957), which emphasize productivity as the predominant growth source.

At this point it is useful to describe the steps required to go from the earlier findings to the results summarized in table 8.1. The first step is to decompose the contributions of capital and labor inputs into

Table 8.1
Sources of economic growth, noneducation sector, 1948–1986

Variable	1948–1986	1948–1953	1953–1957	1957–1960	1960–1966	1966–1969	1969–1973	1973–1979	1979–1986
Value-added	0.0329	0.0521	0.0207	0.0219	0.0486	0.0286	0.0327	0.0266	0.0247
Capital input	0.0334	0.0452	0.0351	0.0218	0.0301	0.0408	0.0363	0.0349	0.0256
Labor input	0.0160	0.0261	0.0028	0.0047	0.0237	0.0202	0.0108	0.0197	0.0128
Contribution of capital input	0.0131	0.0183	0.0137	0.0082	0.0122	0.0164	0.0135	0.0130	0.0103
Contribution of labor input	0.0096	0.0155	0.0015	0.0029	0.0141	0.0121	0.0067	0.0121	0.0074
Rate of productivity growth	0.0102	0.0183	0.0056	0.0109	0.0223	0.0001	0.0125	0.0015	0.0070
Contribution of capital quality	0.0019	0.0033	0.0016	–0.0007	0.0009	0.0025	0.0021	0.0026	0.0023
Contribution of capital stock	0.0111	0.0150	0.0121	0.0089	0.0113	0.0139	0.0114	0.0104	0.0080
Contribution of labor quality	0.0023	0.0072	0.0016	0.0010	0.0023	–0.0003	–0.0012	0.0015	0.0035
Contribution of hours worked	0.0073	0.0083	–0.0001	0.0019	0.0118	0.0124	0.0079	0.0106	0.0039

Table 8.2
Output, input, and productivity, noneducation sector, 1948–1986 (billions of constant dollars)

	Output		Capital input		Labor input		Rate of productivity growth
Year	price	quantity	price	quantity	price	quantity	
1948	0.249	1,065.797	0.027	4,054.481	0.138	1,134.146	
1949	0.246	1,076.599	0.025	4,289.156	0.144	1,095.552	0.0076
1950	0.251	1,171.593	0.027	4,457.063	0.150	1,143.690	0.0434
1951	0.265	1,278.093	0.029	4,730.425	0.163	1,233.235	0.0181
1952	0.268	1,328.518	0.028	4,944.118	0.173	1,266.504	0.0051
1953	0.271	1,382.944	0.028	5,083.360	0.180	1,291.994	0.0172
1954	0.276	1,362.969	0.027	5,257.081	0.187	1,251.960	−0.0077
1955	0.284	1,453.112	0.031	5,404.957	0.190	1,286.933	0.0364
1956	0.291	1,477.838	0.030	5,654.859	0.200	1,311.907	−0.0127
1957	0.301	1,502.588	0.029	5,850.738	0.215	1,306.315	0.0061
1958	0.305	1,485.524	0.027	6,021.056	0.229	1,266.708	−0.0026
1959	0.314	1,580.093	0.032	6,069.450	0.230	1,314.785	0.0354
1960	0.318	1,604.777	0.031	6,246.939	0.240	1,324.775	−0.0002
1961	0.321	1,647.674	0.031	6,402.316	0.247	1,334.175	0.0127
1962	0.329	1,733.329	0.034	6,524.249	0.252	1,380.724	0.0223
1963	0.334	1,806.318	0.036	6,707.688	0.258	1,396.813	0.0233
1964	0.339	1,906.846	0.038	6,921.788	0.267	1,425.858	0.0292
1965	0.349	2,025.082	0.042	7,164.429	0.276	1,471.193	0.0275
1966	0.360	2,148.349	0.043	7,484.444	0.294	1,527.275	0.0190
1967	0.369	2,209.648	0.042	7,831.154	0.310	1,551.371	0.0002
1968	0.384	2,286.968	0.043	8,125.379	0.335	1,585.834	0.0064
1969	0.403	2,341.151	0.042	8,459.672	0.360	1,622.521	−0.0062
1970	0.421	2,353.509	0.041	8,816.794	0.395	1,597.553	−0.0004
1971	0.443	2,411.835	0.044	9,070.631	0.424	1,587.977	0.0179
1972	0.465	2,543.330	0.048	9,378.266	0.451	1,630.242	0.0242
1973	0.492	2,668.337	0.049	9,782.504	0.491	1,693.896	0.0082
1974	0.531	2,643.790	0.048	10,284.073	0.538	1,696.971	−0.0283
1975	0.583	2,637.749	0.053	10,650.143	0.587	1,657.567	0.0002
1976	0.623	2,775.568	0.060	10,835.581	0.631	1,708.765	0.0254
1977	0.666	2,915.021	0.067	11,152.671	0.672	1,766.918	0.0173
1978	0.714	3,071.648	0.073	11,573.787	0.727	1,850.187	0.0098
1979	0.774	3,129.879	0.075	12,060.330	0.798	1,905.881	−0.0152
1980	0.840	3,119.828	0.076	12,494.387	0.878	1,895.752	−0.0129
1981	0.922	3,189.506	0.088	12,744.082	0.951	1,909.137	0.0103
1982	1.000	3,120.697	0.095	13,015.987	1.000	1,880.694	−0.0209
1983	1.040	3,259.378	0.108	13,168.647	1.026	1,922.357	0.0258
1984	1.081	3,502.682	0.120	13,435.873	1.070	2,024.615	0.0336
1985	1.110	3,632.591	0.122	13,929.514	1.124	2,068.691	0.0087
1986	1.135	3,720.172	0.119	14,431.396	1.206	2,084.597	0.0047

the separate contributions of capital and labor quality and the contributions of capital stock and hours worked. Capital stock and hours worked are a natural focus for input measurement, since capital input would be proportional to capital stock if capital inputs were homogeneous, while labor input would be proportional to hours worked if labor inputs were homogeneous. In fact, capital and labor inputs are enormously heterogeneous, so that measurement of these inputs requires detailed data on the components of each input.

The key to understanding the difference between capital stock and hours worked and the measures of capital and labor inputs we have employed is Solow's (1957) distinction between movements along the production function and shifts in the production function. Solow identified movements along the production function with substitution and shifts in the production function with growth in productivity. This distinction gave rise to the famous Solow Residual, which is a measure of growth in productivity. Solow, like Abramovitz and Kendrick, limited consideration to substitution between inputs of capital stock and hours worked.

Although substitution between capital stock and hours worked is important, substitution can also occur among different types of hours worked or different types of capital stock. The growth rate of each input is a weighted average of the growth rates of its components. Weights are given by the shares of the components in the value of the input. This principle was applied to capital stock and hours worked by Abramovitz, Kendrick, and Solow. The same approach can be used to measure the impact of substitution among different types of hours worked or different types of capital stock. Table 8.1 is based on the results of Jorgenson, Gollop, and Fraumeni (1987) for the noneducation sector of the U.S. economy, as revised and extended by Jorgenson (1990).

Our estimate of the contribution of labor input incorporates information on labor market activities. Hours worked for each sex are cross-classified by individual year of age and individual year of education for a total of 2,196 different types of hours worked. Each type of hours worked is weighted by the corresponding wage rate.[5] Similarly, our estimate of capital input involves weighting components of capital input by rental prices. Assets are cross-classified by age of the asset, class of asset, and legal form of organization. Different ages are weighted in accord with profiles of relative efficiency constructed by

Hulten and Wykoff (1981). For the noneducation sector a total of 160 components of capital input are measured separately.[6]

We define growth rates of capital and labor quality as the differences between growth rates of input measures that take substitution into account and measures that ignore substitution. Increases in capital quality reflect the substitution of more highly productive capital goods for those that are less productive. This substitution process requires investment in tangible assets or nonhuman capital. Similarly, growth in labor quality results from the substitution of more effective for less effective workers. This process of substitution requires the massive investments in human capital that we have documented in section 8.4 above.

In the Abramovitz-Kendrick-Solow approach the contributions of substitution among different types of capital stock and different types of hours worked to economic growth are ignored, since these capital and labor inputs are treated as homogeneous. The omission of growth in labor quality severs the link between investment in human capital and economic growth, while the omission of growth in capital quality leads to substantial under-estimation of the impact of investment in nonhuman capital on economic growth. The results presented in table 8.1 reveal that the assumption of homogeneous capital and labor inputs is highly misleading.[7]

In table 8.3 we present an analysis of the growth of the education sector of the U.S. economy. The inputs into this sector include capital, labor, and intermediate goods. Capital input is comprised of educational buildings and equipment. Labor input incorporates the value of the time of teachers and noninstructional employees of the educational system and student time. Intermediate goods include the purchases of educational institutions from other sectors of the economy. These purchases are included in final demand in the U.S. national income and product accounts. Purchases by public institutions are part of government consumption, while purchases by private institutions are part of personal consumption expenditures.

The output of the education sector is a measure of investment in education. This output grows at 2.55 percent per year during the period 1948–1986. Capital input grows at 3.82 percent, labor input at 2.47 percent, and intermediate input at 6.79 percent. As before, the contributions of these inputs are obtained by weighting the growth rates by the corresponding shares of the inputs in educational investment. This produces an allocation of the output of the education

Table 8.3
Sources of economic growth, education sector, 1948–1986

Variable	1948–1986	1948–1953	1953–1957	1957–1960	1960–1966	1966–1969	1969–1973	1973–1979	1979–1986
Output	0.0255	0.0142	0.0264	0.0303	0.0478	0.0435	0.0260	0.0227	0.0066
Capital input	0.0382	0.0519	0.0664	0.0561	0.0517	0.0549	0.0315	0.0225	0.0029
Labor input	0.0247	0.0151	0.0274	0.0290	0.0463	0.0430	0.0236	0.0188	0.0076
Intermediate input	0.0679	0.1836	0.0260	0.0813	0.0661	0.0312	0.0527	0.0669	0.0303
Contribution of capital input	0.0001	0.0002	0.0002	0.0001	0.0001	0.0002	0.0001	0.0001	0.0000
Contribution of labor input	0.0244	0.0150	0.0271	0.0287	0.0458	0.0424	0.0233	0.0185	0.0074
Contribution of intermediate input	0.0007	0.0013	0.0002	0.0006	0.0006	0.0003	0.0005	0.0010	0.0006
Rate of productivity growth	0.0003	−0.0022	−0.0011	0.0008	0.0012	0.0006	0.0021	0.0031	−0.0015
Contribution of capital quality	0.0000	0.0000	0.0000	0.0000	−0.0000	−0.0000	−0.0000	0.0000	0.0000
Contribution of capital stock	0.0001	0.0001	0.0002	0.0001	0.0001	0.0002	0.0001	0.0001	0.0000
Contribution of labor quality	0.0034	0.0020	0.0044	−0.0003	0.0060	0.0060	0.0008	0.0018	0.0051
Contribution of hours worked	0.0209	0.0129	0.0227	0.0290	0.0398	0.0364	0.0224	0.0166	0.0023

sector to its sources. Labor input greatly predominates as a source of educational output; the total of the contributions of capital input, intermediate input, and productivity amount to only one-tenth of the contribution of labor input.

Productivity growth of educational institutions is slightly positive for the period 1948–1986 as a whole, but negative for the subperiods 1948–1953, 1953–1957, and 1979–1986. Positive productivity growth characterizes the remaining five subperiods. Negative growth in productivity during the period 1948–1953 is associated with the relatively sharp contraction of the education sector during this period. Slow growth of output in the subperiods 1953–1957 and 1979–1986 is also associated with negative growth in productivity. Overall, the output of the education sector can be attributed largely to labor input, especially the input of student time that greatly predominates in the total. We present annual data on educational output and inputs into the education sector in table 8.4.

Our final step in analyzing the sources of U.S. economic growth is to define a new measure of aggregate output. This is obtained by including the output of the educational sector along with the outputs of other industries that produce goods and services. We present a new set of growth accounts for the U.S. economy in table 8.5. The growth of value added is 2.93 percent per year for the period 1948–1986, which is slightly lower than the growth of value added in the noneducation sector presented in table 8.1. Capital input grows at 3.35 percent, while labor input grows at 2.20 percent. We obtain the contributions of these inputs to economic growth by weighting the growth rates by the corresponding shares of these inputs in aggregate value added.

The contribution of capital input is 0.65 percent per year, while the contribution of labor input is 1.79 percent per year. Productivity growth is now reduced to 0.50 percent per year and accounts for only a little more than seventeen percent of output growth. Labor input accounts for more than sixty-one percent and capital input accounts for more than twenty-two percent. More than two-fifths of the contribution of labor input is due to labor quality or substitution among different types of hours worked. Substitution among different types of capital stock or capital quality accounts for slightly more than fifteen percent of the contribution of capital input. We present annual data on output, capital and labor inputs, and productivity growth for the U.S. economy as a whole in table 8.6.

Table 8.4
Output, input, and productivity, education sector, 1948–1986 (billions of constant dollars)

	Output		Capital input		Labor input	
Year	price	quantity	price	quantity	price	quantity
1948	0.200	1,073.850	0.013	92.926	0.196	1,086.325
1949	0.213	1,087.643	0.014	96.940	0.209	1,100.997
1950	0.233	1,105.678	0.015	101.762	0.228	1,119.968
1951	0.260	1,128.173	0.015	107.971	0.254	1,144.325
1952	0.284	1,139.493	0.017	114.464	0.277	1,155.400
1953	0.323	1,152.957	0.017	120.481	0.315	1,171.526
1954	0.334	1,168.039	0.017	127.538	0.325	1,186.328
1955	0.360	1,204.181	0.017	137.060	0.350	1,224.160
1956	0.399	1,241.406	0.017	147.812	0.388	1,263.698
1957	0.445	1,281.301	0.019	157.132	0.432	1,307.094
1958	0.457	1,320.186	0.019	167.043	0.444	1,344.572
1959	0.453	1,360.633	0.019	176.782	0.441	1,384.445
1960	0.464	1,403.227	0.018	185.945	0.452	1,425.908
1961	0.458	1,481.479	0.018	195.388	0.446	1,504.080
1962	0.444	1,566.830	0.019	205.951	0.433	1,587.184
1963	0.450	1,642.753	0.019	215.956	0.439	1,662.836
1964	0.448	1,714.201	0.019	227.713	0.438	1,731.557
1965	0.465	1,788.870	0.020	240.218	0.455	1,806.108
1966	0.483	1,868.870	0.021	253.634	0.474	1,883.058
1967	0.501	1,967.926	0.022	269.118	0.491	1,978.778
1968	0.505	2,057.811	0.023	284.389	0.497	2,063.206
1969	0.588	2,129.548	0.024	299.068	0.577	2,142.248
1970	0.629	2,200.554	0.025	311.404	0.620	2,202.727
1971	0.649	2,246.072	0.027	321.780	0.640	2,245.483
1972	0.664	2,292.053	0.029	330.761	0.656	2,286.456
1973	0.675	2,362.968	0.031	339.212	0.667	2,354.288
1974	0.707	2,430.739	0.034	350.301	0.699	2,417.760
1975	0.716	2,504.399	0.037	362.211	0.710	2,477.448
1976	0.711	2,567.221	0.040	375.001	0.708	2,523.510
1977	0.717	2,627.656	0.042	381.420	0.716	2,573.129
1978	0.751	2,652.670	0.045	385.726	0.751	2,591.771
1979	0.781	2,707.057	0.050	388.243	0.782	2,635.970
1980	0.856	2,742.604	0.055	391.282	0.857	2,671.627
1981	0.925	2,720.688	0.060	395.523	0.925	2,651.208
1982	1.000	2,834.856	0.065	396.066	1.000	2,766.105
1983	1.040	2,861.699	0.067	395.437	1.040	2,788.957
1984	1.109	2,859.419	0.069	394.809	1.108	2,788.643
1985	1.186	2,833.546	0.071	394.489	1.184	2,765.863
1986	1.333	2,834.605	0.074	396.159	1.326	2,780.201

Table 8.4 (continued)

Year	Intermediate input price	Intermediate input quantity	Rate of productivity growth
1948	0.163	3.955	
1948	0.163	3.955	
1949	0.169	3.883	−0.0006
1950	0.173	5.362	−0.0026
1951	0.189	6.041	−0.0021
1952	0.197	8.304	−0.0020
1953	0.202	9.903	−0.0035
1954	0.207	10.334	0.0001
1955	0.212	12.097	−0.0021
1956	0.224	12.572	−0.0015
1957	0.235	10.990	−0.0009
1958	0.240	13.841	0.0000
1959	0.246	13.144	0.0015
1960	0.252	14.024	0.0010
1961	0.259	14.556	0.0010
1962	0.267	14.634	0.0026
1963	0.274	14.886	0.0010
1964	0.280	16.558	0.0015
1965	0.288	18.655	−0.0003
1966	0.302	20.844	0.0013
1967	0.320	22.051	0.0020
1968	0.339	21.503	0.0035
1969	0.363	22.890	−0.0036
1970	0.392	25.338	0.0042
1971	0.419	27.428	0.0006
1972	0.444	27.836	0.0022
1973	0.478	28.260	0.0014
1974	0.528	31.000	0.0008
1975	0.581	34.869	0.0041
1976	0.620	38.111	0.0052
1977	0.661	39.191	0.0037
1978	0.711	40.764	0.0016
1979	0.770	42.228	0.0031
1980	0.862	42.557	−0.0003
1981	0.934	43.657	−0.0011
1982	1.000	43.133	0.0000
1983	1.047	45.518	0.0003
1984	1.099	48.074	−0.0018
1985	1.154	49.629	−0.0018
1986	1.193	52.206	−0.0057

Table 8.5
Sources of economic growth, U.S. economy, 1948–1986

Variable	1948–1986	1948–1953	1953–1957	1957–1960	1960–1966	1966–1969	1969–1973	1973–1979	1979–1986
Value-added	0.0293	0.0336	0.0233	0.0257	0.0482	0.0357	0.0294	0.0245	0.0164
Capital input	0.0335	0.0453	0.0356	0.0225	0.0305	0.0411	0.0362	0.0346	0.0252
Labor input	0.0220	0.0194	0.0185	0.0210	0.0388	0.0354	0.0196	0.0197	0.0097
Contribution of capital input	0.0065	0.0099	0.0067	0.0038	0.0057	0.0076	0.0059	0.0065	0.0056
Contribution of labor input	0.0179	0.0152	0.0150	0.0174	0.0317	0.0288	0.0163	0.0159	0.0075
Rate of productivity growth	0.0050	0.0085	0.0016	0.0045	0.0108	−0.0007	0.0072	0.0021	0.0033
Contribution of capital quality	0.0010	0.0018	0.0007	−0.0003	0.0004	0.0011	0.0009	0.0013	0.0013
Contribution of capital stock	0.0055	0.0081	0.0060	0.0041	0.0053	0.0066	0.0051	0.0051	0.0043
Contribution of labor quality	0.0075	0.0038	0.0139	0.0138	0.0142	0.0113	0.0055	0.0022	0.0020
Contribution of hours worked	0.0104	0.0115	0.0011	0.0036	0.0175	0.0175	0.0108	0.0137	0.0056

Table 8.6
Output, input, and productivity, U.S. economy, 1948–1986 (billions of constant dollars)

	Output		Capital input		Labor input		Rate of productivity growth
Year	price	quantity	price	quantity	price	quantity	
1948	0.224	2,148.508	0.027	4,161.488	0.175	2,104.479	
1949	0.230	2,173.316	0.025	4,401.674	0.185	2,090.761	0.0039
1950	0.242	2,285.395	0.027	4,574.551	0.198	2,149.199	0.0203
1951	0.263	2,414.130	0.029	4,855.102	0.219	2,244.429	0.0078
1952	0.276	2,474.365	0.027	5,075.352	0.236	2,281.893	0.0022
1953	0.296	2,541.332	0.028	5,220.004	0.259	2,319.310	0.0081
1954	0.303	2,536.321	0.027	5,400.236	0.269	2,309.389	−0.0050
1955	0.319	2,661.890	0.031	5,555.648	0.283	2,379.647	0.0187
1956	0.341	2,723.923	0.029	5,815.040	0.308	2,445.540	−0.0078
1957	0.368	2,789.816	0.029	6,019.059	0.339	2,497.011	0.0006
1958	0.378	2,810.476	0.027	6,197.879	0.352	2,519.132	−0.0048
1959	0.379	2,946.241	0.031	6,253.140	0.351	2,600.704	0.0192
1960	0.387	3,013.435	0.030	6,438.397	0.362	2,659.208	−0.0009
1961	0.387	3,135.027	0.031	6,601.447	0.362	2,762.475	0.0037
1962	0.384	3,306.819	0.033	6,731.115	0.358	2,896.273	0.0109
1963	0.390	3,456.334	0.036	6,922.651	0.364	2,999.175	0.0106
1964	0.392	3,627.985	0.038	7,146.145	0.367	3,102.528	0.0150
1965	0.404	3,820.328	0.041	7,398.892	0.381	3,224.460	0.0139
1966	0.418	4,023.029	0.043	7,730.674	0.399	3,357.023	0.0107
1967	0.432	4,183.628	0.042	8,090.658	0.417	3,488.037	−0.0005
1968	0.442	4,352.137	0.042	8,397.353	0.431	3,612.701	0.0040
1969	0.492	4,477.900	0.042	8,744.480	0.488	3,732.870	−0.0056
1970	0.522	4,560.447	0.040	9,113.457	0.527	3,785.659	−0.0002
1971	0.543	4,663.418	0.043	9,376.722	0.552	3,828.352	0.0084
1972	0.560	4,841.110	0.047	9,693.535	0.572	3,908.548	0.0146
1973	0.578	5,037.514	0.049	10,107.715	0.595	4,036.824	0.0059
1974	0.616	5,079.495	0.047	10,621.690	0.633	4,110.006	−0.0149
1975	0.648	5,144.950	0.053	10,999.378	0.660	4,140.806	0.0007
1976	0.665	5,343.639	0.059	11,195.389	0.676	4,236.346	0.0160
1977	0.690	5,543.380	0.067	11,520.033	0.698	4,342.905	0.0111
1978	0.731	5,723.890	0.072	11,948.677	0.741	4,442.897	0.0065
1979	0.777	5,835.883	0.074	12,442.080	0.789	4,542.708	−0.0066
1980	0.847	5,861.593	0.076	12,882.250	0.866	4,567.765	−0.0070
1981	0.924	5,907.887	0.087	13,137.175	0.936	4,561.169	0.0050
1982	1.000	5,955.553	0.094	13,412.053	1.000	4,646.799	−0.0110
1983	1.040	6,119.063	0.107	13,565.862	1.034	4,711.207	0.0138
1984	1.094	6,357.458	0.119	13,835.902	1.093	4,811.648	0.0174
1985	1.143	6,459.552	0.121	14,335.599	1.159	4,831.417	0.0044
1986	1.222	6,545.768	0.117	14,844.470	1.275	4,861.424	0.0005

8.3 Conclusion

The revival of the economic growth in the United States will require increasing investments in both human and nonhuman capital. Our measure of economic growth incorporates increments in the national product, as recorded in the U.S. National Income and Product Accounts, compiled by the Bureau of Economic Analysis of the U.S. Department of Commerce.[8] The accumulation of human and nonhuman capital accounts for the predominant share of economic growth.[9] Our new estimates of investment in education will help to bring the role of human capital accumulation in the growth process into proper perspective.

Unfortunately, the information required to measure investment in human capital is not available in standard sources of economic data like the U.S. national accounts. For example, the Bureau of Economic Analysis publishes a great deal of valuable information on investment in physical or nonhuman capital.[10] By contrast the national accounts provide nothing on investment in human capital. The primary reason for this is that the accounts are limited to economic activities recorded through market transactions. While there have been numerous attempts at augmenting the U.S. national accounts to incorporate human capital formation, none of them measures investment in education as an output of the educational system.

Investment in education, which is a major portion of investment in human capital, is produced almost entirely outside the business sector of the economy. Fortunately, participation in schooling is recorded in enrollment statistics. Furthermore, levels of educational attainment are routinely collected for individuals as part of the Census of Population. Transmission of education from schools and universities to their students involves increases in educational attainment that are not evaluated in the marketplace, at least not initially. However, the economic value of these increases can be traced through their impact on the lifetime labor incomes of individuals with higher levels of educational attainment.

The most common approach to compiling data on educational investment is to measure the inputs, rather than the output, of the educational system.[11] Data on outlays by educational institutions for teachers and other personnel, buildings and equipment, and materials can be compiled from accounting records. This information can be supplemented by estimates of the value of time spent by students (and their parents) as part of the educational process. Costs of schooling and the value of the time spent by students can be used to measure the flow of resources into schools and universities.

While outlays on education are highly significant in economic terms, the outlay-based approach to measurement of educational investment ignores a fundamental feature of the process of education. This is the lengthy gestation period between the application of educational inputs—mainly the services of teachers and the time of their students—and the emergence of human capital embodied in the graduates of educational institutions. Furthermore, some of the benefits of investment in education, such as greater earning power, are recorded in transactions in the labor market, while others—like better parenting or more rewarding enjoyment of leisure—remain unrecorded.

Estimates of the value of human wealth based on educational outlays have been constructed by Kendrick (1976) and Eisner (1989) for augmented systems of U.S. national accounts. In Jorgenson and Fraumeni (1992) we have presented a comparison of estimates of human wealth with those of Kendrick. Our estimates are greater than Kendrick's by a factor of more than ten with a gradually declining trend from 1948 to 1969. The disparities between the two sets of estimates of human capital are very striking. These disparities provide a quantitative demonstration of the graphic differences between the outlay-based approach and our income-based approach to the measurement of investment in human capital.

While outlay-based estimates of investment in education reflect the current flow of resources into educational institutions, they do not capture the crucial time dimension of educational investment. The lengthy gestation period between the current outlays of educational institutions and the emergence of human capital embodied in their graduates implies that a very substantial proportion of educational investment is attributable to the time value of money, applied to previous investments in the education of individuals who are still enrolled in school. This feature of investment in education is entirely disregarded in estimates limited to current educational outlays.

We conclude that the appropriate value of investment in education is given by its impact on the individual's lifetime labor income. The relevant concept of labor income must not be limited to market activities alone, since many of the benefits of education accrue in the form of enhanced value for nonmarket activities. Our estimates of investment in education incorporate the impact of higher educational attainment on the value of nonmarket activities such as parenting or enjoyment of leisure, as well as the effect of increased education on earning power in the labor market. The time scale appropriate for measuring human capital formation is given by the lifespan of an educated individual.

There are important opportunities for new research on economic policy within our new framework for analyzing the sources of economic growth. We have identified investments in human and nonhuman capital as the primary sources of growth. These investments should now become the main focus of economic policies to enhance growth opportunities. Educational policies obviously deserve much higher priority in discussions of long term growth, which have been excessively preoccupied with policies that affect nonhuman investment. However, the impact of policies, such as tax and labor market policies, that redistribute income within the lifetime of an individual on investment in education also deserves much more careful examination. These policies are often appraised solely in terms of their effects on the distribution of incomes among individuals.

Notes

1. Rates of return to investment in human capital are discussed by Becker (1964) and Mincer (1974). Welch (1979) presents estimates of relative rates of return for different age cohorts of the U.S. population. Murphy and Welch (1989) give estimates of rates of return for higher education. Surveys of different aspects of the literature are provided by Griliches (1977) and Rosen (1977).
2. In this context we employ the notion of "output" as the economic value produced within the educational sector. The measurement of educational output is described in detail in Jorgenson and Fraumeni (1992).
3. Jorgenson, Gollop, and Fraumeni (1987, especially chapter 8), present estimates of the contribution of education to U.S. economic growth. In Jorgenson and Fraumeni (1989) we give a complete set of U.S. national accounts, incorporating estimates of market and nonmarket labor time and investment in education. Surveys of the contribution of education to economic growth are presented by Dean (1984), Griliches (1988, especially pp. 220–226), Mincer (1984), and Murnane (1988).
4. Overviews of research on sources of economic growth, including alternative data sources and methodologies are provided by the Rees Report to the National Research Council (1979) and Jorgenson (1990).
5. Additional details are given by Jorgenson (1990, esp. pp. 32–41). Measures of labor input incorporating substitution among different types of hours worked were presented for agriculture by Griliches (1960), for the U.S. economy as a whole by Denison (1962), and for all sectors of the U.S. economy by Gollop and Jorgenson (1980, 1983).
6. Additional details are given by Jorgenson (1990, esp. pp. 41–54). Measures of capital input incorporating substitution among different types of capital stock were first

developed at the aggregate level by Jorgenson and Griliches (1967) and Christensen and Jorgenson (1969) and at the sectoral level by Fraumeni and Jorgenson (1980, 1986) and Gollop and Jorgenson (1980).

7. Denison (1969) and Solow (1988) continue to adhere to capital stock as a measure of capital input. This approach ignores the substitution among different types of capital stocks reflected in table 8.2. The measure of capital quality in this table does not incorporate the effects of technical progress. That appears in the Solow Residual.

8. See, for example, Bureau of Economic Analysis (1986).

9. See Jorgenson, Gollop, and Fraumeni (1987, especially chapters 1 and 9).

10. See Bureau of Economic Analysis (1987), which gives investment and capital stocks for 61 industries broken down by 72 categories of physical assets.

11. The cost-based approach to measuring investment in human capital was originated by Machlup (1962) and Schultz (1961b). Campbell and Peskin (1979) and Eisner (1988) survey augmented accounting systems, including those containing cost-based estimates of investment in human capital.

9 Productivity Growth in U.S. Agriculture: A Postwar Perspective

Dale W. Jorgenson and
Frank M. Gollop

9.1 Introduction

There has been a long-standing fascination with productivity trends in U.S. agriculture. In part, this stems from the historical importance of agriculture to the economy but it also reflects economists' early and continued interest in quantifying the rate of return to society's sizable investment in agricultural R&D.

The sum of government sponsored and private sector R&D investment in agriculture has been estimated to have equaled $268 million in 1953.[1] In that year, total R&D investment in the economy from all sources amounted to $5.1 billion.[2] Excluding defense and space-related R&D which accounted for approximately half of the U.S. total in the early fifties,[3] R&D expenditures dedicated to agriculture equaled approximately 10 percent of total U.S. investment in R&D from all sources. The considerable interest in measuring the sector's productivity growth is understandable.

Moreover, early research concluded that the return to this investment was extremely large. Griliches (1958, p. 228), for example, reported that the rate of return earned on dollars invested in hybrid-corn research was at least 700 percent per year as of 1955. The corresponding annual rate of return on hybrid sorghum (p. 238) was nearly 400 percent. In a later paper Griliches (1964b, p. 298) reported that the gross social rate of return to agricultural research dollars averaged 300 percent per year between 1949 and 1959. The need for monitoring the industry's productivity performance was clear.

The U.S. Department of Agriculture (USDA) heeded the call and in 1960 became the first Federal agency to introduce a multifactor productivity measure. Today, incorporating recommendations made by an American Agricultural Economics Association task force, USDA's Economic Research Service bases its official productivity statistics on a sophisticated system of total factor productivity (TFP) accounts. Its TFP model is based on the translog transformation frontier. It relates the growth rates of multiple outputs to the cost-share weighted growth rates of labor, capital and intermediate inputs.[4]

The applied USDA model is quite detailed. The changing demographic character of the agricultural labor force is used to build a quality-adjusted index of labor input. Similarly, much asset-specific detail underlies the measure of capital input. The index of land, for example, includes the base value of land as well as the contribution of improvements to land. The contributions of feed and seed, chemicals, and energy are captured in the index of intermediate input. An important innovation is that livestock is treated as an investment good as well as an agricultural output. The result is a USDA time series of total factor productivity indexes now spanning the 1948–1989 period.

The primary objective of this paper is to compare the postwar productivity performance of U.S. agriculture with sectors in the private nonfarm economy. The analysis is based on the total factor productivity model of sectoral production developed in Jorgenson, Gollop and Fraumeni and on data updated through 1985 as described in Jorgenson and Fraumeni. The model of agriculture and its data accounts are wholly consistent with the USDA model though, given the intersectoral comparison objectives of this project, the treatment of detailed data elements in the Jorgenson, Gollop, and Fraumeni data accounts (especially within output and capital goods) is not nearly as detailed as in the USDA model.

First, we contrast the productivity trends in agriculture and various sectors in the nonfarm economy, and compare the contributions of input growth and productivity growth to economic growth in agriculture and the private nonfarm economy. The important role of productivity growth in agriculture, both in absolute and relative terms, becomes immediately apparent.

Second, we examine the importance of changing input quality as a source of economic growth. The trend, first observed by Griliches (1964b) nearly 30 years ago, that improved labor quality of the agricultural labor force is an important determinant of the sector's economic growth is confirmed in the analysis.

The paper's major conclusion is that productivity growth has been a much more important source of economic growth in agriculture than it has been in the private nonfarm economy. The average annual rate of TFP growth over the postwar period in agriculture (1.58 percent) is nearly four times the corresponding rate in the nonfarm economy (0.44 percent). Moreover, productivity growth explains more than 80 percent of agriculture's postwar growth while it accounts for less than 15 percent of the growth in the private nonfarm economy.

9.2 Patterns of Productivity Growth

The measured rates of productivity growth reported in this paper are formed from Törnqvist indexes of outputs and inputs. A sector's total factor productivity growth over some period is defined as the growth rate in output less the cost-share weighted growth rate of inputs. The relevant inputs for this study are labor, capital, energy and materials. Each input is itself an aggregate that depends, respectively, on quantities of individual labor inputs, capital inputs, energy inputs and material inputs. A complete discussion of the economic theory of production underlying this model of productivity growth, relevant data sources, and steps taken to construct the productivity data accounts is presented in Jorgenson, Gollop, and Fraumeni.

Table 9.1 presents average annual rates of TFP growth for agriculture and nine nonfarm sectors for the complete 1947–1985 period and eight subperiods.[5] It should be noted that the data identified in the table by the heading "Private Nonfarm Economy" do not correspond to TFP growth for the private nonfarm economy viewed as an aggregate but to TFP growth in a representative nonfarm sector within that aggregate.[6] This permits a convenient summary comparison between agriculture and similarly disaggregated nonfarm sectors.

The average annual rate of TFP growth in agriculture over the 1947–1985 period exceeded the corresponding rate for the private nonfarm economy by more than three and one-half times. It was more than double the rate of TFP growth in manufacturing. Agriculture's rate averaged 1.58 percent per year. Productivity in the private nonfarm economy and in manufacturing increased at 0.44 and 0.72 percent annual rates, respectively.

Agriculture's 1.58 percent annual rate in the 1947–1985 period is second only to communications (2.04 percent). It is interesting to note, however, that only communications and agriculture achieved average annual TFP growth rates larger than one percent.

Table 9.1
Total factor productivity growth

	Average Annual Rates of Growth								
Industry	1947–1985	1947–1953	1953–1957	1957–1960	1960–1966	1966–1969	1969–1973	1973–1979	1979–1985
Agriculture	.0158	.0137	.0233	.0135	.0063	.0119	−.0067	.0206	.0358
Private nonfarm economy	.0044	.0049	.0041	.0095	.0096	.0032	.0066	−.0009	.0006
Mining	−.0114	.0056	−.0039	.0075	.0097	.0062	.0029	−.0675	−.0264
Construction	.0029	.0129	.0170	.0266	.0022	−.0119	−.0114	−.0111	.0032
Manufacturing	.0072	.0051	.0011	.0107	.0099	.0080	.0110	.0021	.0115
Transportation	.0096	.0049	.0200	.0100	.0185	.0026	.0257	.0098	−.0093
Communication	.0204	.0175	.0170	.0407	.0194	.0248	.0208	.0393	−.0007
Public utilities	.0087	.0289	.0167	.0147	.0169	.0198	.0017	−.0173	−.0029
Trade	.0090	.0098	.0126	.0105	.0215	−.0008	.0126	−.0042	.0080
Finance, insurance and real estate	.0024	.0014	.0066	.0100	.0088	.0097	.0028	.0076	−.0187
Other services	−.0013	−.0011	−.0036	−.0020	.0031	−.0025	.0011	.0003	−.0065

Furthermore, agriculture outperformed the private nonfarm economy and even aggregate manufacturing in all but two subperiods, 1960–1966 and 1969–1973. In fact, TFP growth in agriculture turned negative in only one subperiod (1969–1973) and fell below one percent only then and in the 1960–1966 period. This is to be contrasted with the private nonfarm economy for which TFP never exceeded an average one percent growth rate in any subperiod spanning 1947 to 1985. Manufacturing registered positive productivity growth in every subperiod, but even then had TFP rates of less than one percent in five of eight subperiods. Only communications can boast of a better postwar record than agriculture.

Perhaps the most striking result reported in table 9.1 is the absolute and relative performance of agriculture since 1979. Agriculture's average rate of TFP growth in the 1979–1985 period equaled 3.58 percent per year. The corresponding rate for the private nonfarm economy equaled only 0.06 percent. Six of the nine aggregate sectors within the private nonfarm economy exhibited negative average annual growth rates in this subperiod. Positive rates were recorded only for manufacturing (1.15 percent), trade (0.8 percent) and construction (0.32 percent).

Table 9.2 focuses on the growth rates of output and each input over the 1947–1985 period in both agriculture and the private nonfarm economy. The contrasting patterns for labor input are striking. Labor input in agriculture decreased at an average rate of 1.81 percent per year over the full 38-year period. In the private nonfarm economy, labor input increased at an annual 1.93 percent rate. While space considerations prevent reporting similar data for the disaggregated sectors within the private nonfarm economy, the underlying data reveal that labor input increased throughout the postwar period at positive rates in all nonfarm sectors and, with only two exceptions (mining and transportation), increased at average rates exceeding one percent per year.

Table 9.2 makes clear that the negative average growth rate for agricultural labor persisted throughout the postwar period. The reported average annual growth rate is negative in every subperiod. Contrast this with the private nonfarm economy where the growth rate of labor input is not only positive in every subperiod but exceeds one percent per year in all but one subperiod (1957–1960). The disaggregated sectoral detail reveals that only agriculture experienced a persistent decline in labor input in every subperiod.

Table 9.2
Postwar trends: Agriculture and the private nonfarm economy

	Average Annual Rates of Growth								
Industry	1947–1985	1947–1953	1953–1957	1957–1960	1960–1966	1966–1969	1969–1973	1973–1979	1979–1985
Agriculture									
Output	.0192	.0127	.0219	.0258	.0104	.0259	.0176	.0231	.0231
Inputs:									
Labor	–.0181	–.0218	–.0415	–.0207	–.0336	–.0086	–.0035	–.0039	–.0105
Capital	.0083	.0127	.0166	–.0010	.0026	.0222	–.0099	.0233	–.0014
Energy	.0211	.0440	.0324	.0524	.0165	.0182	.1075	.0092	–.0644
Materials	.0123	.0034	.0160	.0337	.0213	.0203	.0464	–.0025	–.0131
Total factor productivity	.0158	.0137	.0233	.0135	.0063	.0119	–.0067	.0206	.0358
Private nonfarm economy									
Output	.0335	.0476	.0274	.0271	.0490	.0370	.0367	.0280	.0127
Inputs:									
Labor	.0193	.0275	.0111	.0060	.0293	.0225	.0145	.0220	.0120
Capital	.0418	.0599	.0447	.0248	.0404	.0448	.0460	.0394	.0297
Energy	.0286	.0483	.0392	.0220	.0424	.0546	.0392	.0392	–.0394
Materials	.0323	.0461	.0215	.0240	.0478	.0364	.0366	.0287	.0132
Total factor productivity	.0044	.0049	.0041	.0095	.0096	.0032	.0066	–.0009	.0006

A comparison of the patterns for capital input is equally revealing. Capital input in agriculture generally increased over the 1947–1985 period but at an average annual rate (0.83 percent) equaling only one-fifth the rate for the private nonfarm economy (4.18 percent) and only one-fourth the rate for aggregate manufacturing (3.38 percent). Agriculture is clearly the outlier. With only one exception, transportation (1.34 percent), all private nonfarm sectors had average growth rates for capital input exceeding 3.38 percent per year.

Though less dramatic, both energy and material inputs in agriculture increased at rates less than their private nonfarm economy counterparts. Over the 1947–1985 period, material and energy inputs in agriculture increased at rates equal to 38 percent and 74 percent, respectively, of the corresponding rates in the nonfarm economy.

In spite of the decline in labor input and, by nonfarm economy standards, the modest growth rate in capital input, the agricultural sector managed to record nearly a two percent growth (1.92 percent) in output per year over the postwar period. Moreover, production increased at greater than a one percent annual rate in every subperiod. Output growth in the private nonfarm economy was understandably higher. However, it is important to note that the average 1947–1985 growth rate of output in agriculture equaled 57 and 66 percents of the corresponding growth rates in the private nonfarm economy and manufacturing, respectively. The sources of growth story for agriculture and the rest of the economy appear to be very different. Table 9.3 makes that difference explicit.

Output growth results from input growth and/or productivity growth. The collective contribution of all inputs to output growth is defined as the cost-share weighted average growth rate of all inputs or, stated more simply, the growth rate of aggregate input. The source decomposition of output or economic growth in agriculture, the private nonfarm economy, and its disaggregated sectors is displayed in table 9.3.

There is little doubt that productivity growth is the principal factor responsible for postwar economic growth in agriculture, accounting for more than 80 percent of the sector's growth.[7] This contrasts with 13 and 25 percent levels for productivity's contribution to economic growth in the private nonfarm economy and manufacturing, respectively.

Growth in inputs is typically identified as the primary driving force of the economy's economic growth. That, as reported in Jorgenson,

Table 9.3
Contributions to economic growth

	Average Annual Rates of Growth, 1947–1985			TFP Growth as Percent
Industry	Output	Aggregate Input	TFP	of Output Growth
Agriculture	.0192	.0034	.0158	.82
Private nonfarm economy	.0335	.0291	.0044	.13
Mining	.0147	.0262	−.0114	(—)
Construction	.0308	.0279	.0029	.09
Manufacturing	.0292	.0220	.0072	.25
Transportation	.0223	.0128	.0096	.43
Communication	.0637	.0433	.0204	.32
Public utilities	.0475	.0388	.0087	.18
Trade	.0354	.0264	.0090	.25
Finance, insurance and real estate	.0405	.0381	.0024	.06
Other services	.0403	.0416	−.0013	(—)

Gollop, and Fraumeni (pp. 197–201 and 310–311) and Jorgenson (pp. 22–28) is certainly the case for both the economy taken as a whole as well as most of its sectors. In agriculture, however, 1.58 percentage points of the sector's 1.92 percent annual growth rate are accounted for by productivity growth. Input growth explains only 0.34 percentage points. In contrast, 2.91 percentage points of the nonfarm economy's economic growth (3.35 percent per year) are explained by increased inputs. Only 0.44 percentage points are accounted for by productivity growth. The roles of input growth and productivity growth are almost exactly reversed in the two sectors.

9.3 Input Quality

Few today would disagree that changing input quality, as defined by Jorgenson and Griliches, should be treated as a distinct source of economic growth. Disagreement persists, however, about whether to assign changing input quality to the input growth or productivity growth categories. Economic theory, however, offers clear guidelines.

The growth rate of an index of aggregate input must reflect changes in the levels of disaggregated inputs (for example, labor or capital) as well as substitution possibilities among those inputs. The familiar cost-share weights in the TFP formula explicitly account for these substitution possibilities. The derivative corollary is equally important. A properly formed measure of aggregate input must incorporate substitution possibilities not only among the broadly defined input categories of labor, capital, energy and materials but also among disaggregated input classes within the labor, capital, energy and material aggregates. Treating an hour worked by a highly educated, skilled worker as equivalent to an hour worked by a less educated, unskilled worker is tantamount to assuming that one constant dollar of labor input equals one constant dollar of capital input.

Most economists would agree that such a constant dollar sum leads to a biased measure of aggregate input. Excluding from a measure of aggregate input growth substitution possibilities among hours worked by laborers having different marginal products or substitution possibilities among different capital stocks similarly leads to biased measures of input growth and, worse, productivity growth.

The measures of aggregate input growth reported in table 9.3 correctly account for all substitution possibilities—not only among but within the labor, capital, energy and material aggregates. In table 9.4,

Table 9.4
Input quality

	Average annual rates of growth, 1947–1985	
	Agriculture	Private nonfarm Economy
Aggregate input	.0034	.0291
Contribution of input stocks:	−.0014	.0254
Labor hours	−.0074	.0056
Capital stocks	−.0009	.0064
Energy	.0005	.0008
Materials	.0064	.0126
Contribution of input quality:	.0048	.0037
Labor	.0026	.0013
Capital	.0023	.0024
Energy	.0001	.0000
Materials	−.0002	.0000

aggregate input growth for both agriculture and the private nonfarm economy in the 1947–1985 period is decomposed among its unweighted stock and input quality components. The contribution to aggregate input growth of each unweighted stock and input quality is measured as the product of each component and its input cost share.

The important observation is that compositional shifts within labor and capital inputs have made significant contributions to input growth and therefore economic growth in both agriculture and the private nonfarm economy. In agriculture, the net effect of quality change in all four inputs has resulted in a 0.48 percent per year contribution to economic growth. The corresponding contribution in the private nonfarm economy equaled 0.37 percent per year.

Although small in size, the contributions through input quality are quite significant. Agriculture's 0.48 percent contribution each year equals roughly one-third the annual contribution of productivity growth in agriculture and actually exceeds the annual average rate of productivity growth in the private nonfarm economy. Moreover, quality change in agriculture is the sole reason for any positive contribution arising through growth in aggregate input. Had it not been for quality change, average annual growth in aggregate input would have been negative. The contribution of changing input quality is equally significant in the private nonfarm economy. Its annual average 0.37

percent contribution to economic growth nearly equaled the 0.44 percent contribution of productivity growth.

The important conclusion from a pure measurement perspective is that if input quality is either ignored or inappropriately assigned to productivity growth, the postwar rate of TFP growth in agriculture would be upward biased on average by 0.48 percentage points or 30 percent per year. The corresponding bias in the private nonfarm economy would be 0.37 percentage points or 84 percent per year.

9.4 Conclusion

There is little doubt that the role of productivity growth in agriculture is quite different than it is in the rest of the economy. Although productivity growth explains 82 percent of agriculture's postwar economic growth, it accounts for less than 13 percent in the private nonfarm economy. Moreover, agriculture's average annual rate of TFP growth has been nearly four times as large as the corresponding rate in the rest of the economy. Stated alternatively, had the average annual postwar rate of productivity growth in agriculture equaled the private nonfarm economy average of 0.44 percent, economic growth in agriculture would have proceeded at a 0.78 percent annual rate instead of its actual 1.92 percent rate.

This paper does not identify the sources of productivity growth in agriculture. However, the results reported here are not inconsistent with earlier findings suggesting significant returns to R&D.

Notes

1. Mighell (1955, p. 130).
2. U.S. National Science Foundation (1990, table B-5, p. 47).
3. *Ibid.*
4. See Ball (1985) for a complete description of the USDA model.
5. The "Other Services" sector includes private households and government enterprises.
6. Operationally, this means that transactions in intermediate goods and services among nonfarm sectors enter the calculation of TFP growth reported for the representative nonfarm sector. In contrast, the measurement of TFP growth for the nonfarm aggregate would be net of these transactions.
7. The contribution of productivity growth to agriculture's economic growth remained stable throughout the postwar period. In the 1947–1966 period, productivity explained 83 percent of the sector's economic growth. In the post-1966 period, productivity growth accounted for 82 percent of output growth.

References

Abramovitz, Moses. 1956. Resource and Output Trends in the United States since 1870. *American Economic Review* 46, no. 2 (May): 5–23.

———. 1962. Economic Growth in the United States. *American Economic Review* 52, no. 4 (September): 762–782.

Ando, Albert, and E. Cary Brown. 1963. The Impacts of Fiscal Policy. In *Stabilization Policies*, ed. E. Cary Brown *et al.* Englewood Cliffs, NJ: Prentice-Hall.

Arrow, Kenneth J. 1962. The Economic Implications of Learning by Doing. *Review of Economic Studies* 29(3), no. 86 (June): 155–173.

———. 1964. Optimal Capital Policy, the Cost of Capital, and Myopic Decision Rules. *Annals of the Institute of Statistical Mathematics* 16, nos. 1/2: 16–30.

Arrow, Kenneth J., Hollis B. Chenery, Bagicha S. Minhas, and Robert M. Solow. 1961. Capital-Labor Substitution and Economic Efficiency. *Review of Economics and Statistics* 43, no. 3 (August): 225–250.

Ball, V. Eldon. 1985. Output, Input, and Productivity Measurement in U.S. Agriculture, 1948–1979. *American Journal of Agricultural Economics* 67, no. 3 (August): 475–486.

Barzel, Yoram. 1964. The Production Function and Technical Change in the Steam-Power Industry. *Journal of Political Economy* 72, no. 2 (April): 133–150.

BEA. *See* Bureau of Economic Analysis.

Becker, Gary S. 1964. *Human Capital*, 2nd ed. 1975. New York: Columbia University Press.

———. 1965. A Theory of the Allocation of Time. *Economic Journal* 75, no. 299 (September): 493–517.

Beckerman, Wilfred. 1978. *Measures of Leisure, Equality, and Welfare.* Paris: Organization for Economic Cooperation and Development.

Binswanger, Hans P. 1978. Issues in Modeling Induced Technical Change. In *Induced Innovation*, eds. Hans P. Binswanger and Vernon W. Ruttan, 128–163. Baltimore, MD: Johns Hopkins University Press.

Board of Governors of the Federal Reserve System. 1970. *Flow of Funds Accounts, 1945–1968*. Washington, DC: U.S. Government Printing Office.

———. 1976. *Flow of Funds Accounts, 1946–1975*. Washington, DC: U.S. Government Printing Office.

Bruno, Michael. 1984. Raw Materials, Profits, and the Productivity Slowdown. *Quarterly Journal of Economics* 99(1) (February): 1–30.

Bureau of the Census. *Current Population Reports*, ser. P-60, no. 43, table 22. Washington, DC: U.S. Department of Commerce.

———. 1940. *Census of Population*. Washington, DC: U.S. Government Printing Office.

———. 1950. *Census of Population*. Washington, DC: U.S. Government Printing Office.

———. 1960. *Census of Population*. Final Report PC(2)–7B. Washington, DC: U.S. Government Printing Office.

———. 1963a. *Census of Manufactures*, MC63(1)–6. Washington, DC: U.S. Government Printing Office.

———. 1963b. *Census of Mining*. Washington, DC: U.S. Government Printing Office.

———. 1963c. *Continuation to 1962 of Historical Statistics of the U.S.* 93. Waxhington, DC: U.S. Government Printing Office.

———. 1965. *Survey of Manufactures*, no. 65. Washington, DC: U.S. Government Printing Office.

———. 1966. *Cotton Production and Distribution*, Bulletin 202. Washington, DC: U.S. Government Printing Office.

———. 1967a. *Current Population Reports*, ser. P-50, nos. 14, 49 and 78. Washington, DC: U.S. Department of Commerce.

———. 1967b. *Trends in Income of Families and Persons*, Technical Paper no. 17. Washington, DC: U.S. Government Printing Office.

———. 1968. *Current Population Reports*, ser. P-60, no. 56. Washington, DC: U.S. Government Printing Office.

———. 1970. *Census of Population*. Washington, DC: U.S. Government Printing Office.

———. 1980. *Census of Population*. Washington, DC: U.S. Government Printing Office.

Bureau of Economic Analysis. 1966. *The National Income and Product Accounts of the United States, 1929–1965, Statistical Tables, A Supplement to the Survey of Current Business*. Washington, DC: U.S. Government Printing Office.

———. 1974. Gross National Product by Industry, work file 1205-04-06. Washington, DC: U.S. Department of Commerce.

———. 1976. *The National Income and Product Accounts of the United States, 1929–1974, Statistical Tables, A Supplement to the Survey of Current Business.* Washington, DC: U.S. Government Printing Office.

———. 1977. *The National Income and Product Accounts of the United States, 1929–1974: Statistical Tables.* Washington, DC: U.S. Government Printing Office.

———. 1986. *The National Income and Product Accounts of the United States, 1929–1982: Statistical Tables.* Washington, DC: U.S. Government Printing Office.

———. 1987. *Fixed Reproducible Tangible Wealth in the United States, 1925–1985.* Washington, DC: U.S. Government Printing Office.

Bureau of Labor Statistics. *Special Labor Force Reports.* Washington, DC: U.S. Department of Labor.

———. Various monthly issues. *Consumers' Price Index.* Washington, DC: U.S. Department of Labor.

———. 1983. *Trends in Multifactor Productivity, 1948–1981.* Washington, DC: U.S. Government Printing Office.

Cagan, Phillip. 1965. Measuring Quality Changes and the Purchasing Power of Money: An Exploratory Study of Automobiles. *National Banking Review* 3 (December): 217–36. Reprinted in Z. Griliches, ed., 1971, *Price Indexes and Quality Change*, 215–239. Cambridge, MA: Harvard University Press.

Campbell, Beth, and Janice Peskin. 1979. *Expanding Economic Accounts and Measuring Economic Welfare: A Review of Proposals* (October). Washington, DC: U.S. Department of Commerce, Bureau of Economic Analysis.

Chinloy, Peter T. 1981. *Labor Productivity.* Cambridge, MA: Abt Books.

Christensen, Laurits R. 1971. Entrepreneurial Income: How Does It Measure Up? *American Economic Review* 61, no. 4 (September): 575–585.

Christensen, Laurits R., Dianne Cummings, and Dale W. Jorgenson. 1980. Economic Growth, 1947–1973: An International Comparison. In *New Developments in Productivity Measurement*, eds. John W. Kendrick and Beatrice Vaccara, 595–698. NBER Studies in Income and Wealth, vol. 41. New York: Columbia University Press.

Christensen, Laurits R., and Dale W. Jorgenson. 1969. The Measurement of U.S. Real Capital Input, 1929–1967. *Review of Income and Wealth*, ser. 15, no. 4 (December): 293–320.

———. 1970. U.S. Real Product and Real Factor Input, 1929–1967. *Review of Income and Wealth*, ser. 16, no. 1 (March): 19–50.

———. 1973a. Measuring Economic Performance in the Private Sector. In *The Measurement of Economic and Social Performance*, ed. Milton Moss, 233–251. NBER Studies in Income and Wealth, vol. 37. New York: Columbia University Press.

———. 1973b. U.S. Income, Saving and Wealth, 1929–1969. *Review of Income and Wealth*, ser. 19, no. 4 (December): 329–362.

Christensen, Laurits R., Dale W. Jorgenson, and Lawrence J. Lau. 1973. Transcendental Logarithmic Production Frontiers. *Review of Economics and Statistics* 55, no. 1 (February): 28–45.

Clemhout, Simone. 1963. The Ratio Method of Productivity Measurement. *Economic Journal* 73, no. 290 (June): 358–360.

Cobb, Charles W., and Paul H. Douglas. 1928. A Theory of Production. *American Economic Review* 18, no. 1 (March): 139–165.

Coen, Robert. 1968. Effects of Tax Policy on Investment in Manufacturing. *American Economic Review* 58 (May): 200–211.

Council of Economic Advisors. 1989. *Economic Report of the President*. Washington, DC: U.S. Government Printing Office.

Creamer, Daniel. 1971. The Value of Rented Capital in the United States. Unpublished manuscript.

Creamer, Daniel, Sergei P. Dobrovolsky, and Israel Borenstein. 1960. *Capital in Manufacturing and Mining: Its Formation and Financing*. Princeton, NJ: Princeton University Press.

Cremeans, John E. 1977. Conceptual and Statistical Issues in Developing Environmental Measures — Recent U.S. Experience. *Review of Income and Wealth*, ser. 23, no. 2 (June): 97–115.

Dacy, Douglas C. 1964. A Price and Productivity Index for a Nonhomogeneous Product. *Journal of the American Statistical Association* 59, no. 306 (June): 469–480.

Dean, Charles R., and Horace J. DePodwin. 1961. Product Variation and Price Indexes: A Case Study of Electrical Apparatus. *Proceedings of the Business and Economic Statistics Section of the American Statistical Association*: 271–279.

Dean, E., ed. 1984. *Education and Economic Productivity*. Cambridge, MA: Ballinger.

de Leeuw, Frank. Undated memorandum.

Denison, Edward F. 1961. Measurement of Labor Input: Some Questions of Definition and the Adequacy of Data. In *Output, Input, and Productivity Measurement*, 347–372. NBER Studies in Income and Wealth vol. 25. Princeton, NJ: Princeton University Press.

———. 1962. *Sources of Economic Growth in the United States and the Alternative Before Us*. New York: Committee for Economic Development.

———. 1964. The Unimportance of the Embodied Question. *American Economic Review* 54, no. 1 (March): 90–94.

———. 1967. *Why Growth Rates Differ*. Washington, DC: The Brookings Institution.

———. 1969. Some Major Issues in Productivity Analysis: An Examination of Estimates by Jorgenson and Griliches. *Survey of Current Business* 49, no. 5, pt. 2 (May): 1–27.

———. 1971. Welfare Measurement and the GNP. *Survey of Current Business* 51, no. 1 (January): 13–16, 39.

———. 1972. Final Comments. *Survey of Current Business* 52, no. 5, pt. 2 (May): 95–110.

———. 1985. *Trends in American Economic Growth, 1929–1982*, Washington, DC: The Brookings Institution.

Diamond, Peter A. 1965. Technical Change and the Measurement of Capital and Output. *Review of Economic Studies* 32(4), no. 92 (October): 289–298.

Diewert, W. Erwin. 1976. Exact and Superlative Index Numbers. *Journal of Econometrics* 4, no. 2 (May): 115–145.

Divisia, Francois. 1925. L'indice monétaire et la théorie de la monnaie. *Revue d'Economie Politique* 39: 842–61, 980–1008, 1121–1151.

———. 1926. *Revue d'Economie Politique* 40, no. 1: 49–81.

———. 1928. *Economique rationnelle*. Paris: Gaston Doin.

———. 1952. *Exposés d'économique* 1. Paris: Dunod.

Domar, Evsey. 1961. On the Measurement of Technological Change. *Economic Journal* 71, no. 284 (December): 709–729.

———. 1963. Total Productivity and the Quality of Capital. *Journal of Political Economy* 71, no. 6 (December): 586–588.

Eisner, Robert. 1978. Total Incomes in the United States, 1959 and 1969. *Review of Income and Wealth*, ser. 24, no. 1 (March): 41–70.

———. 1980. Capital Gains and Income: Real Changes in the Value of Capital in the United States, 1946–1977. In *The Measurement of Capital*, ed. Dan Usher, 175–342. Chicago, IL: University of Chicago Press.

———. 1988. Extended Accounts for National Income and Product. *Journal of Economic Literature* 26, no. 4 (December): 1611–1684.

———. 1989. *The Total Incomes System of Accounts*. Chicago, IL: University of Chicago Press.

Engerman, Stanley, and Sherwin Rosen. 1980. New Books on the Measurement of Capital. In *The Measurement of Capital*, ed. Dan Usher, 153–170. Chicago, IL: University of Chicago Press.

Fabricant, Solomon. 1959. *Basic Facts on Productivity Change*, Occasional Paper no. 63. New York: National Bureau of Economic Research.

Feller, William. 1957. *An Introduction to Probability Theory and its Applications*, vol. 1, 290–293, 2nd ed. New York: Wiley.

Fettig, Lyle. 1963. Adjusting Farm Tractor Prices for Quality Changes, 1950–1962. *Journal of Farm Economics* 45 (August): 599–611.

Finegan, T. Aldrich. 1960. Hours of Work in the U.S.: A Cross-Sectional Analysis. Ph.D. Dissertation, University of Chicago, June 1960.

Fisher, Irving. 1922. *The Making of Index Numbers*. Boston, MA: Houghton-Mifflin.

Flueck, John A. 1961. A Study in Validity: BLS Wholesale Price Quotations. In *Price Statistics of the Federal Government*, ed. George J. Stigler, 419–458. Washington, DC: U.S. Government Printing Office.

Folger, John K., and Charles B. Nam. 1964. Educational Trends from Census Data. *Demography* 1, no. 7: 247–257.

Foss, Murray. 1963. The Utilization of Capital Equipment: Postwar Compared with Prewar. *Survey of Current Business* 43, no. 6 (June): 8–63.

Fox, Karl A., and Syamal K. Ghosh. 1981. A Behavior Setting Approach to Social Accounts Combining Concepts and Data from Ecological Psychology, Economics, and Studies of Time Use. In *Social Accounting Systems*, eds. F. Thomas Juster and Kenneth C. Land, 132–217. New York: Academic Press.

Frane, Lenore, and Lawrence R. Klein. 1953. The Estimation of Disposable Income by Distributive Shares. *Review of Economics and Statistics* 35, no. 4 (November): 333–337.

Fraumeni, Barbara M., and Dale W. Jorgenson. 1980. The Role of Capital in U.S. Economic Growth, 1948–1976. In *Capital, Efficiency and Growth*, ed. George M. von Furstenberg, 9–250. Cambridge, MA: Ballinger.

———. 1986. The Role of Capital in U.S. Economic Growth, 1948–1979. In *Measurement Issues and Behavior of Productivity Variables*, ed. Ali Dogramaci, 161–244. Boston, MA: Martinus Nijhoff.

Frisch, Ragnar. 1936. Annual Survey of General Economic Theory: The Problem of Index Numbers. *Econometrica* 4, no. 1 (January): 1–38.

Froomkin, Joseph, Dean Jamison, and Roy Radner, eds. 1976. *Education as an Industry*. Cambridge, MA: Ballinger.

Gates, John A. 1982. Education and Training Costs: A Measurement Framework and Estimates for 1965–1979. In *Measuring Nonmarket Activity*, ed. Janice Peskin, 107–135. Washington, DC: U.S. Government Printing Office.

Gates, John A. and Martin Murphy. 1982. The Use of Time: A Classification Scheme and Estimates for 1975–1976. In *Measuring Nonmarket Activity*, ed. Janice Peskin, 3–22. Washington, DC: U.S. Government Printing Office.

Goldsmith, Raymond W. 1951. A Perpetual Inventory of National Wealth, 5–61. NBER Studies in Income and Wealth, vol. 14. New York: National Bureau of Economic Research.

———. 1955. *A Study of Saving in the United States.* Princeton, NJ: Princeton University Press.

———. 1962. *The National Wealth of the United States in the Postwar Period.* New York: National Bureau of Economic Research.

———. 1965. *The Flow of Capital Funds in the Postwar Economy.* New York: National Bureau of Economic Research.

Goldsmith, Raymond W., Robert E. Lipsey, and Morris Mendelson. 1963. *Studies in the National Balance Sheet of the United States.* Princeton, NJ: Princeton University Press.

Gollop, Frank M. 1985. Analysis of the Productivity Slowdown: Evidence for a Sector-Biased or Sector-Neutral Industrial Strategy. In *Productivity Growth and U.S. Competitiveness,* eds. William J. Baumol and Kenneth McLennan, 160–186. New York: Oxford University Press.

Gollop, Frank M., and Dale W. Jorgenson. 1980. U.S. Productivity Growth by Industry, 1947–1973. In *New Developments in Productivity Measurement and Analysis,* eds. John W. Kendrick and Beatrice Vaccara, NBER Studies in Income and Wealth, vol. 41, 17–136. Chicago, IL: University of Chicago Press.

———. 1983. Sectoral Measures of Labor Cost for the United States, 1948–1978. In *The Measurement of Labor Cost,* ed. Jack E. Triplett, 185–235, 503–520. NBER Studies in Income and Wealth, vol. 44. Chicago, IL: University of Chicago Press.

Gordon, R.A. 1961. Price Changes: Consumers' and Capital Goods. *American Economic Review* 51, no. 5 (December): 937–957.

Gordon, Robert J. 1968. A New View of Real Investment in Structures, 1919–1966. *Review of Economics and Statistics* 50 (November): 417–428.

———. 1971. Measurement Bias in Price Indexes for Capital Goods. *The Review of Income and Wealth* 17, no. 2 (June): 121–174.

Gorman, John A., John C. Musgrave, Gerald Silverstein, and Kathy A. Comins. 1985. Fixed Private Capital in the United States. *Survey of Current Business* 65, no. 7 (July): 36–59.

Graham, John W., and Roy H. Webb. 1979. Stocks and Depreciation of Human Capital: New Evidence from a Present-Value Perspective. *Review of Income and Wealth,* ser. 25, no. 2 (June): 209–224.

Griliches, Zvi. 1958. Research Costs and Social Returns: Hybrid Corn and Related Innovations. *Journal of Polictical Economy* 64 (October): 414–431.

———. 1960. Measuring Inputs in Agriculture: A Critical Survey. *Journal of Farm Economics* 42, no. 5 (December): 1411–1427.

———. 1961. Capital Theory: Discussion. *American Economic Review* 51, no. 2 (May): 127–130.

———. 1963. Capital Stock in Investment Functions: Some Problems of Concept and Measurement. In *Studies in Mathematical Economics and Econometrics in Memory of Yehuda Grunfeld*, eds. Carl Christ, Milton Friedman, Leo Goodman, Zvi Griliches, Arnold Harberger, Nissan Liviatan, Jacob Mincer, Yair Mundlak, Marc Nerlove, Don Patinkin, Lester Telser, and Henri Theil, 115–137. Stanford, CA: Stanford University Press.

———. 1964a. Notes on the Measurement of Price and Quality Changes. In *Models of Income Determination*, 381–404. NBER Studies in Income and Wealth, vol. 28. Princeton, NJ: Priceton University Press.

———. 1964b. Research Expenditures, Education, and the Aggregative Agricultural Production Function. *American Economic Review* 54 (December): 961–974.

———. 1967. Production Functions in Manufacturing: Some Empirical Results. In *The Theory and Empirical Analysis of Production*, ed. Murray Brown, 275–322. New York: Columbia University Press.

———. 1970. Notes on the Role of Education in Production Functions and Growth Accounting. In *Education and Income*, ed. Lee Hansen, 71–115. NBER Studies in Income and Wealth, vol. 35. New York: Columbia University Press.

———. 1973. Research Expenditures and Growth Accounting. In *Science and Technology in Economic Growth*, ed. Bruce R. Williams, 59–83. London: Macmillan.

———. 1977. Estimating the Returns to Schooling: Some Econometric Problems. *Econometrica* 45, no. 1 (January): 1–22.

———. 1988. *Technology, Education, and Productivity*. New York: Basil Blackwell.

Griliches, Zvi, and Dale W. Jorgenson. 1966. Sources of Measured Productivity Change: Capital Input. *American Economic Review* 56, no. 2 (May): 50–61.

Griliches, Zvi, and Will Mason. 1972. Education, Income and Ability. *Journal of Political Economy* 80(3), no. 2, pt. 2 (May): S74–S103.

Grose, Lawrence, Irving Rottenberg, and Robert Wasson. 1966. New Estimates of Fixed Business Capital in the United States, 1925–1965. *Survey of Current Business* 46, no. 12 (December): 34–40.

———. 1969. New Estimates of Fixed Business Capital in the United States. *Survey of Current Business* 49 (February): 46–52.

Haavelmo, Trygve. 1960. *A Study in the Theory of Investment*. Chicago, IL: University of Chicago Press.

Hall, Robert E. 1968. Technical Change and Capital from the Point of View of the Dual. *Review of Economic Studies* 35(1), no. 101 (January): 35–46.

———. 1971. The Measurement of Quality Change from Vintage Price Data. In *Price Indexes and Quality Change*, ed. Zvi Griliches, 240–271. Cambridge, MA: Harvard University Press.

———. 1973. The Specification of Technology with Several Kinds of Output. *Journal of Political Economy* 81(4) (July/August): 878–892.

Hall, Robert E., and Dale W. Jorgenson. 1967. Tax Policy and Investment Behavior. *American Economic Review* 57, no. 3 (June): 391–414.

———. 1971. Application of the Theory of Optimum Capital Accumulation. In *Tax Incentives and Capital Spending*, ed. Gary Fromm, 9–60. Washington, DC: The Brookings Institution.

Hanushek, Eric A. 1986. The Economics of Schooling. *Journal of Economic Literature* 24, no. 3: 1141–1177.

———. 1989. The Impact of Differential Expenditures on School Performance. *Educational Researcher* 18: 45–51.

Hardy, Godfrey H., John E. Littlewood, and George Polya. 1952. *Inequalities*. 2d ed. Cambridge: Cambridge University Press.

Haveman, Robert, and Barbara L. Wolfe. 1984. Schooling and Economic Well-Being: The Role of Nonmarket Effects. *Journal of Human Resources* 19, no. 3 (Summer): 377–407.

Hickman, Bert G. 1965. *Investment Demand and U.S. Economic Growth*. Washington, DC: The Brookings Institution.

Hicks, John R. 1932. *The Theory of Wages*. London: Macmillan (2nd ed., 1963).

———. 1946. *Value and Capital*, 2nd edition. Oxford: Oxford University Press (1st ed., 1939).

———. 1961. The Measurement of Capital in Relation to the Measurement of Other Economic Aggregates. In *The Theory of Capital*, eds. Friedrich A. Lutz and Douglas C. Hague, 18–31. New York: Macmillan.

Hotelling, Harold S. 1925. A General Mathematical Theory of Depreciation. *Journal of the American Statistical Association* 20, no. 151 (September): 340–353.

House, James S. 1981. Social Indicators, Social Change, and Social Accounting: Toward More Integrated and Dynamic Models. In *Social Accounting Systems* eds. F. Thomas Juster and Kenneth C. Land, 421–452. New York: Academic Press.

Houthakker, Hendrik S. 1959. Education and Income. *Review of Economics and Statistics* 41, no. 1 (February): 24–27.

Hulten, Charles R. 1978. Growth Accounting with Intermediate Inputs. *Review of Economic Studies* 45(3), no. 141 (October): 511–518.

Hulten, Charles R., and Frank C. Wykoff. 1981. The Estimation of Economic Depreciation Using Vintage Asset Prices: An Application of the Box-Cox Power Transformation. *Journal of Econometrics* 15, no. 3 (April): 367–396.

Internal Revenue Service. 1963. *Statistics of Income, 1963, Corporation Income Tax Returns*. Washington, DC: U.S. Government Printing Office.

Jack Faucett Associates, Inc. 1975. *Output and Employment for Input-Output Sectors*. Washington, DC: U.S. Bureau of Labor Statistics.

Jaszi, George, Robert Wasson, and Lawrence Grose. 1962. Expansion of Fixed Business Capital in the United States. *Survey of Current Business* 42, no. 11 (November): 9–18.

Johansen, Leif, and Å. Sorsveen. 1967. Notes on the Measurement of Real Capital in Relation to Economic Planning Models. *Review of Income and Wealth*, ser. 13 (June): 175–197.

Johnson, Harry Gordon. 1964. Comment. In O.E.C.D. *The Residual Factor and Economic Growth*: 219–227.

Joint Equipment Committee Report. 1968. Costs of Railroad Equipment and Machinery. Washington, DC: Association of American Railroads.

Jorgenson, Dale W. 1966. The Embodiment Hypothesis. *Journal of Political Economy* 74, no. 1 (February): 1–17.

———. 1973. The Economic Theory of Replacement and Depreciation. In *Econometrics and Economic Theory*, ed. Willy Sellekaerts, 189–221. New York: Macmillan.

———. 1980. Accounting for Capital. In *Capital, Efficiency and Growth*, ed. George M. von Furstenberg, 251–319. Cambridge, MA: Ballinger.

———. 1984. The Role of Energy in Productivity Growth. In *International Comparisons of Productivity and Causes of the Slowdown*, ed. John W. Kendrick, 270–323. Cambridge, MA: Ballinger. Earlier, less detailed versions of this material appeared in *American Economic Review* 74(2) (May 1978): 26–30; and in *The Energy Journal* 5, no. 3 (July 1984): 11–25.

———. 1986a. Econometric Methods for Modeling Producer Behavior. In *Handbook of Econometrics* 3, eds. Zvi Griliches and Michael D. Intriligator, 1841–1915. Amsterdam: North-Holland.

———. 1986b. The Great Transition: Energy and Economic Change. *Energy Journal* 7, no. 3 (July): 1–13.

———. 1990. Productivity and Economic Growth. In *Fifty Years of Economic Measurement*, eds. Ernst R. Berndt and Jack E. Triplett, 19–118. Chicago, IL: University of Chicago Press.

Jorgenson, Dale W., and Barbara M. Fraumeni. 1981. Relative Prices and Technical Change. In *Modeling and Measuring Natural Resource Substitution*, eds. Ernst R. Berndt and Barry C. Field, 17–47. Cambridge, MA: M.I.T. Press.

———. 1989. The Accumulation of Human and Nonhuman Capital, 1948–1984. In *The Measurement of Saving, Investment, and Wealth*, eds. Robert E. Lipsey and Helen S. Tice, 227–282. Chicago, IL: University of Chicago Press.

———. 1992. The Output of the Education Sector. In *Output Measurement in the Services Sector*, ed. Zvi Griliches. Chicago, IL: University of Chicago Press.

Jorgenson, Dale W., Frank M. Gollop, and Barbara M. Fraumeni. 1987. *Productivity and U.S. Economic Growth*. Cambridge, MA: Harvard University Press.

Jorgenson, Dale W., and Zvi Griliches. 1967. The Explanation of Productivity Change. *Review of Economic Studies* 34(3), no. 99 (July): 249–280.

———. 1972a. Issues in Growth Accounting: A Reply To Edward F. Denison. *Survey of Current Business* 52, no. 5, pt. 2 (May): 65–94.

Jorgenson, Dale W., and Alvaro Pachon. 1983a. The Accumulation of Human and Nonhuman Wealth. In *The Determinants of National Saving and Wealth*, eds. Richard Hemmings and Franco Modigliani, 302–352. London: Macmillan.

———. 1983b. Lifetime Income and Human Capital. In *Human Resources, Employment, and Development*, eds. Paul Streeten and H. Maier, vol. 2, 29–90. London: Macmillan.

Jorgenson, Dale W., and Kun-Young Yun. 1986. Tax Policy and Capital Allocation. *Scandinavian Journal of Economics* 88, no. 2: 355–377.

———. 1990. Tax Reform and U.S. Economic Growth. *Journal of Political Economy* 98, no. 5, pt. 2 (October): S151–193.

Juster, F. Thomas, Paul N. Courant, and Greg K. Dow. 1981a. A Theoretical Framework for the Measurement of Well Being. *Review of Income and Wealth* ser. 27, no. 1 (March): 1–31.

———. 1981b. The Theory and Measurement of Well-Being: A Suggested Framework for Accounting and Analysis. In *Social Accounting Systems*, eds. F. Thomas Juster and Kenneth C. Land, 23–94. New York: Academic Press.

Juster, F. Thomas, Paul Courant, Greg J. Duncan, John Robinson, and Frank P. Stafford. 1978. *Time Use in Economic and Social Accounts*. Ann Arbor, MD: Institute for Social Research, University of Michigan.

Juster, F. Thomas, and Kenneth C. Land, eds. 1981a. *Social Accounting Systems*. New York: Academic Press.

———. 1981b. Social Accounting Systems: An Overview. In *Social Accounting Systems*, eds. F. Thomas Juster and Kenneth C. Land, 1–21. New York: Academic Press.

Juster, F. Thomas, and Frank P. Stafford. 1991. The Allocation of Time: Empirical Findings, Behavioral Models, and Problems of Measurement. *Journal of Economic Literature* 29: 471–522.

Kendrick, John W. 1956. Productivity Trends: Capital and Labor. *Review of Economics and Statistics* 38, no. 3 (August): 248–257.

———. 1961a. *Productivity Trends in the United States*. Princeton, NJ: Princeton University Press.

———. 1961b. Some Theoretical Aspects of Capital Measurement. *American Economic Review* 51, no. 2 (May): 102–111.

———. 1972. The Treatment of Intangible Resources as Capital. *Review of Income and Wealth* 18, no. 1 (March): 109–125. The paper was presented in early September 1971, at the meetings of the International Association for Research in Income and Wealth at Ronneby, Sweden.

———. 1973. *Postwar Productivity Trends in the United States, 1948–1969.* New York: National Bureau of Economic Research.

———. 1976. *The Formation and Stocks of Total Capital.* New York: Columbia University Press.

———. 1979. Expanding Imputed Values in the National Income and Product Accounts. *Review of Income and Wealth,* ser. 25, no. 4 (December): 349–364.

———. 1983. Interindustry Differences in Productivity Growth. Washington, DC: American Enterprise Institute.

Kendrick, John W., and Ryuzo Sato. 1963. Factor Prices, Productivity, and Economic Growth. *American Economic Review* 53, no. 5 (December): 974–1003.

Kravis, Irving B. 1959. Relative Income Shares in Fact and Theory. *American Economic Review* 49, no. 5 (December): 917–949.

Kroch, Eugene, and Kriss Sjoblom. 1986. Education and the National Wealth of the United States. *Review of Income and Wealth* 32, no. 1 (March): 87–106.

Kurtz, E. B. 1930. *Life Expectancy of Physical Property Based on Mortality Laws.* New York: Ronald Press.

Kuznets, Simon. 1961. *Capital in the American Economy.* Princeton, NJ: Princeton University Press.

———. 1971. *Economic Growth of Nations.* Cambridge, MA: Harvard University Press.

Land, Kenneth C., and Marilyn M. McMillen. 1981. Demographic Accounts and the Study of Social Change, with Applications to Post-World War II United States. In *Social Accounting Systems,* eds. F. Thomas Juster and Kenneth C. Land, 242–306. New York: Academic Press.

Levhari, David. 1966a. Further Implications of Learning by Doing. *Review of Economic Studies* 33(1), no. 93 (January): 31–38.

———. 1966b. Extensions of Arrow's "Learning by Doing." *Review of Economic Studies* 33(2), no. 94 (April): 117–132.

Machlup, Fritz. 1962. *The Production and Distribution of Knowledge in the United States.* Princeton, NJ: Princeton University Press.

Maddison, Angus. 1987. Growth and Slowdown in Advanced Capitalist Economies: Techniques of Quantitative Assessment. *Journal of Economic Literature* 25(2) (June): 649–698.

Malinvaud, Edmond. 1953. Capital Accumulation and the Efficient Allocation of Resources. *Econometrica* 21 (April): 233–268.

Marston, Alfred, R. Winfrey, and J. C. Hempstead. 1953. *Engineering Evaluation and Depreciation*, 2nd ed. New York: McGraw-Hill.

Mansfield, Edwin. 1965. Rates of Return from Industrial Research and Development. *American Economic Review* 55, no. 2 (May): 310–322.

Massell, Benton F. 1961. A Disaggregated View of Technical Change. *Journal of Political Economy* 69, no. 6 (December): 547–557.

McMillen, Marilyn M. 1980. *The Demographic Approach to Social Accounting*, Ph.D. Dissertation, University of Illinois, Urbana-Champaign.

McMillen, Marilyn M., and Kenneth C. Land. 1980. Methodological Considerations in the Demographic Approach to Social Accounting. *1979 Proceedings of the Social Statistics Section*. Washington, DC: American Statistical Association.

Mendelowitz, Allan I. 1971. The Measurement of Economic Depreciation. *Proceedings of the Business and Economic Statistics Secion*, 140–148. Washington, DC: American Statistical Association.

Meyer, John, and Edwin Kuh. 1957. *The Investment Decision*. Cambridge, MA: Harvard University Press.

Michael, Robert T. 1982. Measuring Nonmonetary Benefits of Education: A Survey. In *Financing Education*, eds. W.W. McMahon and T.G. Geske, 119–149. Urbana, IL: Univeristy of Illinois Press.

Mighell, Ronald L. 1955. *American Agriculture: Its Structure and Place in the Economy*. New York: John Wiley & Sons.

Miller, Herman P. 1960a. Annual and Lifetime Income in Relation to Education: 1939–1959. *American Economic Review* 50, no. 5 (December): 962–986.

———. 1960b. Income Distribution in the U.S. 1960 Census Monograph. Washington, DC: U.S. Government Printing Office.

———. 1965. Lifetime Income and Economic Growth. *American Economic Review* 55, no. 4 (September): 834–844.

Miller, Herman P., and Richard A. Hornseth. 1967. Present Value of Estimated Lifetime Earnings, Technical Paper No. 16. Washington, DC: Bureau of the Census, U.S. Department of Commerce.

Mills, Frederick C. 1952. *Productivity and Economic Progress*, Occasional Paper 38. New York: National Bureau of Economic Research.

Minasian, Jora. 1962. The Economics of Research and Development. In Universities-National Bureau Committee for Economic Research, *The Rate and Direction of Inventive Activity*, 93–141. Princeton, NJ: Princeton University Press.

Mincer, Jacob. 1974. *Schooling, Experience, and Earnings*. New York: Columbia University Press.

———. 1984. Human Capital and Economic Growth. *Economics of Education Review* 3, no. 3: 195–205.

———. 1989a. Human Capital and the Labor Market. *Educational Researcher* 18: 27–34.

———. 1989b. *Job Training: Costs, Returns, and Wage Profiles.* New York: Department of Economics, Columbia University.

Murnane, Richard J. 1988. Education and the Productivity of the Work Force: Looking Ahead. In *American Living Standards: Threats and Challenges*, eds. Robert E. Litan, Robert Z. Lawrence, and Charles L. Schultze, 215–245. Washington, DC: The Brookings Institution.

Murphy, Kevin, and Finis Welch. 1989. Wage Premiums for College Graduates: Recent Growth and Possible Explanations. *Educational Researcher* 18: 27–34.

Murphy, Martin. 1980. The Measurement and Valuation of Household Nonmarket Time. Washington, DC: Bureau of Economic Analysis, U.S. Department of Commerce.

———. 1982. The Value of Household Work for the United States, 1976. *Measuring Nonmarket Economic Activity*, ed. Janice Peskin, 23–41. Washington, DC: U.S. Government Printing Office.

National Center for Education Statistics. 1988. *Digest of Education Statistics.* Washington, DC: National Center for Education Statistics, U.S. Department of Education.

National Center for Health Statistics. Various annual issues. *Vital Statistics of the United States.* Washington, DC: Public Health Service, U.S. Department of Health, Education and Welfare.

National Research Council. 1979. *Measurement and Interpretation of Productivity.* Washington, DC: National Academy of Sciences.

Nordhaus, William D., and James Tobin. 1972. *Economic Research: Retrospect and Prospect*, vol. 5, *Economic Growth.* New York: National Bureau of Economic Research.

O'Neill, D.M., and P. Sepielli. 1985. *Education in the United States: 1940–1983.* Washington, DC: U.S. Government Printing Office.

Office of Business Economics. 1966. *Capital Stock Study.* Washington, DC: U.S. Department of Commerce.

———. 1966. *The National Income and Product Accounts of the United States, 1929–1965, A Supplement to the Survey of Current Business.* Washington, DC: U.S. Department of Commerce. See Bureau of Economic Analysis (1966).

Okun, Arthur M. 1962. Potential GNP: Its Measurement and Significance. *Proceedings of the Business and Economic Statistics Section of the American Statistical Association*: 98–104.

Peskin, Henry M., and Janice Peskin. 1978. The Valuation of Nonmarket Activities in Income Accounting. *Review of Income and Wealth*, ser. 24, no. 1 (March): 71–91.

Peskin, Janice, ed. 1982. *Measuring Nonmarket Activity*. Washington, DC: U.S. Government Printing Office.

Phelps, Edmond S., and Charlotte Phelps. 1966. Factor-Price-Frontier Estimation of a "Vintage" Production Model of the Postwar U.S. Nonfarm Business Sector. *Review of Economics and Statistics* 48, no. 3 (August): 251–265.

Richter, Marcel K. 1966. Invariance Axioms and Economic Indexes. *Econometrica* 34, no. 4 (October): 739–755.

Rosen, Sherwin. 1977. Human Capital: A Survey of Empirical Research. In *Research in Labor Economics*, ed. R. G. Ehrenberg, vol. 1, 3–39. Greenwich: JAI Press.

Ruggles, Nancy, and Richard Ruggles. 1970. *The Design of Economic Accounts*. New York: Columbia University Press.

———. 1973. A Proposal for a System of Economic and Social Accounts. In *The Measurement of Social and Economic Performance*, ed. Milton Moss, 111–146. New York: Columbia University Press.

Ruggles, Richard. 1981. The Conceptual and Empirical Strengths and Limitations of Demographic and Time-Based Accounts. In *Social Accounting Systems*, eds. F. Thomas Juster and Kenneth C. Land, 453–476. New York: Academic Press.

Ruggles, Richard, and Nancy Ruggles. 1982. Integrated Economic Accounts for the United States, 1947–1980. *Survey of Current Business* 62, no. 5 (May): 1–52.

Sametz, Arnold W. 1968. Production of Goods and Services: The Measurement of Economic Growth. In *Indicators of Social Change*, eds. Eleanor B. Sheldon and Wilbert Moore. New York: Russell Sage Foundation.

Samuelson, Paul A. 1950. Evaluation of Real National Income. *Oxford Economic Papers*, N.S. 2 (January): 1–29.

———. 1953. Prices of Factors and Goods in General Equilibrium. *Review of Economic Studies* 21(1), no. 54: 1–20.

———. 1961. The Evaluation of "Social Income": Capital Formation and Wealth. In *The Theory of Capital*, eds. Friedrich A. Lutz and Douglas C. Hague, 32–57. New York: Macmillan.

———. 1962. Parable and Realism in Capital Theory: The Surrogate Production Function. *Review of Economic Studies* 29(3) no. 86 (June): 193–206.

Schmookler, Jacob 1952. The Changing Efficiency of the American Economy, 1869–38. *Review of Economics and Statistics* 34 (August): 214–231.

Schultz, Theodore W. 1961a. Education and Economic Growth. In *Social Forces Influencing American Education*, ed. Nelson B. Henry. Chicago, IL: University of Chicago Press.

———. 1961b. Investment in Human Capital. *American Economic Review* 51, no. 1 (March): 1–17.

———. 1971. *Investment in Human Capital*. New York: The Free Press of Glencoe.

Siegel, Irving H. 1952. *Concepts and Measurement of Production and Productivity*. Washington, DC: U.S. Bureau of Labor.

———. 1961. On the Design of Consistent Output and Input Indexes for Productivity Measurement. In *Output, Input and Productivity Measurement*, 23–41. NBER Studies in Income and Wealth, vol. 25. Princeton, NJ: Princeton University Press.

Solow, Robert M. 1956. A Contribution to the Theory of Economic Growth. *Quarterly Journal of Economics* 70(1) (February): 65–94.

———. 1957. Technical Change and the Aggregate Production Function. *Review of Economics and Statistics* 39, no. 3 (August): 312–320.

———. 1960. Investment and Technical Progress. In *Mathematical Methods in the Social Sciences, 1959*, eds. Kenneth J. Arrow, Samuel Karlin, and Patrick Suppes, 89–104. Stanford, CA: Stanford University Press.

———. 1962. Technical Progress, Capital Formation, and Economic Growth. *American Economic Review* 52, no. 2 (May): 76–86.

———. 1964. *Capital Theory and the Rate of Return*. Chicago, IL: Rand-McNally.

———. 1988. Growth Theory and After. *American Economic Review* 78: 307–317.

Statistical Office of the United Nations. 1968. A System of National Accounts. *Studies in Methods*, ser. F, no. 2, rev. 3. New York: Department of Economics and Social Affairs, United Nations.

Stigler, George J. 1947. *Trends in Output and Employment*. New York: National Bureau of Economic Research.

Stone, Richard. 1971. *Demographic Accounting and Model Building*. Paris: Organization for Economic Cooperation and Development.

———. 1981. The Relationship of Demographic Accounts to National Income and Product Accounts. In *Social Accounting Systems*, eds. F. Thomas Juster and Kenneth C. Land, 307–376. New York: Academic Press.

Terborgh, George 1960. *Sixty Years of Business Capital Formation*. Washington, DC: Machinery and Allied Products Institute.

Terleckj, Nestor E. 1981. A Social Production Framework for Resource Accounting. In *Social Accounting Systems*, eds. F. Thomas Juster and Kenneth C. Land, 95–129. New York: Academic Press.

Theil, Henri. 1965. The Information Approach to Demand Analysis. *Econometrica* 33, no. 1 (January): 67–87.

———. 1967. *Economics and Information Theory*. Amsterdam: North-Holland.

Tice, Helen S. 1967. Depreciation, Obsolescence, and the Measurement of the Aggregate Capital Stock of the United States, 1900–1962. *Review of Income and Wealth*, ser. 13 (June): 119–154.

Tinbergen, Jan. 1942. Zur Theorie der langfristigen Wirtschaftsentwicklung, *Weltwirtschaftliches Archiv*, Bank 55, no. 1, pp. 511–549; English translation (1959), "On the Theory of Trend Movements," in *Jan Tinbergen, Selected Papers*, eds. Leo H. Klaassen, Leendert M. Koyck, and Hendrikus J. Witteveen, 182–221. Amsterdam: North-Holland.

Tobin, James. 1955. A Dynamic Aggregative Model. *Journal of Political Economy* 63, no. 2 (April): 103–115.

Törnqvist, Leo. 1936. The Bank of Finland's Consumption Price Index. *Bank of Finland Monthly Bulletin*, no. 10: 1–8.

United Nations. 1975. *Towards A System of Social and Demographic Statistics*. New York: Department of Economic and Social Affairs, United Nations.

———. 1977. *The Feasibility of Welfare-Oriented Measures to Supplement the National Accounts and Balances: A Technical Report*. New York: Department of Economic and Social Affairs, United Nations.

U.S. Council of Economic Advisors. 1989. *Economic Report of the President*. Washington, DC: U.S. Government Printing Office.

U.S. Department of Education. 1988. National Center for Education Statistics, *Digest of Education Statistics*. Washington, DC: U.S. Department of Education, National Center for Education Statistics.

U.S. Department of Labor, Bureau of Labor Statistics. 1983. *Trends in Multifactor Productivity, 1948–1981*. Washington, DC: U.S. Department of Labor, Bureau of Labor Statistics.

U.S. National Science Foundation. 1990. *National Patterns of R&D Resources 1990, Final Report*, NSF90–316, by J.E. Jankowski. Washington, DC: U.S. Government Printing Office.

Wales, Terence J. 1966. Estimation of an Accelerated Depreciation Learning Function. *Journal of the American Statistical Association* 61 (December): 995–1009.

Wasson, Robert C. 1964. Some Problems in the Estimation of Service Lives of Fixed Capital Assets. *Measuring the Nation's Wealth*, Joint Economic Committee, Congress of the United States, 367–374. Washington, DC: U.S. Government Printing Office.

Wehle, Elizabeth S. 1979. Unpaid Household Work: Methodology and Sources. Unpublished manuscript.

Weisbrod, Burton A. 1961. The Valuation of Human Capital. *Journal of Political Economy* 69, no. 5 (October): 425–436.

Welch, Finis. 1979. Effect of Cohort Size on Earnings: The Baby Boom Babies' Financial Bust. *Journal of Political Economy* 87, no. 5 (October): S65–S98.

Wold, Herman. 1953. *Demand Analysis*. New York: John Wiley & Sons.

Wykoff, Frank C. 1970. Capital Depreciation in the Postwar Period: Automobiles. *The Review of Economics and Statistics* 52(2) (May): 168–172.

Young, Allan. 1968. Alternative Estimates of Corporate Depreciation and Profits: Part I. *Survey of Current Business* 48 (April): 17–28.

Index

Abramovitz, Moses, 1, 26, 39, 53, 101, 143, 374
Accounting systems
compared, 179, 194–197, 291–223, 328–330
components of complete, 176
constructing for measuring performance, 175–178
consumption and, 330
extending to human capital, 89, 166–167, 178, 268–269, 273–331
extending to research and development, 268, 270
total factor productivity and, 140–142
unified social accounting, 88
See also individual accounts; U.S. National Income and Product Accounts
Accumulation account, 176
accounting identity for, 246, 255
capital formation in, 189, 192, 193
capital stock in, 214–215, 314, 315
components of, 189, 314
depreciation in, 197, 211, 214
disaggregating, 178–179
human capital in, 314
investment goods in, 59, 214
link to other accounts, 194, 246
replacement in, 215
revaluation in, 189, 191–192, 193, 197, 211, 314
saving in, 189, 193, 194, 258, 314
"Advance of Knowledge," 52, 85, 163
Aggregate production models, 8–12
Aggregate productivity, 2
capital input and, 8–11
data development for, 21–22
labor input and, 8–11
productivity growth and, 8–11
sectoral output and, 7–12, 21–22
shifts in, 25
and time coefficients, 13
value added and, 8–10
Aggregation
errors arising from, 11–12, 62–63, 65–67, 68–69, 76–84
over sectors, 7–9, 21–22, 89
quality change and, 65–67, 159–160
Agriculture
capital input in, 390
demographic data for, 390
economic growth, 395, 396
input compared with nonfarm, 393–394
input quality and, 397–399
intermediate input in, 390
inventories, 109, 152
labor input in, 393, 394
output of, 393, 394
productivity compared with nonfarm economy, 390–393
productivity growth in, 389–399
research and development for, 389
total factor productivity in, 390–393, 399
value of dwellings, 118–119
Ando, Albert, 189
Arrow, Kenneth J., 87, 114, 143

Becker, Gary S., 333, 354, 371
Brown, E. Cary, 189
Bureau of Economic Analysis (BEA), 20, 255
  human capital and, 360, 385
  See also U.S. National Income and Product Accounts (NIPAs)
Bureau of Labor Statistics (BLS), 20, 71
Business sector. *See* Corporate sector

Cagan, Philip, 218
Capital
  accumulation, 314, 315
  growth rates of, 40–41
  human and nonhuman, 89, 273–277, 281, 328
  intangible, 166
  relative utilization of, 75, 88, 91–93, 124–130, 132
  "surrogate," 36–37, 40–41, 45, 87
  weights for components of, 152–160
Capital assets
  capital services and, 101, 113
  capital stock and, 234, 235
  categories of, 78, 109, 152
  depreciable, 160–161
  Divisia index of, 216
  of government bodies, 185
  investment in, 100
  owner-utilized, 232–233
  perpetual inventory and, 192
  price index of, 110–111, 230, 231, 236–237
  replacement in, 154–158
  tangible, 100, 192
  vintage accounts for, 216
  in wealth account, 101, 192
Capital consumption allowances, 93, 104–105, 181
  measuring, 157–158, 221–222
Capital formation
  in accumulation account, 189, 192, 193
  calculating, 189, 191, 314, 315
  components of, 255
  deflators for, 255
  expanded concept of, 273–274
  indexes of, 255–259, 320
  investment and, 214, 215, 246
  property compensation and, 181
  revaluation compared, 318
  saving and, 189, 260
  in U.S. national accounts, 273–274
  value defined, 177, 214
  wealth and, 180, 258–260
Capital gains
  in allocation of property income, 154
  excluding from value of input, 62
Capital goods
  depreciation on, 212, 213, 215, 260
  Divisia index of, 214, 215
  perpetual inventory and, 210–211
  relative efficiency of, 206–208, 219–220
  retirement distributions for, 218
  value of, 214, 216
  vintage accounts for, 212–213, 216
  wealth and, 258–261
Capital input, 263
  adjusting quantity for quality change, 36–37, 397
  aggregate productivity and, 8–11
  in agriculture, 390
  annual growth, 393–395
  by sector, 240, 241
  capital gains excluded from, 62
  categories of, 109, 152
  consumers' durables and, 109
  contribution to economic growth, 1–4, 143–144, 373–385
  in education sector, 378–382
  efficiency decline and, 155–159, 228
  elements in, 245, 378
  equipment and, 78, 109, 151
  estimates of, 90, 102, 228
  growth rates, 3–5, 374–375, 378, 380, 383, 393–395
  indexes of, 59–60, 78–79, 384
  land as, 78, 109, 152
  measuring, 29–30, 61–62, 109–124, 158
  as output growth source, 1–4
  price and quantity indexes of, 125, 228–241
  relative utilization and potential, 130, 132
  rental value and, 22
  sectoral output and, 4–7, 13–15, 21–22
  in sectoral productivity growth, 13–15
  separating into quality and stock, 376–377
  stock concept of, 140–142
  structures in, 78, 109, 152

taxes in, 250
See also Capital services; Input
Capital services
accounting identity for, 122–124
actual and potential, 130
aggregation error in, 76–79
capital assets and, 101, 113
capital stock and, 75–76, 91, 113–114, 250
components of, 110–113
deflators for, 71
Divisia index of, 240
estimating prices for, 93, 236–237
factor input and, 100–101
factor outlay as, 104
in income and expenditure account, 214
investment goods and, 59–62, 179
measuring, 29, 59, 75–79, 84, 104–106
potential, 122–124, 125
prices by asset class, 236–237
prices by vintage, 213
property income and, 118
relative utilization of, 75, 88, 124–130
rental value of, 117–118, 232–233
separating into price and quantity, 117–118, 122–124
taxes and, 77–78, 93, 118–119, 151
used by households and institutions, 118–119, 236–237
value of, 234
value shares of, 34–35
See also Capital input
Capital stock
in accumulation account, 214–215, 314, 315
benchmarks for, 110–111, 230–231
by asset class, 234–235
by sector, 109, 234–235
capital services and, 75–76, 91, 113–114, 250
decline in efficiency and, 218
deflators in estimating, 110–111
depreciation and, 215, 233
Divisia index of, 130, 132
measuring productivity growth with, 140–142
past investments and, 209
perpetual inventory and, 110–114, 210, 228–232, 250
price index of, 110–111, 230, 231
in production account, 214
proportions by asset class and sector, 234, 235
replacement and, 209, 230, 231
revaluation for, 215
value of, 91, 93
vintage accounts of, 214, 216
in wealth account, 216
Capital Stock Study (Office of Business Economics), 230–232
Census unit value indexes, 115, 117
Chenery, Hollis B., 143
Christensen, Laurits R., 1, 17, 22, 130, 139–140, 151, 374
on measuring economic performance, 175–271
Cobb, Charles W., 12
Consolidated income and expenditure accounts, 261–263, 264
accounting identity for, 177
accumulation account in, 176
See also Income and expenditure account
"Constant cost 2" price index, 230, 255
Consumer outlays
components of, 275
full, 275, 303–308, 311–312, 313
labor income and, 247–248
price and quantity indexes of, 247–249
in U.S. national accounts, 275
value of, 177
Consumer receipts, 177
Consumers' durables
as capital input category, 109
deflators for, 71–73, 114–117
price index of, 110–111, 112, 230, 231
as saving, 186
services of, 180
See also Durables
Consumers' price index (CPI), 71–73, 114–116
Consumption, 91
defined, 90, 186, 274
expenditures, 247–249
full, 274, 275, 286, 287–289, 303
investment and, 274
in measuring economic welfare, 330
Consumption goods
components of, 224
defined, 181–183

Consumption goods (*cont.*)
deflators for, 38
investment goods and, 25, 35, 37–38, 104
measuring, 29–30, 63, 104–106
price and quantity indexes of, 106–108, 213–214, 224–225, 226
separating into price and quantity, 29–30, 63
taxes and, 247
total factor productivity and, 42–43
value shares of, 34–35
Corporate sector
capital input in, 130, 131
potential capital services in, 124, 125
price and quantity indexes of, 122–124, 125, 240–241
property compensation in, 238–240, 256–259
rate of return in, 121–123, 151, 238–240, 251–253
taxes in, 109–110, 121–123, 151, 152, 238–239
See also Noncorporate sector; Sectors
CPI. *See* Consumers' price index
Cummings, Diane, 17

Dacy, Douglas C., 70–71
Dean-DePodwin study, 115
Deflators
for capital formation, 255
for capital services, 71
for capital stock, 110–111
comparisons of, 71–74, 114–117
for consumers' durables, 71–73, 114–117
for consumption goods, 38
for equipment investment, 71–74, 114–116
GNP component, 115
for investment, 38, 71–74, 91
in national accounts, 161, 230
prices and, 54
for producers' durables, 71–74, 114–118
See also Price indexes
Demographic data
for agricultural labor input, 390
for human capital, 277–281, 328–330, 335–337
for labor input, 390
for lifetime labor income, 277–281, 328–330, 335–337
Denison, Edward F., 2, 11, 26, 76, 83, 85, 204, 219–223, 228, 245
reply to growth accounting issues raised by, 99–174
Depreciation
in accumulation account, 197, 211, 214
in both input and output, 146
capital stock and, 215, 233
confused with replacement, 99–100, 145, 157–158, 220–221
decline in efficiency and, 19, 154–157, 168–169, 218, 228
determinants of, 122
estimates of, 189–191, 222, 314–317
excluding from input, 62, 154
expressions of, 211–212
full, 276, 318, 319
growth rates, 318–319
inclusion in product, 145, 148, 157–158
index for, 262
on capital goods, 212, 213, 215
on capital services, 154–158, 161, 213
on human and nonhuman capital, 275–276, 314
on vintages of capital goods, 212–213
in postwar period, 318
price and quantity indexes of, 261, 262
saving and, 189, 314
for tax purposes, 152–153
Diewert, W. Erwin, 21–22
Disaggregation. *See* Aggregation
Disembodied technical change. *See* Embodied and disembodied technical change
Divisia indexes
advantages for social accounting, 199–100
characteristics of, 198–201
eliminating errors with, 68
factor and time reversal tests for, 150–151, 201
Laspeyres indexes compared, 203–204
reproductive property of, 28
See also Index numbers; Price indexes
Domar, Evsey, 22
Douglas, Paul H., 12
Durables
capital services from, 103–104

inclusion of, 149, 183
price index of, 110–111, 112, 230, 231
property compensation and, 180
relative biases in, 71, 73
in services output, 104
used by nonprofits, 180
See also Consumers' durables; Producers' durables
Dwellings
value of services of, 118–119
See also Structures

Econometric modeling of production, 2, 11–13, 16, 90
Economic growth
for agricultural and nonfarm sectors, 395, 396
educational investment and, 371–388
growth accounts, 380, 384
new measurement of, 372
relative contributions of sources, 1–4, 143–144, 245–246, 373–385
research methodology for, 17–22
revival of, 373, 385
in sectors, 4–7, 395, 396
slowdown in, 2, 11, 12, 14, 16
sources of, 1–4
theoretical bases for, 16
Economic performance accounting system, 175–271
Economic theory of production
components of, 51, 52, 54, 57–58
data development and, 21
factor price frontier and, 58
relative utilization and, 88–89
Education
cost-based estimates of, 334, 335
higher income from, 371–372
importance in economic growth, 372–373
as investment, 89, 166–167, 333–334, 371
labor services and, 227–228
policies in relation to, 373
school enrollment data, 361, 385
value of labor market activities, 334, 337–340
worker effectiveness and, 372
See also Educational investment; Education sector
Educational investment, 233
assumptions in estimating, 346–351
comparison of estimates, 361–363, 386
cost-based approach to, 363, 385–386
earnings by school level, 95
economic growth and, 371–388
future income factors in, 346, 349–351
gestation period in, 345–346, 363, 386
human wealth and, 354–360, 361–363, 386
lifetime labor income and, 335, 344–345, 363, 372, 386
nonmarket activities and, 346–354, 355, 361, 363, 386–387
output as a measure of, 378, 385–386
outside business sector, 360–361, 385
school enrollment and, 346–355
taxes and, 373
value compared to work time, 346, 351
value of, 346–348
women and, 346, 351, 355
See also Education; Education sector
Education sector
analysis of growth in, 378–382
human capital and, 268, 333
incorporating into accounts, 89, 166–167, 178, 268, 330
investment by sex and schooling level, 346–355
measuring inputs of, 372, 378–382
measuring output of, 333–335, 363, 364–367, 378–382
percent of national product, 333, 373
productivity growth in, 380–382
time in, 372
See also Education; Educational investment; Sectors
Efficiency, 5, 17
of capital goods, 206–208, 219–220
capital input and, 155–159, 228
capital stock and, 218
decline in, 154–157, 168–169, 218, 222, 228
depreciation and, 19, 154–157, 168–169, 218, 228
geometric decline in, 159
perpetual inventory method and, 206–208, 218
replacement and, 206–208, 228
wealth and, 265

Eisner, Robert, 386
Embodied and disembodied technical change, 25–42
  calculations based on, 26
  factual assumptions in, 39–40
  growth rate of output for, 33–36, 41–42
  indexes of, 34, 36, 38
  interchangeability of, 25–26, 33–37, 39–40
  models for, 41–42
  theoretical framework for, 27–28
  total factor productivity and, 52
Energy
  conservation, 5
  growth and prices of, 2, 14
Energy input
  annual growth, 394, 395
  as output growth source, 2
  in sectoral productivity growth, 13–15
Equipment
  as capital input category, 78, 109, 151
  deflators for, 71–73, 114–116
  measuring stock of, 61
  price index of, 71–73
Expenditures, 183–189, 190
  calculating, 185–187
  defined, 185
  full, 305, 308, 311–312, 313
  See also Income and expenditure account

Fabricant, Solomon, 85
Factor input
  capital services and, 100–101
  components of, 138–139
  Divisia index of, 242–244
  estimating, 88
  growth sources in, 139–140
  human and nonhuman capital in, 281
  measuring, 100–102, 138–140
  price index of, 242–243
  quantity index of, 225, 242–243
  See also Real factor input
Factor outlay
  calculating, 181, 182, 282, 283
  as capital and labor services, 104
  components of, 282
  full, 274, 290, 293–296
  measuring, 104–106
Factor price frontier, 58
Factor productivity. *See* Total factor productivity
Factor supplies, 16
Farm. *See* Agriculture
Federal Reserve System, 192
Fisher, Irving, 200
Foss, Murray, 91–93
Frane, Lenore, 187–188
Fraumeni, Barbara M., 14–15, 22, 390, 397
  on constructing new accounting system, 273–331
  on education investment, 371–388
  on education sector output, 333–369
Full consumer outlays, 303–308, 311–312
  defined, 275
  growth rates, 313
  See also Consumer outlays
Full consumption, 286, 287–289
  defined, 274, 275, 286, 303
  expenditures, 275
  See also Consumption
Full depreciation
  defined, 276
  growth rates, 318, 319
  See also Depreciation
Full expenditures, 308, 311–312
  allocating, 303, 305
  estimating, 308
  growth rates, 308, 313
  See also Expenditures
Full factor outlay, 290, 293–296
  defined, 274
  See also Factor outlay
Full income, 298, 301–305
  allocating, 303, 305
  defined, 275
  growth rates, 303, 304
  See also Income
Full investment, 282–289
  defined, 274
  See also Investment
Full labor compensation, 274–275
Full labor income, 298–304
  defined, 275
  See also Labor income
Full labor outlay, 290–296
Full product, 286–290
  defined, 274
  See also Product

Full property compensation, 274
  See also Property compensation
Full property income, 298, 301–304
  defined, 275
  See also Property income
Full property outlay, 290, 293–296
Full revaluations, 276
  See also Revaluations
Full saving, 303–310, 311–312, 314–318
  defined, 275, 303
  estimating, 303–308
  growth rates, 313, 318, 319
  See also Saving
Full wealth, 318, 321–324
  defined, 276, 318
  growth rates, 324, 325
  See also Human wealth; Wealth

Goldsmith, Raymond W., 91, 192, 230
Gollop, Frank M., 22, 277, 329, 337
  on productivity growth in agriculture, 389–399
Gordon, R. A., 37–38
Government sector
  capital assets in, 185
  claims on, 192–194
  in growth measurements, 89, 330, 372
  income and expenditure accounts for, 185
  labor services and, 103
  property compensation in, 256–259
  rate of return in, 251–253
  U.S. national accounts and assets of, 185
  See also Sectors
Griliches, Zvi, 22, 90, 160, 227–228, 389, 390, 397
  on growth accounting, 99–174
  on productivity change, 51–98
Grose, Lawrence, 90–91, 161
Growth accounting, 144–167
Growth periods, 1, 374, 375
Growth rates, 101
  capital input, 374–375, 378, 380, 383, 393–395
  depreciation, 318–319
  embodied and disembodied technical change, 33–36, 41–42
  full consumer outlays, 313
  full depreciation, 318, 319
  full expenditures, 308, 313
  full income, 303, 304
  full saving, 313, 318, 319
  full wealth, 324, 325
  input, 79
  labor input, 34–35, 374–375, 378–382
  noneducation sector, 373–375
  output, 41–42, 79
  real factor input, 53
  real income, 346, 349–350
  "surrogate" capital, 40–41
  total factor productivity, 53, 79, 391–392
  value shares and, 34–35

Haavelmo, Tygve, 114
Hall, Robert E., 110, 159, 218
"Hedonic" price indexes, 67
Hickman, Bert G., 159, 218
Highway construction, price index of, 70–71
Household sector
  capital services in, 118–119, 236–237
  inclusion in gross product, 148–149
  potential capital services in, 124, 125
  price and quantity indexes of, 122–124, 125, 240–241
  property compensation in, 256–259
  rate of return in, 119–120, 251–253
  taxes in, 109–110, 119–120, 152
  See also Sectors
Housing, owner-occupied, 103–104
Hulten, Charles R., 22, 378
Human capital
  accounting systems for, 89, 166–167, 178, 268–269, 273–331
  accumulation account in, 314
  Bureau of Economic Analysis (BEA) and, 360, 385
  comparison of estimates of, 281, 361–363, 386
  cumulating into stock, 89
  definition of, 273–274, 328
  demographic data for, 277–281, 328–330, 335–337
  depreciation on, 275–276, 314
  education sector and, 268, 333
  in factor input, 281
  formation measured over lifespan, 363, 386–387
  forms of investment in, 354, 361, 364

Human capital (*cont.*)
  labor input as, 89, 166–167
  revaluations of, 276, 314
  as similar to nonhuman, 89, 273–276, 281, 328, 371
  U.S. national accounts and, 360–361, 385
  See also Labor income; Labor input; Labor services
Human wealth
  by sex and educational level, 354, 356–360
  comparison of estimates, 361, 362
  defined, 354
  educational investment and, 354–360, 361–363, 386
  estimates of, 318; 321
  excluding nonmarket time, 355, 360
  nonhuman wealth compared, 318, 322–328
  percentage of total, 276–277
  See also Wealth

Income, 183–189, 190
  calculating, 185–187
  components of, 194
  defined, 185–186, 188
  disposable income and, 188
  education and, 344–345, 346, 349–351, 371–372
  full, 275, 298, 301–305
  human and nonhuman services and, 281
  to individuals, 275
  measuring, 179–198
  productivity measurement and accounts for, 99
  real, 346, 349–350
  taxes and, 185
  See also Income and expenditure account
Income and expenditure account
  accounting identity for, 183, 188, 246
  capital service input in, 214
  components of, 179, 183, 296
  constant prices in, 206, 208, 209, 223–224
  link to other accounts, 194, 246
  nonmarket activity in, 296
  property compensation in, 183, 188
  relation to production accounts, 194
  See also Consolidated income and expenditure account; Income
Index numbers
  Diewart's theory of, 21–22
  factor and time reversal tests for, 150–151, 201
  Laspeyres, 203–204
  Paasche, 203–204
  selecting system of, 198
  from translog production function, 22
  in U.S. national accounts, 203–205
  See also Divisia indexes; Price indexes
Industries. *See* Sectoral output
Inflation, 153–154
Input
  agricultural and nonfarm compared, 393–394
  annual growth, 393–396
  equal to output, 55, 81, 83–84, 85, 103, 146–147
  growth rates, 78–79
  indexes of total, 68–84
  measuring, 58–63
  national output and, 102
  in noneducation sector, 374–376
  prices for structures, 70–72, 110–111, 112, 230, 231
  quality of, 397–399
  See also by individual category
Intangible capital, 166
Intermediate input
  in agriculture, 390
  components of, 17
  in education sector, 378–382
  as energy and materials, 13
  measuring, 20
  sectoral output and, 2, 4–7
Internal Revenue Act of 1954, 153
Inventories
  agricultural and nonfarm, 109, 152
  estimates of, 91, 160–161
  price index of, 73–74, 110–111, 112, 230, 231
  See also Perpetual inventory method
Investment, 100
  in capital assets, 100
  capital formation and, 214, 215, 246
  computing, 91
  consumption and, 274

data for, 90–91
defined, 90
discrepancies in private and social, 87
economic revival and, 373, 385
education as, 89, 166–167, 333–334, 371
full, 274, 282–289
in human capital, 277, 354, 361, 364
measuring, 26–27, 39–42, 104–106
as product, 100
proportion of economic growth, 372
"surrogate," 36–37, 45, 46, 87
in U.S. national accounts, 274, 275, 277
See also Educational investment; Investment goods

Investment goods
adjusting quantity for quality change, 36–37
capital services and, 59–62, 179
classes of, 78
components of, 224
consumption goods and, 25, 35, 37–38, 104
defined, 181, 274
deflators for, 38, 71–74, 91
Divisia index of, 214
index quality of, 33, 44–46
measuring, 29–33, 42–47, 52–53, 63–65, 69–74, 84, 104–106
price and quantity indexes of, 106–108, 213–214, 224–225, 226
prices of, 42–47, 69–74, 214
private and social returns in, 87
in production account, 214
property compensation and, 180
replacement rate for, 60–62
separating into price and quantity, 29–30, 59, 63–65
standards in pricing, 88
stock and, 59, 209, 214
total factor productivity and, 42–43
value of, 214
value shares of, 34–35
See also Investment

Investment tax credit, 121–122, 153

Jack Faucett Associates, 20
Jaszi, George, 90–91

Kendrick, John W., 62–63, 140–143, 154, 225–227, 324–328, 361–363, 386
Klein, Lawrence R., 187–188
Kuh, Edwin, 159, 218
Kuznets, Simon, 16

Labor income
calculating, 296–298
consumer outlays and, 247–248
data base for, 277–278
full, 275, 298–304
life cycles in, 279–280, 344–345
for nonmarket activities, 274, 275, 278–279, 328, 372
projecting into future, 342–344, 346
schooling in, 279–280
taxes and, 296–298, 373
time allocation in, 278
women and, 337–340, 341, 342
See also Human capital; labor services; Lifetime labor income

Labor input
aggregate productivity and, 8–11
agricultural and nonfarm compared, 393, 394
annual growth, 393–394
compensation of self-employed, 104, 151
components of, 17
contribution to economic growth, 1–4, 373–385
data for, 377–378
demographic data for, 390
Divisia index of, 80, 225–227
in education sector, 378–382
estimating, 183
exploiting data on, 88
growth rates, 3–5, 374–375, 378–382, 383
hours per week, 133–135
hours per year, 228, 229
as human capital, 89, 166–167
indexes of, 22, 80–82
initial estimate of, 90–91, 134
measuring, 17–20, 29–30, 59, 80–82, 130–138, 163–164
number of people, 228, 229
as output growth source, 1–4
population growth and, 16
price and quantity indexes of, 225–229, 337, 384
quality adjustments for, 166, 377–378
sectoral output and, 4–7, 18

Labor input (*cont.*)
  in sectoral productivity growth, 13–15
  separating into quality and hours worked, 376–377
  total factor productivity and, 42–43
  unpaid family workers in, 166
  weeks per year, 134, 136
  See also Input; Labor services
Labor outlay, 290–296
Labor services
  compensation, 247, 249
  distribution of labor force, 81–82, 94–95, 130–133, 227, 277
  education and, 227–228
  factor outlay as, 104
  government sector and, 103
  labor stock and, 75–76, 89, 91, 134–136
  man-hours and, 80, 133–138, 225–229, 248
  measuring, 29–30, 58–59, 75–76, 80–82, 104–106, 134–138
  relative utilization of, 75, 88, 124
  separating into price and quantity, 29–30, 59
  taxes and, 188–189, 248
  value shares of, 34–35
  See also Labor income; Labor input
Labor stock, 75–76, 89, 91, 134–138
Land
  as capital input category, 78, 109, 152
  price index of, 112
  shifts in use of, 160
  weights for components of, 152–154
Laspeyres index numbers, 203–204
Lau, Lawrence J., 17, 22
Life cycles, 279–280, 344–345
Lifetime labor income
  data base for, 337–340
  demographic data for, 277–281, 328–330, 335–337
  educational investment, 335, 344–345, 363, 372, 386
  life cycle and, 344–345
  measuring, 277–281, 335, 336, 337–345
  See also Labor income
Lipsey, Robert E., 192
Livestock, 390

Machlup, Fritz, 324
Maddison, Angus, 17, 374
Market activities, value of, 334, 337–340
  by sex and educational attainment, 337, 338–339
  nonmarket activities compared, 334–335, 342
  percentage of human wealth, 360
  See also Nonmarket activities
Market equilibrium, 8
Massell, Benton F., 89
Materials input
  annual growth, 394, 395
  as output growth source, 2
  in sectoral productivity growth, 13–15
Measurement, errors of, 51, 58
  capital services, 75–79, 84
  consumption goods, 29–30, 63
  eliminating, 68–84, 85
  incorrect aggregation, 11–12, 62–63, 65–67, 68–69, 76–84
  investment goods, 29–33, 42–47, 52, 59, 63–65, 69–74, 84
  labor services, 30, 63, 75, 80–82, 84
  in relative utilization figures, 75, 84, 126–128
  through separating into price and quantity, 29–33, 52, 63–65
  total factor productivity and, 68
  unified social accounting and, 88
Mendelson, Morris, 192
Meyer, John, 159, 218
Miller, Herman P., 132
Mills, Frederick C., 85
Mincer, Jacob, 333, 354, 371
Minhas, Bagicha S., 143
Models of production
  aggregate, 8–12
  econometric, 2, 11–13, 16
  economic slowdown and, 11, 12, 16
  sectoral, 4–5, 12–16
Mortality distributions, 207–208
Motors. *See* Power sources, relative utilization of

National accounting systems. *See* Accounting systems
National Center for Health Statistics, 342
National Research Council, 17
Neoclassical model of economic growth, 16

Noncorporate sector
  capital input in, 130, 131
  potential capital services in, 124, 125
  price and quantity indexes of, 122–124, 125, 240–241
  property compensation in, 238–240, 256–259
  rate of return in, 115, 119–120, 237–238, 251–253
  taxes in, 109–110, 119–120, 152
  See also Sectors
Noneducation sector
  analysis of growth sources in, 373–376
  components of, 373
  growth rates, 373–375
  output, 374, 376
  See also Sectors
Nonmarket activities
  comparison of estimates, 361, 362
  educational investment and, 346–354, 355, 361, 363, 386–387
  evaluating time spent in, 334–335, 340–343, 346, 363–364
  labor income and, 274, 275, 278–279, 328, 372
  types of, 340
  value of, 340–342, 343
  value of market activities compared, 334–335, 342
Nonprofits
  durables used by, 180
  real estate of, 180
  in U.S. national accounts, 103–104
Nonresidential structures. *See* Structures
Nordhaus, William D., 340, 361, 362

Office of Business Economics (OBE), 68, 71, 104, 122, 160–161, 230–232
  census unit value indexes compared, 115, 117
  data on full-time equivalent employees, 130
  producers' durables investment deflators, 115, 117
Okun, Arthur M., 75, 124
Output
  aggregating with education, 380
  agricultural and nonfarm compared, 393, 394
  annual growth, 393–396
  by sources, 2–7
  components of, 180
  defined, 103, 181
  in education, 378–382
  equal to input, 55, 81, 83–84, 85, 103, 146–147
  growth rates, 41–42, 79
  indexes of total, 68–84
  initial estimate of, 90
  input growth and, 102
  measuring, 58–63, 103–108, 237
  in noneducation sector, 374–376
  price and quantity indexes of, 225, 226, 227
  in producing sector, 225
  services, 104
  taxes and, 101, 146, 181, 225
  value of, 225
  See also Economic growth; Sectoral output
Owner-occupied real estate, 103–104, 180, 232–233

Paasche index numbers, 203–204
Perpetual inventory method
  for assets, 192
  capital goods and, 210–211
  capital stock and, 110–114, 210, 228–232
  correspondence with price counterpart, 209–210
  data on prices and, 178, 205, 209–214
  quantities estimated by, 208–209, 212–213
  relative efficiency and, 206–208, 218
  wealth accounts and, 178, 206, 208, 209
  See also Inventories
Personal disposable income, national income and, 188
Personal income tax
  allocating between labor and property compensation, 188–189
  See also Taxes
Population growth, 16
Power sources
  capital utilization and, 75, 91–93, 124–128
  relative utilization of, 91–93

Price functions, 13
Price indexes
  "constant cost 2," 115, 230, 255
  consumers' price index (CPI), 71–73, 114–116
  data for, 205
  "hedonic," 67
  using Divisia numbers, 124, 150–151, 199, 202–203
  wholesale price index (WPI), 71–73, 114–116
  See also Index numbers; Prices
Prices
  of capital services, 93, 117–118, 122–124, 213, 236–237
  deflators and, 54
  in economic theory of production, 54
  errors in measuring, 29–33, 42–47, 52–53, 69–74
  perpetual inventory method for, 178, 209–214
  separating from quantity, 29–33, 63–65, 117–118, 122–124
  See also Price indexes
Producer equilibrium, 51
  economic theory of production and, 58
  total factor productivity and, 57
Producers' durables
  deflators for, 71–73, 114–118
  price index of, 110–111, 112, 230, 231
  See also Durables
Producers' point of view, 146–148, 151
Product
  calculating, 181–182, 282, 283
  concept of, 103
  consumption and investment in, 104, 282
  depreciation and, 145, 157–158
  full, 274, 286–290
  investment as, 100
  measuring, 100–101, 104–105
  net, 99–100, 157
  price and quantity indexes of, 106–108, 226
  from producer's point of view, 146–148, 151
  replacement and net, 145, 157–158
  scope of measure, 145–149, 175
  total, 104, 282
  value of, 282
  See also Full product; Real product
Production account, 179–182
  accounting identity for, 176, 179–180, 181
  capital stock in, 214
  components of, 178, 179–180, 194
  constructing in constant prices, 223–246
  disaggregating, 178
  investment goods in, 214
  link to other accounts, 194, 246
  price and quantity in, 176
  relationship to income and expenditure account, 194
  separating price and quantity components for, 224
  values in, 282–283
Production functions
  movements along, 51
  returns to scale in, 57, 58
  shifts in, 51, 53, 57
Productivity, defined, 177
Productivity growth, 384
  aggregate productivity and, 8–11
  in agricultural sector, 389–399
  capital input in, 13–15
  capital stock and, 140–142
  as coefficient of time, 13
  contribution to economic growth, 1–4, 373–383
  in education sector, 380–382
  growth rates, 380, 383
  including government sector, 89
  labor input in, 13–15
  measuring product and factor input in, 100
  in noneducation sector, 374–376
  as output growth source, 1–4
  patterns of biases in, 13–15
  real product and, 145–149
  scope of product in, 145–149
  sectoral output and, 4–7, 148
  See also Total factor productivity
Property compensation
  by sector, 251–257
  capital formation and, 181
  capital services and, 113
  components of, 180
  in corporate sector, 238–240
  durables and, 180

full, 274
in income and expenditure account, 183, 188
indexes for, 250–254
investment goods and, 180
in noncorporate sector, 238
rates of return in, 251–252
saving and, 183–185, 188
taxes and, 188–189, 250–254
value of, 214
Property income
allocation of, 154
calculating, 296–298
capital gains and, 154
capital services and, 118
components of, 101, 250
full, 275, 298, 301–304
saving and, 154
taxes on, 151, 152–153
wealth and, 154
Property outlay, 290, 293–296

Quality
capital input and, 36–37, 376–377, 397
of investment goods, 33, 44–46
See also Quality change
Quality change
adjusting quantity for, 36–37, 397
aggregation errors and, 65–67, 159–160
assignment of, 397–399
measuring, 168
vintages and, 160
See also Quality
Quantity
adjusting for quality change, 36–37, 397
separating from price, 29–33, 63–65, 117–118, 122–124

Rates of growth. *See* Growth rates
Rates of replacement. *See* Replacement
Rates of return
by industry and asset type, 166
by sector, 251, 253
calculating for given sector, 152
calculating in periods, 213
capital service prices and, 118, 153–154
in corporate sector, 122–123, 151, 238–240, 251–253
formula for, 235–236
in household sector, 119–120, 251–253
in noncorporate sector, 115, 151, 237–238, 251–253
in property compensation, 251–253
tax rates and, 122–123
Real estate, 103–104, 180, 223–233
Real factor input
contribution to economic growth, 99, 143–144, 245–246
Divisia index of, 138–140
estimating for economy, 138–140
growth rate in, 53
measuring, 51, 52–53, 101–102
real product growth and, 99, 143–144, 245–246
social accounts for, 52, 54
social production possibility frontier and, 177
total factor productivity and, 138, 242, 245–246
See also Factor input
Real income
future growth rate for, 346, 349–350
See also Income
Real product
alternative concepts of, 145–149
contribution to economic growth, 143–144, 245–246
growth by changes in productivity, 145
growth rate defined, 53
measuring, 51, 52–53, 145–149
productivity growth and, 145–149
real factor input and, 99, 143–144, 245–246
scope of measure in, 175
social accounts for, 52, 54
social production possibility frontier and, 177
total factor productivity and, 138, 242, 245–246
See also Product
Rees Report to National Research Council, 17
Relative utilization
alternative estimates of, 164–165
of capital, 75, 88, 124–130, 132
changes in, 91–93, 101–102, 126–129, 132
economic theory of production and, 88–89

Relative utilization (*cont.*)
  issues in determining, 88, 161–163
  of labor services, 75, 88, 124
  measuring, 75, 84, 91–93, 101, 124–129
  in mining, 126–127
  of power sources, 75, 91–93, 124–128
  in textile subindustries, 126, 128
Rental value
  capital input and, 22
  of capital services, 117–118, 232–233
  determining, 18–19, 22
Renter-occupied real estate, 180
Replacement
  in accumulation account, 215
  in capital assets, 154–158
  in *Capital Stock Study*, 230, 231
  decline of efficiency and, 206–208, 228
  depreciation confused with, 99–100, 145, 157–158, 220–221
  of investment goods, 60–62
  net product and, 145, 157–158
  rates of, 110–111, 114, 230–232
  in vintages, 209
Research and development
  for agriculture, 389
  amounts invested in, 389
  cumulating into stock, 89
  incorporating into accounts, 166–167, 178, 268, 270
Residential structures. *See* Structures
Retirement distributions, 218
Return rates. *See* Rates of return
Revaluations
  in accumulation account, 189, 191–192, 193, 211, 314
  capital formation compared, 318
  for capital stock, 215
  estimates of, 192, 193, 318, 320
  full, 276
  of human and nonhuman capital, 276, 314
  index for, 261, 262
  omission of, 222
Revenue
  defined, 181
  measuring, 103
Rottenberg, Irving, 160

Saving
  in accumulation account, 189, 193, 194, 258, 314
  calculating, 189, 191, 314, 315
  capital formation and, 189, 260
  consumers' durables as, 186
  defined, 183–185, 186, 314
  depreciation and, 189
  determinants of, 330
  full, 275, 303–310, 311–312, 314–318, 319
  growth rates, 318–319
  of human and nonhuman capital, 275, 314
  indexes for, 261, 262, 314, 316–318, 320
  integrating with wealth, 314
  investment as, 100
  net and gross, 255, 314–319
  price and quantity indexes of, 261, 262
  productivity measurement and accounts for, 99
  property compensation and, 183–185, 188
  property income and, 154
  rates of, 275
  in U.S. national accounts, 275
Schmookler, Jacob, 85
School enrollment
  data on, 361, 385
  educational investment and, 346–355
Schultz, Theodore W., 16, 89, 324, 333, 371
Sectoral output, 1–2
  aggregate productivity and, 7–12, 21–22
  capital input and, 4–7, 13–15, 21–22
  energy and, 13–15
  growth by sources of, 4–7
  intermediate input and, 2, 4–7
  labor input and, 4–7, 18
  measuring, 20
  patterns of biases in, 13–15
  productivity growth and, 4–7, 148
  See also Output; Sectors
Sectors
  aggregation over, 7–9, 21–22, 89
  capital stock in, 109, 234–235
  economic slowdown and, 12, 16
  production models using, 4–5, 12–16
  property compensation in, 251–257
  rates of return in, 152, 251–252
  taxes in, 109–110, 119–124, 152, 234–235
  total factor productivity in, 390, 391
  See also by individual name; Sectoral output
Self-employed workers, 104, 151
Slowdown in growth (since 1973), 2, 11, 14

aggregate modeling and, 11, 12
energy prices and, 2, 14
research for understanding, 16
sectoral modeling and, 12, 16
Social accounts, 88
aggregation of inputs and outputs in, 53
Divisia indexes and, 199–100
in economic theory of production, 52, 54
notation representing, 54–55
for real factor input, 52, 54
for real product, 52, 54
Social insurance
in private sector, 192
treatment of, 186–188, 298
Social production possibility frontier, 177
Social welfare function, 177
Solow, Robert M., 1, 16, 25–26, 35–37, 124, 140–141, 143, 245, 374
Solow's Residual, 377
Sorsveen, A., 114
Standard of living
defined, 177, 263
index for, 261–263, 264
social welfare function and, 177
Structures
as capital input category, 78, 109, 152
price index of, 70–72, 110–111, 112, 230, 231
Subsidies, 181
"Surrogate" capital, 36–37, 40–41, 45, 87
"Surrogate" investment, 36–37, 45, 46, 87

Taxes
in capital input, 250
capital services and, 77–78, 93, 118–119, 151
consumption goods and, 247
depreciation and, 152–153
educational investment and, 373
in gross product, 148–149, 151
income and, 185
index numbers for, 201–203
in input and output accounts, 101, 146, 181
Investment credit, 121–122, 153
labor income and, 296–298, 373
labor services and, 188–189, 248
national income and, 185
on property income, 151, 152–153
output and, 101, 146, 181, 225
personal income tax allocation, 188–189
property compensation and, 188–189, 250–254
in sector divisions, 109–110, 119–124, 152, 234–235
Theil, Henri, 200–201
Theory of production. *See* Economic theory of production
Tinbergen, Jan, 1, 8, 12, 16, 17, 25
Tobin, James, 16, 340, 361, 362
Tövrnqvist, Leo, 200, 391
Total factor productivity
agricultural and nonfarm compared, 390–393, 399
alternative accounting variants for, 140–142
alternative estimates of, 140–142, 143, 164–165
based on flow of services, 140–142
consumption goods and, 42–43
contribution to economic growth, 99, 143–144, 245–246
correction of biases and, 161
cyclical changes in, 88–89
defined, 53, 55–57, 138, 242
Divisia indexes and, 28, 56, 58, 242
econometric functions in measuring, 90
embodied and disembodied technical change and, 52
as function of a form, 25
growth rates, 3–5, 391–392
growth rates of, 53, 79
indexes of, 25, 68–84, 244
investment goods and, 42–43
labor input and, 42–43
measuring, 51, 55, 68, 88, 99–100, 138–144
price and quantity indexes for, 242, 244
producer equilibrium and, 57
real factor input and, 138, 242, 245–246
real product and, 138, 242, 245–246
relationship to time series, 42–44
residual change in, 85
in sectoral production, 390, 391
social production possibility frontier and, 177
See also Productivity growth
Total product, 104, 282
Translog production functions, 17, 21

Translog production fuctions (*cont.*)
in agricultural measurement, 390
index numbers and, 22

Unemployment, 248
Unified social accounting, 88
United Nations System of National Accounts, 179, 223
compared with proposed system, 197
U.S. Department of Agriculture (USDA), 389–390
U.S. national accounts. *See* U.S. National Income and Product Accounts (NIPAs)
U.S. National Income and Product Accounts (NIPAs), 88, 179
assets of government bodies and, 185
capital formation in, 273–274
compared with proposed system, 194–197
consumer outlays in, 275
division of output in, 104, 180
government services in, 103
human capital and, 360–361, 385
index numbers in, 203–205
investment in, 274, 275, 277
labor compensation in, 274
property compensation in, 113
rooted in market transactions, 277
saving in, 275
treatment of nonprofits in, 103–104
wealth in, 277
USDA. *See* U.S. Department of Agriculture
Utilization adjustment. *See* Relative utilization

Value added, 8–10
See also Productivity growth
Vintage accounts, 160, 212–214, 216, 222

Wasson, Robert, 90–91, 161
Wealth
calculating, 194, 195, 318, 321
capital formation and, 180, 258–260
capital goods and, 258–261
change in, 217–218, 314, 315, 318, 320, 322–328
components' indexes, 194, 196, 266–267
decline in efficiency and, 265
determinants of, 330
estimates compared, 281, 324, 326–328
full, 276, 318, 321–324, 325
human and nonhuman, 275–277, 281, 318, 322–328
indexes for, 265–267
integrating saving with, 314
measuring, 179–198
productivity measurement and accounts for, 99
property income and, 154
in U.S. national accounts, 277
value of, 217
See also Human wealth; Wealth accounts
Wealth accounts
accounting identity for, 192
capital assets in, 101, 192
capital stock in, 216
components of, 192
constant prices in, 206, 208, 209, 223–224
disaggregating, 178–179
link to other accounts, 194, 246
perpetual inventory method and, 178, 206, 208, 209
See also Wealth
Wholesale price index (WPI)
consumers' price index and, 71–73
drift in, 114–116
as equipment investment deflator, 71–73, 114–116
Women
educational investment and, 346, 351, 355
labor income and, 337–340, 341, 342
WPI. *See* Wholesale price index
Wykoff, Frank C., 218, 378

Yung, Kun-Young, 296, 340